GREATEST
BASEBALL
PLAYERS
OF ALL TIME

Publications International, Ltd.

CONTENTS

Luis Aparicio

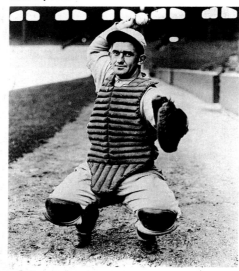

Mickey Cochrane

Andre Dawson

Picture Credits

Allsport USA: Robert Beck, C. Bernhardt, P. Brouillet, John Cordes, Jonathon Daniel, Tim DeFrisco, Brian Drake, Stephen Dunn, Stephen Green, Otto Gruele Jr., Will Hart, T. Inzerillo, Allan Kaye, V.J. Lovero, James Perez, Mike Powell, J. Rettlaiata, Bob Rosato, Kirk Schlea, Bruce L. Schwartzmann, Don Smith, Alan Steele, John Stewart, Rick Stewart, Dave Stock, John Swart, Budd Symes, Fred Vulch; Associated Press: Dean Bapes; George Brace; Chicago Historical Society: Dennis Goldstien; Barry Halper Collection; National Baseball Library. Cooperstown, New York; Anthony Neste; Michael Ponzini; TV Sports Mailbag, Inc.; United Press International; Ron Vesely; Bryan Yablonsky.

Contributing Writer: Tom Owens

Consultant: David Nemec

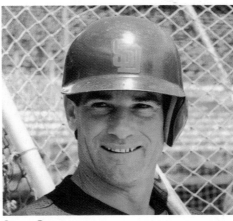
Steve Garvey

Carl Hubbel

Jack Morris

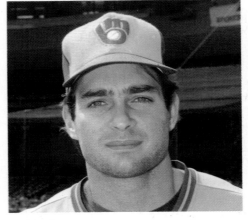
Paul Molitor

CONTENTS

Joe Niekro

Pee Wee Reese

Tom Seaver

INTRODUCTION

Any baseball fan can make a list of great players. Some might single out the gifted pitchers who consistently outwitted opposing hitters; others might emphasize the sluggers whose magic bats conjured up homers in clutch situations. Different fans have different criteria for what makes a player good, or even great—and each set of criteria is certainly valid. But how many would dare define the GREATEST players? Who would dare determine the best of the best, the superstars among the All-Stars?

Greatest Baseball Players of All Time tackles such a challenge. This book details the careers of 300 past and present players who have raised the sport to a new level of excellence. A solid reference source, *Greatest Players* provides a wealth of material on each athlete, including lifetime statistics, a comprehensive biography, and entertaining anecdotes. Full-page action photographs—many of them in beautiful, rich color—accompany each profile.

This guide to the greatest includes yesterday's unforgettable pioneers as well as today's newest sensations. In profiling the hottest athletes on the diamond today—including Rickey Henderson, Roger Clemens, and Darryl Strawberry—*Greatest Baseball Players of All Time* looks to the future by predicting which stars will hold lasting places in sports history. Of course, any analysis of current sports stars is a speculative venture. Injuries, playing for losing teams, and other factors can extinguish even the brightest baseball potential. But if the contemporary players profiled in this book maintain their current caliber of play, they have the ability to rewrite baseball's record books.

Retired stars and baseball legends make up the largest portion of *Greatest Players*, and selecting which of those former greats to profile from the hundreds of possibilities was no easy task. An obvious solu- tion, one that other reference sources have used in the past, would be to simply profile all members of the Baseball Hall of Fame. After all, the Hall of Fame has been enshrin- ing baseball legends since 1936, when Ty Cobb, Babe Ruth, Walter Johnson, Honus Wagner, and Chris- ty Mathewson became the first class of Cooperstown elite. More than 200 notables have gained member- ship into baseball's temple of honor so far. Yet featuring only Hall of Famers would not tell the complete story of baseball; such an approach would omit some of the sport's most accomplished players.

For example, all the qualified players and worthy candidates have not yet been inducted into the Hall of Fame. Members of the Baseball Writers Association of America vote yearly on prospective enshrinees, who have been nominated by sportswriters across the country. Members of the voting committee, like fans, have differing opinions on which nominees are entitled to Co- operstown acclaim. Some voters insist that such borderline players as Don Larsen, a pitcher whose sole glory was a no-hitter in the 1956 World Series, should be elected to the Hall. Many others opt for the true superstars, the players who sta- tistically rank among the tops in baseball history. Thus, some accom- plished baseball players wait many years before their selection into Cooperstown.

In addition, those who vote for future Hall of Famers often neglect certain players, particularly those whose career totals are not out- standing or awe-inspiring. For ex- ample, an unwritten requirement for Hall of Fame membership for bat- ters seems to be a career total of 400-plus home runs. Expert singles hitters or great defensive players aren't taken seriously by many vot- ers, who tend to overlook the intan- gible benefits ball clubs received from these types of stars. Shortstop Phil Rizzuto and second baseman Bill Mazeroski—both defensive mas- terminds—provide two examples of major leaguers who have been slighted in terms of Hall of Fame membership. Although they did not drive in many runs during their careers, their slick glovework robbed opponents of hundreds of scoring opportunities. In addition, they could always be counted on for a base hit in a clutch situation. Maz- eroski won the 1960 World Series for Pittsburgh in the bottom of the ninth during the seventh game by hitting a home run. That homer gave the Pirates their first world championship in 35 years. Maz was not known for offensive prowess but for fielding leadership. He had 1,706 double plays, the most for any second sacker in baseball histo- ry. He is remembered as one of the greatest-fielding second baseman.

The book also covers legendary personal achievements like Joe DiMaggio's 56-game hitting streak in 1941, Nolan Ryan's modern-day single-season record of 383 strike- outs in 1973, Hank Aaron's memo- rable 715th home run in 1974, Bob Gibson's 17 Ks in game one of the '68 Series, Carlton Fisk's home run in game six of the 1975 Series, and Willie Mays' catch to save game one of the '54 Series.

Included in this source then are not only the Hall of Fame legends but also those pitchers and players who worked consistently and quietly to help their teams win.

Greatest Baseball Players of All Time attempts to be a new voice in baseball literature—one that accu- rately details the careers of many hardworking heroes of the diamond yet goes beyond the cold statistics to intimate why baseball is America's national sport. Whether reading about the natural power of Babe Ruth, the inner strength of Jackie Robinson, or the courage of Lou Gehrig, we understand why baseball signifies America.

HANK AARON

Everyone knows Hank Aaron as baseball's all-time home run king. Fewer people remember that this graceful slugger played four positions and won two batting titles during his 23-year career.

Aaron began his pro baseball career as a shortstop in the Milwaukee Braves farm system in 1952. When he made the big leagues two years later, he was converted to the outfield. Although he won a Gold Glove there in 1958, Aaron also played first, second, and third base during his reign in the majors. One of the last of baseball's superstars to get his start in the old Negro Leagues, Aaron was recruited from the Indianapolis Clowns. His first pro experience came at age 16 with the Mobile Black Bears, a semiprofessional team. In 1954, when the Braves' Bobby Thomson broke his ankle in spring training, the 20-year-old Aaron was moved to his spot in right field.

In the majors, Aaron shattered the image of the musclebound homer hitter by winning two batting titles. He led the National League with a .328 mark in 1956 and a .355 average in 1959. Aaron compiled a lifetime batting average of .305 and a slugging percentage of .555. His batting average for 14 World Series games (1957-58) was .364. Aaron belted 3 homers and 7 RBI to lead the Braves to the 1957 championship against the Yankees. During his career Aaron batted above .300 in 14 different seasons.

Aside from playing on a divisional winner in 1969, Aaron's nine years in Atlanta were obscured by playing on mediocre teams that never finished higher than third place. Even in 1969, the Braves were swept in baseball's first-ever divisional playoffs by the "Miracle Mets." Aaron can't be faulted for the defeat, however: He hit .357 with 3 homers and 7 RBI in the three-game set.

His record-setting 755 home runs are Aaron's biggest claim to fame. Ironically, he led the National League in round-trippers only four times (1957, 1963, 1966, and 1967). The highest yearly homer total Aaron ever achieved was 47, in 1971. However, consistency was the hallmark of "Hammerin' Hank." During the 20-year period from 1955-74, Aaron actually averaged 36 homers a season. He topped 40 homers eight times and hit 30 or more four-baggers for 15 seasons.

Aaron started reaching historic milestones in 1970, when he earned his 3,000th hit. He became the first player ever to slug more than 500 homers and 3,000 hits. In 1971 he clubbed his 600th career homer off Gaylord Perry in a home game. He finished the 1973 season with 713 homers. On his first swing of the bat on April 4, 1974, Aaron tied Babe Ruth's record while batting against Cincinnati's Jack Billingham. Four days later he hit his record-shattering 715th against Dodgers lefty Al Downing. The monumental blast came in front of a home crowd of 53,775.

Aaron was traded to the Brewers for journeyman outfielder Dave May and minor league pitcher Roger Alexander on November 2, 1974. He played in Milwaukee, the town where his career started, in 1975-76. He hit his final 22 homers in the American League, giving a dismal Brewers team something to remember.

For his career, Aaron broke more records than any other player in the game's history. Some of his achievements include 24 All-Star game appearances (including the years 1959-61, when two games were played); most lifetime RBI (2,297); most lifetime long hits (1,477); most total bases (6,856); and his home run mark. Additional honors bestowed upon Aaron included the 1957 N.L. Most Valuable Player award and Player of the Year from *The Sporting News* in 1956 and 1963. In 1963 Aaron had the unique distinction of hitting more than 30 home runs and stealing 31 bases.

Even after Aaron departed for Milwaukee, the family name was still represented in Atlanta. Tommie Aaron, five years younger than his brother Hank, played three years in Milwaukee (1962-63, '65) and four years in Atlanta (1968-71) with Hank. The younger Aaron had only 13 homers and a .229 average in seven seasons. However, he continued to coach in Atlanta until his death in 1984.

At the end of his playing days, Hank Aaron returned to the Atlanta Braves. He became the team's director of player development and helped remold the Atlanta minor league system. In his current job, Aaron oversees a farm system that has produced current Braves stars like Dale Murphy, Gerald Perry, and Andres Thomas. Lary Aaron, one of Hank Aaron's five children, was a minor league outfielder in the Braves system.

Aaron became the first-ballot selection at the National Baseball Hall of Fame in 1982, missing by only nine votes the chance to become Cooperstown's first unanimous selection.

CAREER HIGHLIGHTS
HENRY LOUIS AARON

Born: February 5, 1934   Mobile, AL
Height: 6'0"   **Weight:** 180 lbs.   **Batted:** Right   **Threw:** Right
Outfielder: Milwaukee Braves, 1954-65; Atlanta Braves, 1966-74; Milwaukee Brewers, 1975-76.

- ★ Broke more records than any other player in baseball history
- ★ Played in 24 All-Star games
- ★ Ranks second in lifetime at-bats and runs
- ★ Ranks first in lifetime home runs with 755
- ★ Elected to the Hall of Fame in 1982
- ★ Ranks first in lifetime RBI with 2,297

MAJOR LEAGUE TOTALS

G	AB	H	BA	2B	3B	HR	R	RBI	SB
3,298	12,364	3,771	.305	624	98	755	2,174	2,297	240

Hank Aaron, primarily known as a home run hero, was underrated as an all-around player. He won Gold Gloves from 1958 to 1960, and between 1960 and 1968, he averaged 22 stolen bases. Aaron batted at least .300 during 14 seasons.

JOE ADCOCK

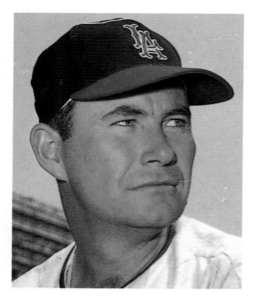

Joe Adcock was an awesome counterpart to the home run punch of Eddie Mathews and Hank Aaron during the glory years of the Milwaukee Braves in the 1950s. Adcock began his career as a first baseman when he entered Louisiana State University in 1944. He entered organized baseball in 1947 with Columbia of the Southern League. Three seasons later Adcock signed with the Cincinnati Reds. He spent the first three years of his big league career primarily as a Reds outfielder due to Ted Kluszewski's solid presence at first.

For the next ten seasons, however, Adcock was a fixture at first base for the Milwaukee Braves. The Braves landed Adcock early in 1953 after moving from Boston to Milwaukee. The trade for Adcock involved the Braves, Phillies, Brooklyn Dodgers, and Cincinnati, with Rocky Bridges, Jim Pendleton, Earl Torgeson, Russ Meyer, and cash rounding out the complex swap. Adcock paid immediate dividends for the Braves in 1953. He played in a career-high 157 games at first base, hitting .285 with 18 homers and 80 RBI.

The following year, Adcock achieved one of baseball's most notable records. On July 31, 1954, versus the Dodgers, Adcock treated an Ebbets Field crowd to a real spectacle: He collected 18 total bases in a 7 RBI, 5-for-5 performance. Adcock says he didn't even take batting practice that day before hitting 4 home runs and a double off four different Brooklyn pitchers. His record could have been even greater if his double off the top of the center field wall of Ebbets had been inches higher or if he had gotten a final at-bat in the top of the ninth when the Braves were finally retired. Adcock was waiting in the on-deck circle when the last out was recorded. With Adcock's homer the day before, he tied the record for the most homers in two consecutive games. During his career, Adcock became the only player to homer over the left field grandstands at Ebbets Field. He ended the 1954 season with 23 home runs, 87 RBI, and a career-best .308 batting average in 133 games.

Exactly one year later, Adcock suffered a severe injury while batting against Giants hurler Jim Hearn. Hearn's pitch was coming straight for Adcock's face, and Adcock tried to shield himself with his right arm. The result was a fractured right forearm that ended his season. Before the injury Adcock had belted 15 homers.

Adcock rebounded in 1956 to hit a career-high 38 homers, along with 103 RBI and a .291 average. Unfortunately the Dodgers edged the Braves out of the National League pennant by just one game. That year Adcock topped the league with an 8.4 percentage of home runs per at-bats.

Even though injuries limited Adcock to part-time status during the 1957 season, he participated in the Braves' first world championship. In the seven-game World Series win over the Yankees, Adcock had 3 hits and 2 RBI. His sixth-inning single against Whitey Ford gave the Braves a 1-0 win in the fifth game of that Series. During the regular season Adcock had 12 homers, 38 RBI, and a .287 average in 65 games.

The Yankees got their revenge in 1958 in a World Series rematch with the Braves. Adcock's regular season totals included 19 homers, 54 RBI, and

a .275 average. In four World Series games Adcock batted .308. Although he boosted his 1959 statistics to 25 homers, 76 RBI, and a .292 average, the Braves lost the National League pennant in a two-game playoff to the Los Angeles Dodgers. One of Adcock's most notable accomplishments in 1959 was a homer that broke up a 12-inning perfect game by Pittsburgh's Harvey Haddix. Because Adcock passed teammate Hank Aaron on the base paths, his three-run homer was ruled by N.L. commissioner Warren Giles as a run-scoring double. Instead of a 3-0 outcome, the final score was 1-0.

Appearances in both All-Star games highlighted Adcock's 1960 season. He played in 138 games (his highest total in four years), hitting .298 with 25 homers, 91 RBI, and a .298 average. In 1961 Adcock tallied 108 RBI (a personal best) to complement 35 homers and a .285 average. He finished his Braves career in 1962 with 29 homers, 78 RBI, and a .248 average. On November 27, 1962, Adcock was traded with Jack Curtis to the Cleveland Indians for Ty Cline, Don Dillard, and Frank Funk. After being a part-timer for one year with the Tribe, Adcock was swapped with Barry Latman to the fledgling Los Angeles Angels for Leon Wagner. From 1964 through 1966, Adcock contributed a total of 53 homers and 159 RBI to the Angels' cause.

Adcock ended his playing career for a shot at big league managing. He skippered the 1967 Indians to a 75-87 mark, good enough for eighth place in the American League. Adcock moved on to manage the minor league Seattle Rainers of the Pacific Coast League in 1968 before ending his baseball career.

CAREER HIGHLIGHTS
JOSEPH WILBER ADCOCK

Born: October 30, 1927   Coushatta, LA
Height: 6'4"   **Weight:** 210 lbs.   **Batted:** Right   **Threw:** Right
First baseman, outfielder: Cincinnati Reds, 1950-52; Milwaukee Braves, 1953-62; Cleveland Indians, 1963; Los Angeles/California Angels, 1964-66.
Manager: Cleveland Indians, 1967.

★ Tallied the best N.L. home run percentage in 1956
★ Played in both All-Star games in 1960
★ Tied the record for most homers in two consecutive games in 1954
★ Played in two World Series

MAJOR LEAGUE TOTALS

G	AB	H	BA	2B	3B	HR	R	RBI	SB
1,959	6,606	1,832	.277	295	35	336	823	1,122	20

Joe Adcock belted more than 20 home runs during six different seasons in his 17-year career. From 1953 to 1962 for the Milwaukee Braves, Adcock averaged 24 homers. He also had a .500 or higher slugging percentage during nine different seasons.

GROVER ALEXANDER

Known as "Old Pete" or "Old Low-and-Away," Grover Cleveland Alexander was one of baseball's most unappreciated talents during the early part of this century.

During his 20-year major league career, Alexander won an incredible 373 games, ranking only behind Cy Young and Walter Johnson. He threw 90 lifetime shutouts, second on the all-time list. Alexander won more than 30 games during three consecutive seasons in his career and topped 20 wins on six occasions. Alexander hurled an incredible 5,189 total innings.

Sadly, Alexander never led a charmed life. During World War I he suffered hearing loss from gunfire and was plagued by epilepsy. He also suffered from alcoholism. Nevertheless, he continued in the majors for 12 more years. Even though he earned a spot in the Baseball Hall of Fame in 1938, Alexander continued to earn a living by pitching for various semipro and independent clubs. He never earned more than $17,500 as a player, which came following his 21-10 season with the 1927 St. Louis Cardinals team.

Alexander, who had been working as a telephone lineman, started his pro career in 1909 with Galesburg of the Illinois-Missouri League. His salary was just $50 a month. He had won 15 games for Galesburg when a freak injury prematurely ended his season — and almost his career. Accidentally struck in the head by a thrown ball, Alexander lay unconscious for two days. He suffered from double vision for several months but recovered to pitch for Syracuse in 1910. His 29 wins won him a promotion to the Philadelphia Phillies in 1911.

His first season in the majors was a classic. He led the National League with a 28-13 mark, 367 innings pitched, 31 complete games, and 7 shutouts. Four of Alexander's shutouts were back-to-back. He rounded out the season with 227 strikeouts and a 2.57 ERA.

Through constant improvement, Alexander led the Phillies to the 1915 World Series. The team was sparked by his league-leading 31-10 record (for a .756 winning percentage). Add to those totals a sterling 1.22 ERA (ninth lowest ever for a single season), 376 innings pitched, 241 strikeouts, and 12 shutouts—all league bests. Although the Phillies lost the World Series in five games to the Boston Red Sox that fall, it was, of course, Alexander who pitched Philadelphia's only victory, winning the Series opener 3-1. His World Series record was 1-1 with a 1.53 ERA.

After he reached the 30-win plateau for the third straight season in 1917, the Phillies traded Alexander and his favorite catcher, Bill Killefer, to the Cubs for Mike Prendergast, Pickles Dillhoefer, and $55,000. The Phillies feared that Alexander would be lost to military service anyway.

Although Alexander didn't enjoy the same success in Chicago that he'd known with the Phillies, he was still a 20-game winner in 1920 (27-14) and 1923 (22-12). For his seven full seasons in Chicago, he always won in double figures and never had a losing record. Still, the Cubs cut Alexander loose during the 1926 season.

The St. Louis Cardinals got one of their biggest bargains ever when they decided to acquire the 39-year-old Alexander on waivers, despite rumors about his drinking problems. He gave them the pitching experience they needed to capture the National League championship.

One of the most dramatic baseball moments of the 1920s came in the 1926 World Series match-up between the Cardinals and the Yankees. In the second Series game Alexander tossed a four-hitter as he downed the Yanks 6-2. He consecutively retired the last 21 batters he faced, and he struck out 10 for the game. After Old Pete evened the Series at one game apiece, he tossed a second complete game in game six, defeating the Yankees 10-2.

The following day, Alexander returned to clinch the Series for St. Louis. He relieved Jesse Haines with two out and the bases loaded in the seventh inning. Alexander needed only four curve balls to strike out New York's mighty Tony Lazzeri, protect a one-run lead, and preserve the victory. He hurled the final two innings to earn the save.

Alexander enjoyed just one more masterful season (a 21-10 performance in 1927) before his career began to slide downhill. He was traded back to his old team, the Phillies, for the 1930 season. He pitched in just nine games, going 0-3 with a 9.14 ERA, before his major league career ended.

During his long career, Alexander achieved many other little-known feats. Twice he won two games in one day. He was one of the finest fielding pitchers of all time, amassing a .985 average. He slugged 11 homers and had a .209 average for his career—not bad for any hurler.

CAREER HIGHLIGHTS
GROVER CLEVELAND ALEXANDER

Born: February 26, 1887 Elba, NE **Died:** November 4, 1950
Height: 6'1" **Weight:** 185 lbs. **Batted:** Right **Threw:** Right
Pitcher: Philadelphia Phillies, 1911-17, 1930; Chicago Cubs, 1918-26; St. Louis Cardinals, 1926-29.

★ Ranks third among lifetime pitching leaders with 373 wins

★ Ranks second in lifetime shutouts with 90

★ Had two wins and one save in 1926 World Series for St. Louis

★ Elected to Baseball Hall of Fame in 1938

★ Twice won two games in the same day

MAJOR LEAGUE TOTALS

G	IP	W	L	Pct.	SO	BB	ERA
696	5,189	373	208	.642	2,198	951	2.56

Grover Cleveland Alexander hurled more than 300 innings in nine seasons during his 20-year career. He had 438 lifetime complete games and 90 lifetime shutouts. Alexander kept his ERA below 2.00 in five different seasons and below 3.00 in ten seasons.

DICK ALLEN

Known as "Richie" or "Dick," this talented slugger is remembered more for his fiery personality than his hitting exploits. Allen, who served four years in the minors before getting his first shot with the Philadelphia Phillies in late 1963, was the National League Rookie of the Year in 1964. The Pennsylvania native's award-winning season with the Phillies consisted of a .318 average, 29 home runs, and 91 RBI. Allen played in every game of the season and led the league with 13 triples and 125 runs scored. Conversely, he struck out 138 times. Also, his fielding at third base was less than spectacular. He made a league-high 41 errors and compiled a dismal .921 fielding average.

Allen's offensive presence was a lift to the Phillies, who finished with a surprising 92-70 record, which tied for second with the Cincinnati Reds. Both the Phillies and the Reds missed the league championship by only one game to the St. Louis Cardinals' 93-69 record.

Although his stats dipped a bit the following season, Allen still managed to hit .302 with 20 four-baggers and 85 RBI. Unfortunately, he eclipsed his previous strikeout mark by fanning 150 times. Allen maintained a .300-plus average through 1967 and always hit at least 20 home runs and 77 RBI. The Phillies, however, had little offense to speak of besides Allen. Therefore, even Allen's heavy hitting couldn't keep the team winning. Slumps and injuries compounded the problems of Allen and the also-ran Phillies.

The Phillies tried to cover up Allen's shaky defense by moving him around to different positions. He got a brief taste of playing second base and shortstop for a couple of seasons and was mainly an outfielder in 1968. In 1969, in what seemed like his final year in Philadelphia, Allen got his first crack at a starting first baseman's role. Even at his new spot, Allen was the second-worst fielder in the league, with 16 errors and a .985 average. Even though Allen belted 32 homers (the third-highest home run percentage in the league at 7.3), 89 RBI, and .288, the Phillies still finished with a dismal 63-99 record.

Allen's frequent personality conflicts with team management got him traded to the St. Louis Cardinals with Cookie Rojas and Jerry Johnson for Curt Flood, Tim McCarver, Joe Hoerner, and Byron Browne on October 7, 1969. Incidentally, Allen wasn't the only controversial

figure in the trade. Flood refused to report to the Phillies, so the Cardinals sent Willie Montanez and Bob Browning to complete the trade in April 1970.

Despite hitting .279 with 34 homers and 101 RBI in just 122 games, Allen didn't fare much better with the Cardinals brass. After just one year he was shipped on to the Los Angeles Dodgers on October 5, 1970, for Ted Sizemore and Bob Stinson. History repeated itself: Allen gained few front office supporters, even by hitting .295 with 23 homers and 90 RBI in 155 games. Allen was unable to crack the team's youthful starting lineup and was saddled with a utility role. That meant yet another trade, this one involving the Chicago White Sox.

Former White Sox general manager Roland Hemond once said that the smartest trade he ever made was on December 2, 1971, when he sent veter-

an pitcher Tommy John and utility man Steve Huntz to the Dodgers for Allen. Hemond said that Allen's awesome power and outgoing nature drew hoards of fans into Comiskey Park.

Allen's team-hopping seemed over when he became a pet project of manager Chuck Tanner. Tanner governed Allen by a separate set of rules and didn't force the free-spirited slugger to take batting practice and follow other team rules. This new management style worked for both Allen and the White Sox. The Allen-powered White Sox moved from their previous season's losing record to a second-place 87-67 finish in the American League Western Division. In 148 games Allen hit .308 with a league-high 37 homers and 113 RBI. Impressively, he committed only 7 errors at first base for a .995 fielding average (tying Kansas City's first sacker John Mayberry as the league's best).

Although he still hit above .300 for the next two seasons for the White Sox, injuries limited his playing time to 72 games in 1973 and 128 games in 1974. In 1974 he still lead the American League with 32 homers (and a 6.9 percentage) along with a .563 slugging percentage.

Allen showed why he was known for his temperament in 1974. The White Sox traded him to the Atlanta Braves, but Allen refused to play. The baffled Braves obliged Allen and traded him back to the Phillies. Although he never matched his original accomplishments, Allen's part-time efforts helped the Phillies to the 1976 divisional title. Allen signed as a free agent with the 1977 Oakland Athletics and then retired from baseball in 1978.

CAREER HIGHLIGHTS
RICHARD ANTHONY ALLEN

Born: March 8, 1942   Wampum, PA
Height: 5'11"   **Weight:** 187 lbs.   **Batted:** Right   **Threw:** Right
First baseman, third baseman, outfielder: Philadelphia Phillies, 1963-69, 1975-76; St. Louis Cardinals, 1970; Los Angeles Dodgers, 1971; Chicago White Sox, 1972-74; Oakland Athletics, 1977.

★ Won the 1964 N.L. Rookie of the Year award

★ Named 1972 A.L. MVP

★ Led the league in triples in 1964

★ Led the league in home runs in 1972 and 1974

★ Scored a league-high 125 runs in 1964

★ Played in the 1976 N.L. playoffs

MAJOR LEAGUE TOTALS

G	AB	H	BA	2B	3B	HR	R	RBI	SB
1,749	6,332	1,848	.292	320	79	351	1,099	1,119	133

In three seasons Dick Allen led the league in home run percentage and slugging percentage. He slugged over .600 three times, and he slugged over .500 in nine seasons. His .534 lifetime slugging percentage is 20th on the all-time list.

CAP ANSON

Cap Anson was baseball's first genuine superstar. He was the greatest player of the 19th century and was one of the most influential figures during the early days of the game.

In a stunning 22-year big league career, Anson batted over .300 for 20 seasons, including two years quite near the magic .400 mark. He ended his career with 2,995 base hits for a lifetime batting mark of .329.

Anson began his baseball career playing with his father and brother on a team in his hometown of Marshalltown, a small community in mid-state Iowa. Anson, whose father, Henry, founded the town, was born ten years after Iowa achieved statehood and ten years before the Civil War. He attended Marshalltown public schools and played second base for his school's state championship team in 1867. Attending Notre Dame as a student in 1869, Anson is credited with organizing the university's first baseball team.

He played with both Rockford and Philadelphia of the National Association (then a major league) before moving to the Chicago White Stockings of the newly formed National League in 1876. Three years later he became player/manager of the club, a position he held for 20 years. Five times (in 1880, 1881, 1882, 1885, and 1886) he guided the Chicago club to the league title. His first pennant winner in 1880 had a stunning winning percentage of .798 (and a 67-17 record), a mark unlikely ever to be broken. Anson's 1886 squad won 90 games to gain the pennant — the most victories in any single season of his managerial career.

An innovative manager, Anson played all the positions for his team at some time, including three games as a pitcher. In 1886 Anson was one of the first managers to embrace the idea of spring training. Anson sent his team by train down to Hot Springs, Arkansas, for preseason warmups. The team, which was housed in a dollar-a-day boarding house, limbered up by walking up to 20 miles a day. One of Anson's players on that team was another Iowa native named Billy Sunday. Sunday was a fair outfielder who only lasted eight seasons in baseball, but he later achieved fame as one of America's most flamboyant evangelists. Anson shared Sunday's views on morality: He insisted that his players refrain from drinking alcohol and smoking tobacco.

Much that Anson accomplished may never show up in any statistics. He was

known as one of the first brilliant managers of the game. He succeeded Albert Spalding as manager in 1879. He promoted many modern ideas, such as base coaches, basestealing, the hit-and-run, and pitching rotations. From the start, Anson insisted that his players get to stay in fashionable quarters and insisted that the team receive carriage rides to the ballpark each day. Sadly, Anson was intolerant when it came to racial issues. He protested against playing teams with black players, and he encouraged the league to bar blacks from organized baseball.

When coaching players on hitting, Anson advised simply making contact with the ball and being content with short hits. Despite his hitting philosophy, Anson did possess power. When he hit 5 home runs during two consecutive games, the record stood until Ty Cobb equalled it 41 years later.

When Anson's career first began, first basemen were used mostly as marks to be thrown to; other infielders took care of active fielding. In the mid-1880s, Anson and Charles Comiskey were the first to decide that first basemen should have a more active role in the game and field their position wide of the bag. Anson insisted that pitchers act as fielders too. Previously, most pitchers were too concerned about the possibility of injuring their pitching hand to risk doing any fielding.

Despite the responsibility of managing, Anson didn't let his playing performance suffer. During the first 20 seasons of his career Anson never hit less than .308. In 1886 he led the league with 147 RBI. Twice he flirted with the elusive .400 mark, narrowly failing on both occasions. During his career, he won two batting crowns. At age 45, Anson closed out his career with a .302 average.

Anson was an aggressive runner as well, swiping 247 bases in his career. Note that stolen base stats were only kept during his last 12 years as a player. Other stats, such as RBI, were sometimes overlooked also.

Although Anson is practically forgotten in his Iowa hometown today, his stardom among baseball fans was perpetuated by his 1900 biography, *A Ball Player's Career*.

Cap Anson finished as one of the N.L.'s top five statistical leaders in RBI for 14 seasons, in batting average for ten seasons, and in slugging percentage, doubles, and base hits for three seasons.

CAREER HIGHLIGHTS
ADRIAN CONSTANTINE ANSON

Born: April 11, 1852 Marshalltown, IA **Died:** April 14, 1922
Height: 6'0" **Weight:** 202 lbs. **Batted:** Right **Threw:** Right
Infielder, outfielder: Chicago White Stockings/Colts, 1876-97. Manager: Chicago White Stockings/Colts, 1879-97; New York Giants, 1898.

* The first player in baseball to compile 3,000 hits
* Batted over .300 for 20 seasons
* Among the first players elected to the Hall of Fame
* Led his club to five pennants

MAJOR LEAGUE TOTALS

G	AB	H	BA	2B	3B	HR	R	RBI	SB
2,276	9,101	2,995	.329	528	124	97	1,719	1,879	247

LUIS APARICIO

Dazzling fielding and electrifying baserunning were the two strengths that propelled Luis Aparicio into the Hall of Fame in 1984. At 5-foot-9 and no more than 160 pounds, the native Venezuelan wasn't a typical-looking player.

Aparicio's father was the guiding light in his son's career. Luis Aparicio, Sr., was one of Venezuela's best-known players. Young Luis took over his father's shortstop job with a hometown team in 1953. The next year, the White Sox discovered young Aparicio and signed him for $6,000. After two years in the minor leagues, he replaced fellow countryman Chico Carrasquel as the starting shortstop of the White Sox in 1956. Aparicio responded with a performance that won him American League Rookie of the Year honors. His first-year statistics in 152 games included a .266 average and a league-leading 21 stolen bases. Aparicio's baserunning and fielding exploits also provided fans with a new kind of excitement.

In the years that followed, Aparicio revived the lost art of basestealing in the majors and became the first player since Ty Cobb to steal at least 50 bases for three straight seasons. "Little Looie" led the American League in stolen bases for nine consecutive seasons from 1956 to 1964. His total of 56 stolen bases in 1959 helped his team acquire the nickname "Go-Go White Sox."

It didn't matter that Aparicio never hit better than in the .270s for the first 13 seasons of his career, finally topping .300 with a .313 effort with the 1970 Chicago White Sox. (Although critics sometimes forget that Aparicio could hit in clutch situations, as evidenced by his .308 average in the 1959 World Series.) Despite his less than spectacular hitting, Aparicio was a defensive wizard long before Ozzie Smith came along. Second baseman Nellie Fox and Aparicio gave the ChiSox one of the best double play combinations in baseball during the 1950s. For his career, Aparicio earned Gold Gloves for fielding excellence from 1958 to 1962 and in 1964, 1966, 1968, 1970, and 1972. Aparicio was also one of baseball's most durable players: During his first 11 years he played in at least 143 games a season.

Incidentally, Fox and Aparicio were involved in one of the wackiest promotions that Chicago team owner Bill Veeck ever staged. Veeck hired three midgets dressed as aliens to parachute onto the field just before a game to

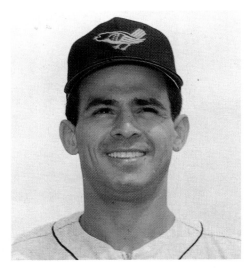

"capture" the keystone combo. Then both players were made honorary Martians in a pregame ceremony. The aliens stated that they had come to earth to aid Fox and Aparicio in their battle against "giant" earthlings.

Out-of-this-world things happened when Aparicio got on base. He could change the whole shape of a game with a single stolen base or hit-and-run play. A team short on power could survive in a game when Aparicio was on the base paths. The Orioles saw a need for Aparicio's talents in 1963, and on January 14, 1963, the O's parted with Hoyt Wilhelm, Pete Ward, Ron Hansen, and Dave Nicholson in exchange for Aparicio and Al Smith. Baltimore's new shortstop registered two more stolen base titles in his first two years, including a career-high 57 in 1964. That same season Aparicio had his greatest year as a power hitter, clubbing 10 round-trippers.

In 1966 Aparicio was a key member

of the world champion Baltimore Orioles. Baltimore compiled a 97-63 mark, winning the league title by nine games. Aparicio led the league in three categories: at bats (659), fielding average (.978), and putouts (303). During the O's four-game sweep of the Dodgers in the Series, Aparicio hit .250.

The White Sox saw the void Aparicio's departure had created on their team, and on November 29, 1967, they reacquired Aparicio in a trade that also landed Russ Snyder and John Matias for Don Buford, Bruce Howard, and Roger Nelson. Although these teams weren't as strong as the Al Lopez-managed Chicago squads Aparicio developed with in the 1950s, Aparicio still played like a winner. He started at shortstop for Chicago for three seasons, gaining All-Star berths in 1969 and 1970. On December 1, 1970, the Boston Red Sox gave up two infielders—Luis Alvarado and Mike Andrews—to obtain Aparicio. Unlike some players, who retire when their careers reach an all-time low, Aparicio's final season was admirable. His .271 average, 135 hits, and 49 RBI were all highs during his stay in Boston.

By the end of his career, Aparicio had appeared in a record number of games for shortstops, having played no other position during his 18 years in the major leagues. He paced A.L. shortstops in appearances for a record five straight seasons and was a member of eight All-Star squads. Aparicio was also the A.L.'s top-fielding shortstop for eight straight seasons, leading in assists for a record six consecutive years. Even without home run heroics or enormous batting averages, Aparicio was a true star.

CAREER HIGHLIGHTS
LUIS ERNESTO APARICIO, JR.

Born: April 29, 1934 Maracaibo, Venezuela
Height: 5'9" **Weight:** 160 lbs. **Batted:** Right **Threw:** Right
Shortstop: Chicago White Sox, 1956-62, 1968-70; Baltimore Orioles, 1963-67; Boston Red Sox, 1971-73.

- ★ Earned nine straight stolen base titles
- ★ Elected to the Hall of Fame in 1984
- ★ Established a major league record for most games at shortstop

- ★ Won nine Gold Gloves
- ★ Participated in two World Series
- ★ Named A.L. Rookie of the Year in 1956

MAJOR LEAGUE TOTALS

G	AB	H	BA	2B	3B	HR	R	RBI	SB
2,599	10,230	2,677	.262	394	92	83	1,335	791	506

Small but powerful, Luis Aparicio led A.L. shortstops in fielding average in seven seasons, assists in six seasons, and putouts in four seasons. His totals of 8,016 assists, 1,553 double plays, and 2,581 games are all-time records for shortstops.

17

LUKE APPLING

Luke Appling won as much of a reputation for his real and imagined injuries as he did for his polished playing abilities. Known as "Old Aches and Pains," Appling always seemed to have a sore back, knee problems, or some other ailment. During his 20-year career Appling also suffered a broken finger and a broken leg, but his physical condition didn't stop him from becoming one of the finest shortstops in American League history.

After playing two years on the Oglethorpe University team in Atlanta, Georgia, Appling entered organized baseball. He hit .326 in his only season of Southern League ball and then was purchased by the Chicago White Sox for $20,000. Appling hit .308 in 26 plate appearances in his 1930 debut with the Sox. He appeared in 96 games the following season but hit just .232. In 1932 Appling spent time at shortstop, second base, and third and upped his average to .274.

Appling gained the team's starting shortstop job in 1933, hitting .322 (second on the team only to the .331 average of outfielder Al Simmons). For the next eight seasons, Appling's average remained above .300; however, the Georgia native didn't adjust immediately to his full-time position at shortstop. Although he led the American League with 534 assists in 1933, he also topped the league with 55 errors.

Appling improved his fielding dramatically over the years. Although he always committed a substantial number of errors, Appling was always among league leaders in both assists and chances. He'd get to grounders most shortstops would never touch.

Hitting was never a problem for Appling, and his average reached a career-high .388 in 1936, when he had 204 hits, 6 homers, and 128 RBI. Never again would Appling exceed 100 RBI or 200 hits. Behind Appling's hitting, the White Sox finished third in the American League, 11 games above .500. (Appling claimed that he was paid only $18,000 after leading both leagues in hitting the previous year.) In 1937, Appling played in all 154 games, hitting .317 with 4 homers and 77 RBI. Again Appling led the league in assists (541) and errors (49). Despite his accomplishments, he never got to participate in a World Series. The Detroit Tigers and New York Yankees were two reasons why Appling's club never saw postseason play.

One more batting title was in the

cards for Appling. In 1943, his 11th full season as a starter, Appling batted a league-best .328 with 3 homers and 80 RBI. Due to military service, Appling missed nearly all of the next two seasons. He returned in time for 18 late-season games in 1945 and proved he hadn't lost his stroke, hitting .362 with 1 homer and 10 RBI. Appling served in a utility role for the White Sox for his last three seasons before retiring in early 1950.

If baseball historians kept track of lifetime foul balls hit, Appling might be near the top in that category. Appling was a noted contact hitter who was at his best when the count reached two strikes. Legend has it that Appling once fouled 14 straight pitches into the stands to get even with a team owner who wouldn't give him a box of baseballs to pass out to fans.

Appling's lifetime hitting feats include a hefty .444 average in four All-Star game appearances. In his final full sea-

son (at age 42), he still hit a respectable .301 in 141 games. His 2,749 hits rank second to Honus Wagner among all-time leaders for shortstops.

Even at age 74, Appling proved he could still hit. In a 1983 Cracker Jacks Old-Timer's Game in Washington, D.C., Appling homered into the seats off Warren Spahn.

Appling has been active in organized baseball as a coach since the end of his playing days. He served as a coach for the Detroit Tigers, Cleveland Indians, Baltimore Orioles, Kansas City Athletics, Oakland A's, Chicago White Sox, Minnesota Twins, and Atlanta Braves during the 1960s and 70s. He was interim manager for the 1967 Kansas City Athletics after Alvin Dark was fired. Appling had a 10-30 record managing. "I wasn't a manager, I was a baby-sitter," Appling jokingly says of his role in the development of many A's stars like Bert Campaneris and Jim "Catfish" Hunter, a situation aggravated by the constant meddling of team owner Charlie Finley.

Although Appling is no longer a regular-season team coach, he has been a minor league roving instructor and spring training coach in the Atlanta Braves farm system through the 1980s. "I have more fun working with these kids than I ever did in baseball," he said in 1988. With his dedication to the game, fans could see Appling coaching right into the next century.

Luke Appling hit over the .300 mark nine seasons in a row from 1933 to 1941, and six seasons in a row from 1943 to 1949, while taking 1944 and most of 1945 off for military service. He scored 1,319 runs and drove in 1,116 during his career.

CAREER HIGHLIGHTS
LUCIUS BENJAMIN APPLING

Born: April 2, 1909   High Point, NC
Height: 5'10"   **Weight:** 183 lbs.   **Batted:** Right   **Threw:** Right
Shortstop: Chicago White Sox, 1930-50.

* Elected to the Hall of Fame in 1964
* Batted over .300 in 16 seasons, including nine straight

* Led A.L. in batting in 1936 and 1943
* Has been active in professional baseball for six decades

MAJOR LEAGUE TOTALS

G	AB	H	BA	2B	3B	HR	R	RBI	SB
2,422	8,856	2,749	.310	440	102	45	1,319	1,116	179

RICHIE ASHBURN

Because he wasn't a power hitter, many fans have underestimated the accomplishments of Richie Ashburn during his 15-year career.

Granted, Ashburn hit only 29 homers in his years with the Philadelphia Phillies, Chicago Cubs, and New York Mets; such a feat would have required only a year's effort from sluggers of the 1950s like Mickey Mantle, Willie Mays, or Hank Aaron. Still, Ashburn proved himself a potent offensive weapon for any team.

The man also known as "Whitey" or "Put-Put" hit an impressive .333 during his debut in 1948. In 117 games he tallied 154 hits and a league-leading 32 stolen bases. He immediately proved his fielding prowess with a .980 average and a league-best 3.5 chances per game. Fans who remember his outfield grace may be unaware that Ashburn started his pro career as a catcher.

More improvement marked Ashburn's second season in 1949. He tied shortstop teammate Granny Hamner for the league lead in at-bats with 662. Ashburn's average dipped to .284, but he had a league-best 514 putouts.

Ashburn and his Phillies club enjoyed the ultimate success in 1950. Manager Eddie Sawyer, who had skippered Ashburn during his final year of minor league ball in 1945, was the pilot of the upstart team. Ashburn hit .303 and again paced the National League in fielding putouts and total chances. On the last day of the season, the youthful Phillies (nicknamed "The Whiz Kids") won the pennant from the rival Brooklyn Dodgers. The rifle-armed Ashburn saved the game and the league title for the Phillies when he threw out Brooklyn's Cal Abrams trying to score in the ninth inning. Philadelphia won the game in the tenth to advance to the World Series.

The Phillies were swept in the 1950 World Series by the New York Yankees. Ashburn hit only .176 in the Series, but the entire Philadelphia team batted only .203 against their A.L. foes. Still, the four-game set was anything but a blowout: The Yankee victories were 1-0, 2-1, 3-2, and 5-2.

Ashburn was a center field fixture for the Phillies during the 1950s. He compiled a consecutive game streak of 730 and never played in fewer than 109 games a season. Even though he was a sixth- or seventh-place hitter in many lineups he played in, Ashburn continued to be a consistent contact hitter. He won his first of two batting crowns in

1955 with a .338 mark that far outdistanced the second-place efforts of Willie Mays and Stan Musial, both of whom batted .319. Ashburn's discipline as a hitter was reinforced by his 105 walks that season. In 1958 Ashburn captured his second batting title with a .350 mark, edging Mays by 3 percentage points.

Ashburn's average sank to .266 in 1959 as the Phillies continued to finish near the bottom of the National League. The needy Phils managed to get three players—Jim Woods, Alvin Dark, and John Buzhardt—for Ashburn in a January 11, 1960 trade with the Chicago Cubs. Ashburn started for the Cubs in center field and hit a team-leading .291. Ironically, only the Phillies had a record worse than the Cubs.

In an effort to supply more power to the lineup, the Cubs made Ashburn a part-timer in 1961 and his average skidded to an uncharacteristic .257. At the end of the season he was sold to the expansion New York Mets. That first Mets team had a woeful 40-120 record. Ashburn provided one of the team's bright spots, hitting .306 with a career-high 7 homers—quite a feat for a guy who had only 22 homers during the previous 14 seasons.

For years many baseball historians have been baffled over Ashburn's omission from the Hall of Fame. This is probably because, despite his lengthy success in baseball, Ashburn didn't hit hundreds of homers like Hank Aaron or Ernie Banks. And players like Frank Robinson and Al Kaline, who outmatched Ashburn only in long-ball skill, got more attention from baseball writers due to their muscle. Yet Ashburn has an on-base percentage of nearly .400 when his lifetime walks are calculated. His numerous fielding achievements are further proof of his worthiness for the Hall. The Nebraska native was capable of reaching hits that other fielders couldn't approach, and his outfield wizardry helped lower the earned run average of many grateful pitchers.

Even young fans who aren't lucky enough to have seen Ashburn play may recognize his name instantly, for upon retirement, Ashburn was named to the Phillies broadcasting team. For more than a quarter-century a whole new generation of fans has been treated to Ashburn's witty and insightful views on the game he mastered decades ago.

CAREER HIGHLIGHTS
DON RICHARD ASHBURN

Born: March 19, 1927 Tilden, NE
Height: 5'10" **Weight:** 170 lbs. **Batted:** Left **Threw:** Right
Outfielder: Philadelphia Phillies, 1948-59; Chicago Cubs, 1960-61; New York Mets, 1962.

- ★ Participated in the 1950 World Series with the "Whiz Kids" team
- ★ Led the league in hits three times
- ★ Won the N.L. stolen base title in rookie season of 1948
- ★ Led the league in batting average twice, including a .350 mark
- ★ Led the league in triples twice
- ★ Led N.L. batters in walks four times

MAJOR LEAGUE TOTALS

G	AB	H	BA	2B	3B	HR	R	RBI	SB
2,189	8,365	2,574	.308	317	109	29	1,322	586	234

Richie Ashburn scored at least 80 runs in 12 consecutive seasons and at least 90 runs in nine seasons. He led N.L. center fielders in total chances per games ten times and in putouts nine times during his 12 years with the Philadelphia Phillies.

HAROLD BAINES

The lackluster Chicago White Sox have won only one division title in the last 20 years. Although the 1980s hasn't been a memorable decade for the club from Comiskey Park, Harold Baines provided Chicago fans with some moments to remember. During home games the fans showed their admiration for Baines with chants of "Har-old! Har-old!" A White Sox regular from 1980 to 1989, Baines became the team's full-time designated hitter in 1987. The 30-year-old slugger was moved to the DH role in hopes of preventing layoffs like his stint on the disabled list from April 7 to May 8 in 1987. Obviously the White Sox treasured Baines' hitting ability and figured that the new role would help prolong his career.

The move seemed to work out to everyone's satisfaction. In 1988 designated hitter Baines led the White Sox with 158 games played, 599 at-bats, 166 hits, 81 RBI, and a .277 average. He had a team-best 67 bases on balls, helping him to lead the team in on-base percentage. Teammates Carlton Fisk and Dan Pasqua tied for second in that category with 50 each.

White Sox fans knew that despite those impressive statistics Baines could do more. His average remained close to .300 from 1983-87. And he always hit in double figures for home runs before 1988, clobbering a career-high 29 homers in 1984, the year after the Sox won their division. His RBI totals were also always substantial: 113 in 1985, 105 in 1982, and 99 in 1983. Imagine what the totals might have been if his White Sox teammates had better on-base percentages.

Baines' 1985 performance won him an outfield spot on that year's *Sporting News* All-Star team. He also appeared on three American League All-Star teams, in 1985-87. Although he just made pinch-hitting appearances each year, he singled in the 1985 midseason classic.

Baines has never courted attention from the baseball press, and writers have often failed to give him his due. Perhaps he has been perpetually overlooked because he never played in a World Series. Nevertheless, he has shown constant growth both offensively and defensively every season. Baines learned a lot of his hitting mastery from the late Charlie Lau, a celebrated coach who also influenced such talented hitters as George Brett and Willie Wilson. Through Lau's tutelage, Baines gained

an ability to hit to the opposite field. Unlike many lefthand pull hitters, Baines has an uncanny knack for stroking outside pitches into left field.

Baines needed only three years in the minor leagues to develop into a major talent. In his second pro season with Knoxville in 1978, Baines was tested as a first baseman. The next year, Baines was the star of the Triple-A Iowa Oaks. Back in the outfield full-time, Baines tied American Association outfielders for the lead in assists with 16. His 1979 hitting marks included 22 homers, 87 RBI, and a .298 average. Other graduates of the 1979 Iowa Oaks team include pitchers Steve Trout and Britt Burns, and outfielder Thad Bosley. Their manager was Tony LaRussa, who now pilots the Oakland A's.

In his rookie season with the White Sox in 1980, Baines played in 141 games, hitting .255 with 13 homers and 49 RBI. Ironically, he lost the league's Rookie of the Year award to Cleveland Indians outfielder Joe Charboneau, who lasted in baseball for only three seasons. Baines' first long-ball success came in 1982, with 25 home runs, followed by 20 in 1983, 29 in 1984, 22 in 1985, 21 in 1986, and 20 in 1987. Despite his consistency, Baines has never been able to seriously challenge for a homer or RBI title in the American League. Some good reasons for this include banner seasons by Hal McRae, Don Mattingly, and Tony Armas—all in years in which Baines could have been a king in the National League.

With a little bit of math and some speculation, it's possible to imagine what Baines could achieve in the next decade. For instance, if Baines equals his totals from his first nine years by age 40, he'll have nearly 2,800 hits, which would surpass the totals of Joe DiMaggio or Ted Williams. If Baines does match his 1980s output in the 90s, it will not be for the White Sox. In 1989, the Sox traded Baines to the Texas Rangers, a move that stunned the fans. Still, Harold Baines will always be remembered as a bright spot from the dark days of White Sox baseball.

Harold Baines drove in at least 80 runs in seven consecutive seasons from 1982 to 1988. He also had at least 23 doubles in eight different seasons, with a career-high of 39. Baines, always a fan favorite, had a slugging percentage of over .450 in six seasons.

CAREER HIGHLIGHTS
HAROLD BAINES

Born: March 15, 1959 Easton, MD
Height: 6'2" **Weight:** 175 lbs. **Bats:** Left **Throws:** Left
Outfielder, designated hitter: Chicago White Sox, 1980-89; Texas Rangers, 1989.

- ★ Led the A.L. with a .541 slugging percentage in 1984
- ★ Hit a career-high .309 in 1985
- ★ Led the 1988 White Sox regulars in batting average, RBI, and hits
- ★ Set an A.L. record for game-winning RBI in a season (22 in 1985)
- ★ Record 12 at-bats in one game in 1984
- ★ Tied the A.L. lead in outfielder double plays with four in 1979

MAJOR LEAGUE TOTALS

G	AB	H	BA	2B	3B	HR	R	RBI	SB
1,428	5,363	1,547	.288	276	44	189	679	835	29

FRANK BAKER

It would seem ludicrous today to tag the nickname "Home Run" onto a player who hit only 96 round-trippers in his entire career and never had more than 12 in a single season. But to sportswriters back in 1911, the label seemed a natural for Frank "Home Run" Baker. At the time he earned his nickname, Baker was finishing his third full season in the big leagues and had accumulated just 17 career home runs. However, this was the era of the "dead ball" in baseball, and Baker's 11 homers led the league in 1911. Baker wasn't christened Home Run until after the 1911 World Series, in which he and his Philadelphia Athletics battled John McGraw's mighty New York Giants. After losing the opener, the A's came back to win the second and third games—both on dramatic home runs by Baker—and eventually went on to take the Series. It was an especially astounding display considering that Baker's home runs were surrendered by two of the National League's top hurlers—Rube Marquard and Christy Mathewson.

Although named for his hitting, Baker played a solid third base for Connie Mack's legendary "$100,000 Infield." The dollar amount did not reflect Baker's salary; it referred to Mack's statement to a reporter that he wouldn't give up infielders Baker, Eddie Collins, Stuffy McInnis, and Jack Barry for $100,000! Mack relented partially on his pledge in 1915, when he sold Baker to the New York Yankees for $37,500. Mack's decision was made in an effort to cut expenses by dealing high-salaried stars like Baker.

Baker needed only one year of minor league baseball with a team in Reading, Pennsylvania, before reaching stardom. The Athletics purchased Baker in 1908. In 1910, Baker got his first taste of World Series play, when the Athletics won the World Series against the Cubs in five games. Baker's 3 hits and 2 RBI gave the A's a 4-1 win in the opener, and he registered 9 hits and a .409 average in the five Series games. The next season, Baker guaranteed Philadelphia a return engagement in the fall classic. Although he had never before hit more than 4 homers in a season, Baker belted a league-leading 11 four-baggers, 115 RBI, and a .334 average. As the A's won their second straight championship in 1911 (this time in six games), Baker hit .375 with 9 more hits. His 2 dramatic homers were high points in the Series.

It can be said that Baker was the first-ever "All-Star" third baseman in American League history. In the spring of 1911 pitcher Addie Joss died, and a special exhibition game was organized to raise money for his widow. A team of all-stars was assembled to play for the first time, with Baker covering the hot corner.

Baker became the American League's muscle man in 1912. He powered out 10 homers and a career-high 130 RBI—both bests in the junior circuit. He was also the American League champion in 1913 with 12 home runs and 126 RBI and in 1914 with 9 round trippers. Baker spent the 1915 season in a semipro league and then joined the Yankees in 1916.

Playing with the 1917 Yankees, the agile Baker led American League third

basemen with 202 putouts and 317 assists. His fielding average in 1918 was .972 (best in the A.L.), with 175 putouts. Baker produced his final home run spurt in 1919, when he hit 10. He finished second in the league behind Babe Ruth's 29 homers. At that time, Ruth was a Boston Red Sox pitcher and outfielder.

In 1920 Ruth was traded to the Yankees and Baker retired temporarily due to the death of his wife. Meanwhile, Ruth bashed 54 homers, becoming the new home run king to replace Baker. In 1921 Ruth erased Baker's record by hitting a then-record 59 homers, compared to Baker's 9 for the year. Baker concluded his career after the 1922 season, when he hit 7 homers, 36 RBI, and .278.

Baker didn't achieve any lasting milestones in the home run department; but after all, he used a 52-ounce bat and had to deal with a baseball with little zip. He finished his career with a stunning postseason record, having hit .363 in six World Series contests—the sixth-best record in history.

The Hall of Fame finally recognized Baker's accomplishments by electing him in 1955. Baker returned to his birthplace, Trappe, Maryland, to farm after his retirement, where he died at age 77.

Frank "Home Run" Baker earned his nickname by being in the A.L. top five for home runs seven times, for total bases six times, and for slugging percentage and runs batted in five times during his 12 full seasons. He led A.L. third basemen in putouts during seven seasons.

CAREER HIGHLIGHTS
JOHN FRANKLIN BAKER

Born: March 13, 1886 Trappe, MD **Died:** June 28, 1963
Height: 5'11" **Weight:** 173 lbs. **Batted:** Left **Threw:** Right
Infielder: Philadelphia Athletics, 1908-14; New York Yankees, 1916-19, 1921-22.

★ Played in the Philadelphia Athletics "$100,000 Infield"
★ Was tops in the A.L. twice in RBI
★ Led the A.L. in home runs four times
★ Elected to the Hall of Fame in 1955
★ Played in six World Series

MAJOR LEAGUE TOTALS

G	AB	H	BA	2B	3B	HR	R	RBI	SB
1,575	5,984	1,838	.307	313	93	96	887	987	235

ERNIE BANKS

Baseball fans of the 1950s think of Ernie Banks as a homer-hitting shortstop; fans of the 1960s remember him as an All-Star first baseman; but everyone recognizes Banks as one of the premier sluggers in baseball history and a great goodwill ambassador for the game. Although he played his entire career with the hapless Chicago Cubs—a team that was forever stuck in the second division—Banks never lost his enthusiasm for the game. "Let's play two!" is one classic quote attributed to the ever optimistic Banks.

The Cubs discovered the Dallas native playing for the Kansas City Monarchs of the Negro League in 1953. At the time, he was hitting .386 with 20 homers for the Monarchs. (Previously he had spent two years in the military.) He broke in with Gene Banker in 1953, and the two men were the first blacks ever to play for the Cubs (some six years after Jackie Robinson broke the color barrier with the Brooklyn Dodgers). Banks was a rare commodity in baseball: a slick-fielding shortstop who could hit home runs. In 1954, the man with the droop-shouldered stance and ever present smile connected for 19 round-trippers, 79 RBI, and a .275 average.

Brooklyn Dodgers second baseman Jim "Junior" Gilliam beat out Banks for the 1954 Rookie of the Year award in a close race. In the following season, Banks blasted 44 homers (including a record-setting total of 5 grand slams). He finished his 19 seasons with the Cubs with 12 career grand slams. Twice he led the National League in homers, including 1958, when he hit a career-high 47 and won the first of back-to-back Most Valuable Player awards. Banks set a major league record for most single-season homers for shortstops in 1958, with an astounding 7.6 homer percentage. The jovial Cub added 129 RBI and a .614 slugging percentage to his feats that year—also league bests. In 1959 Banks' MVP stats were 45 homers, a career-high 143 RBI, and a .304 average.

In 1967 manager Leo Durocher named Banks a player-coach in anticipation of his retirement. Banks' hitting had declined in the previous three seasons ("down" to 15 homers and 75 RBI in 1966), and some people thought he might retire soon. In preseason, Durocher named John Boccabella the starting first baseman, and after the season started, a rookie named Clarence Jones got a brief chance at the job.

Both failed. Banks, however, quietly faced the competition and responded with 23 homers and 95 RBI, hitting .276. His play helped the Cubs register a winning record of 84-78 for a third-place finish.

A lifetime total of 512 home runs ties Banks with Eddie Mathews for 11th place on the all-time list. Five times Banks exceeded the 40-homer plateau. Today Banks is the all-time Cubs leader in virtually every offensive category. Banks hit 290 of his 512 homers at Wrigley Field. Only Mel Ott, who hit 323 of his 511 homers at the Polo Grounds, had more homers in one place.

In 1962 Banks was moved to first base because of a chronic knee injury and finished his brilliant career as one of the best at that position. The Cubs had tested Banks at third base (where he logged 58 games) in 1957 and in the outfield in 1961. Despite his bad knees, Banks proved a rugged competitor. His 717 consecutive games played is the 14th-longest stretch in history.

Banks nearly had his one chance to perform in a World Series in 1969. The Cubs were favored to win all that year, and the team occupied first place for most of the season. Only a last-minute surge by the "Miracle Mets" of New York changed things, and the Cubs finished at 92-70, eight games short of a pennant. That year, Banks hit 23 homers, 106 RBI, and .253 in 155 games. Banks was also the league's top-fielding first baseman in 1969, tallying a .997 average and 1,419 putouts.

For his career, Banks earned a place on 14 All-Star squads (including years when the leagues played two All-Star games). When his playing career ended, jobs in the Cubs front office and in the minor league coaching ranks followed, along with various business ventures in California. He was dubbed "Mr. Cub" and "Mr. Sunshine" by his followers in Chicago. *Mr. Cub* was the title of a 1971 biography co-written by Banks and Jim Enright. In 1977, Banks became the eighth player in history to enter the Hall of Fame during his first year of eligibility. And on August 22, 1982, Banks became the first Cubs team member to have his uniform number (14) retired.

Talent wasn't the only key to Banks' stardom; his dauntless loyalty to the sport was always uplifting. Chicago Cubs pitcher Ferguson Jenkins once said, after being traded to the Texas Rangers in 1973, "I don't think people at Wrigley Field ever saw but two players they liked: Billy Williams and Ernie Banks. Billy never said anything and Ernie always said the right thing."

CAREER HIGHLIGHTS
ERNEST BANKS

Born: January 31, 1931   Dallas, TX
Height: 6'1"   **Weight:** 180 lbs.   **Batted:** Right   **Threw:** Right
Infielder: Chicago Cubs, 1953-71.

- ★ Named to the N.L. All-Star team 14 times
- ★ Led the N.L. in RBI twice
- ★ Hit a major league high of five grand slams in 1955

- ★ Won consecutive MVP awards in 1958 and 1959
- ★ Played in 717 consecutive games
- ★ Elected to the Hall of Fame in 1977

MAJOR LEAGUE TOTALS

G	AB	H	BA	2B	3B	HR	R	RBI	SB
2,528	9,421	2,583	.274	407	90	512	1,305	1,636	50

Ernie Banks hit over 40 homers a season five times during his career. He also drove in at least 100 runs in eight seasons. Banks, always a favorite among Chicago Cub fans, set a record for highest fielding percentage by a shortstop with a .985 mark in 1958.

JESSE BARFIELD

One of Canada's most popular players, Jesse Barfield was a mainstay in the Toronto Blue Jays outfield for nearly a decade. Barfield's 1988 accomplishments were uncharacteristically modest. His health was questionable, and he played in only 137 games. As a result, he hit just .244 with 18 homers and 56 RBI. This was quite a comedown from 28 homers and 84 RBI in 1987. In 1986 Barfield had the greatest season of his career, with a league-leading 40 homers, 108 RBI, and a .289 average. In the outfield, Barfield led flyhawkers with 20 assists, and his .992 fielding average was one of the finest in the majors. It was the second of three straight years in which the strong-armed Barfield would either lead or tie outfielders for the league lead in assists.

Barfield's 1986 feats earned him a spot on the American League All-Star team (and three at-bats in the game). *The Sporting News* placed Barfield on the American League Silver Slugger team in 1986.

Few fans ever would have predicted that a ninth-round selection in the June 7, 1977, free-agent draft would pay such big dividends for the Blue Jays. The yields weren't immediate, though. Barfield served nearly five complete seasons in the minors before getting his big break with Toronto in 1981. He didn't exactly set the world ablaze in the early years of his pro career. In 1977 Barfield batted just .226 at Utica, and his 13 errors were tops in the New York-Penn League. The next year at Dunedin of the Florida State League, Barfield's average withered to .206 and he led the league with 15 errors, but he paced all outfielders with 22 assists.

In 1979 Barfield moved to the Kinston outfield in the Carolina League, where his power production increased to 8 homers, 71 RBI, and a .264 average. Another promotion in 1980 placed Barfield with Knoxville, where he continued to show promise both as an outfielder and as a slugger. In his first season at Knoxville, he hit 14 homers and 65 RBI with a .240 average. The next year he registered 16 homers, 70 RBI, and a .261 mark in 141 games before his late-season call-up to Toronto.

The Blue Jays gave Barfield a chance because they needed help fast. In 1981 Toronto was battling Cleveland for last place in the American League Eastern Division. The Blue Jays were still taking shape from their 1976 expansion and

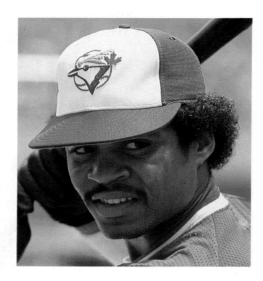

weren't considered a serious contender for the early 80s. Barfield and fellow rookie George Bell (acquired from the Philadelphia Phillies minor league organization) both debuted in 1981. Barfield enjoyed his first full season in the bigs in 1982 and responded with 18 homers, 58 RBI, and a .246 average. That respectable but unspectacular showing earned him Rookie of the Year honors from the Toronto Baseball Writers Association. His totals climbed to 27 homers, 68 RBI, and a .253 average the next season.

Teammate Bell had spent nearly two seasons in the minors before securing his place in the Blue Jays starting line-up. By 1984, both Bell and Barfield were faring well in the homer department. In fact, seven Blue Jays topped double figures in home runs that year. In only 110 games, Barfield pounded 14 homers and 49 RBI. The Blue Jays finished at 89-73, trailing only the pennant-winning Detroit Tigers.

The Blue Jays turned the tables on the Tigers in 1985, partially due to Barfield's 27 homers, 84 RBI, and .289

average. Teammate Bell socked another 28 homers and 95 RBI. Barfield and Bell were dubbed the "B and B" combination. (If the "B and B" nickname sounds familiar, perhaps it's because it recalls the "M & M Boys"—Mantle and Maris—from the legendary Yankees teams of the early 1960s.) The Blue Jays won their division with a tidy 99-62 record. Although the team didn't manage to advance to the World Series, Barfield did his share in the 1985 playoffs, batting .280 with 1 homer and 4 RBI in seven full games.

Since then, "B and B" have continued their power production. In 1987, the duo combined for 75 homers and 218 RBI. (This followed Barfield's best season as a hitter in 1986.) Barfield's improved hitting against all pitching helped him avoid the platoon system, which previously had limited his playing time when righthand pitchers were working.

Another impressive stat for Barfield reveals why he is rated by some as the best right fielder in the American League. He made 8 outfield double plays in both 1985 and 1986, and he has made more than 20 double plays since the 1975 season. To put that in perspective, consider that most teams don't have 8 outfield double plays in one season. Roberto Clemente, who was annually among National League outfield leaders in assists, never had more than 5 double plays in a season or more than 8 in any given three-year stretch.

Surprisingly, Jesse Barfield is not a household name in America; but his move to the New York Yankees during the 1989 season may change that. Barfield, who is barely 30 years old, might well earn some memorable offensive marks if he stays healthy for another decade.

CAREER HIGHLIGHTS
JESSE LEE BARFIELD

Born: October 29, 1959   Joliet, IL
Height: 6'1"   **Weight:** 180 lbs.   **Bats:** Right   **Throws:** Right
Outfielder: Toronto Blue Jays, 1981-89; New York Yankees, 1989.

- ★ Led the A.L. in homers in 1986
- ★ Twice led A.L. outfielders in double plays
- ★ Played in the 1985 A.L. playoffs
- ★ Started for the 1986 All-Star team

MAJOR LEAGUE TOTALS

G	AB	H	BA	2B	3B	HR	R	RBI	SB
1,161	3,904	1,025	.263	181	28	197	601	583	60

In his seven full seasons from 1982 to 1988, powerful Jesse Barfield slugged over .450 five times and averaged 25 home runs, 72 RBI, and 74 runs. He is considered to have the strongest outfield arm in the A.L., leading the league in outfield assists three times.

DON BAYLOR

It took more than luck for Don Baylor to play for five different pennant-winning teams during his major league career. Talent, versatility, and determination are just three reasons why Baylor has appeared in seven different American League Championship Series.

Recently, Baylor had the distinction of playing in three straight World Series contests with three different teams. In 1986 he served as the first baseman and designated hitter for the Boston Red Sox. He led the Sox with 31 homers and added 94 RBI. He hit .182 with 1 RBI and 1 double in 1986 postseason play. Baylor was traded to the Minnesota Twins on August 31, 1987, for minor league pitcher Enrique Rios. The Twins wanted last-minute pinch-hitting help and knew that a wily veteran like Baylor could help win some crucial ballgames. The deal paid off for everyone. The Twins clinched their division with an 85-77 record, beating the second-place Kansas City Royals by two games.

In the 1987 playoffs Baylor went 2-for-5 with 1 RBI for a .400 average. In the 1987 Series against the St. Louis Cardinals, Baylor hit .385 with 1 homer, 3 runs scored, and 3 RBI.

Concerned about Baylor's age and typically large veteran's salary, the Twins released him in December of 1987, despite winning the world championship. The Oakland Athletics realized that Baylor had brought needed leadership to two pennant contenders in two straight seasons. Oakland signed the free agent and gained more than just a part-time player in the deal. Some called him an unofficial coach because of the guidance and constant encouragement he gave to younger players. Baylor's 7 homers and 34 RBI in 92 games also helped the Athletics.

Baylor wasn't always a part-time designated hitter. For the first part of the 1970s, Baylor was a regular in the Baltimore Orioles outfield. After two brief appearances in 1970 and 1971, Baylor became the O's fourth outfielder in 1972. In 102 games, he hit .253 with 11 homers and 38 RBI. He also swiped 24 bases.

The next season, the 1973 Orioles won their division. Baylor aided the pennant drive with 11 homers, 51 RBI, a .286 average, and 32 stolen bases. Baltimore won the A.L. East with a 97-65 mark, eight games past second-place Boston. Although the Oakland A's stopped the Orioles in five games,

Baylor batted .273 in the matchup.

While the Orioles repeated as A.L. East champions in 1974, Baylor sustained his offensive accomplishments. He had 59 RBI, 29 stolen bases, and a .272 average. Although the Athletics repeated their playoff victory over Baltimore, Baylor hit a respectable .267 in four playoff games.

The Red Sox took the pennant away from the Orioles in 1975, but the turnaround was no fault of Baylor's. He had the offensive success everyone had predicted for him. He led the O's with 25 homers and added 76 RBI, 32 steals, and a .282 average. Despite those accomplishments, Baylor made the most news during the off-season. He was traded with Mike Torrez and Paul Mitchell in exchange for Reggie Jackson, Ken Holtzman, and minor leaguer Bill Van Bommell.

Obviously, expectations were large for any player who was slated to fill the shoes of a legend like Jackson. Baylor

didn't match Jackson's home run totals, but he did have 15 homers, 68 RBI, and a .247 average. Most impressively, Baylor pilfered a career-high 52 stolen bases.

Baylor's peak performance made him a hot commodity in the American League that fall. California Angels team owner Gene Autry signed Baylor to a large multiyear contract in hopes of buying a quick pennant. Playing designated hitter, first base, and outfield, Baylor produced 25 homers, 75 RBI, and a .251 average. In 1978, Baylor upped his offensive output to 34 homers, 99 RBI, a .255 average, and 22 stolen bases. It was the seventh straight season he stole 20 bases.

Owner Autry's bankrolled Angels did get their pennant in 1979. Baylor became the American League's Most Valuable Player with a phenomenal season that included a major league-leading 139 RBI, a career-best 36 homers, 22 stolen bases, and a .296 average.

In 1982, his final season with the Angels, Baylor and his teammates won another pennant. Baylor's 24 homers, 93 RBI, and .263 average propelled California to a 93-69 record. The Brewers topped the Angels in a five-game playoff, but Baylor was a one-man demolition crew for the Angels. He set a record with 10 RBI for the series, including a record 5 RBI in the playoff opener.

Free agency gave Baylor a new team in 1983. The Yankees got three straight years of 20-plus homers and 85 or more RBI. In 1983, Baylor hit .303 to top that elusive plateau for the only time in his career.

CAREER HIGHLIGHTS
DON EDWARD BAYLOR

Born: June 28, 1949 Austin, TX
Height: 6'1" **Weight:** 190 lbs. **Batted:** Right **Threw:** Right
First baseman, outfielder, designated hitter: Baltimore Orioles, 1970-75; Oakland Athletics, 1976, 1988; California Angels, 1977-82; New York Yankees, 1983-85; Boston Red Sox, 1986-87; Minnesota Twins, 1987.

★ Established a major league record for being hit by pitches
★ Drove in a league-best 139 RBI in 1979
★ Named minor league player of the year in 1970 by *The Sporting News*
★ Had 21 game-winning RBI in 1982, tops in league
★ Won the 1979 A.L. MVP award
★ Played in three straight World Series in 1986-88

MAJOR LEAGUE TOTALS

G	AB	H	BA	2B	3B	HR	R	RBI	SB
2,292	8,198	2,135	.260	366	28	338	1,236	1,276	285

Don Baylor topped the 20-homer mark in nine seasons during his 19-year career, and he had 80 or more RBI in seven seasons. From 1975 to 1986, he averaged 25 doubles, 24 homers, 86 RBI, and 81 runs. Baylor had more than 20 homers and 20 steals four times.

JAKE BECKLEY

More than 50 years after his death, the player, manager, and umpire known in baseball as "Old Eagle Eye" finally got the recognition he deserved all along.

Jake Beckley was one of baseball's greatest first basemen at the turn of the century. His career spanned 20 seasons, from 1888 to 1907, for five different teams. In those two decades Beckley proved himself as a clutch hitter and adept fielder. After just two seasons with minor league teams, the young Missourian won his first major league job with Pittsburgh in 1888 and hit .343. His average was only 1 point behind superstar Cap Anson. Beckley would hit .300 or better 12 more times in his distinguished career.

The next season, Beckley clubbed 9 homers and 97 RBI to balance a .301 average. His power was remarkable considering that he was playing in the dead-ball era. Beckley also became one of the best-fielding first basemen in the league that year. In 1890 Beckley was part of a historical movement: He was one of many mavericks who participated in the Players' League, an ill-fated attempt to stop team owners from monopolizing the profits from games. Although the league lasted just one year, Beckley had a notable season there. He was among the league leaders in virtually every category: His 10 homers tied him for fourth in the league behind Roger Conner's award-winning 13 dingers; his .541 slugging percentage was second best in the league; and his 120 RBI and 279 total bases ranked third. Ironically, Beckley's Pittsburgh team was 60-68, which was only good enough for a sixth-place finish in the eight-team league.

Beckley returned to Pittsburgh's National League team in 1891 and played five and a half more seasons there. His 19 triples in 1891 gave him the second-highest total in the league. Beckley's best average was .343 in 1894, which tied his career-high mark established during his rookie season.

Playing in the days when contracts were flexible guaranteed that rosters would be shaken up frequently. Players were often treated as commodities—being bought, sold, and traded regularly. Few records even exist concerning how teams acquired veteran players. Beckley was no exception to the personnel shuffling of the day. He finished the 1896 season with the New York Giants, where he hit .302 in 46 games. That year Beckley even played

five games in the outfield and one at second base. (Imagine a lefthander trying to handle second today.) After only 17 games with the 1897 Giants, he was off to Cincinnati. The Red Stockings kept Beckley in the starting lineup for six seasons. He hit better than .300 for those final five years, including a .341 mark in 1900.

The 16-year veteran was sold to St. Louis before the 1904 season and spent his final four seasons there. St. Louis was a familiar setting for the first baseman. He had played for a minor league team in St. Louis in 1888 before getting his midseason break with Pittsburgh. The Cardinals never had a winning season while Beckley was there, but the team had only been in the league since 1892. Beckley's best season in St. Louis came in 1904. In 142 games he hit .325 with 1 homer and 67 RBI. His playing career ended after a 32-game stint in 1907.

In his career, Beckley enjoyed several achievements. His total of 243 triples is the fourth highest of any major leaguer

in history. For 14 of his 20 seasons, he racked up 10 or more triples—a feat which would awe any speedster in baseball today. His speed also brought him 315 stolen bases in an era when steals weren't considered a main ingredient of a team's offense. His 88 homers would be a real feat for many of today's hitters. Beckley's total of 2,930 hits ranks 21st in history (tied with Rogers Hornsby), and his record of 1,575 RBI is the 23rd highest. When combined with a .308 lifetime average, Beckley has to be considered one of the best of the early batsmen.

Beckley may also be one of the greatest defensive infielders of all time. His 2,377 games played at first base rank above all other first sackers in the Hall of Fame—bettering players like George Sisler, Jimmie Foxx, Cap Anson, Johnny Mize, and even Lou "The Iron Horse" Gehrig. He led the National League twice in fielding and six times in putouts. During his lifetime, he made a record-setting 23,709 putouts and had 25,505 total chances at first.

Jake Beckley was still active in baseball as late as 1913. He served as a playing manager for a minor league team in 1911 and then had a brief career as an umpire. Beckley died at age 51 in his native state of Missouri. He would have been 104 years old if he had lived to witness his Hall of Fame induction.

Playing at a time when triples were the measure of batting power, Jake Beckley consistently hit three-baggers. He hit more than 30 triples five times in his career.

CAREER HIGHLIGHTS
JACOB PETER BECKLEY

Born: August 4, 1867   Hannibal, MO   **Died:** June 25, 1918
Height: 5'10"   **Weight:** 200 lbs.   **Batted:** Left   **Threw:** Left
First baseman: Pittsburgh Pirates, 1888-89, 1891-96; Pittsburgh (Player's League), 1890; New York Giants, 1896-97; Cincinnati Redlegs, 1897-1903; St. Louis Cardinals, 1904-07.

★ Led the league in triples twice
★ Batted above .300 13 times
★ Fourth among players in lifetime triples
★ Elected to the Hall of Fame in 1971

MAJOR LEAGUE TOTALS

G	AB	H	BA	2B	3B	HR	R	RBI	SB
2,386	9,527	2,930	.308	475	243	88	1,601	1,575	315

STEVE BEDROSIAN

Steve Bedrosian's career is a classic example of how a talented pitcher can become invisible as a result of playing on mediocre teams.

Bedrosian spent the first five years of his career with the Atlanta Braves—a team that has won only one divisional race in the last two decades. The 1982 Braves took the N.L. West, only to be swept in the playoffs by St. Louis. Upon joining Philadelphia in 1986, Bedrosian's fortunes worsened. Even though the team had a second-place finish, the Mets won the division by 21½ games. The Phillies teams of the next two seasons all had losing outcomes.

All of this means that Bedrosian's accomplishments have been handicapped by pitching for average clubs. Just as an average player can look great on a championship team, a gifted athlete may seem ordinary on an also-ran squad. Therefore, Bedrosian's ability can only be truly appreciated by imagining him pitching for a franchise that wins consistently. Relievers get few opportunities to save ballgames when their club seldom has a lead.

Bedrosian didn't get his first chance in the majors until his 1981 debut with Atlanta. Previously the Massachusetts native had toiled for three and a half seasons in the minors, including the 1980 and 1981 campaigns as a starting pitcher. The hard-throwing righty had control problems in Atlanta. In 24 innings of work with the Braves, he walked 15 and struck out 9, while compiling a 4.50 ERA and a 1-2 record.

The 1982 season was memorable both for Bedrosian and the Braves. The team finished with an 89-73 mark, topping the Dodgers by one game for the pennant. Bedrosian was used primarily as a reliever, and the result was Rookie Pitcher of the Year honors from *The Sporting News*. He was part of a bullpen (including Gene Garber) that recorded a league-leading 51 saves. The flame-throwing righty contributed 11 to the cause, along with a much lowered 2.42 ERA in 137 innings of work. His 64 games pitched were second to teammate Garber's 69. Unfortunately, Bedrosian got only one inning of work in the N.L. Championship when the Braves dropped three straight games to the Cardinals.

No one claimed that Bedrosian was just a one-year wonder after seeing him pitch in 1983. He followed up his first successful season with 70 appearances in 1983, pacing Atlanta with 19 saves.

His 9 wins and 114 strikeouts in 120 innings signalled future success for the hurler. Despite Bedrosian's heroics, the Braves missed the pennant by three games.

Too many appearances put Bedrosian on the disabled list and limited him to 40 games in 1984. Injuries didn't slow Bedrosian's strikeout ratio though, as he tallied 81 Ks in 83 innings. He also matched his career best of 9 wins in 1984.

The pitching-thin Braves made a serious mistake in 1985. The year before, the team had slipped to an 80-82 record, and the team brass tried to bolster the mound corps by placing Bedrosian in the starting rotation. The move backfired for everyone. Bedrosian went 7-15 with an inflated 3.83 ERA. He earned a dubious place in the major league record books by hurling no complete games in 37 appearances. Never before had a starting pitcher been removed from the game 37 times in one season. The Braves finished with a dismal 66-96 record.

Bedrosian got a new start in baseball when he was traded to Philadelphia. On December 10, 1986, the Phillies sent catcher Ozzie Virgil and pitcher Pete Smith to Atlanta for Bedrosian and outfielder Milt Thompson.

The Phillies immediately reinstated Bedrosian as a reliever, and he became the team's bullpen ace. In 1986 he collected 29 saves in 68 appearances. He won 8 additional games and struck out 82 men in 90 innings. The Phillies finished second in the National League Eastern Division. Bedrosian's saves tied him for fifth best in the National League that year.

In 1987 Bedrosian had the finest season of his career. He led the league with 40 saves in 65 games. Counting his 5 victories, Bedrosian participated in 56 percent of the team's 80 victories that year. Strikeouts remained Bedrosian's specialty, with 74 in 89 innings. At season's end, the National League departed from tradition and presented Bedrosian with the Cy Young award. Rarely are relievers given this honor.

Statistics proved that the Phillies needed another pitcher besides Bedrosian to survive. Last place and a 65-96 record were the outcomes for Philadelphia in 1988. Bedrosian, nicknamed "Bedrock" in Atlanta, again had a hand in more than half of the team's wins, with 6 victories and 28 saves. He appeared in just 57 games, not because of health problems but because of Philadelphia's inability to create save opportunities for its star stopper.

Bedrosian's future is bright, but his future statistics will depend on the quality of the teams he pitches for. His trade to the Giants in 1989 may be a blessing in that regard. It's conceivable that, if his arm survives, he'll top the elusive plateau of 300 saves in his career.

CAREER HIGHLIGHTS
STEPHEN WAYNE BEDROSIAN

Born: December 6, 1957   Methuen, MA
Height: 6'3"   **Weight:** 200 lbs.   **Bats:** Right   **Throws:** Right
Pitcher: Atlanta Braves, 1981-85; Philadelphia Phillies, 1986-88; San Francisco Giants, 1989.

★ Won the N.L. Cy Young award in 1987   ★ Led the N.L. in saves in 1987
★ Named *The Sporting News* Rookie Pitcher of the Year in 1982

MAJOR LEAGUE TOTALS

G	IP	W	L	SV	SO	BB	ERA
484	909.2	56	61	161	736	395	3.24

During his six seasons as a reliever, from 1982 to 1984 for the Atlanta Braves and from 1986 to 1988 for the Philadelphia Phillies, Steve Bedrosian averaged 23 saves, 7 wins, and 6 losses. His best season came in 1987, when he saved a league-best of 40 and won 6 games.

BUDDY BELL

Seldom has a son of a major league player gone on to duplicate his father's success in professional baseball; David "Buddy" Bell is an exception to that rule.

Buddy Bell is the son of Gus Bell, who served as an outfielder for the Pittsburgh Pirates, Cincinnati Reds, New York Mets, and Milwaukee Braves from 1950 to 1964. Buddy, though born in Pittsburgh, grew up mainly in Cincinnati. He yearned to play, as his father had, for the local Reds someday.

After graduating from a Cincinnati high school (where he played three sports) in 1969, Bell saw his dream take on a new twist. Another Ohio team, the Cleveland Indians, chose him in the 16th round of the June 5 free-agent draft. In his first pro season with Sarasota of the Gulf Coast League, he only hit .229; however, he led all second baseman with a .970 fielding average.

A promotion in 1970 took Bell to Sumter of the Western Carolina League for a full season. He was shuttled from third base to second to shortstop all season long in an effort to find his defensive calling. Bell's hitting was his most notable accomplishment during the trial: He hit .265 with 12 homers and 75 RBI. In 1971 Bell played Triple-A ball with Wichita of the American Association. Even though he played second, third, shortstop, and the outfield, he hit .289 with 1 homer and 59 RBI.

Bell made the Cleveland Indians roster for the first time in 1972, playing 123 games in the outfield and 6 at third base. Bell challenged for Rookie of the Year honors with 9 homers, 36 RBI, and a .255 average but lost out to catcher Carlton Fisk (then with the Boston Red Sox).

In 1973 Bell proved he could hit major league pitching. He pounded out 14 homers, 59 RBI, and a .268 average for the last-place Indians. He led all American League third sackers with 144 putouts and 44 double plays. Bell played in a career-high 156 games that year and made his first All-Star appearance as a pinch hitter. Two stints on the disabled list cost Bell more than 40 games in 1974. Even though he won the Tribe's starting third baseman's job, he was sidelined from mid-May to mid-June and nearly the whole month of August.

Through 1978 Bell remained a solid-hitting member of the Tribe and became one of the league's brightest fielders. The Indians traded Bell on December 8,

1978—the Rangers giving up infielder Toby Harrah in an even swap. The Indians thought Harrah might have more home run muscle than Bell. Cleveland made a too-hasty call by trading Bell for more power. In 1979 Bell debuted with Texas and showed new strength, leading the third-place Rangers with 101 RBI and 200 hits. Bell's 18 homers tied Richie Zisk and Pat Putnam for the club lead, and he hit .299, his best average in 11 professional years. Bell played in all 162 games for Texas, but surprisingly, he was left out of the All-Star game that year.

Bell followed up his 1979 success with 17 homers, 83 RBI, and a .329 average in 1980. Due to an injury, he played in only 129 games. He divided his time between shortstop and third base but led league third sackers with 3.4 chances per game and a .981 fielding average. Bell continued to be a con-

sistent performer for the Rangers, driving in runs and fielding excellently. For six straight seasons, he had at least 10 homers and 60 RBI. A prolonged slump in 1985 convinced the Rangers to trade Bell; after 84 games, he had just 4 homers and a .236 average. A rookie infielder with power potential, Steve Buchele, was emerging to fill Bell's shoes. On July 19, 1985, the Reds gave up outfielder Duane Walker and pitcher Jeff Russell to obtain the veteran infielder. Buddy Bell was coming home.

Bell enjoyed two prosperous seasons with his hometown Reds. In 1986 Bell hit 75 RBI and a career-high 20 homers. In 1987 he added 17 homers and 70 RBI to his league-leading fielding average of .979.

The 1988 arrival of Chris Sabo cost Bell a job. The Houston Astros obtained Bell in midseason to shore up a shaky defense. Bell played out his option and became a free agent at season's end. The Rangers, remembering Bell's past exploits in Texas, signed him for 1989.

Bell will be remembered for his quiet consistency. He has more total hits than Hall of Fame third basemen Frank Baker, Jimmy Collins, Fred Lindstrom, Eddie Mathews, and Pie Traynor. Although he never hit hoards of homers, Bell was one of the finest third baseman of the past two decades.

Buddy Bell found his power stroke when he went to the Texas Rangers in 1979. He averaged 14 homers and 77 runs batted in from 1979 to 1984 for the Rangers and also had at least 150 hits in ten seasons.

CAREER HIGHLIGHTS
DAVID GUS BELL

Born: August 27, 1951 Pittsburgh, PA
Height: 6'1" **Weight:** 180 lbs. **Batted:** Right **Threw:** Right
Infielder: Cleveland Indians, 1972-78; Texas Rangers, 1979-85, 1988-89; Cincinnati Reds, 1985-88; Houston Astros, 1988.

- ★ Led the A.L. with 10 sacrifice flies in 1981
- ★ Played in five All-Star games
- ★ Tied for the A.L. lead in game-winning RBI in 1979

- ★ Led A.L. third basemen in total chances for four seasons
- ★ Played in all 162 games in 1979
- ★ Tied a major league record with two opening-day homers in 1982

MAJOR LEAGUE TOTALS

G	AB	H	BA	2B	3B	HR	R	RBI	SB
2,405	8,995	2,514	.280	425	56	201	1,151	1,106	55

COOL PAPA BELL

Legend is the only remaining evidence of James Bell's reign in the Negro Leagues for nearly 30 years. Because no official statistics were kept for most Negro League games, no one knows exact averages from those forgotten years. Everyone does remember, though, that Bell was one of the greatest center fielders in Negro League history.

Bell debuted with the St. Louis Stars in 1922 at age 18 after serving as a lefty pitcher for a local semipro team. Despite being from a small Mississippi town, Bell seemed unruffled by playing in front of large crowds; hence the nickname "Cool Papa" was born. After two years of pitching, the Stars moved Bell to the outfield to take advantage of his hitting skills. In the 1920s the Negro Leagues prospered. Bell's team installed lights in their ballpark in the late 20s, years ahead of many major league stadiums. Bell's initial salary was $90 per month.

Despite the success of the black teams at the time, circumstances were tough for the players and the schedules were grueling. After the introduction of night baseball by the Negro Leagues, teams played both day and night. Sometimes, one team would appear in two or three ballparks on the same day. The players traveled most of the time by buses, which also served as dressing rooms, dining cars, and even sleeping facilities in towns where there were no hotels for black guests.

When Bell's league disbanded in 1931, he left his St. Louis team for the Homestead Grays. After only one season Bell had to find another team because the Grays ran short on funds and stopped paying their players. He finished the 1932 season with the Kansas City Monarchs, then landed a starting job with the Pittsburgh Crawfords. From 1933 to 1936, Bell's Pittsburgh teammates included many Negro League immortals like Satchel Paige, Josh Gibson, Judy Johnson, and Oscar Charleston.

Paige and Gibson were two of Bell's biggest fans. Both stood in great awe of Bell's grace and speed: "Cool Papa Bell was so fast he could get out of bed, turn out the lights across the room, and be back under the covers before the lights went out," Gibson once said. Paige's tribute was also fitting: "Let me tell you about Cool Papa Bell," he said. "One time he hit a line drive right past my ear. I turned around and saw the ball hit his ass sliding into second."

All the while, Bell was playing winter baseball in places like Mexico, Cuba, Puerto Rico, and the Dominican Republic. In the book *Baseball When the Grass Was Real* by Donald Hoing, Bell recalled that he played 21 winter league seasons along with 29 summer seasons for a total of 50. Because many Negro League teams would play simply for a percentage of the ticket sales, Bell said that teams would play anywhere from 250 to 300 games a season. Sometimes their pay would be as little as $5 per game.

Such conditions explain why Bell agreed to play on an All-Star team for Dominican Republic dictator Rafael Trujillo. Satchel Paige was the first player recruited, and Paige in turn lured Bell and his teammates to come play in the unusual league. Bell's salary for the season was $1,000 for six weeks, $500 paid in advance.

Bell played with two Mexican League teams from 1938 through 1941. He earned $450 a month in Mexico and didn't have to face the racial discrimination that was so commonplace in America. Bell hit a career-high .437 as a Mexican Leaguer in 1940.

Upon returning to the United States, Bell played for five different Negro League teams. He concluded his career in 1950, after a three-year stint as player/manager with the Kansas City Monarchs. In his final season, one of the young players Bell tutored was future Chicago Cubs star Ernie Banks. During that time the Monarchs barnstormed with the House of David team, which featured all bearded ballplayers. Bell declined a chance to play for owner Bill Veeck's St. Louis Browns in 1951. Veeck publicly called Bell one of the finest outfielders of all time.

Bell recalled that he never batted below .308 in his career and estimated that his lifetime average would hover between .340 and .350. Bell played against major leaguers only in exhibition games, but he had a .391 average after 54 contests. The Hall of Fame finally honored Bell in 1974. The city of St. Louis also acknowledged his greatness: the city street on which he lives today bears his name.

Cool Papa Bell was baseball's fastest runner and one of the game's greatest players during his era. In the 1933 season, Bell was credited with stealing 175 bases. Estimates put Bell's lifetime average at about .340.

CAREER HIGHLIGHTS
JAMES THOMAS BELL

Born: May 17, 1903   Starkville, MS
Batted: Right   **Threw:** Left
Negro League player and manager: St. Louis Stars; Pittsburgh Crawfords; Homestead Grays; Kansas City Stars; Kansas City Monarchs.

★ Batted .437 in the Mexican League in 1940   ★ Elected to the Hall of Fame in 1974

NEGRO LEAGUE TOTALS
(accurate statistics not available)

GEORGE BELL

Hard-hitting George Bell has been an offensive mainstay of the Toronto Blue Jays during the 1980s; however, the team has never seemed able to decide what position Bell is meant for.

Bell got lots of media attention in 1988 when he became upset over being made the team's designated hitter. Bell was being moved out of the outfield to give more time to rookies Sil Campusano and Rob Ducey. Anyone who knew Bell's past history with Toronto could understand his dismay. Toronto had used Bell in the outfield, and at first, second, and third in the past. Never had he spent a full season in one spot.

The position juggling affected Bell's offensive output for 1988. He led Blue Jays regulars with 97 RBI, and his 24 homers were second on the club to Fred McGriff's 34. But even though he played in 156 games, Bell's statistics were far below those of his banner season of 1987.

That was the year that Bell collected honors including a spot on the All-Star team and a Most Valuable Player award. His 134 RBI paced the American League, while his 47 homers were second only to Oakland rookie sensation Mark McGwire. Bell hit a healthy .308 (his second straight season above .300) and wound up with Major League Player of the Year honors from *The Sporting News*. He was second in the circuit in runs scored, second in slugging percentage, fifth in game-winning RBI, and sixth in hits. Despite his great hitting, Toronto wound up at 96-66, two games behind the pennant-winning Detroit Tigers.

In 1986 the Blue Jays challenged for the pennant throughout the season before winding up 9 1/2 games behind the first-place Boston Red Sox. Bell and teammate Jesse Barfield had their own competition during the season as well. The slugging tandem ranked among league leaders in nearly every category. Barfield led the American League with 40 homers, but Bell was close behind with 31 of his own. Barfield racked up a .559 slugging percentage, while Bell finished at .532. They tied for the team lead in RBI with 108 apiece. Bell bested Barfield in just one category: game-winning RBI. Bell's 15 tied him for the league lead and erased the old team mark held by Willie Upshaw.

Bell did have a bit of bad luck that year when his famous temper flared up in the last weekend of the season. He

got into an argument with veteran umpire Al Clark and bumped him, resulting in a two-game suspension. The incident probably prevented Bell from having a 200-hit season—he wound up with 198.

The Blue Jays had the second-best record in baseball in 1985 at 99-62 (second only to the 101 wins of the St. Louis Cardinals). Bell's contributions to the first pennant ever won by the Blue Jays included 28 homers, 95 RBI, and a .275 average in 157 games. Although the Royals stopped Toronto's World Series dreams with a seven-game playoff defeat, Bell distinguished himself in postseason play. He hit .321 with 9 hits and 4 runs scored, and he played all seven games in the outfield without making a single error.

Bell and the Blue Jays had their first serious success in 1984, when Bell played his first full season in Toronto, serving at third base or the outfield for 159 games. His hitting feats included 26 homers, 87 RBI, and a .292 average. The Blue Jays finished second in

the division to the Detroit Tigers but posted an impressive 89-73 record.

Bell was drafted by the Toronto Blue Jays out of the Philadelphia Phillies farm system, where he had hit .311, .305, and .309 in his first three seasons. Despite injuries that prematurely ended his 1980 and 1982 seasons, Bell did well for the Phillies farm organization. He was most successful with Spartanburg in 1979, where he led the Western Carolina League with 15 triples and 102 RBI, along with 22 homers and a .305 average. Given Bell's impressive statistics, it's surprising that the farm director for the Phillies had decided not to protect him from the major league draft by promoting him to the big leagues. Thus, the Blue Jays promptly snatched him in 1980. He debuted with Toronto in 1981 and Anglicized his name from Jorge to George upon entering the majors.

Bill James, in his *Baseball Abstract*, the bible of the sport, rates Bell as the best left fielder in the American League and says that next to Don Mattingly, "...he may be the best triple-crown candidate in baseball today." Two other Bells are preparing to continue the tradition of family stardom started by George: Juan Bell is a shortstop in the Baltimore Orioles organization (and was a key to the deal that sent Eddie Murray to Los Angeles), and Rolando is a shortstop in the Dodgers farm system.

George Bell's mark of 134 RBI in 1987 was the best in the A.L., which helped him garner the MVP award. His 15 game-winning RBI in 1986 erased the old Blue Jays record held by Willie Upshaw.

CAREER HIGHLIGHTS
GEORGE ANTONIO BELL

Born: October 21, 1959   San Pedro de Macoris, Dominican Republic
Height: 6'1"   **Weight:** 190 lbs.   **Bats:** Right   **Throws:** Right
Outfielder, infielder, designated hitter: Toronto Blue Jays, 1981, 1983-89.

* Had nine hits and a .321 average in the 1985 Playoffs
* Named A.L. MVP in 1987
* Hit a career-high 47 homers in 1987
* Led the A.L. with 134 RBI in 1987

MAJOR LEAGUE TOTALS

G	AB	H	BA	2B	3B	HR	R	RBI	SB
1,039	3,966	1,145	.289	212	32	181	574	644	56

41

JOHNNY BENCH

Johnny Bench surprised no one by getting elected to the Baseball Hall of Fame in 1989, his first year of eligibility. After all, Bench was *the* premier catcher of the 1970s, displaying consistent fielding brilliance and power-hitting ability.

Pete Rose provided the hustle and Johnny Bench provided the muscle as the "Big Red Machine"—the great Cincinnati teams of the 1970s—won six National League championships and four pennants. Bench was the regular backstop for the Reds during that dynasty. He was the best to play his position since the days of Roy Campanella and Yogi Berra, hitting more home runs than any other catcher in baseball history.

Bench came onto the big league scene with the Reds in 1967. He hit only .163 in 26 games, with just 1 home run and 6 RBI. The Reds maintained their faith in Bench and gave him the starting catcher's job in 1968. He responded in award-winning fashion. His first full season included 15 homers, 82 RBI, and a .275 average. He won the National League Rookie of the Year award and set a major league record for rookie catchers that still stands today by appearing in 154 games.

Bench kept improving with experience. In 1969 he led all National League catchers with 26 homers and 90 RBI. Unlike some streaky power hitters, Bench batted a healthy .293. The best was yet to come for both Bench and the Reds in 1970. New manager George "Sparky" Anderson piloted the Reds to a 102-60 finish, capturing the National League Western Division by 14½ games. Bench played a major part in the team's whirlwind finish. He won league Most Valuable Player honors with 45 homers and 148 RBI (both N.L. bests) and a .293 average. The Reds swept the Pittsburgh Pirates in three straight playoff games before advancing to the World Series. The Baltimore Orioles won the Series against the Reds in five games.

After what some called a subpar 1971 season for Bench (27 homers and 61 RBI), he rebounded to win his second MVP award in 1972. His return to form helped the Reds recapture their divisional title. Bench's 40 homers and 125 RBI were both league highs. The Reds returned to the World Series, only to be stopped by the Oakland Athletics in seven games.

Bench kept on hitting year after year. He drove in 104 RBI in 1973 and

paced the league with 129 RBI in 1974. In 1975 Bench rekindled the fire in the Big Red Machine with 28 homers and 110 RBI. The Reds swept the Pirates in the league playoffs and faced the Boston Red Sox in the World Series. Bench's club beat the BoSox in seven games, bringing Cincinnati its first World Championship since 1940.

The Reds repeated as world champions in 1976. Bench played in just 135 games due to injuries—his lowest total in nine seasons. However, he contributed 16 homers and 74 RBI to the cause. Bench made up for lost time in postseason competition. He hit .333 in the playoffs, and .533 (with 2 homers and 6 RBI) in the Series. His Series efforts helped the Reds sweep the Yankees in

four straight games. Bench's hitting heroics won him Series MVP recognition. The Reds, meanwhile, became the first N.L. team in 50 years to win consecutive World Series crowns.

During his first ten seasons Bench never caught fewer than 120 games, and he won ten straight Gold Gloves in that stretch. The Reds tried to preserve Bench's knees by playing him at first base, third base, or the outfield. After all, his bat was still a welcome addition to the lineup. Bench, however, saw things differently: "When I play the outfield or infield, it's almost like not playing at all," he said. "Catching is the most important job in baseball."

Bench caught only 13 games in his final three seasons with Cincinnati. In 1981 he played in just 52 games—only the second time in his 17-year career that he played in less than 100 games and hit less than 10 homers.

After he retired at age 36, Bench served as a baseball broadcaster for ABC-TV and CBS Radio. In 1989 Bench became one of the team broadcasters for the Cincinnati Reds. He is one of the youngest players ever elected to Cooperstown.

In 1970, Johnny Bench had one of the greatest seasons ever by a catcher. He won N.L. MVP honors by leading the league with 45 homers and 148 RBI while batting .293. He won his second MVP award in 1972 by leading the league with 40 homers and 125 RBI.

CAREER HIGHLIGHTS
JOHNNY LEE BENCH

Born: December 7, 1947   Oklahoma City, OK
Height: 6'1"   **Weight:** 197 lbs.   **Batted:** Right   **Threw:** Right
Catcher, first baseman, third baseman, outfielder: Cincinnati Reds, 1967-83.

★ Established a major league record for most homers for catchers

★ Named N.L. Rookie of the Year in 1968

★ Led the N.L. in homers in 1970 and 1972

★ Elected to the Baseball Hall of Fame in 1989

★ Drove in 100-plus RBI five times

★ Named N.L. MVP in 1970 and 1972

MAJOR LEAGUE TOTALS

G	AB	H	BA	2B	3B	HR	R	RBI	SB
2,158	7,658	2,048	.267	381	24	389	1,091	1,376	68

YOGI BERRA

Today's fans may remember Yogi Berra only as the major league coach with the cartoon character's nickname (even though the ballplayer's name came before the bear's). Berra is a familiar face on television commercials. He's famous for his oft-quoted wacky observations and his childhood friendship in St. Louis with now-famous sportscaster Joe Garagiola.

Current fans may not remember Berra the player. But what a player he was! If the object of baseball is to win championships, then Yogi Berra was the most successful player ever to put on a major league uniform. In a brilliant 18-year career with the New York Yankees, the three-time MVP played on 14 pennant-winning and ten world championship teams. After his playing days were over, the former catcher managed the Yankees and the New York Mets to two more pennants. It's a record of success that has never been matched.

Berra's career began with an ironic twist. He grew up in St. Louis where a boyhood chum nicknamed him Yogi after seeing a movie about India. Berra tried out for the St. Louis Cardinals with Garagiola. The Redbirds offered Garagiola a $500 signing bonus but overlooked Berra. A year later, a Yankees scout discovered Berra on an American Legion team and signed him for $500. After Branch Rickey moved from heading the Cardinals to the Brooklyn Dodgers, he telegrammed Berra and tried to get him to try out with Brooklyn, but he was too late.

Berra spent one year with the Yanks minor league club in Norfolk. Following the 1943 season, he entered the U.S. Navy. He resumed his baseball career in 1946, playing for Newark. The Yankees called Berra up late in 1946 and used him in seven games.

During the next two seasons, Berra was converted from an outfielder to a catcher. He shared catching duties with Aaron Robinson in 1947 and with Gus Niarhos in 1948. Meanwhile, strong tutoring by former Yankee catching great Bill Dickey was turning Berra into a first-rate backstop. "Bill Dickey is learning me his experience," Berra supposedly said during his rookie catching lessons. No one needed to teach Berra how to hit, however. He hit 11 homers and 54 RBI during the regular season and became the first pinch hitter to homer in World Series history in 1947.

The catcher's job belonged solely to Berra starting in 1949. His fielding was top-notch, including a league-leading 18 double plays and an average of 5.6 total chances per game. He led the Yankees with 91 RBI, and his 20 homers trailed only Tommy Heinrich's 24. It was the first of ten straight years in which Berra would surpass 20 homers. He drove in 100-plus runs for four consecutive seasons. For his career, Berra hit 358 homers — a record for A.L. catchers.

Berra became a capable defensive player behind the plate. He once compiled a string of 148 errorless games. Until Elston Howard took over primary catching duties in 1961, Berra was among the best glove men in the league, with a strong, accurate throwing arm. His 175 lifetime double plays tie him for second on the all-time list for catchers.

Most importantly, Berra was one of the greatest clutch hitters in World Series history. His fourth-game home run helped clinch the 1950 championship against the Philadelphia Phillies. He accomplished the rare feat of hitting a grand slam in the 1956 Series against Brooklyn. Berra almost gave the Yankees the fuel to beat the Dodgers in the 1955 Series. Unfortunately, his long fly ball in the sixth inning was flagged down by Dodger left fielder Sandy Amoros.

Berra played in 14 World Series in just 19 years. His records include 75 Series games played, 259 at-bats, 71 hits, and 10 doubles. His 39 RBI and 41 runs scored rank second among all-time leaders, and his 12 home runs and 32 walks are third.

Berra retired in 1965 and managed the 1964 Yankees, piloting the team to a league title only to lose a seven-game World Series to the St. Louis Cardinals. Despite this success, the Yankees fired Berra in 1965. Berra worked as a coach for the crosstown New York Mets from 1965 to 1972. He won his first National League title in 1973, managing the Mets to a World Series. The Yankees regained Berra as a coach from 1975 through 1983. He managed the Yankees in 1984, then obtained his current job as a Houston Astros coach at the end of the 1985 season.

Two of Berra's sons also excelled in athletics: Dale was a utility infielder for the Pirates, Yankees, and Astros from 1977-87; and Tim turned to football and had a brief career in the NFL.

Berra was remembered for his playing accomplishments with Hall of Fame membership in 1972. Many of his clever and amusing statements were immortal long before he retired. "The game's not over 'til it's over" was one of his classic lines. Casey Stengel probably best described Berra as a person and as a player: "He was a peculiar fellow with amazing ability."

CAREER HIGHLIGHTS
LAWRENCE PETER BERRA

Born: May 12, 1925   St. Louis, MO
Height: 5'8"   **Weight:** 185 lbs.   **Batted:** Left   **Threw:** Right
Catcher, outfielder: New York Yankees, 1946-65. Manager: New York Yankees, 1964, 1984-85; New York Mets, 1972-75.

- ★ Was selected as the A.L. MVP in 1951, 1954, and 1955
- ★ Played for 10 World Champions
- ★ Managed the New York Yankees and New York Mets to league titles
- ★ Played in a record 75 World Series games
- ★ Compiled a record 71 Series hits
- ★ Elected to the Hall of Fame in 1972

MAJOR LEAGUE TOTALS

G	AB	H	BA	2B	3B	HR	R	RBI	SB
2,120	7,555	2,150	.285	321	49	358	1,175	1,430	30

From 1949 to 1958, the colorful Yogi Berra slugged at least 20 homers each season and had more than 100 RBI in four consecutive seasons. A fine defensive player, he had 175 lifetime double plays, tying him for second on the all-time list for catchers.

VIDA BLUE

Although his performance was never consistent, Vida Blue ranked as one of the best pitchers of the 1970s.

A solid lefthander from Louisiana, Blue was a football and baseball star in high school. Blue turned to professional baseball instead of college at the urging of the Kansas City Athletics. His large signing bonus was rumored to be in the $50,000 range. It took just two and a half seasons before Blue was wearing an Oakland A's uniform. After winning one game in 1969 in a late-season trial with Oakland, Blue pitched for the Iowa Oaks of the American Association for most of the 1970 season. He was the hit of the minor leagues, leading all Association teams in wins and strikeouts before getting a late-season call-up to Oakland.

Blue was in the majors to stay when he came in late 1970. He tossed a one-hitter in his first decision. For an encore, he threw a 6-0 no-hitter against the Minnesota Twins on September 21. His arrival was too late to help the A's escape a second-place (89-73) finish, and the Twins won the division by nine games.

All it took was one full season for Blue's impact to be felt. He joined Oakland's starting rotation in 1971 and finished the year with a sparkling 24-8 record—only 1 win behind league leader Mickey Lolich. Blue highlighted the season with 301 strikeouts and paced the American League in two categories: ERA (1.82) and shutouts (8). Because he had pitched more than 50 innings in his first two call-ups in previous seasons, Blue wasn't eligible for the Rookie of the Year award. However, the Athletics pitching ace won both the league MVP and Cy Young awards, along with A.L. Pitcher of the Year honors from *The Sporting News*.

The season ended on a sour note, however, as the Orioles swept the A's in a three-game divisional playoff. Blue started the first game of the playoffs and limited Baltimore to just 1 run in six innings, but the O's staged a four-run rally in the seventh to defeat Blue and company.

Tight-fisted Oakland team owner Charlie Finley locked horns with Blue over contract terms following the season. Blue refused to play until he got a suitable contract and didn't reach an agreement with Finley until mid-May. Blue's late start threw him into a lengthy slump, and he finished the year at 6-10. Although the Athletics won the

World Series against the Cincinnati Reds in seven games, Blue participated in the event only as a relief pitcher.

Blue rebounded to form and became a 20-game winner for the second time in 1973. His 20-9 record was the perfect complement to 21-win seasons by teammates Catfish Hunter and Ken Holtzman. The Athletics won their second straight world championship, this time over the New York Mets.

The crafty lefty won in double figures for the A's during the next four seasons. He won 17 games in 1974, 22 in 1975, 18 in 1976, and 14 in 1977. In 1975 Blue was the instigator of a "mass" no-hitter. During the last week of the season, the Athletics took on the Angels in what seemed like a meaningless contest. Blue started the game and pitched five hitless innings; relievers Glenn Abbott and Paul Lindblad each pitched hitless innings; then Rollie Fingers hurled the final two innings without a hit as well. It was the only time in the major leagues that four

pitchers had combined on a no-hitter.

By the late 1970s, team owner Finley was dumping his high-priced stars due to declining attendance and other fiscal woes. In Blue, he had a hot commodity, and the San Francisco Giants thought so too. On March 15, 1978, the Giants gave up Gary Alexander, Dave Heaverlo, Mario Guerrero, Phil Huffman, John Henry Johnson, Alan Wirts, Gary Thomasson, and $390,000 just to get Blue.

The nine-year veteran handled the transition to another league with ease. He went 18-10 in 1978, then won 14 games in each of the following two years. After he won just 8 games in 1981, the Giants traded Blue to the Kansas City Royals. On March 30, 1982, Kansas City gave up Renie Martin, Craig Chamberlain, Atlee Hammaker, and Brad Wellman for Blue and Bob Tufts. Blue had a respectable 1982 season with Kansas City, winning 13 games. In August 1983, after going winless in 14 starts, Blue was released from the Royals. Subsequently, he was suspended from baseball for one year for alleged drug use.

After spending that off-year in the Puerto Rican League, Blue returned to the majors in 1985 with his old team, the Giants, where he proved he could still pitch by winning 18 games in two seasons. The 1985 Giants had invited Blue to spring training as a non-roster player, and he earned his way back onto the team by showing that he could still throw hard, even after a long career. Blue ended his career in 1986. Blue's lifetime totals include more wins than Hall of Famers Dizzy Dean, Lefty Gomez, or Sandy Koufax. Blue will get his first chance at induction into Cooperstown in 1992.

CAREER HIGHLIGHTS
VIDA ROCHELLE BLUE

Born: July 28, 1949   Mansfield, LA
Height: 6'0"   **Weight:** 189 lbs.   **Batted:** Both   **Threw:** Left
Pitcher: Oakland Athletics, 1969-77; San Francisco Giants, 1978-81, 1985-86; Kansas City Royals, 1982-83.

★ Named A.L. MVP in 1971   ★ Played in three World Series
★ Won the A.L. Cy Young award in 1971   ★ Named to six All-Star teams
★ Pitched a no-hitter against the Minnesota Twins in 1970

MAJOR LEAGUE TOTALS

G	IP	W	L	Pct.	SO	BB	ERA
502	3,344	209	161	.565	2,175	1,185	3.26

Oakland A's lefthander Vida Blue had a great 1971 season, going 24-8 with a league-leading
1.82 ERA. He also threw eight shutouts and racked up 301 strikeouts, winning both the
league MVP and Cy Young awards. In six different seasons, Blue had an ERA under 3.00.

BERT BLYLEVEN

After 20 seasons, Bert Blyleven is quietly becoming one of the most accomplished pitchers in baseball history. Among the biggest winners in history, Blyleven has relied on consistency to eclipse record after record in the late 1980s.

Born Rik Aalbert Blyleven in The Netherlands in 1951, Bert Blyleven completed his 20th major league season in 1989, extending a career that began in 1970 with Rookie Pitcher of the Year honors for the American League. Even though many fans consider Blyleven one of baseball's seasoned veterans, the gifted righthander was only 38 years old when the 1989 season began.

Blyleven was traded back to the Twins at the close of the 1985 season, having played for the Rangers, Pirates, and Indians in the interim. At first glance, a team that plays its home games in a stadium known as the "Homerdome" would seem to have little use for a pitcher with the reputation as one of baseball's most frequent home run victims. For although Blyleven set a major league record in 1986 by serving up 50 home runs in a season, it was also his eighth season at striking out more than 200 batters, setting a league record.

Drafted by the Twins in 1969, Blyleven pitched only 21 minor league games before coming to the major leagues permanently in 1970. After compiling 99 wins with Minnesota, he was traded with Danny Thompson on June 1, 1976, to the Texas Rangers for Bill Singer, Roy Smalley, Mike Cubbage, Jim Gideon, and $250,000. Blyleven was in the midst of what would be his sixth consecutive season striking out more than 200 batters. Dealt to Pittsburgh in December 1977 for Al Oliver and Nelson Norman, Blyleven had a 12-5 record in the Pirates 1979 world championship season, including 1 win each in the League Championship Series and the World Series. After going 8-13 the following season—only the second losing record of his career—Blyleven was traded with catcher Manny Sanguillen to the Cleveland Indians for Gary Alexander, Victor Cruz, Rafael Vasquez, and Bob Owchinko.

He rebounded with an 11-7 record and 2.89 ERA in 1981 but spent virtually the entire 1982 season on the disabled list with his first major injury in 13 seasons. He was in fine shape in 1984, however, leading the Indians with a 19-7 mark. The team finished in sixth place with a 75-87 mark.

Blyleven went back home to Minnesota in a trade on August 1, 1985. It cost the Twins three minor league prospects to get their one-time pitching ace back, but it was worth it. He immediately put together back-to-back strikeout seasons of 206 (tops in the American League) and 215. Blyleven won 17 and 15 games in his first two seasons back with Minnesota. The veteran hurler picked up his second World Series ring with the 1987 Twins. He won two games during Minnesota's five-game trouncing of the Tigers, then won the second game of the World Series.

The 1989 California Angels probably saw many benefits in acquiring Blyleven. He joined a young pitching staff that could benefit from his wisdom and his competitiveness. His knowledge makes him an unofficial "coach" available to less experienced hurlers. Blyleven still maintains four different pitches—an above-average fastball, a changeup, a slider, and the awesome curveball that has been his ticket to success. He helped the surprising Angels to 91 wins in 1989 by going 17-5 with a 2.73 ERA, 8 complete games, 5 shutouts, and 131 strikeouts.

It's hard to imagine what Blyleven's totals could have been with higher-quality lineups to support him. As it is, Blyleven's 254 wins tie him for 34th place on the all-time list. Last year he passed Phil Niekro for seventh place on the all-time strikeout list. It's conceivable that Blyleven could approach 300 wins and 4,000 strikeouts before his career ends. Such feats would guarantee him a place in the Hall of Fame. His stats already surpass a whole crop of current HOF members. Because he has just one 20-game season to savor, such post-career honors might be the most fitting reward Blyleven could earn after pitching for so many mediocre clubs.

Righthand pitcher Bert Blyleven, has won in double figures 16 times in 19 seasons. He started his major league career in 1970 by winning 10 games and being named A.L. Rookie Pitcher of the Year. Blyleven has hurled at least 250 innings in nine seasons.

CAREER HIGHLIGHTS
RIK AALBERT BLYLEVEN

Born: April 6, 1951   Zeist, The Netherlands
Height: 6'3"   **Weight:** 200 lbs.   **Bats:** Right   **Throws:** Right
Pitcher: Minnesota Twins, 1970-76, 1985-88; Texas Rangers, 1976-77; Pittsburgh Pirates, 1978-80; Cleveland Indians, 1981-85; California Angels, 1989.

★ Pitched a no-hitter against California Angels on September 22, 1977
★ A.L. Rookie Pitcher of the Year in 1970
★ Pitched in two World Series
★ In 27th place for lifetime wins
★ Seventh-highest career strikeout total

MAJOR LEAGUE TOTALS

G	IP	W	L	Pct.	SO	BB	ERA
644	4,702.2	271	231	.540	3,562	1,268	3.22

WADE BOGGS

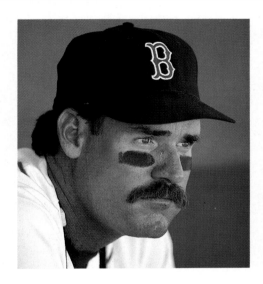

ade Boggs, a seventh-round draft pick by the Boston Red Sox in 1976, batted .263 for Elmira in the New York-Penn League that year—the only year of his entire career in which he hit less than .300. The next year he hit .332 at Winston-Salem in the Carolina League. When he won the International League batting title with a .335 effort in 1980, the Red Sox finally gave Boggs his chance. Since the Nebraska native had no reputation as a collegiate diamond star to build on, he had to do some mighty slugging to earn a spot on the offensively loaded Boston club.

Boggs practically arrived on the major league scene as a superstar, hitting .349 for the Red Sox in his rookie season of 1982.

Boggs' career in the major leagues has been marked by high averages and record-breaking accomplishments. From his rookie season through 1989, his worst batting average was .325, in 1984! As of the 1989 season, his lifetime average was .352. He won five American League batting titles in his first seven years in the majors. For seven consecutive years (1983-89) he produced 200 or more hits. Even more incredible is the fact that he is the first major leaguer to have 200 or more hits plus 100 or more walks in the same season since power hitter Stan Musial accomplished the feat back in 1953.

In addition to his offensive prowess, Boggs' fielding at third base is outstanding, making him the complete player. He led American League third basemen in the 1986 season with 121 putouts. Twice he has led A.L. third basemen in double plays. Bill James in his *Baseball Abstract* rates Boggs, who bats leadoff and had an on-base percentage of .445 after the 1989 season, as the best third baseman in the American League. Because he wasn't a full-time third basemen until he joined Boston, Boggs has worked extra hard to perfect his defensive skills. He has a strong, accurate throwing arm and can handle anything hit his way.

In the 1986 American League playoffs, he batted only .233, which was quite a slump for Boggs. His hitting improved for the World Series, though, where he averaged .290. A torn right hamstring, which had kept him on the bench for the last four games of the regular season, undoubtedly contributed to these disappointing postseason statistics. Boggs reestablished his fame during the 1988 American League playoffs

versus the Oakland Athletics. Even though the A's swept Boston in four straight games, Boggs had a .385 average—the highest for any player on either team.

Perhaps Boggs' only weakness has been his inability to club the ball out of the park. In his first five seasons of play, he managed only 32 home runs, with never more than eight per season. In the 1987 campaign, however, he proved he had the power, smashing a total of 24 round-trippers for the year. During 1988 his homers dropped again, to five. Nor is Boggs a typical speedy leadoff hitter who swipes tons of bases. For his career, Boggs has just 14 stolen bases, and never more than three per season. In 1988 he grounded into 23 double plays, an A.L. high.

Boggs has maintained his batting eye through the years. After winning four batting titles during his first six seasons, some fans may have wondered if he could continue such a pace. In 1988

Boggs and Minnesota's Kirby Puckett dueled for the batting crown all year long. Puckett finished with a .356 average, but Boggs compiled a spiffy .366 mark to claim the title. Such high averages are commonplace for Boggs; he's topped the .360 barrier four times.

Additionally, Boggs led the junior circuit in several other categories in 1988: runs (128), doubles (45), walks (125), intentional walks (18), and on-base percentage (.480, 64 points higher than second-place Mike Greenwell at .416). Rumors of Boggs' marital problems following the 1988 season made some skeptics believe that his off-the-field difficulties would hamper his career. Boggs answered with a 2-for-4 opening day performance to start the 1989 season, silencing most of his detractors.

Astonishingly, Boggs spent six years in the minor leagues before making the Red Sox team at the start of the 1982 season. In the minors he played all of the infield positions before whittling down his choices to first and third base in his 1980 and 1981 seasons with Triple-A Pawtucket. When Boggs first made the Red Sox in 1982, he played first base, third base, and outfield for 104 games. Because his .349 average far outdistanced anyone else on the team, he earned the starting third baseman's job the next season.

Boggs has become one of the premier hitters in baseball. He's a disciplined batsman in the mold of Ted Williams, seldom chasing pitches that aren't strikes. He has long-ball power but has conserved it in favor of being on base regularly. At age 30 when the 1989 season began, Boggs should be a major star in baseball for at least another decade.

CAREER HIGHLIGHTS
WADE ANTHONY BOGGS

Born: June 15, 1958   Omaha, NE
Height: 6'2"   **Weight:** 185 lbs.   **Bats:** Right   **Throws:** Right
Third baseman: Boston Red Sox, 1982-89.

* Hit .290 with nine hits in the 1986 World Series
* Hit .385 in the 1988 playoffs
* Had 200-plus hits for a record seven seasons
* Established a major league record for highest rookie batting average in 1982
* Four-time All-Star
* Five-time A.L. batting champion

MAJOR LEAGUE TOTALS

G	AB	H	BA	2B	3B	HR	R	RBI	SB
1,183	4,534	1,597	.352	314	36	64	823	523	14

After the 1988 season, Wade Boggs had a lifetime .356 batting average and five A.L. batting titles in his first seven years. He has also scored at least 100 runs in six consecutive seasons. Boggs has led A.L. third baseman in double plays in two seasons.

BOBBY BONDS

Bobby Bonds may be best-known today as the father of Pittsburgh Pirates star outfielder Barry Bonds; however, during the early 1970s the senior Bonds was baseball's best example of how a player can successfully mix power and speed.

Giants scout Evo Pusich discovered Bonds at Riverside City College. Other scouts had viewed Bonds in collegiate play but felt he couldn't hit breaking pitches. Scout Pusich told the team's farm system director that he'd stake his job on Bonds' ability.

The gamble paid off. It took only two and a half seasons for Bonds to reach the big leagues. He debuted with the Giants in mid-1968, playing in 81 contests. During that rookie season he hit .254 with 9 homers, 35 RBI, and 16 stolen bases. One highlight of Bonds' inaugural campaign was a grand slam homer in his first game. He pounded the historic blast off Dodgers pitcher John Purdin on June 25, 1968, for his first major league hit.

Bonds earned a starting outfield berth on the 1969 team. He played right field, beside immortal center fielder Willie Mays. In his first full season, Bonds established himself as a multi-faceted offensive weapon. He reached the "30/30" club with 32 homers and 45 stolen bases. Although he hit .259 with 90 RBI, Bonds was also the victim of 187 strikeouts, then a record. In 1970 Bonds racked up a record 189 strikeouts, which overshadowed his 26 homers and 48 stolen bases. His totals included a career-high 134 runs scored (a team record at that time) and a .302 average.

The 1969 Giants won 90 games, but the Atlanta Braves clinched the pennant with three more victories. But in 1971, the Giants posted a 90-72 record to win the Western Division over the Dodgers by one game. Bonds was a major asset in the pennant drive, hitting .288 with 33 homers and 102 RBI. He narrowly missed the "30/30" club, stealing just 26 bases. Impressively, he cut his strikeouts from 189 to 137. That year, Bonds led all National League right fielders with a .994 fielding average. Although the Giants lost the playoffs to the Pirates in four games, Bonds hit .250 in the Series.

In 1972 Bonds scored 118 runs, the fourth straight year he had crossed the plate at least 100 times. He batted .259 with 26 homers and 80 RBI with 44 stolen bases (fourth highest in the league). Bonds repeated his success in

1973 by scoring a league-high 131 runs. Until the final days of the season, fans thought Bonds would break the "40/40" barrier. He fell short of his quest, however, finishing with 39 homers (fifth best in the league), 96 RBI, 43 stolen bases, and a .283 average.

One of the most talked-about trades following the 1974 season involved Bonds. He was swapped to the Yankees for slugger Bobby Murcer on October 22. Bonds was an immediate success in New York, hitting 32 homers, 85 RBI, and .270. He stole 30 bases, which made him the first player ever to achieve the "30/30" combination in both leagues. But the stats don't tell the full story of Bonds' season. On June 7, he fell in the outfield while making a game-saving catch against the White Sox at Comiskey Park. He played hurt

the rest of the season. At the time of the injury, Bonds was leading the American league with 15 homers and 45 RBI after just 51 games. After being injured, Bonds never regained his hitting form that year.

Following the 1975 season, Bonds returned to California through another trade. The pitching-hungry Yankees sent Bonds to the Angels on December 11, 1975, for hurler Ed Figueroa and outfielder Mickey Rivers.

Injuries haunted Bonds again in 1976. He injured the middle finger on his right hand during an April 3 exhibition game with the Dodgers. He had only partial use of the hand for the rest of the season and had to have surgery in early August to remove a bone chip. Bonds played in only 99 games.

Bonds was the unsung hero on the 1977 Angels team. Team owner Gene Autry recruited free agents Joe Rudi, Don Baylor, and Bob Grich in hopes of a quick pennant; but all three were riddled with injuries. Meanwhile, Bonds was healthy for the first time in three seasons. He set several club records and tied the Angels homer mark with 37 (once held by Leon Wagner).

On December 5, 1977, Bonds was part of a six-player trade between the Angels and the White Sox. After just 26 games with the White Sox, Bonds was shipped to the Texas Rangers for Claudell Washington and Rusty Torres. Bonds played his final full season in 1979 with the Cleveland Indians. He finished his career as a part-time player with the 1980 St. Louis Cardinals and the 1981 Chicago Cubs. Bonds retired after an unsuccessful comeback in 1982.

CAREER HIGHLIGHTS
BOBBY LEE BONDS

Born: March 15, 1946   Riverside, CA
Height: 6'1"   **Weight:** 190 lbs.   **Batted:** Right   **Threw:** Right
Outfielder, designated hitter: San Francisco Giants, 1968-74; New York Yankees, 1975; California Angels, 1976-77; Chicago White Sox, 1978; Texas Rangers, 1978; Cleveland Indians, 1979; St. Louis Cardinals, 1980; Chicago Cubs, 1981.

★ First player to have 30 steals and 30 home runs in both leagues

★ Hit a grand slam in his first big league game

★ Bobby and son Barry are the all-time father/son home run duo

★ Led the N.L. in runs scored twice

MAJOR LEAGUE TOTALS

G	AB	H	BA	2B	3B	HR	R	RBI	SB
1,849	7,043	1,886	.268	302	66	332	1,258	1,024	461

Bobby Bonds slugged at least 30 home runs and stole at least 30 bases in four seasons. He is the first player to have had a 30/30 season in both leagues. In 1973, Bonds almost reached the 40/40 mark, getting 39 home runs and 43 stolen bases.

BOB BOONE

If anyone wants to bet on a long-shot for eventual membership in the Baseball Hall of Fame, Bob Boone is a good choice.

Boone's hitting stats don't jump off the page like those of fellow catchers Yogi Berra or Gary Carter. He has never been a defensive dynamo like Johnny Bench or Roy Campanella. Still, Boone has remained a quality backstop through the years with both the glove and the bat. Most importantly, he's been behind the plate for an incredible 2,093 games—the most in history.

Boone is the son of Ray Boone, who played the infield in 1948-60 for six different teams. The younger Boone has been active in the majors since his 1972 debut with the Philadelphia Phillies. Boone was signed by the Phillies organization as a third baseman in 1969, after he received a Bachelor of Arts degree in psychology from Stanford University. Being a player who graduated from college before starting his pro career made Boone an oddity from the start. Furthermore, he didn't take up catching until 1971, when he was a member of the Double-A Reading Phillies.

The Phillies promoted Boone in 1972 to Eugene in the Pacific Coast League. That year Boone distinguished himself as a fine catcher and capable batsman.

Boone got a late-season call-up to the Phillies in 1972 and appeared in 16 games. The following year he became the club's regular catcher, replacing Tim McCarver. In 1973 Boone played in 145 games and batted .261 with 10 homers and 61 RBI. In the same year Phillies pitcher Steve Carlton won only 13 games (down from a career-high 27 wins the previous season). It wasn't long before Boone and Carlton began to clash both on and off the field, with the talented lefthander blaming Boone for his pitching problems. Eventually the dilemma was resolved by assigning McCarver, Carlton's old teammate from St. Louis, as Carlton's "designated catcher." After a few seasons, the rift was mended and Boone resumed catching for everyone on the pitching staff.

Throughout the 1970s, Boone remained a steady presence in the Phillies lineup. Johnny Oates shared some of the starting catcher's duties for the 1975 club and Boone only appeared in 92 games behind the plate that year. Boone won his position back in 1976 and landed on *The Sporting*

News All-Star team as the Phillies won the Eastern Division pennant. Boone fielded flawlessly in Philadelphia's playoff loss to Cincinnati, while hitting .286.

Boone and the Phillies were division winners for three of the next four seasons. In 1980 Philadelphia downed Houston in a five-game playoff series. The Phillies went on to the World Series against the Kansas City Royals, with Boone hitting a team-leading .412 with 4 RBI and 3 runs scored. Boone was behind the plate for every game and fielded errorlessly.

During the 1981 baseball season, which was drastically shortened by the baseball strike, Boone experienced his worst year—hitting just .211 in 76 games. This was shocking considering that his average was in the .280s for 1977-79. Some fans assumed that his career was finished—that he was washed up at age 34. Boone, on the other hand, believed he had a lot more to give to the game of baseball, and his

career picked up again when the California Angels purchased his contract on December 6, 1981.

Angels manager Gene Mauch and Boone worked well together, and the two of them have gotten more than could have been expected from the Angels pitching staff over the past several seasons. In his first season in his native state of California, Boone hit .256 with 7 homers and 58 RBI. Boone was the American League's top catcher with 87 assists and 650 putouts. The Angels won their division for the first time ever in 1982.

In 1986 Boone had a minor falling-out with the Angels when he declared himself a free agent during a salary squabble that reportedly involved less than $50,000. As there is a limited market for 39-year-old backstops, Boone soon found himself on the outside of the major leagues looking in. Boone kept the Angels interest, however, with a strong showing in the 1986 playoffs and re-signed with California in May 1987. The division-winning Angels lost the 1986 playoffs to the Boston Red Sox in seven games, but Boone tied three postseason records and established another. He hit a league record .455 with 10 hits. Nine of those hits were singles and one was a homer. Five of the hits came consecutively. Again, Boone had a perfect fielding average in the playoffs.

Following the 1987 season the Angels acquired catcher Lance Parrish, making Boone expendable. As a free agent, Boone was gobbled up by the Kansas City Royals, who saw his ability to shape young hurlers into winners. Boone celebrated his 18th major league season in 1989.

CAREER HIGHLIGHTS
ROBERT RAYMOND BOONE

Born: November 19, 1947   San Diego, CA
Height: 6'2½"   **Weight:** 195 lbs.   **Bats:** Right   **Throws:** Right
Catcher: Philadelphia Phillies, 1972-81; California Angels, 1982-88; Kansas City Royals, 1989.

- ★ Established a major league lifetime record for the most games caught
- ★ Hit .412 in the 1980 World Series
- ★ Set a major league record by catching 100-plus games for 15 seasons
- ★ Has played in four All-Star games
- ★ Played in six league championships

MAJOR LEAGUE TOTALS

G	AB	H	BA	2B	3B	HR	R	RBI	SB
2,224	7,128	1,810	.254	300	26	105	668	817	37

Catcher Bob Boone has been behind the plate for well over 2,000 games. After the 1989 season, his longevity mark may actually be untouchable. Although not a great hitter, Boone's stats are comparable to those of several backstops who have made it into the Hall of Fame.

JIM BOTTOMLEY

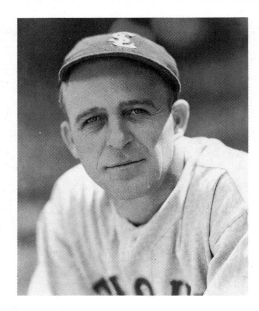

One of the longest-standing records in major league baseball history belongs to Jim Bottomley. In an awesome display of hitting skill, Bottomley set a record in 1924 that stands to this day—12 RBI in one nine-inning game. Playing for the St. Louis Cardinals, "Sunny Jim" (as he was known because of his sparkling personality) accomplished the amazing feat against the Dodgers in Brooklyn's Ebbets Field on September 16. He was perfect—6 hits in six trips to the plate, including 2 home runs (one a grand slam), 1 double, and 3 singles. The Cardinals enjoyed a 17-3 victory. Bottomley exploded for another 6-for-6 game seven years later.

Bottomley drove a grocery truck in Nokomis, Illinois, during his youth, playing semipro baseball mainly on Sundays. He earned $5 a game. After Bottomley started his pro career with the 1922 St. Louis Cardinals, he still returned to Nokomis and served as a town policeman during the off-season. At the beginning of his baseball career, Bottomley hoped to be a lefthand pitcher, but coaches encouraged Bottomley to try first base or the outfield instead. He played for a Witt, Illinois, semipro team in September 1919, earning $7.50 for each game. On Labor Day he thumped 3 triples and 2 homers. A St. Louis policeman who attended the game contacted Cardinals scout Charley Barrett. In 1920 Barrett signed Bottomley, and he joined a minor league affiliate in Sioux City, Iowa.

Bottomley finished the 1920 season in Mitchell, South Dakota, where he hit .312 in 97 games. In 1921 Bottomley moved to a Texas League club in Houston. Although he hit just .227 in 130 games, he was promoted to Syracuse the following year. The Illinois native tore up International League pitching in 1922. In just 119 games he tallied 160 hits with 14 homers and a whopping .348 average. Bottomley stole 13 bases and added a .992 fielding average.

A late-season promotion brought Bottomley to the Cardinals where he hit .325 with 5 homers in 37 games. In 1923, his first full season, Bottomley hit a blistering .371 with 8 homers and 94 RBI. Bottomley's impressive offensive stats in 1924 included 14 homers, 111 RBI, and a .316 average. Bottomley said that his 12-RBI day was the greatest thrill in his career.

Bottomley's average soared in 1925: He played 153 games, hitting .367 with

21 homers and 128 RBI. The big first sacker paced the National League with 44 doubles and 227 hits. However, even though Bottomley posted large averages in 1923 and 1925, he didn't lead even his own team in hitting. Teammate Rogers Hornsby won five straight batting titles from 1920-25, hitting more than .400 three times.

During the 1926 season Bottomley played in all 154 games and led the National League with 40 doubles, 120 RBI, and 305 total bases. His 19 homers were second only to league leader Hack Wilson's 21. In his first-ever World Series, Bottomley hit .345 with 10 hits and 5 RBI as the Cardinals won the Series against the Yankees in seven games.

Perhaps Bottomley's greatest power-hitting season ever came in 1928. He was first in the National League with 31 homers and 136 RBI to match a .325 average. Even though he hit only .214

in the 1928 World Series (a four-game sweep by the New York Yankees), Bottomley was named the National League's Most Valuable Player. Bottomley's highest RBI total ever was 137, which came in 1929.

The Cardinals finished the 1931 season as world champions, defeating the Philadelphia Athletics in seven games. Bottomley hit just .160 in the Series, so St. Louis replaced Sunny Jim with a player named James "Ripper" Collins. The Cardinals traded Bottomley to the Cincinnati Reds on December 17, 1932, for Estel Crabtree and Ownie Carroll. Few people could criticize Bottomley's cumulative performance during his first 11 seasons in St. Louis: He hit .325 with 177 homers throughout his reign as a Cardinal. Only twice did Bottomley hit less than .300.

Cincinnati's newly acquired first baseman made news before the 1933 season by marrying Betty Brawner on February 4. *Who's Who in Major League Baseball* for 1933 stated: "For years James LeRoy [Bottomley] was the choice of Mound City diamond fannettes, but just before reporting to the Cincinnati training camp he up and committed matrimony."

Bottomley led his Reds with 13 homers in 1933, but his accomplishments didn't come close to his achievements as a Cardinal. The Reds posted two last-place finishes in his three years in Cincinnati. The St. Louis Browns acquired him for the 1936 season.

In mid-1937 Bottomley managed the Browns but was saddled with a 21-58 record. Upon retirement, Bottomley was listed among the top ten hitters in every offensive category for the Cardinals. Bottomley was honored by the Hall of Fame in 1974.

CAREER HIGHLIGHTS
JAMES LEROY BOTTOMLEY

Born: April 23, 1900   Oglesby, IL   **Died:** December 11, 1959
Height: 6'   **Weight:** 180 lbs.   **Batted:** Left   **Threw:** Left
First baseman: St. Louis Cardinals, 1922-32; Cincinnati Reds, 1933-35;
St. Louis Browns, 1936-37.

★ Twice went 6-for-6 at the plate
★ Played in four World Series
★ Selected as the N.L. MVP in 1928
★ Elected to the Hall of Fame in 1974
★ Established a record 12 RBI in one nine-inning game

MAJOR LEAGUE TOTALS

G	AB	H	BA	2B	3B	HR	R	RBI	SB
1,991	7,471	2,313	.310	465	151	219	1,177	1,422	58

Jim Bottomley's most noteworthy achievement was the record he set in 1924 for racking up 12 RBI in a single nine-inning game. He hit six times in six trips to the plate. Sunny Jim's feat was accomplished in Ebbets Field as Bottomley's St. Louis Cardinals beat the Dodgers 17-3.

LOU BOUDREAU

Thanks to cable TV and his long tenure as a Chicago Cubs broadcaster, Hall of Famer Lou Boudreau may be more widely known now than he was during his 22-year major league career as a player and manager.

Boudreau began his career in organized baseball in 1938 with a team in Cedar Rapids, Iowa. He was called up to Cleveland for one game that season. After starting the year in Buffalo, the Illinois native played in 53 games for the Indians in 1939. He hit a respectable .258 and proved to be a solid fielder. The Indians awarded Boudreau the starting shortstop job in 1940. Cleveland finished at 89-65 but lost the American League pennant to the Tigers by just one game. Boudreau hit .295, with 9 homers and a team-leading 101 RBI. He paced the American League with 116 double plays, 454 putouts, and a .968 fielding average. Before his playing career ended, Boudreau would lead the league in fielding eight times.

Long before Bo Jackson made news by playing both pro football and baseball, Boudreau was working in two sports as well. He played for a National Basketball Association franchise in Hammond, Indiana, in 1940 and 1941. Boudreau had been a basketball star both in high school and at the University of Illinois. Serving as a basketball team captain in school had been Boudreau's first test of leadership.

Boudreau landed his first skipper's job in Cleveland when he was a 24-year-old shortstop with just two full seasons under his belt. Over the next five years, the Indians struggled to a 450-464 win-loss record. New team owner Bill Veeck considered trading Boudreau to the St. Louis Browns, but a loyal following of fans in Cleveland protested the move. Veeck relented, and Boudreau repaid the loyalty with a world championship the following year. With Boudreau as their spark plug, the Indians clinched the American League pennant in a one-game playoff victory over the Boston Red Sox—a game in which Boudreau went 4-for-4 with a pair of homers, 2 singles, and a walk. The Indians won the game 8-3.

In the 1948 World Series, Boudreau's team downed the Boston Braves in six games. Boudreau's shrewd piloting and .273 batting average for the Series made the difference for the Indians. His many accomplishments that year included a career-high 18 homers, 106 RBI, and a .355 batting average, along with 199 base hits and 106 runs scored—all of which earned him the American League Most Valuable Player award.

One reason Boudreau enjoyed such mass adoration in Cleveland was that he was both a manager *and* a player. During the 1949 season Boudreau filled in around the infield. In earlier years, he had even served the Indians as a backup catcher. After playing only part-time during the 1950 season, Boudreau moved to the Boston Red Sox in 1951. In 1952, he hung up his bat and glove for good after only four games to assume managerial duties for Boston.

In his three seasons in Boston, Boudreau's best team came in 1953—finishing at 84-69. Today's clubs might win a pennant with such a high-quality record, but Boudreau's Red Sox could only get fourth place with those totals.

The fledgling Kansas City Athletics appointed Boudreau as manager in 1955, but even an experienced pilot like Boudreau couldn't coax a winning record out of the hapless A's. Boudreau's final managerial turn came in 1960, for the Chicago Cubs. Boudreau had started broadcasting Cubs games in 1958. In early 1960 he replaced Charlie Grimm as manager and Grimm became the team broadcaster. After one losing season, Boudreau stuck to full-time announcing duties for Chicago.

During his managerial career in the 1940s, Boudreau became famous for "the Williams shift." This strategy repositioned infielders toward the right side of the infield to combat the Boston Red Sox pull hitter Ted Williams. All infielders would play to the right of second base; only the left fielder would remain on the left side of the diamond by playing a deep shortstop. The plan was usually successful; however, in late 1946 Williams collected an inside-the-park homer by hitting to a vacant left field to beat the shift. Not only did the Red Sox win the game, they won the pennant as well.

Baseball seems to run in the Boudreau family's blood. Lou's father (Louis Boudreau, Sr.) was a semipro baseball player. One of Lou's children had a brief career in organized baseball. Boudreau's daughter married former Detroit Tigers pitcher Denny McLain.

Boudreau was elected to the Hall of Fame in 1970. His noteworthy records include a league-leading .327 batting average in 1944 and a lifetime average of .295 with 1,779 hits. When he retired, his fielding average was the best for any shortstop up to that time.

CAREER HIGHLIGHTS
LOUIS BOUDREAU

Born: July 17, 1917   Harvey, IL
Height: 5'11"   **Weight:** 185 lbs.   **Batted:** Right   **Threw:** Right
Infielder: Cleveland Indians, 1938-50; Boston Red Sox, 1951-52. Manager: Cleveland Indians, 1942-50; Boston Red Sox, 1952-54; Kansas City Athletics, 1955-57; Chicago Cubs, 1960.

★ Served as a player/manager at age 24   ★ Selected as the A.L. MVP in 1948
★ Elected to the Hall of Fame in 1970   ★ Led 1948 Indians to World Championship
★ Youngest person ever to manage a full season in the majors

MAJOR LEAGUE TOTALS

G	AB	H	BA	2B	3B	HR	R	RBI	SB
1,646	6,030	1,779	.295	385	66	68	861	789	51

Lou Boudreau, who played the bulk of his 22-year career as a shortstop for the Cleveland Indians, has been uniquely honored by the Tribe and the fans of Cleveland. The street outside that city's Municipal Stadium has been named Boudreau Boulevard in his honor.

LARRY BOWA

Larry Bowa was known for his fielding talent during his 16-year career in the major leagues. In fact, he is remembered as one of the best glove men of all time. His .980 lifetime fielding percentage is the highest for any shortstop in baseball history.

Bowa was signed by the Philadelphia Phillies organization on October 16, 1965, after attending Sacramento City College. His first season was at Spartanburg of the Western Carolina League in 1966 where the wiry infielder hit a tidy .312 and led the league in fielding with a .972 mark.

Bowa hit .316 the next year at San Diego, but military obligations limited him to only 29 games. In 1968 Bowa hit .242 in a full season with the Reading (Pennsylvania) team. His fielding dominance continued as he tied for the league lead with 395 assists. Bowa was promoted to Philadelphia's top minor league club in Eugene in 1969. He tried playing a bit of second base in hopes of making his skills more attractive to the Phillies.

The Phillies liked Bowa and brought him up to stay in the 1970 season. The talented rookie was given the starting shortstop job immediately. Bowa hit .250 and gave the Phillies high quality defense. In 1971 Bowa played in 159 games and led the National League with a .987 fielding percentage, 560 assists, 843 total chances, 97 double plays, and 650 at-bats. Bowa would lead the National League in fielding a record six times during his career.

In 1972 Bowa kept his league lead in shortstop fielding with an identical .987 average. This tied a National League record for the highest single-season fielding percentage. He also topped the National League with 13 triples and belted 1 homer (the first of only 15 in his major league career). Bowa's average stayed at a consistent .250, but his stolen base totals slipped from 28 in 1971 to a modest 17. The following season, Bowa was injured and spent nearly five weeks on the disabled list.

A comeback was in the works for Bowa in 1974, when he played a full slate of 162 games. He tallied the best offensive totals of his career, with a .275 average and 39 stolen bases. His .984 fielding percentage was a National League high.

Unfortunately, Bowa was injured for the second time in three seasons in 1975. He missed nearly a month of competition and played in only 136 games. The missed time didn't harm

Bowa's hitting, however; he hit .305, which would be the best average of his major league career.

Bowa and the Phillies had a lot to look forward to beginning in 1976. Philadelphia would win four division titles in the next five seasons, including three consecutive flags from 1976-78. During the 1976 season, the stalwart shortstop provided his usual tidy defense. Even though his average was down, Bowa drove in 49 runs—a career best. The season ended with the Reds sweeping the Phillies in the league play-offs.

Everything worked out for both Bowa and the Phillies in 1980. Bowa hit .267 with 2 homers and 39 RBI. The Phillies compiled a 91-71 record, won the five-game playoff against the Houston Astros, and captured their first National League championship since 1950. Bowa hit .316 in the playoffs, then batted a sparkling .375 in the World Series. It took only six games for Bowa and his teammates to capture the

championship against the Royals.

In an attempt to get a younger, faster shortstop, Philadelphia shipped Bowa to the Chicago Cubs in exchange for Ivan DeJesus on January 27, 1982. The Cubs wound up getting the best of the trade. In addition to the veteran shortstop, the Phillies threw in an extra player to sweeten the deal—an untested infielder named Ryne Sandberg. The Phillies lived to regret it.

The fact that Bowa had three decent seasons in Chicago was somewhat eclipsed by Sandberg's quick climb to fame. Bowa's fielding average was a league-leading .984 in 1983. The Cubs put Bowa into his fifth career National League playoff in 1984, but his opportunity for a second trip to the World Series got nipped by the San Diego Padres.

Bowa was released in midseason 1985 by the Cubs and finished his career with the New York Mets.

The San Diego Padres hired Bowa in 1986 to manage their top minor league team. Bowa was an immediate success, managing the Las Vegas Stars to the Pacific Coast League crown with an 80-62 record. Surprisingly, the Padres immediately promoted Bowa to pilot the major league club the next year. Bowa didn't last long. In 1987 San Diego finished sixth at 65-97. In 1988, after the team got off to a 16-31 start, the Padres fired Bowa. Since then, Bowa has coached for the Philadelphia Phillies.

In addition to his high seasonal and lifetime fielding percentages, Bowa holds the notable record of 2,222 games at shortstop. Despite his .260 lifetime batting average, Bowa did get 2,191 hits, more than several Hall of Fame shortstops.

CAREER HIGHLIGHTS
LAWRENCE ROBERT BOWA

Born: December 6, 1945 Sacramento, CA
Height: 5'10" **Weight:** 155 lbs. **Batted:** Right **Threw:** Right
Shortstop, second baseman: Philadelphia Phillies, 1970-81; Chicago Cubs, 1982-85; New York Mets, 1985. Manager: San Diego Padres, 1987-88.

- ★ Set a major league record for best fielding percentage for a shortstop
- ★ Hit .375 in the 1980 World Series
- ★ Set an N.L. record for most games at shortstop
- ★ Played in five All-Star games

MAJOR LEAGUE TOTALS

G	AB	H	BA	2B	3B	HR	R	RBI	SB
2,247	8,418	2,191	.260	262	99	15	987	525	318

Though fielding stars often have a difficult time getting into the Hall of Fame, Larry Bowa's stats show that he deserves consideration. Despite a mediocre .260 average, he accumulated 2,191 hits during his career and holds a record for appearing in 2,222 games as a shortstop.

KEN BOYER

Ken Boyer was a member of a baseball-loving family. All six of Ken's brothers played professional baseball, and two of them reached the major leagues. Older brother Cloyd Boyer had a five-year career pitching in the early 50s. Younger brother Clete played third base with the Kansas City Athletics, New York Yankees, and Atlanta Braves for 16 years.

Ken Boyer played third base, too. He was known for his combined fielding talent and power-hitting ability. Naturally, having two brothers play third base for two different teams during the same 15-year stretch brought lots of comparisons.

When the St. Louis Cardinals and the New York Yankees took the field in the 1964 World Series, some casual baseball fans may have been surprised to see that a Boyer was playing third base for both teams. It was an unusual situation that the baseball press delighted in dramatizing: brother against brother. The Cardinals won in a seven-game Series that saw both Boyers hit home runs—the only time two brothers homered in the same World Series.

Both of the Boyers made their baseball debuts in 1955. Clete played for the Kansas City Athletics that year, and Ken started at third base for the Cards. In his first year of minor league baseball, the Cardinals had used Boyer as a pitcher but then gave him the chance to play every day because of his .455 batting average. Boyer missed two seasons of minor league play due to service in the U.S. Army. Following his 1954 season at Houston (in which he hit .319 with 21 homers and 116 RBI), the Cardinals traded regular third baseman Ray Jablonski to the Cincinnati Reds. Boyer's rookie season was a success as he hit .264 with 18 homers and 62 RBI. The Cardinals, trying to find a long-term job for this native Missourian, gave him an 18-game trial at shortstop.

In 1956 Boyer's hitting improved to .306 with 26 homers and 98 RBI. His 37 double plays and 309 assists were tops for National League third basemen. Despite his fielding accomplishments, the Cardinals moved Boyer to center field in 1957 to make room for rookie Eddie Kasko (who later became a Boston Red Sox manager). The sure-handed Boyer made the adjustment easily, pacing center fielders with a dazzling .996 average. The defensive pressure didn't bother Boyer's hitting either as he supplied the Redbirds with 19 homers and 62 RBI.

Kasko moved to shortstop in 1958 to allow Boyer's return to the hot corner. The veteran third baseman remained one of the best in the business, pacing the National League in putouts (156), double plays (41), and total chances per game (3.7). Boyer's first-class hitting, including 23 homers and 90 RBI, was the best among any Cardinals regular.

Boyer hit right around .300 from 1958-62. He drove in at least 90 runs in each of those seasons and always hit 20-plus homers. All the while, the Cardinals lacked the stamina to win a National League title. Things were different in 1964, though. The Cardinals won a down-to-the-wire dogfight with the Philadelphia Phillies and the Cincinnati Reds to claim the pennant, finishing at 93-69—one game better than the Phils or Reds. Boyer's contributions to the pennant were numerous: He won the league's RBI crown with 119 and hit .295 with 24 homers and 100 runs scored.

Boyer's .222 average in the World Series doesn't reflect the assistance he provided in his team's world championship drive. Boyer had 6 hits (including 1 double and 2 homers), scored 5 runs, and drove in 6 more.

Boyer slumped in 1965 to a .260 average, partly because of an ailing back. The Cardinals traded Boyer to the New York Mets on October 20, 1965, in exchange for Al Jackson and Charley Smith. In just 136 games with the New York Mets, Boyer had a team-leading 61 RBI to complement 14 homers and a .266 average. Boyer divided his 1967 season between the Mets and the Chicago White Sox, then spent 1968 with the White Sox and the Los Angeles Dodgers. Boyer ended his career in 1969 as a pinch hitter for Los Angeles.

Beginning in 1970, Boyer started a career as a minor league manager. In 1971 and 1972 he was a coach in St. Louis for former teammate and manager Red Schoendienst. In 1974-76 Boyer managed Tulsa, the Cardinals top minor league affiliate, winning the American Association championship in 1974. As manager of the St. Louis Cardinals from 1978-80, Boyer had a career mark of 166-191.

Boyer was supposed to manage the Cardinals minor league club in Louisville in 1982, but he was diagnosed with lung cancer. He died before the season was over, at the age of 51. He finished his career with 282 homers, 1,141 RBI, 2,143 hits, and a .287 average.

Ken Boyer was one of six brothers to play pro baseball. In an unusual twist, the 1964 World Series pitted third baseman Ken Boyer of the Cardinals against third baseman Clete Boyer of the Yankees.

CAREER HIGHLIGHTS
KENTON BOYER

Born: May 20, 1931 Liberty, MO **Died:** September 7, 1982
Height: 6'1" **Weight:** 190 lbs. **Batted:** Right **Threw:** Right
Third baseman: St. Louis Cardinals, 1955-65; New York Mets, 1966-67; Chicago White Sox, 1967-68; Los Angeles Dodgers, 1968-69. Manager: St. Louis Cardinals, 1978-80.

★ Won the 1964 N.L. MVP award
★ Led N.L. center fielders in fielding in 1957
★ Played in the 1964 World Series
★ Won five Gold Gloves at third base

MAJOR LEAGUE TOTALS

G	AB	H	BA	2B	3B	HR	R	RBI	SB
2,034	7,455	2,143	.287	318	68	282	1,104	1,141	105

GEORGE BRETT

One of the top major league players for the past decade and a half, George Brett had accumulated a lifetime average of .310 by the end of the 1989 season. He has come closer to batting .400 than any player since Ted Williams in 1941. His leadership and high quality play have brought Kansas City six division titles in 17 years. Unfortunately, this great player's aggressiveness makes him injury-prone.

Brett first experienced the major leagues in 1973 when he was called up late in the season by the Royals, ultimately playing in only 13 games. He managed only 5 hits in 40 trips to the plate for a .125 batting average and began the following season back in the minors. After a brief stint for Triple-A Omaha in the American Association, he was again called up to the majors and has since remained in the big leagues. Ironically, Brett had a less-than-stellar minor league career. He hit .268 with 10 home runs and 68 RBI in 1972 for San Jose, and he led the league with 30 errors. His average never passed .300 for any minor league team.

The 1975 season gave the first hint of Brett's upcoming stardom. He led the American League with 195 hits and 634 at-bats, and his .308 average was the best in the Royals starting lineup. Brett displayed some welcome speed along with his hitting—topping the A.L. with 13 triples and 13 stolen bases. For the first time, he achieved power totals of 11 homers and 89 RBI.

More success followed in 1976. Brett won his first batting crown at age 23 with a .333 mark. He appeared in his first of ten All-Star games. He also tied a major league record by leading the league in triples for the second straight year. In the 1976 playoffs, the division-winning Royals were squeezed out by the Yankees in five games. Brett battered New York pitchers at a .444 clip (with 1 homer and 5 RBI) for the playoffs. Brett's three-run homer came in the eighth inning of the fifth game, and only a ninth-inning blast by Chris Chambliss saved the pennant for the Bronx Bombers.

With the aid of Brett's heavy hitting, the Royals won their division again in 1977 with a 102-60 mark (best in the American League). Although his average shrank to .312, Brett's run production soared. He clobbered 22 homers and 88 RBI to lead Kansas City into the A.L. playoffs. Brett batted .300 against the Yankees, but the Royals lost the series in five games.

Both teams won their divisions again in 1978. Brett missed 34 games due to injuries and wound up hitting .294 for the year; still, his 45 doubles gave him the league lead in that category. Brett made up for lost time by recovering for the playoffs where he hit .389 and belted 3 homers in game three. Five of Brett's seven hits in the playoffs went for extra bases.

Brett was the American League leader in both hits and triples in 1979. He wound up the year with 23 homers, 107 RBI, and a .329 average. His efforts were in vain, as the Angels took the divisional title away from Kansas City. Brett stepped up his efforts in 1980 and won both the league MVP award and Man of the Year honors from *The Sporting News*. Brett's award-winning totals included 24 homers, 118 RBI, and a league-best .390 average. The Royals finally defeated the Yankees in the playoffs, this time in three straight games. The final 4-2

victory was iced by a clutch three-run homer by Brett off ace Yankee reliever Goose Gossage. Although the Royals lost the Series to Philadelphia in six games, Brett collected 9 hits for a .375 average.

The Royals won their first world championship in 1985 against the St. Louis Cardinals. Brett chipped in with 30 homers for the season, 112 RBI, and a .335 average (his highest in five seasons). Brett had 3 homers, 5 RBI, and a .348 average as the Royals whipped the Toronto Blue Jays in the playoffs. The Royals rallied from a three-games-to-one deficit to win the Series. Brett's World Series exploits included 10 hits, 5 runs scored, and a .370 average.

Brett became Kansas City's regular first baseman in 1987 when he began to have chronic shoulder problems. Kevin Seitzer took over at third and became an instant hit. Meanwhile, Brett put in two stints on the disabled list. For the third time in his career, he was unable to appear in the All-Star game due to an injury. He finished the season at .290 with 22 homers and 78 RBI.

The 1988 season saw Brett back in high gear. He played in 157 games and led the Royals with a .306 average and 103 RBI. His 300 total bases ranked fourth in the American League, and his 42 doubles were second. For fans who think Brett isn't feared by league pitchers anymore, consider that he received 15 intentional walks in 1988; only Wade Boggs, Mike Greenwell, and Greg Brock had more.

George Brett could have his 3,000th hit in three more seasons. Regardless of whether he achieves that milestone or not, Brett's eventual Hall of Fame membership is a sure bet.

CAREER HIGHLIGHTS
GEORGE HOWARD BRETT

Born: May 15, 1953   Glen Dale, WV
Height: 6'0"   **Weight:** 185 lbs.   **Bats:** Left   **Throws:** Right
Third baseman, first baseman, designated hitter: Kansas City Royals, 1973-89.

- ★ Named A.L. MVP in 1980
- ★ Won batting titles in 1976 and 1980
- ★ Has a lifetime .373 batting average for two World Series
- ★ Three-time A.L. leader in triples
- ★ Led the A.L. in hits three times
- ★ Holds a .340 mark for six A.L. playoffs

MAJOR LEAGUE TOTALS

G	AB	H	BA	2B	3B	HR	R	RBI	SB
2,137	8,148	2,528	.310	514	120	267	1,300	1,311	175

A powerful hitter, George Brett has come the closest to batting .400 since Ted Williams last accomplished the feat in 1941. Brett won batting titles in 1976 and 1980, with a .333 and .329 average respectively. Brett was also named the A.L. MVP in 1980.

LOU BROCK

At the time, it appeared to be an equal trade—a 29-year-old pitcher who had averaged 15 wins a year for the St. Louis Cardinals over his past four seasons, for a 25-year-old Chicago Cubs outfielder who showed promise but had batted only .260 during his first two years in the majors. Almost immediately after the Cubs had traded away Lou Brock for Ernie Broglio, they discovered they had made a big mistake. Playing the rest of his career in St. Louis, Brock went on to record over 3,000 base hits, steal a record 938 bases, and lead the Cardinals to three pennants and two world championships. Broglio, on the other hand, won only seven more games the rest of his career.

The Cardinals got a good deal in Brock. Upon joining the Cardinals in 1964, he entered the starting lineup. By season's end, Brock had 12 homers, 44 RBI, and a blistering .348 average. Most importantly, Brock had 33 stolen bases.

Brock led the National League with 74 stolen bases in 1966, the first of eight seasons in which he'd accomplish the feat. Brock also set a modern record by stealing at least 50 bases during 12 seasons. In 1967 Brock was a motivating force in the team's world championship against the Boston Red Sox. During the regular season Brock hit .299 with 21 homers and 76 RBI (career highs). His National League bests included 689 at-bats, 113 runs scored, and 52 stolen bases. In the 1967 Series, Brock collected 7 more stolen bases to go with 12 hits, 8 runs scored, and a .414 average.

In 1968 the Cardinals easily defended their National League title, winning 97 games. Brock duplicated his success as well, leading the National League with 46 doubles, 14 triples, and 62 stolen bases. While the Tigers nipped the Cardinals in a seven-game World Series in 1968, Brock provided some bright spots for the Cardinals: He hit .464 with a record 13 hits (two of them home runs), 5 RBI, and 7 stolen bases against Detroit.

The Cardinals fell on hard times with two straight fourth-place finishes in 1969 and 1970. But Brock's 1970 season was his best in three years—with 13 homers, 57 RBI, a .304 average, and 51 stolen bases. However, Cincinnati's Bobby Tolan swiped six more bases than Brock to lead in that department (the only time from 1966-74 that Brock didn't win a stolen base title).

The following season brought about Brock's second All-Star berth. He earned the trip with a .313 average, 200 hits, and 64 stolen bases. The Cardinals wound up winning 90 games, only seven games short of a pennant. A fourth-place finish awaited the Cardinals in 1972. Brock's 193 hits were second highest in the league as he ended with a .311 mark. St. Louis, even at 81-81, missed a pennant by just one game in 1973. Brock ended the year at .297 with 7 homers and 63 RBI. At that time, his 70 steals were the second highest of his career.

Brock earned a permanent place in history in 1974 by stealing 118 bases in a single season. Rickey Henderson has since broken the mark, but Brock's achievement will always be remembered. Chants of "Lou-Lou-Lou" greeted Brock all year long in his quest for the new milestone. Finally, on September 10 in front of a home crowd, Brock shattered Maury Wills'

previous record of 104 steals. He tied the mark with a first-inning steal, also setting a new National League record with 739 pilfers. In the seventh inning against Philadelphia pitcher Dick Ruthven, Brock led off with a single. He waited only one pitch before taking off and completing his second steal.

Brock's 118 steals moved him from ninth to second on the all-time list for stolen bases. It seemed possible that Brock could pass both lifetime leader Ty Cobb at 892 and all-time leader Billy Hamilton at 937. Hamilton's mark was due to an old rule: Prior to 1898, a runner was credited for a stolen base for each extra base advanced on another player's hit.

At the same time, fans wondered just how many hits Brock could achieve before his retirement. When he singled off Phillies pitcher Jim Kaat on September 27, 1976, Brock collected his 2,700th career hit. On August 29, 1977, Brock stole second base against the San Diego Padres in the seventh inning to break Cobb's record. The National League announced that in the future the Lou Brock award would be given to the league's top basestealer. This was the first time an award was named for an active player.

Disappointment met Brock in 1978. He collected just 66 hits (batting .221). He ended the year with 100 less than the 3,000-hit mark he coveted.

Brock returned for one last season in 1979, and staged a memorable comeback—hitting .304, his best in four years. On August 13 versus Chicago Cubs pitcher Dennis Lamp, Brock got his 3,000th hit. He also stole 21 bases that year, just enough to pass Hamilton's 1800s mark and earn the undisputed title of baseball's stolen base king.

CAREER HIGHLIGHTS
LOUIS CLARK BROCK

Born: June 18, 1939   El Dorado, AR
Height: 5'11½"   **Weight:** 170 lbs.   **Batted:** Left   **Threw:** Left
Outfielder: Chicago Cubs, 1961-64; St. Louis Cardinals, 1964-79.

- ★ Ranks first in lifetime stolen bases with 938
- ★ Established a record of 12 straight seasons with more than 50 steals
- ★ Named to the N.L. All-Stars six times
- ★ Batted .391 in three World Series
- ★ Elected to the Hall of Fame in 1985

MAJOR LEAGUE TOTALS

G	AB	H	BA	2B	3B	HR	R	RBI	SB
2,616	10,332	3,023	.293	486	141	149	1,610	900	938

Lou Brock's best seasons came after he was traded to the St. Louis Cardinals by the Chicago Cubs. Much to the dismay of the Cubs, Brock stole 33 bases his first year as a Redbird. He went on to lead the N.L. in stolen bases for eight years.

THREE-FINGER BROWN

You might say that Mordecai Brown reached the Hall of Fame by accident—a childhood farm accident that cost him part of two fingers and led to his distinctive nickname, Three-Finger Brown. He won 20 or more games for six straight seasons between 1906 and 1911, notching a career-high 27 victories in 1909.

Mordecai Peter Centennial Brown was born in 1876 as America was celebrating its 100th birthday, which accounts for his extra middle name. The farm accident came seven years later, when he stuck his right hand into a feed chopper. To complicate matters, before his fingers had fully healed, he fell down chasing a pig and broke the third and fourth fingers of the same hand. Throughout his 14-year career, Brown always claimed that his apparent handicap allowed him to throw the wicked curveball that baffled the best batters.

Brown's first taste of organized baseball was playing for a small Indiana semipro team consisting mostly of minors. He played third base for this club, but pitched for Terre Haute in 1901 and went 23-8. The following season, Brown posted a 27-15 mark. His success led to a big league career that began with the 1903 St. Louis Cardinals. After a 9-13 rookie year, the Redbirds shipped Brown and Jack O'Neill to the Chicago Cubs in exchange for Jack Taylor and Larry McLean. Brown immediately blossomed for the Cubs. In 1904 he went 15-10 with a 1.86 ERA. Brown led National League relievers with a 2-0 mark that year. Following an 18-12, 2.17 ERA outing in 1905, Brown soon became one of the dominant pitchers in baseball. A 26-6 record with an incredible league-best 1.04 ERA was Brown's season in 1906, the first of six straight years in which the Indiana native would win 20 or more decisions. His 10 shutouts were tops in the National League. Brown had a 1-2 record in the World Series. Chicago's two teams, the Cubs and the White Sox, met in the fall classic. The Sox won in six games.

The Cubs won the 1907 World Series with Brown hurling a shutout for the decisive win. During the regular season, Brown was 20-6 with a 1.39 ERA. In 1908 the Cubs won it all again. Brown had a career-best 29-9 record with a 1.47 ERA and 5 saves. The sly righthander beat the Tigers twice in the 1908 Series, throwing 11 scoreless innings.

Brown was one of baseball's first

"swing men," alternating between the starting rotation and the bullpen. From 1908-11, Brown led the National League in saves with a total of 32. This was in addition to a league-leading 27-9 record in 1909, 25 wins in 1910, and 21 in 1911. Brown's ERA was only 1.31 in 1909 and reached 1.86 in 1910. In 1911 Brown paced the league with 13 saves and 53 appearances.

After posting a losing season with the Cubs in 1912 and with Cincinatti in 1913, Brown became a star in the short-lived Federal League. He played with teams in St. Louis and Brooklyn in 1914, amassing a 14-11 mark. The next season, he helped the Chicago Whales to a league title. Brown's efforts included a 17-8 record with a 2.09 ERA and 18 complete games. At the season's end, the financially strapped team sold nearly its entire roster to the Chicago Cubs.

In his heydey, Brown's only mound rival in the league was the great New York Giants pitcher Christy Mathewson, and the two were famous for their pitching duels. In 24 such contests, Brown came out on top 13 times, including nine in a row. His most dramatic win came in 1908, when Brown defeated Mathewson in a replay of a game against the New York Giants. The original contest had ended after Fred Merkle failed to touch second base as the potential winning run scored. Thousands of fans stormed the field, and the umpires were forced to call the game a 1-1 tie and start from scratch. Brown came in during the first inning and went the rest of the way, winning the pennant for the Cubs 4-2.

Brown's major league career ended in 1916, but he spent four more years in the minor leagues before retiring in 1920. Brown compiled the third-best ERA in history at 2.06. He was an iron-man hurler in baseball's early years, tossing 272 complete games. Brown was also a first-class fielder, once handling 108 chances without an error. Amazingly, Brown won nearly two-thirds of his career decisions. He lived in Terre Haute, Indiana, until his death in 1948 at age 71. The next year he was elected to the Baseball Hall of Fame.

Pitcher Three-Finger Brown claimed that the childhood accident that cost him two fingers on his right hand allowed him to throw his wicked curveball. Brown's claims could be true as his ERA of 2.06 is the third best in baseball history.

CAREER HIGHLIGHTS
MORDECAI PETER CENTENNIAL BROWN

Born: October 19, 1876 Nyesville, IN **Died:** February 14, 1948
Height: 5'10" **Weight:** 175 lbs. **Batted:** Both **Threw:** Right
Pitcher: St. Louis Cardinals, 1903; Chicago Cubs, 1904-12, 1916; Cincinnati Reds, 1913; St. Louis Minors, 1914; Brooklyn Tiptops, 1914; Chicago Whales, 1915.

★ Won 20 or more games for six straight seasons
★ Had 57 career shutouts
★ Pitched five complete-game World Series wins
★ Led N.L. in saves four times
★ Elected to the Hall of Fame in 1949

MAJOR LEAGUE TOTALS

G	IP	W	L	Pct.	SO	BB	ERA
481	3,172	239	130	.648	1,375	673	2.06

TOM BRUNANSKY

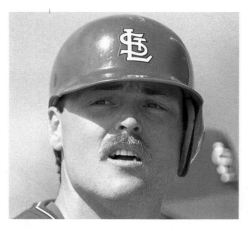

Power. That's one resource the St. Louis Cardinals have seen little of in recent years. With the 1988 loss of Jack Clark to free agency, the Cardinals found themselves in dire need of another player who could pop the ball out of the park. They turned to Tom Brunansky for an answer.

The Cardinals traded popular second baseman Tom Herr to the Minnesota Twins to acquire Brunansky on April 22, 1988. At the time, Brunansky had hit just .183 in his first 14 games, and the Twins thought they had little to lose. The Twins did wind up as big losers in the trade, however. Herr, dogged by injuries, played in just 86 games, became a free agent at season's end, and signed with Philadelphia. Brunansky, meanwhile, socked a team-leading 22 homers and 79 RBI for the Cardinals. He provided steady defense in right field, a position that had posed problems ever since Andy Van Slyke went to Pittsburgh. Brunansky's defensive skill is no secret to American League fans. Both in 1983 and 1984 he had led junior circuit outfielders in double plays.

Brunansky distinguished himself mostly as a power hitter during his six seasons with the Minnesota Twins. Some skeptics believed Brunansky was simply a lucky hitter who benefited from playing in a stadium nicknamed "The Homerdome" because of its short fences. Brunansky refuted those doubts with a fine long-ball season in St. Louis' spacious Busch Stadium.

The California Angels had been high enough on Brunansky back in 1980 to give him an estimated signing bonus of $100,000 after making him a first-round draft pick. After a banner 1980 season with El Paso (.323, 24 homers, and 97 RBI), Brunansky got into the opening lineup for California in 1981. His debut lasted for only 11 games. After a year back at Salt Lake City, the Angels swapped "Bruno" and pitcher Mike Walters for pitcher Doug Corbett and second baseman Rob Wilfong on May 12, 1982. During Brunansky's debut with Minnesota he hit 20 homers with a career-high .272 average.

Brunansky got into 151 games in 1983 and responded with even more clutch hitting—ending the year with 28 homers and 82 RBI. He set a Twins team record with 15 game-winning RBI. The Red Sox learned about Brunansky's hitting the hard way: He racked up 6 RBI in a single game versus Boston on September 1. Brunansky led all major

league outfielders by having a hand in 8 double plays. His 16 assists were second in the American League. Again in 1984, Brunansky topped the Twins in homers. His 32 round-trippers were complemented by 85 RBI and a .252 average. No one since Harmon Killebrew had hit so many home runs for the Twins in one season. In August Brunansky put together a 15-game hitting streak.

Membership on the American League All-Star team highlighted Brunansky's 1985 season. He hit 27 homers and logged a career-high 90 RBI. At the All-Star game Brunansky also won a pregame home run contest. Due to a late-season slump, Brunansky finished the season at .242. He led the Twins in homers, slugging percentage (.448), walks (71), and game-winning hits (10); his 13 sacrifice flies tied a team record.

In 1986, for the second straight year, Brunansky played in 157 games—no easy feat for a slugger with a history of recurring wrist, back, and knee prob-

lems. Brunansky's totals included 23 homers, 75 RBI, and a .256 average. His 152 hits were a career high. On May 27, Brunansky had the third four-hit game of his career. He led the Twins with 10 outfield assists and a .750 success rate when stealing bases. He also had 3 two-run homer games to give him 10 for his career.

In 1987 Brunansky tied his career best with 32 homers. His .259 average was his best in five full major league seasons. Other career highs included 83 runs scored and 74 walks. The California native had 40 multi-hit games and belted his third career grand slam versus Tom Candiotti on May 20 in Cleveland. Brunansky banged out 56 extra-base hits—41 percent of his hit total. The 1987 Twins nosed out the Oakland A's for the Western Division pennant and then took on the Detroit Tigers in the American League Championship Series. The Twins defeated the Tigers in five games, partly due to Brunansky's hitting feats. He tied a major league record with 6 extra-base hits in the Series, and his 1.000 slugging average established another A.L. record.

When the Cardinals acquired Brunansky in 1988, many American League hurlers must have been relieved. Brunansky's 166 home runs rank fourth on the all-time Twins list. For five straight years, Brunansky had 10 or more outfield assists for the Twins.

Brunansky's power makes him a cornerstone in the Cardinal lineup. At age 28, Tom Brunansky has a lot more slugging to do, and he could well become one of the best-known home run hitters of the 1990s.

CAREER HIGHLIGHTS
THOMAS ANDREW BRUNANSKY

Born: August 20, 1960   West Covina, CA
Height: 6'4"   **Weight:** 216 lbs.   **Bats:** Right   **Throws:** Right
Outfielder: California Angels, 1981; Minnesota Twins, 1982-88;
St. Louis Cardinals, 1989.

* Has hit at least 20 home runs for seven consecutive seasons
* Played in the 1985 All-Star game
* Led the 1988 Cardinals in homers and RBI

* Set a team record for game-winning RBI with the 1983 Twins
* Hit .412 in the 1987 A.L. playoffs
* Member of the major league all-rookie team in 1982

MAJOR LEAGUE TOTALS

G	AB	H	BA	2B	3B	HR	R	RBI	SB
1,228	4,425	1,095	.247	205	20	208	593	639	58

In 1984 Tom Brunansky slammed 32 homers, more than any other Minnesota Twins player. Not since Harmon Killebrew had anyone hit so many homers for the Twins in one season. Currently with St. Louis, Brunansky is a cornerstone in their offensive lineup.

BILL BUCKNER

It seems as though Bill Buckner has been in major league baseball forever. Buckner got his first at-bat with the Los Angeles Dodgers in 1969, and he continued in baseball until 1989. Near the end of his career, Buckner chased the 3,000-hit milestone, but the goal ultimately eluded him. Currently, only 16 players in history have reached the 3,000-hit plateau. In 1988 Buckner moved into 43rd place on the all-time hit list passing Ted Williams, Jimmie Foxx, and Steve Garvey. Buckner advanced little beyond that mark, however, because the hardworking veteran hung up his spikes during the following season. Few were surprised at his decision, but many hated to see him go.

Buckner's first hit in organized baseball came in 1968 with Ogden, Utah, of the Pioneer League. Buckner, who was a second-round draft pick in 1968, topped the league in games played, at-bats, hits (88), triples (8), and fielding average for first basemen (.992). Most impressively, Buckner won the league batting title with a .344 mark. After a one-game trial with the 1969 Dodgers, Buckner played in 28 games in 1970, hitting .191. His first full season was in 1971; in 108 games, Buckner hit .277 with 5 homers and 41 RBI.

The following year, Buckner surpassed the .300 level for the first of seven times in his career. His .319 average was supplemented by 5 homers and 37 RBI. Buckner hit .314 in 1974 to spark the Dodgers to a National League championship. His 83 runs scored, 182 hits, and 58 RBI were all personal bests in Buckner's young career.

Injuries haunted Buckner in 1975, and he played in just 92 games. A badly sprained ankle plagued him for the rest of the season and eventually required surgery in the fall. Buckner had stolen 31 bases in 1974, but his speed would never be the same after the operation. Leg problems forced Buckner to concentrate on a full-time job at first base.

In 1976 Buckner rebounded with a .301 average, 7 homers, and 60 RBI in 154 games. Despite his comeback, the Dodgers sent Buckner, shortstop Ivan DeJesus, and pitcher Jeff Albert to the Chicago Cubs for outfielder Rick Monday and pitcher Mike Garman. Buckner spent the first three weeks of the season on the disabled list, but he still played in 122 games. He hit .284 with 11 homers and 60 RBI. More injuries followed in 1978, when he played in just 117 games. His average

soared to .323, however, and he drove in 74 runs, the most in his major league career.

Buckner played in 149 games in 1979, slamming a career high of 14 homers to go with 66 RBI and a .284 average. In 1980 Buckner won the National League batting title with a .324 average. His achievement was one bright spot in Chicago's 64-98 last-place finish. Buckner had 10 homers, 68 RBI, and 187 total hits. He was named N.L. Player of the Week (for the fourth time during his stint with the Cubs), and earned Player of the Month honors in August.

Buckner was the National League's top doubles hitter in 1981 with 35. Ten homers, 75 RBI, and a .311 average were other season high points despite playing in just 106 games. Buckner missed only one game in 1982, hitting 15 homers, 105 RBI, and a .306 average. His 201 hits were the most by a Cub since Billy Williams passed 200 hits

in 1970. Buckner delivered again in 1983 with 16 homers, 66 RBI, and a .280 average. He set a major league record for assists by a first baseman with 159 in 1982, only to break that record with 161 assists in 1983.

Leon Durham won the Cubs first baseman job in 1984. After just 21 games, Buckner was swapped with outfielder Mike Brumley to the Boston Red Sox for pitcher Dennis Eckersley on May 25, 1984. In the American League, Buckner enjoyed two of his greatest seasons ever. In 1985 Buckner played in all 162 games, swatting 16 homers and 110 RBI with a .299 average. His career-high 46 doubles were second in the A.L., while his 201 hits finished third in the league. In 1986 Buckner helped the Red Sox get to the World Series by hitting .267 with 18 homers and 102 RBI.

Unfortunately, his fine season was blighted by his World Series performance. Buckner hit just .188 against the New York Mets, and his error allowed the winning run to score in the sixth game. His critics ignored the fact that Buckner was laboring with leg injuries and a strained Achilles' tendon. The Red Sox released him in July of 1987.

Buckner had a reputation for clutch hitting and for always making contact. He never walked much, but he seldom struck out, either. At age 39 when the 1989 season started, Buckner tried not to let past injuries slow him down. He still ran the bases aggressively, and he played effectively as a pinch hitter/designated hitter. But the past caught up with him eventually, and Buckner retired from baseball before the end of that season.

CAREER HIGHLIGHTS
WILLIAM JOSEPH BUCKNER

Born: December 14, 1949   Vallejo, CA
Height: 6'0"   **Weight:** 185 lbs.   **Batted:** Left   **Threw:** Left
First baseman, outfielder: Los Angeles Dodgers, 1969-76; Chicago Cubs, 1977-84; Boston Red Sox, 1984-87; California Angels, 1987; Kansas City Royals, 1988-89.

★ Played in three different decades
★ Has topped 200 hits twice
★ First in the N.L. in doubles in 1981 and 1983

★ Played in two World Series
★ Won the 1980 N.L. batting title
★ Led first basemen in assists four times

MAJOR LEAGUE TOTALS

G	AB	H	BA	2B	3B	HR	R	RBI	SB
2,495	9,354	2,707	.289	498	49	172	1,073	1,205	183

Steady hitter Bill Buckner decided to end his 20-year career during the 1989 season. Adept at hitting doubles, Buckner led the N.L. in two-baggers in 1981 with 35, though his career high occurred in 1985 with 46.

JIM BUNNING

Out of baseball for more than 15 years, Jim Bunning hasn't been elected to the Baseball Hall of Fame, so he tried for the U.S. House of Representatives instead—and won! Bunning, who compiled 224 wins in his big league career, is now a Congressman in Washington, D.C., representing his home state of Kentucky.

During his 17 years in the majors, from 1955 to 1971, Bunning was a precision pitcher who won in double figures every season without much fanfare. He won 20 games one year and 19 games on four other occasions. Even though he pitched 2 no-hitters—one in each league, and one of them a perfect game—he never put together the really spectacular season that baseball writers look for when filling out their annual Hall of Fame ballots. Strangely enough, Bunning's only 20-win season came with the Detroit Tigers in 1957, his first full year in the majors. Because he never pitched for a pennant-winning team, Bunning never got the national exposure that a World Series provides for star players.

Bunning did not have an easy entry into the major leagues. He toiled in the minors for six years, from 1950 through 1955. During that time, he earned an economics degree from Xavier University in Cincinnati. After brief trials in the majors in 1955 and 1956, Bunning pitched his first full season in 1957 and posted a 20-8 record with a league-leading 267 innings. Bunning won in double figures for the Tigers for the next six seasons. He struck out 201 batters in 1959 and 1960 to win consecutive American League strikeout crowns. The Tigers traded Bunning and Gus Triandos to the Philadelphia Phillies for Don Demeter and Jack Hamilton on December 4, 1963. The trade paid immediate dividends for the Phillies.

In 1964 Bunning helped the Phillies mount a valiant but ultimately unsuccessful charge at the National League pennant. Bunning went 19-8 with a 2.63 ERA. The Kentucky native hurled 5 shutouts and 219 strikeouts to highlight his season. Unfortunately, Philadelphia finished the season at 92-70, missing the title by a single triumph.

Bunning had three more spectacular seasons with the light-hitting Phillies. His 19-9 record in 1965 was just short of the elusive 20-win circle. In 1966 Bunning got a league-best 41 starts, and won 19 of them, and his 5 shutouts were tops in the N.L. Bunning's record

slipped to 17-15 in 1967, but he remained one of the best pitchers in baseball. (Many blame Philadelphia's offensive ineptitude for Bunning's low win-loss percentage.) League bests for Bunning included games started (40), innings pitched (302), shutouts (6), and strikeouts (253).

The Pittsburgh Pirates needed pitching so badly that they gave up four players to get Bunning. On December 15, 1967, the Bucs sent Don Money, Woodie Fryman, Bill Laxton, and minor leaguer Hal Clem to Philadelphia for the veteran righthander. Bunning had his worst-ever season with Pittsburgh, going 4-14. He rebounded to a 10-9 record with Pittsburgh in 25 games in 1969. However, on August 15, 1969, the Los Angeles Dodgers gave up two minor leaguers and cash to obtain Bunning. He wound up the season with a cumulative 13-10 record.

Bunning found work with his old club, the Phillies, to start the 1969 sea-

son and he suffered through losing records in 1969 and 1970 before retiring.

One of Bunning's most impressive career statistics is his strikeouts/bases on balls ratio. In 17 years, Bunning struck out 2,855 hitters and walked only 1,000. Bunning was a rare breed: a powerful strikeout pitcher with pin-point control. He tallied more than 200 strikeouts six times (including four straight seasons in 1964-67). Bunning had success in both leagues, winning more than 100 games both as an American and National Leaguer. He tossed a no-hitter in each league as well, including a perfect game against the 1964 New York Mets. In his career Bunning had 16 saves, and his 224 wins tie him for 54th on the all-time list with Jim "Catfish" Hunter, a Hall of Fame member.

Bunning managed for the Philadelphia minor league organization for two years following retirement, and then entered private business. He began his political career in 1982 by winning a U.S. House seat on the Republican ticket. He was later nominated by his party to run for governor of Kentucky. After suffering a defeat, Bunning was reelected to the House in 1986.

Former pitcher Jim Bunning may top his baseball accomplishments with a career in the political arena. Bunning, who compiled 224 lifetime wins and won three strikeout crowns, is currently a Congressman from his home state of Kentucky.

CAREER HIGHLIGHTS
JAMES PAUL DAVID BUNNING

Born: October 23, 1931   Southgate, KY
Height: 6'3"   **Weight:** 190 lbs.   **Batted:** Right   **Threw:** Right
Pitcher: Detroit Tigers, 1955-63; Philadelphia Phillies, 1964-67, 1970-71; Pittsburgh Pirates, 1968-69; Los Angeles Dodgers, 1969.

- ★ Pitched a no-hitter against the Boston Red Sox in 1958
- ★ Hurled a perfect game against the New York Mets in 1964
- ★ Led the A.L. with 20 wins in 1957
- ★ Won three league strikeout crowns
- ★ Has 40 lifetime shutouts

MAJOR LEAGUE TOTALS

G	IP	W	L	Pct.	SO	BB	ERA
591	3,760	224	184	.549	2,855	1,000	3.27

LEW BURDETTE

Lew Burdette teamed up with Warren Spahn to create one of the greatest pitching combinations in baseball in the 1950s. The two Milwaukee Braves hurlers haunted National League hitters for years. While Spahn (who earned 363 lifetime wins) usually got more headlines, Burdette grabbed the nation's attention during the 1957 World Series against the New York Yankees.

Burdette started his career as a Yankees farmhand, but only got to pitch in two games for New York in 1950. The Yankees threw in Burdette when they purchased Johnny Sain from the Boston Braves in 1952. In the World Series five years later, the deal came back to haunt the Bronx Bombers. When star pitcher Spahn was sidelined by the flu, Burdette hurled three games for the Braves. Three times he threw complete games and three times he claimed victories. Two of his victories were shutouts, and two wins came in Yankee Stadium. Burdette won the second game of the Series 4-2 on a seven-hitter. A string of 24 consecutive scoreless innings followed for Burdette's next two appearances.

Burdette was a repeat winner in game five with a seven-hit, 1-0 victory. Club ace Spahn was slated to start the decisive seventh game, but was still too sick to play. So the team called upon Burdette one more time. Despite having just two days to rest, the West Virginia native handcuffed the Yankees again with a seven-hitter, and the Braves won 5-0. Burdette finished the Series with an amazing 0.67 ERA.

The 1957 World Series was only one memorable moment in Burdette's long career. Because Burdette was mired in the New York Yankees farm system, he didn't pitch a full season in the major leagues until age 26. Therefore, his records are a bit misleading; with a few more seasons in the majors, Burdette might have come closer to matching Spahn's statistics. Instead, his prime years were hidden in the minors. Burdette's first full year, with the 1952 Boston Braves, ended with a 6-11 record; but Burdette did gain 7 saves in relief that year. When the Braves relocated to Milwaukee in 1953, Burdette's fortunes changed. He posted a 15-5 mark with 8 saves. He won 15 games again in 1954 and hurled 13 complete games.

After slumping to a 13-8 win-loss record in 1955, Burdette had his best season ever in 1956. His 19-10 record

was accentuated by a league-leading 2.70 ERA and 6 shutouts. The Braves weren't so lucky, losing the pennant by just one game. In 1957 Burdette won 17 games, just 4 less than Spahn's Cy-Young-award-winning exploits that season. Burdette, however, posted a .654 winning percentage in that championship year. "We got paid bonuses for complete games," he said in a 1988 interview explaining part of his success.

The Braves defended their National League crown in 1958 but fell to the Yankees in that year's fall classic. Burdette gained 20 wins for the first time in his career (with an additional win in the Series), and his .667 winning percentage was the best in the league. In 1959 Burdette led all N.L. hurlers with a 21-15 mark and 4 shutouts. Because only one Cy Young award was given for both leagues, Early Wynn of

the Chicago White Sox nosed Burdette out for the honor. The Braves, meanwhile, lost the pennant to the Dodgers only after a special two-game playoff was staged to break the deadlock. Burdette nearly won 20 for three straight seasons, but ended 1960 with a 19-13 record and a league-high 18 complete games.

Burdette won in double figures every year he was with the Milwaukee Braves (including 18 wins in 1961 and 10 in 1962). In early 1963 the Braves traded Burdette to the St. Louis Cardinals for Bob Sadowski and Gene Oliver. In June, 1964, Burdette was shipped to the Chicago Cubs. Stops with the Philadelphia Phillies in 1965 and the California Angels in 1966-67 rounded out his career. Burdette worked solely as a reliever in his last two years with the Angels.

Besides becoming a successful reliever late in his career, Burdette was noted for his hitting. He had 12 lifetime home runs and twice hit 2 round-trippers in a single game.

Burdette's lifetime record includes a 203-144 mark with 31 saves in 3,068 innings. He was accused for years by batters of throwing an illegal spitball, but he denies using it. He claims that some of his success came from hitters who were distracted waiting for the supposed trick pitch. Also, Burdette always yielded a high number of hits and a low number of strikeouts each season. "The only thing that meant anything to me was winning the ball game," Burdette says. "I didn't care how I did it, even if every batter hit a line drive at someone. I still won."

CAREER HIGHLIGHTS
SELVA LEWIS BURDETTE

Born: November 22, 1926 Nitro, WV
Height: 6'2" **Weight:** 180 lbs. **Batted:** Right **Threw:** Right
Pitcher: New York Yankees, 1950; Boston Braves, 1951-52; Milwaukee Braves, 1953-63; St. Louis Cardinals, 1963-64; Chicago Cubs, 1964-65; Philadelphia Phillies, 1965; California Angels, 1966-67.

★ Had a record-setting three complete-game wins in the 1957 World Series

★ Threw two shutouts in the 1957 World Series

★ Pitched a league-leading 18 complete games in 1960

★ First in N.L. shutouts in 1956 and 1959

★ Led the N.L. in wins in 1959

MAJOR LEAGUE TOTALS

G	IP	W	L	Pct.	SO	BB	ERA
626	3,068	203	144	.585	1,074	628	3.66

Lew Burdette and Warren Spahn became one of baseball's deadliest pitching combinations during the Eisenhower Era. Burdette's career highlight is the record-setting 3 complete-game wins pitched against the Yankees in the 1957 World Series.

ROY CAMPANELLA

Although his major league career was tragically cut short by a paralyzing automobile accident, Roy Campanella squeezed more baseball into his seasons than most players could into 20.

Campanella played with the Brooklyn Dodgers from 1948 to 1957. In that time, the husky catcher won three MVP awards. He was the National League's premier backstop—the complete handler of pitchers, a power hitter with a respectable batting average, and a deceptively quick and agile catcher.

Before Campanella made his big league debut with the Brooklyn Dodgers in 1948, he had already played in the Mexican and Negro Leagues for nine seasons. He was a star for the Baltimore Elite Giants of the Negro National League. When Branch Rickey called him up to the Dodgers, Campanella became the first black catcher in major league baseball. The Dodgers signed Campanella in 1945 following Jackie Robinson, and he played two years in their minor league system. For one game in 1948, Campanella substituted for ejected Nashua manager Walter Alston, becoming the first black manager in the white minor leagues.

In ten seasons as a player, Campanella set a large number of slugging and fielding records for catchers that stood for many years. He was the first catcher to slug more than 20 home runs in five consecutive seasons. Until Johnny Bench came along, Campanella held the league record for most career home runs by a catcher (242). A model of durability, Campanella caught in 100 or more games for nine straight seasons, often performing with injuries that would have sidelined other players. He led the league's catchers in putouts, fielding percentage, and other defensive categories on many occasions.

"Campy" played in just 83 games in 1948, hitting .258 with 9 homers and 45 RBI. Originally, the Dodgers organization planned to start Campanella as an outfielder, with Gil Hodges as the primary catcher, but manager Leo Durocher insisted that Campanella serve as the team's starting catcher. The Dodgers, however, wanted the stocky backstop to play in St. Paul of the American Association to break that league's color barrier. He did, but returned to the Dodgers in June.

In 1949 Campanella served his first full year with the Dodgers. He responded with 22 homers, 82 RBI, and a .287 average. He caught the entire All-Star game, as he did in 1950-53. The Dodgers won the National League championship but lost the Series to the Yankees in five games.

In both 1950 and 1951, Campanella broke the 30-homer barrier. His average climbed to .325 by 1951, fourth highest in the National League (behind Stan Musial's leading .355 mark). The Dodgers catcher was third in the National League with RBI (108), slugging percentage (.590), and doubles (33). Campanella won his first Most Valuable Player award that year, but it was a small consolation as the New York Giants won a three-game playoff to advance to the World Series.

In 1952 the Dodgers returned to the top of the National League. Playing in just 128 games, Campanella still had 22 homers and 97 RBI. He hit just .214 in the World Series, however, as the Yankees again whipped Brooklyn in the fall classic. Campanella improved in 1953, hitting 41 homers, a league-leading 142 RBI, and a .312 average. He became only the fourth man in National League history to win two MVP awards. Campy batted .273 in the World Series

loss to New York but was hampered after being hit in the hand with a pitch by Allie Reynolds. His only home run gave the Dodgers their first win in the Series.

A broken hand plagued Campanella throughout 1954, when he played just 111 games. Although he had 19 homers and 51 RBI, his average sank to .207. Even after surgery, Campanella didn't have total control of the hand. Only with postseason surgery did he fully recover. In 1955 Campanella won his third MVP award (matching National League rival Stan Musial's accomplishment) with an impressive season: 32 homers, 107 RBI, and a .318 average.

In 1957, which would prove to be his final season, Campanella hit .242 with 13 homers and 62 RBI.

On January 28, 1958, Campanella was seriously injured in a car accident. Returning to his Glen Cove, N.Y., home in the early morning hours, his car crashed into a telephone pole. He was subsequently paralyzed. Even after his crippling accident, Campanella never lost his zest for life. His uplifting autobiography, *It's Good to Be Alive,* has inspired thousands and was made into a TV movie. The Dodgers moved to Los Angeles in 1958, and the following May, 93,000 adoring fans watched as the Dodgers and the New York Yankees played a benefit exhibition to honor the Dodgers beloved catcher. The lights in the Memorial Coliseum were shut off, and fans held up lit matches in a stunning tribute to the man called Campy.

Campanella was elected to the Baseball Hall of Fame in 1969 and now serves on the board of directors for the Hall. He's also a member of the Old Timers Voting Committee.

CAREER HIGHLIGHTS
ROY CAMPANELLA

Born: November 19, 1921 Philadelphia, PA
Height: 5'9" **Weight:** 190 lbs. **Batted:** Right **Threw:** Right
Catcher: Brooklyn Dodgers, 1948-57.

★ Selected N.L. MVP in 1951, 1953, and 1955
★ Played in five World Series
★ Led N.L. catchers in putouts six times
★ Hit 242 home runs as a catcher
★ Elected to the Hall of Fame in 1969

MAJOR LEAGUE TOTALS

G	AB	H	BA	2B	3B	HR	R	RBI	SB
1,215	4,205	1,161	.276	178	18	242	627	856	25

Signed to the Brooklyn Dodgers after playing in both the Mexican and the Negro Leagues,
Roy Campanella was respected for his scouting abilities as well as for his playing talent.
Monty Irvin and Larry Doby were among those players Campanella discovered.

BERT CAMPANERIS

Although his statistics probably won't warrant Hall of Fame consideration, Bert Campaneris will be remembered as a great baserunner and good defensive shortstop. His speed and glovework helped spark the Oakland Athletics to five consecutive division titles and three straight world championships.

Campaneris began his big league career in 1964, when the A's still had a Kansas City mailing address. He moved into the starting shortstop role the following season and remained a fixture there for the next dozen years—except for one unusual day. On September 8, 1965, Campaneris made baseball history as the first player to play nine different positions in one game (a different position each inning). It was a publicity stunt dreamed up by team owner Charles O. Finley to boost attendance for his sagging A's, who were hopelessly cemented in the American League basement. When it came his turn on the mound, Campaneris struggled, yielding 1 hit and 1 earned run, 2 walks and a strikeout. He ended his brief pitching career with an ERA of 9.00. Perhaps one reason the accomplishment didn't receive more attention is that the California Angels beat the A's, 5-3.

Campaneris is one of five players in baseball history to steal over 30 bases in ten straight seasons. He got his first chance to steal in the majors in 1964. He began the season at Birmingham, stinging minor league pitchers for 6 homers, 40 RBI, and a .325 average. The Athletics called up Campaneris in midseason, and he got to play in 67 games. His .257 average, 4 homers, and 22 RBI were enough to keep him on the roster the following year. In 1965 he was used in 109 games at shortstop, and he also filled in as a fourth outfielder and utility infielder. The Athletics loved Campaneris more for his baserunning than for his .270 average, 6 homers, and 42 RBI. He swiped 51 bases (in 70 attempts) to lead the American League.

Three more consecutive stolen base crowns awaited the Cuban speedster in 1966-68, with Campaneris winning the starting shortstop job from incumbent Wayne Causey in 1966. Still, his inspired play was masked by the team's continual losing records. When the Athletics moved to Oakland in 1968, things began to change. Campaneris paced the junior circuit with 177 hits and stole a career-high, league-leading 62 bases. Even though "Campy"

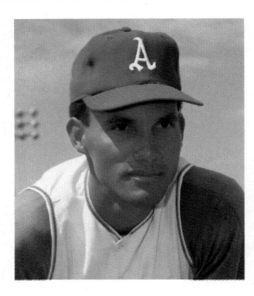

matched that stolen base total again in 1969, Seattle Pilot Tommy Harper stole the league lead with 73 pilfers.

Campaneris stunned the baseball world with his hitting exploits in 1970. In his six previous major league seasons, Campaneris had never hit more than 6 home runs in a year, and his highest RBI total was 42. But in 1970 Campaneris broke loose with 22 homers, 64 RBI, and a .279 average. He also regained the league stolen base title with 42 swipes.

In 1972 Campaneris earned his sixth stolen base crown with 52. His 625 at-bats were also tops in the American League. The once erratic shortstop led his league with 283 putouts. The A's advanced to the American League Championship Series against the Detroit Tigers. During game two, Campaneris became one of the most flamboyant Athletics: Tigers pitcher Lerrin LaGrow brushed back Campaneris with a tight pitch, and in retaliation Campa-

neris threw his bat at LaGrow and charged the mound. American League president Joe Cronin suspended Campaneris for three games and fined him $500. Baseball commissioner Bowie Kuhn ruled that Campaneris could play in the World Series, but that he'd be suspended for the first seven games of the following season.

Despite missing those seven games, Campaneris still led his division-winning team in at-bats in 1973. He played in 151 games, hitting .250. He played in all five playoff games versus the Baltimore Orioles without incident. He hit a team-leading .333 and won game three of the playoffs with an 11th-inning home run off Mike Cuellar. Of Campaneris' 7 hits, 2 were homers and 1 was a double. In the 1973 World Series, Campaneris hit .290 with 1 homer, 3 RBI, and 3 stolen bases. His 11th-inning single won game three for the A's, 3-2. His two-run homer in the seventh game was a key hit in Oakland's clinching the championship.

Campaneris made a small part of baseball history following the 1976 season, when he became one of six Oakland players to play out their options to try the newly created method of free agency. The A's lost the nucleus of their winning team when Campaneris signed a five-year contract with the Texas Rangers for $950,000. He had little success compared to his glory days with the Oakland teams but stuck in baseball for five more years. His last year was with the 1983 Yankees, hitting .322 in 60 games.

Besides ranking eighth overall in lifetime stolen bases, Campaneris was one of the most active shortstops in history. His 2,097 games at shortstop put him seventh on the all-time list.

CAREER HIGHLIGHTS
DAGOBERTO BLANCO CAMPANERIS

Born: March 9, 1942   Pueblo Nuevo, Cuba
Height: 5'10"   **Weight:** 160 lbs.   **Batted:** Right   **Threw:** Right
Shortstop: Kansas City Athletics, 1964-67; Oakland Athletics, 1968-76; Texas Rangers, 1977-79; California Angels, 1979-81; New York Yankees, 1983.

- ★ Led the A.L. in stolen bases six times
- ★ Led the A.L. in triples in 1965
- ★ Led the A.L. in hits in 1968
- ★ Played in three World Series
- ★ Has the eighth-highest stolen base total in history

MAJOR LEAGUE TOTALS

G	AB	H	BA	2B	3B	HR	R	RBI	SB
2,328	8,684	2,249	.259	313	86	79	1,181	646	649

Fleet-footed Bert Campaneris may have been one of the smallest catchers in baseball history. Campaneris enjoyed his banner year in 1970 when he slammed 22 home runs, racked up 64 RBI, earned a .279 average, and captured the A.L. stolen base title.

JOHN CANDELARIA

One of the tallest pitchers in baseball, John Candelaria is known as "The Candy Man." The New York Yankees valued Candelaria as an addition to their fragile pitching staff in 1988. Signed as a free agent, he instantly became the team's ace with a club-best 13-7 record. His 3.38 ERA was tops in the starting rotation for the Yanks, as was his total of 121 strikeouts. Candelaria became one of the few players who has seen service with both New York teams—the Yankees and the Mets.

The Mets acquired Candelaria as a backup pitcher for their unsuccessful pennant run of 1987. On September 15, 1987, the Mets sent two minor league prospects, Shane Turner and Jeff Richardson, to the California Angels for Candelaria. The native New Yorker returned home and went 2-0 in a three-game stint. Unfortunately, the Mets finished in second place, just three games behind the pennant-winning St. Louis Cardinals. The Mets wanted Candelaria back in 1988, but the crosstown Yankees outspent their N.L. rivals to sign the veteran hurler.

Candelaria had spent the previous two and a half seasons on the California Angels staff. His best year in Anaheim did not start off well. He was sidelined due to an injury from April 15 to July 8, 1986, then spent a week's rehabilitation with California's minor league team in Palm Springs to prove his soundness. He returned to compile a 10-2 record with a 2.55 ERA, and the Angels went on to win their division with a 92-70 record. In the American League playoffs, Candelaria had a 1-1 record with a 0.84 ERA, yielding only 9 hits in seven innings to earn the win in game three. Candelaria started the seventh game and lost mostly due to bad luck. Two Angels errors led to 7 unearned runs by the Red Sox in their 8-1 defeat. More injuries marred Candelaria's 1987 season with California. He pitched in just 20 games for the Angels, going 8-6 before being traded to New York.

Despite his 1988 success with the Yankees, Candelaria's best years came as a member of the Pittsburgh Pirates. Candelaria earned a reported $40,000 to sign with the Pirate organization in 1973. His first year with Charleston was the talk of the Western Carolina League. He went 10-2 with a league-leading win-loss percentage of .833. Candelaria earned a reputation as a power pitcher with Salem in 1974. He was 11-8 in 25 games, but he struck

out an impressive number of batters—147 in 154 innings. Candelaria didn't even spend a full season in Triple-A ball in 1975 before getting his promotion to Pittsburgh. Candelaria was 7-1 in ten games in Triple-A, and his 1.78 ERA and 48 strikeouts in 61 innings were the primary reasons the Pirates brought him up so early. Most of all, the Pirates needed help in winning the National League Eastern Division.

Candelaria started the third game of the National League Championship Series against the Cincinnati Reds. The Reds had a two-game lead in the best-of-five series. The 22-year-old rookie had gone 8-6 with a 2.75 ERA in his first 18 games in the majors, striking out 95 batters in 121 innings. In the playoffs Candelaria struck out 14 batters in 7.2 innings, allowing just 3 hits; but one of those was a two-run homer

by Pete Rose that enabled the Reds to squeeze out a 5-3 win to clinch the National League title.

The 1976 Pirates finished second in their division, but Candelaria pitched like a champion. He was first on the Pirates in wins with a 16-7 record, and his .696 winning percentage was second only to Steve Carlton in the National League. Candelaria allowed only 7.08 hits per nine innings, ranking only behind James Rodney Richard and Tom Seaver. A 3.15 ERA and 138 strikeouts were other highlights in Candelaria's season, along with a 2-0 no-hit victory against the Los Angeles Dodgers on August 9.

In 1977 Candelaria won the National League ERA crown with a 2.34 effort, while his 20-5 mark gave him a league-best .800 win-loss percentage. However, the Pirates remained stuck in second place behind the Phillies even after winning 96 games. Candelaria gave up just 1.95 walks per nine innings, the best ratio in the league. The Pirates had yet another second-place finish in 1978, but Candelaria slumped to 12-11 with a 3.24 ERA.

The Pirates returned to the top of the National League East in 1979, and Candelaria rebounded to a 14-9 record—the best among Pittsburgh starters. He also kept his reputation as one of the N.L.'s best control pitchers.

Candelaria missed nearly the entire 1981 season due to injuries. On August 2, 1985, the Angels traded Bob Kipper, Mike Brown, and Pat Clements for Candelaria, George Hendrick, and Al Holland. After playing for the Mets in 1987 and the Yankees in 1988, he was traded to the Montreal Expos in 1989.

CAREER HIGHLIGHTS
JOHN ROBERT CANDELARIA

Born: November 6, 1953   New York, NY
Height: 6'7"   **Weight:** 250 lbs.   **Bats:** Left   **Throws:** Left
Pitcher: Pittsburgh Pirates, 1975-85; California Angels 1985-87; New York Mets, 1987; New York Yankees, 1988; Montreal Expos, 1989.

★ Pitched in three league championships
★ Named to the 1977 All-Star team
★ Pitched a no-hitter vs. the Dodgers in 1976

★ Went 1-1 in the 1979 World Series
★ Won 20 games with the 1977 Pirates
★ Led the N.L. in ERA in 1977

MAJOR LEAGUE TOTALS

G	IP	W	L	Pct.	SO	BB	ERA
410	2,318	164	104	.617	1,495	527	3.27

Currently pitching for the New York Yankees, John Candelaria is one of the few players who has seen service with both New York teams. Candelaria pitched for the New York Mets at the end of the 1987 season in their unsuccessful bid for the pennant.

JOSE CANSECO

Jose Canseco was the talk of the American League in 1988 when he became the league's Most Valuable Player—just two seasons after being named A.L. Rookie of the year.

In 1988 the Cuban-born, Miami-raised star became the first player in history to hit 40 home runs and steal 40 bases in one season, finishing the year at .307 with 42 homers, 124 RBI, and 40 steals. Canseco and teammate Mark McGwire, nicknamed "The Bash Brothers," made up one of the most prodigious home run twosomes since Mickey Mantle and Roger Maris powered the New York Yankees teams of the early 1960s. Canseco and McGwire's combined totals include 74 homers and 223 RBI. They are two reasons why the Athletics had a 104-58 record, the best in baseball in 1988.

Check any American League offensive category for 1988 and it's likely that Canseco's name will pop up among the leaders. He was first in homers, RBI, and slugging percentage (.569); he was second in runs scored (120) and total bases (347); and he was fourth in stolen bases, game-winning RBI (16), and times hit by a pitch (10). Canseco also worked hard to improve his baserunning and fielding skills. Former Oakland outfield great Joe Rudi has been Canseco's defensive mentor.

In the '88 American League playoffs versus Boston, the A's cruised to victory in four straight games. Canseco was a major force in Oakland's domination against the Red Sox, with a .313 average, 3 homers, 4 RBI, and 1 stolen base. He also earned the game-winning RBI in the decisive fourth game. But Canseco, and the rest of the A's had little luck against the Los Angeles Dodgers in the World Series. Canseco hit .053 in five games. His only hit was a grand slam homer in the first game, which the Dodgers won 5-4.

In 1986 Canseco played his first full season with Oakland. He contended for the league homer crown with 33 round-trippers, and his 117 RBI finished second only to Cleveland's Joe Carter. At one point, before a late-season slump set in, Canseco was driving in so many runs that Ted Williams' rookie RBI mark of 145 was in danger. During his first trip to Chicago, Canseco was able to homer over the Comiskey Park roof, a rare feat for even a seasoned slugger. Canseco struck out 175 times during his first season and hit just .240. However, his average climbed and his strikeout totals went down each year

from then on. Canseco won a close vote for the 1986 Rookie of the Year award, with Wally Joyner coming in second.

Canseco's sophomore season in 1987 proved that the young slugger was for real. Skeptics wondered if he could match the success of his Rookie of the Year season in 1986. Canseco came through and exceeded most people's expectations: He played in 159 games, thumping 31 homers and 113 RBI to go with a .257 average. The A's wound up in second place in the A.L. West, only slightly behind the Minnesota Twins. Many have overlooked Canseco's accomplishments in 1987 because McGwire was busy winning the 1987 Rookie of the Year award. One of Canseco's most notable achievements was driving in over 100 runs in each of his first two seasons. Even Reggie Jackson, the A's last great slugger, couldn't match that feat during his first two years in Oakland.

Canseco's first year in organized baseball was 1982. After being selected

in the 15th round of the free-agent draft in June, Canseco played both for Miami of the Florida State League and Idaho Falls of the Pioneer League. His first full season in the minors came in 1983. He split his time between Madison of the Midwest League and Medford of the Northwest League. In Medford, Canseco showed his first signs of power, blasting 11 homers and 40 RBI in 59 games. He spent the 1984 season at Modesto, hitting .276 with 15 homers.

The following year, Canseco made the jump from Double-A to the major league club in just one season. He started out with the Huntsville Stars in the Southern League. In just 58 games, Canseco had 25 homers, 80 RBI, and a .318 average. Even though he missed nearly three weeks due to injuries, he was still Southern League MVP at the season's end. Huntsville heroics were just a small part of Canseco's banner 1985 season. He was promoted to the Tacoma Tigers, Oakland's Triple-A minor league affiliate, where he registered a .348 average in 60 games, hitting 11 homers and 47 RBI. More than a third of his 81 hits went for extra bases. *The Sporting News* named Canseco the Minor League Player of the Year for his efforts. All of this doesn't even include the 29 games he played during his late-season call-up to Oakland. In his major league debut, Canseco hit .302 with 5 homers and 13 RBI. The starting left fielder's job was his the following season.

After just a few seasons of major league play, Canseco commands superstar attention from both the media and the public. Once during the off-season Canseco received a speeding ticket in Florida and made national headlines.

CAREER HIGHLIGHTS
JOSE CANSECO

Born: July 2, 1964   Havana, Cuba
Height: 6'3"   **Weight:** 185 lbs.   **Bats:** Right   **Throws:** Right
Outfielder, designated hitter: Oakland Athletics, 1985-89.

★ Had 40 stolen bases and 42 homers, first member of the "40/40" club
★ Led the A.L. with a .569 slugging percentage in 1988
★ Named A.L. Rookie of the Year in 1986
★ Named to the All-Star team in 1986-89
★ Hit a grand slam in the 1988 World Series
★ Named A.L. MVP in 1988

MAJOR LEAGUE TOTALS

G	AB	H	BA	2B	3B	HR	R	RBI	SB
568	2,163	583	.270	110	5	128	342	424	128

Barring serious injury, Jose Canseco has an exciting future in baseball. Named the A.L. Rookie of the Year in 1986 for slugging 33 homers and accumulating 117 RBI, Canseco won A.L. MVP honors just two years later with his 42 home runs and 40 stolen bases.

ROD CAREW

In 1977 Rod Carew appeared to be on the verge of doing what no hitter had done in 36 years—bat more than .400 for a season. The slender contact hitter attracted national media attention after batting an amazing .486 in mid-June. By mid-July, he was still above the magic .400 mark. Carew's average dipped to .374 by the end of August, but the lefthand slugger hit .439 in September to finish the incredible season with a .388 mark—the highest batting average in two decades.

In addition to his league-leading average that year, Carew topped the circuit in hits (239), runs (128), and triples (16) and finished the season with 100 RBI and 351 total bases for a .570 slugging percentage. In each category, he achieved a career high and demonstrated that he was definitely more than just a singles hitter. For his extraordinary efforts, he won the league's Most Valuable Player award.

It was the best season in a career filled with outstanding seasons. In his 19-year career, Carew won seven batting titles, compiled a .328 lifetime average, and led the league several times in various fielding categories. He established a major league record by stealing home 7 times in one season and tied another by swiping 3 bases in one inning. Throughout the 1970s, Carew was the best contact hitter in baseball. In his final season in the majors, he joined the exclusive group of batters who have rapped out more than 3,000 base hits. The fleet batsman finished his career with 3,053 hits for the 12th-best total in history. His .328 lifetime average places him 27th on the all-time list.

Despite his quick success in the majors, Carew had not broken into the big leagues overnight. Carew got a $5,000 signing bonus to ink a contract with Minnesota in 1964, and then he labored in the minor leagues perfecting his craft before getting his chance at stardom. As a 21-year-old rookie second baseman in 1967, Carew batted .292 with 8 homers and 51 RBI to capture the Rookie of the Year award.

In 1969, at the tender age of 24, Carew won his first American League batting title with a .332 effort. Carew then got an early taste of postseason play as the Twins won the Western Division. The Orioles handcuffed Carew in the league playoffs, allowing him only 1 hit in 14 at-bats for an .071 average. Without Carew's offense, the Twins

were swept in three games. Although the Twins defended their league title in 1970, the Orioles proved to be Minnesota's undoing again in the playoffs. Saddled with injuries in 1970, Carew appeared in just 51 games. His average was an electrifying .366 for the shortened season.

Carew posted consecutive .300-plus seasons during his next eight seasons with the Twins. He was named to the American League All-Star team during his first 12 seasons in the majors. In one of the most incredible hitting displays in history, Carew won six batting titles in seven years, with averages of .318 in 1972, .350 in 1973, .364 in 1974, .359 in 1975, .388 in 1977, and .333 in 1978. Carew's only "off" year was in 1976, when he finished with a .331 average. Kansas City's George Brett finished 2 percentage points higher at .333 to edge out the Twins veteran for the title.

In what seems like one of the most baffling trades in history, the Twins sent

Carew to the California Angels on February 3, 1979, in exchange for outfielder Ken Landreaux, pitchers Brad Havens and Paul Hartzell, and catcher Dave Engle. Carew had undoubtedly grown tired of being a member of an also-ran team, and team owner Calvin Griffith had probably grown tired of Carew's large salary. Since it seemed possible that Carew might escape Minnesota via free agency, leaving the Twins with no compensation at all, a trade probably seemed like the best option.

The trade benefited California immediately. Although Carew participated in just 110 games due to an injury, he hit .318 with 3 homers and 44 RBI. The Angels won their first pennant in their short history with an 88-74 record. The Baltimore Orioles downed California in four games in the playoffs, but Carew remained a bright spot for the Angels, his .412 average (with 7 hits and 4 runs scored) sparking the Angels anemic offense. Carew's other disappointment during the year was that he was injured and unable to participate in the All-Star game that season. Although he missed a total of three All-Star games due to injuries, he hit .244 in 10 midseason contests.

Carew batted above .300 for the next four seasons. In 1982 the Angels returned to the top of their division, only to be bested in a five-game duel with the Milwaukee Brewers in the playoffs. His average led the Angels through 1984. The Angels gave Carew an unconditional release after the 1985 season in order to make room for rookie Wally Joyner. For his career, Carew hit below .300 only four times in 19 years. Carew will be eligible for Hall of Fame membership in 1991.

CAREER HIGHLIGHTS
RODNEY CLINE SCOTT CAREW

Born: October 1, 1945 Gatun, Canal Zone, Panama
Height: 6'0" **Weight:** 170 lbs. **Batted:** Left **Threw:** Right
Second baseman, first baseman: Minnesota Twins, 1967-78; California Angels, 1979-85.

★ Named A.L. Rookie of the Year in 1967 ★ Selected as A.L. MVP in 1977
★ Won seven batting titles ★ Led the A.L. in hits three times
★ Played in four league championships

MAJOR LEAGUE TOTALS

G	AB	H	BA	2B	3B	HR	R	RBI	SB
2,469	9,315	3,053	.328	445	112	92	1,424	1,015	353

Rod Carew will most likely be inducted into the Hall of Fame in his first year of eligibility in 1991. Carew hit .300 or above 15 times for a career average of .328. In 1977, he hit .388, which was the highest player average in two decades.

MAX CAREY

Long before stolen base king Lou Brock or today's speedsters like Vince Coleman or Rickey Henderson, there was Max Carey. Carey was a basestealing demon for 20 National League seasons. He was one of the first to transform baserunning from a chore into an art form.

Born Maximilian Carnarius in Terre Haute, Indiana, he was studying to become a minister before he took up baseball. While he was at Concordia College in Fort Wayne, Indiana, the Pirates signed him (under the name of Max Carey) to a contract. After playing at shortstop and third base in the minors, Carey joined the Pittsburgh Pirates near the end of the 1910 season. His two-game debut was a big success: He went 3-for-6 with 1 triple, 2 RBI, and 2 runs scored. He earned a starting job in the Pirates outfield in 1911. In his first full major league season, Carey hit .258 with 5 homers and 43 RBI. Most importantly, he swiped 27 bases. For 18 straight seasons, Carey would have double-figure totals in steals.

Despite Pittsburgh's mediocre record throughout most of his years as a Pirate, Carey remained a model of consistency. He improved to .302 in 1912, with 5 homers and 66 RBI. He scored 114 runs and stole 45 bases. Carey became the National League's stolen base leader in 1913 with 61 pilfers. He also led the league in at-bats and runs scored (99) that year. In 1914 Carey's 17 triples were tops in the National League.

All the while, Carey was gaining a reputation as a gifted outfielder. He was dubbed "Scoops" for his defensive wizardry. In 1916 Carey had one of his brightest seasons, winning his third stolen base crown with a career-high 63 steals. In the outfield, Carey led all league center fielders with 419 putouts, 32 assists, 10 double plays, and an average of 3 chances per game. Today's outfielders are praised for having even a third of the assists that Carey accumulated in just one season!

The following season, Carey cut his strikeout totals from 58 to 38. The Indiana native was perfecting the fine art of contact hitting, a feat that seldom shows up in statistics. His average showed the improvement, jumping to .296. In 1918 Carey's average dipped to .274, and he played in 126 games. Nevertheless, he managed to win another stolen base title with 58. Carey saw action in only 66 contests in 1919, but

he pumped his average up to .307. Carey's decreased strikeouts helped him hit above .300 five more times in the next ten seasons.

Carey achieved true stardom in the 1920s. In 1920 he had a league-leading 52 steals. In 1921 he batted .309 and once more led National League center fielders in putouts and total chances. In 1922 his hitting blossomed into a .329 average with a career-high 207 hits. His 10 homers and 70 RBI were also personal bests. His 51 bases (in 53 attempts) and 80 walks were first in the league. During one extra-inning game in 1922 Carey went 6-for-6 and stole 3 bases (including home). The gifted flyhawker paced the league in putouts (450) and assists (28) in 1923. A .308 average and league titles in stolen bases (51) and triples (19) were other high points in Carey's season.

The Pirates gained new respect in 1923. They finished in third place with an 87-67 record, only eight and a half games behind John McGraw's pennant-winning New York Giants. Pittsburgh's record improved to 90-63 in 1924, but the Giants won the pennant again,

although by only three games. In 1924 Carey was again the league leader in putouts and stolen bases, and he hit .297 with 7 homers and 55 RBI. Incredibly, Carey struck out just 17 times in 599 at-bats. During the next three seasons, Carey's strikeouts would remain under 20.

Years of struggle paid off for Carey and the Pirates in 1925 when the team coasted to the World Series with a 95-58 record. Carey helped his team with a .343 average and led the league with 46 stolen bases. The Pirates faced the Washington Senators in the fall classic and won the Series after being behind three games to one. Their comeback was the first of such magnitude in baseball history. Carey was instrumental in the Pirate world championship.

Carey became embroiled in a contract dispute with the Pittsburgh management in 1926. The Pirates released Carey after he played just 86 games that season. The Brooklyn Dodgers eagerly claimed Carey on waivers on August 13, 1926.

He played two more full seasons with the Dodgers, stealing 32 bases in 1927 and 18 in 1928. His average was .266 in 1927 and .247 in 1928. Carey retired from active duty after just 19 games in 1929, concluding his final season with a .304 mark in 23 at-bats.

Carey managed the Dodgers in 1932-33, piloting the team to a third-place finish his first season. In the 1940s, Carey was a manager and later a Commissioner of the All-American Girls Professional Baseball League. The Hall of Fame elected Carey in 1961. His modern National League record of 738 steals (which was fifth highest in history) would stand for nearly five decades before Lou Brock erased the mark.

CAREER HIGHLIGHTS
MAX GEORGE CAREY

Born: January 11, 1890   Terre Haute, IN   **Died:** May 30, 1976
Height: 5'11"   **Weight:** 170 lbs.   **Batted:** Both   **Threw:** Right
Outfielder: Pittsburgh Pirates, 1910-26; Brooklyn Dodgers, 1926-29. Manager: Brooklyn Dodgers, 1932-33.

★ Hit .458 in the 1925 World Series   ★ Led the N.L. in stolen bases ten times
★ Topped the N.L. in runs scored in 1912 ★ Elected to the Hall of Fame in 1961

MAJOR LEAGUE TOTALS

G	AB	H	BA	2B	3B	HR	R	RBI	SB
2,476	9,363	2,665	.285	419	159	69	1,545	800	738

An early basestealing talent, Max Carey set an N.L. record of 738 career stolen bases that stood for almost fifty years before Lou Brock shattered it. A true star during the Roaring Twenties, Carey batted above .300 in eight seasons.

STEVE CARLTON

The consummate pitcher of the past two decades, Steve Carlton is a sure-fire Hall of Fame selection. Although Carlton's reputation and popularity are widespread now, he was just another good young pitcher in the late 1960s.

In 1967, his first full season, he won 14 games and lost 9 for the world champion St. Louis Cardinals. Carlton struck out 168 in 193 innings, giving the Redbirds a powerful one-two strikeout punch with team ace Bob Gibson. It's hard to believe that Carlton had to struggle to make the St. Louis roster. After his first year of minor league baseball in 1964, Carlton went 10-1 at Rock Hill with a 1.03 ERA and 91 strikeouts in 79 innings. He made it to the Cardinals in 1965 for 15 games but spent the rest of the season at Tulsa. Carlton started the fifth game of the 1967 World Series against the Boston Red Sox, where he yielded just 3 hits in six innings but was tagged for a loss due to 1 unearned run.

Carlton won 13 games in 1968 as the Cardinals defended their National League crown. In 1969 the tall flamethrower notched a 17-11 record with a team-best 2.17 ERA (second best in the league). He was the winning pitcher in the All-Star game with three innings of work. An unexpected slump dropped Carlton's record to 10-19 in 1970. When Carlton bounced back to a 20-9 record in 1971, he wanted a fitting pay raise. Team owner August Busch balked, remembering the pitcher's previous-season slump. Because of the contract dispute, Carlton was traded to the Philadelphia Phillies on February 25, 1972, for Rick Wise.

Carlton delivered for his new team immediately, soothing local critics and fans who missed Wise, a club favorite. Carlton was dubbed "The Franchise" for his heroics with the last-place Phillies. He won his first Cy Young award with a 27-10 record. Carlton accounted for an incredible 45.8 percent (setting a modern record) of Philadelphia's 59 victories. He was the National League leader in wins, ERA (1.97), starts (41), complete games (30), innings pitched (346), and strikeouts (310). Only Hall of Famer Sandy Koufax had broken the 300-strikeout barrier in the National League before. Only five other pitchers had ever won 20 or more for a last-place club. During Carlton's stunning 1972 season, he had a 15-game winning streak. He was rewarded with a $150,000 contract to

start the 1973 season, the highest salary paid to a Phillies player at that time.

Carlton went into a decline in 1973, though his 13-20 record was partly due to the anemic Phillies offense that gave him little support. He improved to 16-13 in 1974, winning the league strikeout title with 240. Carlton was 15-14 in 1975. Philadelphia won its first pennant since 1950 the following season, and Carlton contributed a 20-7 mark to the effort. His winning percentage was the highest in the National League that year.

The National League presented Carlton with his second Cy Young award in 1977. His 23-10 record was his best since his 1972 debut with the Phils. He won just 16 games in 1978, but had a 1-0 mark in the playoffs. In 1979 the Phillies failed to defend their pennant. Carlton ended the year at 18-

11. It took a league-leading performance of 24 wins from Carlton in 1980 to send the Phillies to their first World Series in 30 years. He won his third Cy Young award and struck out a league-best 286 batters.

In 1982 the Phillies faltered despite Carlton's achievements. He won an unprecedented fourth Cy Young award, going 23-11 with league highs in strikeouts (286) and innings pitched (295). Carlton slipped to 15-16 in 1983, but he sent the Phillies to another World Series with two playoff victories.

Carlton's last winning season came in 1984. He won 13 games, but the sore-shouldered hurler had to cope without his once-wicked slider, the pitch that made him famous. In 33 starts, the one-time workhorse of the Phillies staff had just 1 complete game. The Phillies released Carlton in June 1986. He pitched one month with the San Francisco Giants, then finished the year with the Chicago White Sox. Carlton played a half-season with the Indians before being traded to the Minnesota Twins. The Twins released Carlton after just four games in 1988.

During his career, Carlton accumulated six 20-win seasons and earned seven All-Star game selections. He ranks ninth overall in career victories and has the second-highest strikeout total in history. He'll be remembered as one of baseball's greatest lefthanders.

Lefthander Steve Carlton won the coveted Cy Young award an unprecedented four times during his remarkable career. His banner year came in 1972 when he won 27 games for the Philadelphia Phillies, including a 15-game winning streak.

CAREER HIGHLIGHTS
STEPHEN NORMAN CARLTON

Born: December 22, 1944   Miami, FL
Height: 6'4"   **Weight:** 210 lbs.   **Batted:** Left   **Threw:** Left
Pitcher: St. Louis Cardinals, 1965-71; Philadelphia Phillies, 1972-86; San Francisco Giants, 1986; Chicago White Sox, 1986; Cleveland Indians, 1987; Minnesota Twins, 1987-88.

★ Had the best ERA in the N.L. in 1972   ★ Topped the N.L. in wins four times
★ Led the N.L. in strikeouts five times   ★ Pitched in five All-Star games
★ Won the Cy Young award in 1972, 1977, 1980, and 1982

MAJOR LEAGUE TOTALS

G	IP	W	L	Pct.	SO	BB	ERA
741	5,217	329	244	.574	4,136	1,833	3.22

GARY CARTER

New York Mets catcher Gary Carter, one of the best National League backstops of the 1980s, is tracking down some historic milestones. In 1988 Carter hit the 300th home run of his distinguished career, and he is also approaching his 2,000th lifetime hit. However, any upcoming plateaus will be reached with another team as the wily catcher was not picked up by the Mets after the 1989 season.

Carter was a savior on offense for the needy Mets in 1985. They hadn't had a dependable catcher since Jerry Grote patrolled behind the plate in the 1970s. The Mets seemed ready to challenge for a National League title, but they needed one more good hitter and a capable catcher to guide a talented but inexperienced pitching staff. Dreams came true for Mets fans on December 10, 1984, when New York shipped Hubie Brooks, Mike Fitzgerald, Herm Winningham, and Floyd Youmans to the Montreal Expos for Carter. In 149 games, Carter topped the Mets in homers (32) and RBI (100). He hit an impressive .281 and led National League backstops in putouts (956) and chances per game (7.2). Unfortunately, the Mets finished at 98-64, three games behind the pennant-winning St. Louis Cardinals.

Another superb season by Carter helped the Mets win their first divisional crown since 1973. The Mets finished with a stunning 108-54 record, while Carter posted some snappy statistics of his own: 24 homers, 105 RBI, and a .255 average. Although he hit just .148 in the National League playoffs against Houston, Carter was one of the stars of the team's seven-game World Series triumph. He hit 2 homers in the fourth game of the Series as the Mets triumphed 6-2 and evened the match at two games each. Carter wound up his first fall classic with 8 hits for a .276 average, including 4 runs scored and a team-leading 9 RBI.

Carter's stats dropped off in 1987 to 20 homers and 83 RBI. In 1988 he had just 11 homers and 46 RBI but provided the game-winning RBI in the first game of the National League Championship Series against the Los Angeles Dodgers.

When looking at Carter's defensive accomplishments over the last 15 years, it's amazing to realize that he began his major league career as an outfielder. A third-round draft pick by the Montreal Expos in 1972, Carter played catcher, first base, third base, and outfield in

three minor league seasons before making the big leagues. Carter's brief nine-game trial in 1974 with the Expos was a walloping success, as he hit .407 with 1 home run. In 1975, however, Carter played 92 of his 144 games in the Expos outfield. Carter did well enough there, making only 4 errors. He was stuck in left field because defensive whiz Barry Foote had the starting catcher's job locked up. Carter's first-year hitting included 17 homers, 68 RBI, and a .270 average.

Six weeks on the disabled list blighted Carter's 1976 sophomore season. He played in only 91 games, and his average sank to .219. An admirable comeback was in the works for 1977. His play was so inspired that the Expos traded Foote in June and presented the starting job to Carter.

The new responsibilities brought out the best in Carter, and he hit .284 with 31 homers and 84 RBI. Carter proved that he could handle the defensive expectations of a full-time major league

catcher. He paced the league with 101 assists, 811 putouts, and 14 double plays. Despite hitting 20 homers and 72 RBI, he had what some critics considered an off-year in 1978. In 1979 his totals improved to .283 with 22 homers and 75 RBI. He went 1-for-2 in the All-Star game with 1 RBI. Again, Carter was first among league catchers in assists, putouts, and double plays.

The 1980 season was one of Carter's most memorable. The Expos, once the laughingstock of the N.L., finished second in the East with a 90-72 record (only one game behind the division-winning Phillies). Carter was partly responsible for his team's prosperity. He sparked Montreal with 29 homers and 101 RBI. Defensively, he led N.L. catchers in putouts, assists, and fielding percentage (.993). In 1981 the Expos came within inches of the National League Championship Series. In a special divisional playoff, the Expos nipped the Phillies in five games. Although he played in just 100 games during the regular season, Carter led both playoff teams in hitting with 2 homers, 6 RBI, and a .421 average. The Dodgers denied the Expos the chance at the World Series in the N.L. Championship Series. Carter, however, was the leading hitter of the series with a .438 mark.

Carter hit 29 homers and 97 RBI in 1982, while recording a spiffy .293 average. Although he hit just 17 homers in 1983, Carter had a league-best .995 fielding average. Carter's last year in Montreal, 1984, was a memorable one: He hit .294 with 27 homers and a league-leading 106 RBI.

In his mid-thirties, Carter may not have the stamina to catch much longer, but his bat remains a potent weapon. His talent, wits, and leadership make him a valuable asset to any team.

CAREER HIGHLIGHTS
GARY EDMUND CARTER

Born: April 8, 1954   Culver City, CA
Height: 6'2"   **Weight:** 205 lbs.   **Bats:** Right   **Throws:** Right
Catcher: Montreal Expos, 1974-84; New York Mets, 1985-89.

★ Led the N.L. in RBI with 106 in 1984   ★ Named to 11 All-Star teams
★ Hit .276 in the 1986 World Series   ★ Played in four N.L. Championship Series
★ Named Rookie of the Year by *The Sporting News* in 1975

MAJOR LEAGUE TOTALS

G	AB	H	BA	2B	3B	HR	R	RBI	SB
1,958	7,041	1,879	.267	321	30	302	941	1,128	36

Steady slugger Gary Carter was a powerful asset to the Montreal Expos during the early 1980s. Often last in the N.L. East during the 1970s, the Expos consistently improved as a team with the help of Carter's home run and RBI totals.

JOE CARTER

Joe Carter is a player on the verge of baseball stardom as the result of discovering a home run swing during the 1986 season. In his three prior major league seasons, Carter had never hit more than 15 round-trippers, but in 1986 he powered 29 over the wall. Also that year, he stole 29 bases, hit .302, and placed sixth in the American League with a .514 slugging average. In addition, he led both leagues with 121 RBI, becoming the first Indians hitter to achieve that feat since Al Rosen scored 145 RBI in 1953. Carter highlighted his success with a 21-game hitting streak, the second longest in the league. He was baseball's top run producer in 1986: Tallying RBI plus runs scored (108) minus home runs, Carter had a score of 200, outdistancing Don Mattingly, Jim Rice, and Kirby Puckett in that category. Carter finished in ninth place for the MVP balloting with 72 points.

Carter's potent new offense bolstered the Cleveland Indians 1987 pennant hopes, but the Tribe fell far short on pitching. Carter himself regressed in batting average, dropping 38 points from his 1986 total by the end of the 1987 season. The power remained, however, and by season's end he had hit 32 home runs and had managed a second consecutive 100-plus RBI performance. He also became a member of the exclusive "30/30" club in 1987 with 32 home runs and 31 stolen bases.

The 1988 season found Carter in top form. He paced the Indians with 27 homers and 98 RBI, hitting .271. He struck out just 82 times in 1988, his lowest total in three seasons. Carter continued to be an aggressive baserunner, swiping a club-high 27 bases. Inferior pitching sank Cleveland again and the Tribe finished at 78-84 in fifth place in the American League Eastern Division.

Playing for a struggling team has kept Carter from receiving the recognition he deserves as one of the American League's finest sluggers. His speed and power make him a future candidate for the "40/40" club.

Carter was first obtained by Cleveland in a controversial trade with the Chicago Cubs. The Indians gave up catcher Ron Hassey and pitchers George Frazier and Rick Sutcliffe in exchange for Darryl Banks, Don Schulze, Mel Hall, and Carter. Sutcliffe had gone 17-11 with the Indians in 1983. After the Indians traded him, Sutcliffe went 16-1, pitching the Cubs

to a division pennant. Meanwhile in Cleveland, angry fans wanted to know what their team got in return for their star hurler. Carter, despite spending a month on the disabled list, responded by delivering 13 homers, 41 RBI, and a .275 average in 66 games.

Due to a groin injury and a sprained left wrist, Carter got into only 143 games in 1985. He played first base, second, third, and the outfield. He batted .262 with 15 homers and 59 RBI. One four-bagger was an inside-the-park job at Seattle on September 10. Carter stole 24 bases in 30 attempts, including home twice.

It seems that both the Indians and the Cubs benefited from that 1984 trade. Carter began his pro career with

the Chicago Cubs organization, pocketing a $150,000 signing bonus after being named College Player of the Year in 1981 at Wichita State. The Cubs made Carter the second choice of the 1981 draft. (Mike Moore was the first player chosen, by Seattle.) Carter played in the Cubs minor league system for four seasons. At the Triple-A minor league level in 1983, Carter hit .307 with 22 homers and 83 RBI; he was named the American Association Rookie of the Year. The Cubs apparently gave up on Carter after his September 1983 call-up to the majors, in which he hit a dismal .176 in 23 games, with no home runs and only a single RBI. At the time of his trade, Carter was hitting .313 with 14 homers and 66 RBI in 61 games with the Iowa Cubs (Chicago's Triple-A affiliate).

One of Carter's biggest problems early on with Cleveland was his lack of one full-time position. His bat was too valuable to keep out of the Indians line-up, but he was shuttled from designated hitter to first base to the outfield with regularity. However, he remained primarily in the Cleveland outfield in 1988 due to the presence of Willie Upshaw. And with the 1988 off-season acquisition of Pete O'Brien, Joe Carter spent most of the 1989 season in the outfield. Such a move made sense. Carter has a strong throwing arm, and he has the jumping ability to snatch a potential home run from the top of the outfield fence.

Carter got a late start in the big leagues, and he didn't play his first full season until age 25. However, he's making up for lost time with his current statistics. If the Indians ever make it to a division pennant, Carter will finally be acclaimed as one of baseball's best.

CAREER HIGHLIGHTS
JOSEPH CHRIS CARTER

Born: March 7, 1960   Oklahoma City, OK
Height: 6'3"   **Weight:** 210 lbs.   **Bats:** Right   **Throws:** Right
Outfielder, first baseman: Chicago Cubs, 1983; Cleveland Indians, 1984-89.

- ★ Named to the All-American baseball team in 1980-81
- ★ Led the A.L. in RBI in 1986
- ★ Topped the 1988 Indians in homers and RBI
- ★ Played in all 162 games in 1986
- ★ Hit three home runs in one game on August 29, 1986, and May 28, 1987

MAJOR LEAGUE TOTALS

G	AB	H	BA	2B	3B	HR	R	RBI	SB
700	2,656	727	.274	133	19	116	378	426	114

Playing for the struggling Cleveland Indians has kept Joe Carter from receiving the media attention he deserves. Carter's biggest year to date was 1986, when he slammed 29 home runs, hit .302, stole 29 bases, and led both leagues with 121 RBI.

NORM CASH

When the Detroit Tigers traded Steve Demeter to the Cleveland Indians on April 12, 1960, little did anyone suspect that the Bengals would get their second greatest homer hitter ever in return. Norm Cash would be a star for the Tigers for 15 years.

From 1955-59, Cash labored in the Chicago White Sox minor league system and spent a year in the military. Cash had a 13-game introduction to the majors with the 1958 White Sox. In 1959 he saw part-time action for Chicago, hitting 4 homers, 16 RBI, and a .240 average in 58 games. The native Texan went 0-for-4 as a pinch hitter in the 1959 World Series versus the Dodgers. The White Sox traded Cash, Johnny Romano, and Bubba Phillips to Cleveland in exchange for Minnie Minoso, Jake Striker, Don Ferrarese, and Dick Brown on December 6, 1959. The Indians then traded Cash for Detroit's Steve Demeter when the 1960 season opened, partly because Demeter had the added appeal of playing third base. While Cash lasted 15 seasons with the Tigers, the Indians came up empty-handed from the trade; Demeter played only four games in 1960 before his career ended.

The player nicknamed "Stormin' Norman" was an immediate hit in Detroit. In his first season with the Tigers, Cash hit .286 with 18 homers and 63 RBI in 121 games. In 1961 Cash had one of the best offensive seasons in Tiger history. He won the American League batting title with a .361 average and added a league-leading 193 hits. Cash displayed awesome batting power, clobbering 41 homers and 132 RBI. Cash's average would be the highest of any major leaguer during the entire decade. Cash was selected for the 1961 All-Star game, but he was overlooked in Most Valuable Player balloting because Roger Maris was busy hitting a record 61 homers.

Cash followed up his momentous 1961 season with 39 homers and 89 RBI in 1962. He would hit in double digits for homers for 14 of his 15 seasons in Detroit. Cash was also a fixture at first base. He wasn't the slickest-fielding first sacker the Tigers ever had, but he provided the kind of consistency they hadn't known for years.

The 1963 season saw Cash's power output drop somewhat. He hit 26 round-trippers, second on the Tigers only to superstar Al Kaline. Kaline and Cash proved to be a solid long-ball combination throughout the 1960s for

Detroit. In 1964 Cash hit 23 home runs and led the team with 83 RBI. He paced the American League with a 6.4 home run percentage in 1965, hitting 30 dingers and 82 RBI. Cash came close to winning his first home run crown, only to be edged out by Boston rookie Tony Conigliaro's 32 homers. He did have a fine year with the glove, making only 4 errors all year long. Although Cash didn't have a reputation as a fielding great, his .997 fielding percentage was the best for any first sacker in the majors in 1964.

Cash got his second All-Star game invitation in 1966. That year he hit .279 with 32 homers and 93 RBI in a career-high 160 games. Cash finished fourth in the home run race behind Frank Robinson's league-best 49 with Baltimore.

The Detroit Tigers jumped from a third-place finish in 1966 to a 91-71 record in 1967. The Red Sox beat the Bengals out of the pennant by only one game. Cash had a typically solid year at the plate, with 22 homers and 72 RBI. He topped American League first basemen with 112 assists and a .995 fielding percentage.

The Tigers turned the tables on the Red Sox in 1968, winning the American League title with a dazzling 103-59 record. Even though he missed 35 games, Cash hammered 25 homers and 63 RBI. The veteran first baseman led the Tigers in hitting throughout the seven-game Series. His .385 average was tops among Tiger regulars. Cash had 10 hits, 1 homer, 5 RBI, and 5 runs scored in the fall classic.

Cash continued his slugging prowess in 1969 with 22 homers, 74 RBI, and a .280 average. An uncharacteristic slump left Cash with only 15 homers and 53 RBI in 1970. His comeback in 1971 brought him another All-Star appearance. He banged out 32 homers and 91 RBI, batting .283. Cash's homer percentage (7.1) was the highest in the American League. Cash narrowly missed yet another home run title, this time to Bill Melton of the Chicago White Sox, who hit 33. Cash's .531 slugging percentage was the third highest in the junior circuit.

Cash was back on the American League All-Star roster in 1972. He powered the Billy Martin-managed Tigers to a division title with 22 homers and 61 RBI. Although the Tigers never advanced beyond the American League Championship Series, Cash batted .267 with 1 home run and 2 RBI. Cash played his last full season in 1973, hitting 19 homers and 40 RBI.

Cash retired with 377 career home runs, to rank 29th on the all-time list and second highest for any Detroit Tiger. Cash served as a broadcaster for the Tigers after retirement.

CAREER HIGHLIGHTS
NORMAN DALTON CASH

Born: November 10, 1934   Justiceburg, TX   **Died:** October 12, 1986
Height: 6'0"   **Weight:** 185 lbs.   **Batted:** Left   **Threw:** Left
First baseman, outfielder: Chicago White Sox, 1958-59; Detroit Tigers, 1960-74.

- ★ Topped the A.L. in home run percentage in 1965
- ★ Led the A.L. in hits in 1961
- ★ Ranks second on the Tigers all-time home run list
- ★ Won the A.L. batting title in 1961
- ★ Hit .385 in the 1968 World Series

MAJOR LEAGUE TOTALS

G	AB	H	BA	2B	3B	HR	R	RBI	SB
2,089	6,705	1,820	.271	241	41	377	1,046	1,103	43

"Stormin' Norman" Cash was traded by the Cleveland Indians to the Detroit Tigers for Steve Demeter. The Indians lived to regret their decision as Cash went on to hit .286 that season, while Demeter played in only four games before his career ended.

ORLANDO CEPEDA

He was known as "Cha-Cha" or "The Baby Bull" to baseball fans throughout the 1960s; National League pitchers knew him as Orlando Cepeda, one of the most dangerous power hitters in the league.

Cepeda earned his Baby Bull nickname long before he started clubbing major league home runs. His father, Peruchio Cepeda, was a famous hitter in Puerto Rican baseball known as "The Bull." Naturally, Cepeda's son needed a similar moniker, hence The Baby Bull. Young Cepeda signed his first contract in the U.S. at age 17 and immediately became the talk of minor league baseball. In 1955 he won his first batting crown with a .393 average at Salem, Virginia (where he was paid $225 per month). In 1956 he had a league-leading .355 mark with Minneapolis. The transition to America was more difficult for Cepeda off the field, however. He spoke no English when he first arrived in America, and even though Jackie Robinson had broken baseball's color barrier nearly a decade earlier, many small towns still refused to allow minorities into restaurants or movie theaters.

Soon, Cepeda began pounding National League pitching. He won National League Rookie of the Year honors in 1958 with 25 home runs, 96 RBI, and a .312 average. Cepeda led the National League with 38 doubles. Although he was first among National League first basemen in errors, he also topped them with 1,322 putouts and an average of 9.8 chances per game. Cepeda's average rose to .317 in 1959, and he smashed 27 home runs and drove in 105 runs.

Due to the arrival of Willie McCovey, Cepeda was reassigned to the Giants outfield in 1960. The shuffling didn't seem to bother his hitting, and he reeled off 24 homers, 96 RBI, and a .297 mark. In 1961 Cepeda exceeded everyone's expectations with 46 homers and 142 RBI, both National League highs. His .311 rounded out a sparkling season.

Cepeda topped 100 RBI again in 1962 by driving in 114 runs. He played in all 162 games and thumped 35 homers. Cha-Cha followed with 30-plus homers and 97 RBI in both 1963 and 1964. He missed nearly the entire 1965 season after having knee surgery. The Giants management, which had had constant money squabbles with Cepeda, happily traded him to St. Louis for pitcher Ray Sadecki on May 8, 1966. With that one trade, the Cardi-

nals obtained the offensive fuel for two National League titles.

In 1967 Cepeda won the league MVP award with 25 homers, a league-best 111 RBI, and a .325 average. The Cardinals wound up as world champions. The Cards returned to the World Series in 1968 with Cepeda's help. St. Louis traded Cepeda to Atlanta in 1969. The Braves won their first division title that year, with The Baby Bull contributing 22 homers, 88 RBI, and a .257 average. Cepeda hit .455 in the fateful playoffs against the "Miracle Mets" from New York.

Cepeda's last great season was in 1970, in which he hit 34 homers and 111 RBI. Cepeda's weak knees needed surgery again in 1971. Following the surgery, he found work as a pinch hitter/designated hitter in the American League for three seasons. Cepeda was

used as an example by defenders of the new designated hitter rule established in 1973. Here was a great veteran who was physically unable to meet the demands of a full-time position, but thanks to the DH spot, he was able to extend his career a few more seasons. When he earned 20 home runs, 86 RBI, and a .289 average for the 1973 Red Sox, he showed how a designated hitter could add offensive fireworks to any game.

Throughout his 17 big league seasons, Cepeda was often criticized and misunderstood by the press. Many reporters labeled him as "hot-tempered." When Giants manager Alvin Dark ordered Cepeda and his foreign teammates to speak only English in the clubhouse, Cepeda refused. The Giants even tried to cut Cepeda's salary after he hit 35 home runs and 114 RBI in 1962.

Following his distinguished career, Cepeda returned to Puerto Rico a local hero. He shocked baseball fans everywhere when he was arrested at the San Juan airport with a trunkload of marijuana in his car. He served less than a year in jail after being sentenced to five years on the charges. This unfortunate incident may keep this truly gifted player from ever being elected to the Hall of Fame.

Orlando Cepeda was used by supporters of the designated hitter rule—established in 1973—as an example of a player who could extend his career by becoming a DH. As a DH for the BoSox, Cepeda socked 20 homers and 86 RBI in the '73 season.

CAREER HIGHLIGHTS
ORLANDO MANUEL CEPEDA

Born: September 17, 1937   Ponce, Puerto Rico
Height: 6'2"   **Weight:** 210 lbs.   **Batted:** Right   **Threw:** Right
First baseman, designated hitter: San Francisco Giants, 1958-66; St. Louis Cardinals, 1966-68; Atlanta Braves, 1969-72; Oakland Athletics, 1972; Boston Red Sox, 1973; Kansas City Royals, 1974.

★ Selected N.L. Rookie of the Year in 1958

★ Led the N.L. in homers and RBI in 1961

★ Batted over .300 nine times

★ Played in three World Series

★ Named N.L. MVP in 1967

MAJOR LEAGUE TOTALS

G	AB	H	BA	2B	3B	HR	R	RBI	SB
2,124	7,927	2,351	.297	417	27	379	1,131	1,365	142

RON CEY

Consistency was always Ron Cey's strong point. Although he never hit .300 in the major leagues, Cey could be counted on to hit in the .260s or .270s. Likewise, he'd sock some 25 balls into the seats each season and would occasionally lead the league in a fielding stat of some sort. During his dozen years in the Dodger-blue livery, Cey contributed to four National League West division titles and league pennants with timely extra-base hits.

Cey was the New York Mets 24th-round draft pick in 1966 but turned it down. His third-round selection by the Dodgers in 1968 was more to his liking, but he toiled for five years in the minor leagues, unable to displace rising Dodger star Steve Garvey from his third-base post in Los Angeles. In 1969 with Bakersfield, Cey smashed out 22 homers and 56 RBI for a .331 average. With the 1971 Spokane club, Cey had another banner year with 32 homers, 123 RBI, a .328 average, and a league-leading fielding percentage of .940. Though Cey played two games in the big leagues in 1971 and 11 in 1972, the Dodgers tested Cey one more year with Albuquerque before bringing him up to stay in 1973.

Cey's consistency in the field and with the bat earned him a permanent spot with the 1973 Dodgers, where his relatively short stature and unusual baserunning style earned him the nickname "Penguin." Cey took over third base from Steve Garvey, who moved to first. With Davey Lopes manning second base and Bill Russell at shortstop, the Dodgers sported what would become the longest-running infield in baseball history.

In his 1973 rookie season, Cey played in 152 games, hitting .245 with 15 home runs and 80 RBI. Cey's 328 assists were tops in the National League, but outfielder Gary Matthews of the San Francisco Giants beat him out for the N.L. Rookie of the Year award.

Cey was a major contributor to the Dodgers' 1974 division pennant and league championship, their first in eight years. He got his first of six consecutive trips to the All-Star game with a banner season at the plate: His totals included 18 homers, 97 RBI, and a .262 average. Cey had a two-run double for the National Leaguers in the midseason matchup. In the 1974 playoffs versus Pittsburgh, Cey hit .313.

In 1975 Cey upped his power production by clubbing 25 homers and 101 RBI for a .283 average. Cey missed 17

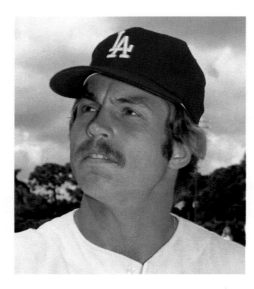

games in 1976, so his totals slipped to .277 with 23 homers and 80 RBI. Both Cey and the Dodgers rebounded in 1977. The Dodgers regained their division title, and Cey thumped a career-high 30 homers and 110 RBI. Cey hit .308 in the National League Championship Series, including a grand slam in the opening game.

The Dodgers repeated as both Western Division and National League champions in 1978, with the aid of 23 homers, 84 RBI, and a .270 average by Cey. Cey sizzled in postseason play: He hit .313 with 1 homer and 3 RBI in the playoffs and scored the winning run in the deciding fourth game of the competition. Los Angeles lost to the New York Yankees in the six-game World Series, but Cey still managed a .286 average. All of his clutch hitting came in the team's 4-3 win in game two. Cey battered Yankee starter (and eventual Hall of Famer) Jim "Catfish" Hunter for a

three-run homer and an RBI single.

Cey had 28-homer seasons in 1979 and 1980. In 1979 he led National League third sackers in fielding for the first time ever with a .977 percentage. In 1980 Cey had a league-high 127 putouts. He saw action in just 85 games in 1981, when the Dodgers earned their first world championship since 1965. Even with limited appearances, Cey hit .288 (his best-ever average) with 13 homers and 50 RBI. Cey hit .278 with 3 RBI in the playoffs versus Montreal, then batted .350 in the World Series against the Yankees. The highlight of Cey's Series had to be his three-run homer off Dave Righetti to help with the third game (after the Yankees had jumped out to a two-game lead).

Cey's last season with the Dodgers was in 1982, when he hit .254 with 24 homers and 79 RBI. The emergence of Pedro Guerrero gave the Dodgers the chance to have a power-hitting third baseman with a higher average. Cey was traded to the Cubs and hit 20-plus homers for Chicago for three straight years, helping them to their 1984 division title. Cey joined the Athletics in 1987 but got lost in the team's youth movement and retired in midseason.

Ron Cey ended his career in style in mid-1987, sending his new teammates on the Oakland Athletics a telegram wishing them the best of luck in their chase for the pennant and apologizing for not being able to do more to help their cause. Though his career totals are unlikely to ever earn him serious Hall of Fame consideration, Cey's contribution to the Los Angeles Dodgers dynasty of the 1970s and to the Chicago Cubs one-year-wonder pennant in 1984 will not be forgotten by fans.

CAREER HIGHLIGHTS
RONALD CHARLES CEY

Born: February 15, 1948   Tacoma, WA
Height: 5'10"   **Weight:** 185 lbs.   **Batted:** Right   **Threw:** Right
Third baseman: Los Angeles Dodgers, 1971-82; Chicago Cubs, 1983-86; Oakland Athletics, 1987.

★ Hit a grand slam in the first game of the N.L. Championship Series in 1977
★ Scored the winning run in the N.L. Championship Series in 1978
★ Drove in 100-plus runs twice
★ Hit 20 or more homers for 10 seasons
★ Played on four World Series teams

MAJOR LEAGUE TOTALS

G	AB	H	BA	2B	3B	HR	R	RBI	SB
2,073	7,162	1,868	.261	328	21	316	977	1,139	24

Ron "the Penguin" Cey was a part of the Chicago Cubs team that captured
not only the 1984 division title but the hearts of baseball fans everywhere. Cey did
well during his stint with the Cubs, hitting over 20 homers for three straight years.

FRANK CHANCE

Baseball fans usually think of Frank Chance as just one part of the famous infield triumvirate, "Tinker to Evers to Chance." But the Chicago Cubs first baseman could easily stand on his own as one of the finest hitters of his day, and as a player/manager in the early 1900s, he achieved unequaled success.

Chance grew up in California and was attending the University of California to become a dentist when he was discovered by a Chicago Cubs scout in 1898. With only semipro experience, Chance made a quick adjustment to the big leagues. He served as a Cubs catcher and outfielder in 1898, appearing in 53 games. His playing time grew slowly through the next four seasons, and he didn't appear in more than 100 games until 1903.

Manager Frank Selee made Chance a full-time baseman for the Cubs in 1902. That same year, shortstop Joe Tinker and second baseman Johnny Evers arrived, and together they formed the most famous infield in baseball history. Chance responded with his best offensive season ever in 1903. In 125 games, Chance had 2 homers, 81 RBI, and a .327 average. He also won the National League stolen base crown with 67 swipes. Chance hit a career-high 6 homers in 1904 and hit .310 with 49 RBI and 42 stolen bases. The Cubs management appointed Chance as a player/manager in 1905, when ill health forced Selee to retire. "The Peerless Leader," as he was dubbed by a Chicago sportswriter, led the Cubs to four pennants in five years. His 1906 Cubs won an incredible 116 games—still a major league record—and finished the season a staggering 20 games in front of the second-place New York Giants. He hit .319 in 1906 and stole a league-best 57 bases. His 103 runs scored were a National League high, too. Chance and his Cubs were defeated in the World Series by the crosstown White Sox in six games.

The next year the Chance-piloted Cubs were even more successful, finishing at 107-45. The man who was nicknamed "Husk" hit .293 and led first sackers in fielding with a .992 percentage. In the 1907 World Series, the Cubs swept the Detroit Tigers in four straight games.

The Cubs defended their world championship in 1908, again beating the Tigers in the fall classic. As a player, Chance hit .272 with 2 homers and 55 RBI. He was the leading hitter in the

1908 Series with a .421 average, including 8 hits, 4 runs scored, and 5 stolen bases. Chance's Cubs missed out on postseason play in 1909 but returned to the World Series in 1910 against the Philadelphia Athletics. Connie Mack's team prevailed, although Chance was one of the hottest hitters in the event. He sparked his Cubs with a .353 average in the five-game affair.

Chance hit .298 in 88 games in 1910, which was his last productive year as a player. He suffered from continual headaches (possibly from getting beaned by several pitches). He needed surgery for blood clots following the 1912 season. The Cubs and Chance parted in 1912 over several financial issues. Chance wanted to obtain more quality players; the Cubs ownership didn't want to spend the money. After quitting the Cubs, Chance managed the New York Yankees in 1913 and 1914. Neither of his teams had winning records, and Chance and company stayed mired in seventh place for two years. After managing a Pacific Coast

League team in Los Angeles in 1916 and 1917, Chance reentered the major leagues as manager of the Boston Red Sox in 1923, but the BoSox wound up in last place with a 61-91 mark. Less than a year later, Chance died.

Chance ended his playing career with a .296 average. He had 1,273 hits in 17 years. His 401 stolen bases made him one of baseball's greatest speedsters during the early years of the game. His 10 steals in four World Series rank third in history. Tinker, Evers, and Chance—the immortal double play trio—were all inducted into the Hall of Fame in 1946.

Franklin P. Adams, a writer for the New York *Mail* in 1910, made the infield trio famous with the following verse:

"These are the saddest of possible words—
   Tinker to Evers to Chance.
Trio of Bear Cubs and fleeter than birds—
   Tinker to Evers to Chance.
Ruthlessly pricking our gonfalon bubble,
   Making a Giant hit into a double,
Words that are weighty with nothing but trouble—
   Tinker to Evers to Chance."

Frank Chance's role as a manager was ultimately more significant to baseball history than his career as a first baseman. Chance played only 11 seasons as a full-time player, possibly due to injuries from frequent beanings.

CAREER HIGHLIGHTS
FRANK LEROY CHANCE

Born: September 9, 1877 Fresno, CA **Died:** September 14, 1924
Height: 6'0" **Weight:** 190 lbs. **Batted:** Right **Threw:** Right
First baseman: Chicago Cubs, 1898-1912; New York Yankees, 1913-14. Manager: Chicago Cubs, 1905-12; New York Yankees, 1913-14; Boston Red Sox, 1923.

★ As a player/manager, led the Chicago Cubs to four penants in five years
★ Won two stolen base titles
★ Hit .310 in four World Series
★ Guided the Cubs to a record 116 wins in 1906
★ Led the N.L. with 103 RBI in 1906
★ Elected to the Hall of Fame in 1946

MAJOR LEAGUE TOTALS

G	AB	H	BA	2B	3B	HR	R	RBI	SB
1,287	4,297	1,273	.296	200	79	20	797	597	401

OSCAR CHARLESTON

Like so many who grew up near the turn of the century, Oscar Charleston believed that earning his own living was a far more pressing matter than a formal education. Thus he dropped out of school at the age of 15 and joined the army. He was promptly shipped to the Philippines.

Charleston learned many things during his tour of duty, but perhaps most importantly, he learned a new pastime: the game of baseball. He also learned that a profitable, enjoyable living could be made as a baseball player. By the time he was 18, he was the first black player in the Manila League.

Upon his 1915 return to Indianapolis, Charleston signed with the ABCs. By 1916 the scrawny, dominating center fielder was leading his team to a Negro League Championship. Playing shallow, almost breathing down the second baseman's neck, Charleston had the speed to fade in or out in time to make the play. His theatrical catches sometimes featured spontaneous choreography, with Charleston turning once or twice en route to the catch, backhanding a snag, and never taking his eye off the ball.

Clocked by the army as traveling close to 10 yards per second when on a tear, it's a small wonder Charleston was a terror on the base paths. He was truly every pitcher's nightmare; he was as mean at the plate as he was in the field. A fastball was pabulum to him, and he had a knack for putting it anywhere in the park.

His long stay with the ABCs was interrupted when he spent 1919-21 with Rube Foster's Chicago American Giants. Foster's high-strung, take-charge personality apparently struck some kind of chord in Charleston, for after his time with the Giants, Charleston was a manager or player/manager for all but one season of his career.

Back with the ABCs in 1921, Charleston batted .430, stole 35 bases, and paced the circuit in home runs, triples, and doubles. Baseball scholars still talk about the 4 home runs he hit in a single exhibition game against the St. Louis Cardinals. In 1922 he again was the league's best in homers, and his .399 average wasn't too shabby either.

By 1930 he was part of one of history's all-time great teams: the Homestead Grays, featuring superstars such as Smokey Joe Williams, Josh Gibson, and manager Judy Johnson. In 1932 Johnson jumped to the Pittsburgh Crawfords and induced many of his Grays teammates to do the same. Charleston also skipped to the Crawfords where he became a teammate of the great Satchel Paige. Although Charleston was 36 when he joined the Crawfords, he slammed an astonishing .363 his first year there, topping it with .450 the next.

By the time he reached the Crawfords, Charleston had all but retired from the outfield, staying instead at first base where his diminishing speed was not so noticeable. With foresight for the day when his speed would be gone, he began managing his teams and from 1933 to 1935 started in the first three Negro League All-Star games. It was no surprise to those who had followed his career that he was an excellent manager. On barnstorming tours he had often played all nine positions in a single game to add a little flair to the proceedings.

His career as a manager lasted until 1954, with such teams as the Toledo Crawfords, the Indianapolis Crawfords, the Philadelphia Stars, and the Indianapolis Clowns, whom Charleston led to the 1954 Negro world championship, his first as a manager.

The Clowns had an interesting place in baseball history, dating back to the first effort in the 1890s to segregate the game. The disenfranchised players turned to clowning—mixing humorous antics with legitimate play in order to attract an audience, much like the Harlem Globetrotters in the 1950s.

Even though Charleston himself scouted the Negro Leagues for a player for Branch Rickey to thrust into the majors (Jackie Robinson undertook the task in 1947) it would be many years before blacks would be sought out and accepted by the white major leagues. Eventually Charleston got the recognition he deserved: In 1976 he was fittingly enshrined in baseball's Hall of Fame.

Oscar Charleston was a great center fielder who was able to play quite shallow because of his great speed, which allowed him to bolt back for deep fly balls. It is said that in 1921 he batted .434 and led the Negro League in home runs.

CAREER HIGHLIGHTS
OSCAR McKINLEY CHARLESTON

Born: October 12, 1896 Indianapolis, IN **Died:** October 6, 1954
Height: 6'1" **Weight:** 180 lbs. **Batted:** Left **Threw:** Left
First baseman, outfielder, manager: Indianapolis ABC's, 1915-23; Harrisburg Giants, 1924-29; Hilldale and Homestead Grays, 1930-31; Pittsburgh Crawfords, 1932-40; Philadelphia Stars, 1940-44; Brooklyn Brown Dodgers, 1945-49; Indianapolis Clowns, 1950-54.

★ Led the National Negro League, the Eastern Colored League, and the American Negro League in batting average, doubles, and homers
★ Compiled an estimated .376 lifetime batting average
★ Batted .405 in his rookie season in the Cuban winter league
★ Elected to the Baseball Hall of Fame in 1976

MAJOR LEAGUE TOTALS

(no accurate statistics available)

JACK CHESBRO

History is sometimes cruel. Such is the case with Hall of Fame pitcher Jack Chesbro, who won a staggering 41 games in 1904. It's a modern-day record that will probably stand forever, but the mark was overshadowed by a wild pitch that Chesbro unleashed in his final appearance of the season, costing his New York Highlanders the pennant. Few people remember that Chesbro had pitched his 41st victory on the previous Friday. He was forced to pitch again the next day and lost. With only a day's rest, the Highlanders started him again on Monday, October 10, when the fatigued hurler lost the finale by just one run due to his wild pitch.

The wild pitch was a sour ending to what should have been the pitcher's sweetest season. Chesbro, coming into the game with an incredible 41-11 record, was making his 51st (and most important) start of the year. It was the first game of a season-ending doubleheader between the Highlanders (who later became the Yankees) and the Boston Red Sox, who held a game-and-a-half lead over the New York club. The Highlanders had to win both games to capture the pennant, and they went with their ace in the opener. It was a classic confrontation, with Chesbro and Boston pitcher Bill Dinneen battling to a 2-2 tie into the ninth. The Red Sox were batting, with two outs and Lou Criger on third as the potential winning run. Chesbro was a master of the spitball. (At the turn of the century, the spitball was a legal pitch.) Chesbro threw two strikes past the batter, Fred Parent, then wound up with another wet one. The ball sailed over the head of catcher Jack Kleinow, allowing the winning run to score. Although New York won the second half of the twin bill, Boston won the pennant.

Chesbro played sandlot ball in Massachusetts as a youth and was discovered as the star of a baseball team composed of workers from the New York State Mental Hospital. Chesbro labored at his craft in the minors for several years. The first three minor league teams he played for suffered financial collapse in 1895-96. In 1896 Chesbro pitched as a semipro in Cooperstown, New York, long before the Hall of Fame was an institution in that town. After he pitched for a Richmond, Virginia, team for two seasons, the Pittsburgh Pirates found Chesbro and acquired him in July 1899 for $1,500. He appeared in 19 games that

first season, going 6-10; however, he showed tremendous durability, hurling 15 complete games in 17 starts. In 1900 Chesbro was 14-13 with 3 shutouts and 1 save. He continued to be a team workhorse, logging 20 complete games in 26 starts.

In the seven years between 1901 and 1907, Chesbro won 154 games. His 1901 season consisted of a 21-10 record and a league-best .677 winning percentage. His ERA and 26 complete games (in 28 starts) were also season highlights. Chesbro even handled himself well at the plate: In 1901 he had 25 hits (including 1 homer) for a .216 average. His 28-6 record, 8 shutouts, and .824 winning percentage were tops in the National League in 1902.

Chesbro chose to sign with a new American League team, the New York Highlanders, when it entered the league in 1903. While he made more money in New York, his timing wasn't the greatest. The Pirates finished first in the National League for the third straight year and participated in the first World Series in 1903.

Chesbro entered the 20-win circle again in 1903 with the Highlanders. His record-setting season of 1904 saw him lead the American League in wins (41), winning percentage (.774), games (55), games started (51), complete games (48), innings pitched (454.2), and wins in relief (3). As if all that weren't enough, Chesbro also had a great year with the bat, helping his own cause with 41 hits (including 1 homer) for a .236 average.

In 1905 Chesbro won 19 games. His record could have been higher if the Highlanders had provided him with some support, but New York had the third-worst record in the league at 71-78. Chesbro's last winning season was a 23-17 outing in 1906. He was first in the league in games (49) and starts (42).

Known as "Happy Jack" because of his outgoing personality, Chesbro began to decline as a pitcher in 1907. He went 10-10, then slipped to 14-20 in 1908. He finished his career with the Boston Red Sox in 1909.

For his short 11-year career, Chesbro piled up some mighty statistics: He pitched 2,898 innings and notched 261 complete games along with 198 wins. He retired in Conway, Massachusetts, after briefly coaching the Amherst College baseball team. The Baseball Hall of Fame inducted Chesbro in 1946, almost 15 years after his death.

Though unfairly remembered as the pitcher who lost the pennant for the Yankees in the final game of the 1904 season, Jack Chesbro was elected to the Hall of Fame on the strength of his entire career.

CAREER HIGHLIGHTS
JOHN DWIGHT CHESBRO

Born: June 5, 1874   North Adams, MA   **Died:** November 6, 1931
Height: 5'9"   **Weight:** 180 lbs.   **Batted:** Right   **Threw:** Right
Pitcher: Pittsburgh Pirates, 1899-1902; New York Highlanders, 1903-09; Boston Red Sox, 1909.

- ★ Won a record 41 games in 1904
- ★ Led the N.L. with 28 wins in 1902
- ★ Elected to the Hall of Fame in 1946
- ★ Pitched 454 innings in 1904
- ★ Topped the N.L. in winning percentage in 1901 and 1902

MAJOR LEAGUE TOTALS

G	IP	W	L	Pct.	SO	BB	ERA
392	2,898	198	132	.600	1,265	690	2.68

JACK CLARK

When Jack Clark was traded from the New York Yankees to the San Diego Padres with Pat Clements in exchange for Lance McCullers, Jimmy Jones, and Stan Jefferson, both Clark and the Padres were seeing their wishes come true. Clark wanted to return to the National League and California, where he had played for so many years, and the Padres wanted a veteran slugger who could be their long-needed offensive powerhouse. The Padres were so delighted to gain Clark's services that they tore up his old $1.5 million Yankees contract and signed him to a new two-year pact worth $4 million.

Clark's ability and reputation as an awesome power hitter made him well-worth such a truckload of money. Clark had had a fine 1988 season with the New York Yankees. Serving as the team's designated hitter, Clark led the Yanks with 27 homers, 93 RBI, and a .242 batting average. Playing in 150 games, he was second in the American League in walks with 113 and tied for fourth in game-winning RBI with 16. Despite his unqualified success with the Yankees, Clark had always said that he felt more like a National Leaguer. Also, by joining the Padres, Clark found a way to become a full-time player again.

The beginning of Jack Clark's career in organized baseball dates back to 1973. Clark was a dandy high school pitcher at Gladstone High in Azusa, California. He went 11-3 with a 1.25 ERA as a prep pitcher and batted .517 to lead his school squad to a league title. After graduation he briefly tried pitching with Great Falls in 1973 but then concentrated on becoming an accomplished hitter. He was drafted by San Francisco in the 13th round of the June free-agent draft as a hurler. However, he went 0-2 with a 6.00 ERA. The Giants then tried grooming Clark as a third baseman. He played third off and on for four minor league seasons, but he only played the hot corner four times in his major league career.

In 1974, Clark's first full season in organized ball, he notched 19 homers and a league-leading 117 RBI, hitting .315. Moving to Lafayette of the Texas League in 1975, Clark hit 23 homers, 77 RBI, and a .303 mark. By season's end, Clark advanced from Double-A to the Giants. He went 4-for-17 in his major league trial at the conclusion of 1975 and the Giants placed Clark with Triple-A Phoenix in 1976 for more seasoning.

Clark's first great season came in 1978 with the Giants. He was named to *The Sporting News* All-Star team with totals of 25 homers, 98 RBI, and a .306 average. He also tied for the league lead in double plays by outfielders with five. In 1979 Clark was named to his second straight All-Star team, having smashed 26 homers and 86 RBI to complement a .273 average. Clark was dogged by injuries in 1980 and appeared in only 127 games. Nevertheless, he finished with 22 homers and 82 RBI. More time on the disabled list was in store for Clark in 1981, limiting his service to just 99 games.

Clark regained his classic form in 1982: Playing in 157 games, he registered 27 homers and earned a career-high 103 RBI. In 1983 Clark started part-time duty at first base for the Giants. Clark was saddled with more physical woes in 1984. He appeared in just 57 games after tearing cartilage in his right knee on June 26. Clark had been off to one of his best starts, with 11 homers, 44 RBI, and a .320 average.

The St. Louis Cardinals pulled off one of the best deals of the century when they obtained Clark on February 1, 1985. The Redbirds gave up David Green, Dave LaPoint, Jose Uribe, and Gary Rajsich to obtain Clark. The trade was clouded by mystery. Was Clark hard to get along with in San Francisco? Did his string of injuries make him damaged goods? Some of the sparkle was disappearing from Clark's stardom.

The mighty righthander erased all doubts with his momentus performance with the 1985 Redbirds. Although hobbled by some pulled rib cage muscles in August, Clark still managed to play in 126 games. In his limited action, Clark clubbed 22 homers and 87 RBI (third best in the league). Clark reached base during each of the six games of the National League Championship Series. His two-out, three-run homer in the ninth inning of the final game of the playoffs gave the Cardinals a 7-5 come-from-behind victory over the Los Angeles Dodgers. Dodger reliever Tom Niedenfuer had tried to pitch to Clark instead of walking him—with devastating results.

Undoubtedly, Clark's biggest offensive season ever came in 1987. He clobbered a career-best 35 homers and 106 RBI, leading the Cardinals to their second National League championship in three seasons.

If Jack Clark remains injury-free for the remainder of his career, he could accumulate some remarkable offensive stats. When he has been healthy, he has been one of the most fearsome hitters of the past decade.

CAREER HIGHLIGHTS
JACK ANTHONY CLARK

Born: November 10, 1955   New Brighton, PA
Height: 6'2"   **Weight:** 185 lbs.   **Bats:** Right   **Throws:** Right
Outfielder, first baseman: San Francisco Giants, 1975-84; St. Louis Cardinals, 1985-87; New York Yankees, 1988; San Diego Padres, 1989.

- ★ His homer won the 1985 N.L. Championship Series for St. Louis
- ★ Played in four All-Star games
- ★ Had 16 game-winning RBI in 1988
- ★ Hit .381 in the 1985 N.L. Championship Series
- ★ Led the N.L. in game-winning RBI in 1980
- ★ Hit 20 or more homers seven times

MAJOR LEAGUE TOTALS

G	AB	H	BA	2B	3B	HR	R	RBI	SB
1,658	5,775	1,563	.271	291	37	282	952	998	72

Though sometimes plagued with injuries, power hitter Jack Clark has been an asset to any team he has played with. Clark's best season occurred in 1987 when he belted 35 home runs and racked up 106 RBI for the pennant-winning St. Louis Cardinals.

FRED CLARKE

One of the lesser-known player/ managers at the turn of the century was Fred Clarke. Cap Anson and Frank Chance got the most attention for pulling double duty with major league teams, but Clarke was one of the most proficient personalities in baseball at holding down the dual responsibility of playing and managing.

Clarke, who was elected to the Baseball Hall of Fame in 1945, was one of many great players who were born in Iowa. He was 19 years old and playing with an Iowa semipro team in 1891 when he found an ad in *The Sporting News* that changed his life. The Hastings team in the Nebraska State League was looking for players. Clarke responded to the advertisement and found early success. He advanced rapidly through the minor leagues, playing for teams in St. Joseph, Missouri, Montgomery, Alabama, and Savannah, Georgia. After hitting .311 with Savannah, Clarke was accepted by the Louisville Colonels (then considered a major league team) in 1894. In his June 30 debut with the Colonels, the speedy outfielder went 5-for-5. It was just an indication of what was to follow. During an outstanding 21-year career, Clarke excelled as a batter, baserunner, outfielder, and manager. For Louisville, any help was welcome. The team finished in last place with a 36-94 mark in 1894.

The talented Iowan hit .347 in his first full season with Louisville in 1895, and he paced his team in both average and RBI (82). Clarke struggled some in the field that first year, leading the league with 49 errors. In 1896 the Colonels stayed in last place with a 38-93 outcome, but Clarke compiled a .327 average and paced his team with 9 homers and 79 RBI. His hitting blossomed into a .390 average in 1897. Despite his stunning average, Clarke came in second in the race for the batting crown; Wee Willie Keeler hit a whopping .424 that same year. During his banner hitting season, Clarke also showed dynamic leadership skills. He was appointed player/manager of the Colonels late in the 1897 season. He was just 24 years old at the time.

In 1898 Clarke made huge strides in Louisville's progress. The team had never really been a serious contender; however, with young Clarke at the helm, the Colonels advanced to a 70-81 record—nearly twice the number of victories the team achieved two years earlier. As a player, Clarke continued as a

mainstay of the Colonels, hitting .307. In his last year with the Colonels in 1899, Clarke lifted Louisville's record to 75-77 and batted a team-leading .342 with 5 homers and 70 RBI.

The National League reduced its teams from 12 to 8 in 1900, and Louisville closed up shop. Most of its players were sold to Pittsburgh, and Clarke went with them as their player/manager. Clarke and his Colonels turned the Pirates, usually an annual second-division finisher, into a true contender. Clarke's 1900 Pirates finished second in the league at 79-60. Clarke used a gifted young player in right field named Honus Wagner, who hit .381 that year. Wagner would play his best years under Clarke's guidance, later earning Hall of Fame credentials as a Pirates shortstop.

The next season, Clarke and the Pirates won their first title with a 90-49

record. Clarke played left field, hitting .324 with 6 homers and 60 RBI. The team repeated in 1902 as league champions, with Clarke hitting .316. The Pirates played the Red Sox in the first official World Series in 1903. Clarke hit .351 (with a league-leading 32 doubles) to help his squad advance to the Series. The Boston Red Sox, however, won five of eight games to capture the championship.

Clarke couldn't get his Pirates back in first place until 1909. The Chicago Cubs (with player/manager Frank Chance) and the New York Giants (piloted by the fiery John McGraw) monopolized the top standing in the league. The 1909 Pirates returned to the top of the N.L. heap with a 110-42 record. Wagner led the National League with a .339 average, while Clarke batted .287 with 3 homers and 68 RBI. Clarke was first in the National League with 362 putouts in left field and a .987 fielding percentage.

The Pirates defeated the Tigers in seven games to claim the World Series crown that year. Clarke's Series average was only .211, but he paced his club with 7 runs scored and 7 RBI. In the fifth game of the Series, after each team had won twice, Clarke's two-run homer in the seventh inning was the winning difference in the Pirates 8-4 triumph. In the decisive seventh game, Clarke drew 4 walks as the Pirates strolled to an 8-0 win. As manager, Clarke charted an aggressive course against the Tigers, and his Bucs stole a Series record 18 bases (including 3 by Clarke himself).

Clarke ended his career with a .312 average, 2,672 career hits, and 220 triples (seventh highest in history). The Hall of Fame inducted Clarke in 1945.

CAREER HIGHLIGHTS
FRED CLIFFORD CLARKE

Born: October 3, 1872 Winterset, IA **Died:** August 14, 1960
Height: 5'10" **Weight:** 165 lbs. **Batted:** Left **Threw:** Right
Outfielder: Louisville Colonels, 1894-99; Pittsburgh Pirates, 1900-15. Manager: Louisville Colonels, 1897-99; Pittsburgh Pirates, 1900-15.

* Went 5-for-5 in his major league debut on June 30, 1894
* Became a player/manager at age 24
* Elected to the Baseball Hall of Fame in 1945
* Had a 31-game hitting streak in 1895
* Ranks seventh in career triples

MAJOR LEAGUE TOTALS

G	AB	H	BA	2B	3B	HR	R	RBI	SB
2,242	8,568	2,672	.312	361	220	67	1,619	1,015	506

Though a solid hitter and a sure-handed outfielder, Fred Clarke made his most significant contributions as a player/manager. While managing the Pittsburgh Pirates, Clarke guided the legendary Honus Wagner for most of Wagner's best years.

JOHN CLARKSON

Contemporary major league pitchers get lots of praise (and lots of money) if they pitch even 300 innings in one season. Can you imagine any of today's hurlers pitching more than 600 innings in just one year? That's what John Clarkson did for the 1885 Chicago White Stockings.

Clarkson had one of the most incredible years in pitching history under the guidance of manager Cap Anson. One reason that Clarkson pitched so many games was that Chicago didn't have any relief pitchers. That's right, the White Stockings had a two-person pitching staff. Clarkson handled the workload in fine style, going 53-16 in 623 innings of work. Besides leading the league in wins and innings pitched, Clarkson was first in games started (70), complete games (68), strikeouts (318), and shutouts (10). A no-hitter thrown against the rival Providence Grays on July 27, 1885, highlighted Clarkson's accomplishments. Incredibly, Clarkson was in fine shape following this momentous season, and he pitched for nine more years in organized baseball. Clarkson was no one-year wonder, either: He won 209 games from 1885-1889.

Clarkson's first year in baseball was with a Worcester, Massachusetts, team in 1882. He moved to a club in Saginaw, Michigan, in 1883 and was sold to Chicago in 1884. In his debut with the White Stockings (then a National League club), Clarkson won 10 games and lost 3 with a 2.14 ERA. He also played the outfield, first base, and third base that year, due to his fine hitting ability. Clarkson's average was .262. (He had hit .364 previously with Worcester.) During his record-setting season of 1885, Clarkson had continued success with the bat: He slugged 61 hits (including 4 homers) for a .216 average. As if Clarkson wasn't busy enough, Anson put him in the outfield for three games and at third for another.

In 1886, Clarkson won "just" 36 games in 467 innings of work. Still, he was second in the league with 313 strikeouts and completed 50 of the 55 games he started.

In 1887 Clarkson reclaimed his reputation as the league's most accomplished pitcher. He topped the National League with 38 wins, 59 starts, 56 complete games, 523 innings pitched, and 237 strikeouts. At bat he hit .242 with 52 hits, including 6 homers and 25 RBI. Clarkson was even credited with 6 stolen bases that year. At this time, however, baseball rules stated that a

player could earn a stolen base each time he advanced an extra base on another player's hit.

A new chapter in Clarkson's career began in 1888 when he joined the Boston Beaneaters. The Chicago team ownership sold Clarkson and teammate Mike "King" Kelly to Boston. Clarkson retained his position as the league leader in innings pitched with 483. He went 33-20 as a member of a four-man pitching rotation, but Boston finished with a fourth-place 70-64 record. The team improved in 1889, thanks to a sterling effort from Clarkson. Clarkson won a league-high 49 games and also led the league in innings pitched (620), ERA (2.73), strikeouts (284), games started (72), and complete games (68). The Beaneaters finished in second place with an 83-45 record.

Clarkson continued to be a winning pitcher for the next three seasons, but the excessive demands on his pitching arm seemed to finally catch up with

him. He won 25 games in 1890 and had 33 wins (and 3 saves) in 1891. After just 16 games, Boston traded Clarkson to the Cleveland Spiders in early 1892. Clarkson won 17 games before the season was through to come up with a cumulative 25-16 record. His record slipped to 16-17 in 1893, and when he won just 8 games in 1894, Clarkson knew it was time to retire.

For his relatively brief 12-year career, Clarkson was a sensational pitcher, averaging more than 27 wins a year. His 326 victories (11th best in history), 485 complete games (eighth best in history), and 37 shutouts are memorable, as is his sparkling .648 winning percentage. Furthermore, he was a fair hitter. Clarkson filled in the outfield, first base, or third base for 31 games in his career. Lifetime, he had a .219 average with 432 hits (24 of them home runs) and 214 RBI.

Two of Clarkson's brothers also pitched in baseball. Arthur "Dad" Clarkson was active from 1891-96, while Walter Clarkson pitched from 1904-08. John Clarkson moved back to his hometown of Cambridge, Massachusetts, after retirement. He died there of pneumonia at age 47. The Hall of Fame posthumously inducted Clarkson in 1963.

John Clarkson was one of the greatest pitchers of the 19th century, once pitching over 600 innings in one season. A temperamental player given to extreme mood swings, Clarkson spent his last years in an asylum.

CAREER HIGHLIGHTS
JOHN GIBSON CLARKSON

Born: July 1, 1861 Cambridge, MA **Died:** February 4, 1909
Height: 5'10" **Weight:** 155 lbs. **Batted:** Right **Threw:** Right
Pitcher, outfielder: Worcester, 1882; Chicago White Sox, 1884-87; Boston Beaneaters, 1888-92; Cleveland Spiders, 1894-96.

★ Won 53 games in 1885
★ Pitched 623 innings in 1885
★ Won 49 games in 1889
★ Elected to the Hall of Fame in 1963
★ Ranks eighth in lifetime complete games for pitchers

MAJOR LEAGUE TOTALS

G	IP	W	L	Pct.	SO	BB	ERA
531	4,537	327	178	.648	1,978	1,191	2.81

ROGER CLEMENS

Even off the field, Roger Clemens sets records. In February 1989, the Boston Red Sox deluxe pitcher signed one of the most amazing contracts in baseball history. He became one of the youngest players ever to receive a $2 million salary. With only four years and 142 days of major league experience, Clemens beat fellow $2-million-earner Kirby Puckett by five days to become the least-seasoned baseball millionaire. Clemens signed a three-year pact that pays him at least $7.5 million. The contract includes $2.2 million in 1989 and then $2.5 million in 1990 and 1991. Other incentives include a $300,000 signing bonus, plus $100,000 if he wins another Cy Young (to go with the awards he won in 1986 and 1987), or $50,000 if he finishes second in the balloting. The contract includes a similar bonus if he wins a Most Valuable Player award (as he did in 1986).

What makes Clemens worth so much money? Well, he's one of the best moundsmen to have worn a Red Sox uniform in more than a decade. His fastball remains one of the best in the league. With the addition of a curveball, forkball, and change-of-pace, Clemens has become a complete hurler.

Clemens could have started in baseball as early as 1981 but decided to go to college instead. He was a 12th-round choice in the June 1981 free-agent draft by the New York Mets but turned the team down. (Imagine how powerful the current Mets pitching staff could be with Clemens as a member.) Instead, Clemens helped the University of Texas to the NCAA World Series. In 1985 he was much more popular, becoming the 19th player selected in the draft when the Red Sox made him a first-round pick.

The Red Sox rushed Clemens through their minor league system. He spent only four games with Winter Haven of the Florida State League before finishing the 1983 season with New Britain.

Clemens' rookie season was blighted by an injury during September. He missed nearly a month of 1984 due to a forearm muscle pull. Nevertheless, he went 9-4 with 5 complete games and a shutout. Clemens showed a glimpse of his future potential by fanning 126 batters in 133.1 innings. In 1985 Clemens was hampered by a bad shoulder and needed surgery at season's end. He had an unspectacular 7-5 record with a 3.29 ERA.

Clemens returned healthy and revitalized for the 1986 season and helped Boston coast to its first World Series in a decade. The hurler called "The Rocket" (for his blazing fastball) had the best season of his young career. Clemens had a 24-4 record, creating a league-leading .857 winning percentage. His wins included 10 complete games and a shutout. He struck out 238 batters, second in the league only to Mark Langston's 245 Ks. Clemens led the league in ERA at 2.48. He also set a new major league record against the Seattle Mariners by striking out 20 in one game on April 29, 1986.

Clemens threw seven shutout innings against the California Angels in the decisive seventh game of the American League Championship Series to send the Red Sox to the World Series. Clemens struck out 17 Angels during three starts and established an A.L.

record by pitching 22.2 innings in the A.L.C.S. He was winless in two World Series starts against the Mets as the New York club won the Series in seven games.

In 1987 the Red Sox tumbled to fifth place, but Clemens contributed another stellar season with 20 victories. He became the first Red Sox pitcher to have back-to-back 20-win seasons since Luis Tiant manned the mound in Fenway in 1973-74. Besides his league lead in victories, Clemens' 20-9 record gave him a league-best .690 winning percentage. His 18 complete games and 7 shutouts were also American League highs. Again Clemens was the second-best strikeout artist in the league. His 256 strikeouts were just 6 short of Mariner Mark Langston's record.

Clemens had mixed success in 1988. A late-season slump stopped him from earning his third straight 20-win season. However, his yearly efforts for the league strikeout championship finally paid off. He whiffed 291 batsmen to pace the American League. His 18-12 record tied him for fourth in wins and he tied Oakland's Dave Stewart for the high in complete games with 14. Clemens was first in the league in shutouts with 8 and was third in innings pitched at 264. Although he lost the second game of the American League Championship Series, he gave up just 3 runs and 6 hits in seven innings.

It may be too early to reserve a spot in the Hall of Fame for a pitcher who was just 26 years old when the 1989 season started. However, if Clemens stays healthy, he could assemble some incredible statistics.

CAREER HIGHLIGHTS
WILLIAM ROGER CLEMENS

Born: August 4, 1962   Dayton, OH
Height: 6'4"   **Weight:** 205 lbs.   **Bats:** Right   **Throws:** Right
Pitcher: Boston Red Sox, 1984-89.

* Won back-to-back Cy Young awards in 1986 and 1987
* Went 1-1 with 17 strikeouts in the 1986 A.L. Championship Series
* Established a major league record with 20 strikeouts in one game in 1986
* Had two straight 20-win seasons in 1986 and 1987
* Struck out a career-high 291 batters to lead the A.L. in 1988
* Was named 1986 A.L. MVP

MAJOR LEAGUE TOTALS

G	IP	W	L	Pct.	SO	BB	ERA
175	1,284	95	45	.679	1,215	371	3.06

Roger Clemens, one of the highest-paid players in baseball, has already passed 1,000 strikeouts in his six-year career. Providing his powerful arm remains unhampered by injury, the young hurling ace could soar through the American League for years to come.

ROBERTO CLEMENTE

Roberto Clemente was not just a national hero, but an international one. When Clemente joined the exclusive 3,000-hit club by rapping out a double for his final hit of the 1972 season, everyone looked forward to next year and hit number 3,001. But three months later, on New Year's Eve, the 38-year-old Pirates star was killed in a plane crash while on a mercy mission to Nicaragua. Clemente was one of five people aboard the cargo plane airlifting food, clothing, and emergency medical supplies to a country ravaged by a devastating earthquake. Three months later, the Hall of Fame waived the usual five-year waiting period and enshrined Clemente immediately.

The 12-time Pirate All-Star got his major league start thanks to the Brooklyn Dodgers. Dodgers scout Al Campanis—the same man who would be driven out of baseball in 1988 due to alleged racist remarks he made on a late-night television program—discovered Clemente playing winter ball in Santurce, Puerto Rico. Following the 1953-54 season, Clemente received a $10,000 bonus to sign with the Dodgers.

Why didn't Clemente ever play for the Dodgers? Possibly because the Dodgers were well-stocked with outfielders that season. Sandy Amoros, Duke Snider, and Carl Furillo had their positions locked up. Besides, the Dodgers were known for overstocking their minor league teams with capable rookies. Also, Clemente didn't have an incredible first year in the minors. In Montreal of the International League, Clemente batted .257 with 2 homers and 12 RBI in 87 games. He played both outfield and third base. Pirates scouts spotted Clemente's long-range potential and drafted him at the end of the season.

He found immediate work in Pittsburgh. Clemente, then known as "Bob" instead of Roberto, played in 124 games. In 1956 the Pirates auditioned Clemente at second and third base for three games. He stayed in the outfield for the rest of the year, however, and hit .311 (only 17 points behind league-leader Hank Aaron). His power totals increased to 7 homers and 60 RBI, but he led National League right fielders with 13 errors. Clemente did unveil an awesome throwing arm that season, ringing up 17 assists. He would lead National League right fielders in that category four times during his career. Injuries from a car accident limited Clemente to just 111 games in 1957, and his overall playing performance suffered.

In 1958 Clemente batted .289 with 6 homers and 50 RBI and led the National League with 22 assists. His first truly successful season came in 1960, when he was appointed to the National League All-Star team (for both games). His .314 average was third in the league, only points away from league-leading teammate Dick Groat. Clemente paced the Pirates with 94 RBI, was second with 16 home runs, and again led the National League in outfield assists. America got its first look at Clemente's future greatness in the 1960 World Series. The Pirates, after winning 95 games during the regular season, nipped the Yankees in a seven-game Series. He tied a World Series record by hitting safely in seven straight games.

Clemente was one of baseball's unsung heroes in the 1960s. Because the Pirates weren't consistent winners, Clemente was neglected by the media. In 1961 he finally won his first batting title with a whopping .351 average. He hit 23 home runs and topped the 200-hit plateau for the first time. In two 1961 All-Star games, Clemente went 2-for-6 with 2 RBI. Clemente maintained his high average throughout the decade and won additional batting crowns in 1964 (.339), 1965 (.329) and 1967 (.357). In 1966 Clemente had one of his best years as a run producer, smacking 29 dingers and 119 RBI. He finished second in the league in RBI and total bases (342) and third in triples (11) and hits (202). His .317 average ranked fourth in the league. Clemente earned the National League MVP award for his efforts.

Clemente left his mark on baseball history in 1971 postseason play. In the 1971 playoffs, Clemente hit .333. In the Pirates hard-fought World Series victory in seven games over the Baltimore Orioles, Clemente was superb. He batted .414 with 12 hits (including 2 doubles, 1 triple, and 2 homers). Again, Clemente hit safely in every game. His exploits earned him the Series MVP award.

At the untimely end of his career, Clemente ranked in the top ten for 12 different offensive categories for the Pirates. He racked up 12 Gold Gloves during his 18 seasons in the outfield. His uniform number (21) was retired during the 1973 season in Pittsburgh. Also, the Pittsburgh Chapter of the Baseball Writers' Association of America instituted "The Roberto Clemente Award," given yearly to a Pirate who exemplifies the standard of excellence established by the superstar. Clemente's memory lives on in Puerto Rico as well, through an athletic complex he sponsored to help underprivileged children.

CAREER HIGHLIGHTS
ROBERTO WALKER CLEMENTE

Born: August 18, 1934   Carolina, Puerto Rico   **Died:** December 31, 1972
Height: 5'11"   **Weight:** 175 lbs.   **Batted:** Right   **Threw:** Right
Outfielder: Pittsburgh Pirates, 1955-72.

- ★ Led the N.L. in hits during two different seasons
- ★ Selected N.L. MVP in 1966
- ★ Named to 12 All-Star teams
- ★ Compiled 3,000 career hits and a .317 lifetime average
- ★ Won four N.L. batting titles
- ★ Elected to the Hall of Fame in 1973

MAJOR LEAGUE TOTALS

G	AB	H	BA	2B	3B	HR	R	RBI	SB
2,433	9,454	3,000	.317	440	166	240	1,416	1,305	83

The second baseball player to be honored on a U.S. stamp, Roberto Clemente was a great humanitarian. Though many recall his ill-fated mercy flight to Nicaragua, few realize that he often spoke out against the prejudice experienced by Latin players in the big leagues.

TY COBB

Ty Cobb, the man known as "The Georgia Peach," ranks as one of the greatest overall players in the history of baseball. For 24 seasons, Cobb earned his fame at bat, on the base paths, and in the outfield.

When Pete Rose set his all-time hit record in the mid-1980s, he was chasing the awesome record of the native Georgian. While Rose played enough seasons to break Cobb's mark of 4,190 hits, it seems unlikely that any player will ever be be able to match his lifetime batting average. Cobb began amassing his stunning statistics in 1905 at age 18 with the Detroit Tigers. Cobb played in 98 games the next season and hit .316, the first of 23 straight years in which he'd top the .300 barrier.

Cobb's first great season came in 1907, and the Tigers rode his success all the way to the World Series. The gutsy outfielder banged out a league-best .350 average. Other league bests included hits (212), RBI (119), stolen bases (49), and slugging percentage (.468). The Cubs swept the Tigers in the Series, as Cobb was limited to just 4 hits in 20 at-bats.

Cobb won nine consecutive batting titles starting in 1907. Cobb powered the Tigers back into the World Series (again against the Cubs) with a .324 average and 108 RBI. The Cubs won the Series in five games, but Cobb avenged his previous downfall against Chicago by hitting .368.

The Tigers put together their third straight league title in 1909. Cobb won his first homer title with 9 round-trippers, and he topped the league with a .377 average, 107 RBI, 216 hits, 116 runs scored, and 76 stolen bases. It was only the second time in American League history that a player had won the triple crown. No one would match Cobb's feat for another 24 years, when Jimmie Foxx turned the trick.

Cobb continued accumulating offensive milestones, and his season highs are still astounding. He exceeded .400 three times: with .420 in 1911, .410 in 1912, and .401 in 1922. He logged 248 hits in 1911, and he stole a career-high 96 bases in 1915. The master batsman won the league's Most Valuable Player award in 1911. Cobb never concentrated on power hitting, but he hit as many as 12 homers in a single season. He was the first player in modern history to hit 5 homers in two consecutive games.

Cobb was undoubtedly the fiercest competitor the game has ever known.

Always searching for a winning edge, Cobb would intimidate his opponents mercilessly. His pregame ritual of sitting on the dugout steps and sharpening his spikes with a file has been well documented. And with sharpened spikes flying, Cobb was a notoriously daring base runner who swiped 892 bases in his career. Because of his reckless style and frequent brawling, Cobb was not personally liked by many of his contemporaries, but he was universally respected. He was the first player elected to the Baseball Hall of Fame, and six years later, when *The Sporting News* asked former major league managers and players to name the greatest player of all time, Ty Cobb was the runaway winner. Cobb once told a reporter, "The baseline belongs to me!"

Later in life, the retired Cobb didn't like admitting he had played with such reckless abandon. He denied deliberately spiking dozens of rival players but showed scars from the numerous spikings he suffered. Cobb claimed that most of his aggressiveness came from the nonstop jockeying he received from Tiger teammates when he became a well-publicized rookie.

Cobb served as a player/manager during his final six seasons in Detroit. He never piloted his Bengals to a pennant, but the team did wind up with a .519 winning percentage under Cobb's reign. Detroit's best season under Cobb was a second-place finish at 83-71 in 1923. The Tigers released Cobb on November 2, 1926. A major criticism of Cobb as manager was that although he knew the game inside out, he couldn't communicate with the players. Hall of Famer Charlie Gehringer, who broke into the majors on Cobb's team, once said that Cobb couldn't understand why other players couldn't perform as well as he did.

In 1927 the dauntless Cobb joined the Philadelphia Athletics, determined to continue playing. Even at age 40, Cobb proved he could still compete with the best of them. He hit .357 (with 93 RBI) in 134 games for Connie Mack's club. He concluded his career in 1928 by hitting .323 in 95 games.

It's no wonder that Cobb was among the first inductees in the Baseball Hall of Fame. He held more than 40 offensive records at the time of his retirement. Brooklyn Dodgers executive Branch Rickey paid perhaps the greatest of tributes to one of baseball's first superstars by saying, "Ty Cobb lived off the field as though he wished to live forever. He lived on the field as though it was his last day."

CAREER HIGHLIGHTS
TYRUS RAYMOND COBB

Born: December 18, 1886 Narrows, GA **Died:** July 17, 1961
Height: 6'1" **Weight:** 175 lbs. **Batted:** Left **Threw:** Right
Outfielder: Detroit Tigers, 1905-26; Philadelphia Athletics, 1927-28. Manager: Detroit Tigers, 1921-26.

- ★ His .366 batting average ranks first in history
- ★ Batted over 300 in 23 consecutive seasons
- ★ Elected to the Hall of Fame in 1936
- ★ Has the second-highest stolen base total ever at 892
- ★ First in lifetime runs scored with 2,245
- ★ Won 12 A.L. batting titles

MAJOR LEAGUE TOTALS

G	AB	H	BA	2B	3B	HR	R	RBI	SB
3,034	11,434	4,190	.366	724	294	118	2,245	1,933	892

Ty Cobb's lifetime batting average of .366 remains the highest in history. Cobb, possibly baseball's best all-around player, won 12 A.L. batting titles during his career, hit over .400 three times, led in steals six times, and led in runs scored five times.

MICKEY COCHRANE

Mickey Cochrane was one of baseball's greatest catchers during the late 20s and early 30s. If he hadn't suffered a serious beaning at the height of his career, Cochrane could have compiled statistics to rival any catcher in history.

While playing (and managing) with the Detroit Tigers in 1937, Cochrane was struck on the temple by a pitched ball by New York Yankee hurler Bump Hadley. Unconscious for ten days, he recovered well enough to manage the team from the bench, but he never played again. Tiger second baseman Charlie Gehringer, on deck at the time of the beaning, said that the ball hit Cochrane's skull so hard that it bounced all the way back out to the pitcher's mound. Only 34 years old at the time and hitting .306, Cochrane might have played for several more seasons if he had been healthier.

Cochrane first demonstrated his gritty competitiveness playing football at Boston University. Besides being a star halfback, Cochrane also participated in basketball, boxing, track, and baseball on the collegiate level. He played third base in a semipro league under an assumed name to protect his athletic eligibility in college. Upon graduation from Boston University, Cochrane decided to attempt a pro baseball career.

The first pro team that Cochrane played for (in Saranac Lake, New York) soon went bankrupt. Through a teammate, he learned that the Dover, Delaware, club in the Eastern Shore League needed a backstop. So Cochrane switched to catcher in 1923 to get the job. By 1924, he was playing so well in the Pacific Coast League that Connie Mack gave up five players and $50,000 to obtain Cochrane for his Philadelphia Athletics.

Cochrane had hoped to return to playing the outfield in Philadelphia, but Mack immediately installed him as his full-time catcher. In 134 games Cochrane delivered 6 homers, 55 RBI, and a .331 average. Most importantly, Cochrane warmed up to his catching duties and handled the Athletics pitching staff with the hand of a veteran. He soon became skilled at blocking home during plays at the plate. A faster runner than most catchers, Cochrane batted in the second or third spot for most of his 13-year career and finished with a .320 lifetime average. He was also one of the hardest catchers in history to strike out.

By 1927, Cochrane was an accomplished hitter. He batted .338 with 12 homers and 80 RBI. Defensively he was first in the American League in putouts and total chances per game. In 1928 Cochrane was at the top of his game, winning the American League MVP award. He hit .293 with 10 homers and 57 RBI, but he was most brilliant in the field, again leading the league in putouts and total chances per game. With his award, Cochrane also received a $1,000 check. Although Philadelphia won 98 games in 1928, the Tigers won the league championship by two and a half games.

Cochrane and the Athletics were runaway winners in the American League in 1929. Their 104 wins outdistanced second-place New York by 18 games. The scrappy A's catcher hit .331 with 7 homers and 95 RBI and paced the league in fielding average and putouts.

Philadelphia won the 1929 World Series with the help of Cochrane's .400 average. In 1930 Cochrane hit a career-high .357 average (fourth in the league), with 10 homers and 85 RBI. He pounded two more homers in the World Series, as the Athletics successfully defended their World Series crown against the St. Louis Cardinals.

The Athletics reached their third straight World Series in 1931, only to lose to the St. Louis Cardinals. Cochrane was one of the finest players in Philadelphia all season long, posting a .349 average.

In 1932 Cochrane had a career-best 23 homers and 112 RBI. He also led the league in putouts, assists, double plays, and fielding percentage for yet another year.

At the start of the 1933 season, Cochrane and Bill Dickey, the famed New York Yankees catcher, were appointed to the first All-Star game. For years, these two men were considered the elite backstops in baseball. The debate over which man had the best catching skills rages eternally, but many felt that Cochrane had a better arm.

On December 12, 1933, Connie Mack traded Cochrane to the Detroit Tigers for Johnny Pasek and $100,000. Immediately, Cochrane was appointed manager. He was a smart baseball man, and he convinced the team ownership to trade for slugger "Goose" Goslin, a vital member of the team. In 1934 he coached the Tigers to their first pennant in 25 years. The next season, Cochrane's club went to their second straight World Series, beating the Cubs in six games.

Only ten years after his playing career ended, Cochrane was elected to the Baseball Hall of Fame.

CAREER HIGHLIGHTS
GORDON STANLEY COCHRANE

Born: April 6, 1903 Bridgewater, MA **Died:** June 28, 1962
Height: 5'10" **Weight:** 180 lbs. **Batted:** Left **Threw:** Right
Catcher: Philadelphia Athletics, 1925-33; Detroit Tigers, 1934-37. Manager: Detroit Tigers, 1934-38.

★ Compiled a .320 lifetime average   ★ Played in five World Series
★ Named A.L. MVP in 1928   ★ Elected to the Hall of Fame in 1947
★ Caught 100-plus games for 11 consecutive seasons

MAJOR LEAGUE TOTALS

G	AB	H	BA	2B	3B	HR	R	RBI	SB
1,482	5,169	1,652	.320	333	64	119	1,041	832	64

Mickey Cochrane, whose playing career met an untimely end in 1937, had a combative temperament on the field that was ideal for a catcher. His hard-nosed attitude was an asset to his defense and in his coaching of pitchers.

ROCKY COLAVITO

In 1959 both Rocky Colavito and Harvey Kuenn enjoyed exceptional seasons. Kuenn, the dependable Detroit Tigers shortstop, led the American League with a sparkling .353 average; Colavito, the Cleveland Indians slugging outfielder, led the league in home runs with 42. Despite their fine seasons, both Kuenn and Colavito were traded—for each other. When the deal was made just before the 1960 season, it left fans of both teams astonished. It was one of the most dramatic trades in baseball history—swapping the reigning batting champ for the reigning home run champ, an even trade at best.

The Indians kept Kuenn only one year, dealing him to the San Francisco Giants in 1961. Colavito, meanwhile, had four very productive years in Detroit—averaging 35 home runs a season, including a career high of 45 dingers in 1961—before he was traded to the Kansas City Athletics.

Colavito was a popular performer. Although he didn't command as much attention or hit as many home runs as some other American League sluggers of his day, he was consistently near the top of the list. He was always a threat to break a game wide open. On June 10, 1959, he clubbed 4 home runs in a single game against the Baltimore Orioles.

The Cleveland Indians signed Colavito as a pitcher/outfielder at age 18. His signing bonus in 1951 was $3,000. Colavito toiled for five and a half seasons in the Indians minor league farm system before getting his long-deserved shot at the majors. He pitched only one four-inning stint during his first year with Daytona Beach, but his 23 home runs and 111 RBI convinced the Cleveland organization that his bat would be more valuable than his arm. Surprisingly, Colavito did make use of his pitching skills twice in his career: In 1958 he pitched three scoreless innings of relief for the Indians, even striking out one batter, and during his final season with the 1968 New York Yankees, Colavito actually gained a victory! He pitched 2.2 innings, giving up 1 hit and 2 walks and striking out 1. Colavito's feat became a trivia question in 1988, when Cardinal infielder Jose Oquendo lost a game against the Atlanta Braves as a relief pitcher. For more than 20 years, Colavito has been the only "non-pitcher" ever to win a major league game.

Even three incredible seasons in the minor leagues didn't win Colavito a spot on the Indians roster. With the Indianapolis Indians, Colavito led the American Association in 1954 with 28 homers and 121 RBI but couldn't advance to the big leagues. In 1955 he upped his totals to a league-best 38 homers and 116 RBI. Colavito finally got to play the last five games of the season with Cleveland and hit .444. Nevertheless, the next year he was back in the minors. However, after just 35 games with San Diego of the Pacific Coast League, Colavito was back in the majors to stay.

The 23-year-old slugger enjoyed his first season with Cleveland in 1956 and responded with 21 homers and 65 RBI. In 1957 Colavito's totals climbed to 25 round-trippers with 84 RBI. Colavito exceeded those stats in 1958 with 41 homers, 113 RBI, and a .303 average. Yankee great Mickey Mantle hit only 1 additional homer to edge out Colavito for the home run title that year.

Baseball recognized Colavito's accomplishments by naming him to both All-Star games in 1959. He went 2-for-5 with 1 home run in the pair of contests. During the regular season, Colavito was the league leader in home runs with 42. He drove in 100-plus runs for the second straight season as well.

Colavito adapted his long-ball stroke to Tiger Stadium with ease. One of his greatest years at the plate came as a Tiger in 1961, when he hit a personal best of 45 homers and 140 RBI. On November 18, 1963, the Tigers sent Colavito, Bob Anderson, and an estimated $50,000 to the Kansas City Athletics for Ed Rakow, Jerry Lumpe, and Dave Wickersham. Colavito had 34 homers and 102 RBI for the A's. Kansas City traded Colavito back to his original home team of Cleveland in 1965. The big slugger was first in the American League that year with 108 RBI and 93 bases on balls. He played in all 162 games (for the first and only time on the Indians roster), hitting 26 homers.

Colavito's last great year was with the 1966 Indians, hitting 30 homers. He bounced around with the White Sox, Dodgers, and Yankees until 1968 and then coached with the Indians and Kansas City Royals for five years before retiring to his Pennsylvania farm.

The Cleveland Indians have always tended to make bad trades. Perhaps the worst occurred when the Tribe traded popular Rocky Colavito, who led the A.L. in homers that year, to Detroit for singles-hitter Harvey Kuenn.

CAREER HIGHLIGHTS
ROCCO DOMENICO COLAVITO

Born: August 10, 1933   New York, NY
Height: 6'3" **Weight:** 190 lbs. **Batted:** Right **Threw:** Right
Outfielder: Cleveland Indians, 1955-59, 1965-67; Detroit Tigers, 1960-63; Kansas City Athletics, 1964; Chicago White Sox, 1967; Los Angeles Dodgers, 1968; New York Yankees, 1968.

- ★ Led the A.L. in homers in 1959
- ★ Led the league in RBI in 1965
- ★ Hit four homers in one game in 1959
- ★ Played in eight All-Star games
- ★ Topped the league in slugging percentage in 1958

MAJOR LEAGUE TOTALS

G	AB	H	BA	2B	3B	HR	R	RBI	SB
1,841	6,503	1,730	.266	283	21	374	971	1,159	19

EDDIE COLLINS

Eddie Collins was one of the most mysterious rookies in baseball history. Collins was a successful quarterback at Columbia University when he got his first chance to play professional baseball for the Philadelphia Athletics in 1906. Long before the collegiate athletic corruption scandals of the 1980s, Eddie Collins was involved in his own tale of campus intrigue.

At that time, Collins liked football better than baseball, so he didn't want to risk his collegiate eligibility by signing a pro contract for any other sport. So while still attending college, Collins played six games for the A's in 1906, using the name of "Eddie Sullivan" to shield his future in college football. A's manager Connie Mack had offered to take the 19-year-old infielder along on a western road trip to pick up some experience. Mack also suggested the phony name. The guise was unsuccessful and Collins lost his eligibility. In 1907 Eddie "Sullivan" Collins played 14 more games with Philadelphia and 4 games with Newark of the Eastern League. Collins graduated in 1907. The following season, Collins (using his real name) got a full-time job from the Athletics.

He had his first full season with the A's in 1909, getting to play in 153 games. The man nicknamed "Cocky" hit .346 and stole 67 bases. In 1910 Collins sparked the Athletics to their first of four pennants in five years. The steady second baseman was the A.L. leader in stolen bases with 81 and hit .322 with 3 homers and 81 RBI. Collins hit a team-leading .429 with 9 hits as the Athletics won the World Series in five games. In 1911 the Athletics repeated as world champions with the help of more timely hitting from Collins. He batted .365 during the regular season and contributed 6 hits to the team's World Series domination of the New York Giants.

Collins was first in the league with 137 runs scored in 1912, hitting .348 with 64 RBI. By developing his talent as a contact hitter, Collins kept his average at .300 or better 18 times in his career. In 1913 Collins helped the Athletics regain their world championship. He batted .345 and starred in Philadelphia's World Series triumph by hitting .421.

With Collins at second, Frank "Home Run" Baker at third, Jack Barry at shortstop, and Stuffy McInnis at first, the Philadelphia A's had a "$100,000 infield." Manager Mack had boasted to reporters that he wouldn't part with his

four star players for $100,000. (Mack eventually changed his mind.) Collins was named the American League's Most Valuable Player in 1914, hitting .344 with 2 homers, 85 RBI, and 58 stolen bases. The A's returned to the World Series, only to lose to the Boston Braves in four straight games. On December 8, 1914, the Chicago White Sox purchased Collins' contract for $50,000.

Chicago would get good use out of Collins for the next 12 years. Starting immediately in 1915, Collins gave the White Sox their money's worth: He hit .332 and led the American League with 119 walks. He surpassed .300 again in 1916. In 1917 Collins hit an uncharacteristic .289, but he rebounded to hit .409 in the World Series as the White Sox beat the New York Giants in six games. Collins' eighth-inning single in

the fifth game provided the game-winning hit in an 8-5 victory.

Collins and the White Sox returned to the World Series in 1919. Although he hit .319 for the season and led the league with 33 steals, his efforts were obscured by the "Black Sox" scandal during the fall classic. Collins was one of the Chicago players honestly trying to beat the rival Cincinnati Reds. The World Series ended with Cincinnati as the victors, and eight White Sox players were accused of purposely losing to earn bribes from mobsters. The eight players were suspended from baseball for life.

The following season, Collins hit a career best of .369 and 222 hits. His lowest average from 1920 to 1926 was a .324 mark in 1922. He also won consecutive stolen base titles in 1923 and 1924. Collins served as the White Sox player/manager in 1925-26. Although both of his teams had winning records, they finished fifth both times.

After Collins was released by the White Sox in 1926, he signed with the A's. In 1927 he was the league's leading pinch-hitter with a 12-for-34 record. Collins retired after the 1930 season. In 1933 Collins became vice-president of the Boston Red Sox and held the post until his death in 1951.

Collins held numerous offensive and defensive records at the time of his retirement. He led the league in fielding nine times and set a major league longevity record by playing for 25 years. His 14 stolen bases in World Series play remained a record for nearly 50 years, until Lou Brock equaled the feat in 1967-68. Only Brock, Rickey Henderson, and Ty Cobb have more stolen bases in modern baseball history.

CAREER HIGHLIGHTS
EDWARD TROWBRIDGE COLLINS

Born: May 2, 1887 Millerton, NY **Died:** March 25, 1951
Height: 5'9" **Weight:** 175 lbs. **Batted:** Left **Threw:** Right
Infielder: Philadelphia Athletics, 1906-14, 1927-30; Chicago White Sox, 1915-26.
Manager: Chicago White Sox, 1925-26.

★ Compiled a .333 batting average over 25 major league seasons
★ Played in six World Series
★ Fourth-highest total for lifetime steals
★ Ranks eighth in career hits
★ Elected to the Hall of Fame in 1939

MAJOR LEAGUE TOTALS

G	AB	H	BA	2B	3B	HR	R	RBI	SB
2,826	9,948	3,310	.333	437	186	47	1,819	1,299	743

Eddie Collins played for 25 years in the major leagues—19 of those years at second base, which is a position that lends itself to injuries. Collins led the A.L. in fielding nine times, more than any other second baseman.

JIMMY COLLINS

Baseball's rich free agents of today may have taken their inspiration from Jimmy Collins. The talented infielder was lured to the new American League in 1901 with the promise of big money by a new franchise—the Boston Red Stockings. (Because he was a popular crosstown star, Collins was an appealing name in Boston.) The Red Stockings offered Collins $4,000, which seemed like an enormous sum back then. Collins held out for $5,500, along with a promise of 10 percent of the team's profits.

Collins told the press that he had been thinking about his family's needs in accepting the offer from a rival league. Collins even demanded that he'd be paid the same amount to serve solely as manager, in case his former team legally stopped him from playing for the Red Stockings.

Everything turned out well for Collins, who did get to serve his new team as player/manager for six seasons. In 1901 Collins hit .332 in 138 games to spark his team on the field. His average was fifth highest in the new league. At the hot corner, Collins led the league with 328 assists and 4.2 chances per game. At 79-57, the Red Stockings were strong second-place finishers—only four games behind the Chicago White Stockings.

In 1902 the Red Stockings continued to be consistent winners, and their 77-60 record was third best in the league. Collins was the leading third baseman in the league with a .954 average, hitting .322 with 6 homers and 61 RBI in 108 games.

Collins couldn't have found a better year than 1903 to pilot his Red Stockings squad to a 91-47 finish for the American League title. For the first time, the top club from each league would go on to compete in a unique championship called the World Series. Manager Collins had made a significant on-field contribution to his team's first-place finish, hitting .296 and pacing league third basemen in putouts, double plays, and fielding percentage.

In the World Series, Boston, the pride of the junior circuit, won five of eight games against the favored Pirates. Collins had 9 hits (3 for extra bases) for a .250 average, as his team became the first entry into a new page of baseball history. The embarrassment of having the world championship claimed by the upstart junior circuit caused the National League club owners considerable irritation. The 1904 World Series was cancelled, and the fall classic was restructured into a seven-game event more acceptable to National League executives.

The veteran third baseman played in a career-high 156 games in 1904. Collins batted .271 with 3 homers and 67 RBI. As a manager, Collins had a great season with a first-place record of 95-59. Unfortunately, there was no World Series to be played in 1904. He hit .276 with 4 homers and 65 RBI in 1905. After seeing his team slip to a 44-92 record in mid-1906, Collins was traded on June 7, 1907, to the Philadelphia Athletics for Jack Knight. At age 37, Collins was near the end of his career. He played in just 37 games in 1906 and in 143 games in 1907, hitting .279. Collins retired after playing 115 games with the A's in 1908.

Collins enjoyed his greatest accomplishments as a player before the turn of the century. During those years, he was one of the game's best defensive third baseman but he got there by way of the outfield.

It happened back in 1895. The Baltimore Orioles were playing the struggling Louisville Colonels, and with great contact hitters like Willie Keeler and Hughie Jennings on their roster, the Orioles were frustrating the Louisville infield by laying down bunt after bunt. Especially ineffective at defending against the slow rollers was Louisville third baseman Walter Preston, who was mercifully removed from the contest. Colonels manager John McCloskey called in outfielder Jimmy Collins to replace him, and third base hasn't been played the same since. With sure-handed confidence and daring, Collins revolutionized the position, developing the modern technique of playing away from the bag and charging home plate in bunting situations. He was the first to scoop up bunts barehanded and fire the balls over to first base in one continuous motion. Collins had to contend with constant bad-hop grounders. Unlike today's well-manicured fields, baseball diamonds at the turn of the century were bumpy and hazardous.

Collins was also an effective clutch hitter, batting .346 in 1897 and leading the league in home runs the following year with 15. He hit for a lifetime average of .294 and ended his major league career at exactly the 2,000 mark. Collins was also a heavy hitter, notching 352 career doubles and 983 RBI. During his years as a Red Sox manager, he won 455 games, mostly due to the help of legendary hurler Cy Young. Collins died in 1943 and was inducted into the Hall of Fame in 1945.

CAREER HIGHLIGHTS
JAMES JOSEPH COLLINS

Born: January 16, 1870 Buffalo, NY **Died:** March 6, 1943
Height: 5'9" **Weight:** 178 lbs. **Batted:** Right **Threw:** Right
Infielder: Louisville Colonels, 1895; Boston Beaneaters, 1895-1900; Boston Red Sox, 1901-07; Philadelphia Athletics, 1907-08. Manager: Boston Red Sox, 1901-06.

★ Led the league in home runs in 1898
★ Winning manager of the first World Series in 1903
★ Topped the league in at-bats in 1900
★ Elected to the Hall of Fame in 1945

MAJOR LEAGUE TOTALS

G	AB	H	BA	2B	3B	HR	R	RBI	SB
1,726	6,796	2,000	.294	352	117	65	1,055	983	194

Though third baseman Jimmy Collins had a relatively short playing career, he managed to revolutionize how his position was played, securing himself a place in baseball history. Collins was also a heavy hitter, notching 352 career doubles and a .294 average.

EARLE COMBS

Earle Combs was a school teacher before he started his professional baseball career, and he was known as much for his intelligent, articulate persona as for his on-field accomplishments. Fans called him "The Kentucky Colonel."

Combs attended Eastern Kentucky University, graduating in 1921. He starred in collegiate track and basketball, as well as baseball, where he played both shortstop and outfield. In his final prep season, Combs batted .591. To finance his education, he worked for a local coal company and taught in one-room schoolhouses. Combs taught 40 students from ages 6 to 16 during his first teaching assignment, earning $60 a month. His parents wanted Combs to be a school teacher. However, he started playing semipro baseball partially to help pay his college tuition more quickly. Baseball had always been his dream. As a youngster growing up with six brothers and sisters on a farm near the Cumberland Mountains, Combs practiced by throwing stones at chipmunks. Even while teaching school, he encouraged his students to play ball.

Finally, Combs convinced his father that he could earn a better living as a ballplayer. In 1922 Combs signed his first contract, with the Louisville Colonels of the American Association. Combs batted .344 his first season, playing 130 games. In 1923 he electrified the American Association with a .380 average and 241 hits in 166 games. In 1924 he played 157 games with Louisville. His .368 average and 233 hits caught the attention of major league scouts everywhere. The New York Yankees needed $50,000 and two players to pry Combs from the Colonels.

In 1924 Combs compiled a .400 average after just 24 games with the Yankees and had a perfect fielding mark. He went 5-for-8 as a pinch hitter. A broken ankle ended what might have been an incredible rookie season. Combs showed courage rarely seen in rookies when he skipped spring training in 1924. He insisted on getting a percentage of the purchase price the Yankees paid to obtain him, as the Louisville front office had promised. Combs insisted that he'd go back to teaching if the problem wasn't solved to his satisfaction.

A recovered Combs played in 150 games in 1925, hitting .342 with 203 hits, 117 runs scored, and 61 RBI. His

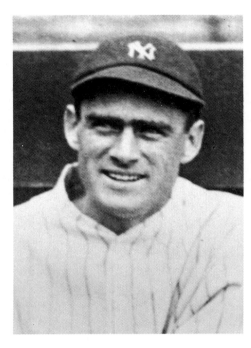

speed gave him great range in the outfield, and he was soon taking extra bases on many hits. The following season, the Yankees cruised all the way to the World Series. While Babe Ruth and Lou Gehrig were clubbing home runs, Combs was becoming baseball's star leadoff man. While his average dipped to .299, he scored 113 runs. In the 1926 World Series, Combs had 10 hits for a .357 average.

Combs never matched the long-ball talents of his Yankee teammates, but he was a key member of the 1927 New York "Murderers' Row" team. He would get on base and wait for Ruth, Gehrig, or Bob Meusel to drive him home. The plan worked to perfection in 1927, when Combs batted a career best of .356 with a league-leading 231 hits. He also topped the American League in at-bats (648) and triples (23) that year. In

the Yankee four-game World Series sweep, Combs batted .313 with 6 runs scored. In 1927 Ruth earned $70,000, while Combs had the second-highest salary on the team at $19,500.

As a full-time player, Combs never hit under .299. He batted just .310 in 1928 but led the league in triples for the second straight year with 21. His average soared to .345 in 1929, and he surpassed the 200-hit barrier for the third time in his career. In 1930 Combs tallied 22 triples to pace the league. His 82 RBI were a personal best.

Combs batted .318 during the 1931 season. In 1932 he hit 30 or more doubles for the eighth straight year, while his .321 average marked the sixth straight year he had stayed above .300. In the 1932 World Series (which the Yankees won against the Cubs in four straight games), Combs hit .375 with 1 home run, 4 RBI, and 8 runs scored. The lanky Kentuckian (now with prematurely gray hair) was slowing down a bit by 1933. The Yankees had moved him to left field, and his average, still a respectable .298, was low by Combs' standards. In August 1934 while playing outfield in St. Louis, Combs fractured his skull. He retired following the 1935 season.

Combs stuck with the Yankees through the 1943 season as a coach, influencing the early career of Joe DiMaggio. He also served as a coach with the St. Louis Browns, Boston Red Sox, and Philadelphia Athletics before retiring to his Kentucky farm in 1954.

The Gentleman from Kentucky ended his playing days with a lifetime .325 average, 1,866 hits, 154 triples, and 1,186 runs scored. His cumulative World Series batting average is .350 with 21 hits. Combs was elected to the Hall of Fame in 1970.

CAREER HIGHLIGHTS
EARLE BRYAN COMBS

Born: May 14, 1899 Pebworth, KY **Died:** July 21, 1976
Height: 6'0" **Weight:** 185 lbs. **Batted:** Left **Threw:** Right
Outfielder: New York Yankees, 1924-35.

★ Led the A.L. in triples three times ★ Played in four World Series
★ Had a league-leading 231 hits in 1927 ★ Elected to the Hall of Fame in 1970
★ Compiled a .325 lifetime batting average

MAJOR LEAGUE TOTALS

G	AB	H	BA	2B	3B	HR	R	RBI	SB
1,455	5,746	1,866	.325	309	154	58	1,186	633	96

Earle Combs' contribution to baseball was as the leadoff man for the New York Yankees "Murderers' Row" team of the mid-1920s. His job was to get on base and then get home with the help of power hitters Babe Ruth, Lou Gehrig, or Bob Meusel.

DAVE CONCEPCION

When baseball fans talk about fixtures on the Cincinnati Reds baseball club, they usually cite such well-known stars as Johnny Bench or Pete Rose. While these men were long-standing heroes for the Ohio-based ballclub, neither served as much time on the team as Davey Concepcion.

Concepcion ended his career with Cincinnati after being released in late 1988. This marked the end of 19 straight seasons in a Reds uniform for the native Venezuelan. During his career, Concepcion was known for flashy fielding, clutch hitting, and fleet baserunning. The Reds signed Concepcion as a free agent on September 12, 1967. He began his pro career in 1968 with Tampa of the Florida State League. He hit just .234 but was promoted to Asheville in 1969. Concepcion was the Southern League's top shortstop—leading in putouts, assists, and fielding average. A promotion to Triple-A Indianapolis concluded Concepcion's 1969 season. After hitting .341 for the Reds' top minor league farm club, Concepcion won a spot on Cincinnati's roster to open the 1970 season.

Concepcion wore number 13 on his uniform. "The players tell me not to take 13, that it is a bad number," Concepcion once told reporters, "but number 13 is my lucky number..." Concepcion was quite lucky in 1970, hitting .260 in 101 games. He didn't get any at-bats in the National League Championship Series against the Pirates but hit .333 with 3 RBI in the World Series against the Baltimore Orioles. Concepcion's luck didn't hold out in 1971, when his average slipped to .205. He did help the Reds defensively, playing shortstop, second base, third base, and outfield—wherever he was needed.

In 1972 Concepcion shared the shortstop position with Darrel Chaney. Concepcion's average was .209 with 2 homers and 29 RBI. The Reds, nicknamed "The Big Red Machine," steamed to another National League title. Concepcion redeemed himself in the World Series by hitting .308 with 4 hits, 2 runs scored, and 2 RBI, but the Reds lost the Series in seven games to the Oakland A's.

Year by year, Concepcion improved both at bat and in the field. He pumped his average up to .287 in 1973, slugging 8 homers and 46 RBI. He stole 22 bases and made a career-low 12 errors. Concepcion was having a banner sea-

son before he was injured on July 22 and missed the remainder of the season. In 1974 Concepcion played in a career-high 160 games. He batted .281 and led all N.L. shortstops with 536 assists. Most impressively, Concepcion clubbed an amazing 14 homers and 82 RBI (and swiped 41 bases), nearly doubling his previous season's totals.

He hit .274 in 140 games, with 5 homers and 49 RBI and made his first All-Star team in 1975. In the All-Star game, Concepcion went 1-for-2. The flashy shortstop was active in postseason play, hitting .455 with 1 homer versus the Pittsburgh Pirates. The Reds needed seven games to defeat the Boston Red Sox and win their first world championship in 35 years. In the second game of the Series, Concepcion singled in Johnny Bench for the tying run, stole second, and scored the winning run on a Ken Griffey double.

In 1976 Concepcion continued his fielding prowess, topping the National League in both putouts and assists. His 9 homers, 69 RBI, and .281 average maintained his standing as one of the best-hitting shortstops in the league. In the 1976 World Series, Concepcion contributed a .357 effort as the Reds swept New York in four games. In 1978 he batted .301 with 6 homers and 67 RBI. While his average slipped a bit in 1979, Concepcion hit a career-best 16 homers to complement his 84 RBI and .281 average. The Reds won their division pennant and faced the Pirates in the Championship Series. While the Pirates sailed to three straight wins, Concepcion provided a majority of the Reds' offense. He hit .429 in three games and fielded flawlessly.

In 1980 Concepcion fell victim to elbow problems. He never had a great throwing arm, but he compensated by getting a good jump on hits. Concepcion was a master at one-hopping throws deep in the hole to first base (on artificial grass) just in time to nip batters. After off-season surgery, Concepcion was at his best in 1981. He played in just 106 games but hit .306 (the second time he batted above .300 in regular-season play). Though not noted for his long-ball ability, Concepcion was one of a handful of players to hit a home run into the "red seats" at Cincinnati's Riverfront Stadium. Concepcion had 101 career homers.

Although he spent his final three seasons as a utility player, Concepcion could still show flashes of brilliance in the field. As late as 1987, he delivered a .319 average in 104 games of part-time duty. He has established a tradition of excellence that 1990s shortstops may have to struggle to match.

CAREER HIGHLIGHTS
DAVID ISMAEL CONCEPCION

Born: June 17, 1948   Aragua, Venezuela
Height: 6'2"   **Weight:** 155 lbs.   **Batted:** Right   **Threw:** Right
Shortstop, utility infielder: Cincinnati Reds, 1970-88.

★ Topped N.L. shortstops in fielding percentage in 1977
★ Played in four World Series
★ Has a lifetime .351 average in five N.L. Championship Series
★ Played in seven All-Star games
★ Led the N.L. in game-winning RBI in 1981

MAJOR LEAGUE TOTALS

G	AB	H	BA	2B	3B	HR	R	RBI	SB
2,488	8,723	2,326	.267	389	48	101	993	950	321

A key member of the Big Red Machine, Dave Concepcion played his entire 19-year career for the Reds. Concepcion was a dynamite postseason player, averaging over .400 in the 1975 and 1979 playoffs and over .300 in the 1970, 1972, and 1976 World Series.

CECIL COOPER

Cecil Cooper was an unsung hero for the Milwaukee Brewers for nearly a decade. While today's fans might claim that Paul Molitor and Robin Yount are the only two real stars the Wisconsin team has ever had, they forget that Cooper's fine defense and timely hitting kept Milwaukee afloat for years.

Actually, Cooper didn't get his start with Milwaukee. He came from the Boston Red Sox on December 6, 1976. The Brewers gave up first baseman George "Boomer" Scott and outfielder Bernie Carbo to get Cooper. He promptly hit an even .300 in 1977 —the first of seven straight years that Cooper topped the .300 mark. During that stretch, the big first baseman was among the league leaders in virtually every offensive category. In his initial season with Milwaukee, Cooper played in 160 games, hitting 20 homers and 78 RBI.

Cooper missed six weeks of the 1978 season due to injuries; nevertheless, he logged a fine .312 average in 107 games. Cooper was revitalized in 1979, hitting .308 with 24 homers and 106 RBI. He tied Chicago's Chet Lemon for the league lead in doubles with 44. The Brewers were second-place finishers in the American League Eastern Division with a 95-66 record. Cooper's continued accomplishments earned him his first spot on an A.L. All-Star team in 1979.

Fans outside of Milwaukee never realized the full extent of Cooper's achievements. In 1980, for example, Cooper batted .352 with 25 home runs and a league-leading 122 RBI—statistics that should almost guarantee an MVP award. To top it all off, Cooper had a sensational year in the field: He paced all A.L. first basemen by making just 5 errors all year long, and his .997 fielding percentage, 160 double plays, and 106 assists were all league highs. Cooper's best season was all but ignored, however, because Kansas City Royals star George Brett set the league on fire with an incredible .390 average.

In Milwaukee only since 1970, the Brewers won their first division title in 1981. Both leagues played under a split season due to a players' strike. Milwaukee won a second-half pennant with a 31-22 record. Cooper was a major contributor to the Brewers' success. He batted .320 with 12 homers and 60 RBI in the shortened season and missed a batting title by just 6 percentage points. He was the league lead-er in doubles (35) and was third in hits (133), total bases (206), and runs scored (70). Defensively, he led the league in double plays (111) and total chances (10.6). Milwaukee lost a special five-game divisional playoff to the New York Yankees.

The following season was a different story for Cooper's Brewers. He hit a personal best of 32 homers, along with 121 RBI and a .313 average. Cooper remained among the league leaders in several categories, placing second in RBI, hits (205), and total bases and fifth in batting average. In the field, Cooper made just 5 errors for a .997 average (trailing only Baltimore's Eddie Murray). Cooper was first in double plays, how-ever.

The Brewers needed a full five games to defeat the California Angels in the A.L. Championship Series. Cooper bat-ted only .150, but he was the man who put the Brewers in the World Series. With the Brewers trailing 3-2 in the sev-enth inning, Cooper singled in both the tying and winning runs to give the Brewers a 4-3 victory. The St. Louis Cardinals downed the Brewers in a seven-game World Series. Cooper, how-ever, was a tough out against the Cardinals. He had 8 hits with 1 homer and 6 RBI.

Cooper's last great season as a hitter came in 1983, when he tied for the league lead in RBI with 126 (with Boston's Jim Rice) and hit 30 homers and a .307 average. As late as 1985 he still had 99 RBI and an average close to .300. Cooper lost his first baseman's job to Greg Brock in 1987 and wound up as the club's designated hitter. When rookie Joey Meyer arrived, Cooper became expendable and was released after sitting on the bench for much of the 1987 season.

The lifetime stats of Cooper are even more amazing in light of the fact that he didn't get his first full-time job in the majors until 1974. He toiled in the Boston Red Sox minor league organiza-tion before getting to play in 121 games during the 1974 season, when he batted .275. He progressed to .311 with 14 homers and 44 RBI in 1975. Cooper batted .400 in the 1975 Championship Series but had only 1 hit in the World Series against Cincinnati. In 1976, Cooper batted .282 with 15 homers and 78 RBI.

Cooper's lifetime stats compare favorably with several Hall of Fame first basemen. He wound up with just 1 hit less than Bill Terry, and his stats outdis-tance those of George "High Pockets" Kelly in nearly every category. Still Cooper may be overlooked for Coop-erstown membership. Cooper would be eligible for the Hall of Fame starting in 1993.

CAREER HIGHLIGHTS
CECIL CELESTER COOPER

Born: December 20, 1949 Brenham, TX
Height: 6'2" **Weight:** 165 lbs. **Batted:** Left **Threw:** Left
First baseman: Boston Red Sox, 1971-76. First baseman, designated hitter: Milwaukee Brewers, 1977-87.

★ Batted over .300 in eight seasons, including seven straight
★ Hit a career high of .352 in 1980
★ Topped A.L. hitters in doubles twice
★ Led the league in RBI in 1980 and 1983
★ Played in five All-Star games
★ Played in two World Series

MAJOR LEAGUE TOTALS

G	AB	H	BA	2B	3B	HR	R	RBI	SB
1,896	7,349	2,192	.298	415	47	241	1,012	1,125	89

The Milwaukee Brewers marched to the 1982 World Series only with the help of Cecil
Cooper's smooth batwork—32 homers, 121 RBI, and a .313 average. Though the Brewers
were defeated in the Series by the Cardinals, Cooper had 8 hits, 1 homer, and 6 RBI.

STAN COVELESKI

Stan Coveleski was a self-taught major league star. As a youth, he didn't have access to any organized leagues to learn baseball fundamentals. In fact, Coveleski dropped out of school after the fourth grade to work in the Pennsylvania coal mines. While working six days a week during most of the daylight hours, he developed his pitching style and talent by throwing rocks at tin cans during his limited free time. Born Stanislaus Kowalewski to Polish immigrant parents, Coveleski claimed that in his youth he could hit tin cans at 40 to 50 feet away.

Older brother Harry Coveleski had made the big leagues in 1907 with the Philadelphia Phillies. After six years in the mines, Stan Coveleski got his chance at a baseball career at age 18. The local semipro team, realizing that he was the brother of a major leaguer, asked Coveleski to sign a contract. He pitched four years for Lancaster in the Tri-State League before getting a shot with the Philadelphia Athletics in 1912. Coveleski pitched in five games, going 2-1 with 2 complete games. His debut was a five-hit shutout victory, one of the few times a rookie had accomplished this feat so quickly. Still, the Athletics were well-stocked with star pitchers like Eddie Plank, Chief Bender, and Herb Pennock, so Connie Mack shipped him out to a minor league team in Spokane, where he spent two years. During his 1915 season with Portland of the Pacific Coast League, Coveleski learned how to throw a spitball—then a legal pitch.

The spitter was Coveleski's ticket back to the big leagues. The Cleveland Indians discovered Coveleski's newfound talent and made him a regular member of their 1916 pitching rotation. In his first year with the Tribe, Coveleski was 15-13 with 3 saves. In 1917 Coveleski improved to a 19-14 mark with a sparkling 1.81 ERA. Coveleski's season of success was highlighted by 9 shutouts, 24 complete games, and 4 saves.

Coveleski helped Cleveland to a second-place 73-54 finish in 1918, just two games behind the pennant-winning Boston Red Sox. Coveleski ranked among American League leaders in several pitching categories. With a 22-13 record, he trailed only Walter "The Big Train" Johnson by 1 victory for the league lead. Coveleski's winning percentage (.629) was third best in the league, while his dazzling 1.82 ERA was second only to Johnson's. Addi-

tionally, Coveleski was third best in the American League with 311 innings pitched and fourth in complete games with 25.

Again in 1919, Coveleski remained one of the American League's most dominant pitchers. He won 24 games, second only to Chicago White Sox star Ed Cicotte's 29. His .667 winning percentage was fourth best in the A.L. Other notable accomplishments by Coveleski that year included fourth in strikeouts (118), third in games pitched (43), third in complete games (24), and second in saves (4). This time the Indians finished three and a half games behind the 1919 Chicago White Sox, the team that would be forever known as the "Black Sox" for deliberately losing the World Series.

The 1920 World Series was a talent showcase for the 31-year-old veteran. Cleveland finally won an American League pennant, going 98-56. Coveleski's 24-14 record was among

the best in the junior circuit that year. In the World Series against the Brooklyn Dodgers, Coveleski pitched three complete game victories. Coveleski won the first game 3-1 with a five-hit effort. Pitching with three days' rest, Coveleski won 5-1, again with a five-hitter. Then, with only two days of rest, he hurled a shutout to clinch the world championship for Cleveland. Coveleski wound up with 3 wins, 3 complete games, and 3 five-hitters. His ERA was a remarkable 0.67. He walked only 2 men in 27 innings, exhibiting his usual sterling control. At bat, Coveleski even had 1 hit and scored 2 runs.

Coveleski wound up the 1920 season with a 2.49 ERA, 26 complete games, and 3 shutouts in 315 innings of work. The Indians veteran won the only strikeout title of his career by fanning 133 batters.

Major league baseball decided in December 1920 to ban the use of the spitball. Under a "grandfather clause," only Coveleski and 16 other major leaguers were allowed to continue with the pitch. Coveleski said that he could throw three different types of spitters, each curving in a different direction. He said that he'd always go through the motions of preparing a spitball but would throw the pitch only occasionally, in hopes of keeping hitters off balance. Because Coveleski had a solid fastball and curve, the spitter was an effective change of pace.

Coveleski had two more 20-win seasons before retiring. His brother, who pitched for nine years, won 81 games. Together the Coveleskis won 296 games, making them one of the most effective brother combinations of all time.

CAREER HIGHLIGHTS
STANLEY ANTHONY COVELESKI

Born: July 13, 1889 Shamokin, PA **Died:** March 20, 1984
Height: 5'11" **Weight:** 166 lbs. **Batted:** Right **Threw:** Right
Pitcher: Philadelphia Athletics, 1912; Cleveland Indians, 1916-24; Washington Senators, 1925-27; New York Yankees, 1928.

★ Won two ERA titles

★ Won three games in the 1920 World Series

★ Had five 20-win seasons

★ Paced the A.L. with 9 shutouts in 1917 and 5 shutouts in 1923

★ Elected to the Hall of Fame in 1969

MAJOR LEAGUE TOTALS

G	IP	W	L	Pct.	SO	BB	ERA
450	3,081	215	142	.602	981	802	2.89

Spitball ace Stan Coveleski escaped the drudgery of the Pennsylvania coal mines when he opted for a pitching career in professional baseball. "I only saw the sun on Sundays," he once quipped. "I would have been great in night baseball."

SAM CRAWFORD

Playing in the outfield next to superstar Ty Cobb for 13 seasons would obscure the accomplishments of any deserving player. Despite that handicap, however, Sam Crawford distinguished himself as one of baseball's best hitters during the early 1900s.

Crawford was known as "Wahoo Sam" because he was born in the tiny town of Wahoo, Nebraska. Crawford enjoyed the colorful nickname, as it personified his lively style of on-field play. Crawford had been a barber's apprentice, playing baseball in pick-up teams in his free time. He would travel throughout Nebraska with his hometown friends, starting up impromptu games with teams in other towns. He got his first break with a team in Chatham, Ontario, in a small Canadian league. When the league went bankrupt, Crawford's contract was sold to a Grand Rapids, Michigan, team in the Western League. Only a year later, the native Nebraskan was playing for the Cincinnati Reds. He played 31 games with the 1899 Reds, hitting .307.

In 1900 Crawford hit just .267, but he showed what was considered awesome power back then, hitting 7 homers to lead his club. Crawford became the National League home run leader in 1901 with 16 round-trippers, as well as 104 RBI and a .330 average. The following season, Crawford led the league with 23 triples and a .333 average. Playing with a second-division team like the Reds must have been trying for the gifted outfielder. He broke his contract and signed with the Detroit Tigers in the newly formed American League.

Crawford opened his American League career in 1903 by hitting a league-high 25 triples, together with 4 homers, 89 RBI, and a .335 average. Maybe because American League pitchers got to know Crawford's hitting habits, his usually high average didn't climb above .297 for the next three years. Then in 1907 Crawford's career shifted back into high gear. He was a vital spark in the Tigers' American League championship, batting .323 with 4 homers, 81 RBI, and a league-best 102 runs scored. Crawford was limited to only 5 hits in the World Series as the Chicago Cubs swept the Tigers.

In 1908 the Tigers captured their second straight American League crown. Crawford claimed the A.L. homer crown with 7 dingers. This was the first time a player had won home run honors in both leagues. Crawford kept his average above .300 in a league-leading 591 at-bats. Again facing the Cubs in the World Series, Crawford batted .238, as he had in the previous year's fall classic. The Cubs needed five games to top the Tigers this time.

Detroit became a three-time loser when the Pirates defeated the Tigers in the 1909 World Series. Crawford's regular season accomplishments included a .314 average, 6 homers, 97 RBI, and a league-finest 35 doubles. Crawford pumped his postseason batting average up to .250, including a fifth-game homer.

During the next six seasons, Crawford would drive in 100-plus runs five times (leading the league on three occasions). In 1910 he paced the American League both in RBI (120) and triples (19). Crawford registered a career-high .378 average in 1911, third in the league behind teammate Cobb at .420. Cobb also led the league in hits that year, and Crawford was third with 217 (a lifetime best). In 1912 Crawford tallied a .325 average with 4 homers and 109 RBI. He belted 9 homers in 1913, the most since the 16 four-baggers that had won him the National League title in 1901. Crawford played in a career-high 157 games in 1914, batting .314 with the American League RBI lead (104). In 1915 Crawford hit .299 with 4 homers and 112 RBI.

Crawford retired as baseball's lifetime triples champion with 309—a number that may never be topped even by today's stars. Because he played in the dead-ball era, many of Crawford's ferocious drives fell in for triples. The three-base hit was an art form Crawford mastered, getting 20 or more triples in five seasons. He never had the speed of Cobb, but he had baserunning savvy and wound up with 366 steals.

It's no secret that Tiger teammates Crawford and Cobb were never the best of friends off the field. Cobb blamed Crawford and other Tiger veterans for unmercifully hazing him when he was a rookie with the team. Crawford said that Cobb had a belligerent attitude and took offense too easily. Crawford later said that Honus Wagner, not Ty Cobb, should be considered the most gifted player in history.

Nonetheless, Cobb insisted after his retirement that Crawford was worthy of Hall of Fame membership. His wish became reality in 1957, when Crawford was enshrined at Cooperstown.

Sam Crawford was probably the best triples hitter in the history of baseball, ending his career with a record-setting 312. Crawford, who was overshadowed by teammate Ty Cobb for much of his career, surpassed Cobb in that category by 15.

CAREER HIGHLIGHTS
SAMUEL EARL CRAWFORD

Born: April 18, 1880 Wahoo, NE **Died:** June 15, 1968
Height: 6'0" **Weight:** 190 lbs. **Batted:** Left **Threw:** Left
Outfielder: Cincinnati Reds, 1899-1902; Detroit Tigers, 1903-17.

- ★ Compiled a .309 lifetime average with 2,961 hits
- ★ Topped the N.L. in homers in 1901
- ★ Led the league in triples for six seasons
- ★ Hit 309 triples in lifetime–first on the all-time list
- ★ First in the A.L. in RBI three times
- ★ Elected to the Hall of Fame in 1957

MAJOR LEAGUE TOTALS

G	AB	H	BA	2B	3B	HR	R	RBI	SB
2,517	9,580	2,961	.309	458	309	98	1,391	1,525	366

JOE CRONIN

Baseball has no other rags-to-riches story that can compare with Joe Cronin's. The son of Irish immigrants, the industrious Cronin worked his way up from scrub infielder to perennial All-Star, then to pennant-winning manager, respected front-office executive, and finally to president of the American League. In his 20-year playing career, Cronin was one of the most consistent hitters and fielders in baseball.

It's probably fitting that Cronin came into the world in San Francisco shortly after the famous 1906 earthquake, for Cronin would cause opposing pitchers to tremble throughout his long big league career. From the time he first put on a Pittsburgh Pirates uniform in 1926, Cronin was a determined batsman. The Pirates signed Cronin in 1924. He played just over two full seasons in the minors before getting a chance to play in Pittsburgh. He didn't win a starting job in 1926 with the Pirates, but he hit .265 in 38 games. After keeping Cronin on the bench for all but 12 games in 1927, the Pirates sold him to the Washington Senators where he served as a backup shortstop in 1928, playing in 63 games. His .242 average and steady defense were enough to earn a starting job the next year.

Cronin blossomed in 1929, his first year as a regular in Washington. Playing for manager (and immortal hurler) Walter Johnson, Cronin hit .281 and led American League shortstops in assists. In 1930 Cronin exceeded all expectations by winning the American League Most Valuable Player award. The fiery, slender righthander hit .346 with 13 home runs and 126 RBI. He was also an awesome glove man, leading his American League contemporaries in putouts, assists, double plays, and total chances per game. Unfortunately, the Senators finished at 94-60, eight games behind the pennant-winning Philadelphia Athletics.

Cronin hit .306 in 1931 and .318 in 1932. In 1933, he hit .309 and drove in 100-plus runs for the fourth straight season. At age 26, Cronin took on an even greater task: serving as a player/manager. He was a natural leader who inspired his team by his own determined brand of play. That first year, he piloted the Senators to a league-leading 99-53 record. Although his club lost the World Series in five games to the New York Giants, Cronin hit a respectable .318 in what would

prove to be his only postseason experience.

Although he was a fan favorite in Washington, the Senators couldn't refuse an offer from the Red Sox to purchase Cronin for $225,000 and Lyn Lary after the 1934 season. Not only did Cronin become Boston's starting shortstop, he also assumed managerial duties. The square-jawed Irishman was an instant hit in Boston. Even though he never put his team in a World Series while he was an active player, he always performed with ferocious dedication.

One of Cronin's greatest achievements during his years with the Red Sox was his acquisition of a home run stroke. Only twice had he hit in double figures for homers before joining Boston. However, as the short left field wall known as "the Green Monster" beckoned, Cronin answered. He hit 94 home runs from 1937-1941 (his last full season in the majors). His best year was in 1940, when he hit 24 homers and 111 RBI.

Cronin kept playing until 1945, when a broken leg ended his playing career. He prolonged his career mostly

out of necessity. As team manager, Cronin had to try to patch together lineups during the years of World War II, when most able-bodied men were in the military. Nevertheless, Cronin performed admirably. In 1943 he set an American League record with 5 pinch-hit home runs.

The New York Yankees were one reason why the Red Sox never won a pennant during the 1930s. Their dynasty teams stopped the Red Sox, the Detroit Tigers, and any other team. Furthermore, the Red Sox seldom gave Cronin the best pitchers to work with. Finally, the year after he retired as a player, the Red Sox won the American League pennant (only to lose the World Series to the St. Louis Cardinals). When the Red Sox hired Joe McCarthy as manager in 1948, they promoted Cronin to general manager. He held that post until he became American League president in 1959. This was the first time a former player had gained such a position of responsibility in the front office. He was in charge of the junior circuit until 1973, when he became chairman of the American League board. He held that title until his death.

Cronin retired with a lifetime average of .301. A seven-time All-Star, Cronin was remembered for his warm, outgoing personality and his eternal gratitude to the game that made him famous. Cronin was elected to the Hall of Fame in 1956.

Though best known for his leadership, Joe Cronin was a competent hitter. He led the league in triples in 1932 with 18, and in doubles in 1933 and 1938 with 45 and 51.

CAREER HIGHLIGHTS
JOSEPH EDWARD CRONIN

Born: October 12, 1906 San Francisco, CA **Died:** September 7, 1984
Height: 5'11" **Weight:** 180 lbs. **Batted:** Right **Threw:** Right
Infielder: Pittsburgh Pirates, 1926-27; Washington Senators, 1928-34; Boston Red Sox, 1935-45. Manager: Washington Senators, 1933-34; Boston Red Sox, 1935-47.

★ Led the A.L. with 18 triples in 1932
★ Topped the league with 18 pinch hits
★ Hit .318 in the 1933 World Series
★ Elected to the Hall of Fame in 1956

MAJOR LEAGUE TOTALS

G	AB	H	BA	2B	3B	HR	R	RBI	SB
2,124	7,579	2,285	.301	515	118	170	1,233	1,424	87

KIKI CUYLER

If you were saddled with the given name of Hazen Shirley Cuyler, you'd probably welcome the nickname "Kiki" too. In his youth, Hall of Famer Kiki Cuyler went by "Cuy" (rhymes with "guy"). Early in his career, when he was playing center field for Nashville of the Southern League, the shortstop and second baseman would both call out his name when the ball was hit toward center. The cries of "Cuy, Cuy" were echoed by the fans. Spelled phonetically, it came out "Kiki," the name by which Cuyler would be known for the remainder of his distinguished career.

Cuyler didn't really start his career in organized baseball until after serving a two-year hitch in the military. He was active in nearly all sports in high school, and he played semipro baseball throughout Canada. Meanwhile, he was working as an automobile builder at a plant in Flint, Michigan. Only when the plant closed down did he sign a contract with the nearby Bay City team. In his first year, Cuyler served as a righthand pitcher until he was spiked sliding into second base. For rehabilitation, he was told to play the outfield. He played there the rest of his career. In 1920 he hit .258 in 69 games. The next year, Cuyler played in 116 games, hitting .317 with 8 homers and 32 stolen bases. The Pittsburgh Pirates brought him up for just one game in 1921 and 1922.

In 1922 Cuyler moved on to Charleston. He earned 151 hits in 131 games, notching 12 homers and 35 steals. Cuyler became the Most Valuable Player in the Southern Association in 1923 while playing for the Nashville Volunteers. His fine season, which included league highs in six different categories (including a .340 average and 68 steals), secured him a permanent place in the Pirates outfield. Cuyler was the starting left fielder for the 1924 team. He batted an impressive .354 in 117 games. He was fourth in the league in average, second in stolen bases (32), and fourth in slugging percentage (.539). The rifle-armed Cuyler gunned down 19 runners from his left field post during his first year, but he also led his contemporaries with 16 errors. Cuyler played beside another great fielder in the Pittsburgh outfield, center fielder Max Carey. Carey and Cuyler were two of the best basestealers in baseball.

Cuyler's sophomore season in 1925 exceeded even his rookie season success. The Michigan native hit .357

(fourth in the N.L.), with 17 homers and 102 RBI. Cuyler stole 41 bases, second only to teammate Carey's 46. Cuyler was first in the league with 26 triples and 144 runs scored. He upstaged Carey in the World Series, batting .269 with 1 homer and 6 RBI. Cuyler's eighth-inning, bases-loaded double off Walter Johnson won the World Series for the Pirates.

In 1926 Cuyler played in a career-high 157 games, hitting .321 with 8 homers, 92 RBI, and a league-best 113 runs scored. Cuyler won his first of four stolen base crowns in five seasons, leading the league with 35 swipes. His title-winning totals for steals included 37 in 1928, 43 in 1929, and 37 in 1930. A leg injury and a broken foot had curtailed his basestealing aspirations earlier in his career.

Cuyler's 1927 season is shrouded in mystery. He batted .309 in only 85 games. Following a run-in with Cuyler, Pirates manager Donie Bush left his star outfielder sitting on the bench for nearly the entire final two months of the season. Even though the Pirates won the

National League title with a 94-60 record, Cuyler didn't see a single at-bat in the 1927 World Series. The "Murderers' Row" New York Yankees team, meanwhile, easily swept the Pirates in four straight games.

Cuyler was traded to the Chicago Cubs on November 28, 1927, for Sparky Adams and Pete Scott. The Pirates, willing to unload Cuyler, gave the Cubs a bargain. Cuyler was a Cubs regular for the next seven and a half seasons. In 1928 Cuyler pounded 17 homers, 79 RBI, and a .285 average. He upped his totals to .360, 15 homers, and 102 RBI in 1929. The Cubs, under manager Joe McCarthy, strolled to a 98-54 record. In the 1929 World Series, Cuyler hit .300 for a losing cause. His two-run single provided the team with its only postseason win in the third game.

Cubs fans were treated to another awesome season from Cuyler in 1930. He batted .355 with 13 home runs and a career-best 134 RBI. In 1932 the Cubs won another pennant with the assistance of 10 homers, 77 RBI, and a .291 average from Cuyler.

Following his release by the Cubs, Cuyler played for the Cinncinnati Reds for two and a half seasons, then closed out his career with the 1938 Brooklyn Dodgers. Following his retirement, Cuyler had mixed success managing in the minor leagues. He coached on the major league level for the Cubs and was a coach with the Boston Red Sox at the time of his death.

Cuyler retired with a .321 average, 2,299 hits, and 328 career steals. Some fans, impressed with his awesome line-drive hitting, fleet baserunning, and fine fielding, dubbed him a right-handed Ty Cobb.

CAREER HIGHLIGHTS
HAZEN SHIRLEY CUYLER

Born: August 30, 1899 Harrisville, MI **Died:** February 11, 1950
Height: 5'10" **Weight:** 180 lbs. **Batted:** Right **Threw:** Right
Outfielder: Pittsburgh Pirates, 1921-27; Chicago Cubs, 1928-35; Cincinnati Reds, 1935-37; Brooklyn Dodgers, 1938.

★ Compiled a lifetime .321 batting average ★ Batted over .350 for four seasons
★ Played in three World Series ★ Elected to the Hall of Fame in 1968
★ Led the league in stolen bases four times

MAJOR LEAGUE TOTALS

G	AB	H	BA	2B	3B	HR	R	RBI	SB
1,879	7,161	2,299	.321	394	157	128	1,295	1,065	328

Kiki Cuyler played on the same Pittsburgh Pirates team as the famed Max Carey. Cuyler and Carey were two of the best basestealers in baseball. Though Carey's stats became the record setters, Cuyler did lead the N.L. in stolen bases four times.

RAY DANDRIDGE

His teammates called him "Hooks" for his fine fielding ability, or "Squat" for his husky resemblance to a fire hydrant. Baseball historians have called Ray Dandridge "the best third baseman never to make the major leagues." Dandridge was a key member of the Newark Eagles in the 1930s.

In another time, he would have garnered Gold Gloves with his agility and ability to anticipate a play. As it was, Dandridge was a Golden Glove boxer before being discovered on a sandlot team by barnstorming Candy Jim Taylor in 1933. Taylor, manager of the Detroit Stars of the National Negro League, studied the stocky, short-legged, long-armed outfielder and saw talent that needed nurturing—and rearranging, too. He took away Dandridge's spindly stick and replaced it with a big bat. He encouraged him to hit for average and not to try to pull every pitch. These hallmarks of Taylor's style stayed with Dandridge throughout all of his playing days. But whereas Candy Jim, a shortstop himself, had assigned his favorite pupil to that position, Dandridge's next coach assigned him to third.

Dick Lundy (who, like Taylor, had played short) originally placed Dandridge at third as an emergency measure, but Dandridge acclimated so well that he stayed on after the crisis.

He liked his new position—studying other third sackers, seeking advice, and testing his own limits against the batters' talents. He memorized runners' speeds to gauge how fast to get rid of the ball. Although troubled by a bad knee (an amateur football injury), he played far in to be ready for bunts.

Six years after his professional debut, Dandridge left the Negro Leagues for the higher pay of the Mexican League. He had offered to stay if his manager could match the Mexican price, but as much as his employers wanted to comply, the Negro Leagues had little cash to spend freely. Furthermore, black players who played in Mexico didn't have to suffer non-stop prejudice; they could live stable, happy lives in an integrated society. Dandridge traveled south.

Dandridge's new manager was former great shortstop Willie "Diablico" Wells. He changed Dandridge's position again—but only because Dandridge was hard of hearing on his left side and couldn't hear instructions from his shortstop/manager. Dandridge began playing at second base. At first the double play pivot was a sore point for his

team, but when Dandridge finally got it down, he was just about unstoppable.

Although records were rarely kept for players of the Negro or Mexican Leagues, those available seem to indicate that Dandridge hit his stride south of the border. Although he batted over .300 from the start, he peaked at .370 in the Mexican Leagues, maintaining that average upon his 1949 return to the states.

Before his return, he served as player/manager for a Mexican team, winning the pennant and personal acclaim. He raised his average when playing against barnstorming whites—including the New York Yankees and their fearsome future Hall of Famer, Whitey Ford.

Dandridge was 34 when Jackie Robinson crossed baseball's color line in 1947, and he hoped to join Robinson in the majors. Dandridge lied about his age to get into the minor leagues when

he was 36. While playing for the Minneapolis Millers, the New York Giants minor league affiliate, Dandridge was named the American Association's Rookie of the Year in 1949. He hit a home run in his first game with his new team, winning instant loyalty from teammates and fans.

As the Giants raced for the pennant in 1950, Sal Maglie and Monte Irvin pleaded for Dandridge's call-up—a call that never came. No one ever knew why. Did the Giants know that Dandridge was seven years older than he claimed? Was he more valuable in the minors, boosting attendance in Minneapolis as a fan favorite? Was there a secret quota among league owners, limiting the number of blacks per team? The theories are endless. Baseball historians still speculate how Dandridge might have affected the major leagues if only he'd been given a chance. As it is, Dandridge won a lasting tribute in the respect, affection, and devotion of Willie Mays, to whom Dandridge was a surrogate father when both were on the Millers.

By 1953, Dandridge could no longer conceal his age. After a season-long arm injury healed, he played one last year in South Dakota before accepting the fact that fate had passed him by. He retired, tending bar in Newark and scouting for the Giants.

Fate came calling in 1987 and this time stayed for a cup of coffee. He got the very thing he had wanted from the majors: He was elected to the Baseball Hall of Fame, calling it "one of the happiest days of my life." Since then, Dandridge has been a frequent guest at sports collector shows across the country.

CAREER HIGHLIGHTS
RAYMOND DANDRIDGE

Born: 1913   Richmond, VA
Height: 5'7"   **Weight:** 175 lbs.   **Batted:** Right   **Threw:** Right
Shortstop, second baseman, third baseman: Negro Leagues, Mexican Leagues, minor leagues. Teams include: Newark Eagles, Detroit Stars, 1933-39; Vera Cruz, 1939-49; Minneapolis Millers, 1949-53; Oakland, Pacific Coast League, 1953; Bismark, 1955.

★ Named American Association Rookie of the Year in 1949
★ Named A.A. MVP in 1950

★ Hit as high as .370 in the Mexican League
★ Elected to the Hall of Fame in 1987

MAJOR LEAGUE TOTALS
(no accurate statistics available)

Third baseman Ray Dandridge was one of the greatest players in the Negro Leagues. He also played on integrated teams in the Mexican League in the 1940s, where he batted as high as .370. Sadly, Dandridge never got to play in the U.S. major leagues.

WILLIE DAVIS

Willie Davis was a fixture in the Los Angeles Dodgers outfield for more than a decade. He brought so much raw speed to the Dodgers lineup, both on the base paths and in the field, that a visiting clubhouse attendant gave him the nickname "Comet."

The Arkansas native reached the Dodgers after only two seasons of minor league baseball. Davis had been a star pitcher in high school in Los Angeles. The Dodgers, realizing Davis' speed, converted him into an outfielder. In 1959 Davis played just seven games with Green Bay, Wisconsin, before being reassigned to a minor league team in Reno, Nevada. In 117 games Davis tore up the California League with an awesome display of offensive prowess. He topped the league in six categories: batting average (.365), runs scored (135), hits (187), doubles (40), triples (16), and outfield putouts (302).

Davis played the 1960 season with Spokane in the Pacific Coast League. He became *The Sporting News* minor league player of the year with another incredible season. Davis earned a spot on the Triple-A All-Star team and a late-season call-up to the Los Angeles Dodgers.

Davis quickly adapted to major league pitching, hitting .318 with 2 homers and 10 RBI in 22 games in 1960. His blazing speed earned him a starting job in the Dodger outfield in 1961. Davis hit .254 with 12 homers and 45 RBI in 128 games. Tommy Davis moved from center to right field to make room for the newest Davis, and Frank Howard was squeezed out of a job to make room for the new Dodger speedster. Willie Davis was one of eight Dodgers to hit in double figures for home runs that year. Although Davis had a respectable first season, he had some stiff competition for the National League Rookie of the Year award. Another young outfielder named Billy Williams had broken in that year with the Chicago Cubs. Williams ran off with the top rookie honors.

In 1962 Davis upped his average to .285. He clubbed 21 homers and 85 RBI and led the National League with 10 triples. He also established himself as one of the league's premier baserunners, swiping 32 bases. A highlight of Davis' sophomore season was a grand slam homer against Philadelphia on July 2, 1962.

Davis had a subpar 1963 season, hitting just .245. The Dodgers, however, marched to the 1963 World Series. In the Series, Davis batted only .167, but his average doesn't tell the full story of his contribution to the team's world championship. In the second game his two-run double staked the Dodgers to a first inning lead and an eventual 4-1 win. In the decisive fourth game of the sweep by Los Angeles, a seventh-inning sacrifice fly by Davis drove in Junior Gilliam with the winning run in the Dodgers 2-1 triumph.

In 1964 Davis rebounded to hit .294 with 12 homers, 77 RBI, and a career-high 42 stolen bases. His steals ranked third in the league behind Maury Wills and Lou Brock. Davis led the 1964 Dodgers with 91 runs scored, 7 triples, and 180 hits. His 400 putouts were tops among National League center fielders. The Dodgers regained their world championship in 1965 against the Minnesota Twins, and Davis tied a major league record set by Honus Wagner by stealing 3 bases in one

World Series game. Davis and the Dodgers had another banner season in 1966 but suffered a humiliating four-game sweep at the hands of the Baltimore Orioles in the World Series. Orioles pitching gave up no Dodger runs in the final three Series games. Davis earned a dubious pair of records by making 3 errors in the fifth inning of the second game (during Sandy Koufax's last game) —the most errors ever made by one player in a single game or in a single inning.

Davis finally surpassed the .300 barrier for the first time in 1969, batting .311 with a team-leading slugging percentage of .456. The Dodger veteran became the talk of the National League with a 31-game hitting streak.

In 1970, for the second time in his career, Davis led the National League with 16 triples. His three-base hits set a single-season Dodger club record. He batted .305 in 146 games with 8 homers and a personal best of 93 RBI. Davis also stole 38 bases, his best effort since 1964. In 1971, Davis won his first Gold Glove and gained his first N.L. All-Star selection. He finished the season at .309 with 10 homers and 74 RBI. Defensively, he was a league leader with 404 putouts.

Davis was named Dodger captain in 1973. Starting in 1974, he bounced around with four different teams and played two years in the Japanese League. His last season was with the 1979 Angels. He ended his career in the top ten of virtually every Dodger offensive category, and he was only the third player in team history to record more than 2,000 hits—a feat Steve Garvey, Gil Hodges, and Duke Snider couldn't match.

CAREER HIGHLIGHTS
WILLIAM HENRY DAVIS

Born: April 15, 1940   Mineral Springs, AR
Height: 5'11"   **Weight:** 180 lbs.   **Batted:** Left   **Threw:** Left
Outfielder: Los Angeles Dodgers, 1960-73; Montreal Expos, 1974; Texas Rangers, 1975; St. Louis Cardinals, 1975; San Diego Padres, 1976; California Angels, 1979.

★ Hit in 31 straight games for the 1969 Los Angeles Dodgers
★ Led the league in triples twice
★ Played in three World Series

★ Tied a World Series record with three steals in one game
★ Won three Gold Gloves
★ Stole 42 bases in 1964

MAJOR LEAGUE TOTALS

G	AB	H	BA	2B	3B	HR	R	RBI	SB
2,429	9,174	2,561	.279	395	138	182	1,217	1,053	398

Despite some impressive statistics during his first year in the majors, including a .254 batting average and 12 home runs, Willie Davis lost the Rookie of the Year award to another young outfielder, Billy Williams of the Chicago Cubs.

ANDRE DAWSON

Andre Dawson, the man called "Hawk," is one of the most pleasant surprises the Cubs have had since winning their last pennant in 1984. He has been one of the team's most dependable outfielders since Hall of Famer Billy Williams patrolled the ivy-covered walls of Wrigley Field.

Dawson played out his free agency with the Montreal Expos in 1986, after spending his first 11 major league seasons there. Although Dawson had sterling lifetime hitting statistics, some teams were concerned about the questionable condition of his knees. Other clubs were hesitant about throwing big bucks at other team's players, especially players over age 30. Thus, Dawson found no takers for his services. Anxious to play in a homer-friendly ballpark like Wrigley Field, he presented himself to the Cubs with a "fill-in-the-blank" contract. Dawson welcomed the idea of playing more day games on a grass field (which would be kinder to his ailing knees).

Dawson had an incredible inaugural season with the Cubs, becoming the first player in history on a last-place club to win a Most Valuable Player award. He was also the first player in 40 years to win an MVP award during his first season with a club. Cubs broadcaster Harry Caray dubbed him "Awesome Dawson" for his league-leading 49 homers and 137 RBI. He led the Cubs in nine offensive categories, winning his seventh Gold Glove and fourth Silver Slugger award along the way. Only Hack Wilson, who clubbed 56 homers in 1930, had hit more single-season homers in a Cubs uniform. Dawson captured America's heart by keeping the mediocre Cubs afloat with his spectacular brand of play. He received more than a million votes to be named a National League starter in the All-Star game.

In 1988 Dawson didn't match his momentous debut season with the Cubs; however, he exceeded 20 homers and 75 RBI for the ninth time in his career, and his 24 homers and 79 RBI were Cubs highs. Dawson batted .303, the fourth time in 13 seasons he broke the .300 barrier. The Cubs right fielder was second in the league in hits (179) and total bases (298). He ended the season only 2 homers short of 300, just 4 runs away from 1,000, and 68 hits shy of 2,000.

Looking back, it seems incredible that Dawson didn't get drafted by the Montreal Expos until the 11th round of

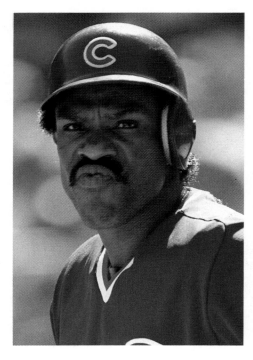

the June 1975 free agent draft. Coming from Florida A & M University, Dawson was an immediate success in the minor leagues, playing less than two full seasons before winning a job in the majors. In 1975 he hit .330 in 72 games with a league-leading 13 homers with the Lethbridge team. Dawson began the 1976 season at Quebec of the Eastern League (Double-A), hitting .357 with 8 homers and 27 RBI in 40 games. Dawson was then promoted to Denver (Triple-A) of the American Association, where he had 14 homers and 28 RBI in his first month, earning player of the month honors. After 74 games, Dawson had 20 homers, 46 RBI, and a .350 average. The Expos took notice, giving Dawson a 24-game trial at season's end.

Rookie of the Year honors awaited Dawson in 1977 after hitting .282 with 19 homers and 65 RBI. Dawson set a Montreal team record by making just 4 errors all season long. Sixteen of Dawson's homers came after June 10, when his bat shifted into high gear. In 1978 Dawson made the "25/25" club in both homers and stolen bases. He exhibited fine defense throughout the season, compiling a career-high 17 assists.

Dawson hit .308, the best in his career, in 1980. The multitalented Expo highlighted his season with 17 game-winning RBI and a 19-game hitting streak. In 1981 Dawson nearly won the league MVP award, finishing second in voting to Mike Schmidt. Dawson's 24 homers, 64 RBI, and .302 average helped the Montreal Expos to the Eastern Division title. Another typically fine season followed for Dawson in 1982: He hit .301 with 23 homers and 83 RBI, while scoring a career-high 107 runs. The Florida native was an MVP runner-up again in 1983, with 189 hits, 32 homers, 113 RBI, and 104 runs scored.

After a subpar season at the plate in 1984, Dawson rebounded to hit 23 homers and 91 RBI in 1985. He tied a record on September 23 with 2 three-run homers in one inning against the Chicago Cubs. Dawson missed nearly a month of 1986 because of a hamstring pull, but he still socked 20 homers and 78 RBI.

If his knees stay in good shape, Dawson should be around for a long time. While Cooperstown may not be ready to welcome him yet, his hometown of South Miami has already honored its native son by renaming a street "Andre Dawson Drive."

CAREER HIGHLIGHTS
ANDRE FERNANDO DAWSON

Born: July 10, 1954   Miami, FL
Height: 6'3"   **Weight:** 180 lbs.   **Bats:** Right   **Throws:** Right
Outfielder: Montreal Expos, 1976-86; Chicago Cubs, 1987-89.

- ★ First in the league in homers and RBI in 1987
- ★ N.L. Rookie of the Year in 1977
- ★ Won the N.L. MVP award in 1987
- ★ All-time Montreal Expos home run leader
- ★ Led the N.L. with 189 hits in 1983
- ★ Played in five All-Star games

MAJOR LEAGUE TOTALS

G	AB	H	BA	2B	3B	HR	R	RBI	SB
1,753	6,840	1,932	.282	350	77	298	996	1,054	276

In 1987 Andre Dawson of the Chicago Cubs became the first player in baseball to win the MVP award while playing on a last-place team. Two years later, Dawson was instrumental in the Cubs hard-fought drive to a first-place division win.

DIZZY DEAN

No one is quite sure how the gifted Arkansas-born pitcher named Jay Hannah Dean acquired the nickname "Dizzy." While many fans suspected that the moniker referred to the star hurler's crazy off-the-field behavior, legend has it that a Chicago White Sox coach attached the label to Dean when he rendered numerous players "dizzy" by striking them out. Dean said to a reporter in reference to the nickname, "I may be dizzy here in the hotel lobby, but I'm not dizzy out there on the mound."

That comment illustrates how Dean became almost a dual personality during his short, 12-year career in the major leagues. Although he was a tough competitor on the mound, he was also a happy-go-lucky boaster known for his outlandish public statements and practical jokes. "If you can do it, it ain't braggin'," he said simply, to defend his behavior. Dean had only a second-grade education in Chickalah, Arkansas, and spent his youth picking cotton in the fields. Later the Cardinals claimed that Dean had attended high school in Holdenville, Oklahoma, and went on to Oklahoma Teacher's College (playing baseball for the college team).

Because his parents were farm laborers, they moved frequently. Supposedly, when a neighbor's son died, young Dean promised that he'd adopt the late son's name of Jay Hannah and make the name famous. Dean played baseball whenever he could, gaining a lot of his experience in sandlot baseball in San Antonio, Texas. Whatever the true story of Dean's childhood may be, it is a fact that he became a Depression-era hero who gained a following to rival Babe Ruth's. The events in Dean's life gained mythic proportions. When he was hit on the head with a baseball during the 1934 World Series, a newspaper headline read: "X RAYS OF DEAN'S HEAD SHOW NOTHING."

Dean's first professional season was 1930. He was 17-8 with St. Joseph before moving to the Texas League with Houston, going 8-2. Dean got a late-season call-up to St. Louis but didn't get a starting assignment until the last day of the season. When summoned, he threw a complete game, three-hit win against the Pittsburgh Pirates.

Because the Cardinals had a wealth of pitchers, Dean was sent back to Houston for some fine-tuning in 1931. He won 26 games there with a 1.53 ERA. The young flamethrower racked up 303 strikeouts in 304 innings. He

struck out 18 batters in one game and won the Texas League pennant for Houston, pitching on one day's rest. Dean later credited Houston coach Joe Schultz with valuable coaching assistance in the areas of pitching, batting, and baserunning during that season.

Dean was 18-15 in his first season with St. Louis. The following year he went 20-18, taking the National League lead in games, complete games, and strikeouts. In 1934 younger brother Paul Dean joined the Cardinals staff. Paul, of course, was nicknamed "Daffy." The younger Dean was 19-11 as a rookie, while Dizzy Dean led the league with a 30-7 record (and his third straight strikeout title). He publicly claimed that he and his brother Paul would beat their World Series foes, the Detroit Tigers, by themselves. They did just that: Each won two games in the Series.

Daffy Dean won another 19 games in 1935, while Dizzy Dean again paced the league with 28 wins. Twenty-nine complete games and a fourth consecu-

tive strikeout title highlighted Dean's season. In 1936, Dizzy Dean compiled a 24-13 mark, while his brother had problems with a sore arm and won just 5 games. (He would win only 7 more games in the final six years of his career). Dizzy Dean continued his winning ways, earning 13 victories in 1937. During the 1937 All-Star game, Dean suffered a broken toe from a line drive off the bat of Earl Averill. Dean changed his pitching motion to compensate for the injury but aggravated his arm and forever lost his ability as a master moundsman.

The Cardinals shipped the sore-armed superstar to the Chicago Cubs for Tuck Stainback, Curt Davis, Clyde Shoun, and $185,000. The dividends were minimal for the Cubs. Dean was 7-1 in 1938 for the Cubs but was 0-1 in the World Series. He won only 9 more games in three seasons with Chicago. Dean's last major league appearance was a 1947 publicity stunt with the St. Louis Browns, when he pitched a four-inning stint for just one game but allowed no runs.

Dean's record was blighted by the sore arm that prematurely ended his career at age 29. Nevertheless, he won 150 games and registered 30 saves. A whole new generation of fans became acquainted with Dean in the 1940s, 50s, and early 60s, when he did radio and television baseball broadcasts for CBS and NBC. His fractured English, including the constant use of "ain't," provoked some criticism. However, his folksy observations and constant singing of "The Wabash Cannonball" provided a new brand of entertainment for baseball fans. The Hall of Fame elected Dean in 1953.

CAREER HIGHLIGHTS
JAY HANNA DEAN

Born: January 16, 1911 Lucas, AR **Died:** July 17, 1974
Height: 6'2" **Weight:** 182 lbs. **Batted:** Right **Threw:** Right
Pitcher: St. Louis Cardinals, 1930-37; Chicago Cubs, 1938-41; St. Louis Browns, 1947.

- ★ Led the N.L. in complete games for four consecutive years
- ★ Won two games in the 1934 World Series
- ★ Won a career-high 30 games in 1934
- ★ Earned four league strikeout titles
- ★ Elected to the Hall of Fame in 1953
- ★ Three-time 20-game winner

MAJOR LEAGUE TOTALS

G	IP	W	L	Pct.	SO	BB	ERA
317	1,966	150	83	.644	1,155	458	3.04

Colorful Dizzy Dean prematurely ended his pitching career when he returned to the mound too early following an injury. His later antics as an announcer pushed the limits of English grammar, inciting the wrath of some listeners while amusing others.

BILL DICKEY

Many baseball historians call Bill Dickey the greatest catcher in baseball history. The few who rank Yogi Berra as even greater should remember that it was Dickey's personal coaching of young Berra from 1957-59 that helped produce yet another superb Yankees catcher.

Bill Dickey grew up in Arkansas and played his first game in organized baseball there. Lena Blackburne, who eventually became a manager of the Chicago White Sox, discovered Dickey. Blackburne convinced the 17-year-old Dickey to sign a contract with the Little Rock team of the Southern Association in 1925.

Dickey says that he got his first baseball instruction from his father, a former minor league catcher. The instruction was so good that brother George "Skeets" Dickey also made the big leagues, serving as a backstop for the Red Sox in 1935-36 and for the White Sox in the 1940s.

Bill Dickey sharpened his skills playing with minor league teams in Jackson, Muskogee, and Minneapolis. His development was so impressive that the Yankees scout who discovered him in 1928 wired back to New York, "If this boy doesn't make it, I'll quit scouting." Dickey did make it, stepping in as the full-time catcher in 1929. He stayed there for 15 more years, helping the Bronx Bombers to eight pennants and seven world championships.

Despite his youth, the rookie catcher handled the Yankee pitching staff like a wise old veteran. At the plate, Dickey tallied 10 homers, 65 RBI, and a .324 average in 1929. Defensively, Dickey led the league in assists and double plays. Although the Yankees won 88 games, they finished a distant second behind the Philadelphia Athletics' 104 victories.

Soon Dickey had helped mold the Yankees pitching staff into the foundation of a dynasty. Eight Yankee teams went to the World Series with Dickey behind the plate. In 1931 Dickey's magic glovework included a string of 322 consecutive chances without an error. From April 19 to July 2, 1931, Dickey handled 255 putouts and 31 assists without an error. The 1932 season was the first time Dickey reached postseason play. He had hit .310 with 15 homers and 84 RBI during the regular season. The usually quiet Yankees catcher gained some dubious fame that year when he broke the jaw of Washington outfielder Carl Reynolds

during a squabble at the plate. Dickey got a 30-day suspension and a stiff fine for his rowdiness. In the World Series, Dickey batted .438.

Year after year, Dickey continued to field exceptionally and hit for both power and average. His home run totals climbed from 14 in 1933 to 22 during the team's championship season of 1936. Dickey also contributed 107 RBI and 99 runs scored to the winning effort. Dickey repeated his offensive success in 1937, belting a career high of 29 homers and 133 RBI with a .332 average. In 1938 Dickey had 27 home runs and 115 RBI. Throughout much of the 1930s, Dickey would race with Detroit Tigers catcher Mickey Cochrane, both contending annually for the lead in various defensive departments. In 1938 Dickey was tops in both assists and putouts. After having two subpar seasons batting in the World Series,

Dickey rebounded to a .400 average in the 1938 fall classic.

The 1939 New York Yankees won their fourth straight world title. Dickey was a team leader again at bat and on the field, hitting .302 with 24 homers and 105 RBI. In the first game of the World Series against the Cincinnati Reds, Dickey singled the winning run home in a 2-1 victory. His homers in the third and fourth games assured a Yankee sweep in the Series. Dickey finished the competition with 5 RBI and a .267 average.

In 1941 Dickey played his last full season as a starting catcher. In 109 games the Yankee veteran hit .284. The 1941 World Series saw the Yankees claim yet another world championship, this time against the Brooklyn Dodgers. The 1942 St. Louis Cardinals burst the Yankee bubble by winning that year's World Series. The following year, Dickey settled the score. He hit .351 during the regular season, with 4 homers and 33 RBI. In the World Series, the Yankees regained their world championship by defeating the Redbirds in five games. In the fifth game, the 16-year veteran catcher smashed a two-run homer to win the Series for New York. Following the Series, Dickey served 1944 and 1945 in the U.S. Navy.

Dickey returned to baseball in 1946 for his final season with the New York Yankees. He played in 54 games, hitting .261, and he managed the Yankees to a 57-48 record. After retiring, Dickey served as a Yankees coach from 1948 through 1957.

Dickey retired with several fielding records and an impressive .313 mark. His 24 World Series RBI rank eighth in history. He was well loved by both fans and teammates. Dickey was elected to the Hall of Fame in 1954.

CAREER HIGHLIGHTS
WILLIAM MALCOLM DICKEY

Born: June 6, 1907 Bastrop, LA
Height: 6'1½" **Weight:** 185 lbs. **Batted:** Left **Threw:** Right
Catcher: New York Yankees, 1928-43, 1946. Manager: New York Yankees, 1946.

★ Compiled a lifetime average of .313   ★ Played in 38 games in eight World Series
★ Served as player/manager in 1946   ★ Elected to the Hall of Fame in 1954
★ Slugged grand slams in two straight games in 1937

MAJOR LEAGUE TOTALS

G	AB	H	BA	2B	3B	HR	R	RBI	SB
1,789	6,300	1,969	.313	343	72	202	930	1,209	36

Though time and two generations of great catchers have taken the edge off of Bill Dickey's accomplishments, some historians still rank him as the best, along with Mickey Cochrane. His lifetime stats and World Series performances are proof.

JOE DiMAGGIO

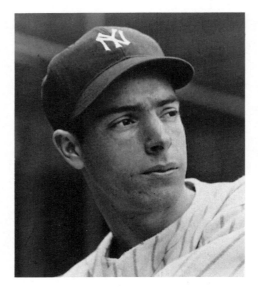

To this day, former New York Yankees outfielder Joe DiMaggio retains his image as America's ultimate hero. In the 1960s Simon and Garfunkel included the baseball star in the song "Mrs. Robinson." In the 1970s, DiMaggio was famous for his "Mr. Coffee" TV commercial endorsements. In the 1980s, a book was written about his marriage to movie star Marilyn Monroe. All the while, no one has forgotten that DiMaggio was one of baseball's greatest stars.

The Hall of Fame outfielder got his start in pro ball in 1932 with the San Francisco Seals of the Pacific Coast League. DiMaggio's first position with the team was at shortstop. He spent three seasons with that PCL team. In 1933 he compiled a 61-game hitting streak, a sample of what he would accomplish in the major leagues just nine years later. In November 1934 the New York Yankees gave the Seals $25,000 plus five well-traveled players to obtain DiMaggio.

Because DiMaggio had injured his knee during the 1934 season, the Yankees wanted him to play in San Francisco in 1935. He proved his health with a .398 average, 34 homers, and 154 RBI in his final PCL season. With Babe Ruth gone, the Yankees needed a new power hitter for 1936. DiMaggio responded to the challenge with 206 hits for a .323 average, including 29 home runs and 125 RBI. He proved his worth in the outfield as well, leading the league with 22 assists. Most importantly, DiMaggio helped the Bronx Bombers win their first pennant in four years. The Yankees took their first of four straight world championships by defeating the New York Giants in six games. For the Series, DiMaggio hit .346. After the Series, DiMaggio received a $6,000 raise, bringing his salary up to $14,000.

During his sophomore season of 1937, DiMaggio hit .346 with league highs of 46 homers, 151 runs scored, and a .673 slugging percentage. DiMaggio missed the RBI title because Detroit Tigers star Hank Greenberg knocked in 183 runs.

In 1939 DiMaggio won his first of two straight batting titles with a .381 average. He followed with a league-best .352 mark in 1940. His success was marred when the Detroit Tigers edged out his club for the pennant.

In 1941 DiMaggio performed one of the greatest feats in sports history. Starting on May 15 of that year, he got

at least one hit in 56 straight games. He broke the National League record of 33 straight games by Rogers Hornsby, then smashed the American League mark of 41 games by George Sisler. Later, the all-time record of 44 straight games by Willie Keeler was discovered and DiMaggio broke that too. The entire country was following the streak. The Les Brown orchestra released a song called "Joltin' Joe DiMaggio." Finally, on July 17, 1941, DiMaggio's streak ended. Indians third baseman Ken Keltner became famous for successfully fielding two hot grounders that were hit by DiMaggio.

Later, it was revealed that DiMaggio could have gained a lucrative endorsement contract from the Heinz 57 company if his streak had continued just one more game. After being stopped that night in Cleveland, DiMaggio safely hit in 17 more games, finishing the season at .357 with 30 homers and 125 RBI in

139 games. With brothers Vince and Dom also playing in the majors in the 1940s, the DiMaggio name became the most famous in baseball circles.

In 1942 DiMaggio had an off year, hitting only .305 with 21 homers and 114 RBI. Although he hit .333 in the World Series, the Yankees lost to the St. Louis Cardinals. In 1943 DiMaggio enlisted in the military and missed three seasons worth of prime playing time due to World War II. DiMaggio returned in 1946 and hit under .300 for the first time in his career. In 1948 DiMaggio proved he hadn't lost his incredible talent during the war: He hit 39 home runs and 155 RBI to lead the league, and his average climbed back up to .320. Unfortunately, heel problems began bothering DiMaggio. In 1949 he played in only 76 games but hit .346.

Aches and pains were catching up with DiMaggio by 1950, although he hit .301 with 32 homers and 122 RBI to lead the Yankees to yet another pennant.

DiMaggio's last season was 1951, when he batted .263 with 12 homers and 71 RBI in 116 games. Although he could have held on for a couple of more seasons, DiMaggio wanted to retire before he started struggling. He announced his retirement in December, after his Yankees beat the Giants in the 1951 World Series. DiMaggio's final conquest was a two-run homer that won the fourth game of the fall classic.

DiMaggio retired with a .325 average (hitting over .300 eleven times), and the knowledge that he sparked the Yankees to ten American League pennants and nine world championships during his career. DiMaggio was elected to the Baseball Hall of Fame in 1955.

CAREER HIGHLIGHTS
JOSEPH PAUL DiMAGGIO

Born: November 25, 1914   Martinez, CA
Height: 6'2"   **Weight:** 195 lbs.   **Batted:** Right   **Threw:** Right
Outfielder: New York Yankees, 1936-51.

- ★ Named A.L. MVP in 1939, 1941, and 1947
- ★ Compiled a 56-game hitting streak in 1941
- ★ Won two batting titles
- ★ Selected for the league All-Star team 11 times
- ★ Elected to the Hall of Fame in 1955
- ★ Played in ten World Series

MAJOR LEAGUE TOTALS

G	AB	H	BA	2B	3B	HR	R	RBI	SB
1,736	6,821	2,214	.325	389	131	361	1,390	1,537	30

It has been almost 40 years since Joe DiMaggio retired, and his off-the-field experiences tend to overshadow his contributions to baseball. Yet, Joltin' Joe's 56-game hitting streak, his graceful fielding, and his mighty bat testify to his greatness as a player.

LARRY DOBY

Larry Doby could be considered the Jackie Robinson of the American League. While the Brooklyn Dodgers first broke the color barrier by inserting Robinson in their infield, the Cleveland Indians were setting an historic precedent in the American League. Flamboyant Cleveland team owner Bill Veeck realized that the Indians were going nowhere. He spotted Doby as a Negro National League All-Star and paid $15,000 to obtain him from the Newark Eagles. Doby had been the league's homer and RBI leader before joining the Indians.

Doby made his debut with the Indians on July 5, 1947. If Veeck hadn't moved quickly, Doby might have been playing with Robinson in the Brooklyn Dodgers lineup. Roy Campanella, in his biography *It's Good to Be Alive*, stated that Branch Rickey paid him to scout Negro League players in 1945. When Campanella saw Doby playing second base for the Eagles, he recommended that the Dodgers sign him. Rickey was interested in Doby, too, but he passed when he learned that the Indians might sign Doby. Rickey wanted all the teams to follow the Dodgers lead of including black players on their rosters. A year later Rickey's wish started coming true when the Indians inked a contract with Doby.

Unfortunately, Doby's first year with the Indians wasn't memorable. He played in 29 games, but he hit just .156. Undoubtedly, the pressure of bringing racial integration to the American League was overwhelming. Doby had much more success during his sophomore season of 1948, when the Indians put him in the outfield. He hit .301 with 14 homers and 66 RBI, and his 9 triples were tops on the Cleveland squad. The Indians finished with a 97-58 record, winning the American League pennant by one game over the Boston Red Sox. Doby batted a team-high .318 with 7 hits in the 1948 World Series against the Boston Braves.

In 1949 Doby led the Indians with 24 homers, 85 RBI, and 106 runs scored. The Indians dropped to third place at 89-65, eight games behind the pennant-winning New York Yankees. Doby increased his output in 1950 to .326, the fourth-highest batting average in the league. Doby was also fourth in the league in slugging percentage with a .545 effort. He hit 25 homers and 102 RBI and scored 110 runs. Every year the converted outfielder was perfecting his flyhawking craft. The Indians called

upon Hall of Famer Tris Speaker to tutor Doby on proper outfield technique. The Cleveland Baseball Writers named Doby "Man of the Year," and the Baseball Writers Association of America named Doby to their All-Star team. Doby was also the starting center fielder for the American League All-Stars for the midseason classic. On August 2, 1950, before a hometown crowd, Doby tied an exclusive club record when he became the sixth Indian in team history to hit 3 homers in one game and only the fourth to hit 3 homers in consecutive at-bats.

Doby slipped to 20 homers, 69 RBI, and a .295 average in 1951 but returned to the ranks of the league's best hitters in 1952. He hit a league-high 32 homers to complement his 104 RBI and .276 average. Never before had a black player captured a major league home run title. Doby also set an Indians record for most homers by a center

fielder. Teammate Al Rosen had just 1 more RBI than Doby to win the American League RBI title.

Doby maintained his All-Star status in 1953 with 29 homers, 102 RBI, and a .263 average. In 1954 Doby became the league's top power hitter by winning both the home run and RBI categories with 32 dingers and 126 RBI. Only two Indians in history (including Rosen in 1950) had won A.L. homer crowns before Doby, and only Nap Lajoie, Hal Trosky, and Al Rosen had previously led the league in RBI.

Doby departed from Cleveland after the 1955 season, when he hit 26 homers, 75 RBI, and a .291 batting average. The Chicago White Sox gave up outfielder Jim Busby and infielder Chico Carrasquel in exchange for Doby on October 25, 1955. With the White Sox Doby hit 24 homers and 102 RBI in his first season. In 1957 Doby played in only 119 games, hitting 14 homers and 79 RBI. The Indians got Doby back in a roundabout fashion. Doby was traded to the Baltimore Orioles in the off-season in a seven-player swap; however, on April 1, 1958, the Indians sent Dick Williams, Gene Woodling, and Buddy Daley to Baltimore in exchange for Doby and Don Ferrarese.

Doby played with Cleveland in 1958, then concluded his career with the Tigers and White Sox in 1959. Doby's last professional season was in the Japanese League in 1962. He later became baseball's second black manager with the 1978 White Sox. As an Indian, Doby wound up ranking in the team's top ten for virtually every offensive category. Today he's a front office executive for the New Jersey Nets basketball team.

CAREER HIGHLIGHTS
LAWRENCE EUGENE DOBY

Born: December 13, 1924 Camden, SC
Height: 6'1" **Weight:** 180 lbs. **Batted:** Left **Threw:** Right
Outfielder: Cleveland Indians, 1947-55, 1958; Chicago White Sox, 1956-57, 1959; Detroit Tigers, 1959. Manager: Chicago White Sox, 1978.

- ★ Led the A.L. in homers and RBI in 1954
- ★ Was the first black player in the A.L.
- ★ First in the A.L. in homers in 1952

- ★ Was the second black manager in the major leagues
- ★ Batted .318 in the 1948 World Series
- ★ Topped the A.L. in runs scored in 1952

MAJOR LEAGUE TOTALS

G	AB	H	BA	2B	3B	HR	R	RBI	SB
1,533	5,348	1,515	.283	243	52	253	960	970	47

Larry Doby was not only an excellent center fielder but was also known for his prowess with a bat. He was one of the few players, along with Ruth, Williams, and Mantle, to hit a homer over the distant center field wall in Washington's Griffith Stadium.

BOBBY DOERR

oerr began his career at the age of 16 with the Hollywood club in the Pacific Coast League in 1934. Growing up in California gave the youngster a year-round climate for ball-playing. He had an active American Legion baseball program to participate in, along with a supportive father. Doerr hit .259 his first year, then improved to a .317 mark with 4 homers and 74 RBI in 1935. He played 172 games that year, accumulating 205 hits. After another banner season in 1936 with San Diego (the Hollywood club's new home), Doerr was making headlines for his steady batwork and consistent defense. In 1936 he batted .342 with 12 homers and 77 RBI. His 238 hits and 504 assists at second base were PCL highs. Doerr attracted the attention of Eddie Collins, who starred as a Philadelphia Athletics second baseman for more than two decades. Collins, who was then the general manager of the Boston Red Sox, personally traveled to San Diego to scout and eventually sign Doerr. In 1937 the 19-year-old Doerr made his debut with the Red Sox.

In his first season in the majors, Doerr played in 55 games, batting .224 with 2 homers and 14 RBI. While his rookie season wasn't memorable, Doerr showed enough potential to win the starting second baseman's job from Eric McNair, who hit .292 with 12 homers and 76 RBI that year. In 1938, Doerr's sophomore season, he batted .289 with 5 homers and 80 RBI. The fiery Californian led A.L. second sackers with 118 double plays.

Doerr continued to improve with every campaign. In 1939 he hit .318 with 12 homers and 73 RBI and averaged a league-high 6.2 chances per game. The Red Sox, meanwhile, seemed like constant second-place finishers behind the Yankees. In 1940 Doerr gained more fame in the junior circuit. Not only did he lead the league in putouts and double plays, but he also hit 22 homers, 105 RBI, and had a .291 average.

The 1941 season featured more heavy hitting by Doerr. He clubbed 16 homers and 93 RBI, hitting .282. Again Doerr produced more run-scoring hits than any other second baseman. In 1942 Doerr registered a league-leading .975 fielding average and batted .290 with 15 homers and 102 RBI. Only Ted Williams had a more productive offensive season with the BoSox. Doerr played in his second All-Star game in 1943 and quickly became the American

League hero. His three-run homer in the second inning gave the junior circuit a 5-3 victory over the National League. The game drew international interest because military personnel stationed in Europe during World War II were tuned in. During the regular season, Doerr played in a career-high 155 games. While he hit just .270 with 16 homers and 75 RBI, Doerr was stunning in the field. He led the American League in fielding percentage and putouts and tied for the lead in assists. Doerr handled 349 chances without an error to set a record.

Doerr racked up a league-leading .528 slugging percentage in 1944, batting .325 with 15 homers and 81 RBI. Doerr nearly won his first batting title, but Lou Boudreau batted 2 percentage points higher (.327) to win the crown. No other second baseman in either league came close to his offensive totals. On May 14, 1944, Doerr hit for the cycle for the first time.

After spending 1945 in military service, Doerr returned to baseball in fine form in 1946. He was tops in the

league in putouts, assists, double plays, and fielding percentage. Offensively, Doerr pounded out 18 homers and 116 RBI with a .271 average, and he was fourth in the league in RBI. In the 1946 World Series, the St. Louis Cardinals downed the Red Sox in seven games, though Doerr personally had a sensational Series, hitting .409 with a team-leading 9 hits.

In 1947 Doerr hit 17 homers and 95 RBI. His totals climbed to .285 with 27 homers (fifth highest in the league) and 111 RBI in 1948. Another career highlight for Doerr came on May 13, 1947, when he hit for the cycle for the second time in his career. In 1948 Doerr surpassed even his previous defensive achievements by playing 73 straight games of errorless baseball. He handled 414 straight chances without a miscue, making 177 putouts and 227 assists. Again in 1949 Doerr was among league leaders in RBI, driving in 109 runs, fourth highest in the league. Doerr batted .309 with 18 home runs. This marked the tenth straight season in which Doerr had a double-digit effort in homers. Doerr achieved another first in 1950 when he led the league with 11 triples.

Time caught up with Doerr in 1951. While his hitting was as strong as ever, Doerr had injured his back and didn't have the stamina of his earlier years. He did play in 106 games, hitting .289 with 13 homers and 73 RBI. To have back surgery in order to keep playing was too much for Doerr; instead, he opted for retirement at age 33.

Upon retirement, Doerr coached in the Red Sox minor league system and later served the Blue Jays as a hitting coach in the 1970s. He was elected to the Hall of Fame in 1986.

CAREER HIGHLIGHTS
ROBERT PERSHING DOERR

Born: April 7, 1918 Los Angeles, CA
Height: 5'11" **Weight:** 175 lbs. **Batted:** Right **Threw:** Right
Second baseman: Boston Red Sox, 1937-51.

★ Led A.L. second basemen in fielding percentage for six seasons
★ Batted .409 in the 1946 World Series
★ Led the A.L. with a .528 slugging percentage in 1944
★ Eight-time All-Star
★ Elected to the Hall of Fame in 1986

MAJOR LEAGUE TOTALS

G	AB	H	BA	2B	3B	HR	R	RBI	SB
1,865	7,093	2,042	.288	381	89	223	1,094	1,247	54

Bobby Doerr played his entire career for the Boston Red Sox. A great all-around player, Doerr was also good in the clutch. In the Sox's successful run for the '46 Series, he hit .409 and singled the scoring run into position in the do-or-die seventh game.

BRIAN DOWNING

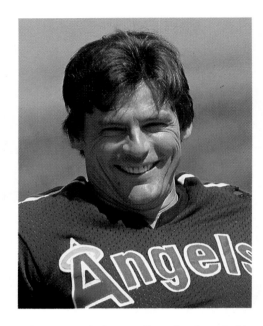

The comic-strip character Charlie Brown is a Little Leaguer who has never won a game and has little hope of winning one in the future. If he were to look at California Angels designated hitter Brian Downing, he might find inspiration. The player who now leads the Angels in six all-time offensive categories was turned down for membership on his high school varsity baseball team.

At 5-foot-10 and 170 pounds, Downing even looks like the famous "round-headed kid" from the funny pages. Fellow major leaguers have said Downing makes up for what he lacks in natural ability with heart, and a look at the record book proves the point.

By 1982 Downing had been in professional baseball for a dozen years, yet it wasn't until then that he suddenly materialized in major league record books. Always an exemplary fielder, Downing broke the barrier in 1982 with 158 games—a full season's worth—of errorless baseball. He racked up a perfect fielding average, tying two major league records. Ironically, his stellar year also saw him tie another fielding record—no double plays registered in an entire season. In 1984 the Los Angeles native again served donuts instead of errors, logging yet another perfect fielding average in 156 games.

In the 1987 season Downing made 118 appearances as a designated hitter and notched career highs in homers (29) and runs scored (110), while leading the American League in bases on balls (106). Seven of his homers came while batting as the Angels leadoff hitter, setting a team record. In 1988 DH Downing racked up his sixth season of 20-plus home runs. Even with three weeks spent on the disabled list, Downing garnered 80 runs, 117 hits, and 64 RBI.

Downing is positive proof that hard work and persistence can pay off. He has always played the game with dedication. His wide-open batting stance with feet straddled (he almost faces the pitcher while pointing his left foot toward the third-base dugout) illustrates his determination.

Though not a naturally gifted runner, Downing barrels down on infielders with no mercy. This same attitude in the outfield has led some writers to claim that Downing never met a wall he didn't like and that sometimes the walls take the meeting harder than Downing. Born with an average arm, Downing acquired the correct anticipation and quick release needed to collect flawless fielding marks.

As a fielder, Downing almost had two careers. In his first full season with the Chicago White Sox in 1974, Downing caught, but he also spent a little time in the pasture, just as he would in 1977 during his last year with the ChiSox. In between, he did nothing but catch, as he did for three years after being obtained by the Angels. On December 5, 1977, Downing and pitchers Dave Frost and Chris Knapp were sent from the White Sox to California for outfielders Thad Bosley and Bobby Bonds and pitcher Rich Dotson.

Few fans probably remember Downing's strange major league debut in 1973. He opened his first game at third base on May 31. On the first pitch, he injured his knee as he dove to catch a pop foul. The disability kept him out of action until August 10. The next day, Downing had an inside-the-park homer versus star Tigers hurler Mickey Lolich for his first major league hit.

In 1979 Downing played in his first and only All-Star game. He had his best offensive performance of the 70s that year with 12 homers and 75 RBI.

After a fractured left ankle took him out of commission from April 20 to September 1, 1980, the Angels started moving him into left field, hoping to prolong his slugging career. It seemed not only to work but to have a miraculous effect. While catching in the majors, Downing had never hit more than a dozen homers; in 1981 he hit just 9. But the following year, after taking his new spot in left field, his homers more than tripled for an astonishing 28.

Although his average has always been in the high .200s (with the exception of 1979, when he peaked out at .326 during the club's first pennant season), he reached career highs in hits (175) and doubles (37) in 1982, the year he stopped catching. His career high in RBI came in 1986 when he chased in 95 runs.

The Angels star has remained offensively dependable throughout the 1980s. He helps his club in many ways, as evidenced by his team-leading on-base percentage of .366 in 1988. It was the fifth straight year that Downing collected double-digit totals in game-winning RBI.

Because Downing has forsaken streaky success in favor of consistent achievement, it might be easy to take this team mobilizer for granted. But wisely, the Angels still respect Downing's ability. There could be a lot more hits in this veteran's bat yet.

CAREER HIGHLIGHTS
BRIAN JAY DOWNING

Born: October 9, 1950   Los Angeles, CA
Height: 5'10"   **Weight:** 170 lbs.   **Bats:** Right   **Throws:** Right
Catcher, outfielder, designated hitter: Chicago White Sox, 1973-77; California Angels, 1978-89.

- ★ Ranks first among career Angels in six offensive categories
- ★ Hit a career-high 29 homers in 1987
- ★ Has hit 20 or more homers six times
- ★ Played in three League Championship Series
- ★ All-time Angels leader in home runs
- ★ Played in the 1979 All-Star game

MAJOR LEAGUE TOTALS

G	AB	H	BA	2B	3B	HR	R	RBI	SB
2,018	6,796	1,807	.266	307	24	234	1,012	934	48

In 1987 Brian Downing achieved career highs with 29 homers, 110 runs scored, and a league-leading 106 walks. He is the all-time leading home run hitter for the Angels. Downing has cracked 20 or more home runs in six different seasons for California.

DON DRYSDALE

Don Drysdale capped an incredible career by pitching 58 consecutive scoreless innings during his last full season in baseball. Drysdale began pitching for the Brooklyn Dodgers in 1956 and ended with the Los Angeles Dodgers in 1969. During that time, the man known as "Big D" gained a reputation for a fearsome fastball and a willingness to throw at batters who inched too close to the plate.

The 6-foot-5 hurler was an awe-inspiring sight on the mound even before he threw the ball. When he did, he notched 209 wins (including 49 shutouts) and 2,486 strikeouts with a 2.95 ERA. Had he not been forced out of the game by a sore shoulder at the age of 33, the numbers could have been even more impressive. For a ten-year period from 1957 to 1966, Drysdale teamed with fellow Dodger Sandy Koufax to form one of the most incredible pitching tandems in baseball history. They both have plaques in Cooperstown to prove it.

Drysdale eventually became one of the best pitchers in baseball. He started out with Bakersfield of the California League in 1954, compiling a modest 8-5 record. A promotion to Montreal followed in 1955, where he went 11-11 in 28 games. Drysdale didn't begin pitching until he was 16 years old. His father, who also coached him in American Legion baseball, wanted him to save his arm.

Drysdale got his first chance in the majors in 1956. He was used both as a starter and reliever, starting in 12 games and relieving in 13. His record was 5-5. The Dodgers faced the Yankees in the 1956 Series, and so Drysdale got to appear in his first postseason contest. In two innings of relief, the Yankees nailed him for 2 runs.

In 1957, the Dodgers' last year in Brooklyn, Drysdale started 29 games and posted a team-best 17-9 record. The Dodgers dropped to third that year, 11 games behind the Milwaukee Braves.

It took five years for Drysdale to become a big winner in Los Angeles. The move had to be exciting, however, because he had grown up in nearby Van Nuys. He won in double figures from 1958-1962, but he never earned more than 17 victories. His 17-13 record in 1959 included a league-leading 242 strikeouts and appearances in two All-Star games (back then, leagues played two All-Star games per season). The Dodgers beat the White Sox in the

1959 World Series. Despite giving up 11 hits in the third game of the Series, Drysdale pitched seven innings to gain his first win in the fall classic.

Drysdale's record dropped to 15-14 in 1960, but he still led his club in triumphs. His 246 strikeouts were tops in the National League for the second straight season. He won just 13 games in 1961 but accomplished a feat most pitchers only dream about. On August 9, at home versus Milwaukee, the Dodger righty clubbed a second-inning grand slam against Don Nottebart. "Big D" finished his career with 29 home runs (including 7 round-trippers in 1958 and 1965), an impressive achievement for any pitcher.

Drysdale was ready for the biggest season of his career in 1962. The Dodgers had a brand new ballpark, and Drysdale had the experience needed to become a major winner. He dazzled batters with a league high of 25 victories against just 9 losses. He also paced

N.L. pitchers in innings pitched (314) and strikeouts (232). Despite his efforts, the Dodgers still finished in second place, one game behind the San Francisco Giants.

The Dodgers were world champions in 1963, and Drysdale contributed a 19-17 record to the effort. Los Angeles swept the Yankees in four straight games in the World Series. Drysdale all but closed the door on New York in game three by tossing a three-hit complete game against the American League champs, walking just 1 and striking out 9. Drysdale outdueled Jim Bouton as the Dodgers won 1-0.

In 1965 Drysdale topped the 20-win plateau for the second time in his career, going 23-12. Although Drysdale was shelled by the Minnesota Twins in the opening game of the World Series (going only 2.2 innings), he avenged himself in the fourth game by throwing a five-hit complete game, striking out 11 Twins batters.

A similar pattern developed in 1966. Drysdale won just 13 games during the regular season, but he was still summoned to start the first game of the World Series against the Baltimore Orioles. He lasted just two innings as the O's scored 4 quick runs. Drysdale returned for the fourth game and gave up just 4 hits in nine innings, but because of a Frank Robinson home run, Drysdale lost 1-0.

Drysdale's crowning glory was his scoreless streak of 58 innings in 1968. He threw 6 straight shutouts to achieve the mark. Two decades later, fellow Dodger Orel Hershiser broke the once-untouchable record. Drysdale, now a Los Angeles Dodgers radio announcer, watched from the broadcast booth as his record shattered.

CAREER HIGHLIGHTS
DONALD SCOTT DRYSDALE

Born: July 23, 1936 Van Nuys, CA
Height: 6'5" **Weight:** 190 lbs. **Batted:** Right **Threw:** Right
Pitcher: Brooklyn Dodgers, 1956-57; Los Angeles Dodgers, 1958-69.

- ★ Led the N.L. in strikeouts three times
- ★ 1962 Cy Young award winner
- ★ Pitched in five World Series
- ★ Hurled 58 consecutive scoreless innings in 1968
- ★ Won 20 games twice
- ★ Elected to the Hall of Fame in 1984

MAJOR LEAGUE TOTALS

G	IP	W	L	Pct.	SO	BB	ERA
518	3,432	209	166	.557	2,486	855	2.95

Batters quaked in their spikes at Don Drysdale's 90-plus m.p.h. fastball delivered with a big sidearm motion. And their fears were justified. Drysdale set a record for hitting batters during his career, striking 154—or about 1 per 22 innings.

DEL ENNIS

One of the most surprising teams in history was the 1950 Philadelphia Phillies. Nicknamed "The Whiz Kids," the Phillies team came out of nowhere to win the National League pennant with 91 victories. The leading power hitter on that team was right fielder Del Ennis.

Nothing could be more fitting than seeing a Philadelphia-born player rise to stardom with his hometown Phillies. That thrill belonged to Ennis, who paced the Phillies to the pennant with 31 homers, a league-leading 126 RBI, and a .311 average. Ennis was the Phillies individual leader in all three categories. During the month of August he set a team record with 41 RBI. Ennis also submitted a .551 slugging percentage, the fifth best in the National League. His batting average was the fourth best in the senior circuit. No Phillies player since Chuck Klein in 1933 had led the league in RBI. (Greg Luzinski in 1977 was the next Philly to turn the trick.) Ennis and the Phillies had their Cinderella season end abruptly when the Yankees won four straight World Series games. Ennis batted .143 in the Series, but the entire team's batting average amounted to just .203.

The 1950 storybook season was Ennis' fifth in the big leagues. He began his pro career in 1943 with Trenton. Ennis tallied impressive stats, including a .346 average with 18 homers and 93 RBI. His career was sidetracked for two seasons when he served in the U.S. Navy during World War II. During that time many major leaguers were in the military. Ennis used the situation to his best advantage and was able to prepare himself for a quick climb to the majors. It was no secret that some roster spots on nearly every team were up for grabs because most clubs were using makeshift lineups during the war years. The well-prepared Ennis was able to earn an immediate roster spot with the 1946 Phillies. His first season was a major success, with 17 homers, 73 RBI, and a .313 average. Ennis won the Rookie of the Year award from *The Sporting News* that season.

In 1947 Ennis slipped to .275 with 12 homers, but his RBI total climbed to 81. The following season Ennis hit 30 homers and 95 RBI, batting .290. In 1949 the strong-armed Ennis was first in the league with 16 assists. Ennis also kept growing as a hitter. He batted .302 with 25 homers and 110 RBI (fifth highest in the league). His 39 doubles were second in the league, while his

slugging percentage (.525) and total bases (320) were fourth.

When the Phillies dropped to fifth in the National League with a 73-81 record in 1951, Ennis suffered a letdown, too. He batted .267 with 15 homers and 73 RBI. Ennis staged a major comeback in 1952, hitting .289 with 20 homers and 107 RBI. Ennis was third in the league in RBI and fourth in total bases with 281. The veteran kept producing runs in 1953. He drove in 125 runs—the fourth-highest total in the league—and topped the Phillies with 29 homers.

Twenty-five homers and 119 RBI highlighted Ennis' 1954 season. As usual, Ennis ranked high in the league RBI race, finishing fifth. Again in 1955 Ennis provided the majority of Philadelphia's offense, batting in 120 runs (third in the league) and 29 homers. Ennis spent his final season with the Phillies in 1956, when he hit .260 with 26

homers and 95 RBI. It was the first time in five seasons that Ennis failed to make the 100-RBI club. On November 19, 1956, the Phillies traded Ennis to the St. Louis Cardinals for Bobby Morgan and Rip Repulski. Ennis paid immediate dividends for the Redbirds, hitting .286 with 24 homers and 105 RBI in 136 games. Ennis was second in the league in RBI, trailing only Hank Aaron's 132.

Ennis declined in 1958, hitting only 3 homers and 47 RBI for the Cardinals. St. Louis sent Ennis, Bob Mabe, and Eddie Kasko to the Cincinnati Reds for George Crowe, Alex Kellner, and Alex Grammas on October 3, 1958. Ennis played only one month for the Reds, and then was traded to the Chicago White Sox for Don Rudolph and Lou Skizas on May 1, 1959. After just 26 games with Chicago, Ennis ended his major league career.

The Philadelphia native had entered the select group of players with 2,000 hits in their careers. Ennis finished his 14-year career with 288 homers—259 of those round-trippers were in Philadelphia. Until Mike Schmidt came along, Ennis was the team's all-time homer champ. Ennis was also a durable performer, playing in more than 140 games for 10 of his 14 seasons. He compiled a lifetime batting average of .284 and drove in 1,284 runs. Today Ennis still ranks in the top 10 in various Phillies offensive categories. At the start of the 1988 season, Ennis ranked 150th on the all-time hit list with 2,063, a total that ranks above several Hall of Famers.

For nearly three decades after his retirement, Ennis operated a bowling alley carrying his name in Huntington Valley, Pennsylvania.

CAREER HIGHLIGHTS
DELMER ENNIS

Born: June 8, 1925   Philadelphia, PA
Height: 6'0"   **Weight:** 195 lbs.   **Batted:** Right   **Threw:** Right
Outfielder: Philadelphia Phillies, 1946-56; St. Louis Cardinals, 1957-58; Cincinnati Reds, 1959; Chicago White Sox, 1959.

★ Played for the "Whiz Kids" Phillies in the 1950 World Series
★ Named *The Sporting News* Rookie of the Year in 1946
★ Led the N.L. in RBI in 1950
★ Drove in 100-plus runs seven times
★ Hit a career-high 31 homers in 1950

MAJOR LEAGUE TOTALS

G	AB	H	BA	2B	3B	HR	R	RBI	SB
1,903	7,254	2,063	.284	358	69	288	985	1,284	45

Outfielder Del Ennis played the bulk of his career with his hometown Philadelphia Phillies. As one of the 1950 Phillies "Whiz Kids," Ennis led his team to the pennant with 31 home runs, a league-leading 126 RBI, and a .311 batting average.

DARRELL EVANS

If the fable of the tortoise and the hare were told as a baseball parable, it would be hard to decide which role to assign to Darrell Evans. His career took off with rabbit-like speed as he drew interest in free-agent drafts from the Cubs, Yankees, Tigers, and Phillies before finally signing a pro contract with the Kansas City Athletics in 1967. After just two seasons in the A's minor league organization, the Atlanta Braves snatched him from oblivion in the minor league reentry draft in 1969. He had a 12-game audition in Atlanta (hitting .231) that year before spending the remainder of the season in the Braves minor league system. In 1970 with Triple-A Richmond, Evans hit .307 with 20 home runs and 83 RBI. After hitting .318 during his second 12-game trial in Atlanta in 1970, Evans was in the majors to stay.

Eighteen years later, he has moved back to Atlanta: The 1989 season found Evans back in the South, where he can continue his slow but steady pace into the baseball record books. He had a triumphant return. The Detroit Tigers refused to offer the 41-year-old slugger a new contract after the 1988 season, so the unemployed veteran accepted a minor league contract from his old team, the Braves. Coming to Atlanta's spring training as a non-roster invitee, Evans waged a successful battle to win a roster spot with the 1989 Braves. As a pinch hitter and substitute infielder, Evans batted in the low .200s for much of the season, ending the year with a .207 average, 57 hits, 11 home runs, and 39 RBI.

Evans' major league average has only once gone above .300, and that was in his 12-game rookie season in Atlanta. Since then, he has averaged .250 from season to season, dipping to .208 in 1988. But that included 22 homers, the fourth consecutive year he had slammed more than 20, making for a lifetime total of 403 going into the 1989 campaign.

An All-Stater in both baseball and basketball in the late 1960s, the lifelong California resident was the Gulf Coast League's Player of the Year only two seasons out of high school. It was as a third sacker that Atlanta originally hired him. More than a decade later, he began steady work at first base with the Detroit Tigers, dropping his claim to third for the first time.

He logged his first full season with the Braves in 1972, with 19 homers and 71 RBI. In 1973 he blasted 41 homers—a career high—the same year fellow Braves Hank Aaron and Davey Johnson smashed 40 and 43, respectively. They are history's only trio of teammates to achieve such a feat. In his sophomore year, Evans found himself leading the N.L. in bases on balls with 124—a tribute to his fearsome bat.

Evans was traded to the San Francisco Giants on June 13, 1976, with shortstop Marty Perez in exchange for infielders Mike Eden and Craig Robinson, outfielder Jake Brown, and first baseman Willie Montanez. Although the stats he posted in 1977, his first full year in San Francisco, were modest except for his 17 home runs, the Giants picked up his free-agent contract without delay at year's end. Evans repaid their faith with two consecutive seasons of league-leading defense, with highs in putouts, chances, and assists.

A year of milestones occurred for Evans in 1981—his 1,500th major league game, his 200th double, and his 750th RBI. His long-lived records grew slowly until 1983, when the 36-year-old startled baseball watchers with 30 homers and 82 RBI. Yet the Giants let him go. The Tigers got out their checkbooks and signed the slugging free agent to a four-year deal on December 19, 1983. Evans posted a near perfect fielding average the following season at first and third base that helped take Detroit to a five-game world championship over the San Diego Padres.

Then came 1985, when the 38-year-old walloped a homer for each of his birthdays plus two. Prior to 1989, Evans was the only player ever to hit that many homers in each league. During the Tigers' division-pennant-winning season of 1987, Evans chipped in with 34 homers and 99 RBI (the most he had driven in since 1973). The selective hitter drew 100 walks, the fifth time he's exceeded that plateau.

A utility man in the best sense of the word, Evans has played third base, first base, designated hitter, outfield, and shortstop. He's known for his accurate arm and an eye for action. In a career that has spanned 22 years (and still counting), Evans has never spent time on the disabled list.

Darrell Evans slugged 20 or more homers in ten different seasons, and he averaged 15 round-trippers a season during the seven years that he did not reach the 20-homer mark. Evans led the A.L. with 40 home runs in 1985, while notching 94 RBI.

CAREER HIGHLIGHTS
DARRELL WAYNE EVANS

Born: May 26, 1947   Pasadena, CA
Height: 6'2"   **Weight:** 200 lbs.   **Bats:** Left   **Throws:** Right
Third baseman, first baseman, outfielder, designated hitter: Atlanta Braves, 1969-76, 1989; San Francisco Giants, 1976-83; Detroit Tigers, 1984-88.

★ Became the only 40-year-old to hit 30 homers in a season in 1987

★ Had a career-high 41 homers in 1973

★ Has had 10 seasons of 20 or more homers as of 1989

★ Played in two All-Star games

★ Hit a homer versus every A.L. team in 1986

★ Played in the 1984 World Series

★ Only player to hit 40-plus homers in a season in both major leagues

★ Led the N.L. in walks twice

MAJOR LEAGUE TOTALS

G	AB	H	BA	2B	3B	HR	R	RBI	SB
2,687	8,973	2,223	.248	329	36	414	1,344	1,354	98

DWIGHT EVANS

There are five names that top almost every category of the all-time team leaders for the Boston Red Sox. Three of those names are Carl Yastrzemski, Ted Williams, and Bobby Doerr. The other two belong to current players Jim Rice and Dwight Evans. Not bad company to keep—especially considering that such BoSox notables as Jimmie Foxx and Dom DiMaggio often rank behind the two current sluggers. While Rice has shown some signs of slowing down in recent years, Evans looks as good as ever.

Evans has chalked up an impressive array of firsts, leads, and awards in his career. One of the most unusual statistics is likely to be ignored, however: the feat of digging in so deep with his team and making a mark so indelible, that in 18 years of major league play the team has never abandoned him.

Evans may be buried with Red Sox on his feet; he's spent enough of his life in them to warrant it. The tall California native's season statistics reflect his yearly migration from the West Coast to the East Coast. Spring finds his swing slow and his average dismal. But by the time the season warms up, Evans has built up a head of steam. It has resulted in a handful of Gold Gloves; almost yearly recognition on *The Sporting News* All-Star team; and an afternoon in 1984 when he hit for the cycle, winning an 11-inning game with a three-run homer.

It may be that Evans was born in Red Sox as well. Progressing through the Little, Colt, Pony, and Connie Mack leagues while growing up in Northridge, California, Evans showed prowess at third base and on the mound, winning All-Star status at each position. But it was for his work on the gridiron that he was awarded two letters.

The Sox had a hunch about the 17-year-old, and they made him their fifth selection in the draft of June 1969. Evans' three and a half years in the minors saw him lead the league in games, giving notice of his future tenacity, and also in RBI, showing there is more to "Dewey" as a player than mere patience.

His ability on the field is demonstrated by his consistently high fielding averages and his renown in containing bloopers. His low number of assists has been attributed to the fact that few runners dare to tempt his shotgun arm. A bad knee keeps Evans from wildly running the bases, but he compensates with power at the plate. Each season

finds Evans virtually starting from scratch with his swing, but dedicated attention from coaches such as Walt Hriniak brings quick results.

So far Evans shows few, if any, signs of age. In 1987, after 15 years in the majors, he not only spent time at first base for the first time in the bigs, but he posted his highest batting average ever at .305, with 34 homers and 123 RBI. His 1988 marks were almost as good in the BoSox's race for the pennant, with 21 four-baggers, 111 RBI, and an average of .293 (one of his highest in five years). Evans seems to be part of the new trend of well-conditioned players who are able to make contributions into their 40s.

His big league career started with a

191-game errorless streak in 1973 and 1974. By 1982 he was going strong, with a .403 on-base average and personal bests in runs (122), hits (178), homers (32), extra-base hits (76), total bases (325), RBI (98), and walks (112). The only thing that could stop him was an injury, and 1983 found him languishing on the disabled list with hip, ligament, and knee cartilage problems.

The next year Evans made up for lost time, with three multi-homer games, his first career grand slam, and his second recognition as Boston's MVP. In 1985 Evans experienced another slow start and another amazing finish (which included yet another Gold Glove). During the Sox's pennant-winning season of 1986, Evans contributed 26 homers and 97 RBI. Versus the Mets, Evans batted .308 with 2 homers and 9 RBI.

Evans has never been showered with acclaim for his efforts. He played in the shadow of the legend called "Yaz" in the early 70s. In 1975 the arrival of Rice and Fred Lynn diverted more attention away from Evans' quiet, consistent success. In 1988 all eyes were on new Red Sox rookie sensations like Ellis Burks and Sam Horn. Evans has always put the Red Sox first. His dedication is evidenced by his recent willingness to shuttle between first base and right field. Despite his lack of experience at first, he has played the position like a pro.

In the 1989 season Evans continued to climb in many Red Sox all-time categories. He will soon be a solid third in several departments, trailing only the dazzling careers of Ted Williams and Yastrzemski. While other stars quickly fade, Evans should continue to be a constant bright spot in Boston's future.

CAREER HIGHLIGHTS
DWIGHT MICHAEL EVANS

Born: November 3, 1951   Santa Monica, CA
Height: 6'2"   **Weight:** 180 lbs.   **Bats:** Right   **Throws:** Right
Outfielder, first baseman: Boston Red Sox, 1972-89.

★ Ranks in the all-time top 10 in 11 Red Sox offensive categories
★ Paced the Red Sox with 9 RBI in the 1986 World Series
★ Has played in two World Series
★ Led the A.L. in homers in 1981
★ Topped the A.L. in walks three times

MAJOR LEAGUE TOTALS

G	AB	H	BA	2B	3B	HR	R	RBI	SB
2,382	8,281	2,262	.273	456	69	366	1,369	1,283	73

Dwight Evans' strength as a player is not reflected in his batting average. A good defensive outfielder, Evans was a poor hitter in his early career. Slowly, he has learned to draw walks, leading the A.L. three times, and to hit his share of home runs.

JOHNNY EVERS

Johnny Evers, the middleman in the Chicago Cubs Tinker-to-Evers-to-Chance infield, was 125 pounds of grit and determination; but it was his detailed knowledge of the baseball rule book that won the Cubs their third straight pennant in 1908. Evers kept baseball charts, researched statistics, recorded observations, and tested theories, always searching for the winning edge. And it was Evers' passion for the rules that changed the outcome of the 1908 pennant race. In one game the Cubs were playing the Pirates, with two outs in the bottom of the ninth inning and Pittsburgh runners on first and third. The batter stroked a ball that was obviously going to drop for a hit, allowing the winning run to score. As was frequently the custom in those days, the runner on first base, Warren Gill, headed for the dugout instead of going to second. Evers complained to umpire Hank O'Day that Gill had to touch second, avoiding the force play, for the run to count. Although the rule was not usually enforced, O'Day realized that Evers was correct and decided to make the correct call if the situation came up again.

Two weeks later, it did. The Cubs were playing the Giants in a crucial game. In the bottom of the ninth inning, New York's Fred Merkle failed to touch second base on an apparent game-winning hit by Al Bridwell. Instead, seeing the winning run cross the plate, Merkle cut across the diamond to get to the clubhouse (because hundreds of fans were running onto the field to celebrate). Evers retrieved the ball and forced Merkle out at second. This time O'Day ruled in favor of the Cubs. The game was declared a 1-1 tie, since the field could not be cleared of the mulling spectators, and the two teams were forced to play a playoff game, which the Cubs won 4-2. What was known for years after as "Merkle's Boner" should have been dubbed "Evers' Rescue."

Evers played less than one season of organized baseball (with Troy of the New York State League) before making the Chicago Cubs team in late 1902. In his first season he batted just .225 with 2 RBI in 26 games. Evers quickly picked up two different nicknames. His aggressive style of play earned him the title "The Trojan," and he was also dubbed "The Crab," possibly because of his diminutive stature or foul temperament. During his sophomore season Evers became the starting second base-

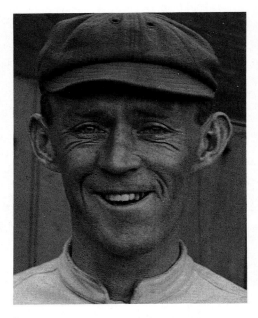

man for the Cubs, hitting .293 with 52 RBI. The Tinker-Evers-Chance infield double play combination was born in 1903. Although Evers made a league-leading 54 errors in his second full season at second base, he also topped the league in putouts, assists, and total chances.

The pencil-thin second baseman hit his first career homer in 1905. In 1906 Evers stole 49 bases, the fifth-highest total in the senior circuit. He played in all 154 games. The Cubs won the National League pennant, only to be defeated by the crosstown White Sox in the World Series. The Cubs won only two games in Series play, and Evers had only 3 hits, but one was a run-scoring single in game four, which provided the Cubs with a 1-0 victory.

In 1907 Evers hit .250 with 2

homers and 51 RBI. The Cubs defended their National League title and trounced the Detroit Tigers in the World Series in four straight games. Evers had 7 hits in the Series for a .350 average, plus 3 stolen bases.

Evers batted an even .300 in 1908, his best average in six seasons. The Cubs and the Tigers had a rematch in the 1908 World Series, and the Cubs downed the Bengals in five games. Again Evers had 7 hits and a .350 average in the fall classic.

Evers had identical .263 averages in 1909 and 1910. In 1911 he played in only 46 games due to injuries. He bounced back in 1912 with an amazing .341 average, fourth highest in the league and 41 points higher than any of Evers' previous averages. He belted 163 hits and 63 RBI, more than his RBI totals for the three previous seasons put together. The Cubs traded Evers to the Boston Braves for Bill Sweeney and cash in February 1914.

Despite notions that the veteran was past his prime, the 33-year-old infielder was a key member of the 1914 Boston Braves, batting .279 with 1 homer and 40 RBI in 139 games. Evers batted .438 with 7 hits in the World Series and the Braves needed only four games to defeat the Philadelphia Athletics. Evers clinched the Series with a dramatic two-run single in the fifth inning against Bob Shawkey, giving the Braves a 3-1 triumph.

Evers had little success as a manager, but he coached for the Giants, White Sox, and Braves. He retired in Albany, New York. Evers was elected to the Hall of Fame in 1946, one year before his death.

CAREER HIGHLIGHTS
JOHN JOSEPH EVERS

Born: July 22, 1883 Troy, NY **Died:** March 28, 1947
Height: 5'9" **Weight:** 125 lbs. **Batted:** Left **Threw:** Right
Second baseman: Chicago Cubs, 1902-13; Boston Braves, 1914-17, 1929; Philadelphia Phillies, 1917; Chicago White Sox, 1922. Manager: Chicago Cubs, 1913, 1921; Chicago White Sox, 1924.

- ★ Played on three consecutive pennant-winning teams
- ★ Batted .438 in the 1914 World Series
- ★ Stole home 21 times, fourth highest in history
- ★ Named the 1917 MVP
- ★ Elected to the Hall of Fame in 1946

MAJOR LEAGUE TOTALS

G	AB	H	BA	2B	3B	HR	R	RBI	SB
1,784	6,137	1,659	.270	216	70	12	919	538	324

Johnny Evers was immortalized as the middle player in the "Tinker-to-Evers-to-Chance" infield combination, which fueled the Chicago Cubs to many victories. Evers was a good player in his own right, however, and consistently hit above league average.

BUCK EWING

William "Buck" Ewing was the best catcher of the 19th century. His talent was so great that many baseball historians have called him the best all-around player of his era. Connie Mack once proclaimed him the best catcher of all time.

Ewing, who was given the nickname Buck as a youngster, witnessed firsthand the birth of professional baseball. Born in Hoaglands, Ohio, he was ten years old when the Cincinnati Red Stockings became baseball's first professional team in 1869. Just nine years later Ewing himself was in organized ball, playing with the Cincinnati Mohawk Browns. By 1880 he had moved up to Rochester of the National Association and the Troy Haymakers for the start of an 18-year baseball career that would take him all the way to Cooperstown.

In his first year with the newly born New York Giants in 1883, Ewing played in 88 games. The 5-foot-10, 188-pound player accomplished quite a feat by leading the National League with 10 homers. (In the dead-ball era, anyone hitting 10 homers had achieved something special.) Ewing proved to be a multitalented asset to the Giants. In his first year Ewing caught 63 games, then filled in as an outfielder, second and third baseman, and shortstop. Before his career was over, Ewing had played all nine positions (including nine games as a pitcher). As a hurler Ewing did well; for his career, he was 3-3 with a 3.45 ERA, 4 complete games, and 23 strikeouts in 47 innings.

In Ewing's second season with the Giants, he batted .277 in 94 games, and his 20 triples were first in the National League. In 1885 Ewing's average climbed to .304 with 6 home runs. In 1886 Ewing hit a respectable .309 with 4 homers and 31 RBI in 73 games.

The Ohio native was deceptively fast considering his size. In 1887, the first year that stolen base statistics from the National League were available, Ewing was credited with 26 steals. The next year he stole a career-high 53 bases, while batting .306 with 6 homers and 58 RBI. Ewing cemented his National League stardom in 1889 with 34 stolen bases and a .327 effort, including 4 homers, 87 RBI, and 91 runs scored.

Ewing was a central character in the birth of a new league in 1890. The players, unhappy over low salaries, decided to form their own organization, the Players' League. Ewing served as a player/manager with the New York

franchise, leading the team to a third-place 74-57 outcome. Ewing had a league-leading fielding percentage for catchers, and he hit .338 with 8 homers, 72 RBI, and 98 runs scored.

Meanwhile, panic-stricken National League owners started trying to buy back players, offering inflated salaries and three-year contracts. Ewing had seemed ambivalent when he jumped to the new league, feeling sorry for the Giants team owner. The National League owners used Cap Anson to set up a secret meeting with Ewing and tried to get him to sign a statement declaring that he'd return to the National League in 1891 because he had no faith in the future of the Players' League. Ewing declined the offer because no other players were willing to

join him. Later, Ewing claimed that he never intended to cooperate, but that he was merely spying for the Players' League. Many players doubted him and shunned him after the incident.

Ewing did return to the Giants in 1891 when the Players' League disbanded after financial difficulties. In 1892 Ewing played in 105 games, hitting .310 with 7 homers and 76 RBI. The Cleveland Spiders of the National League dealt for Ewing in 1893. In 116 games for the Spiders, he hit a career-best .344 with 6 homers, an astounding 122 RBI, and 117 runs scored.

The Cincinnati Red Stockings offered Ewing the chance to manage the team in 1895. He served as a player as well, hitting .318 in 105 games. Ewing's club wound up in eighth place with a 66-64 record. In 1896 Ewing played his last full season, batting .278 in 69 games, with 1 homer and 38 RBI. Ewing's troops improved to 77-50, taking third place in the league that year. Ewing managed the Reds through 1899. His teams were usually contenders with winning records, but none won pennants. The Reds were fourth at 76-56 in 1897, came in third at 92-60 in 1898, and finished sixth at 83-67 in 1899.

Ewing retired after playing just one game with the 1897 Reds. He managed the 1900 Giants for the first half of the season, but the team remained stuck in eighth place with a 21-41 record.

Ewing retired with a .303 average, including 1,625 hits in 1,315 games. Ewing is considered to be the first catcher to adopt the current squatting stance behind the plate. The iron-armed catcher was able to throw out runners from his crouch.

CAREER HIGHLIGHTS
WILLIAM EWING

Born: October 17, 1859 Hoaglands, OH **Died:** October 20, 1906
Height: 5'10" **Weight:** 188 lbs. **Batted:** Right **Threw:** Right
Catcher: Troy Haymakers, 1880-82; New York Giants, 1883-89; New York (Players' League), 1890; New York Giants, 1891-92; Cleveland Spiders, 1893-94; Cincinnati Reds, 1895-97. Manager: New York (Players' League), 1890; Cincinnati Reds 1895-99; New York Giants, 1900.

★ Batted .300 or better for 11 seasons   ★ Led the N.L. in homers in 1883
★ Was first in triples in 1884   ★ Elected to the Hall of Fame in 1939
     ★ Played on three consecutive pennant-winning teams

MAJOR LEAGUE TOTALS

G	AB	H	BA	2B	3B	HR	R	RBI	SB
1,315	5,363	1,625	.303	250	178	71	1,129	833	354

Perhaps the best all-around player of the 19th century, Buck Ewing was a fierce baserunner as well as a strong-armed catcher. His biggest rival was King Kelly, who—like Ewing—could play most of the positions on the field and bat over .300.

ELROY FACE

One of the first great relievers of the 1950s was Elroy Face. At 5-foot-8 and 155 pounds, he was hardly an imposing figure on the mound; but for 15 seasons he was one of the best bullpen stoppers in the majors.

Using a forkball as his "out" pitch, Face gained his fame as a big league reliever. It was a long road to the major leagues, however. Face served in the U.S. Army in 1946 and 1947, then signed a contract with the Philadelphia Phillies. He had two sensational seasons with Bradford of the Pony League. In 1949 Face won 14 and lost just 2, leading the league with an .875 winning percentage. The following season Face was 18-5 with 150 strikeouts and a league-best 2.58 ERA.

The Brooklyn Dodgers spotted Face's talent and drafted him. In 1950 Face hurled with Pueblo and led the Western League with a 23-9 record. Face moved to Fort Worth of the Texas League in 1952. Although he was just 14-11, Face got his big break. He advanced to the Dodgers top farm club in Montreal but was stuck there because Brooklyn already had a well-stocked pitching staff. Pittsburgh discovered Face and drafted him on December 1, 1952, placing him on the roster immediately. In 1953 Face was 6-8 with a 6.58 ERA in 41 games, all but 13 in relief. As a reliever, Face was 3-2.

Face was demoted to New Orleans of the Southern League in 1954, where he went 12-11 in 40 games. His most important accomplishment there was learning how to throw the forkball.

Back with the Pirates in 1955, Face was a new pitcher. Although the Pirates were stuck in last place with a 60-94 record, Face was first on the team with 5 saves. In 1956 Face led the National League in games pitched (68). He won 12 games and saved 6 more. The 1957 Pirates stayed mired in last place, but Face contributed 4 relief wins and 10 saves, along with a 3.07 ERA.

Face started an incredible streak in 1958. From May 30, 1958, to September 11, 1959, he went without a defeat in 98 straight appearances. Face ended 1958 with a 5-2 record, a 2.89 ERA, and a league-leading 20 saves. The Pirates, meanwhile, finished in second place with an 84-70 record.

In 1959 relief ace Face didn't start a single game. Yet, pitching entirely in relief, he compiled an amazing record of 18 wins (including 17 straight) and 1 loss for a winning percentage of .947—

a mark that has never been matched. That record, combined with 10 saves and a sparkling 2.70 ERA, adds up to one of the most memorable pitching performances in major league history. What's astonishing is that Face didn't win the Cy Young award. Back then there was only one award for both leagues, and Early Wynn of the American League Chicago White Sox won it that year.

Along with contemporary Hoyt Wilhelm, Face revolutionized the role of the relief specialist. During baseball's first 75 or 80 years, it was considered almost a disgrace if a pitcher failed to complete a game. Relief pitchers were seldom used and never celebrated. But in the period following World War II, the role of the relief pitcher developed, and his special talents came to be appreciated. Wilhelm and Face were responsible for showing baseball the

vital contributions relievers could make.

In 1960 Face paced the Pirates to a world championship. Pittsburgh was 95-59 during the regular season and easily rolled to the World Series against the New York Yankees. Pitching exclusively in relief, Face was 10-8 with 24 saves (second in the league only to Lindy McDaniel's 26). The Yankees pummeled all Pirates pitching in the World Series, and Face wound up with a 5.23 ERA in four appearances. However, he earned saves in the first, fourth, and fifth games, hurling a total of 10.1 innings.

Face topped the National League with 17 saves in 1961. In 1962 Face was 8-7 with a career-best 1.88 ERA and 28 saves. After coming up with 16 saves in 1963, Face suffered through a slump, gaining only 4 saves in two years. In 1966 Face rebounded to his usual level, compiling a 6-6 record with 18 saves in 54 games. The New York native won 7 games and saved 17 in 1967. After 43 games in 1968, Face was purchased by the Detroit Tigers. Face's last major league season was in 1969, with the expansion team Montreal Expos.

A four-time All-Star, Face appeared in 848 games during a 16-year career played almost entirely with the Pirates. During that time, he started only 27 games but made 821 appearances in relief, recording 96 wins and 193 saves. He brought home an additional 8 victories when he was used infrequently as a starter early in his career. Even though relief pitchers were used less often in those pioneering days, Face still ranks among career leaders in games, wins, and saves. His 547 games finished is still a National League record.

CAREER HIGHLIGHTS
ELROY LEON FACE

Born: February 20, 1928   Stephentown, NY
Height: 5'8"   **Weight:** 155 lbs.   **Batted:** Both   **Threw:** Right
Pitcher: Pittsburgh Pirates, 1953-68; Detroit Tigers, 1968; Montreal Expos, 1969.

- ★ Compiled a record 18-1 mark (.947 winning percentage) in 1959
- ★ Led the N.L. in saves three times
- ★ Ranks in the all-time top ten in games, wins, and saves for relievers
- ★ Pitched in the 1960 World Series
- ★ Led the N.L. in games pitched twice

MAJOR LEAGUE TOTALS

G	IP	W	L	Pct.	SV	SO	BB	ERA
848	1,375	104	95	.523	193	877	362	3.48

Reliever Elroy Face was known for his forkball pitch, which is called the split-fingered fastball in modern baseball. Even though relievers were used less often in Face's era, he still ranks near the top in games, wins, and saves.

BOB FELLER

For 20 years Bob Feller was called "Bullet Bob" and "Rapid Robert" by baseball fans because of the sheer power he displayed when pitching for the Cleveland Indians. Feller achieved dazzling success with a team that won only two pennants during his career. The most impressive aspect of Feller's accomplishments is that he compiled such stunning statistics after missing nearly four seasons to military service.

The talented righthander enlisted in the U.S. Navy on December 8, 1941, the day after the Japanese attack on Pearl Harbor. At the time, Feller was a 23-year-old star pitcher in the major leagues. He had just finished the 1941 season by leading the American League with a 25-13 record, the third straight season he had topped the junior circuit in wins. Feller was the league leader in games, games started, innings pitched, strikeouts, and shutouts. Upon entering the military, Feller accepted duty as an anti-aircraft gunner aboard the U.S.S. *Alabama* and came out a highly decorated war hero. However, he missed nearly four complete seasons. Before joining the Navy, Feller had won 107 games in six years. In 1945 he pitched in nine games, going 5-3 with 7 complete games. All of America wondered if the once-great moundsman could regain his form.

Feller seemed better than ever in 1946. When he pitched in Washington, Senators owner Clark Griffith set up a primitive speed gun to clock Feller. His fastball was timed at 98.6 miles per hour. He led the league with a 26-15 record that year and was also first in games (48), games started (42), complete games (36), innings pitched (371.1), strikeouts (a career-high 348, the fifth-highest mark in history), and shutouts (10). He pitched in his fourth All-Star game, getting his first midseason classic win with three innings of shutout hurling against the National League. Feller's season highlight came on April 30, when he tossed a no-hit gem against the archrival New York Yankees.

In 1947 Feller won 20 games for the fifth time in his career, leading the league in games started, innings, strikeouts, and shutouts. The Indians won their first pennant in 28 years in 1948, but Feller "slumped" to a 19-15 record. Despite Feller's lack of wins, he still won his seventh league strikeout crown. Feller was winless in the World Series, although he allowed just 2 hits in a con-troversial 1-0 opening game loss.

Feller earned 15 wins in 1949 and 16 wins in 1950. His final great season came in 1951, when he topped the league with a 22-8 record and .733 winning percentage. In 1952 Feller suffered through his first losing season, going 9-13. The veteran pitcher was a clutch performer for the 1954 Indians, who won their second pennant in seven seasons. Feller pitched in just 19 games, but he compiled a 13-3 record. That year the Indians won a record 111 games. Feller retired in 1956 after pitching in 19 games.

The rise to stardom came quickly for Bob Feller. His father, an Iowa farmer, provided constant encouragement. A diamond was constructed on the family farm, and teams from surrounding towns would play there. By age 14, Feller was attracting crowds of 1,000 or more when he pitched. He played four years of American Legion baseball, and it was Legion umpires who urged Cleveland Indians scout Cy Slapnicka to observe Feller. In 1934 he saw Feller personally and promptly signed him to a $75-a-month contract. Because Feller had a sore arm in 1935, he never pitched minor league baseball. He earned a big league roster spot with the 1936 Indians at age 17.

Feller's first game was a three-inning exhibition stint against the St. Louis Cardinals. He struck out 8 batters in three innings and gained national attention. Feller didn't get his first start with the team until August. He struck out 15 Philadelphia Athletics in one game that season, setting what was then an American League record.

In 1938 Feller joined the starting rotation on a full-time basis. He was 17-11 with a league-leading 240 strikeouts in 277.2 innings. On October 2, 1938, Feller struck out 18 Detroit Tigers, setting a record at that time. In 1939 Feller was the leading A.L. winner with a 24-9 record and a league-best 246 strikeouts. Feller's 1940 season started with a bang. He pitched the first opening-day no-hitter in American League history against the Chicago White Sox on April 16, walking 5 and fanning 8.

Feller ranks 28th in history with 266 wins. He remains the Indians all-time leader in shutouts (46), strikeouts (2,581), innings (3,828), and All-Star appearances (8). Even today, historians still speculate that Feller might have won 350 games and registered nearly 3,500 strikeouts if he hadn't missed four seasons in the military. The Indians have since retired his uniform number (19), making him one of only three Cleveland players in history to earn the honor.

CAREER HIGHLIGHTS
ROBERT WILLIAM ANDREW FELLER

Born: November 3, 1918   Van Meter, IA
Height: 6'0"   **Weight:** 185 lbs.   **Batted:** Right   **Threw:** Right
Pitcher: Cleveland Indians, 1936-56.

- ★ Struck out 15 batters in one game as a rookie
- ★ Led the A.L. in strikeouts seven times
- ★ Led the A.L. in victories for six seasons
- ★ Struck out a career-high 348 batters in 1946
- ★ Pitched three no-hitters
- ★ Elected to the Hall of Fame in 1962

MAJOR LEAGUE TOTALS

G	IP	W	L	Pct.	SO	BB	ERA
570	3,828	266	162	.621	2,581	1,764	3.25

Bob Feller was just a teenager during his rookie year, but he still managed to set an A.L. record by striking out 17 batters in one game. Feller experienced his banner year in 1946 when he struck out 348 batters and led the league with a 26-15 record.

RICHARD FERRELL

Rick Ferrell was a slick-fielding, contact-hitting catcher for 18 major league seasons. Along with New York Yankee Bill Dickey and Detroit Tiger Mickey Cochrane, Ferrell was considered one of the finest back-stops in the A.L. However, Ferrell was best known as part of a duo of brothers who excelled during the 1930s.

Ferrell grew up in North Carolina with six brothers. Younger brother Wes Ferrell actually beat Rick to the major leagues by two seasons (getting his start as a pitcher with the 1927 Cleveland Indians). As youngsters, the brothers were a natural pitcher-catcher combination. In 1921 the Ferrell family (with Wes pitching and Rick behind the plate) led a team to the Guilford County championship. Rick Ferrell was attending Guilford College in 1924, playing catcher for the collegiate club. He had been involved in boxing when he was younger and once won the North Carolina state boxing championship in the 135-pound lightweight category. In 1925 St. Louis Cardinals scout Charley Barrett spotted Ferrell's ability. Even with the offer of a $1,000 bonus, Ferrell decided to bypass professional baseball for a year. The Detroit Tigers successfully signed Ferrell in 1926 and assigned him to Kinston of the Virginia League.

The slim catcher played with Columbus of the American Association in 1927, hitting .249. He increased his batting average to .333 in 126 games in 1928. He was named to the league All-Star team in 1928. Just when the Tigers thought they might have a future catcher, Ferrell became a free agent. The Tigers had left Ferrell off draft lists that fall without notifying the young catcher, which kept other teams from obtaining the hot prospect. Ferrell complained to baseball commissioner Judge Kenesaw Mountain Landis. The Judge sided with Ferrell and ruled that he should become a free agent. The New York Giants and the St. Louis Browns got into a bidding war for Ferrell, which the Browns won. Ferrell settled for a $25,000 bonus and a $12,500 contract for 1929.

In his first year with the Browns, Ferrell caught in 45 games and had 16 pinch-hitting assignments. He ended the year with a .229 average. Ferrell won a starting job as the Browns top backstop in 1930 and hit .268 with 1 homer and 41 RBI. In 1931 Ferrell batted .306 with 3 homers and 57 RBI. He was the leading A.L. catcher, topping the league

in double plays (11) and assists (86). Ferrell's brother threw a no-hitter against the Browns in 1931. Rick almost took the no-hitter away from his brother with a hard shot to the short-stop on which he was ruled safe. The scorers ruled it an error, however, preserving Wes's hitless gem.

Ferrell's average climbed to .315 in 1932, the best average among Browns regulars that year. He had a .986 field-ing average, making only 8 miscues all season. After just 22 games in 1933, Ferrell was traded to the Boston Red Sox. On May 9 the Browns sent Ferrell and Lloyd Brown to Boston for Merv Shea and cash. Ferrell finished at .297 for the season with 4 homers and a career-high 77 RBI. In 1934 the Red Sox traded Bob Weiland, Bob Seeds, and $25,000 to the Cleveland Indians for Dick Porter and Rick's brother Wes. Catcher Ferrell batted .297 in 1934.

Ferrell and Ferrell were both success-ful for the Red Sox in 1935. Wes

Ferrell won 25 games with his brother behind the plate. Rick Ferrell hit .301 with 3 homers and 61 RBI. Despite the success of the Ferrell brothers, the Red Sox finished the season in fourth place at 78-75.

In 1936 Ferrell batted .312 and was first in the American League in putouts (556) and fielding percentage (.987). Boston sent both Ferrells packing on June 11, 1937. Rick Ferrell, Mel Almada, and Wes Ferrell were traded to the Washington Senators in exchange for infielder Ben Chapman and pitcher Bobo Newsom. Rick Ferrell quickly adjusted to his new surroundings in Washington, hitting .292 with the 1938 Senators. He was traded back to the Browns in 1941, but the Senators reac-quired him in 1944.

Ferrell retired as a player following the 1947 season. In 18 seasons Ferrell caught in 1,805 games, which ranks fourth in history. Ferrell was a gifted defender, making 139 career double plays (11th best in history). His fielding skills were considered just as good as Dickey's, or Cochrane's, although the latter two catchers landed more fame through their power hitting. The six-time All-Star had the distinction of play-ing in the first midseason battle between the leagues in 1933. Ferrell batted .281 lifetime and showed incredible discipline while hitting. He never struck out more than 26 times in one season and fanned just 277 total times in 6,028 at-bats.

Following his retirement, Ferrell was a Detroit Tigers coach from 1950 to 1953. He was promoted to general manager in 1960. He became vice-president in 1962 and held that job until 1975. In 1974 Ferrell became a member of the Baseball Hall of Fame.

CAREER HIGHLIGHTS
RICHARD BENJAMIN FERRELL

Born: October 12, 1905 Durham, NC
Height: 5'10" **Weight:** 160 lbs. **Batted:** Right **Threw:** Right
Catcher: St. Louis Browns, 1929-33, 1941-43; Boston Red Sox, 1933-37; Washington Senators, 1937-41, 1944-45, 1947.

- ★ Set an A.L. record for games caught
- ★ Batted over .300 for five seasons
- ★ Struck out fewer than 20 times a season during 14 seasons
- ★ Named to six All-Star teams
- ★ Elected to the Hall of Fame in 1974
- ★ Caught more than 100 games for nine straight years

MAJOR LEAGUE TOTALS

G	AB	H	BA	2B	3B	HR	R	RBI	SB
1,884	6,028	1,692	.281	324	45	28	687	734	29

Rick Ferrell served as the catcher for the Boston Red Sox during the same years that brother Wes pitched for them. The Ferrell Brothers were supposedly so in tune to each other that Rick could catch an entire game without signs.

WES FERRELL

No one had ever dreamed of a designated hitter rule when Wes Ferrell pitched in the 1930s. In fact Wes Ferrell was one of the best-hitting pitchers of all time and could have been a designated hitter himself in today's American League. Although he stuck to pitching for 15 years, Ferrell was a frequent pinch hitter and even played 13 games as an outfielder for the 1933 Cleveland Indians.

Ferrell had grown up on a North Carolina farm with his brother Rick. The Ferrell brothers, like many farm youngsters, had very few nearby playmates. Because of chores, the kids could play in organized teams only on weekends. So they formed a childhood battery, with Wes pitching and Rick catching. With five other brothers in the family, the Ferrells could almost field an entire team. (Brothers George and Marvin went on to minor league baseball careers.) Wes Ferrell began his career in 1927 with a semipro team in East Douglas, Massachusetts, in the Blackstone Valley League. At age 18 he made his debut with the 1927 Cleveland Indians, pitching one inning.

Ferrell was demoted to Terre Haute in 1928, where he was 20-8. He got a late-season recall to Cleveland, going 0-2, and he was in the majors to stay.

He began the first of four consecutive 20-win seasons in 1929, when the big righthander won 21 games and lost just 10. Ferrell led the third-place Indians in victories and was third in the league in winning percentage (.677), games pitched (43), and victories. Only George Earnshaw and Lefty Grove of the pennant-winning Philadelphia Athletics entered the 20-win circle in 1929 with Ferrell.

In 1930 Ferrell won 25 games for the fourth-place Indians. The North Carolina native ranked second in the league behind Grove's 28 victories. Ferrell was fourth in the league in winning percentage (.658) and strikeouts (143) and second in innings pitched (296.2), earned run average (3.31), and complete games (25). The 1931 Indians remained mired in fourth place with a 78-76 record. Ferrell kept on winning for the mediocre club, notching 22 victories and leading the league with 27 complete games. Ferrell's record might have been greater if he hadn't missed 14 days in midseason due to a suspension. Indians manager Roger Peckinpaugh, who never got along well with Ferrell, forced the star pitcher to throw out of the rotation on less rest than he

usually got. When Peckinpaugh tried to relieve Ferrell in the second inning of a game at Boston, Ferrell refused to go. The argument resulted in a $1,500 fine and a two-week suspension.

The secret was getting out around the American League that Ferrell was a surprisingly talented hitter. While most pitchers would be worried about injuring themselves at bat or on the base paths, Ferrell would take his cuts as mightily as any player. In 1930 he was 3-for-7 as a pinch hitter before finishing the year with 35 hits, a .297 average, and 14 RBI. The following season Ferrell had his record-setting 9 homers, along with 30 RBI, a .319 average, and a wondrous .621 slugging percentage.

In 1932 Ferrell won 23 games for the Indians, who remained in fourth place. He ranked fourth in the league in wins and second in complete games.

The 1933 Indians, under new manager Walter Johnson, even used Ferrell as a part-time outfielder. He played the outfield in 13 games and hit .271 for the season, with 7 homers and 26 RBI. On the mound, however, Ferrell dropped to 11-12. Ferrell was a member of the first American League All-Star team in 1933.

Ferrell got a childhood wish the following season. On May 25, 1934, Ferrell and Dick Porter were traded to the Boston Red Sox for Bob Weiland, Bob Seeds, and $25,000. The catcher on the Boston Red Sox was five-year veteran Rick Ferrell. The brothers were reunited. The trade had a rejuvenating effect on Wes Ferrell's career, and he rebounded to a 14-5 mark in 1934. In 1935 Ferrell topped the American League with a 25-14 record. Ferrell was first in games started (38), complete games (31), and innings pitched (322.1).

The following season Ferrell was 20-15, his sixth 20-win season in eight years. Again he paced the American League in innings pitched, games started, and complete games. Ferrell had his most prestigious season as a hitter in 1935. He batted .347 with 52 hits, ending the year with 7 homers and 32 strikeouts. The 21 walks he received that season is more evidence of his offensive reputation.

Ferrell won 14 games in 1937 and 15 in 1938. His major league career ended in 1941 with the Boston Braves. Throughout the 1940s, he served as a playing manager for several southern minor league teams. Playing the outfield, he won two minor league batting titles. Ferrell died at age 68.

CAREER HIGHLIGHTS
WESLEY CHEEK FERRELL

Born: February 2, 1908 Greensboro, NC **Died:** December 9, 1976
Height: 6'2" **Weight:** 195 lbs. **Batted:** Right **Threw:** Right
Pitcher: Cleveland Indians, 1927-34; Boston Red Sox, 1934-37; Washington Senators, 1937-38; New York Yankees, 1938-39; Brooklyn Dodgers, 1940; Boston Braves, 1941. Outfielder: Cleveland Indians, 1933.

- ★ Topped the A.L. in innings pitched three times
- ★ Hit 38 career homers, a record for pitchers
- ★ Led the A.L. in complete games four times
- ★ Posted 20-win seasons six times

MAJOR LEAGUE TOTALS

G	IP	W	L	Pct.	SO	BB	ERA
374	2,623	193	128	.601	985	1,040	4.04

Wes Ferrell was a fine pitcher in his day, posting six 20-win seasons in eight years. He was also a skilled batsman, particularly for a hurler, and boasts a .280 lifetime batting average. His 38 career homers are a record for pitchers.

179

ROLLIE FINGERS

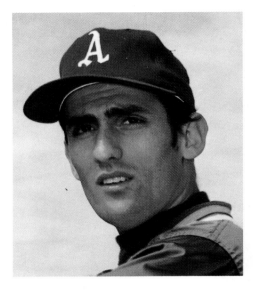

Over a stunning 17-year career that was often hampered by injuries, Rollie Fingers hurled a record 341 saves — a mark that is likely to stand long beyond Fingers' almost certain induction into the Baseball Hall of Fame.

Fingers was the competent closer on the awesome Oakland Athletics teams that won five consecutive division titles and three straight world championships between 1971 and 1975. Toward the end of his career, Fingers went to Milwaukee. In 1981 he won the American League Cy Young and Most Valuable Player awards, then helped the Brewers to their first league championship in 1982. The relief pitcher with the distinctive handlebar moustache was so effective that he led the league in saves three times.

Fingers began his professional career in 1965 pitching in the Kansas City Athletics farm system. He toiled for four seasons in the minors before getting his big chance with the 1969 Athletics team, which had moved to Oakland the previous year. During his rookie season, the 6-foot-4 190-pounder tied Paul Lindblad for the team lead in appearances with 60, and he topped the A's with 12 saves. His record was 6-7 with a 3.71 ERA.

In 1970 the A's made Fingers into a swing man, alternating him between the bullpen and the starting rotation. He pitched in 45 games, 19 of them as a starter. As a result of his dual duties, Fingers fell to 7-9 with 2 saves. The A's won their first divisional title in 1971 behind Fingers' 4 wins and 17 saves.

The A's shook off their 1971 American League Championship Series defeat to the Baltimore Orioles and won the pennant in 1972. Fingers topped American League relievers with 11 wins. Combined with his 21 saves, Fingers was responsible for nearly a third of the team's 101 wins. In the 1972 League Championship Series, Fingers was 1-0 in three appearances. Versus the Cincinnati Reds in the World Series, Fingers appeared in six games, earning 1 win and 2 saves.

Fingers appeared in 62 games in 1973, winning 7 and saving 22 while posting a 1.92 ERA. In the 1973 World Series, Fingers' ERA was a mere 0.66. He pitched in six games against the New York Mets, saving 2.

Oakland earned a third consecutive world championship in 1974. Fingers remained the team's bullpen ace, appearing in a league-high 76 games,

logging 9 wins and 18 saves. He saved the team's final win in the fourth game of the American League Championship Series against Baltimore.

Going against the Dodgers in the World Series, Fingers gave a performance that equaled the 1959 accomplishment of Los Angeles reliever Larry Sherry. Fingers won the first game with 4.1 innings of relief, then supplied 3 more saves as the A's took the Series 4-1. Fingers played a role in every one of the A's Series victories, earning the World Series Most Valuable Player award for his achievement.

Fingers led the league in relief wins (10) again in 1975. He appeared in a league-leading 75 games and earned 24 saves. Fingers and the A's won their fifth straight division.

Fingers won a career-high 13 games and earned 20 saves in 1976. That season, Fingers, Reggie Jackson, Bert Campaneris, Don Baylor, Sal Bando, and Joe Rudi were playing out their contracts. Team owner Charlie Finley, unable to agree to financial terms with the six, saw the end coming, so he tried to sell off three of his stars: Rudi, Vida Blue, and Fingers. On June 15, 1976, Finley tried to sell Fingers to the Boston Red Sox, who were willing to pay $1 million. Commissioner Bowie Kuhn immediately voided the deal, claiming that the move wasn't in the best interests of baseball.

Stranded with the A's until season's end, Fingers signed a free-agent contract with the San Diego Padres, a five-year pact estimated at $1.5 million. In 1977, his first season in the National League, Fingers appeared in a league-best 78 games and was first in the National League with 35 saves. In 1978 he won his second straight Fireman of the Year award with 37 saves.

Fingers was traded to the Cardinals in the off-season of 1980 but was sent to the Milwaukee Brewers before the 1981 season began. After all, the Cardinals had Bruce Sutter and had no need for two stoppers. With the 1981 Brewers, Fingers had yet another banner year. Figuring his 6 wins and 28 saves, Fingers had a hand in 55 percent of the team's victories. In 1982 Fingers earned 29 saves but was on the injured list during the playoffs and World Series.

The Brewers released Fingers after the 1985 season, when he had 17 saves. For his career, Fingers earned a record 341 saves plus a record 6 saves in World Series competition. He'll be eligible for induction into the Hall of Fame in 1991.

CAREER HIGHLIGHTS
ROLAND GLEN FINGERS

Born: August 25, 1946   Steubenville, OH
Height: 6'4"   **Weight:** 190 lbs.   **Batted:** Right   **Threw:** Right
Pitcher: Oakland A's, 1968-76; San Diego Padres, 1977-80; Milwaukee Brewers, 1981-85.

- ★ Compiled a major league career record of 341 saves
- ★ Won both the Cy Young award and the MVP award in 1981
- ★ Led the league in saves three times

- ★ His 107 wins in relief ranks third best in baseball history
- ★ His six saves in World Series play set a major league record
- ★ Pitched in three World Series

MAJOR LEAGUE TOTALS

G	IP	W	L	Pct.	SV	SO	BB	ERA
944	1,701	114	118	.491	341	1,299	492	2.90

Reliever Rollie Fingers saved a record-setting 341 games during his career, and his 107 relief wins rank third on the list. Fingers experienced his two top save seasons while with the San Diego Padres, saving 35 games in 1977 and 37 in 1978.

CARLTON FISK

In 1987 the 39-year-old catcher Carlton Fisk smashed 3 consecutive homers, one after the other, off Boston pitching whiz Roger Clemens. In 1988 he sat out a chunk of the season with a broken thumb.

That says pretty much all there is to say about Carlton Fisk: Either he's playing at 150 percent, or he isn't playing at all.

It is almost unbelievable that Fisk has lasted 19 years (and counting) as a catcher, a position that requires physical abuse reminiscent of the Spanish Inquisition. It certainly is not surprising that he has been injured so often. What is surprising are his consistently exemplary stats, especially in fielding, where he continues to prove that his playing days are far from over. He has been quoted as saying, "If the human body recognized agony and frustration, people would never run marathons, have babies, or play baseball."

His long and consistent career was preceded by a long, consistent stint in the minors. After spending a little time at college on a basketball scholarship, Fisk began his baseball career at age 19 in 1967, playing for four different teams in as many seasons (and spending ten months in the military).

After his debut minor league season, when he had a .338 batting mark and .982 fielding average, Fisk's hitting plummeted to the low .200s. Then, upon his permanent call-up to the Boston Red Sox in 1971, Fisk notched a .313 batting average in 14 games, the first of three times in the majors when he would hit .300 or better.

With only 16 big league games under his belt, Fisk embarked upon his official rookie season in 1972. He immediately distinguished himself in offense and defense, rallying circuit contenders with 9 triples and 846 putouts—both top achievements for the righty. He also paced the league with 72 assists and 15 errors.

This wasn't a big enough gaffe to keep Fisk from snaring American League Rookie of the Year accolades. It was a happy beginning to what turned into a ten-year relationship with Boston, lasting through three injury layoffs and one thrilling World Series.

In 1975 Fisk created an image in the minds of baseball fans that remained engraved on the inside of their eyelids for years as surely as it aired each week at the top of nationally televised baseball games for weeks. With the score tied at 6 in the 12th inning of the sixth

game, Fisk banged a game-winning solo homer off losing Reds pitcher Pat Darcy. The image of Fisk swinging, watching the ball sail, and waving his arms to encourage it to stay in fair territory is truly memorable. He was one of the few hitters in World Series history to literally bounce around the bases instead of run. During the regular season Fisk had spent three months on the disabled list, and he had missed nearly the entire 1974 season as well. His 1975 regular season stats included a career high .331 batting average in 79 games, 10 home runs, and 52 RBI.

Following a subpar 1976 season (a .255 average, 17 homers, and 58 RBI) Fisk rebounded in 1977, hitting .315 with 26 homers and 102 RBI. All three marks were the second-highest totals in his career. That season he tied a major league record for most long hits in an inning (2) on June 30, 1977. He had reached that record once before in May 1975. Both times, he did it in the

eighth inning. Also he tied the A.L. record for fewest passed balls in a season of 150 games or more (4). Three weeks on the disabled list in 1979 blighted his accomplishments, which included .272 with 10 homers and 42 RBI in just 91 games.

Fisk became a free agent when the Red Sox failed to offer him a new contract before the December signing deadline. The Chicago White Sox secured Fisk's services with a five-year, $2.9 million deal. The White Sox were desperate not only for offense, but for an on-field general with some major league experience. Fisk was just what they were looking for.

He helped the Sox to a 1983 divisional title by hitting .289 with 26 homers and 86 RBI, leading the league in putouts as well. In the League Championship Series, he had perfect fielding but only 3 hits. His finest season in Chicago came in 1985. After being plagued by injuries in 1984, he came back the next season with career highs in homers (370 and RBI (107). He credited his comeback to pumping iron through the winter.

In 1989 Fisk fractured his right hand only six games into the season. (At the time, he already had 2 homers and had seemed ready for a banner season.) Fans wondered how many more injuries the talented backstop could take and when the rigors of catching would sideline him permanently. But by midsummer, he was back in the lineup, and in the middle of July he connected with his 2,000 career hit. "Pudge" was indisputably healthy again. When he's healthy, he's one of the finest hitters and fielders in the American League.

CAREER HIGHLIGHTS
CARLTON ERNEST FISK

Born: December 26, 1947   Bellow Falls, VT
Height: 6'3"   **Weight:** 220 lbs.   **Bats:** Right   **Throws:** Right
Catcher: Boston Red Sox, 1969, 1971-80; Chicago White Sox, 1981-89.

- ★ Established a record for the most season home runs by a catcher in 1985
- ★ Named 1972 Rookie of the Year
- ★ Named to ten All-Star teams and played on nine squads
- ★ Hit dramatic home run in sixth game of 1975 World Series
- ★ Has topped 20 homers eight times
- ★ Hit for the cycle on May 16, 1984

MAJOR LEAGUE TOTALS

G	AB	H	BA	2B	3B	HR	R	RBI	SB
2,141	7,603	2,063	.272	371	46	336	1,155	1,161	117

A ten-time All-Star, Carlton Fisk had his best season in 1985, with a career-high 37 homers and 107 RBI. One of the most durable catchers in history, Fisk set the A.L. record for most games caught in 1988, breaking Rick Ferrell's record of 1,805.

CURT FLOOD

Despite an impressive 15-year career that included smooth hitting and consistent defense, Curt Flood may be best remembered for his off-the-field courage, taking a stand on behalf of players everywhere.

Flood had played 12 stellar seasons with the St. Louis Cardinals, but on October 7, 1969, Flood, catcher Tim McCarver, reliever Joe Hoerner, and outfielder Byron Browne were traded to the Philadelphia Phillies in exchange for first baseman Dick Allen, infielder Cookie Rojas, and pitcher Jerry Johnson. Flood refused to report to his new team. Why? "After 12 years in the major leagues, I do not feel I am a piece of property to be bought and sold irrespective of my wishes," Flood explained. "I just decided that there comes a time in a man's life when he should have a say in where he goes to work."

Even though the Phillies offered him a $100,000 contract, Flood decided to sit out the season. He filed a lawsuit against Commissioner Bowie Kuhn challenging baseball's reserve clause. The suit went all the way to the U.S. Supreme Court. Although Flood lost the case, his efforts influenced owners to adopt a more equitable arbitration system for working out contract disputes.

The legal action overshadowed Flood's fine career with the St. Louis Cardinals. Although Willie Mays got more national attention as a center fielder, Flood was regarded in many circles as the finest defensive center fielder in the National League.

Flood didn't begin his career with the Cardinals. He started as a Cincinnati Reds farmhand with Thomasville of the Carolina League in 1956. He led the league in batting (.340) and runs scored (133), and he tied for the lead in games played (154) and hits (190). Flood led outfielders with a .983 fielding percentage, the first of many years that he'd be racking up defensive accomplishments. The Reds summoned Flood near the end of the season, and he appeared in five games but got only one at-bat. In 1957 Flood was assigned to Savannah of the Sally League. The Reds tinkered with the idea of making Flood into a third baseman, but he suffered through the season, making 41 errors. The Reds brought up Flood for three games at the end of the season, and he played at second and third base.

The Reds packaged up Flood and outfielder Joe Taylor, sending the pair to the St. Louis Cardinals for pitchers Marty Kutyna, Willard Schmidt, and Ted

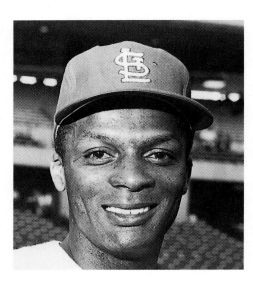

Wieand on December 5, 1957. In his first season with St. Louis, Flood hit just .261 with 10 homers and 41 RBI in 121 games.

By 1960 Flood was still struggling as a hitter, batting just .237 with 8 homers and 38 RBI. However, he paced N.L. center fielders with a .993 fielding percentage. In 1961 Flood's average soared to .322. The Texas native cultivated even more new-found power in 1962: He socked 12 homers and 70 RBI to complement a .296 average and led the Cardinals with 99 runs scored.

The 1963 Cardinals were second in the league, finishing six games behind the pennant-winning Dodgers. Flood contributed a .302 average, registering 200 hits for the first time. He also scored a career-high 112 runs. In the field Flood was tops in the league in putouts and chances accepted. Flood gained his first All-Star game appearance in 1964 as the Cardinals cruised to their first world championship since 1946. He batted .311, leading the

league with 211 hits. Flood won his first Gold Glove with only 5 errors in center field all season. In the World Series Flood scored 5 runs, and his run-scoring triple was a key to the Redbirds' opening victory against the New York Yankees.

Flood batted a team-leading .310 in 1965, driving in a career-high of 83 runs and scoring 90 runs as well. Another Gold Glove highlighted Flood's season. Flood returned to the N.L. All-Star roster in 1966, hitting .267 with 10 homers and 78 RBI. Flood hit safely in 19 straight games in 1966, the longest streak of his career. The fleet center fielder also compiled a spotless 1.000 fielding average in 160 games. In both 1965 and 1966, Flood was the leading RBI man for the Cardinals.

The Cardinals won 101 games in 1967, then won a seven-game World Series against the Boston Red Sox. Flood batted .335 (fourth in the league) to pace the Cardinal attack. In the World Series Flood hit just .179 with 5 hits. However, the Gold Glove winner played errorless baseball in seven games.

In 1968 the Cardinals defended their National League title. Flood hit .301 (fifth highest in the senior circuit) and was the only Cardinals regular to surpass the .300 mark. Flood, now the team co-captain, notched 186 hits, another club high. He was one of four Redbirds chosen to play in the All-Star game. The Cardinals suffered a seven-game defeat at the hands of the Detroit Tigers, but Flood had his best World Series output ever, batting .286 with 8 hits, 4 runs scored, and 2 RBI.

In 1969 Flood won his seventh Gold Glove. He played in 153 games, logging a .285 average.

CAREER HIGHLIGHTS
CURTIS CHARLES FLOOD

Born: January 18, 1938 Houston, TX
Height: 5'9" **Weight:** 165 lbs. **Batted:** Right **Threw:** Right
Outfielder: Cincinnati Reds, 1956-57; St. Louis Cardinals, 1958-69; Washington Senators, 1971.

★ Won seven Gold Gloves
★ Played in three World Series
★ Tied for the N.L. lead in hits in 1964
★ Hit a career-high .335 in 1967
★ Batted over .300 six times

MAJOR LEAGUE TOTALS

G	AB	H	BA	2B	3B	HR	R	RBI	SB
1,759	6,357	1,861	.293	271	44	85	851	636	88

Curt Flood excelled as a center fielder, garnering seven Gold Gloves during his career. He was also a competent hitter who banged a career-high of .335 in 1967—two years before the controversy over the reserve clause virtually ended his career.

WHITEY FORD

The greatest dynasty in the history of baseball had to be the incredible New York Yankees teams of the 1950s and early 1960s. The backbone of their pitching staff was Whitey Ford.

Ford, who was called "Eddie" in his early years, apparently picked up the moniker Whitey at the Yankees minor league training camp in 1947. Lefty Gomez, who was managing the Binghamton team, had trouble remembering all the players' names, so he gave everyone a nickname. First he called Ford "Blondie," then later switched to "Whitey," which stuck throughout Ford's career. He had a couple of other nicknames, too. Teammates Billy Martin and Mickey Mantle first called Ford "City Slicker" because he was born in New York City. Later the title was shortened to "Slick." (Ford used that nickname as the title of his recent autobiography.) After Ford became a clutch World Series winner for the Yankees, he was dubbed "The Chairman of the Board" for his ability to rule in pressure situations.

Ford started pitching in his senior year of high school when his coach ran short on hurlers. After high school, Ford played amateur baseball as a pitcher/first baseman. He attracted considerable attention from baseball scouts. The Boston Red Sox were the first team to try to snare Ford with a contract. Then the New York Giants became involved in the bidding war. Finally, the New York Yankees hooked Ford with a $7,000 signing bonus in 1946.

It was nearly a four-year wait before Ford made his first appearance in Yankee Stadium. In 1947, with Butler of the Mid-Atlantic League, Ford was 13-4. He advanced to Norfolk in 1948, leading the Piedmont League with 171 strikeouts while winning 16 games. In 1949 Ford played in Binghamton where he was 16-5 with a league-leading 1.61 ERA. Ford kept on winning with Kansas City in the American Association in 1950, going 6-3 in 12 appearances.

Ford finally joined the Yankees in mid-1950. After several relief outings, Ford finally broke into the starting rotation and posted an impressive 9-1 record with a 2.81 ERA. The 21-year-old lefty won the fourth and decisive game of the World Series against the Philadelphia Phillies, allowing just 7 hits and 2 runs in 8.2 innings. At the time, Ford was the youngest pitcher ever to win a World Series game.

His career was interrupted for two seasons when he was drafted for military duty in the early stages of the Korean War. When Ford returned to the Yankees in 1953, he produced a team-best 18-6 record. Team manager Casey Stengel began calling Ford his "banty rooster," for the gutsy determination he showed on the mound.

Ford led the American League with an 18-7 record and 18 complete games in 1955. His ERA was second in the league at 2.63, and his 254 innings pitched ranked second as well. Ford was yielding an average of 6.67 hits per nine innings, the third-best total in the junior circuit. During the month of September, Ford hurled back-to-back one-hitters against the Washington Senators and Kansas City Athletics. He was only the fifth pitcher in history to accomplish the feat. Although 1955 is remembered for the Brooklyn Dodgers' exciting World Series win over the Yanks, few people may remember that

Ford won both the opening game of the Series and the sixth game (with a four-hitter, allowing just 1 run).

In 1956 Ford won 19 games against just 6 losses and paced the league with a 2.47 ERA. In both the 1956 and 1957 World Series, Ford registered a win and a complete game. In 1958 Ford's ERA was a league-leading 2.01, the lowest in his career. Only five times in his 16-year career did his ERA exceed 3.00. His 7 shutouts were also highest in the league.

Ford's record dropped to 12-9 in 1960, but he was still first in the league with 4 shutouts. Ford increased his productivity in the World Series, throwing shutouts in the third and sixth games of the fall classic. His first 20-win season came in 1961 when Ford was baseball's Cy Young award winner with a league-leading 25-4 mark. In the World Series, Ford registered 2 more victories (one a shutout), helping the Yankees recover the world championship from the Cincinnati Reds.

He had his last great year in 1963, leading the league with a 24-7 record. In 1964 the Yankees made Ford a pitcher/coach. He retired after just seven games in 1967 due to arm problems.

Ford ended his career with a 236-106 record (with the second-best winning percentage in history). The New York City Slicker had 14 straight winning seasons during his career. His 10 wins and 94 strikeouts rank first in World Series history. Ford is the only pitcher in Yankee history to have had his uniform number retired. Perhaps his greatest thrill was getting elected into the Hall of Fame in 1974 along with Mantle, his best buddy.

CAREER HIGHLIGHTS
EDWARD CHARLES FORD

Born: October 21, 1928 New York, NY
Height: 5'10" **Weight:** 178 lbs. **Batted:** Left **Threw:** Left
Pitcher: New York Yankees, 1950, 1953-67.

★ Has the second-best winning percentage in baseball history
★ Was a 20-game winner twice
★ Pitched for 11 World Series teams, winning 10 games

★ Established eight career pitching records in World Series play
★ Led the league in victories three times
★ Won the A.L. Cy Young award in 1961

MAJOR LEAGUE TOTALS

G	IP	W	L	Pct.	SO	BB	ERA
498	3,171	236	106	.690	1,956	1,086	2.75

Whitey Ford's World Series performances rank among the best of any pitcher. Pitching in 11 Series, Ford started the most games (22), hurled the most innings (146), struck out the most batters (94), and won the most games (10).

GEORGE FOSTER

Once the highest-paid player in baseball (at more than $2 million a season), George Foster ended his 18-year major league career at the end of the 1986 season. Although his career numbers fell short of the milestones that would have earned him a plaque at Cooperstown, Foster will always be remembered by Cincinnati fans as an integral part of the "Big Red Machine" teams of the 1970s. Foster's 52 home runs in 1977 was the last time anyone has broken out of the 40s in that most impressive of baseball stats. By virtue of his constant threat to earn a home run title and his membership on winning teams, Foster will always be a star in the eyes of many fans.

Foster was plucked out of junior college in California by the San Francisco Giants in the third round of the 1968 free-agent draft. Following his second season of minor league ball, he got a September trial with San Francisco. In the nine-game trial, the robust slugger hit an even .400. In another nine-game audition with the Giants at the close of the 1970 season, he hit .316 and earned a spot on the opening day roster for 1971. However, there were three good reasons why Foster didn't earn a starting outfield berth, namely Ken Henderson, Bobby Bonds, and Willie Mays. His career was going nowhere until he got traded to the Cincinnati Reds.

On May 29, 1971, the Giants sent Foster to Cincinnati in exchange for Frank Duffy and Vern Geishert. Despite the two-for-one nature of the deal, historians have called this one of the most one-sided trades in baseball history. Foster wasn't an immediate success for Cincinnati, however. In 104 games he finished the year with a .234 average and a combined 13 homers and 58 RBI. The following season he hit just .200 with 2 homers and 12 RBI in 59 games. After only 17 games in 1973, Foster was demoted to the Reds Triple-A team, Indianapolis in the American Association. Finally in 1974, a rejuvenated Foster began to make his mark in the National League. That year Foster hit .264 with 7 homers and 41 RBI.

Foster's totals soared to 23 homers, 78 RBI, and a .300 average in 1975. The Reds won the National League Western Division and swept Pittsburgh in the three-game N.L. Championship Series. Foster batted .364 versus the Pirates, then had 8 hits in the World Series triumph against the Boston Red Sox. The Reds moved Pete Rose to

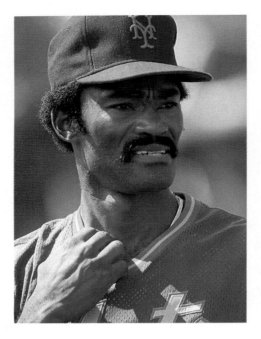

third base in order to keep Foster in the lineup full-time.

The Reds got an express ride back to the World Series in 1976, courtesy of Foster's incredible offense. He batted .306 with 29 homers (fourth in the league) and an N.L. best of 121 runs batted in. He also paced left fielders with a .994 fielding average. The Reds whipped the Phillies in the 1976 N.L. Championship Series and then swept the Yankees in the World Series, where the man who earned the nickname "The Destroyer" batted .429 with 4 RBI.

Foster's greatest season came in 1977. He led the league in homers (52), RBI (149), total bases (388), runs scored (124), and slugging percentage (.631). He set club records for homers, RBI, and total bases. Only nine players

before Foster had ever hit 50 or more homers in a season. That season Foster won the National League MVP award and his second Player of the Year honors from *The Sporting News*. In 1978 Foster encored his previous season by leading the senior circuit in homers and RBI for a second straight year with 40 dingers and 120 RBI.

The Alabama native (who had been a Little League opponent of Dave Kingman while growing up in California) continued to be a heavy hitter for the Reds. His homer totals include 30 in 1979, 25 in 1980, and 22 in 1981, along with 90-plus RBI each year. His seven-figure salary, his advancing age (33), and his imminent free-agent status were the primary reasons the Reds swapped Foster to the New York Mets for Alex Trevino, Jim Kern, and Greg Harris on February 10, 1982.

Foster was no longer the run-scoring machine of the 1970s that the Mets had wanted. Although he continued to draw an enormous salary, Foster's best season was a 28 homer, 90 RBI effort with the 1983 team. In 1984 Foster fueled the Mets' pennant hopes with 24 homers and 86 RBI. He hit 21 round-trippers with 77 RBI in 1985 but fell victim to the crop of rookies vying for playing time. The team released Foster after 72 games in August 1986. (Foster had complained to the press about his spotty playing time, which may have hastened his departure from The Big Apple.) After a two-week comeback attempt with the Chicago White Sox in which he hit .216 with 1 home run, Foster retired at age 37. Foster ended his career with a .274 lifetime batting average, 348 homers, and 1,239 RBI.

CAREER HIGHLIGHTS
GEORGE ARTHUR FOSTER

Born: December 1, 1948   Tuscaloosa, AL
Height: 6'1"   **Weight:** 180 lbs.   **Batted:** Right   **Threw:** Right
Outfielder: San Francisco Giants, 1969-71; Cincinnati Reds, 1971-81; New York Mets, 1982-86; Chicago White Sox, 1986.

- ★ Named *The Sporting News* Player of the Year in 1976 and 1977
- ★ Named N.L. MVP in 1977
- ★ Won three RBI titles
- ★ Named to *The Sporting News* Silver Slugger Team in 1981
- ★ Hit a career-high 52 homers in 1977
- ★ Played in three World Series

MAJOR LEAGUE TOTALS

G	AB	H	BA	2B	3B	HR	R	RBI	SB
1,977	7,023	1,925	.274	307	47	348	986	1,239	51

A member of Cincinnati's Big Red Machine in the 1970s, George Foster presented a menacing image at the plate with his black bat and scowling expression. Foster's best season occurred in 1977 when he led the N.L. with 52 homers, 149 RBI, and 124 runs scored.

RUBE FOSTER

As early as 1915, Negro League player-turned-manager Rube Foster was locking horns with organizers of white baseball, urging the integration of the sport, and meeting with resistance. White managers feared player walkouts, fan disapproval, and misbehavior on the part of black players, some of whom were infamous for giving their black managers short shrift.

Never mind that some black managers treated their players with little respect, earning disdain in return. And never mind the healthy attendance figures at Negro League games. Organized white baseball did not choose to look for the positive possibilities of integration. In 1920 Kenesaw Mountain Landis was named commissioner of baseball, and in the aftermath of the 1919 World Series gambling scandal, he was reluctant to stir up more disputes in the world of baseball.

Educated through the eighth grade, Foster was pitching for the Fort Worth Yellow Jackets by the age of 18. In 1902 he spent time with three teams (including the white semipro Otsego, Michigan, team), ending with E.B. Lamar's Philadelphia Cuban X-Giants.

Baseball fans and sports writers were prone to comparing notable black players to their white counterparts. Foster received his nickname because he often outpitched his contemporary, Rube Waddell. Foster pitched 4 of the X-Giants' 5 wins in the 1903 "Colored Championship of the World" against the Philadelphia Giants. In 1904 Foster was in the Series again, this time playing for the Philadelphia Giants, who beat their opponents of the year before. Foster notched 2 wins, whiffing 18 in one confrontation and hurling a two-hitter the next.

A salary dispute took him back to Chicago, where he persuaded Frank Leland to attempt a talent raid on the Philadelphia Giants. Although he was not officially dubbed team manager until 1910, some historians believe Foster began running the team as early as 1908, urging and obtaining membership in the Chicago league, and finishing with a record of 108-18. One year later, Foster put the team into the Park Owners Association, playing in the finest Negro League park in the nation. (It seated 4,400.) In 1909 the Leland Giants played the Chicago Cubs. In 1910 the Giants record under Foster was 123-6.

In 1911 Foster teamed with John Schorling (the son-in-law of Charles

Comiskey) to form his own team, using all the players from Leland's Giants. Schorling leased the old White Sox grounds, and Foster provided the Chicago American Giants. With a handshake, the two agreed to split the profits.

As was his practice, Foster put most of his cut back into the team. Players traveled by private Pullman coach and received more than a living wage. As a result, the Chicago American Giants were the best in the Negro League from 1910 to 1915 and continued their dominance through the early 1920s.

By 1919 Foster had accepted that he might not see integration in his lifetime, and so he began lobbying for a Negro National League patterned after the white major leagues. He wanted all Negro Leaguers to have good pay and self-respect so they would "be ready when the time comes."

He called a 1920 meeting for selected team owners of six Negro League clubs. Upon his election as temporary president, Foster produced a list of rules and bylaws he had compiled, setting the stage for the firm hand he would employ in the next decade.

He set to work acquiring parks, employed a system of bonuses and incentives for players, and created rules discouraging player raids. All the while, he kept managing the Giants to victories.

In 1926 Foster suffered a nervous breakdown and was institutionalized until his death in 1930. Thousands showed up to mourn the manager who had often shared his own pocket money with his players. Ironically, Foster—the man who had fought for good wages and had worked to make his team the best-paid Negro Leaguers (from $2,000 to $5,000 a year)—left his wife and children wanting because he had no written contract from the Negro National League for his life's work. The Negro National League outlived him by only two years.

Foster was elected to the Baseball Hall of Fame in 1981, in recognition of his determination against all odds to develop black baseball players .

In 1920 Rube Foster (one of the greatest pitchers at the turn of the century) created the Negro National League. The N.N.L. broke the stranglehold that a small cabal of white promoters had on black ball, allowing blacks to profit from the game.

CAREER HIGHLIGHTS
ANDREW FOSTER

Born: September 17, 1879   Calvert, TX   **Died:** December 9, 1930
Height: 6'4"   **Threw:** Right
Pitcher: Fort Worth Yellow Jackets, 1897-1902; Chicago Union Giants, 1902; Cuban X-Giants, 1902-04; Philadelphia Giants, 1904-07; Frank Leland's Chicago Giants, 1907-10; Chicago American Giants, 1910-15. Manager: Chicago American Giants, 1910-26.

* Managed the Chicago American Giants to many league titles
* Created the Negro National League
* Won four Colored Championship Series games as a pitcher in 1903
* Elected to the Hall of Fame in 1981

NEGRO LEAGUE TOTALS
(no accurate statistics available)

NELLIE FOX

Second baseman Nellie Fox was not a large man, but he was one of the most durable infielders and scrappiest hitters in baseball during the 1950s. He made such a big contribution to the Chicago White Sox that they retired his uniform number.

Fox was discovered by Philadelphia Athletics manager Connie Mack in 1944. The 16-year-old Fox played with Lancaster, Pennsylvania, in 1944 as a first baseman/outfielder. He finished the season with Jamestown of the Pony League, where he hit .304 with 18 RBI. Back with Lancaster in 1945, Fox was shifted to second base. He led the league with 426 putouts, 400 assists, and a .972 fielding percentage. At bat he led the league in at-bats, hits, and triples. Fox was carried on the Philadelphia roster in 1946, but he missed the entire season due to military service. In 1947 Fox remained with Lancaster, getting to participate in only seven late-season games in Philadelphia. Fox was banished to the Western League in 1948, where he led the league in hits and batted .311. In the field Fox was first in putouts and assists. Philadelphia used Fox in just three games that year. Fox stuck with Philadelphia through 1949.

His big break came on October 19, 1949, when the Chicago White Sox traded catcher Joe Tipton for Fox. Philadelphia got little benefit out of the deal: Tipton served as a second-string catcher for two and a half years before getting traded to the Cleveland Indians. Fox, meanwhile, became a fixture at second base for the White Sox for the next 14 seasons.

The Pennsylvania native quickly adjusted to his new responsibilities in Chicago. In 1951 Fox had 189 hits (only 2 hits under league leader George Kell). His .313 average was fifth in the league. Defensively he was first in the league with 6 chances accepted per game. The fiery second sacker represented the White Sox as an All-Star game starter. In 1952, Fox was the league hit leader with 192 and was second with 10 triples. Fox was the best among A.L. second basemen in putouts (406), assists (433), and fielding percentage (.985).

Fox returned to the All-Star game in 1953, earning his way there with a season of 3 homers, 72 RBI, and a .285 average. He also led second basemen in putouts and chances per game. Fox upped his batting average to .319 in 1954. Fox and Detroit Tiger Harvey

Kuenn shared the A.L. hit lead with 201. Fox had the third-highest league batting average, tying with New York's Irv Noren. In the 1954 All-Star game, Fox won the game for the American League with a two-run single in the eighth. The junior circuit won 11-9 in the highest-scoring All-Star game in history. On August 7, 1954, Fox began a streak of 798 consecutive games that continued through September 3, 1960—the longest streak ever compiled by a second baseman.

In 1955 the little ironman led the league with 636 at-bats and batted .311 with a career-high 6 homers and 59 RBI. His 198 hits were only 2 behind league leader Al Kaline. Fox was first among A.L. fielders in putouts, assists, and chances per game. His average slipped to .296 in 1956. But even if Fox slumped at the plate, the White Sox could count on their second base-

man to be among the finest fielders in the league.

Fox staged a minor comeback in 1957. He was the league's hit leader with 196, and he batted .317, fifth highest in the league. His 110 runs scored trailed only league leader Mickey Mantle. With Fox's aid, the White Sox finished at 90-64, only eight games behind the league champion New York Yankees. Fox was tops in four defensive categories in 1957, including double plays. Teamed with 5-foot-9 shortstop Luis Aparicio, Fox was part of the shortest but most effective keystone combination of the decade.

Fox had a hand in 117 double plays in 1958, tops for A.L. second basemen. He also topped .300 for the fourth time in his career. Again Fox and his teammates were second behind the Yankees.

In 1959 Chicago was nicknamed the "Go-Go White Sox." The team earned the sobriquet by stealing a league-leading 113 bases. Although Fox swiped just 5 bases, he won American League Most Valuable Player honors with one of his best overall seasons ever. He was fourth in batting (.306) and second in doubles (34) and hits (191). Fox drove in 70 runs, second highest on the White Sox. Although the Los Angeles Dodgers downed the White Sox in six World Series games, Fox batted .375 in the Series with 9 hits and 4 runs scored.

Fox's last full season was as the Houston Astros second baseman in 1964. After 21 games in 1965, Fox retired and served as a team coach in 1966 and 1967. His 2,663 hits rank 45th highest in history. Despite his achievements, Fox has been overlooked for Hall of Fame membership for almost two decades.

CAREER HIGHLIGHTS
JACOB NELSON FOX

Born: December 25, 1927 St. Thomas, PA **Died:** December 1, 1975
Height: 5'10" **Weight:** 160 lbs. **Batted:** Left **Threw:** Right
Second baseman: Philadelphia Athletics, 1947-49; Chicago White Sox, 1950-63; Houston Astros, 1964-65.

- ★ Never struck out more than 18 times in one season
- ★ Was named A.L. MVP in 1959
- ★ Led the A.L. in hits four times
- ★ Hit .375 in the 1959 World Series
- ★ Won three Gold Gloves
- ★ Played in 798 straight games

MAJOR LEAGUE TOTALS

G	AB	H	BA	2B	3B	HR	R	RBI	SB
2,367	9,232	2,663	.288	355	112	35	1,279	790	76

A member of the 1959 "Go-Go" White Sox, second baseman Nellie Fox was instrumental in that team's pennant win. Though not a premier hitter early on, Fox learned to bang out short drives to lead the A.L. in singles for seven years and in hits for four years.

JIMMIE FOXX

In an era of great sluggers, Jimmie Foxx was the greatest of them all. He hit his first major league home run in 1927—the same year that Babe Ruth hit 60—and retired two decades later with 534. It was a career record that no righthand slugger could match until Willie Mays did it in 1967. In 1932 Foxx launched a career-high 58 round-trippers, along with 169 RBI, and won his first of two successive MVP awards.

Foxx was molded into a big leaguer by Frank "Home Run" Baker, a star of the old Philadelphia Athletics "$100,000 Infield." Baker, who once held the league home run record with 12 in a season, quickly recognized Foxx's abilities. Foxx, who had initially concentrated on being a track star in high school in Maryland, was spotted by Baker pitching both in high school and semipro games. His first pro contract was with Easton, Maryland, an Eastern Shore League franchise. Foxx batted .296 with 10 homers in 76 games and was impressive enough to earn a shot with Connie Mack's Philadelphia A's in 1925. (Foxx had been with Philadelphia in late 1924, but Mack had kept the strapping youngster on the bench.) Foxx got only nine pinch-hitting at-bats with Philadelphia in 1925 but connected six times, assembling a .667 batting average.

Foxx, nicknamed "Double X" for the unique spelling of his last name, spent the rest of the 1925 season with Providence, Rhode Island, of the International League. At Providence, Foxx hit .327 in 41 games. Manager Mack still refused to give Foxx an immediate berth in the starting lineup. In 1926 Foxx appeared in 26 games, hitting .313. Aside from more pinch-hitting duties, Foxx also caught 12 games. Due to the presence of the legendary Mickey Cochrane behind the plate, Foxx had little hope of winning a position there.

In 1927 Mack shifted Foxx to first base, where he appeared in 32 contests. In a total of 61 games, Foxx batted .323 and was 7-for-20 as a pinch hitter. Foxx's first full season came in 1928. He batted .328 with 13 homers and 79 RBI. That season Foxx played primarily at third base. He couldn't seem to land a position in the field, but his bat was too potent to keep out of the lineup. Finally in 1929 Foxx became the A's starting first baseman, beating Joe Hauser out of a job.

Foxx made the most of his starting opportunity, hitting .354 (fourth in the

league) with 33 homers and 117 RBI. Foxx handled himself well in the field too, making just 6 errors at first base for a .995 fielding percentage. In the 1929 World Series, the Athletics clubbed the Cubs in five games. Foxx batted .350 in the Series, including a crucial home run in each of the first two games to help the A's roar out to a two-game Series lead. In 1930 Foxx contributed 37 homers, 156 RBI, and a .335 average to Philadelphia's second straight title. The Athletics defeated the St. Louis Cardinals in a six-game World Series. Foxx batted .333 in the affair and won the fifth game with a two-run homer.

In 1931 the A's won their third straight pennant but lost to the Cardinals in the World Series. Foxx's offensive totals dropped but remained admirable at 30 homers and 120 RBI. Foxx's greatest season came in 1932,

when he batted .364 with 58 homers and 169 RBI, both American League highs. The good-natured slugger wielded an astounding .749 slugging percentage to lead the league. He scored a league-leading 151 runs and had a total of 100 extra-base hits. Foxx followed up his success with another mammoth offensive show in 1933. The man nicknamed "The Beast" earned the league's triple crown with a .356 batting average, 48 homers, and 163 RBI. Again Foxx's slugging percentage was a league best at .703.

In 1934 he hit 44 homers and 111 RBI, batting .334. In 1935 Foxx won his third homer crown with 36 dingers. His slugging percentage (.636) was another American League high.

In 1935 Mack still hadn't recovered from Depression-era losses, and so he started selling off high-salaried A's players to make ends meet. He shipped Foxx and Johnny Marcum off to the Boston Red Sox in exchange for Gordon Rhodes, George Savino, and $150,000 on December 10, 1935. The trade gave new life to Foxx's 11-year career. "The Green Monster," Fenway Park's short left field wall, made homer-hitting a joy for Foxx. He began his stay with the BoSox in 1936, hitting 41 homers and 143 RBI for a .338 average. After 36 homers and 127 RBI in 1937, Foxx gave Red Sox fans more thrills in 1938. He won the league batting title with a .349 mark, drove in a career-best 175 runs to lead the league, and hit 50 homers.

In 1940 Foxx's homers declined to 36 and his RBI total to 119. Foxx ended his career in 1945 with the Philadelphia Phillies, where he even pitched in nine games.

CAREER HIGHLIGHTS
JAMES EMORY FOXX

Born: October 22, 1907 Sudlersville, MD **Died:** July 21, 1967
Height: 6'0" **Weight:** 195 lbs. **Batted:** Right **Threw:** Right
First baseman: Philadelphia Athletics, 1925-35; Boston Red Sox, 1936-42; Chicago Cubs, 1942, 1944; Philadelphia Phillies, 1945.

★ Has the fourth-highest slugging percentage in history
★ Hit 40 or more homers for five seasons
★ Led the league in homers four times
★ Named A.L. MVP in 1932, 1933, and 1938
★ Played in 18 World Series games
★ Elected to the Hall of Fame in 1951

MAJOR LEAGUE TOTALS

G	AB	H	BA	2B	3B	HR	R	RBI	SB
2,317	8,134	2,646	.325	458	125	534	1,751	1,922	87

With 534 home runs to his credit, Jimmie Foxx ranks as one of the greatest long-ball threats in baseball history. Foxx, who often ripped the sleeves off his shirts to expose his bulging biceps, hit 40 or more homers in five seasons.

FRANKIE FRISCH

Hall of Famer Frank Frisch graduated from Fordham University and burst onto the big league scene as a hustling, switch-hitting infielder who would personify the spirit of the St. Louis Cardinals great "Gashouse Gang" teams. Bypassing the minors, "The Fordham Flash" began his pro career with John McGraw's New York Giants in 1919. When the Giants starting second baseman was injured, Frisch was an instant hit as a substitute infielder. Whether at second base, shortstop, or third, Frisch was always a vital presence in New York's starting lineup.

Frisch played his first full season (110 games) with the Giants in 1920. He served as the starting third baseman, hitting .280 with 4 homers, 77 RBI, and 34 stolen bases. "There's nothing tough about playing third," he said about his new position. "All you need is a strong arm and a strong chest." In 1921 Frisch divided his time between third base and second, batting .341 with 8 homers, 100 RBI, and a league-leading 49 stolen bases. In the 1921 World Series, the Giants took five out of eight games from the New York Yankees. Frisch hit .300 for the Series and had 4 hits in the opener against submariner Carl Mays. The 1922 Giants successfully defended their world championship against the Yankees. Frisch hit .327 in the regular season, then batted .471 in the Series.

Frisch's 223 hits led the National League in 1923. He batted .348, which ranked fourth in the league. Frisch hit 12 homers and 111 RBI. He led Giants regulars with a .400 average in the 1923 World Series.

The speedy infielder continued his offensive exploits in 1924, topping the league with 121 runs scored. Frisch batted .328 during the regular season and .333 in the World Series. In 1925 the Giants' streak of four consecutive pennants snapped. One of the few bright spots on the team was Frisch, who batted .331 with 11 home runs. The Giants continued their downward spiral in the National League standings in 1926. The team wound up with a 74-77 record. McGraw, one of the most combative managers in history, blamed Frisch for part of the team's decline. Frisch, however, batted .314 that season. In spite of his average, the Giants traded Frisch and pitcher Jimmy Ring to the St. Louis Cardinals for second baseman Rogers Hornsby. St. Louis had just beaten the Yankees in the 1926 World Series with Hornsby as manager.

Naturally, St. Louis fans were irate over the trade. Replacing the "Mighty Rajah" in the Cardinals lineup was a challenge, but Frisch did it. He batted .337 with 10 home runs, 78 RBI, 112 runs scored, and a league-best 48 stolen bases. In the field, Frisch was first in fielding percentage, assists, and chances accepted (which set a new record at the time). Frisch set a Cardinals team record in 1927 that may never be broken: In 617 at-bats, he struck out just 10 times. The Cardinals, meanwhile, became instant contenders in the National League. In 1928 Frisch batted .300, leading the Cardinals to the World Series.

Frisch pumped his average up to .334 in 1929. The Cardinals rebounded from their fourth-place 1929 finish to a first-place effort in 1930. Frisch hit .346, his highest average ever. Other personal bests that season included 121 runs scored and 114 RBI. In 1931 Frisch hit .311 with a league-leading 28

stolen bases. This was the third stolen base title Frisch earned and the 11th time he had stolen 20 or more bases. The Cardinals, meanwhile, won a team record 101 games and won the World Series in 7 games. Frisch, who had 7 hits in the World Series, was named the National League Most Valuable Player for his efforts.

In 1932 the Cardinals slid to sixth place. Frisch suffered too, hitting .292 (the first time in 12 seasons that he batted under .300). Manager Gabby Street's problems continued in 1933, and the Cardinals front office appointed Frisch as player/manager on July 24. He finished the season at .303.

In his first full season as a big league skipper, Frisch piloted the 1934 Cardinals to a world championship, directing Dizzy and Daffy Dean to their incredible combined 49 victories. The team won the National League pennant on the final day of the season, posting a 95-58 season total. The high-spirited Gashouse Gang went on to defeat the Detroit Tigers in a seven-game World Series. Frisch had six hits in the 1934 Series victory. As he devoted more time to managing, Frisch's on-the-field performance slipped a bit. He batted .294 in 103 games in 1935, then hit .274 in 93 games in 1936. Frisch ended his playing career after 17 games in 1937.

For his aggressive brand of play and on field leadership, Frisch was touted early-on as prime managerial material. The New York Giants, before they tabbed Bill Terry as successor to manager McGraw, unsuccessfully attempted to reobtain Frisch via trade with the Cardinals. Frisch went on to manage the Pittsburgh Pirates from 1940-46 and the Cubs in 1949-51.

CAREER HIGHLIGHTS
FRANK FRANCIS FRISCH

Born: September 9, 1898 Bronx, NY **Died:** March 12, 1973
Height: 5'11" **Weight:** 165 lbs. **Batted:** Both **Threw:** Right
Infielder: New York Giants, 1919-26; St. Louis Cardinals, 1927-37. Manager: St. Louis Cardinals, 1933-38; Pittsburgh Pirates, 1940-46; Chicago Cubs, 1949-51.

★ Batted over .300 for 11 straight seasons ★ Selected as N.L. MVP in 1931
★ Topped the N.L. in hits in 1923 ★ Captured three stolen base titles
★ Played in eight World Series ★ Elected to the Hall of Fame in 1947

MAJOR LEAGUE TOTALS

G	AB	H	BA	2B	3B	HR	R	RBI	SB
2,311	9,112	2,880	.316	466	138	105	1,532	1,244	419

Hard-hitting Frankie Frisch was a major factor in the New York Giants' four consecutive pennant wins from 1921-1924. Frisch hit over .300 in 13 seasons, racked up over 100 RBI in three seasons, and scored over 100 runs seven times.

CARL FURILLO

One of the most vital but most over-looked members of those hard-hitting Brooklyn Dodgers teams had to be outfielder Carl Furillo. Playing on the same team with such personalities as Jackie Robinson, Pee Wee Reese, Duke Snider, and Roy Campanella tended to overshadow the many accomplishments the dependable outfielder compiled for 13 full seasons.

Furillo got his first big league experience at age 24. He played in 117 games for the Brooklyn Dodgers, hitting .284 with 3 homers and 35 RBI. The following season Furillo batted .295 with 8 homers and 88 RBI. He batted .353 with 3 RBI in the 1947 World Series, but the Yankees downed the Dodgers in seven games. In 1948 Furillo batted .297.

The Pennsylvania native was nicknamed "The Reading Rifle" for his awesome throwing arm. He mastered the numerous caroms that balls hit off the rightfield wall (or scoreboard) in Brooklyn's Ebbets Field would take. The strong-armed outfielder racked up 10 or more assists in 10 different seasons. Twice he was the league leader in assists (18 in 1950 and 24 in 1951). Teammates referred to Furillo as "Skoonj."

The 1949 season saw Furillo bloom into a serious offensive threat in the National League. He batted .322 with 18 homers and 106 RBI. The Dodgers right fielder suffered a concussion when he was beaned in the head by New York Giants pitcher Sheldon Jones. According to Furillo, the beaning was ordered by Giants manager Leo Durocher (who battled with Furillo when managing in Brooklyn). Again in 1949 Furillo and the Dodgers were World Series victims of the New York Yankees. In 1950 Furillo's average dipped to .305, but his power totals stayed at 18 homers and 106 RBI. His totals were all for naught, as the Phillies won the pennant away from the Dodgers on the last day of the season.

The Reading Rifle shot down 24 baserunners from his right field post in 1951, a career high for Furillo. Unfortunately there are no statistics to tell how many times Furillo's arm stopped opposing runners from attempting extra bases on hits. In 1951 Furillo hit 16 homers, 91 RBI, and a .295 average and led the National League with 667 at-bats. Both Gil Hodges and Furillo played in 158 games that season, a club record.

Furillo suffered through a minor

slump in 1952, and his average fell to .247. However, he earned his first spot on a National League All-Star roster. In 1953 Furillo's average skyrocketed 97 points and he won his first batting championship. His .344 average was the highest award-winning Dodger total since Lefty O'Doul hit .368 in 1932. Besides his average, Furillo tallied 21 homers and 92 RBI.

That year Furillo was hit in the hand by a pitch by Giants hurler Ruben Gomez. After his earlier beaning incident, Furillo had vowed to get even if he ever got hit again by New York. He charged the New York Giants bench after being hit, a brawl ensued, and Furillo got his hand broken when he was kicked by a Giants player. Skoonj recovered in time for the World Series, batting .333 with 8 hits.

The Dodgers finally beat the Yankees in the 1955 World Series. Furillo tied Reese and Snider for the club lead of 8 Series hits (batting .296). During the regular season Furillo had a .314 average with 26 homers and 95 RBI.

Furillo ended his career on a sour note. The Dodgers released the veteran outfielder after just eight games in 1960. With outfielder Frank Howard becoming a full-timer, Furillo didn't seem necessary any more. Because Furillo was released while nursing a leg injury, the team claimed that he wasn't entitled to his full salary. Immediately, Furillo filed a lawsuit against the team to recover the rest of his money. He won the lawsuit, but his aggressiveness ruined his chances of getting any kind of baseball-related job for a while. In later years he was an instructor at the Dodger adult fantasy camps in Vero Beach, Florida.

Furillo died of natural causes at age 66. His lifetime batting average was .299, and he hit 192 home runs and drove in 1,058 runs. He still ranks in the top ten in nine different Dodgers offensive categories today.

Steady Carl Furillo ranks in the top ten in nine different Dodger offensive categories, yet his role on that team and his accomplishments are often overshadowed by those of such legendary Dodgers as Jackie Robinson, Duke Snider, and Roy Campanella. Furillo played with the Dodgers his entire career.

CAREER HIGHLIGHTS
CARL ANTHONY FURILLO

Born: March 8, 1922   Stony Creek Mills, PA   **Died:** January 21, 1989
Height: 6'0"   **Weight:** 190 lbs.   **Batted:** Right   **Threw:** Right
Outfielder: Brooklyn Dodgers, 1946-57; Los Angeles Dodgers, 1958-60.

★ Led the league with a .344 batting mark in 1953

★ Batted over .300 five times

★ Tied for first in World Series history with 3 pinch hits

★ Played for seven World Series teams

★ Selected for two All-Star teams

MAJOR LEAGUE TOTALS

G	AB	H	BA	2B	3B	HR	R	RBI	SB
1,806	6,378	1,910	.299	324	56	192	895	1,058	48

GARY GAETTI

Gary Gaetti, an eight-year veteran third baseman with the Minnesota Twins, had both his biggest success and his biggest challenge before the 1989 season. His past performances have been rewarded by a large salary (estimated at $2.4 million for 1989 alone), and the media claimed that Gaetti was indeed one of the highest paid players in 1989. Quite an accomplishment for a player who began his career in the Twins minor league farm system in 1979. However, Gaetti's super salary could be a super headache. If Gaetti doesn't live up to the potential represented by that salary, he'll get considerable heat from both sportswriters and fans.

If fans want to judge Gaetti's financial worthiness, they should look at his finest seasons. He was a spark plug of the 1987 Minnesota Twins, who quietly crept to their first world championship since the team arrived in Minneapolis in 1961. Gaetti batted .257 with 31 homers and career highs of 109 RBI and 95 runs scored. He also led American League third basemen in games played. In the field Gaetti set a club record by playing 47 consecutive errorless games at third base. He tied for the league lead in putouts (with 134) as he won his second straight Gold Glove.

When the Twins won the Western Division, Gaetti was raring to go in the League Championship Series against the Detroit Tigers. He set a major league record when he became the first player in history to hit home runs in his first two postseason at-bats. His 2 homers led the Twins to an opening-game win by an 8-5 margin. In the five-game series Gaetti batted .300 with 6 hits, 1 double, 2 homers, and 5 RBI. Additionally, he tied for the team lead in runs scored with 5. Gaetti won the Lee MacPhail award as Most Valuable Player in the Championship Series. Gaetti was also a prime contributor in Minnesota's seven-game World Series win over the St. Louis Cardinals. He batted .259 with 7 hits (3 singles, 2 doubles, 1 triple, and 1 home run), with 4 RBI and 4 runs scored. Gaetti's big hit was a second-inning home run in game two off Cardinals starter Danny Cox.

Gaetti won his first Gold Glove during the 1986 season. That year he was tops among junior circuit third basemen in games played (156), assists (334), total chances (473), and double plays (36). At the plate Gaetti fared even better. He clobbered a personal best of 34 home runs and 171 total hits in 1986, complemented by 108 RBI and a .287 average. Gaetti, not noted for outstanding speed, even stole a career-high 14 bases. The Twins third baseman hit his 100th career homer off Milwaukee's Chris Bosio on August 28. In June he tied a club record by doubling three times in one game.

Anyone who closely followed Gaetti's gradual climb to excellence in the minors might have predicted that he'd duplicate it in the majors. Gaetti had been drafted by both the St. Louis Cardinals and the Chicago White Sox in 1978, before finally agreeing to sign with the Twins as a first-round choice in the secondary phase of the free-agent draft of June 1979. Gaetti's first pro season was spent at Elizabethton, where he hit 14 homers, 42 RBI, and a .257 average in 66 games. Gaetti was promoted to Wisconsin Rapids in 1980. There in his first full pro season he logged 22 homers, 82 RBI, 24 stolen bases, and a .266 average. He led the Midwest League in home runs as well as three defensive categories (not including a league-best 137 games played). Gaetti's final minor league season came with Orlando in 1981. There he smashed 30 homers, 93 RBI, and a .277 average. He continued to shine defensively as well, leading Southern League third basemen in three departments.

Gaetti's major league debut was record-setting. In his first at-bat with the Twins on September 20, 1981, he became the 47th player in history to homer in his first plate appearance, setting his mark against Texas hurler Charlie Hough.

Since then Gaetti has been a defensive stalwart and consistent power source for the Twins. In 1988 his 28 homers marked the sixth year he's exceeded 20 four-baggers a season. He also tied Eddie Murray for the fourth-highest total in the league. Although he missed more than 30 games after tearing cartilage in his knee in August while sliding, he still batted a career-high .301 with 88 RBI.

Gaetti's contract runs through 1990. Because the Illinois native is a clutch performer, expect a controversy to heat up when salary negotiation time nears.

During the Minnesota Twins' 1987 world championship season, Gary Gaetti batted .257 with 31 homers and had career highs of 109 RBI and 95 runs scored. Gaetti set a club record by playing 47 consecutive errorless games at third base.

CAREER HIGHLIGHTS
GARY JOSEPH GAETTI

Born: August 19, 1958   Centralia, IL
Height: 6'0"   **Weight:** 180 lbs.   **Bats:** Right   **Throws:** Right
Third baseman: Minnesota Twins, 1982-89.

- ★ Hit 20 or more homers in six seasons going into 1989
- ★ Batted a career-high .301 in 1988
- ★ Had 7 hits and 4 RBI in the 1987 World Series
- ★ Named MVP of the 1987 A.L. Championship Series
- ★ Drove in 100-plus runs twice
- ★ Played in the 1988 All-Star game

MAJOR LEAGUE TOTALS

G	AB	H	BA	2B	3B	HR	R	RBI	SB
1,207	4,412	1,144	.259	225	20	185	585	673	68

201

PUD GALVIN

James "Pud" Galvin had to overcome many obstacles to become one of the greatest pitchers of the 19th century. Prior to 1876, baseball rules stated that pitchers could not throw overhand. Until 1888, batters received four strikes before being called out, and hitters were allowed to use any size bat until 1893. Opposing batters were even given the opportunity to request a high or low pitch.

Galvin also had to contend with a shorter distance between home plate and the pitching rubber—just 50 feet. The distance wasn't expanded to its present 60 feet and 6 inches until 1893. Batters having problems with Galvin or any other accomplished pitcher of the day simply had to bunt again and again. Through 1893, foul bunts did not count as strikes.

Galvin succeeded all those years through talent and wits. He began playing in the National Association in 1875. The following year he pitched two no-hitters for his semipro St. Louis team, including one perfect game. The 5-foot-8, 190-pound hurler joined the minor league Buffalo Bisons in 1878. He pitched in all but 10 of the team's 116 games, winning 72 of them. He threw 96 complete games that year.

When the Bisons officially joined the National League in 1879, Galvin got his first widespread recognition. He pitched an incredible 66 complete games and won 37 of them. He supposedly got the nickname "Pud" from sportswriters who said he made pudding out of opposing batters. Some baseball historians, however, suggest that the nickname derived from his portly frame. His weight was always a problem, and he once ballooned from 190 to 320 pounds. When he ran, he jiggled like a bowl of pudding. Players called him "The Little Steam Engine" for his lethal fastball and "Gentle Jeems" for his pleasant personality.

In 1880 Galvin suffered the first of only five losing seasons during his 14-year career. He won 20 games, but lost 37 in 58 appearances. Galvin rebounded with 29 wins in 1881 and 28 in 1882. He then compiled two straight 46-win seasons in 1883 and 1884. After spending late 1885 and 1886 in the American Association with the Pittsburgh Alleghenies, Galvin's club was accepted into the prestigious National League in 1887. The portly righthander won 28 games in 1887, then 23 games in each of the next two seasons.

Galvin and most of his teammates jumped to the Players' (Brotherhood) League in 1890. The league folded after just one season over a dispute regarding low salaries, and Galvin was welcomed back to his old club in 1891. Shortly after that the team was accused of trying to "pirate" away a player from the Philadelphia club. Hence, the team gained its dubious nickname.

The enormous strain of constant pitching caught up with Galvin after his return to the Pirates. He pitched in "only" 33 games in 1891, going 14-13. The next year he pitched just 12 games with Pittsburgh. He tried for a comeback with St. Louis late in the 1892 season but went 5-7. With his playing career ended, Galvin briefly umpired in the National League. Later he opened a saloon in Pittsburgh—a vocation that seemed well suited to his gentle, easy-going personality. Despite the popularity of the establishment, he went broke. Less than ten years after his retirement, Galvin died at age 46.

Galvin finished his career with 361 wins and 307 losses. His wins are sixth highest in baseball history; his losses are second highest. In terms of career innings pitched (5,941) and complete games (639), only the legendary Cy Young had more. Galvin's 56 shutouts give him the eleventh-best all-time total. He struck out 1,799 and walked 744. Galvin walked almost no one when he was pitching. He averaged only 1.13 walks per 9 innings. He also had an effective pick-off move for his day. He once nailed three baserunners in one inning.

A slick fielder, Galvin often served as a replacement in the outfield when he wasn't pitching. In 51 games in the outfield and two at shortstop, Galvin compiled a lifetime .202 batting average with 135 RBI.

In 1965, some 63 years after his death, Galvin was elected to the Baseball Hall of Fame.

One of the hardest-working pitchers in baseball history, Pud Galvin pitched 656 innings in 1883, 636 in 1884, 593 in 1879, and over 400 in six other seasons. In the 19th century most teams carried only two pitchers, who alternated playing days. Despite this, Pud still pitched more than his share.

CAREER HIGHLIGHTS
JAMES FRANCIS GALVIN

Born: December 25, 1856 St. Louis, MO **Died:** March 7, 1902
Height: 5'8" **Weight:** 190 lbs. **Batted:** Right **Threw:** Right
Pitcher: St. Louis Maroons, 1875; Buffalo Bisons, 1878-85; Pittsburgh (American Association), 1885-86; Pittsburgh Alleghenys/Pirates, 1887-89, 1891-92; Pittsburgh (Players' League), 1890; St. Louis Browns, 1892.

★ Won 46 games in two different seasons ★ Won 37 games in his first N.L. season
★ Won 20 games three times ★ Elected to the Hall of Fame in 1965
★ Led the league with 72 games pitched in 1883

MAJOR LEAGUE TOTALS

G	IP	W	L	Pct.	SO	BB	ERA
697	5,941	361	307	.540	1,799	744	2.87

GENE GARBER

Like many veteran pitchers, Gene Garber has had a well-traveled major league career. He has twice been sold or traded in midseason to a team in need of relief pitching, and he has hopped from the majors to minors four times in his 24-year pro career.

In 1975, after a decade of professional ball, Garber tied the major league record for the most consecutive games won by a relief pitcher. His series of 3 straight wins took place May 15, 16, and 17 of 1975, the·same year Garber led the National League in relief games finished with 47.

Most memorable about Garber's career was his delivery. His motion was particularly devastating to rookies who hadn't studied his unorthodox pitching stance. Beginning his windup with his back to the plate, Garber would uncork fast sinkers that would tempt batters beyond restraint and change-ups that were as perplexing as a Houdini escape. His slow curve and sweeping slider were two other weapons he employed in a battle of wits. Variety, not overpowering speed, was Garber's ticket to success. His long, unusual windup didn't do much to hold runners on base, but it provided a spectacle that hadn't been seen since the days of Luis Tiant's herky-jerky pitching style.

Garber's lifetime stats have suffered because of the late start he got in the major leagues. The Pennsylvania native made 14 relief appearances with the Pittsburgh Pirates in 1970 at the age of 23, but he endured an 0-3 record. He floundered in the minor leagues for two more seasons before getting rescued by the Kansas City Royals. On October 25, 1972, the Royals traded Jim Rooker to the Pirates in exchange for Garber. The trade was an immediate boon to the Pirates, who moved Rooker into the starting rotation. The Royals attempted to make Garber a starter. He started 8 times and logged 4 complete games. This would be the only time in his lengthy career that he'd be used in a role besides reliever. Garber finished the season at 9-9. Finally, in his fourth year in the major leagues, he had achieved his first win.

The 1975 Phillies gave Garber his first shot at stardom. That year he topped the National League with 71 appearances. He tied Tug McGraw for the team lead in saves with 14. In 1976 Garber tallied a 9-3 mark with 11 saves. The Phillies won their first pennant since 1950 but got swept in the N.L. Championship Series by the Cincinnati Reds. In 1977 the Phillies defended their division title. Garber led the team with 64 appearances and 19 saves. He gained a win in the opening game of the Championship Series against the Dodgers, but Los Angeles won the final three games.

A low came in 1979 when Garber, newly acquired by the Braves after a five-year stint with the Philadelphia Phillies, established a major league record for the most games lost by a relief pitcher, with 16 debits that season. The Braves had given up successful starting pitcher Dick Ruthven to get Garber from the Phils on June 15, 1978.

Atlanta stood by Garber for seven more seasons and through two lengthy injuries in 1981 and 1983. In 1982 Garber rewarded the faith of Atlanta followers by saving 30 games. The Braves won the National League Western Division. In the National League Championship Series, the St. Louis Cardinals shelled Garber in two appear-ances. He was 0-1 with an 8.10 ERA.

Garber rejoined the Royals in 1987. His career came to a dramatic halt in 1988 when he was released by Kansas City. The Royals had both award-winning bullpen ace Dan Quisenberry and veteran Garber in the pen. Ironically, both men looked similar on the mound, with Quisenberry's submarine motion comparable to Garber's low, sidewinding delivery. Batters would seem to be seeing double, as Garber would sometimes serve as a set-up man while "Quiz" would work as a stopper. Neither man had great success and both got their releases.

Garber's lifetime stats include 931 appearances and 96 victories. Adding his 218 saves, Garber had a hand in 314 team victories in his career. Garber earned double-digit totals in saves ten times, and four times he reached 24 or more saves in a season. Pitching for several mediocre teams not only kept Garber from participating in a World Series, but it also denied him dozens of save opportunities. After all, bullpen aces normally don't get used in one-sided, losing affairs. Although Garber's pitching career was over after his 1988 release from the Royals, his lifetime stats will ensure him a place in baseball lore.

Retiring in 1988, Gene Garber had tallied 96 wins and 212 saves. Unfortunately, pitching for mediocre teams denied him save opportunities and better stats.

CAREER HIGHLIGHTS
HENRY EUGENE GARBER

Born: November 13, 1947   Lancaster, PA
Height: 5'10"   **Weight:** 175 lbs.   **Batted:** Right   **Threw:** Right
Pitcher: Pittsburgh Pirates, 1969-72; Kansas City Royals, 1973-74, 1987-88; Philadelphia Phillies, 1974-78; Atlanta Braves, 1978-87.

* Started only nine games in entire major league career
* Led the N.L. in appearances in 1975
* Stopped Pete Rose's 44-game hitting streak
* Has tallied 20-plus saves four times

★ Pitched in three League Championship Series

MAJOR LEAGUE TOTALS

G	IP	W	L	Pct.	SV	SO	BB	ERA
931	1,509.1	96	113	.459	218	940	445	3.34

STEVE GARVEY

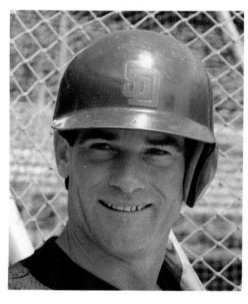

Steve Garvey's rise to the major leagues had a storybook beginning. When Garvey was growing up in Florida during the 1950s, his father was a bus driver and drove the team bus for the Brooklyn Dodgers during their spring training in Florida. Young Garvey got to meet his major league idols up close (even serving as a team batboy), gaining a lasting inspiration that would carry him to stardom in that same Dodger blue some two decades later.

The Minnesota Twins attempted to draft Garvey straight out of high school in 1966, when he was named "athlete of the year" playing both football and baseball. Garvey decided to go to college instead. At Michigan State University he was an All-American baseball player and a starting defensive halfback.

He was the Dodgers' first pick in the special phase of the June 1968 free-agent draft. The Dodgers sent Garvey to their Ogden, Utah, team for the rest of the season. He hit .338 there with 20 homers and 59 RBI (both league bests). In 1969 he advanced to Albuquerque, becoming an All-Star third baseman. In 83 games Garvey socked 14 homers and 85 RBI to complement a .373 batting average. His exploits won him a late-season trial with the Dodgers.

It was back to the minors for more seasoning in 1970 after playing 34 games with Los Angeles. With the parent team, Garvey hit .269. However, the team wanted Garvey groomed as a future third baseman. He labored the rest of the season in Spokane, batting .319 with 15 homers and 87 RBI.

In 1971 Garvey put in his first full season with the Dodgers. He played third base then, due to the presence of Gold Glove man Wes Parker at first. Garvey was adequate at the hot corner but struggled at bat. He hit just .227 with 7 homers. Garvey went back to Michigan State that year, earning a degree in education.

The 1972 season was a bit brighter for Garvey. His average climbed to .269 and he played in 96 games. At season's end Parker retired, allowing Garvey to switch to first base and Ron Cey to take over at third. For the next decade shortstop Bill Russell, second baseman Davey Lopes, Cey, and Garvey would be mainstays in the Dodger infield. The team set a major league record by sticking with the same infield regulars for ten years.

In 114 games Garvey batted .304 with 8 homers and 50 RBI in 1973. In the 1974 campaign Garvey wound up as the National League Most Valuable Player. His .312 average, 21 homers, and 111 RBI were three reasons why the Dodgers coasted all the way to the World Series. Garvey hit .389 versus the Pirates in the N.L. Championship Series (with 2 homers and 5 RBI). Although the Dodgers were outgunned by the Oakland A's in the Series, Garvey hit .381. Garvey was voted his first of seven consecutive All-Star game starts in 1974. He earned 2 hits and scored 1 run.

The graceful first baseman hit a career-high .319 in 1975. In 1976 Garvey played in all 162 games, batting .317. The next four years were major RBI seasons for Garvey. His totals included 115 in 1977, 113 in 1978, 110 in 1979, and 106 in 1980. Garvey was at his best, compiling a consecutive game streak that would reach 1,207 before he was through. At that time, only Everett Scott (1,307) and Lou Gehrig (2,130) had played in more games back-to-back.

Garvey's 33 homers were fifth highest in the league in 1977, helping to put the 1977 Dodgers back on top. They turned back the Phillies in a four-game Championship Series, with Garvey winning N.L.C.S. Most Valuable Player honors. Garvey led the charge in the World Series against the New York Yankees. Although the American Leaguers won in six games, Garvey valiantly batted .375 with 9 hits. In the 1977 All-Star game, Garvey was the game's MVP by way of 2 hits, 2 RBI, and the winning run.

The Dodgers returned to the World Series on the wings of another splendid season by Garvey. He hit .316 with 21 homers and had a league-leading 202 base hits. In the N.L. Championship Series Garvey was a one-man wrecking crew against Philadelphia. He registered a .389 average with 4 homers and 7 RBI as the Dodgers returned to the fall classic. But the Yankees handcuffed Garvey in the Series, allowing him only 5 hits, and the Dodgers were toppled in six games.

Garvey hit .315 with 28 dingers in 1979, then .304 with 26 four-baggers in 1980. He suffered through subpar seasons in 1981 and 1982, hitting in the .280s. In 1982 he signed a five-year, $6.6 million contract with the San Diego Padres. Garvey never matched his Dodger brilliance, but he did help the team to a 1984 National League title.

The smooth-fielding Garvey ended his career following the 1987 season with lifetime stats that include a .294 average with 2,599 hits.

CAREER HIGHLIGHTS
STEVEN PATRICK GARVEY

Born: December 22, 1948 Tampa, FL
Height: 5'10" **Weight:** 192 lbs. **Batted:** Right **Threw:** Right
First baseman: Los Angeles Dodgers, 1969-82; San Diego Padres, 1983-87.

* Won the N.L. MVP award in 1974
* Didn't make a single error in 1984
* Led the N.L. in base hits in 1978 and 1980
* Named to 11 All-Star teams
* Had six 200-hit seasons
* Played on five World Series teams

MAJOR LEAGUE TOTALS

G	AB	H	BA	2B	3B	HR	R	RBI	SB
2,332	8,835	2,599	.294	440	43	272	1,143	1,308	83

At first base, Steve Garvey was a part of the famed Dodger infield that did not change for over a decade. Also a powerful hitter, he slugged over .300 eight times during his career and had six seasons with over 200 hits.

LOU GEHRIG

The story of Lou Gehrig is both triumphant and tragic. He grew up in a modest home in the shadow of Yankee Stadium, went on to one of the most magnificent careers in all of baseball, and then was struck down by a crippling, incurable disease that claimed his life when he was just 37.

Gehrig was born to poor German immigrants in an Upper Manhattan neighborhood. Gehrig's three siblings all died as children. As a child Gehrig excelled in all sports—football, basketball, skating, swimming, and baseball. He graduated in 1920 from the High School of Commerce in New York. In the 1920 intercity championship game played at Wrigley Field in Chicago, the young slugger powered a homer over Wrigley's right field fence.

When Gehrig first attended Columbia University in 1921, he wasn't allowed to play on the baseball team because he had played professionally that summer with a team in Hartford, Connecticut. That spring Gehrig had received an invitation from John McGraw to try out for the New York Giants. The Giants asked Gehrig to play in Hartford that summer. Even though Gehrig played under an assumed name, he was discovered and denied a year of eligibility. The next year, Gehrig played fullback on the Columbia football team. He played first base and served as an alternate pitcher for the 1923 collegiate squad.

The New York Yankees signed Gehrig to a professional contract in June 1923. Gehrig's impoverished parents were so concerned that he make a living that Gehrig jumped at the chance to leave school for a job. Gehrig played at Hartford in 1923 and 1924, hitting .324 with 24 homers in his first year of minor league play. In a brief trial with the Yanks, he hit .423 in 13 games. The man dubbed "Columbia Lou" for his college experience became even more prosperous with the 1924 Hartford team, hitting .369 with 37 homers.

Gehrig was in the majors to stay when he joined the 1925 Yankees. On June 1 he began his incredible streak of 2,130 consecutive games, which continued through 1939. The story behind Gehrig's entrance into the starting lineup is legendary. Starting first baseman Wally Pipp complained of a headache. Young Gehrig was substituted for Pipp and didn't leave the position for the next 15 seasons.

In his first full season Gehrig hit a modest .295 with 20 homers and 68 RBI. He batted .313 with 16 homers and 75 RBI in 1926. Gehrig became known as "Larrupin' Lou" when he was a vital component of the 1927 team known as "Murderers' Row." Gehrig established a major league record with 175 RBI to complement his 47 homers and .373 average. The Yankees swept the Pirates in four straight World Series games, thanks in part to Gehrig's 2 doubles, 2 triples, and 5 RBI in postseason play.

The Yankees defended their world championship in 1928. Gehrig continued his sensational hitting with 27 homers, 142 RBI, and a .374 average. In the 1928 Series, Gehrig hit .545, clubbing 4 homers and 9 RBI. Gehrig's stats dipped in 1929, but he remained one of baseball's best sluggers, hitting .300 with 35 homers and 126 RBI. In 1930 Gehrig won his third RBI crown by batting in 174 runs. He smashed 41 homers and hit a career-best .379. His hit total was a career-high 220. Gehrig broke his own major league RBI record in 1931 with 184, and he also beat teammate Ruth in the home run derby by hitting 46.

Gehrig continued to tear up American League pitching throughout most of the 1930s. But on May 2, 1939, Gehrig took himself out of the lineup after just eight games that year. After playing in a total of 2,164 contests, Gehrig's career was ended. He had been diagnosed with a rare degenerative disease that would later take on his name. During his 17 seasons with the Yankees, the slugger hit .340 with 493 homers and 1,990 RBI. He led the league in runs scored four times, in home runs three times, and in RBI five times. Gehrig had 13 straight seasons of topping 100 RBI. He bettered the .300 mark in batting 12 consecutive years, including six seasons over .350. The man once called "The Iron Horse" won the triple crown in 1934, with 49 homers, 165 RBI, and a .363 average.

After his illness was made public, all of America marveled at Gehrig's courage. On July 4, 1939, Gehrig was honored at Yankee Stadium in front of a crowd of 82,000. At season's end Gehrig was inducted into the Baseball Hall of Fame. Less than two years later Gehrig died. His career was immortalized in the movie *Pride of the Yankees* starring Gary Cooper. Gehrig left behind an impressive list of lifetime records and achievements. But his greatness goes beyond the stats: The secret battle he fought with his illness made Lou Gehrig's life truly memorable.

CAREER HIGHLIGHTS
HENRY LOUIS GEHRIG

Born: June 19, 1903 New York, NY **Died:** June 6, 1941
Height: 6'0" **Weight:** 200 lbs. **Batted:** Left **Threw:** Left
First baseman: New York Yankees, 1923-39.

★ Established an A.L. record of 184 RBI in 1931

★ Compiled a major league record of 23 grand slams

★ Ranks third in lifetime RBI with 1,990

★ Topped the .300 batting mark for 12 straight seasons

★ Played in a record 2,130 consecutive games

★ Elected to the Hall of Fame in 1939

MAJOR LEAGUE TOTALS

G	AB	H	BA	2B	3B	HR	R	RBI	SB
2,164	8,001	2,721	.340	534	163	493	1,888	1,990	102

Lou Gehrig was a remarkable player, but he was overshadowed in his era by Babe Ruth.
When Gehrig hit 47 home runs in '27, Ruth hit 60; though Lou was made MVP that year,
he earned $6000 while Ruth got $80,000; when Gehrig hit .545 in the '28 Series,
Ruth hit .625.

CHARLIE GEHRINGER

Charlie Gehringer was labeled the "Mechanical Man" because of his dependability. Fellow American Leaguer Doc Cramer once stated that all you had to do was wind him up on opening day. Gehringer certainly did not perform like a robot on the field, however. He played smoothly and aggressively for 19 seasons — all with the Detroit Tigers. Perhaps his nickname is evidence that the star second sacker was taken for granted in baseball and that everyone always expected success from him. Hall of Fame pitcher Lefty Gomez once said, "Charlie Gehringer is in a rut. He hits .350 on opening day, and he stays there all season."

Gehringer, whose father died when Charlie was still a youth, was a high school star in football, basketball, and baseball (he even did considerable pitching). Growing up on a farm near Lansing, Michigan, he couldn't help but become a childhood fan of the nearby Tigers. He attended one semester at the University of Michigan, playing football and baseball, then left to find a job.

Gehringer was discovered playing for the local team in Fowlerville. Former Detroit Tigers outfielder Bobby Veach arranged a tryout for him with the Bengals. The Michigan native impressed manager Ty Cobb with his fielding, and Cobb signed him to a contract and sent him to London of the Michigan-Ontario League. There he hit .292 in 112 games. He was shifted from third base to second—the position he'd eventually claim as his own. Gehringer made it to the Tigers for five late-season games in 1924 and then spent the 1925 season in Toronto of the International League for more experience. There he answered his critics by batting .325 with 25 homers and 206 total hits.

Regular Tiger second baseman Marty McManus became ill in 1927. Gehringer subbed at that spot, then took permanent possession of the starting job. After batting a modest .277 during his 1926 rookie season, Gehringer blossomed as a major league hitter the following year. In 1927 he hit .317 with 4 homers and 61 RBI. Gehringer showed surprising speed on the base paths as well, swiping 17 bases. Manager Cobb always remained high on Gehringer: He ranked him behind only Eddie Collins on his list of all-time greats at second base.

The 5-foot-11, 180 pounder registered an even better performance in

1928, hitting .320 with 6 homers and 74 RBI. He scored 108 runs, one of 12 campaigns in which he'd pass the 100-run barrier. In 1929 Gehringer's average was still rising: He batted .339 and his power totals increased to 13 round-trippers and 106 RBI. Gehringer scored the most runs in the junior circuit that year (131) and topped the league in stolen bases with 28.

During the 1930s, Gehringer set the pace for all American League second basemen, topping the league in fielding average five times. He won his only batting title in 1937 with a .371 average. Aside from a .298 in 1932, he kept his average above .300 the entire decade. Gehringer scored more than 100 runs eight times in the 1930s and registered six 200-hit seasons.

He was one of the trio of "G-Men" (with Hank Greenberg and Goose Goslin) who led the Tigers to the World Series in 1934. The St. Louis Cardinals defeated the Tigers in seven games, but

Gehringer blasted a team-best 11 hits for a .379 average. He contributed a .375 effort the following year when the Bengals took the world championship in six games. In Detroit's unsuccessful bid to repeat as world champs in 1940, Gehringer's average dropped to .214.

Gehringer's career stats are truly impressive for a second baseman. While most second basemen were expected to be of the "good field, no hit" variety, Gehringer redefined the limits of what a multitalented middle infielder could do. He ended his career in 1942 with a .320 lifetime batting average, 2,839 hits, 184 homers, and 1,427 RBI.

Gehringer also played every inning of the first six All-Star games. Ironically, he's best remembered in All-Star play for *not* striking out against New York Giants pitcher Carl Hubbell, leading off the game against the great screwballer with a single. After a walk to Heinie Manush, Hubbell struck out Babe Ruth, Lou Gehrig, and Jimmie Foxx in succession, then fanned Al Simmons and Joe Cronin in the following inning, knocking off five of the greatest players in American League history.

Gehringer spent the 1943 and 1944 seasons in the military. It's conceivable that he might have reached 3,000 hits if he had returned for one more year, but he declined, despite his solid physical condition. After retiring, Gehringer worked in private business, then served the Detroit Tigers throughout the 1950s as a general manager and then as a vice president. He was elected to the Baseball Hall of Fame in 1949 and later served on the Veterans Committee to screen the selection of old-timers for membership in Cooperstown. Gehringer still lives in his native state of Michigan.

CAREER HIGHLIGHTS
CHARLES LEONARD GEHRINGER

Born: May 11, 1903 Fowlerville, MI
Height: 5'11" **Weight:** 180 lbs. **Batted:** Left **Threw:** Right
Second baseman: Detroit Tigers, 1924-42.

- ★ Compiled a .320 lifetime average
- ★ Paced the A.L. in hits twice
- ★ Played in three World Series
- ★ Selected A.L. MVP in 1937
- ★ Won the 1929 A.L. stolen base title
- ★ Elected to the Hall of Fame in 1949
- ★ Ranks second in lifetime assists by a second baseman

MAJOR LEAGUE TOTALS

G	AB	H	BA	2B	3B	HR	R	RBI	SB
2,323	8,860	2,839	.320	574	146	184	1,774	1,427	181

Quiet Charlie Gehringer rarely showed emotion or spoke out on anything. Though not as colorful as his contemporaries, he led the A.L. in hits twice, batted over .300 in 13 seasons, and won the MVP award in 1937 with his league-leading .371 average.

BOB GIBSON

Bob Gibson, the fireballing Hall of Fame pitcher, got his start playing professional basketball with the Harlem Globetrotters in 1957. Luckily for baseball fans, he decided that he'd rather throw strikes than shoot free throws. Both teammates and rival players often said that Gibson had the raw determination and physical skills to succeed at any sport. His choice of baseball as a vocation proved a wise one: He carved himself a deep niche in the history of the sport with a sterling 17-year career.

Gibson's rise from a poor childhood in Omaha, Nebraska, is traced in his best-selling biography *From Ghetto to Glory*. His father died before Gibson was born. The youngest of six brothers and sisters, Gibson suffered from a variety of childhood ailments. He recovered and became a respected athlete in baseball, track, and basketball at Omaha Technical High School. Although Gibson got a contract offer from the Negro League Kansas City Monarchs following his 1953 high school graduation, he opted for a basketball scholarship from Creighton University. He was a member of the Blue Jays varsity team before playing a season with the Globetrotters.

Gibson was signed to a contract by Cardinals executive Bill Bergesch and began his pro career with Omaha of the American Association in 1957. He was 2-1 in ten games that first year. Gibson split the 1958 season between Omaha and Rochester of the International League for a combined 8-9 record. After returning for 24 games with Omaha, Gibson got a 13-game tryout in St. Louis in 1959. He went 3-5 with a 3.33 ERA during his rookie season. In 1960 Gibson was farmed out to Rochester but played just six games before coming back to St. Louis to stay.

Gibson's first full season as a Cardinals starter came in 1961. He ranked fifth in the league with a 3.24 ERA and was fourth in the league with 166 strikeouts. In 1962 Gibson was 15-13 with a league-leading 5 shutouts. His ERA dropped to 2.85, and he tallied 15 complete games. The big hurler also demonstrated his all-around ability, batting .263 with 20 hits and 2 homers. By the end of his career Gibson had slugged 24 round-trippers. His batting average soared as high as .303 in 1970.

A broken leg at the end of the 1962 season hampered Gibson's start in 1963. He finished with an 18-9 record,

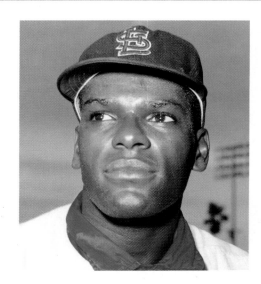

though, tying Ernie Broglio for the team lead in victories. The Cardinals were strong second-place finishers in the National League, giving a sign of what was in store for the next year.

In 1964 the Cardinals won their first pennant since 1946. Gibson contributed a 19-12 record to the pennant run, finishing second in the league in strikeouts (245) and third in innings pitched (287). He won 9 of his last 11 decisions and had a string of 8 straight complete games to seal the title. The man nicknamed "Hoot" (after the Hollywood cowboy) earned 2 World Series victories as the Cardinals toppled the once-mighty Yankees in postseason competition. Gibson went ten strong innings in the fifth game to stop New York 5-2. In the Series finale Cardinals manager Johnny Keane refused to remove Gibson, even when he was struggling. The big righthander responded with a 7-5 complete-game win to clinch the world championship.

Gibson earned his first 20-win sea-

son in 1965 and set a Cardinals record with 270 strikeouts. Even though he spent two weeks on the disabled list in 1966, Gibson was 21-12.

In 1967 the Cardinals won another world championship, this time against the Boston Red Sox. Gibson suffered a shortened season in 1967. On July 15, his right ankle was broken by a line drive off the bat of Roberto Clemente. He missed eight weeks and finished at 13-7. In the World Series Gibson was marvelous. Three complete-game wins, a shutout, a 1.00 ERA, and 26 strikeouts earned Gibson his second Series MVP award (the first was in 1964).

Gibson won both the National League MVP and Cy Young awards in 1968. He won 22 games against just 9 losses and notched an amazing league-best 1.12 ERA. Gibson also topped the league in strikeouts (268) and shutouts (13). In the World Series that year, the Tigers nipped the Redbirds in seven games. Gibson won the opening game on a five-hitter, striking out a record 17 Tigers. He struck out 10 in game four, another complete-game triumph.

In 1969 Gibson defeated every team in the National League at least once and finished the season at 20-13.

Gibson won his second Cy Young in 1970, pacing the league with 23 wins and a .767 winning percentage. In 1971 a thigh injury hampered Gibson's productivity, but he managed to earn his first no-hitter ever, against the Pittsburgh Pirates. In 1972 Gibson won 19 games and struck out 200-plus batters for the ninth season, establishing a new major league record.

Gibson retired following the 1975 season and was later a pitching coach for the Mets and Braves. He was elected to the Hall of Fame in 1981.

CAREER HIGHLIGHTS
ROBERT GIBSON

Born: November 9, 1935   Omaha, NE
Height: 6'1"   **Weight:** 189 lbs.   **Batted:** Right   **Threw:** Right
Pitcher: St. Louis Cardinals, 1959-75.

★ Won two Cy Young awards, in 1968 and 1970

★ Won the N.L. MVP award in 1968

★ Elected to the Hall of Fame in 1981

★ Pitched in three World Series, winning seven games

★ Logged 20-win seasons five times

★ Hit 24 homers in his career

MAJOR LEAGUE TOTALS

G	IP	W	L	Pct.	SO	BB	ERA
528	3,885	251	174	.591	3,117	1,336	2.91

Bob Gibson has been called the best righthand pitcher of the 1960s. In 1968, his 1.12 ERA was the lowest in N.L. history; he threw 13 shutouts, which was second-best in N.L. history; and he struck out a record 35 batters in the Series, including 17 in one game.

JOSH GIBSON

If there had never been a race barrier in baseball, Roger Maris and Hank Aaron might have been chasing Josh Gibson's records rather than Babe Ruth's. Because Gibson spent his entire career in the Negro Leagues (before baseball was integrated), the big slugger never had the chance to display his talents in the majors. Nonetheless, Gibson was one of the biggest drawing cards of his day. Because of his awesome power, he was commonly called "the Babe Ruth of the Negro Leagues."

Born in Buena Vista, Georgia, Gibson moved to Pittsburgh as a youngster and entered pro ball in 1929 as a 17-year-old rookie catcher with the Homestead Grays, perhaps the most dominant of all the Negro League teams. Legend has it that the tall, powerful high school student was called out of the stands to substitute when regular Grays catcher Charles Williams split his finger on a fastball. Gibson was plucked from the crowd because of his prowess on a local department store team, where he had played for three years. He had, by some accounts, played in organized ball for two years before joining the Grays in midseason, logging time with the semipro Pittsburgh Crawfords.

In 1931 the mighty Gibson supposedly belted 75 homers for the Grays. Playing at Yankee Stadium in New York and Forbes Field in Pittsburgh, he hit the longest homers ever measured in either park.

In 1932 he was back with the Pittsburgh Crawfords, teaming with Satchel Paige for one of the most unbeatable batteries of all time. With Cool Papa Bell in the outfield and Judy Johnson at second, it's no wonder the Crawfords were the most fearsome team of the Negro Leagues. Barnstorming against local teams after the regular season, they would actually advertise a promise that Paige would strike out 9 contenders and Gibson would hit 2 home runs.

After the 1934 season the Crawfords played a series of barnstorming games against a team of major leaguers that included Paul and Dizzy Dean. The Crawfords won seven of nine games.

Of the four Crawford Hall of Fame superstars, all but Judy Johnson left in 1936 to play for President Rafael Trujillo of the Dominican Republic. The talent drain dropped the Crawfords to last place.

Like many black players, Gibson did not seek outside employment during the off-season, opting instead to play winter ball in Cuba, Puerto Rico, Mexico, and Venezuela. This he did from 1933 to 1945, earning half of his stateside salary while south of the border. Combining his two salaries produced an annual income of $9,000—riches to a Negro Leaguer, but a drop in the bucket compared to the $80,000 Babe Ruth earned for playing half as many games.

Gibson and other black players were able to gain public acclaim south of the border — something that was denied them in the states because of their exclusion from the big leagues and the lack of money and organization in the Negro Leagues. Another bonus in the winter leagues was the keeping of reliable records, which show Gibson batting an incredible .480. He was named Puerto Rico's Most Valuable Player in honor of that mark.

With the swift fall of the Crawfords, Gibson rejoined the Grays for the 1937 regular season. He spurred them to nine consecutive Negro League titles with his dependable catching and phenomenal throwing arm. He never played for a losing team. He spent two years in the Mexican Leagues in 1940-1942 at a salary increase of $2,000. He was back with the Grays by the end of his career in 1946.

Hall of Famer Roy Campanella played with Gibson in the Negro Leagues, and he has said that Gibson had more ability than any player he had seen before or since. Sadly, there are few or no records to substantiate his ability, although estimates place his lifetime homers at 960 and his batting average at .350. He hit more home runs in Washington's sprawling Griffith Stadium than any other player in history, slamming 4 in 1938 and 11 in 1943.

It is said that Joe DiMaggio patterned his swing after Gibson's, swinging without making a stride into the pitch. Gibson hit flat-footed and was famous for turning up his cap and rolling up his sleeves during every plate appearance.

Historians do not agree on the cause of Gibson's unexpected death at the age of 35. Some say he died from a stroke brought on by alcoholism; others say a brain tumor, for which Gibson refused surgery, was the cause of his death.

In 1972, a quarter of a century after his death, organized baseball acknowledged Gibson's astonishing talent by inducting him into Baseball's Hall of Fame. He was the second Negro Leaguer to win recognition at Cooperstown.

CAREER HIGHLIGHTS
JOSH GIBSON

Born: December 21, 1911 Buena Vista, GA **Died:** January 20, 1947
Height: 6'1" **Weight:** 215 lbs. **Batted:** Right **Threw:** Right
Catcher: Negro Leagues, 1930-46.

★ Member of the Negro League barnstorming team that defeated a squad of major league All-Stars in seven out of nine games in 1934

★ Most powerful slugger in Negro League history

★ May have hit 75 homers in one season

★ Elected to the Hall of Fame in 1972

NEGRO LEAGUE TOTALS

(No accurate statistics available)

Although accurate records were not kept in the Negro Leagues, some historians have estimated that Josh Gibson slugged 960 career home runs and batted .350 lifetime. Roy Campanella said that Gibson had more ability than any player he'd ever seen.

KIRK GIBSON

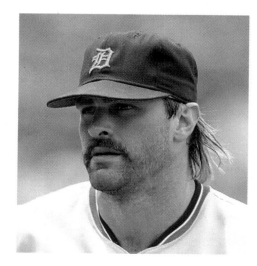

By 1989 Kirk Gibson had a decade of exceptional major league play behind him — all but one year with the Detroit Tigers. But his come-from-behind game-winning homer in the bottom of the ninth inning in the first game of the 1988 World Series may be the memory of him fans will carry for years to come. Gibson rounded the bases for the Dodgers with a jubilant but painful gait, still troubled by the injured knees that had kept him on the bench for weeks. But Gibson's chronic injuries — and his amazing ability to overcome them — are part of the legend behind this hard-hitting right fielder.

The National League's 1988 Most Valuable Player started his minor league career in 1978, the same year *The Sporting News* named him both outfielder on the All-American Baseball Team and wide receiver on the All-American Football Team. In 1979 he was selected by the St. Louis Cardinals of the National Football League in the seventh round of the draft, an opportunity he passed up in favor of a reported $200,000 bonus to sign with the Detroit Tigers.

Gibson progressed rapidly through the minor leagues. In 1978 he hit .240 with 7 homers and 40 RBI in 54 games with Lakeland. The next year, with Evansville, Gibson batted .245 with 9 homers and 42 RBI in 89 games. He joined the Tigers for good at the end of the 1979 season, playing in 12 games. The Michigan native lived up to his promise of excellence, entering the Tigers starting lineup in the 1980 season.

With a blend of speed and power, he has averaged 25 homers and 30 stolen bases for the last five years, despite bench-warming injuries over four of those seasons. His speed — somewhat surprising with such a hulking frame — often gives his hits more mileage, with singles stretching into doubles. A lefty in all aspects, Gibson has his toughest times against lefthand pitchers. Despite his trademark confidence and aggression (fearsome traits in close games and on double plays at second), he often bunts against lefthanders. This is not a choice he favors, however, as evidenced by his many strikeouts, which only slightly exceed his prolific RBI and runs scored.

Gibson is a player who always rises to a challenge, as evidenced by League and World Championship Series stats that rise like mercury in the Bahamas. His first big league homer came for the Tigers in 1979 in Baltimore off Steve Stone. His first N.L. homer for the Dodgers in 1988 was in Atlanta on April 9.

During 1980, his first full year with the Tigers, Gibson was leading his team with 9 round-trippers when a June 18 wrist injury knocked him out of action. The next year found him rehabilitated from surgery, slugging a career-high .328, and snagging A.L. Player of the Week honors twice.

In 1982 Gibson proved that the bigger they come, the harder they fall. Sidelined for all but 69 games with problems ranging from knee, calf, and wrist injuries to stomach complaints, Gibson showed that his greatest strength was also his biggest weakness. His dedication to the game sometimes causes him to push too hard, making him susceptible to injury. Yet this dedication also allows him to rise above the problems he encounters, as he did in his miraculous ten-day recovery from arthroscopic knee surgery in 1983.

That same season he bulleted a homer 523 feet out of Tiger Stadium, across the road and onto a rooftop.

In 1984, after four seasons of major league play, Gibson found himself a respected member of a championship team. Taking the American League Championship Series Most Valuable Player award, Gibson hit .417 in 12 at-bats. During the regular season, Gibson helped the Tigers snag a pennant with a .282 average, highlighting a year that saw Gibson become the first Tiger to hit more than 20 homers and steal 20-plus bases in the same season. It was also the first of five seasons Gibson collected more than 100 hits.

Gibson's 1985 season began on a shocking note: He was beaned by Oakland's Tim Birtsas on May 30. Gibson was back in action the next day with 17 stitches in his mouth. He finished the season with career highs in at-bats (581), hits (167), doubles (37), home runs (29), and RBI (97).

In 1986 Gibson was named A.L. Player of the Week three times. He missed a month due to a sprained ankle but still stole a career-high 34 bases. Gibson set a major league record with 5 consecutive game-winning RBI in 1986.

The Dodgers signed Gibson as a free agent in 1988. Dodger fans were hoping the new star could guarantee a pennant, and Gibson delivered. He played in 150 games, his highest in three seasons. He topped the Dodgers in runs scored (106), doubles (28), home runs (25), total bases (262), and walks (73). He also had a team-leading 6 RBI in the N.L. Championship Series versus the Mets. Gibson may not have been the best player in baseball that year, but he certainly was the most inspirational.

CAREER HIGHLIGHTS
KIRK HAROLD GIBSON

Born: May 28, 1957 Pontiac, MI
Height: 6'3" **Weight:** 215 lbs. **Bats:** Left **Throws:** Left
Outfielder: Detroit Tigers, 1979-87; Los Angeles Dodgers, 1988-89.

★ Won the 1988 N.L. MVP award
★ Homered over the right field roof at Tiger Stadium in 1983
★ Hit .417 in the A.L. Championship Series of 1984
★ Batted .333 in the 1984 World Series
★ Had 75 game-winning RBI through 1988
★ Had a game-winning homer in the first game of the 1988 World Series

MAJOR LEAGUE TOTALS

G	AB	H	BA	2B	3B	HR	R	RBI	SB
1,114	4,005	1,096	.274	176	38	186	669	603	209

Plagued by injuries through much of his career, Kirk Gibson still manages to come through for his team. In 1984, Gibson's .282 average, 20 home runs, and 29 stolen bases helped the Tigers clinch the pennant. Gibson hit .333 in that year's World Series.

JUNIOR GILLIAM

Jim "Junior" Gilliam, the versatile infielder of the pennant-winning Dodgers teams of the 1950s and early 1960s, followed the trail to the major leagues that Jackie Robinson had blazed. He began in the 1940s in the Negro Leagues, moved to the Dodgers top farm club in Montreal, and finally made it to the big leagues in 1953, his Rookie of the Year season in Brooklyn.

The speedy second baseman burst onto the Brooklyn scene the year Robinson moved to the outfield. Gilliam batted .278, leading the league in triples during his first big league campaign. He remained a spark plug on the Dodgers roster for 14 years. He was a multitalented, hustling performer who played second base, third base, and the outfield with equal competence. At the plate he was a disciplined contact hitter who was always among the league leaders in hits, walks, and runs scored.

Gilliam was discovered playing for the Baltimore Elite Giants of the Negro American League. Because he was the youngest player in that club, he was nicknamed Junior. He signed with the Dodgers in 1951, playing his first two seasons in Montreal of the International League. Roy Campanella and Robinson had preceded Gilliam on the route from Montreal to the big leagues, but there were still very few black players in organized baseball in the early 50s. In his first season with Montreal, Gilliam batted .287 with 7 homers and 73 RBI. He led the league with 117 runs scored. In his second season Gilliam batted in 112 runs in 151 games. He remained the International League's top run scorer at 111, while hitting .301 with 9 homers. Gilliam's .987 average topped I.L. second basemen.

The Brooklyn Dodgers called up Gilliam in 1953, moving Robinson to left field to make room for Gilliam at second base. He hit .278 that year with 6 homers and 63 RBI. Gilliam set a National League record for drawing the most walks for any rookie in history, with 100 free passes. Because the Dodgers earned the National League pennant that year, Gilliam had the chance to participate in a World Series during his rookie season. The Yankees wrote an unhappy ending for his rookie season story, but Gilliam batted a respectable .296 with 2 homers in the losing effort.

The swift second sacker gained new found clout briefly in 1954. Gilliam played in 146 games (five less than his first season), but his home run totals rose from 6 to 13 in one season. The most homers he ever belted again were 7 in 1955.

Brooklyn regained its National League pennant from the Giants in 1955. Gilliam had slumped to .249 with 40 RBI, but he perked up in the World Series, hitting .292 (and drawing 8 walks). The Dodgers claimed a seven-game world championship against the Yankees.

In 1956 Gilliam scored 102 runs (the fourth straight season he'd surpassed the 100 mark), and his average reached a career high of .300. He batted just .083 in the World Series, but he reached base safely on 2 hits and 7 walks. In 1957, the team's final year in Brooklyn, Gilliam slumped to .250.

When Gilliam and the Dodgers reached Los Angeles in 1958, he was transferred to outfield duty. He played 75 games as an outfielder, 44 games at third, and 32 at second. Gilliam batted .261 that year with 43 RBI and 18 stolen bases. He earned the starting third baseman's role in 1959 as the Dodgers marched to their first world championship as Californians. Gilliam hit .282 during the regular season with a league-leading 96 bases on balls. In the World Series against the Chicago White Sox, Gilliam batted .240 with 6 hits and 2 runs scored. Four of his hits came in the fifth game, tying a World Series record.

In 1960 Gilliam batted .248. Gilliam became a busy man in 1961: He divided his time around the infield, playing third base 74 times, second base 71 times, and the outfield on 11 occasions. He played in only 144 games, which means that Dodgers manager Walter Alston shuffled Gilliam to more than one position in several games.

In 1962 Gilliam made 113 appearances at second base and 90 at third. His average climbed back to .270 as he tallied 159 hits. Gilliam's hitting improved even more in 1963: He batted .282 with 6 homers and 49 RBI with 19 stolen bases. Gilliam got more time at his old stomping grounds at second base when Dodger rookie third baseman Ken McMullen arrived. In 1964, however, the Dodgers shuttled Gilliam back to third base for most of the season and used rookie Nat Oliver at second. Gilliam's last full season was 1965, when the Dodgers made him a player/coach. The extra title perked up Gilliam's hitting to an average of .280 in 111 games. Gilliam had 1 of only 2 Los Angeles RBI in the 1966 World Series, as the Orioles swept the Dodgers in four straight games.

Gilliam ended his playing career after 88 games in 1966, hitting just .217. Gilliam remained in the Los Angeles Dodgers organization as a team coach until his unexpected death in 1978 at the age of 49. Gilliam's lifetime totals in 1,956 games include a .265 average and 1,889 hits. He scored 1,163 runs (fourth highest in Dodger history), drew 1,036 walks, and stole a total of 203.

CAREER HIGHLIGHTS
JAMES WILLIAM GILLIAM

Born: October 17, 1928 Nashville, TN **Died:** October 8, 1978
Height: 5'10" **Weight:** 175 lbs. **Batted:** Both **Threw:** Right
Infielder: Brooklyn Dodgers, 1953-57; Los Angeles Dodgers, 1958-66.

★ Named N.L. Rookie of the Year in 1953 ★ Led the N.L. in walks in 1959
★ Played on seven pennant-winning Dodgers teams ★ Ranks in the top ten in eight Dodger offensive categories

MAJOR LEAGUE TOTALS

G	AB	H	BA	2B	3B	HR	R	RBI	SB
1,956	7,119	1,889	.265	304	71	65	1,163	558	203

Junior Gilliam played with the Dodgers team his entire career, first in Brooklyn and then in Los Angeles. Playing in both the infield and outfield, Gilliam appeared in 1,956 games in his career—more than Steve Garvey, Maury Wills, or Duke Snider.

LEFTY GOMEZ

When the baseball Veteran's Committee elected Vernon "Lefty" Gomez to the Hall of Fame in 1972 (nearly 30 years after he retired), some fans thought Gomez was being honored for his popularity as a player instead of his career accomplishments. Granted, Gomez had an admirable 14-year career as an American League hurler, but fans remember him most for his off-the-field wit.

Long before reporters clamored to get a clever quip from Yogi Berra, Gomez was baseball's chief philosopher during the 1930s. His funny observations and unique insights earned him the nicknames of "The Gay Castillion" and "Goofy." Because Gomez was of Spanish ancestry, his nickname soon became "El Goofo." If Gomez created a nickname for a player, it stuck. (Just ask Charlie "The Mechanical Man" Gehringer or Edward Charles "Whitey" Ford.) Although Gomez was a tough on-the-field competitor, he never took the game too seriously. He may have been baseball's first official flake. For starters, he'd sometimes interrupt a game he was pitching to watch an airplane passing over the stadium. Because he was so fidgety when he wasn't pitching, it was said that he'd change his clothes three times a day just to stay occupied.

Gomez had plenty of pitching talent, though. Gomez was discovered as a 16-year-old high school star in Richmond, California, by San Francisco manager Nick Williams. He started his career with Salt Lake City in 1928. The next year, in San Francisco, Gomez tallied an 18-11 mark and was purchased for $35,000 by the New York Yankees. The Seals of the Pacific Coast League claimed that the wiry 6-foot-2 hurler weighed 173 pounds, but he actually weighed in at just 146!

Gomez debuted in 1930 with the Yankees but suffered through a forgettable 2-5 season. The Yanks sent him to St. Paul in the American Association to beef up and get more experience. Gomez improved with the tutoring of Cy Perkins, Yankees coach and former star catcher of the Athletics. Perkins helped Gomez fine-tune both his curveball and his control. An older and wiser Gomez was an instant success with the 1931 Yankees: He was 21-9 with a 2.63 ERA. This was the first of four 20-win seasons in his career.

The Yankees reached the World Series in 1932, and Gomez paced the team with a 24-7 record. New York swept the Chicago Cubs, and Gomez assisted in the romp with a complete-game victory in the second game.

Perhaps Gomez registered his greatest season in 1934. He won a league-leading 26 games against just 5 losses. He topped the league in winning percentage (.839), ERA (2.33), complete games (25), innings pitched (281.2), strikeouts (158), and shutouts (6). When Joe DiMaggio first joined the Yankees in 1936, Gomez became a mentor to the gifted rookie. Because both men had played in San Francisco and were California natives, they had a common bond.

Although Gomez won just 13 games during the 1936 season, he earned 2 wins in the 1936 world championship against the New York Giants. Gomez rebounded to a league-leading 21-11 season in 1937, matching his career-low 2.33 ERA. In the 1937 Series the Giants and Yankees had a rematch with the Bronx Bombers winning again. Again Gomez gained 2 of the team's 4 victories with complete-game efforts on both outings.

The California native's record of 189 career wins may not compare favorably with most other Hall of Fame pitchers, but his dominance in the 1930s is demonstrated by the fact that he was the American League's starting pitcher in five of the first six All-Star games. Between 1934 and 1941 Gomez led the league in winning percentage twice, ERA twice, and strikeouts three times. He was especially effective in postseason play, setting a World Series record by winning 6 games without a loss in five fall classics. He pitched all but 4 of his 2,503 innings in a Yankee uniform. After just one game with the 1943 Washington Senators, he retired.

Gomez will be remembered for his humorous anecdotes about the game. He became the Joan Rivers of baseball, making wisecracks that hinted that he wasn't the greatest pitcher of all time. When Mark "The Bird" Fidrych became famous with the Detroit Tigers in the 1970s for talking to baseballs, Gomez claimed he did the same thing during his career. What did he say to his baseballs? "Go foul! Go foul!" When America first explored on the moon, Gomez claimed that a white object one astronaut saw was the home run that Jimmie Foxx had hit off him years ago. Above all, Gomez reminded fans that baseball can be fun.

Lefty Gomez was as rowdy and witty as Charlie Gehringer was quiet and solemn. He was also a solid pitcher. His best year was 1934 when he led the A.L. with 26 wins and a 2.33 ERA.

CAREER HIGHLIGHTS
VERNON LOUIS GOMEZ

Born: November 26, 1908 Rodeo, CA **Died:** February 17, 1989
Height: 6'2" **Weight:** 173 lbs. **Batted:** Left **Threw:** Left
Pitcher: New York Yankees, 1930-42; Washington Senators, 1943.

★ Pitched for five World Series teams
★ Won 20 games four times
★ Set a record by winning six World Series games without a loss

★ Led the league in wins twice
★ Elected to the Hall of Fame in 1972
★ Paced the A.L. in shutouts for three seasons

MAJOR LEAGUE TOTALS

G	IP	W	L	Pct.	SO	BB	ERA
368	2,503	189	102	.649	1,468	1,095	3.34

DWIGHT GOODEN

The problem with child prodigies is that they do everything so quickly — including growing up.

Delivering a steady stream of balls as subtle as an atomic blast, boy wonder Dwight Gooden had a mind-boggling 1984 rookie season. With a 17-9 record, he had a .654 winning percentage and a 2.60 ERA, and he led the Mets and the National League with 276 strikeouts.

Fans immediately awarded him an honorary degree, and "Dr. K" lived up to the title. The following year he paced the league with 268 strikeouts, while becoming the youngest pitcher in modern history to reach the 20-win plateau. At season's end the 20-year-old had a record of 24 wins and 4 losses for a career-high winning percentage of .857, complemented by a career- and league-best ERA of 1.53.

The Sporting News and Baseball Writers Association of America named Gooden Rookie Pitcher and Rookie of the Year. He was named to the All-Star team his freshman year and every active season after. He was 1985's Cy Young award winner and *TSN's* National League Pitcher of the Year.

On top of all of this, the kid was actually getting better. Connoisseurs could see that he had more control of the strike zone, and his curve had more confidence. He also acquired a change-up to save his arm, and his heat only got hotter as the game goes on.

In 1985 Shea Stadium was filled nightly with fans carrying banners, placards, clothing, and posters with prominent letter Ks. Mets outfielders would be booed for catching a foul fly ball and denying the Doctor the chance to practice his craft.

Throughout it all the quiet Florida native seemed to handle himself as admirably off the field as on. He phoned home after every game. He learned to overcome his shyness with the press. He endeared himself to his loony-tune teammates by joining in their antics instead of standing aloof. When outfielder Darryl Strawberry rubbed Heet balm into the seat of Gooden's pants, Gooden slipped some slightly-used gum into his buddy's cap.

Sadly, appearances can be deceptive. The gum-chewing youngster, after a 17-6 record in the 1986 campaign, was found to suffer from drug addiction. Treatment kept him from spring training in 1987, so the Doctor was sent to heal himself in the New York minor league system. His five starts there seemed to indicate all was well. His stats were all normal — vital signs intact. Back with the Mets he tallied an admirable 15-7 season, although his 3.21 ERA was his highest major league mark to date.

Besides his minor league rehabilitation in 1987, Gooden spent only two years in the Mets farm system before earning big league fame. The Mets forked over an estimated $125,000 in a signing bonus to sign Gooden to his first contract when he was 18 years old. In 1982 with Kingsport, he struck out one batter for every inning pitched (66). His debut included a record of 5 wins, 4 losses, and a 2.47 ERA. He finished 1982 with Little Falls, pitching only two games. In 1983 it was on to Lynchburg, where he led the Carolina League with 19 wins, 112 walks, a 2.50 ERA, and a career high of 300 strikeouts, all in only 191 innings of work.

Some of Gooden's success can be attributed to his masterful fastball and curve. He has constantly improved his pitching by targeting specific parts of the plate, and he has whittled down the number of gopher balls served to eight in 1988 (or one every 31 innings). Gooden's pickoff move is also tougher than in previous seasons.

The Mets flamethrower has already seen action in two League Championship Series and one World Series in his young career. In the 1986 Series versus the Boston Red Sox, Gooden lost 2 games. He had come off a subpar season following his 1985 Cy Young award win. His 200 strikeouts and 2.84 weren't up to Gooden's standards, yet other pitchers dream about such numbers. Boston roughed up Gooden in game two for 6 runs (5 earned) on 8 hits over five innings. However, he whiffed 6. In game five Gooden went four innings, allowing 4 runs on 9 hits, walking 2, and striking out 3.

Some of the New York media vowed that they would shave their heads in tribute to Gooden if he could pump his 1989 totals up to 10 straight wins. Unfortunately for Gooden (but luckily for the scribes) he suffered his first loss after 5 consecutive triumphs. Gooden's 1989 season ended on a winning note, if not a particularly spectacular one. Pitching in 19 games, the young hurler won 9 and lost 4 for a 2.89 ERA. Gooden also collected one save. In 119 innings pitched, he struck out 101 batters. Though 1989 was not up to the caliber of Gooden's remarkable 1984 and 1985 seasons, his stats were nothing to be ashamed of either. Teammate Sid Fernandez outshone Gooden that year with his 14-5 record.

Still only in his mid-twenties, Gooden is one of the youngest "old veterans" in baseball. He'll go as far as his magic arm will take him.

CAREER HIGHLIGHTS
DWIGHT EUGENE GOODEN

Born: November 16, 1964   Tampa, FL
Height: 6'2"   **Weight:** 190 lbs.   **Bats:** Right   **Throws:** Right
Pitcher: New York Mets, 1984-89.

- ★ Named N.L. Rookie of the Year in 1984
- ★ Topped the N.L. in wins in 1985
- ★ Established a record for the most strikeouts by a rookie with 276
- ★ Won the Cy Young award in 1985
- ★ Named to four All-Star teams
- ★ Established N.L. record for the most strikeouts in three straight games with 43

MAJOR LEAGUE TOTALS

G	IP	W	L	Pct.	SO	BB	ERA
177	1,290	100	39	.719	1,168	379	2.64

In 1985 20-year-old Doc Gooden had one of the best seasons of any hurler in years. He led the N.L. with 268 strikeouts, had a 24-4 record for an .857 winning percentage, and threw 8 shutouts. Gooden led the league with a 1.53 ERA and 16 complete games.

GOOSE GOSLIN

Cruel as it may seem, Goose Goslin got his nickname because he wasn't very good looking. His features were described by *The Washington Post* in 1933 with little timidity: "He has small, sharp eyes set deeply behind a large proboscis and even resembles a bird by the manner in which he carries his arms while chasing balls hit in his direction." Of all the monikers tagged on baseball players, Goslin's is one of the most appropriate. Granted, Goslin did have a nose that could put Pinocchio's to shame, but his last name (which sounds like gosling, the term for a baby goose) also helped give birth to the nickname.

During his 18-year career with three different teams, Goslin played like a goose on the loose in the American League. During the 1920s and 30s Goslin registered a .316 *lifetime* batting average, including 11 seasons of .300 or better. From 1922 to 1928 Goslin averaged .338 and capped the string with a career-high .379. The Hall of Fame outfielder slashed out 2,735 hits in his career, along with 248 home runs and 1,609 RBI.

Goslin began his professional career in 1920 with Columbia of the South Atlantic League. He started out as a pitcher, but was pinch-hitting and playing the outfield on his off-days. In 1921 in Columbia Goslin batted .390 in 142 games. He had 214 hits, 16 homers, and 20 stolen bases. His long-ball prowess brought Washington team owner Clark Griffith to personally scout Goslin. Griffith was enchanted with Goslin's power potential, but he noticed that Goslin was almost hit on the head by several fly balls. Griffith ordered Goslin to get a pair of sunglasses and prepare to play left field—a tough, sunny chore in Washington. Griffith paid $7,000 to obtain the young slugger. Goslin appeared in 14 games late that season with the Senators, hitting .260 with 1 homer.

Goslin played his first full American League season in 1922. In 101 games he batted .324 with 3 homers and 53 RBI. Unfortunately, Goslin wound up with 15 errors and a paltry .932 average in left field. During his sophomore season of 1923, Goslin's fielding gradually improved. He wound up with at least 10 errors a season throughout the 1920s but was noted for his strong throwing arm. At bat Goslin had 9 homers, 99 RBI, and a .300 average. His 18 triples were tops in the junior circuit that year.

In 1924 Goslin was the leading run producer in the American League with 129 RBI. He compiled a .344 average and socked 12 homers. Goslin's efforts sent the Senators to the World Series, where they beat the New York Giants in seven games. Goslin aided the triumph with a game-winning two-run homer in game four. He finished the Series with 11 hits (including 3 homers and a double), batting .344 with 44 runs scored and 7 RBI. In 1925 Goslin helped put his club back into postseason contention with another fine offensive display. The Goose had a league-best 20 triples, together with 18 homers, 113 RBI, and a .334 average. In the Senators seven-game Series loss to the Pirates, Goslin hit .308 with 3 homers.

While Washington was denied another American League pennant for the rest of the decade, Goslin was busy becoming one of the most celebrated hitters of the 1920s. He didn't have the punch of Babe Ruth; yet Goslin was durable and consistent. The veteran slugger never struck out more than 38

times in one season from 1926 to 1929 (his last full season with the Senators). When he won the batting title in 1928 with a .379 average, he won it with a hit in his final at-bat. The hit came in front of the St. Louis Browns and Heinie Manush, who finished second in the batting race, less than 1 percentage point behind.

The two men crossed paths on June 13, 1930, when General Crowder and Manush were traded from the St. Louis Browns for Goslin. Goslin batted .326 with his new team and ended the year with combined totals of 37 homers, 138 RBI, and 115 runs scored. The Senators regained Goslin for the 1933 season, when they won their third pennant, but team owner Griffith was financially strapped at the end of the season and couldn't afford to keep Goslin. Picked up by the Tigers (at the urging of manager Mickey Cochrane), Goslin was an active participant in two straight pennants. In 1935 Goslin's ninth-inning single drove in the winning run against the Cubs in the decisive sixth game of the World Series.

Following 1938, his final year in the majors, Goslin served as a player/manager in the minors for three seasons. He retired to his native New Jersey and operated a boat rental and fishing tackle business for many years. He was elected to the Hall of Fame in 1968, three years before his death.

Goose Goslin inspired his teams to win pennants. While he was with the Senators, they won the only three pennants they'd ever win. When he was traded to Detroit, the Tigers won two in a row.

CAREER HIGHLIGHTS
LEON ALLEN GOSLIN

Born: October 16, 1900 Salem, NJ **Died:** May 15, 1971
Height: 5'11" **Weight:** 185 lbs. **Batted:** Left **Threw:** Right
Outfielder: Washington Senators, 1921-30, 1933, 1938; St. Louis Browns, 1930-32; Detroit Tigers, 1934-37.

- ★ Played in five World Series
- ★ Had a 30-game hitting streak in 1934
- ★ Led the A.L. in batting with a .379 mark in 1928
- ★ Compiled a .316 lifetime batting average
- ★ Elected to the Hall of Fame in 1968
- ★ Batted .344 in the 1924 World Series with 3 homers and 7 RBI

MAJOR LEAGUE TOTALS

G	AB	H	BA	2B	3B	HR	R	RBI	SB
2,287	8,656	2,735	.316	500	173	248	1,483	1,609	175

RICH GOSSAGE

Throughout his long and distinguished career, relief artist Rich "Goose" Gossage has been more than a damage control specialist.

Fastballs hard down the middle are his forte. If they're hit they can go for miles; but rare is the player who can make contact, especially when Gossage is under pressure. Bunting is a favorite choice for batters, as the Goose's windup leaves him off-balance. But this is only a stop-gap measure, as proved by Gossage's position near the top of the all-time saves list and the impressive number of lifetime victories the reliever has earned to date.

As a 19-year-old minor leaguer, Gossage showed a lack of consistency—posting a 5.91 ERA in Appleton in 1970 but leading the league the next year with a 1.83 ERA, 18 wins, 15 complete games, and 7 shutouts. This was enough to earn him a quick trip to Chicago, for the White Sox had selected him just two years earlier in the ninth round of the June 1970 draft.

It proved to be too much, too soon, for the 21-year-old hurler. Although his win-loss record was a respectable 7-1, his ERA expanded to 4.28 in 80 innings. Things looked even worse in 1973, when Goose started the season with 4 losses and a 7.43 ERA in only 49.2 innings of play. It was back to the Iowa Oaks, Chicago's Triple-A minor league affiliate in the American Association. There Gossage's form and confidence immediately improved.

Early in the 1974 campaign it was back to the bigs. Finally, team management heard the call of Goose's destiny: His 4-6, 4.15 ERA record included 1 save, the first of 4 saves so far in his young career. But 39 appearances as a middle reliever made it obvious where his talents lay. In 1975 Gossage and the White Sox led the league with 26 saves. His ERA fairly matched his stellar years in the minors at 1.84, and his 9-8 record earned him his first Fireman of the Year award. In 1976 the pitching-thin White Sox tried to patch up their starting rotation by yanking Gossage out of the bullpen, but even though he had 15 complete games, he couldn't do better than a 9-17 record.

When it was apparent that Gossage would be playing out his option in search of greener pastures, the White Sox decided to trade him. He was sent to the Pittsburgh Pirates with fellow reliever Terry Forster in exchange for Richie Zisk and Silvio Martinez on December 10, 1976. That season

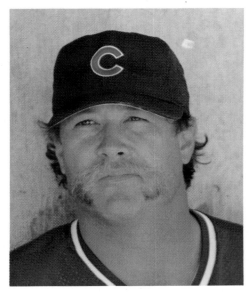

proved to be a transition year for Gossage. He had his first taste of the National League, and he was trying to impress prospective teams who might want to sign him to a big-money, long-term contract.

Pittsburgh got an impressive season out of Gossage in 1977. He logged 26 saves with a dazzling 1.62 ERA. He set a league record for relievers with 151 strikeouts in a career-high 72 games. As a free agent he struck it rich with a multiyear deal with the New York Yankees at season's end. The move proved serendipitous for the meaty flamethrower. As a first-year Yankee Gossage posted a league-high 27 saves in 1978. Two years later he would tie for a league lead with 33 in 37 opportunities.

Despite strikes and injuries, 1981 was good to Gossage. His ERA reached a career low at 0.77 in 32 games, 20 of which were saves. He added 2 more during World Series play, tying the record for most saves in a six-game Series. His five innings on the mound yielded no runs for Los Angeles.

Two more good years with the Yankees ensued before Gossage took up with the San Diego Padres—just in time for another Series. Gossage contributed a save to secure the league championship but pitched only 2.2 innings in the Padres' losing cause in the World Series.

In 1985 his 1.82 ERA was the second lowest of his career. His 50 appearances scarcely show his time out for arthroscopic knee surgery.

Stats and vibes took a turn for the worse in 1986, when Gossage was suspended for two weeks for reported insubordination to the Padres management. Although Goose had an eight-game stretch in July that totaled a 0.87 ERA, the season ended at 4.45, Goose's highest in more than a decade. However, he kept up his 10-year average of 20 annual saves by posting 21.

The yearly addition dropped to 11 saves in 1987, with Gossage on the disabled list. After recovering he was shipped to the Cubs with Ray Hayward in exchange for Keith Moreland and Mike Brumley on February 12, 1988. Gossage mustered just 13 saves and a 4-4 record and was released during 1989 spring training. The San Francisco Giants signed Gossage in April, showing a willingness to hope that the bullpen ace can add a few more saves to one of the most impressive relief-pitching career totals in baseball.

CAREER HIGHLIGHTS
RICHARD MICHAEL GOSSAGE

Born: July 5, 1951   Colorado Springs, CO
Height: 6'3"   **Weight:** 226 lbs.   **Bats:** Right   **Throws:** Right
Pitcher: Chicago White Sox, 1972-76; Pittsburgh Pirates, 1977; New York Yankees, 1978-83; San Diego Padres, 1984-87; Chicago Cubs, 1988; San Francisco Giants, 1989.

- ★ Led the A.L. in saves three times
- ★ Second in lifetime saves after 1988
- ★ Threw 15 complete games for the 1976 Chicago White Sox
- ★ Pitched in three World Series
- ★ Ranked fifth in career relief wins after 1988
- ★ A.L. Reliever of the Year in 1975 and 1978

MAJOR LEAGUE TOTALS

G	IP	W	L	Pct.	SV	SO	BB	ERA
822	1,592	111	97	.534	303	1,355	629	2.93

Reliever Goose Gossage's best season was probably 1977 when he logged 26 saves with a 1.62 ERA. That year he set an N.L. record for relievers with 151 strikeouts. In 1985 he set another record when he finished his fifth All-Star game.

HANK GREENBERG

Despite losing four prime seasons to military service during World War II and another season to injuries, Hank Greenberg put together some awesome offensive statistics in what amounted to just ten full major league seasons. At a time when the bigotry of Nazism cast a pall over the world, Greenberg was a proud Jewish American inspiring others with his determination to be one of baseball's stars.

Greenberg was born in 1911 in New York City, the son of Romanian Jewish immigrants. He played baseball in high school (and lettered in four sports) but didn't play during his semester of schooling at New York University, even though he was attending school on an athletic scholarship. The New York Yankees valiantly tried to sign Greenberg after several other pro teams showed interest as well. Realizing that Lou Gehrig had a monopoly on first base with the Yankees, Greenberg decided to sign with Detroit Tigers scout Jean Dubuc instead.

Greenberg went hitless in 1 at-bat during his 1930 debut with the Tigers. He played 17 games with Hartford of the Eastern League in his first pro season, then advanced to Evansville of the Three-I circuit in 1931. In Evansville, Greenberg batted .318 with 15 homers. His success earned a 1932 promotion to Beaumont of the Texas League, where he hit .290 with 39 homers and 123 runs scored and was voted MVP. Del Baker managed Greenberg at Beaumont and then advanced to Detroit with the gifted young slugger in 1933.

In 1933 Greenberg played in 117 games with Detroit, beating resident first baseman Harry Davis out of a job. Greenberg's rookie season totals included 12 homers, 87 RBI, and a .301 average. In his sophomore campaign of 1934, Greenberg tallied 201 hits (98 of them going for extra bases). His 63 doubles led the league and came only 4 short of Earl Webb's 1931 major league record. Greenberg clubbed 26 homers and 139 RBI in the first of many seasons spent terrorizing American League pitchers. The Tigers won the 1934 A.L. pennant, only to lose the World Series to the St. Louis Cardinals in 7 games. Greenberg topped the Tigers in postseason play with seven RBI, batting .321 in his first fall classic.

The 24-year-old Tiger won the American League Most Valuable Player award in 1935. Detroit used Greenberg's league-leading totals of 36 homers and 170 RBI, along with his .328 average, to return to the World Series, where the Bengals battered the Cubs in six games. Greenberg hit a two-run homer in the second game of the Series but broke his wrist in the matchup and got only 6 at-bats.

Greenberg batted .348 during the first 12 games of 1936. Unfortunately, he rebroke his wrist and missed the remainder of the season.

In 1937 Greenberg rebounded by hitting .337 with 40 homers. His 183 RBI fell only 1 short of the American League record established earlier by Lou Gehrig. Greenberg led the league in 1938 with 58 homers, 144 runs scored, and 119 walks. Ironically, Greenberg's 146 RBI didn't even lead the league. By Greenberg's standards, he slumped during 1939 with "only" 33 homers, 112 RBI, and a .312 average.

Greenberg earned his second MVP award in 1940, leading the league with 41 homers and 150 RBI. He narrowly missed winning a triple crown; his impressive .340 average was 12 points shy of league leader Joe DiMaggio's record. Detroit won the American

League pennant but suffered a seven-game World Series defeat at the hands of the Cincinnati Reds. Greenberg had a team-best 10 hits in the Series, batting .357 with 1 homer and 6 RBI.

The Tigers star left for military duty in early 1941, after playing in just 19 games that season. He returned in mid-1945 after serving in the Army Air Corps, winning four battle stars. Greenberg highlighted his comeback with a memorable 1946 season. That year he led the junior circuit in homers (44) and RBI (127), batting .277. On January 18, 1947, the Tigers shocked the baseball world by selling Greenberg to the Pittsburgh Pirates for $75,000. An understandably shocked Greenberg refused to report to the Pirates but finally agreed to play when presented with a $100,000 contract. Although the Pirates finished in last place with a pitiful 62-92 record, Greenberg finished his final season with 25 homers and 74 RBI in 125 games. His career totals were obscured due to his injuries and time lost in World War II. However, Greenberg's .605 slugging percentage remains the fifth best in history.

Following his retirement as a player, Greenberg served as the Cleveland Indians farm director and general manager. The Indians won pennants in 1948 and 1954 with the aid of Greenberg's front office guidance. The Baseball Hall of Fame enshrined Greenberg in 1956. In 1958 Greenberg became part-owner and vice president of the Chicago White Sox, and the White Sox promptly won a pennant in 1959. Three years later he left baseball and began a long career in banking. He died September 4, 1986, at his home in Beverly Hills, California. The 75-year-old baseball superstar died of cancer.

CAREER HIGHLIGHTS
HENRY BENJAMIN GREENBERG

Born: January 1, 1911 New York, NY **Died:** September 4, 1986
Height: 6'4" **Weight:** 210 lbs. **Batted:** Right **Threw:** Right
First baseman, outfielder: Detroit Tigers, 1930-46; Pittsburgh Pirates, 1947.

★ Slugged 58 home runs in 1938
★ Led the A.L. in RBI four times
★ Batted .318 in four World Series
★ Elected to the Hall of Fame in 1956
★ Selected A.L. MVP in 1935 and 1940

MAJOR LEAGUE TOTALS

G	AB	H	BA	2B	3B	HR	R	RBI	SB
1,394	5,193	1,628	.313	379	71	331	1,051	1,276	58

Despite playing only ten full seasons, Hank Greenberg hit 331 home runs and accumulated 1,276 RBI. In addition to his batting skills, Greenberg helped younger team members, including slugger Ralph Kiner, to reach their full potential.

BOBBY GRICH

Second sacker Bobby Grich split his 20-year career in organized baseball evenly between the Baltimore Orioles and the California Angels before retiring from the game in 1986.

For a recent player, his dedication to only two teams is quite unusual, almost old-fashioned. Yet Grich was a trailblazer for free agency in the late 1970s — one of the first to risk leaving the fold and to land, crowing, on his feet. The readiness of Angels team management and owner Gene Autry to sign him to a five-year contract for $1.7 million also gave players who weren't home run stars or strikeout artists the courage to try to better their financial situations.

Not that Grich was unhappy with the Birds. A first-round pick in 1967, Grich advanced one minor league class a year until he finally got a spot on the Baltimore roster. The talented rookie infielder really had to prove himself, because the Orioles already had veteran second sacker Davey Johnson, shortstop Mark Belanger, and third baseman Brooks Robinson in their lineup.

In his first pro season with Bluefield in 1967, Grich batted .254 with 3 homers and 26 RBI. He advanced to Stockton in 1968, where he hit 8 home runs and 44 RBI, with a withered .228 batting mark and a career high of 126 strikeouts. Nevertheless, he was promoted to Dallas-Fort Worth in 1969, where his average soared to .310. In 1970 with the Triple-A Rochester Red Wings, Grich set the league ablaze. He hit .383 in just 63 games, racking up 9 homers and 42 RBI. A promotion late in the season got Grich a 30-game audition with the Orioles. Playing 20 games at shortstop, 9 at second base, and one at the hot corner, Grich batted an anemic .211.

It took one more year in Rochester (in 1971) before he could gain a permanent spot on the Orioles roster. Grich's final season at Rochester left no doubt about his talent: He hit 32 homers and 83 RBI to complement 124 runs, 159 hits, and a snappy .336 average. *The Sporting News* named him Minor League Player of the Year. He returned for seven games with Baltimore in 1971 and stayed for good.

With Baltimore to stay in 1972, Grich was faced with the problem of finding a full-time position. He played 81 of his 133 games at shortstop and filled in at the other three infield positions. Offensively, he was an Orioles mainstay, with 12 homers, 50 RBI, a .278 batting average, and 13 stolen bases. At the end of the 1972 season, second baseman Johnson was dispatched to the Atlanta Braves in a November 30 trade. The second base job now belonged to Grich.

Playing in every one of Baltimore's 162 games in 1973, his average dipped to .251, but his home run and RBI totals remained the same. Grich was, without a doubt, the finest-fielding second sacker in the junior circuit that year. He led the league in putouts (431), assists (509), double plays (130), chances accepted per game (5.8), and fielding percentage (.995, which included just 5 errors all season). Grich was to become one of the league's best-known glove men during his years with the Orioles, winning four straight Gold Gloves for fielding excellence.

Even though he played in two fewer games in 1974, Grich belted more homers and drove in more runs. He socked 19 round-trippers and notched 82 RBI while hitting .263. The Orioles won their second straight pennant, and Grich was in his second straight League Championship Series. He batted .250 with 1 homer and 2 RBI in the A.L.C.S., but the Orioles lost in four games to the Oakland A's. In 1975 Grich played in 150 games and saw his totals dip to 13 homers and 57 RBI. Still, he matched his career high in bases on balls (107) and continued his fancy fielding.

When Grich signed his lucrative five-year pact with the Angels in 1976, big things were expected. Naturally everyone was shocked when, just 52 games into the 1977 season, Grich underwent back surgery. Although he never regained his full mobility, he still had many fine seasons with the Angels. In 1979 he batted .294 with 30 homers and 101 RBI. In 1981 he tied for the A.L. lead in homers, becoming the first second baseman to lead the junior circuit since Nap Lajoie did in 1901.

Grich's career ended on an unfulfilled note in 1986. He had played well in limited action, hitting .268 in 98 games, and sharing the second base job with Rob Wilfong. Although he batted just .208 in the League Championship Series, he had a homer and 3 RBI. He had the game-winning hit in the fourth game of the A.L.C.S. to give the Angels a three-games-to-one lead over Boston and what looked like a guaranteed World Series appearance. Boston rallied to take the last three games, however, denying Grich his only chance at world championship play.

Grich ranks in the top three in several Angels' career offensive categories. Only Brian Downing and Jim Fregosi have spent more time in an Angels uniform. Grich was the first player elected to the Angels Hall of Fame in 1988.

CAREER HIGHLIGHTS
ROBERT ANTHONY GRICH

Born: January 15, 1949 Muskegon, MI
Height: 6'2" **Weight:** 180 lbs. **Batted:** Right **Threw:** Right
Second baseman: Baltimore Orioles, 1970-76; California Angels, 1977-86.

- ★ Had double-digit homer totals in 12 seasons
- ★ Led the A.L. in homers in 1981 with 22
- ★ First inductee to the Angels Hall of Fame
- ★ Had a record-setting fielding percentage in 1985
- ★ Won four straight Gold Gloves
- ★ Appeared in five League Championship Series

MAJOR LEAGUE TOTALS

G	AB	H	BA	2B	3B	HR	R	RBI	SB
2,008	6,890	1,833	.266	320	47	224	1,033	864	104

Second baseman Bobby Grich won four straight A.L. Gold Gloves from 1973-76. In 1985, he set a record with a .997 fielding percentage. In 1981, Grich tied for the A.L. lead with 22 homers and topped the league with a .543 slugging percentage.

BURLEIGH GRIMES

Burleigh Grimes, the last of the legal spitballers, grew up at the turn of the century in Wisconsin, where it's said he toiled in a lumber camp from morning 'til night for a dollar a day. This began a rough-and-tumble lifestyle that continued throughout his distinguished baseball career.

The Wisconsin native's pro career spanned from 1913 (when he briefly appeared on a Detroit Tigers roster but didn't pitch) to 1934 with the New York Yankees. Playing 19 years with seven teams, Grimes lived up to his reputation as a tough, brash competitor who hated to lose. Grimes was an active advocate of using the beanball to gain control of a game's tempo. He always pitched with a one-day growth of beard to create a fearsome visage on the mound, so he became known as "Ol' Stubblebeard."

The strong righthander will always be remembered as the last legal spitball pitcher in baseball. When baseball's brass outlawed the moist delivery in 1920, they provided a grandfather clause allowing the 17 established spitballers to continue throwing the pitch. Of the 17, Grimes lasted the longest, terrifying and baffling batters for another 14 years. While modern-day pitchers like Phil Niekro claimed that the knuckleball prolonged their careers, Grimes tacked years onto his stay in baseball through his mastery of the wet one.

Grimes graduated from high school in 1911 and immediately took to playing semipro baseball. He pitched for teams in Eau Claire, Wisconsin, Ottumwa, Iowa, Chattanooga, Tennessee, Richmond, Virginia, and Birmingham, Alabama, before making the Pirates club in 1916. His best minor league season was with Birmingham in 1916, when he was 20-11. This success earned him a late-season hookup with the Pittsburgh Pirates.

Grimes was one of the early saliva slingers in baseball history, but he didn't originate the pitch. That honor goes to a minor league outfielder by the name of George Hildebrand. While warming up one day, he noticed that balls picked up out of the wet grass often took on peculiar spins. Was it moisture that made the difference? He tried spitting on the ball to test the theory. He succeeded, and the spitter became an accepted part of baseball for more than three decades.

When Grimes retired from the Yankees in 1934, fans thought that the spitball was gone forever. But all that

happened was that pitchers developed more elaborate schemes for throwing the doctored baseball without getting caught. Grimes declared that he could control his spitter better than a knuckleballer. He said that he hit just one batter with a spitter in 19 seasons, and "only because he was leaning over the plate."

When Grimes made his debut with the Pirates in 1916, he won 2 games and lost 3, with 4 complete games. His rookie season was less than memorable; but his sophomore campaign was a nightmare. The Pirates wound up in last place, and Grimes wasn't any luckier. He suffered through a 13-game losing streak and ended the year with a 3-16 mark.

On January 9, 1918, the Pirates and the Brooklyn Dodgers made a three-for-two swap: Grimes, Chuck Ward, and Al

Mamaux were sent to the Dodgers in exchange for George Cutshaw and Casey Stengel.

The new environment did wonders for Grimes. He was 19-9 with a sparkling 2.14 ERA, 19 complete games, a career-high 7 shutouts, and a league-leading 41 appearances. Grimes slumped to 10-11 in 1919, then rebounded to 23-11 in 1920, leading the Dodgers to the National League title with a 93-61 record. The Cleveland Indians whipped the Dodgers in the World Series, five games to two. Although Grimes won the second game with a 3-0, seven-hit shutout, he lost games five and seven. Indians ace pitcher Stanley Coveleski, a spitballer like Grimes, had 3 complete-game wins in the Series. Organized baseball outlawed the spitter in December of that year.

Two more 20-win seasons came for Grimes with the Dodgers. In 1928 he was 25-14, his best record ever, with the Pittsburgh Pirates. Perhaps Grimes' brightest moment came at age 38, when he won 2 games in the 1931 World Series for the victorious St. Louis Cardinals.

Grimes won 270 games in his career, logged 314 complete games in 495 starts, and earned 18 saves in relief duty. While Grimes was never a long-ball threat, he handled himself well at bat. He hit .321 in 1928 and .306 in 1920, the two winningest years of his career. Following his retirement Grimes managed the Brooklyn Dodgers in 1937 and 1938. Throughout the 1940s he piloted several minor league clubs. In 1955 he was a coach with the Kansas City Athletics. Grimes was elected to the Hall of Fame in 1964.

CAREER HIGHLIGHTS
BURLEIGH ARLAND GRIMES

Born: August 9, 1893 Emerald, WI **Died:** December 6, 1985
Height: 5'10" **Weight:** 175 lbs. **Batted:** Right **Threw:** Right
Pitcher: Pittsburgh Pirates, 1916-17, 1928-29, 1934; Brooklyn Dodgers, 1918-26; New York Giants, 1927; Boston Braves, 1930; St. Louis Cardinals, 1930-31, 1933-34; Chicago Cubs, 1932-33; New York Yankees, 1934. Manager: Brooklyn Dodgers, 1937-38.

★ Led the N.L. in complete games four times

★ Pitched on four World Series teams

★ Won 20 or more games for five seasons

★ Elected to the Hall of Fame in 1964

MAJOR LEAGUE TOTALS

G	IP	W	L	Pct.	SO	BB	ERA
616	4,181	270	212	.560	1,512	1,295	3.53

Burleigh Grimes was a tough old pro from a bygone era. In the final game of the '31 Series, Grimes pitched with an inflamed appendix. He shut out the opposing team for 8 innings before weakening in the ninth. Another pitcher relieved him for the win.

LEFTY GROVE

Long before Steve Carlton landed the nickname, baseball knew only one "Lefty." He was Robert Moses Grove, one of the most talented southpaw hurlers in baseball history. Before he was through Grove would pitch 17 major league seasons and become only the sixth player in baseball history to win 300 games.

Grove never finished high school; instead, he went to work to help support his family. He worked briefly as a coal miner, then became a locomotive mechanic, and later worked in a glass factory. After playing amateur baseball in 1919 in a small Maryland town, Grove signed a contract with a minor league baseball team, Martinsburg of the Blue Ridge League. In 1920 he pitched in just six games before being purchased by Baltimore Orioles team owner Jack Dunn for $3,200. Grove spent the next five seasons with the International League club, which won pennants every year Grove was on the roster. Grove was 12-2 in the 1921 campaign, 25-10 in 1922, and 18-8 in 1923. At that time the leading International League club would meet the top finisher in the American Association in what was called "The Little World Series."

He became nearly invincible after that, winning 27 games in 1924 (with 330 strikeouts in 303 innings). The New York Giants tried to acquire Grove after the season's conclusion, but the Orioles wanted too much money. He earned a 26-6 record in 1925, then was purchased in the off-season by Philadelphia Athletics team owner Connie Mack. The Orioles owner insisted on selling Grove for the strange sum of $100,600. The $600 was added because the Orioles wanted to set a record for getting the most money ever for selling a player to the majors.

Grove didn't have immediate success with the Athletics, but owner/manager Mack was very patient with him. Mack called his new pitcher "Robert," and refused to call him by his nickname. Grove was also called "Mose" because of his middle name. Grove had the only losing season of his career in his 1925 Philadelphia debut, going 10-13. Even then he led the league with 116 strikeouts. In 1926 he was 13-13 with a league-leading 2.51 ERA and 194 strikeouts. He won 20 games for the first time in 1927, then topped the league with a 24-8 effort in 1928.

The Athletics won their first of two consecutive world championships in

1929. Grove won 20 games against just 6 losses, and he was first in the league in winning percentage (.769), ERA (2.81), games started (37), and strikeouts (170). He earned saves in games two and four of the Series, pitching 6.1 innings of shutout relief. Grove fanned 10 Cubs in his short appearances.

In 1930 Grove was the American League's winningest pitcher with 28 triumphs. He was also the league leader in winning percentage, ERA, games, and strikeouts. The Athletics beat the Cardinals in a six-game World Series. Grove was 2-1 in the World Series with 2 complete-game wins and a 1.42 ERA. The Cardinals turned the tables on Philadelphia in the 1931 Series, but Grove again went 2-1 with complete-game wins in the first and sixth games. That year Grove was the American League MVP with a 31-4 season. The

wily lefty earned a career-low ERA (2.06) and a career-high winning percentage (.886). Grove struck out 175 opponents to win his seventh straight strikeout title. In 1932 he won 25 games and led the league in ERA (2.84) and complete games (27).

Grove again dominated A.L. pitching in 1933, topping the league with 24 wins, a .750 winning percentage, and 21 complete games. Grove got the first save in the historic first All-Star game with three innings of spotless relief against the National Leaguers. But he was traded at season's end. Team owner Mack had taken such a severe financial beating during the Depression that he was forced to market some of his biggest, highest-paid stars to other teams. Grove's departure came on December 12, when Mack sent him with Max Bishop and Rube Walberg to the Boston Red Sox for Bob Kline, Rabbit Warstler, and a much-needed $125,000. In the following eight years, Grove won 20 games once and 17 games twice.

For his 17-year career, Grove won exactly 300 games. His .680 lifetime winning percentage is the fourth best in baseball history. Grove grabbed a total of nine ERA titles and seven strikeout crowns in his career. He accumulated a career total of 55 saves and led the junior circuit with 9 in 1930. Grove was the leading winner in the American League on four occasions and was the winner of 20 or more games during eight seasons (seven of those coming in 1927 through 1933).

Grove was elected to the Hall of Fame in 1947. After operating a bowling alley for many years, he died in 1975 at age 75.

CAREER HIGHLIGHTS
ROBERT MOSES GROVE

Born: March 6, 1900 Lonaconing, MD   **Died:** May 22, 1975
Height: 6'3" **Weight:** 190 lbs.   **Batted:** Left **Threw:** Left
Pitcher: Philadelphia Athletics, 1925-33; Boston Red Sox, 1934-41.

- ★ Named A.L. MVP in 1931
- ★ Had four World Series wins for the 1929-31 Philadelphia Athletics
- ★ Earned seven straight league strikeout crowns
- ★ Led the A.L. in wins four times
- ★ Has highest winning percentage of any 300-game winner
- ★ Elected to the Hall of Fame in 1947

MAJOR LEAGUE TOTALS

G	IP	W	L	Pct.	SO	BB	ERA
616	3,940	300	141	.680	2,266	1,187	3.06

In 1920 Connie Mack purchased Lefty Grove from the Baltimore Orioles of the International League for a then record $100,600. Grove was well worth the price as he eventually led the A.L. in wins four times and earned seven consecutive strikeout titles.

PEDRO GUERRERO

Tantalizing talent combined with frequent injury makes Pedro Guerrero's stats look as though they belong to Dr. Jekyll and Mr. Hyde. He has been sidelined for a month or more during one-fourth of his 16 professional seasons. His injuries have sometimes altered his ability upon return.

In 1989, the St. Louis Cardinals hoped that Guerrero could regain his magic batting stroke to help plug the hole at first base resulting from the 1987 loss of Jack Clark. (Like Guerrero, Clark has been cursed with an assortment of physical woes.) This coupling of a needy team and a battered slugger was a long shot: Guerrero was 33 years old, and three of his five injury layoffs occurred within the last six years.

Perhaps the most devastating blow came in 1985, when Guerrero injured his left wrist while chasing a foul off the bat of Mets star Darryl Strawberry in early September. Although he had tied Steve Garvey's record of 33 Los Angeles Dodger homers in a single season before the accident, Guerrero was unable to add to that total after recuperation, much to the Dodgers' detriment during pennant play. By April 3, 1986, he was back on the bench with a ruptured leg tendon.

Having suffered earlier sliding mishaps resulting in a 1977 ankle fracture and a 1980 knee ligament problem, Guerrero very rarely slides feet-first these days. He can't slide head first, either, because of back and shoulder injuries in 1984. The only solution appears to be long hits, which Guerrero managed nicely in 1987, with 25 doubles and 27 home runs.

A comeback in 1986 earned Guerrero standing ovations from Dodger fans. His 1987 return for the whole season netted him UPI's Comeback Player of the Year award, recognizing his team leads in a dozen offensive categories and his personal best of 184 hits — second best in the National League.

Guerrero began the 1988 season with another disability and sadly after 16 years with the Dodgers, he was shuttled from the club only weeks before they would return to postseason play for the first time since 1981. On August 16 the Cardinals gave up top left-hander John Tudor to get Guerrero.

In a sense, Guerrero's trade to the Cards prior to the 1988 World Series may have been the greatest boost he could have given the Dodgers into the postseason. Pitcher Tudor was a much-needed replacement for the prolific but ailing Fernando Valenzuela, helping the Blue Crew win the Western Division.

The Dominican Republic native was a key ingredient in the 1981 Dodgers world championship. In the World Series victory over the Yankees, Guerrero's 21 at-bats in six games netted him a tidy .333 average. His flawless outfield performance included 17 putouts and 1 assist. His 5 RBI in the final game (including 1 single, 1 double, and 1 homer) sparked the Dodgers 9-2 clinching triumph. Guerrero, third baseman Ron Cey, and catcher Steve Yeager were named Most Valuable Players, the first time in history the award was split three ways.

An injury to Cey earlier that season had caused Guerrero to be pulled from his newly acquired starting position in right field to cover third base. He alternated between the two positions (adding first base and sometimes even second) until 1985, when he settled permanently into the first base/outfield mode. It was as a first sacker that the Cardinals acquired him, hoping he could become the first long-time occupant of that spot since Keith Hernandez.

Third base had never been Guerrero's specialty, and his uneasiness in the field often continued to unnerve him when he came to bat. The shorter range needed to cover first base seemed to make defense easier on him. First base was the position Guerrero played exclusively for two years in the minors as well as during his brief call-up to Los Angeles. At that time, however, Garvey held the permanent lease on that spot.

Guerrero was signed as a free agent by the late Reggie Otero (a former Cleveland Indians scout who went on to discover many prospects with the Dodgers). Guerrero was fresh from the Dominican Republic, where he still returns during the off-season. After spending 1973 at shortstop and third, Guerrero honed in on the hot corner after being acquired by the Dodgers in exchange for Bruce Ellingsen on April 3, 1974. There followed three years at third, two at first, and one at both, before his call-up to the bigs. This was interrupted by a brief return to Albuquerque (the Dodgers Triple-A affiliate) where Guerrero, in preparation for his future, alternated between first, third, and the outfield.

With Guerrero's strikeout ratio declining over the past two years and his flexible swing still intact, the Cardinals are hoping for more accomplishments from their new long-ball threat. Playing in cavernous Busch Stadium will be an awesome long-ball challenge to the three-time All-Star.

CAREER HIGHLIGHTS
PEDRO GUERRERO

Born: June 29, 1956   San Pedro de Macoris, Dominican Republic
Height: 5'11"   **Weight:** 176 lbs.   **Bats:** Right   **Throws:** Right
Outfielder, first baseman, third baseman: Los Angeles Dodgers, 1978-88; St. Louis Cardinals, 1988-89.

* Batted .333 during the '81 World Series
* Played in three League Championship Series
* Led the Pacific Coast League in RBI twice
* Played in four All-Star games
* Tied a record with 15 homers in June 1985
* Topped 30 homers in three different seasons

MAJOR LEAGUE TOTALS

G	AB	H	BA	2B	3B	HR	R	RBI	SB
1,242	4,321	1,330	.308	218	26	193	637	732	90

Pedro Guerrero's career is marked by extreme highs and lows as injuries have kept him out of the game for long periods of time. Guerrero was awarded UPI's Comeback Player of the Year award in 1987 for leading his team in several offensive categories.

RON GUIDRY

From his first full season with the New York Yankees in 1977, power-pitching Ron Guidry was known as "Louisiana Lightning."

The Yankees chose the 21-year-old architecture major in the third round of the free-agent draft in June 1971. Nearly six years in the minors gave no clue that the Bronx Bombers had anything special planned for the thin hurler. Guidry was able to earn a brief appearance with the Yankees in late 1975 but posted an 0-1 record in ten games. He surfaced for keeps in mid-1976, after notching a 5-1 record with an 0.68 ERA in 40 innings at Syracuse. He again turned in an undistinguished performance as a Yankee in '76. It became evident that Guidry was a man with promises to keep if he was to remain in the majors.

Used in relief in six of his first seven appearances of 1977, Guidry went on to finish the season with 24 straight starts, tallying 16 wins, 7 losses, 176 strikeouts, and a 2.82 ERA. He pitched a three-hitter to win the second game of the American League Championship Series. The Yankees captured the world championship, with Guidry winning the fourth Series game with a four-hitter against the Dodgers.

This was the country's first glimpse of Louisiana Lightning. The crash of thunder was not far behind. In 1978 Guidry smashed major league records with a 25-3 season and an .893 winning percentage. His 1.74 ERA was rare for a starting pitcher, and his 9 shutouts tied Babe Ruth's 1916 A.L. record for lefties. Guidry's career-high 248 strikeouts set a club record; he acquired 10 or more in each of eight games, and 18 in one memorable game against the California Angels. The Yankees won 30 of the 35 games he started.

A torrent of accolades rained down: *The Sporting News* Man of the Year, *TSN's* Player of the Year, AP Male Athlete of the Year, and election to four All-Star teams. Guidry was the first unanimous choice for the Cy Young award since Denny McLain won it in 1968. The year ended with another world championship for the Yankees. Guidry won the fourth and decisive game of the 1978 American League Championship Series against the Kansas City Royals, then contributed a complete-game victory over the Dodgers in game three of the World Series.

This excellence continued in 1979,

with Guidry's second straight lead in league ERA (2.78). After his first 100 career decisions, Guidry was 72-28. Only four pitchers in history (Sal Maglie, Vic Raschi, Spud Chandler, and Ed Reulbach) had matched this accomplishment. In 1981 Guidry was named A.L. Pitcher of the Month for his August marks of 4 wins, no losses, and a 0.37 ERA. All this came despite breaking a finger on his catching hand on August 23; Guidry never missed a start.

In late 1982 Guidry secured his 100th major league victory and gained his first of five straight Gold Glove awards for his unmarred fielding percentage. An inflamed rib cartilage placed Guidry on the disabled list for the first time in 1984, but not before he struck out a season-high 13 White Sox, blanking them 7-0 on 4 hits. Earlier in 1984 "Gator" had fanned his 1,258th

batter, moving him to fourth place on the all-time Yankees list.

But these were merely rumblings—the quiet before the stormy summer of 1985. His last glorious year included a league-leading 22-6 record and a top .786 winning percentage. At 259 innings, the second-busiest season of his career, Guidry's summer included an early winning streak of 12 games, wih 58 strikeouts and an ERA of 2.18. His career Ks reached 1,500, his fielding percentage still remained among the best in baseball (with just 1 error all year), and he threw 2 consecutive shutouts in June. These, in addition to the career-high 9 shutouts notched in his banner year of 1978, brought his career total to 26.

A lack of work resulted in a dropoff in Guidry's stats in the years following 1985. Injuries kept him inactive in 1986 and 1988. Some of 1987 was spent in the minors when the Yankees dallied in picking up his free-agent contract. The chorus repeated in early 1989: Yankee manager Dallas Green didn't want free-agent Guidry re-signed for 1989, but he was pressured by owner George Steinbrenner to take him back. The Yanks forked over a one-year, $500,000 contract.

Even though Guidry's career was near its end, there was still a spark in the Louisiana Lightning. His pitches no longer traveled their regular paths at 90-plus miles per hour, and his wicked sliders no longer left batters swinging at air. Guidry had acquired a crafty change-up, however, thanks to dedicated coaching by Billy Martin in Guidry's shining season of 1985. Past injuries and time quickly caught up to him, though, and Guidry retired during the 1989 season.

CAREER HIGHLIGHTS
RONALD JAMES GUIDRY

Born: August 28, 1950   Lafayette, LA
Height: 5'11"   **Weight:** 161 lbs.   **Batted:** Left   **Threw:** Left
Pitcher: New York Yankees, 1975-89.

★ Won the Cy Young award in 1978
★ Has a 3-1 record in three World Series
★ Set a major league mark for winning percentage (.893) in 1978

★ Topped 20-wins three times
★ Led the A.L. in ERA twice
★ Won five Gold Gloves from 1982 through 1986

MAJOR LEAGUE TOTALS

G	IP	W	L	Pct.	SO	BB	ERA
368	2,393	170	91	.651	1,778	633	3.29

Ron Guidry retired in 1989 after an illustrious 15-year career. His banner year came in 1978 when he impressed the sports world with his 25-3 record and his .893 winning percentage. He was the unanimous choice for the Cy Young award.

TONY GWYNN

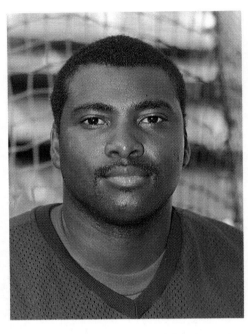

An eight-year veteran of the major leagues and an eight-year son of the Padres, lefthand slugger Tony Gwynn has broken records and broken bones, but he never broke a fan's or a manager's heart.

His 1988 season is a case in point. It started out darkly on March 11, with surgery on his left hand to provide unrestricted tendon movement. He was back in the box in only one week but was troubled by scar tissue. After a May 7 tumble on the astroturf, Gwynn was even more troubled by his right thumb and was out for the rest of the month.

Entering June with only a .237 batting average, Gwynn finished the month with an 18-game hitting streak and two Player of the Week awards. In July he hit .406 for Player of the Month, the third such honor for the 29-year-old. Before the season was out, he collected his 1,000th career hit (off veteran moundsman Nolan Ryan, no less) and went on to become the Padres all-time hit leader (breaking Dave Winfield's mark of 1,134 in 570 fewer at-bats). He was also voted team Most Valuable Player for the third consecutive year (and for the fourth time). He fell only 1 RBI short of his 1984 career best (71) and ripped through his final 73 games with an average of .364.

Even in a bad year, Gwynn looks good. The effect is heightened by his placement on an unspectacular team. Yet Gwynn is far from complacent in his niche as the Padres resident superstar. Each year Gwynn strives to improve some weakness in his playing and, although he may never become a power hitter, he has certainly become an all-around player.

Considered only average on the base paths after 8 stolen bases in 1982 and 7 in 1983, Gwynn streaked to 33 swipes in 1984 and hasn't gone below double digits since. In 1986 he tied the modern National League record for most stolen bases in a game with 5 on September 20. In 1987 he had an impressive 56 steals, his best single-season to date.

With a fielding average that dipped as low as .893 in his 1983 rehabilitation in the minors and with an arm of only average strength, Gwynn was not originally considered much of a threat in the field. In 1984, however, he came back with a .989 fielding percentage for the first of three consecutive seasons. In 1986 he earned his first of two back-to-back Gold Glove awards, finishing with 19 outfield assists (second best in the entire major league) and leading the N.L. in total chances (360) and putouts (337). In 1987 he made his fourth consecutive journey to the All-Star game. He depends upon accuracy and range for his totals and is known for getting a good jump on balls hit to right field.

Despite six straight seasons of .300-plus batting, Gwynn has also worked to improve his average against fellow lefties and against low breaking pitches. His excellent patience is demonstrated by his 1988 mark of only 40 strikeouts in 521 at-bats, a 1-to-13 ratio. Even with the count stacked against him, Gwynn has an uncanny knack for fouling off pitches until he sees the one he wants.

His 1987 average of .370 was the National League's highest since 1948, when Stan Musial bested the mark by only 6 points. In contrast, his 1988 batting title output of .313 was the lowest average ever to win an N.L. batting crown. Only five National League hitters even managed to top the .300 plateau in 1988. Gwynn's modest average was acquired despite a month on the disabled list.

Gwynn has made besting his own efforts a challenge from the start. He still holds the record for most assists in basketball at San Diego State University. He broke his wrist for the first time during his second year of professional baseball, breaking a 15-game debut hitting streak at the same time. Playing winter ball in Puerto Rico, he fractured the wrist again, yet finished the '83 season in San Diego with a .309 effort.

The Los Angeles native has been quietly earning a reputation as one of baseball's purest hitters. From 1984 through 1988 Gwynn amassed a total of 1,057 hits. Only Boston's Wade Boggs has more (just 7 more, at 1,064). Gwynn first gained national recognition in 1984, the year the upstart Padres marched all the way to the World Series. The team's National League championship was fueled by Gwynn's league-leading .351 average and league-best 213 hits (making him the first Padre ever to break the 200-hit barrier). Gwynn got the Padres to the World Series with a .368, seven-hit showing against the Chicago Cubs in the League Championship Series.

Gwynn's younger brother, Chris, is a future outfield star for the Los Angeles Dodgers. Tony Gwynn continues to influence other young stars of the future: He's part owner and an instructor at the famous San Diego School of Baseball, where youngsters from across the nation go for training.

CAREER HIGHLIGHTS
ANTHONY KEITH GWYNN

Born: May 9, 1960   Los Angeles, CA
Height: 5'11"   **Weight:** 185 lbs.   **Bats:** Left   **Throws:** Left
Outfielder: San Diego Padres, 1982-89.

★ Won N.L. batting titles in 1984, 1987, and 1988
★ Played in five All-Star games
★ Led the league in hits three times

★ Batted .368 in the 1984 League Championship Series
★ Hit over .300 for the last seven seasons
★ Named as Silver Slugger three times

MAJOR LEAGUE TOTALS

G	AB	H	BA	2B	3B	HR	R	RBI	SB
1,060	4,078	1,354	.332	192	51	45	617	410	221

Tony Gwynn won N.L. batting titles in 1984, 1987, and 1988. He led the league in hits three times, each time getting more than 200 hits. Gwynn's best season came in 1987, when he had 218 base hits, 36 doubles, 56 stolen bases, and a .370 batting average.

STAN HACK

When a discussion of the Chicago Cubs greatest third basemen arises, 1960s slugger Ron Santo is quickly mentioned. However, Cub fans of the 1930s and 40s may remember another stalwart at the hot corner, a hard-working fellow by the name of Stan Hack.

Hack was a well-liked performer with the Cubs from 1932 through 1947. His popularity was reflected in his nickname, "Smilin' Stan." Hack was a slick-fielding leadoff hitter. Hack was not endowed with the long-ball prowess of Santo, but he was a perennial .300 hitter whose average never slipped below a season total of .289 during his first ten full seasons in the National League. Unlike the Cubs stars from the past four decades, Hack had the pleasure of participating in four World Series with Chicago.

Professional baseball discovered Hack when he was working as a bank clerk and playing ball on a recreational basis for an amateur team in Sacramento, California. The Solons, the local team representing the Pacific Coast League, liked Hack's ability and convinced him to try out for the league in 1931. Hack spent one year with the Sacramento club, batting .352.

In 1932 the Cubs bought Hack off the Solons roster for $40,000. He was given the starting third baseman's job but had trouble holding it due to his erratic hitting. By season's end, he had batted only .236 in 72 games. However, his modest contributions helped the Cubs win their first of three National League pennants during the decade. After appearing in just 20 games the next season, Hack had his first big success in 1934, batting .289 in 111 games.

When the Cubs returned to the World Series in 1935, Hack helped out with a .311 average, 4 home runs, and 64 RBI. Although he batted just .227 in the six-game World Series (won by the Tigers), Hack's single off "Schoolboy" Rowe was a key hit in the Cubs come-from-behind 6-5 win over the American Leaguers in game three. The two following years, Hack hit .298 and .297, respectively. He was named to his first of four All-Star teams in 1938, and his season sparked the Cubs to another National League title. Even though he stole just 16 bases, Hack won his first of two straight National League stolen base titles. He also batted a personal best of .320. While the Yankees swept the Cubs in four straight World Series

games that year, Hack waged his own battle in the fall classic. He battered a tough Yankee pitching staff with a .471 clip, gaining 8 hits in 17 plate appearances.

In the 1945 Series against the Tigers, Hack had a game-winning double in the twelfth inning of game six to send the Series to a seventh game.

Hack retired as a player following the 1947 season, when he hit .271 in 76 games. His lifetime totals include a .301 batting average, 2,193 hits, 363 doubles, 81 triples, 57 homers, and 642 RBI. Two of his most impressive totals are in runs scored (1,239) and bases on balls (1,092), showing his consistent value to the Cubs as a leadoff man. Furthermore, Hack was a solid contact hitter who struck out only 466 times in his career (an average of 29 per season). Hack still ranks in the top ten in nine different all-time hitting categories for the Cubs—in everything except homers, RBI, and batting average. His Cubs records include most career bases on balls (1,092) and most career singles (1,692).

As a fielder, Hack was dependable and sure-handed. In the all-time categories for third basemen, Hack fares well. He ranks 12th in games played (1,836), 14th in career putouts (1,944), and 15th in lifetime chances accepted (5,684). In single-season achievements, Hack led the league twice in fielding percentage and assists. He was first in putouts for five seasons and led in double plays three times.

It's reasonable to say that Hack was one of the most competent third basemen in major league baseball during the 1930s. Considering the assistance he gave to four different pennant-winning Cubs teams, it's baffling that he hasn't received more attention as a possible Hall of Famer. The only thing that has kept Hack from gaining lasting fame has been his lack of home runs, an unofficial past prerequisite needed for recognition in Cooperstown.

Following his retirement as a player, Hack managed for several years in the Cubs minor league organization. He was promoted to manage in Chicago in 1954. Three unsuccessful seasons followed for Hack. His 1954 team finished seventh in the league with a 64-90 mark; the 1955 squad wound up sixth at 72-81; and in 1956 the Cubs fell to a 60-94 mark, coming in eighth.

Hack was a St. Louis Cardinals coach in 1957 and 1958 and was an interim manager for the last ten games of the 1958 season when manager Fred Hutchison was fired. The Cards were 3-7 under Hack. His managerial totals include 199 wins and 272 losses for a .423 winning percentage. Hack managed in the Pacific Coast League, Texas League, and American Association before retiring from the sport in 1966.

After he left baseball, Hack owned and operated a restaurant in Illinois. He died after his 70th birthday in 1979.

CAREER HIGHLIGHTS
STANLEY CAMFIELD HACK

Born: December 6, 1909 Sacramento, CA **Died:** December 15, 1979
Height: 6'0" **Weight:** 170 lbs. **Batted:** Left **Threw:** Right
Third baseman: Chicago Cubs, 1932-47.

* Compiled a career .301 batting average
* Batted over .300 six times
* Led the N.L. in hits twice
* Selected as an All-Star four times
* Scored 100-plus runs seven times
* Appeared in four World Series

MAJOR LEAGUE TOTALS

G	AB	H	BA	2B	3B	HR	R	RBI	SB
1,938	7,278	2,193	.301	363	81	57	1,239	642	165

Four-time All-Star third baseman Stan Hack led the N.L. in putouts for five seasons, double plays three times, and fielding percentage twice. Hack, who played for the Cubs his entire career, also led the N.L. in hits during two seasons.

GABBY HARTNETT

Baseball historians disagree on exactly how Charles Leo Hartnett came to be known as "Gabby," but there has never been any dispute among baseball fans about this gifted backstop's place in the history of the game.

The hard-working Hartnett first captured the attention of major league scouts while playing with Worcester of the Eastern League. His contract was purchased by the Chicago Cubs for $2,500, and in 1922 the young catcher reported to training camp at Catalina Island, where he acquired his nickname. It depends on which story you choose to believe: Some accounts have it that Hartnett was labeled "that gabby guy" for all of his comments; still others claim that he was silent throughout the spring and the nickname was adopted facetiously. Approximately one decade earlier the Cubs had a catcher who was nicknamed "Noisy John" Kling because he was so silent.

Hartnett's explosive bat and powerful arm did plenty of talking during his 20 years in the majors. For 19 years Hartnett was a fixture behind the plate for the Cubs. For 12 seasons the strong, dependable backstop caught 100 or more games—leading the league in fielding percentage seven times. A powerful hitter, Hartnett compiled a lifetime batting average of .297 and hit 236 home runs (once a major league record for catchers). His most famous round-tripper came on September 28, 1938, when his homer defeated the Pittsburgh Pirates and won the Cubs the National League pennant. Hartnett's hit was dubbed the "homer in the gloamin'" because the game had dragged on so long that darkness was descending on unlit Wrigley Field.

In his one minor league season, Hartnett had batted .264 in the New England League. When he advanced to the Chicago Cubs in 1922, he played in just 31 games, hitting .194. In 1923 Hartnett played 39 games behind the plate and 31 more at first base. The Rhode Island native upped his average to .268 with 8 homers and 39 RBI during his sophomore season.

Hartnett soon became known as one of the league's best-hitting catchers. In 1924 he batted .299 with 16 homers. He whacked 24 round-trippers in 1925. Injuries limited Hartnett to 93 games in 1926. He rebounded in 1927 with 10 homers, 80 RBI, and a .294 average. The Cubs became contenders in the late 1920s, partially due to Hartnett's con-

tributions. In 1928 Hartnett's totals included 14 homers, 65 RBI, and a .302 average. While the Cubs won the N.L. pennant in 1929, Hartnett played in only 25 games that year. He was only available for pinch-hitting duty in the World Series, which the Philadelphia Athletics won in just five games.

Hartnett had two of his most noteworthy seasons during the early 1930s. In 1930 he batted .339 with 37 homers and 122 RBI. Hartnett had an average season in 1932 (12 homers, 52 RBI, and a .271 average); however, in the World Series against the Yankees, he batted .313.

The National League elected Hartnett as its Most Valuable Player following the 1935 season, when he hit 13 homers, 91 RBI, and a .344 average (third in the league). Hartnett's efforts helped the Cubs to the 1935 World Series against the Detroit Tigers. Although the Bengals downed Chicago in six games, Hartnett batted .292 with 1 homer. In 1936 Hartnett's average

fell to .307, still an admirable mark for any catcher. He rebounded the next year to a .354 average (third in the league) and hit 12 homers and 82 RBI.

Hartnett limited his playing time during his final three seasons with Chicago because he was also serving the team as manager. After replacing Cubs skipper Charlie Grimm, Hartnett piloted his club to a National League pennant. Besides his managerial duties, Hartnett played in 88 games, hitting .274 with 10 homers and 59 RBI. His luck ended when the World Series started and his club was swept in four straight Series games by the New York Yankees. Hartnett had just 1 hit in 11 appearances.

In 1939 Hartnett played in 97 games. Even at age 38 he could still hit, as evidenced by his 12 homers, 59 RBI, and .278 average. He concluded his career in Chicago after playing 39 games in 1940. Hartnett's final season was with the 1941 New York Giants, where he served as a player/coach. Although he played just 64 games, Hartnett put the icing on a fine career with a final batting average of .300.

Hartnett ranks sixth in history in games caught (1,790). The five-time All-Star accumulated 1,912 lifetime hits and 1,179 RBI. He still ranks in the top ten in nine different all-time Cubs offensive categories, including a fourth-place spot in homers with 236. Only Ernie Banks, Billy Williams, and Ron Santo had more.

After spending three one-year stints as a minor league manager during the 1940s, Hartnett retired from baseball until 1965, when he coached and scouted for the Kansas City Athletics for two years. Hartnett was elected to the Hall of Fame in 1955.

CAREER HIGHLIGHTS
CHARLES LEO HARTNETT

Born: December 20, 1900   Woonsocket, RI   **Died:** December 20, 1972
Height: 6'1"   **Weight:** 195 lbs.   **Batted:** Right   **Threw:** Right
Catcher: Chicago Cubs, 1922-40; New York Giants, 1941.
Manager: Chicago Cubs, 1938-40.

★ Once held the record for most lifetime homers by a catcher
★ Played in four World Series
★ Won the 1938 pennant for the Cubs with a "homer in the gloamin'"
★ Elected to Hall of Fame in 1955
★ Caught 100 or more games for 12 seasons

MAJOR LEAGUE TOTALS

G	AB	H	BA	2B	3B	HR	R	RBI	SB
1,990	6,432	1,912	.297	396	64	236	867	1,179	28

Considered one of the N.L.'s best catchers, Gabby Hartnett led N.L. backstops in fielding
six times, played in over 100 games in 12 seasons, and caught 1,790 games. Hartnett was
a strong-armed catcher who could handle even the most temperamental pitchers.

HARRY HEILMANN

Although he was nicknamed "Slug," outfielder Harry Heilmann was anything but a snail during his 17 years in the major leagues. Known for his slugging ability, Heilmann was a four-time batting champion of the 1920s, and he is also regarded as one of the finest outfielders in Detroit Tigers history.

Heilmann is best remembered as a .400 hitter. He's one of only 31 players in all of baseball history who topped the revered mark during a single season. And what a season it was. Heilmann won his second American League batting title that year with a stunning .403 average, outdistancing Babe Ruth in the race for the best average by a full 10 points. That season Heilmann had 18 home runs (third in the league behind Ruth's 41) and 115 RBI (third behind Ruth and Tris Speaker of Cleveland). He ranked third in the league in hits (211), fourth in total bases (331), and second in slugging percentage (his .632 was topped by Ruth's incredible .764 mark). Heilmann's heavy hitting was of limited use to the Tigers, who finished second in the league with an 83-71 record. The Yankees topped Heilmann and his Tiger teammates in the pennant race by 15 games, posting a 98-54 record.

In retrospect, Heilmann's .400-plus average is even more impressive. He is one of just eight players who have done it in the 20th century, entering the company of such greats as Ty Cobb, Rogers Hornsby, Nap Lajoie, "Shoeless" Joe Jackson, Bill Terry, George Sisler, and Ted Williams.

If the American League had been using designated hitters back in the 1920s, Heilmann would have been the best around. Historians don't discuss his fielding skills—apparently because he didn't have many to speak of. He did have a league high of 31 assists when he played right field with the 1924 Detroit Tigers. The Tigers also tried him at first base to keep his potent bat in the lineup; in 1919 and 1920 he led the A.L. first basemen in errors.

The Tigers signed Heilmann out of college in 1913, but they gave him only limited playing time in 1914. He was forced to spend nearly three seasons in the minors simply because the Tigers outfield was glutted with quality hitters like Cobb, "Wahoo" Sam Crawford, and Bob Veach. At the plate, however, Heilmann had few equals. He was one of the best clutch hitters in the junior circuit. In 18 major league seasons, all

but three of them with the Tigers, Heilmann compiled a .342 lifetime batting average. Between 1921 and 1927 he won four American League batting crowns with averages of .394 in 1921, .403 in 1923, .393 in 1925, and .398 in 1927. In his "off" years during that period he batted .356, .346, and .367. Heilmann batted .300 or better for 11 straight seasons. Unlike some players, Heilmann wasn't always a better hitter in his home ballpark. In 1925, for instance, he seemed better away from Tiger Stadium: His average on the road was a blistering .456 that season.

Throughout most of his years with Detroit, Heilmann had teamed with Ty Cobb to give the Tigers a dynamic one-two punch at the plate. It was Cobb, named manager of the Tigers in 1921, who helped Heilmann develop into a great hitter. In previous seasons Heilmann had been hitting only .296. But when Cobb began working with him in 1921, his average soared to an amazing .394 and never dipped below .340 for the next seven years. Some

baseball followers say that Heilmann was also more successful once the spitball was banned and the dead-ball era was over.

Heilmann closed out his playing days with a two-year stint with the Cincinnati Reds in 1930 and 1932. Heilmann was still a prosperous hitter in 1930, and the Reds made him their center fielder. He hit .333 that year with 19 home runs and 91 RBI in 142 games. Arthritis kept him out of action for all of 1931, and he played in just 15 games in 1932 before retiring.

From 1933 to 1951, Heilmann was a fan favorite as a radio announcer for Detroit Tigers games. Many of his listeners had never seen him play, but they adored his sense of humor and unique understanding of the game. Perhaps much of Heilmann's broadcasting success can be traced to his off-season experience on the vaudeville circuit (along with several other stars of the day). This made him a natural for the booming medium of radio.

Heilmann died of cancer less than a month before his 57th birthday in 1951. The long-time Bengal hero died just one day before the All-Star game, which was hosted by Detroit that year. In a touching display of affection for one of Detroit's greatest players, thousands of fans attended his funeral service. Heilmann was elected to Cooperstown in 1952.

Though a bit slow on the field, Harry "Slug" Heilmann batted a career-high .403 in 1923. He won A.L. batting titles in 1921, 1923, 1925, and 1927. His powerful bat more than compensated for his lack of speed.

CAREER HIGHLIGHTS
HARRY EDWIN HEILMANN

Born: August 3, 1894 San Francisco, CA **Died:** July 9, 1951
Height: 6'1" **Weight:** 200 lbs. **Batted:** Right **Threw:** Right
Outfielder: Detroit Tigers, 1914, 1916-29; Cincinnati Reds, 1930, 1932.

- ★ Won batting titles in 1921, 1923, 1925, and 1927
- ★ Compiled a .342 lifetime average
- ★ Elected to the Hall of Fame in 1952
- ★ Notched a career-high .403 batting mark in 1923
- ★ Batted over .300 during 12 seasons
- ★ Led the A.L. with 237 hits in 1921

MAJOR LEAGUE TOTALS

G	AB	H	BA	2B	3B	HR	R	RBI	SB
2,146	7,787	2,660	.342	542	151	183	1,291	1,538	112

RICKEY HENDERSON

The next two years will be breathless ones for baseball fans with an eye toward history. By the end of that time, Rickey Henderson will almost surely have stolen Lou Brock's title as the all-time stolen base king.

Brock's career record stands at 938 stolen bases and has gone unchallenged for a decade. Behind Brock is Ty Cobb with 892, followed by Rickey Henderson at over 800 and still counting. If he matches Brock's longevity, Henderson has another few years to establish a new pilfering record for future starry-eyed rookies to dream of breaking.

Henderson has topped the league in stolen bases every season since his 1980 rookie appearance, except for 1987, when he spent two months on the disabled list. These season totals range from 56 steals in 1981 to a record-breaking 130 in 1982. In 1988 Henderson logged 93 steals, the best in the league. He dropped to third in the "caught stealing" category, behind Harold Reynolds and Jose Canseco. Five times a leader in unsuccessful steals, Henderson's shrinking number of aborted attempts proves there is more to Henderson than reckless daring. He is a thinking man's larcenist.

It seems as if the temptation has always been there for Henderson. As a high school senior in 1976, he received a reported two dozen scholarship offers to play college football. Instead, Henderson trekked to Idaho for the first of three and a half years in the Oakland A's farm system. A fourth-round pick in the June free-agent draft, Henderson made his debut with a .336 average and 29 steals in 36 attempts. Improvements in these and other vital statistics led to his recognition as an All-Star and MVP.

Even before reaching the majors, Henderson reached the record books by becoming the fourth player in minor league history to steal 7 bases in a single game. In 1978 he led his league in steals as well as double plays and assists. By June of 1979, Henderson was ready for a spot on the A's starting lineup, and although his total of 33 swipes seemed paltry by his own standards, it was by far the best on Henderson's new team.

Henderson settled in for a mutually satisfying stay with the Athletics. In 1980 he became the third major leaguer ever to steal 100 bases in a season, a feat he'd later surpass not once, but twice. The next year brought Henderson's first Gold Glove and league bests in hits (135) and runs (89).

The 1981 A's, under manager Billy Martin, won the second half of the strike-marred split season with a 37-23 record. The A's beat the Kansas City Royals in a special playoff with three straight wins. Oakland was swept by the Yankees in the American League Championship Series, but Henderson paced the losing A's with a .364 batting average.

His steals more than doubled in 1982, when Brock's record of 118 pilfers in a single season was shattered by Henderson's 130. His dedication to catching Brock for good is evident in the league-leading walks posted for Henderson that year (116). He knew that a player couldn't steal if he couldn't get on base. He snatched 108 bases in 1983. At age 24 he became the youngest player ever to steal 400 bases.

Two years later he was the youngest to reach 500.

The New York Yankees gave up five players to get Henderson from Oakland, the town where he grew up. On December 8, 1984, the A's sent Henderson, minor leaguer Bert Bradley, and cash to New York in exchange for Jay Howell, Jose Rijo, Stan Javier, Tim Birtsus, and Eric Plunk. Oakland seemed unable to sign Henderson to a long-term contract, so the team cut its losses and traded him before losing him to free agency (with the team getting nothing). The cash that the A's threw in probably helped the Yankees pay off their new star. Henderson signed a five-year contract worth a reported $8.65 million.

Despite a month's worth of injuries in early 1985, Henderson finished his first Yankee season with personal highs in homers and RBI (24 and 72), which he would surpass the following year with his standing best—28 dingers and 74 RBI. He set two new records: one for most homers from a leadoff batter in a season (9); the other for most leadoff homers in a lifetime (34).

Henderson has been a perennial All-Star since his 1980 rookie season. He's one of the finest fielders in the American League, using his speed to turn the potential base hits of rival batters into routine outs. Most importantly, Henderson is mounting a solid pace to break all existing stolen base marks. During the opening month of the 1989 season, Henderson quickly bagged his 800th career steal and set a new mark with his 36th career leadoff home run. A short time later, he was traded back to his hometown of Oakland.

CAREER HIGHLIGHTS
RICKEY HENLEY HENDERSON

Born: December 25, 1958   Chicago, IL
Height: 5'10"   **Weight:** 185 lbs.   **Bats:** Right   **Throws:** Left
Outfielder: Oakland A's, 1979-84, 1989; New York Yankees, 1985-89.

- ★ Broke the A.L. stolen base mark of 96 with 100 steals in 1980
- ★ Led the A.L. in stolen bases seven consecutive seasons
- ★ Scored 146 runs in 1985, more than any player since the expansion
- ★ Set a record for most stolen bases (130) in one season in 1982
- ★ Topped the 100-steal barrier three times in ten seasons
- ★ Batted .364 in the 1981 Championship Series

MAJOR LEAGUE TOTALS

G	AB	H	BA	2B	3B	HR	R	RBI	SB
1,472	5,524	1,603	.290	261	47	138	1,171	561	871

Perhaps the best base thief in modern baseball, Rickey Henderson will no doubt usurp Lou Brock as the stolen base king before the end of his career. Henderson swiped a remarkable 130 bases in 1982, establishing a record for most stolen bases in one year.

GEORGE HENDRICK

George Hendrick was winding down a long and illustrious major league career in 1988. Even though Hendrick was a talented performer who could hit for power and average, his abilities were often overlooked and misunderstood because of his unwillingness to talk to the press.

Hendrick was leading the Angels in batting average in mid-August of 1987 with a .290 mark before slumping to .241 by the end of the season. Again in 1988, Hendrick was used part-time in just 69 games, batting .244. The Los Angeles native fell a bit short of Hall-of-Fame-quality lifetime statistics. He missed the 300-home-run milestone by 33 and stopped 20 hits shy of the 2,000-hit plateau. His career average of .278 was due to a decline in productivity once he left the National League.

Aside from inadequate numbers, Hendrick will probably never get into Cooperstown for another reason. Throughout most of his career, he suffered from a bad reputation for not talking to the press. Many of the writers whom Hendrick continually avoided were the people who could have given him national recognition. These media are likely to hold Hendrick's silence against him when he is eligible for election to the Hall of Fame.

Hendrick was the first player selected in the free-agent draft of June 1968, when he was chosen by the Oakland Athletics. In his first pro season with Burlington, he led the Midwest League with a .327 batting average and 25 doubles. After three more seasons in the minors, Hendrick played out the end of the 1971 campaign with the A's.

He spent little more than a week in the minors at the start of the 1972 season before being called back to Oakland. In 58 games for the A's that season, he hit just .182. He appeared in the 1972 World Series for the A's, getting 2 hits and scoring 3 runs as the Athletics took the world championship. The A's traded him with catcher Dave Duncan to Cleveland for catcher Ray Fosse and infielder Jack Heidemann on March 24, 1973.

With the Tribe in 1973, Hendrick spent six weeks on the disabled list, which was the only time he has been officially out of action in his major league career until early 1987 — a remarkable feat of endurance for any ballplayer. After his fourth season with the Indians, Hendrick was traded to the San Diego Padres. Early in 1978 he was dealt to the St. Louis Cardinals for

pitcher Eric Rasmussen. The California native was an immediate success with St. Louis and experienced some of his greatest years with the Redbirds, batting over .300 in half his seasons there and posting home run totals in the double digits each year. In 1979 he batted .300 and led the league with 20 outfield assists. In 1980 he tied his career high of 25 homers while knocking in 109 runs with a .302 average.

Hendrick was a major reason why the Cardinals rolled to a World Series win over the Milwaukee Brewers in the 1982 fall classic. During the regular season, the tall slugger batted .282 with 19 home runs and 104 RBI. In the seventh and decisive game of the Series, Hendrick's sixth-inning single put the Cardinals ahead to stay after a three-run rally. The Cards wound up with a 6-3 win and their first world championship since 1967. Hendrick paced the winners in the seven-game affair with 9 hits, 5 RBI, 5 runs scored, and a .321 average. He played flawless defense in

the field with no errors, 10 putouts, and 1 assist.

On December 12, 1984, Hendrick was traded to the Pittsburgh Pirates with catcher Steve Barnard in exchange for pitcher John Tudor and outfielder Brian Harper. It was no secret that Hendrick wasn't happy in Steel City, and he made his feelings known by a lack of determination on the field. Some accused him of not running out hits or pursuing fly balls with any enthusiasm. After just 69 games (and a dismal .230 average), he was traded to the California Angels with pitchers Al Holland and John Candelaria for pitchers Pat Clements and Bob Kipper and outfielder Mike Brown on August 2, 1985. For Hendrick, who lived in Inglewood, California, being with the Angels meant playing close to home, something all veteran players with families appreciate.

Unless he starts granting interviews once his career is over, Hendrick's position in baseball history seems uncertain. Despite his All-Star status and the fact that he was a key performer for several pennant-winning teams in the 1970s and 80s, the man known as "Silent George" may never receive his due recognition.

George Hendrick was a major catalyst in St. Louis' 1982 world championship. For the season he batted .282 with 104 RBI. He paced the Redbirds in the Series with 9 hits, 5 RBI, 5 runs scored, and a .321 average.

CAREER HIGHLIGHTS
GEORGE ANDREW HENDRICK

Born: October 18, 1949   Los Angeles, CA
Height: 6'3"   **Weight:** 195 lbs.   **Batted:** Right   **Threw:** Right
Outfielder: Oakland A's, 1971-72; Cleveland Indians, 1973-76; San Diego Padres, 1977-78; St. Louis Cardinals, 1978-84; Pittsburgh Pirates, 1985; California Angels, 1985-88.

- ★ Hit 19 or more homers for eight seasons
- ★ Appeared in two World Series
- ★ Hit 3 home runs in one game in 1973
- ★ Played in three All-Star games
- ★ Batted .300 or better four times
- ★ Played in three League Championship Series

MAJOR LEAGUE TOTALS

G	AB	H	BA	2B	3B	HR	R	RBI	SB
2,048	7,129	1,980	.278	343	27	267	941	1,111	59

TOMMY HENRICH

It's ironic that a player nicknamed "Old Reliable" should be best-remembered for striking out. That's the case of Tommy Henrich, a popular and talented outfielder and first baseman who played with the New York Yankees for 11 years.

Henrich was always a heads-up type of player who could be counted on to come through, hence his nickname. Even when he struck out during the fourth game of the 1941 World Series, Henrich made the most of the situation. The Dodgers were leading in the game 4-3. With two outs in the top of the ninth, it looked as though reliever Hugh Casey had iced the victory for the hosting Dodgers. After getting two strikes on Henrich, Casey threw the Yankee lefthander a big, breaking pitch. The ball bounced in front of the plate, and Henrich swung and missed; the ball got past Dodgers catcher Mickey Owen for a dropped third strike, allowing Henrich to take first base safely. One of the most famous pictures in World Series history shows Henrich, looking over his right shoulder and running to first base as the Dodger catcher flipped off his mask to hunt for the ball.

Henrich's alert play sparked a crucial Yankee rally. Joe DiMaggio followed with a single. Charlie "King Kong" Keller drove in both of his teammates with a two-run double. Bill Dickey followed with a walk. Second baseman Joe Gordon provided the climactic blow, a two-run double that set the final score at 7-4. The Yankees went on to post a 3-1 win in the fifth game to claim the world championship.

Of course, Henrich contributed more than just a strikeout to New York's World Series triumph. He scored 4 runs and notched 3 hits in the five-game matchup. During the regular season, he had socked a personal best of 31 home runs to complement 85 RBI and a .277 batting average.

Henrich didn't get his start with the Yankees until he was 24 years old. He was discovered playing softball on an amateur team in his hometown of Massillon, Ohio. He originally signed with the Cleveland Indians organization (after turning down an offer from the Detroit Tigers) but languished in their system for three seasons with no hope of promotion to the majors. He was obtained by the Milwaukee Brewers of the American Association at the end of 1936. Henrich became concerned when he started hearing conflicting stories that Milwaukee might sell his con-

tract elsewhere, or that the Indians might include him as a throw-in in a trade with the St. Louis Browns. It was long before the days that agents or unions assisted players, so Henrich went straight to the top with his problem. He wrote Judge Kenesaw Mountain Landis, commissioner of baseball, asking for help. Henrich got a favorable ruling from Landis, who agreed that the Indians had been "covering up" the hard-hitting rookie without allowing him to progress naturally through the farm system. He was declared a free agent.

Eight teams went after Henrich, but the Yankees won his services for two reasons: First, he received a $10,000 contract and a bonus for signing the contract worth $20,000; and second, Henrich had always been a Yankee fan. While he suspected that he might have gotten more money from another team, playing with the Yankees was a childhood dream that no money could buy.

Henrich didn't adjust immediately to playing hardball on the big league level. Major league curveballs posed a particular challenge. But after only a brief

demotion to Newark, the Yankees recalled Henrich and put him in the outfield with Keller and DiMaggio. In his 1937 debut, Henrich batted .320 with 8 homers and 42 RBI in 67 games. His best season was in 1948, when he hit .308 with a league-best 14 triples, 25 homers, and 100 RBI, and a circuit-leading 138 runs scored.

Henrich finished his career with the 1950 Yankees, batting .272 in 73 games. Due to injuries he wasn't able to compete in the 1950 World Series against the Philadelphia Phillies. After retiring at age 37, he spent the next year as a Yankees coach. He then stayed in private business until coaching opportunities with the New York Giants and Detroit Tigers came along later in the decade.

Henrich's career statistics include 1,297 hits in 1,284 games for a .282 lifetime batting average. He socked 183 home runs and 795 RBI, amassing a slugging percentage of .491. His grand totals in five World Series include 22 hits in 21 games, including 4 doubles, 4 home runs, 8 RBI, and 13 runs scored for a .262 average.

While Henrich doesn't have the career stats to warrant nomination to the Hall of Fame, he could have been a definite contender if three years of his career hadn't been sacrificed to military service during the war. With that extra time at the peak of his career, Henrich might have become one of the American League's longest-lasting stars.

Tommy Henrich's best season came in 1948, when he batted .308 with a league-leading 14 triples and 138 runs scored. That season he also had 25 homers, 100 RBI, and 42 doubles.

CAREER HIGHLIGHTS
THOMAS DAVID HENRICH

Born: February 20, 1913 Massillon, OH
Height: 6'0" **Weight:** 180 lbs. **Batted:** Left **Threw:** Left
First baseman, outfielder: New York Yankees, 1937-42; 1946-50.

★ Had double-digit totals for homers in eight seasons
★ Led the A.L. in triples twice
★ Named to four consecutive All-Star teams in 1947-50
★ Played in four World Series
★ Scored a league-leading 138 runs in 1948

MAJOR LEAGUE TOTALS

G	AB	H	BA	2B	3B	HR	R	RBI	SB
1,284	4,603	1,297	.282	269	73	183	901	795	37

BILLY HERMAN

When Billy Herman was first approached to play professional baseball, he was hesitant. He was an athletic youngster, a third baseman in high school baseball, and a star pitcher on his church league team. However, when the business manager of the Louisville Colonels minor league team asked Herman in 1927 if he wanted to play ball full-time, Herman said he needed to earn a living. He had gotten married earlier that year.

Fortunately, Louisville executive Bill Neal persuaded Herman that he had a bright future as a player. Herman finally agreed and went on to be a star second baseman for 15 big league seasons.

Herman had grown up in New Albany, Indiana, just across the river from Louisville, Kentucky. His pro career began in 1928, when he played in 106 games with Vicksburg of the Cotton States League, batting .332 with 4 homers and 18 stolen bases. He advanced to Dayton of the Central League, where he accumulated a .329 average with 13 homers, 174 total hits, and 96 runs scored. The next two and a half years were spent with the Colonels of the American Association. Herman finished up the 1929 season with 24 games in Louisville. In 1930 Herman batted .305 with the Colonels. He earned his ticket to the majors in 1931 by batting .350 in his first 118 games. Herman had 170 hits and 100 runs scored in that short time.

Business manager Neal sold Herman to the Chicago Cubs for $50,000. The Louisville executive claimed that Herman was more advanced at his young age than were Hall of Famers Dave Bancroft or Earle Combs when they joined the majors. Bancroft and Combs had also made the jump from Louisville directly to the big leagues.

The Indiana native broke in with the Cubs in late 1931, playing just 25 games. He batted .327, high enough to earn a starting spot in the Cubs lineup. He inherited second base from Rogers Hornsby, the fiery player/manager who had been sacked by the Cubs for tussles with the team ownership. Herman said that his first year was somewhat painful because the hard-throwing Cubs staff would get into beanball wars with opposing teams. When that happened, every Cubs batter became a prime target at the plate.

The agile second baseman batted .314 in his sophomore season, playing all 154 games. He played another full 154-game season in 1935 and submit-

ted one of his best offensive performances ever, batting .341—fifth highest in the league. He showed considerable bat skill, something uncommon for a middle infielder. Herman was a batting terror in the National League, racking up a league-leading 227 hits and 57 doubles. He also paced second basemen in five defensive categories: putouts, assists, total chances, double plays, and fielding percentage. In the 1935 World Series, the Cubs lost to the Detroit Tigers in six games. Herman batted .333 and a team-leading 6 RBI in the competition. One of his key hits was a run-scoring triple in the fifth game, which helped the Cubs to one of their two victories.

The Brooklyn Dodgers obtained Herman in early 1941 and he stayed with the team until mid-1946. He participated in the 1941 Series with the Dodgers but batted just .125. Like so many other WWII-era players, Herman missed the 1944 and 1945 seasons of

his career due to military service.

As a player/manager with the 1947 Pittsburgh Pirates, Herman played just 15 games while skippering the Bucs to a 61-92 mark. After his release from the Pirates, Herman played in 1948 with Minneapolis of the American Association and then Oakland of the Pacific Coast League in 1950. That last season in the minors, Herman hit .307. Herman was a coach during the glory days of the Brooklyn Dodgers, from 1952 to 1957. He managed the Red Sox for two games in 1964, then for the balance of 1965 and 1966. The BoSox were disappointing under Herman, logging ninth- and tenth-place finishes. His cumulative totals as a manager included 189 wins and 274 losses. Herman's final days as a big league coach came with the San Diego Padres in 1978 and 1979.

In his 13 years as a second baseman, Herman was a noted fielder. He tied a league record in 1933 by making 11 putouts in one game, then set a major league record with 5 more putouts, for an unmatched total of 16 in a double-header. Herman led the N.L. second sackers in putouts for a record seven seasons and accepted 900 or more chances in five years. He topped the senior circuit in fielding percentage three times.

Herman's major league totals include a .304 lifetime average, 2,345 career hits, and a .242 average for four World Series appearances. In ten straight All-Star games from 1934 to 1943, Herman hit .433. He fielded flawlessly in his first nine midseason classics.

Herman was elected to the Hall of Fame in 1975.

CAREER HIGHLIGHTS
WILLIAMS JENNINGS BRYAN HERMAN

Born: July 7, 1909   New Albany, IN
Height: 5'11"   **Weight:** 180 lbs.   **Batted:** Right   **Threw:** Right
Second baseman: Chicago Cubs, 1931-41; Brooklyn Dodgers, 1941-43, 1946; Boston Braves, 1946; Pittsburgh Pirates, 1947. Manager: Pittsburgh Pirates, 1947; Boston Red Sox, 1964-66.

★ Compiled a .304 lifetime batting mark
★ Had a league-best 227 hits in 1935
★ Had a league-best 18 triples in 1939
★ Played in four World Series
★ Had a league-best 57 doubles in 1935
★ Elected to the Hall of Fame in 1975
★ Played five seasons at second base fielding 900 or more chances

MAJOR LEAGUE TOTALS

G	AB	H	BA	2B	3B	HR	R	RBI	SB
1,922	7,707	2,345	.304	486	82	47	1,163	839	67

Brooklyn Dodgers owner Larry MacPhail brought Billy Herman to his club in 1941 and bragged, "I just bought a pennant." MacPhail was correct as Herman and the young Pee Wee Reese played well together, securing the Dodgers their first pennant in 21 years.

KEITH HERNANDEZ

Physicists probably find first baseman Keith Hernandez a bit baffling. Physicists say that every action produces an equal and opposite reaction—Hernandez seems to defy this law. When pushed, he produces an opposite reaction, all right, but seldom an equal one. When Hernandez turns on the power, opponents often wonder what hit them.

When Hernandez is up to bat, his average improves according to the number of teammates on base. He can pull when he needs to or hit for power, as his ten years of two-digit round-trippers proves.

Nobody pushes Hernandez around at first base either. He doesn't think twice about charging the plate on bunt attempts and seems to have radar in his glove. Some scouts have observed that with Hernandez at first a second baseman is superfluous. He has for years displayed perfection in the 3-6-3 double play. In 1988 Hernandez won his 11th consecutive Gold Glove for fielding excellence, which constituted the longest string of award-winning defense for any active player.

Hernandez's father, John, a former minor league infielder, keeps an eye on Keith via cable television. When his son suffered a batting slump in 1985, John phoned to suggest a tighter stance. Byebye slump; hello to Keith's fifth of six years of .300-plus batting in the majors.

Hernandez began his professional baseball career in 1972, having been drafted in the 42nd round by the St. Louis Cardinals the previous year. He was the first athlete at his California high school to make All-League in three major sports: as a quarterback in football, a guard in basketball, and a .500 batter in baseball. After back-to-back .300-plus seasons at Tulsa, Keith got his first trial with St. Louis at the end of the 1974 season. By midseason in 1975, he was in the majors to stay. His breakout season occurred in 1979, when he led National League hitters in batting average (.344), runs (116), and doubles (48). He also topped senior circuit first basemen in putouts (1,489), assists (146), and double plays (145). He was named co-winner of the National League MVP award that season, sharing the honor with Willie Stargell of the Pittsburgh Pirates.

He was *The Sporting News* Player of the Year, and his .995 fielding average landed him a spot on *TSN's* All-Star Fielding team for the second time in ten consecutive years. He also made

his first of five appearances to date in the All-Star lineup. His first All-Star outing was as a pinch hitter, but in his four subsequent games at first he has maintained flawless fielding.

Hernandez has set more major league records than centipedes have feet, including most game-winning RBI in a season (24 in 1985) and in a lifetime (129 through 1988); most years leading the league in double plays by a first baseman (6); and most first sack lifetime assists (1,631). Even when he sets a negative record, he does it in a positive way. In 1983, when Hernandez led the loop in errors, his 13 was the lowest total ever posted as a league lead.

Hernandez's tendency to push too hard has had some unfortunate repercussions, such as his 1985 courtroom confession of a previous drug problem. (He testified to being clean since 1983.) Also infamous is his 1989 spring training scuffle with teammate Darryl Strawberry, when an argument over salaries led to pushing and shoving. The dubious event was captured for posterity because the on-field wrestling started just before the Mets team picture was to be taken.

His teams cannot deny, however, that Hernendez has helped push them to be the best. In 1982 he slugged a .333 average in the National League Championship to pace St. Louis to the World Series. In 1983 he was traded to the Mets for pitchers Neil Allen and Rick Owenby, and by 1986 the Mets were in the Series. This time Hernandez tasted victory, though his 48 putouts and 4 RBI were less than his 1982 Series totals of 62 and 8. Likewise, his 7 hits, 5 RBI, and 57 putouts in the 1988 N.L.C.S. didn't get his Mets the pennant, although they came very close. It may be a while before the premier first sacker, who was 36 in 1989, is through energizing lineups with his hitting and fielding.

As of 1988, Keith Hernandez had won 11 consecutive Gold Glove awards for fielding excellence—the longest streak of award-winning defensive play in baseball history. In addition to his fielding prowess, Hernandez is also a consistent .300 hitter with plenty of line-drive power.

CAREER HIGHLIGHTS
KEITH HERNANDEZ

Born: October 20, 1953   San Francisco, CA
Height: 6'0"   **Weight:** 180 lbs.   **Bats:** Left   **Throws:** Left
First baseman: St. Louis Cardinals, 1974-83; New York Mets, 1983-89.

- ★ Led the N.L. in batting in 1979
- ★ Named to five All-Star teams
- ★ Holds the record for most game-winning RBI in a season and lifetime
- ★ Has won 11 straight Gold Gloves
- ★ Appeared in two World Series
- ★ Co-winner of the N.L. MVP award in 1979
- ★ Hit above .300 six times

MAJOR LEAGUE TOTALS

G	AB	H	BA	2B	3B	HR	R	RBI	SB
2,045	7,240	2,156	.298	424	60	161	1,117	1,063	98

OREL HERSHISER

His reserved manner and lanky, youthful appearance give Orel Hershiser the aura of an overnight sensation—a young pup suddenly thrust into the limelight. The impression is misleading, as batters who tangle with the fresh-faced moundsman have discovered.

Hershiser was 21 before starting out in the minors, and he spent five long years there perfecting his role—as a reliever. Hurling more than a dozen saves per season, Hershiser earned his late 1983 trek to Los Angeles by finishing third in saves in the Pacific Coast League.

With six minor league years under his belt, his first year in the majors is already the stuff of legend. Despite beginning the 1984 season with the James and Dearie Hulvey award as the top Dodger rookie, Hershiser is said to have been intimidated by the big boys around him. Tommy Lasorda, trying to pump up Hershiser's confidence, began calling him "Bulldog." Overnight, so the legend goes, Hershiser became the confident pit bull the Dodger manager foresaw. Hershiser himself is a bit embarrassed by the tale, insisting he is capable of overcoming stress without pop psychology.

Early that year, fate took one of its quietly devastating turns in the form of an injury to starting pitcher Jerry Reuss. Hershiser started just to fill the void in the rotation; by the end of one month, he was a Dodger starting pitcher. He won his first game two days after his official starting debut with a complete-game effort. His season included 4 shutouts in July alone, resulting in Pitcher of the Month accolades and a tie for league leader in season shutouts.

Hershiser began work immediately on an impressive array of shutouts and one-, two-, and three-hit games. His second full year with Los Angeles resulted in 22 consecutive scoreless innings and a string of 29 batters unable to hit out of the infield. His 11-0 record and 1.08 ERA at home challenged and broke Dodger records. Hershiser's league-leading .864 winning percentage and low 2.03 ERA helped the boys in blue to a Western Division title in 1985.

As devoted to his family and faith as he is to the game, Hershiser withdraws from family life the day before a game in order to get properly "zoned." His fastball sinks like an anchored lariat and his hard-breaking curveball has stymied even "The Bash Brothers," Mark McGwire and Jose Canseco of the

Oakland A's, whose 1988 World Series averages shrank before the Dodger ace.

Hershiser has never been known as a slick fielder, so his Gold Glove win was a special achievement. He has always been a decent-hitting pitcher, sending his average as high as .239 in past seasons. In 1989 Hershiser led the National League with 19 sacrifice hits.

After a lackluster 1986, Hershiser opened 1987 in fine fashion. Selected to the National League All-Stars for the first time, he also set new career highs in innings pitched, complete games, strikeouts (including 14 on a June night in Houston), hits, and RBI (2 each on a single day in June versus Atlanta). An appendectomy in the off-season didn't slow him down at all the following year.

Hershiser was an acknowledged league leader in all categories except shutouts entering the 1988 season. Nonetheless, the baseball world—and maybe even Hershiser himself—couldn't have predicted the superstardom that would materialize before the season's end. His streak of 59 scoreless

innings began on May 30 with four scoreless frames against Montreal. Five shutouts later, history was made as former Dodgers hurler Don Drysdale's record was broken. He unofficially ran the mark up to 67 with eight scoreless innings in the opening game of the N.L.C.S. versus the Mets. During the streak (which was broken in his first 1989 appearance), Hershiser struck out 38 and walked 11 while giving up just 31 hits.

No Dodger since Sandy Koufax (who won 27 games in 1966) had matched Hershiser's 23-8 record of 1988. He won 5 straight games during the month of April, winning N.L. Pitcher of the Month honors both in April and September. By season's end, Hershiser had an enormous array of honors and awards. A partial list includes World Series MVP, Championship Series MVP, *Sports Illustrated* Sportsman of the Year, *The Sporting News* Player of the Year, *Baseball America* N.L. Pitcher of the Year, and AP Male Athlete of the Year. Only Cincinnati's Danny Jackson provided Hershiser with any competition for the Cy Young award.

Hershiser immediately gained national recognition following the team's World Series victory. His biography *Out of the Blue* was published at the beginning of 1989. He made several commercial endorsements and even sang a bit of a church hymn on NBC-TV's *The Tonight Show* for Johnny Carson. Only 30 years of age when the 1989 season started, Hershiser can become one of the finest Dodger hurlers in history if his arm stays healthy. He's already climbing into the top ten in many team categories.

CAREER HIGHLIGHTS
OREL LEONARD HERSHISER

Born: September 16, 1958   Buffalo, NY
Height: 6'3"   **Weight:** 192 lbs.   **Bats:** Right   **Throws:** Right
Pitcher: Los Angeles Dodgers, 1983-89.

* Threw a major league record of 59 scoreless innings in 1988
* Won 1988 Gold Glove
* Posted two complete-game victories in the 1988 World Series
* Won 11 straight games in 1985
* Led the N.L. with an .864 winning percentage in 1985
* Earned 1 save and 1 complete-game shutout in the 1988 N.L.C.S.

MAJOR LEAGUE TOTALS

G	IP	W	L	Pct.	SO	BB	ERA
231	1,456	98	64	.605	1,011	434	2.69

Orel Hershiser's popularity soared after pitching a record-breaking 59 scoreless innings in 1988. The young hurler won 23 games that season. In addition to garnering several awards, Hershiser became a popular spokesperson in TV commercials.

GIL HODGES

The New York Mets entered the 1969 season as a 100-to-1 shot to win the National League pennant. Playing with a roster full of over-the-hill veterans and other teams' castoffs, the Mets were the laughing-stock of the league. In their first seven seasons, they had averaged just 66 wins per year, and in five out of seven seasons they had finished in last place.

But 1969 was to be the year of the "Miracle Mets", directed by manager Gil Hodges. After getting off to a good start, the Mets never stumbled and stayed close to the Cubs all summer. They finished strong to take the division by eight games. Then they swept three straight from the Western Division Atlanta Braves (in the first year of division play) to capture their first league pennant. It took just five games for the Mets to win their first world championship against their highly favored American League foes, the Baltimore Orioles. It was the most amazing turnaround in baseball history.

Looking at the statistics of that championship Mets team, much of the credit goes to pitchers Tom Seaver and Jerry Koosman, reliever Tug McGraw, and sluggers Tommie Agee and Cleon Jones. What the numbers can't reveal, however, is the leadership, guidance, and inspiration supplied by manager Hodges, then in his second season as Mets pilot. Baseball writers of the day gave Hodges as much credit for the miracle season as any of the players.

And why not? In a sense, Hodges can be credited with the game-winning RBI in the decisive fifth game of the 1969 World Series. The Mets were trailing 3-0 into the bottom of the sixth inning. Jones claimed that he was hit in the foot by a pitch, but the umpires didn't believe him. The ever-alert Hodges fetched the ball for the umps, showing the shoe polish scuffed on the ball as proof that Jones had been hit. With Jones on first base, Donn Clendenon hit a home run that put the New Yorkers back into contention. A two-run rally in the eighth won the game for the Mets 5-3.

Hodges, who earlier in his career had been the dependable first baseman of the great Dodgers teams of the 1950s, was one of the most admired and respected men in all of baseball—first as a player and later as a manager. During his heyday in Brooklyn, he was a consistent slugger who usually batted around .280 and averaged over 30 homers a year. Hodges finished his career with 370 homers and 1,274 RBI. He helped the Dodgers to seven league titles, six in Brooklyn and one in Los Angeles. As a player and manager, Hodges' career in the big leagues stretched over a period of 24 years.

The Indiana native never played minor league baseball before his big league debut. He was active in all sports in high school and then played baseball for three years at St. Joseph's College. Hodges played one game with the 1943 Brooklyn Dodgers—at third base. Following the season, he was drafted into the U.S. Marines and missed two years of potential playing time during World War II. In 1946 Hodges was sent down to Newport News of the Piedmont League for a year. The Dodgers groomed Hodges to become a catcher and the experiment worked: Hodges led the league in fielding average (.983), assists (90), and putouts (731). The Dodgers brought him up in 1947 to serve as catcher in 28 games. His batting suffered, as he hit just .156.

The next season, Hodges got a big career break. After 38 games at catcher, he was moved permanently to first base. The Dodgers had acquired another catcher by the name of Roy Campanella and needed to make room for their new arrival. The move did Hodges good: In 134 games, he hit 11 homers, 70 RBI, and a .249 average.

Playing in Brooklyn, Hodges had season "lows" of 23 homers and 87 RBI. For seven straight seasons he drove in more than 100 runs. During the 1954 season Hodges enjoyed the greatest offensive output of his career—batting .304 (only the second time in his career that he'd top .300) with career highs of 42 homers and 130 RBI.

In seven World Series, he helped the Dodgers to two championships (in 1955 with Brooklyn and in 1959 with Los Angeles). In the 1955 Series, Hodges had 1 homer, 5 RBI, and a .292 average. In 1959 he had 9 hits and a .391 mark. His fourth-game homer gave the Dodgers a 5-4 win.

The fact that Hodges has not been elected to the Hall of Fame is somewhat surprising. Many followers of baseball feel that had he lived longer his managerial achievements could have matched his accomplishments as a player. Hodges' career was cut short when he suffered a fatal heart attack while playing golf in Florida during spring training. He died less than a week before the 1972 season opened, two days shy of his 48th birthday.

CAREER HIGHLIGHTS
GILBERT RAYMOND HODGES

Born: April 4, 1924   Princeton, IN   **Died:** April 2, 1972
Height: 6'2"   **Weight:** 200 lbs.   **Batted:** Right   **Threw:** Right
First baseman: Brooklyn Dodgers, 1943, 1947-57; Los Angeles Dodgers, 1958-61; New York Mets, 1962-63. Manager: Washington Senators, 1963-67; New York Mets, 1968-71.

- ★ Managed the New York Mets to a world championship in 1969
- ★ Hit 370 home runs
- ★ Won three Gold Glove awards
- ★ Hit over 20 home runs in 11 consecutive seasons
- ★ Played in seven World Series
- ★ Hit 14 career grand slams

MAJOR LEAGUE TOTALS

G	AB	H	BA	2B	3B	HR	R	RBI	SB
2,071	7,030	1,921	.273	295	48	370	1,105	1,274	63

Gil Hodges is known to recent baseball fans as the manager of the 1969 Miracle Mets, yet
his playing career was impressive as well. He slugged over 30 home runs in six seasons,
won three Gold Glove awards, and hit 14 grand slams.

ROGERS HORNSBY

Rogers Hornsby was the greatest righthand hitter in the history of baseball. His batting accomplishments spill out of the record books like a cascading waterfall. During the five years from 1921 to 1925, Hornsby batted .397, .401, .384, .424, and .403. The .424 mark established a record for the 20th century.

"The Rajah," as Hornsby was called because of his wizardry with the bat, led the league in batting seven times. Not just a singles hitter, the big second baseman displayed enough power to twice win the triple crown, first in 1922 when he hit .401 with 42 home runs and 152 RBI, and then again in 1925 when he batted .403 with 39 round-trippers and 143 RBI. Hornsby hit over .300 for 13 straight seasons, making his lifetime batting mark of .358 the best in the N. L.

The slugging righthander grew up in Texas. His first professional baseball experience was in 1914 with teams in Oklahoma and Dallas. After he had played part of 1915 in Dennison, Texas, the St. Louis Cardinals purchased his contract. He made his big league debut at age 19.

His rookie season came in 1916. Playing in 139 games, Hornsby hit .313 with 6 homers and 61 RBI. In 1917 he had a league-leading slugging percentage of .484, playing shortstop full-time. After an off year in 1918, Hornsby moved to third base in 1919 and raised his average from .287 to .318. He didn't become a full-time second baseman (the position at which he became famous) until 1920. That year Hornsby topped the National League in five offensive categories: hits, doubles, RBI, batting average, and slugging percentage. He played in full slates of 154 games both in 1921 and 1922.

Following his triple crown of 1922, Hornsby enjoyed banner years in 1923 and 1924. Though he didn't show as much power at the plate, he tallied slugging percentages of .627 and .696. After his second triple crown in 1925, The Rajah led the Cardinals to a 1926 world championship as a player/manager. His admirable .317 average was his lowest in a decade.

The native Texan lasted only one season under the reign of feisty manager John McGraw. Hornsby's .361 average, 26 home runs, and 125 RBI weren't enough to override his personality conflicts with McGraw. Hornsby was traded to Boston, where he again lasted a single season. With the Braves

in 1928, Hornsby won his seventh and final batting title with a .381 performance. He also led the league with 107 runs scored and a .632 slugging percentage.

Hornsby's last great season came as a Cub in 1929. He scored a career-high 156 runs to lead the league and chalked up a league-best slugging percentage of .679, the third highest in his career. His batting average was a sizzling .380, but that was only third highest in the senior circuit. Philadelphia Phillies star Lefty O'Doul was first with a .398 mark and Chicago teammate Babe Herman came in second at .381.

Hornsby's gruff determination made him an appealing choice for manager with several teams. However, his overbearing need to win at all costs quickly alienated him with many club owners.

Hornsby's first piloting job was with the St. Louis Cardinals in 1925, when he took over for Branch Rickey. As the 1926 player/manager of the Cardinals, his sturdy play and guidance led the Cards to an 89-65 record and a National League pennant. The Redbirds whipped the mighty New York Yankees in a seven-game World Series as Hornsby hit .250. Hornsby's only mistake was angering team owner Sam Breadon by asking for a three-year contract. On December 20, he was traded to the New York Giants.

Hornsby was a player/manager again in 1928 with the Boston Braves. The Chicago Cubs employed Hornsby as a manager from 1930 to 1932. When he was hired on September 30, 1930, he replaced future Hall of Famer Joe McCarthy. Boston got Socks Seibold, Percy Jones, Lou Legett, Freddie Maguire, Bruce Cunningham, and $200,000 from the Cubs in exchange for Hornsby. He was released in August 1932, shortly before the Cubs won the pennant, due to more conflicts with the front office.

Hornsby hooked up with the St. Louis Browns as a manager in 1933 but was fired in 1937 after more battles with team ownership. The Browns were unhappy with Hornsby's off-the-field behavior and gambling debts. During the 1940s he managed several minor league teams. Hornsby's last hurrah in the majors was as Cincinnati Reds skipper in late 1952 and most of 1953.

CAREER HIGHLIGHTS
ROGERS HORNSBY

Born: April 27, 1896 Winters, TX **Died:** January 5, 1963
Height: 5'11" **Weight:** 175 lbs. **Batted:** Right **Threw:** Right
Infielder: St. Louis Cardinals, 1915-26; New York Giants, 1927; Boston Braves, 1928; Chicago Cubs, 1929-32; St. Louis Browns, 1933-37. Manager: St. Louis Cardinals, 1925-26; Boston Braves, 1928; Chicago Cubs, 1930-32; St. Louis Browns, 1933-37, 1952; Cincinnati Reds, 1952-53.

- ★ Batted over .400 three times, including .424 in 1924
- ★ Has the second-highest career batting average (.358) in history
- ★ Led the league in slugging average nine times
- ★ Led the league in batting for six consecutive years
- ★ In 1922 became the first player in N.L. history to hit 40 homers
- ★ Elected to the Hall of Fame in 1942

★ Topped the league in hits four times

MAJOR LEAGUE TOTALS

G	AB	H	BA	2B	3B	HR	R	RBI	SB
2,259	8,173	2,930	.358	541	169	301	1,579	1,584	135

Rogers Hornsby's batting skills have made him a legendary baseball figure. He is the only righthander to hit .400 three times; he won six straight batting titles from 1920-25; and he won two triple crowns and two MVP awards during his career.

WILLIE HORTON

Willie Horton was a non-stop homer factory for the Detroit Tigers for 12 strong years. His fielding was undistinguished and his baserunning was questionable, but those shortcomings didn't matter once Horton started booming long balls over American League fences. In all, Horton compiled 15 straight seasons in the majors (from 1964 through 1979) with double-digit homer totals.

Future stardom as a home run hitter seemed a sure thing for Horton, even when he was playing high school baseball. He was born in Virginia in 1942 but grew up in Detroit. Horton knew what it took to be a good team player long before he started playing sports in school. He was the youngest in his family, preceded by 20 brothers and sisters. Willie was called "Boozie" by his parents, because he was caught as a baby creating havoc with the family's flour and lard canisters.

Detroit's Northwestern High baseball squad won the 1959 city championship with the aid of Horton's offense. The Tigers presented Horton with a $50,000 signing bonus in 1961. At the age of 18, he was a professional ballplayer. He began his first minor league season with Duluth-Superior in 1962. In 123 games Horton hit 15 home runs and 72 RBI while batting .295. He spent most of 1963 with Knoxville of the Sally League. There he tallied 14 homers, 70 RBI, and a .333 average in 118 games. Horton was called up to the Tigers for 15 games at the end of the season. He hit .326 in his brief tryout.

One final season of minor league ball followed before Horton could land a full-time job with Detroit. He proved himself in 1964 with Syracuse of the International League. Playing both outfield and third base, he slammed 28 round-trippers and 99 RBI in 141 games, earning a .288 average. He played the final 25 games of the season with Detroit. Although he hit just .163, Horton was in the majors to stay.

Horton started in left field for the Tigers in 1965. He beat Gates Brown out of a starting job, but the results were beneficial to both men. Horton got a chance to show his power-hitting skills to the world on a regular basis, while Brown became such an accomplished pinch hitter that he was known as the Tigers "super-sub." During his first season as a starter, Horton batted .273 with 29 homers and a team-leading 104 RBI. He was just 3 homers behind league leader Tony Conigliaro of Boston, who had 32 dingers. Rocky Colavito edged out Horton by 4 in the RBI race. Horton's sophomore season was almost as good: His totals included 27 homers and 100 RBI.

Horton missed 40 games in 1967, which cut his totals to 19 homers and 67 RBI. His missing bat from the Tiger lineup may have been one reason the Boston Red Sox won the pennant by just one game. The Bengals did win 91 games, although Horton got into only 122 contests.

Both Horton and the Tigers had dream seasons in 1968. The batsman smacked a career high of 36 homers that year. He was second in the league in homers (36), home run percentage (7.0), slugging average (.543), and total bases (278). His 85 RBI and .285 average were fourth in the league. The Tigers won the World Series in seven highly competitive games. Most games were billed as great pitching showcases for Denny McLain and Mickey Lolich.

All the while, other team members were having a prosperous Series as well. Horton, for example, had 7 hits for a .304 average including 1 double, 1 triple, and 1 home run to complement 3 RBI and 6 runs scored. Horton and each of his teammates who received a full share of the World Series profits earned $10,937 for their efforts.

Just when it seemed that Horton might be nearing the end of his career, he surprised the baseball world with a stellar showing with the 1979 Seattle Mariners. Before he signed with Seattle as a free agent, Horton had been with five different teams in the previous two seasons. He won Comeback Player of the Year honors as the team's designated hitter. He appeared in all 162 games, rapping out a personal best of 180 hits. His 29 home runs and 106 RBI were team bests for the M's.

Horton retired with 325 career homers, which places him among the top 60 sluggers of all time in this category. Horton had 1,993 hits in 2,028 games for a batting average of .273. He tallied 1,163 RBI for his career and scored 873 runs on his own. Horton ranks high among the top ten for several all-time hitting departments on the Detroit Tigers.

He played two years with the Portland Beavers of the Pacific Coast League after being traded back to the Texas Rangers on December 12, 1980. The entire deal involved 11 players, most notably Richie Zisk and Horton. In 1983 he finished his career as a Mexican League player. He served as an Oakland A's coach in 1984. He coached for his old team, the Tigers, in 1985 and was a hitting instructor for the Chicago White Sox in 1986.

CAREER HIGHLIGHTS
WILLIE WATTERSON HORTON

Born: October 18, 1942 Arno, VA
Height: 5'11" **Weight:** 210 lbs. **Batted:** Right **Threw:** Right
Outfielder, designated hitter: Detroit Tigers, 1963-77; Texas Rangers, 1977; Cleveland Indians, 1978; Oakland A's, 1978; Toronto Blue Jays, 1978; Seattle Mariners, 1979-80.

★ Hit 20 or more homers seven times
★ Ranks in the top 60 for lifetime homers
★ Finished second in the league in homers in 1968

★ Batted .304 in 1968 World Series
★ Named Comeback Player of the Year in '79
★ Had double figures in home runs for 15 straight seasons

MAJOR LEAGUE TOTALS

G	AB	H	BA	2B	3B	HR	R	RBI	SB
2,028	7,298	1,993	.273	284	40	325	873	1,163	20

Willie Horton spent most of his playing days as a long-ball hitter for the Detroit Tigers. At the end of his career, he played on five different teams. Everyone assumed he was washed up when he rapped 180 hits, 29 homers, and 106 RBI for the 1979 Mariners.

CHARLIE HOUGH

When the Texas Rangers acquired 42-year-old pitcher Nolan Ryan as a free agent in 1989, they demonstrated their faith in experience on the mound. The Rangers had good reason to put their trust in veteran hurlers: they already owned one of the elder statesmen of the American League—40-year-old knuckleball artist Charlie Hough.

The two accomplished hurlers are true contrasts in style. Ryan huffs and puffs on the mound and baffles batters with barrages of fastballs. Hough has a flowing and effortless delivery and sends showers of fluttering knucklers to unsuspecting hitters. Together, the two graybeards of the junior circuit made the Rangers an interesting team to follow during the 1989 season.

Hough has been a big winner on the Rangers pitching staff for the last several years. In that time span he has won well over 100 games for one of the best totals in baseball (with Detroit's Jack Morris staying ahead). While many might attribute Hough's success to hard work and determination, some say Elvis Presley had a hand in it. It seems that Hough likes to wear an Elvis T-shirt under his team jersey.

Hough perfected his craft with many minor league seasons, becoming a three-time Pacific Coast League All-Star pitcher. He started out in 1966 and had average success in the Los Angeles Dodgers farm system. He was originally a third baseman and took up pitching at the urging of Tommy Lasorda. When Hough adopted the knuckleball in 1970, he gained his first major success with a 1.95 ERA, down more than 2 full points from the previous year. He had 12 wins and 8 losses.

In his major league debut of 1970, Hough highlighted his first season by striking out Willie Stargell with the bases loaded. Hough got his permanent promotion in 1972, and he was used primarily as a reliever for most of his time with the Dodgers. His best year out of the Los Angeles bullpen came in 1977, when he saved 22 games and won 6 others. His contributions helped propel the Dodgers to the National League pennant. In 1976 he posted 12 victories and saved 18. His ERA was 2.20, his lowest in his major league career.

While Hough played on three Dodger pennant-winning clubs, he didn't figure prominently in any of their postseason competitions. Even though he had minor roles in each League Championship Series and World Series,

he never earned a win, loss, or save. In the 1977 World Series, however, he appeared in five innings over two games with an ERA of 1.80 and 5 strikeouts.

In 1977 the Dodgers started using Hough as a starter on a limited basis. In his first start, he allowed just 2 hits and no runs in five innings for a victory. He even blasted his first home run that year. But the Dodgers kept him busy mostly as a reliever. His 22 saves that year ranked him fourth among National League relievers. It wasn't until 1980, when he was sold in midseason to the Texas Rangers, that his career as a starter really began.

After all, being a starting pitcher made more sense for a knuckleball specialist like Hough. He could pace himself better in a starting role and keep a better command of his trick pitch. Because knuckleballers are prone to

wild pitches and passed balls, they aren't always the best solution for clutch relief.

Hough keeps getting better with age. After a month off for disability and rehabilitation in 1986, he finished the season with a 17-10 record (and his first All-Star game appearance). In 1987 he had 18 victories and 13 losses (a career-high win total) and earned another personal best in innings pitched—a career-high 285. His sometimes wacky knuckler also beaned a league-leading 19 batters that year.

Hough's success comes from being able to deliver his knuckler at various speeds. Even though hitters can anticipate his big pitch, they have trouble connecting because they can't always gauge the speed. This is good because his fastball, which never earned any speeding tickets anyway, has gone quickly downhill. He throws a lot of pitches and survives pitching batters to full counts. Hough has missed out on several 20-win opportunities simply because the Rangers couldn't provide much offensive support, but hopefully that situation might reverse itself before Hough retires.

Knuckleball specialist Charlie Hough played for the L.A. Dodgers for almost 11 seasons, but his career as a starting pitcher really didn't soar until he was traded to the Texas Rangers. After 1982 Hough won in double-digits each season, with a career-high of 18 wins in 1987.

CAREER HIGHLIGHTS
CHARLES OLIVER HOUGH

Born: January 5, 1948 Honolulu, HI
Height: 6'2" **Weight:** 190 lbs. **Bats:** Right **Throws:** Right
Pitcher: Los Angeles Dodgers, 1970-80; Texas Rangers, 1980-89.

- ★ Tied the major league record for most strikeouts in one inning (4) in 1988
- ★ Appeared in three World Series with the Dodgers
- ★ Participated in the 1986 All-Star game
- ★ Posted eight double-digit winning seasons in the majors
- ★ Led the league in games started once and tied for the lead once
- ★ Led the league in complete games in 1984

★ Ranked first among Rangers in wins for seven straight seasons

MAJOR LEAGUE TOTALS

G	IP	W	L	Pct.	SV	SO	BB	ERA
713	2,888	174	157	.526	61	1,874	1,263	3.60

267

ELSTON HOWARD

Jackie Robinson shattered baseball's color barrier in 1947; but it took time for others to follow him through the rubble, sweep away the shards of prejudice, and continue the fight for racial integration of America's pastime. The New York Yankees, one of baseball's greatest dynasties during the late 1940s and early 50s, didn't place a black player on its major league roster until 1955. The responsibility of being the team's first black player fell upon the strong shoulders of Elston Howard.

Howard was 21 years old when he was signed by the Yankees in 1950. He began his minor league career in Muskegon in 1950, batting .283 with 9 homers and 42 RBI. The next two years of his career were lost to military service. In 1953 he resumed playing with Kansas City of the American Association. Howard also attempted to play catcher for the first time that year. His offensive production remained consistent, a .286 average with 10 homers and 70 RBI. Howard was promoted to Toronto in 1954. There he was named Most Valuable Player of the International League. He was the top fielder among the league's backstops, with a league-best 588 putouts. Howard was at his best at bat with a league-leading 16 doubles, 22 home runs, 109 RBI, and a .330 average.

Those close to the man nicknamed "Ellie" had every reason to rejoice over his 1963 Most Valuable Player award in the American League, which marked the first time a black player had won the honor. His victory honored the many years of selfless dedication he had given to the game. The only child of a dietitian and a high school principal, Howard excelled in three major sports at his hometown high school in St. Louis. In 1947 he turned down scholarships from 25 different colleges with the hope that he could play professional baseball.

This was not to be for three long years, as team owners waited to see what the aftershock of Robinson's National League debut would bring. Baseball would not be fully integrated until the end of the 1950s.

Howard had been trained as an outfielder in his youth, but the Yankees wanted him to switch to catching. Friends warned him that the Yanks had too many catchers (including the famed Yogi Berra), but Howard's faith in his team could not be shattered.

The Yankees assigned former Yankee backstop Bill Dickey to convert Howard to catching in 1953. Manager Casey Stengel told the youngster to be prepared in case Berra ever became disabled. After his 1954 season in the International League, Howard proved he was ready.

"Thank God I can play more than one position," Howard said to the press. Not only did this keep Howard on the roster while he was waiting for Berra's retirement, but it raised him even higher in Stengel's estimation. Stepping in for an injured Berra during postseason play in his rookie season, Howard was dubbed by Stengel "our most valuable utility man." To be ranked so high in a team that appeared in nine World Series in ten years is no small reward.

The most memorable moment of his many Series contests was surely in 1958. The Milwaukee Braves were leading three games to one. In the fourth game the Yanks led by one, but the Braves were ready to score. Enter Howard, who was playing left field. He made a diving catch of a line drive and doubled a runner off first base to squelch the rally. The Yankees battled back after that and took the world championship.

In 1961 Howard became a full-time catcher. His 21 homers and 77 RBI were the usual accomplishments the Yankees could expect from Howard. Howard upped his average more than 100 points, from his 1960 mark of .245 to a total of .348 in 1961.

Howard's MVP-winning year of 1963 was especially important because it came when teammates Maris and Mickey Mantle were injured throughout the season. Howard helped the team to an American League pennant by tutoring a young pitching staff, and he registered a career high of 28 home runs.

In 1964 Howard hit the peak of his fielding success. For the third straight year, he led the league's catchers in fielding percentage, and he made only 2 errors for a .998 mark.

The Yankees traded Howard to the Boston Red Sox in late 1967 for two minor leaguers. Boston used Howard's veteran wisdom to clinch the league pennant. After his retirement in 1968, Howard coached with the Yankees for a full decade, ending in 1979. He died of heart failure in 1980 at age 51, after one year of working in the Yankee front office. On July 21, 1984, the New York Yankees retired Howard's uniform number (32), making him one of only 12 Yanks to receive the honor.

CAREER HIGHLIGHTS
ELSTON GENE HOWARD

Born: February 23, 1929 St. Louis, MO **Died:** December 14, 1980
Height: 6'2" **Weight:** 196 lbs. **Batted:** Right **Threw:** Right
Catcher, outfielder, first baseman: New York Yankees, 1955-67; Boston Red Sox, 1967-68.

- ★ Won the 1963 MVP award
- ★ Appeared on ten World Series teams
- ★ Was first black player to play with the New York Yankees
- ★ Hit a career-high 28 homers in 1963
- ★ Hit a homer in his first World Series at-bat
- ★ Hit .348 in 1961, one of the highest batting averages by a catcher

★ Had his uniform number (32) retired by the Yankees

MAJOR LEAGUE TOTALS

G	AB	H	BA	2B	3B	HR	R	RBI	SB
1,605	5,363	1,471	.274	218	50	167	619	762	9

A plaque in the outfield of Yankee Stadium honoring Elston Howard reads in part: "A man of great gentleness and dignity....If indeed, humility is a trademark of many great men—Elston Howard was one of the truly great Yankees."

FRANK HOWARD

Frank Howard was one of the most fearsome long-ball threats in baseball during the 1960s and early 70s. He was known as "Hondo" or "The Capital Punisher" (during his homer hitting days with the Washington Senators). Perhaps his most memorable nickname was "The Horse." Those who encountered the 6-foot-7, 255-pound outfielder/first baseman up close understood why Los Angeles Dodgers teammate Bob Lillis dreamed up this moniker. Howard responded by nicknaming the 5-foot-11 Lillis "The Flea."

Whatever you called him, Howard was known as a prolific manufacturer of home runs throughout the 1960s. Big Frank was born in Columbus, Ohio, in 1936 and attended Ohio State University. Although he starred in baseball, he was also captain of the Buckeyes basketball team. As a forward, Howard earned three letters in basketball and was named to the All-Big-Ten Conference team. He considered an attempt at a pro basketball career, but changed his mind when he realized how much money a professional baseball career could bring. The Los Angeles Dodgers signed Howard with a $108,000 bonus in 1958.

Howard played his first professional baseball with Green Bay in 1958. In 129 games he led the Three-I League in homers (37), RBI (119), and runs (104). He even pitched one scoreless inning that year in his only pro experience on the mound. The Dodgers immediately promoted him at season's end. In eight starts Howard hit .241 with 1 homer. He started the 1959 season with Victoria of the Texas League, where he batted .356 with 16 homers and 47 RBI in 76 games. Advancing to Spokane of the Pacific Coast League, he notched 16 homers, 47 RBI, and a .319 batting average. Late in 1959, he played in nine games with Los Angeles, batting .143 with 1 home run.

It only took 26 games with Spokane (hitting .371) to convince the Dodgers to call Howard up for good in 1960. The Dodgers released Carl Furillo to make room for Howard, their new right fielder. Howard returned to Los Angeles and won the National League Rookie of the Year award with 23 homers, 77 RBI, and a .268 average in 117 games. His four-baggers set a new record for Dodgers rookies.

Howard's sophomore season of 1961 included 15 homers, 45 RBI, and a .296 average in just 92 games. The next year, a healthy Howard boomed

31 homers and 119 RBI (fifth in the league), batting .296 again. The Dodgers lost the National League pennant in a special three-game playoff to the San Francisco Giants. In 1963 Howard missed 39 games during the season, so his stats dropped to 28 homers, 64 RBI, and a .273 average.

In 1964 Howard's batting average slid to .226, although he still contributed 24 homers and 69 RBI. On December 4, 1964, the Dodgers traded Howard, pitchers Pete Richert and Phil Ortega, and infielder Ken McMullen to the Washington Senators for infielder John Kennedy, pitcher Claude Osteen, and an estimated $100,000. Beginning in 1965, Howard became the backbone of the struggling Senators. His homer-hitting sideshows helped fans forget that the Washington team was often outmatched by American League rivals. The Ohio native delivered in his first American League season, batting .289 with 21 homers and 84 RBI.

As A.L. pitchers got wise to Howard's strength, he found his second season in the junior circuit a bit tougher. Howard hit .271 with 18 homers and 71 RBI. He bounced back in 1967, socking 36 homers and 89 RBI.

The 1968 season proved to be one of the most productive outings in Howard's career. He led the league with 44 homers and a .552 slugging percentage, and he had a .274 average and 106 RBI. But those stats only tell half the story of Howard's 1968 success. During a 15-day stretch in May, Howard clobbered 12 homers, including a record-setting 10 dingers in six consecutive games. The Senators, however, finished in last place in the American League with a 65-96 record.

With another banner season by Howard in 1969 and the management of Ted Williams, the Senators finished in fourth place with an 88-76 mark. Playing in left field, Howard smashed 48 homers and 111 RBI for a .296 average. Harmon Killebrew hit 49 homers that year to edge out Howard for the long-ball crown. Howard played in 161 games again in 1970, topping the league with 44 homers, 126 RBI, and 132 bases on balls.

Following the 1971 season, in which he hit 26 homers and 83 RBI, Howard was sold to the Detroit Tigers. He spent his last year as a designated hitter.

Howard wanted to play baseball in Japan in 1974 but appeared in only one game due to a chronic knee injury. Since his retirement Howard has coached for several teams and managed the Padres and Mets briefly. He was named a New York Yankees coach prior to the 1989 season.

CAREER HIGHLIGHTS
FRANK OLIVER HOWARD

Born: August 8, 1936   Columbus, OH
Height: 6'7"   **Weight:** 255 lbs.   **Batted:** Right   **Threw:** Right
Outfielder, first baseman: Los Angeles Dodgers, 1958-64; Washington Senators 1965-71; Texas Rangers, 1972; Detroit Tigers, 1972-73. Manager: San Diego Padres, 1981; New York Mets, 1983.

★ Led the A.L. twice in home runs
★ Hit .300 in the 1963 World Series
★ Clubbed 40-plus homers for three straight seasons

★ Named N.L. Rookie of the Year in 1960
★ Topped the A.L. in RBI and walks in 1970
★ Drove in 100-plus runs for four seasons

MAJOR LEAGUE TOTALS

G	AB	H	BA	2B	3B	HR	R	RBI	SB
1,895	6,488	1,774	.273	245	35	382	864	1,119	8

Frank Howard was a long-ball specialist for many teams during his career. He began with the L.A. Dodgers in 1960, winning N.L. Rookie of the Year honors and setting a Dodger record for home runs by a rookie (23).

WAITE HOYT

Despite his misleading nickname, "Schoolboy" Waite Hoyt was already a veteran of sorts when he made his debut with the 1918 New York Giants at the age of 18. Hoyt had signed his first pro contract at age 15 and had logged three minor league seasons before he reached the majors.

Hoyt graduated from a Brooklyn High School at age 15, then briefly attended Middlebury College before opting for a pro career. He bounced around with minor league teams in Mt. Carmel, Hartford-Lynn, Memphis, Montreal, and Nashville before getting a brief one-inning shot with the Giants (gaining no decision). Hoyt would later become one of baseball's most celebrated hurlers of the 1920s although he had losing records with five of his six minor league squads. His only success in the minors was a 5-1 mark with Mt. Carmel of the Pennsylvania State League in 1916.

The Boston Red Sox obtained Hoyt in 1919, but he turned in unremarkable performances in two straight seasons. On December 15, 1920, the Red Sox traded Hoyt, Harry Harper, Wally Schang, and Mike McNally to the New York Yankees for Muddy Ruel, Del Pratt, Sammy Vick, and Hank Thormahlen.

Hoyt immediately made the trade worthwhile for the Yanks, going 19-13 in 21 complete games. The Yankees rode Hoyt's success straight to the World Series. The Giants whipped the Bronx Bombers in five out of eight Series games. In the second game of the Series, Hoyt beat the Giants on a two-hitter. In game five, he scattered 10 hits and gave up just 1 unearned run, nipping the National League rivals 3-1. Hoyt nearly won the eighth game but was victimized by a first-inning error by Yankee shortstop Roger Peckinpaugh. Hoyt held the Giants scoreless through the rest of the game, but the Yankees still lost 1-0.

In the next eight years, Hoyt and the Yankees would play in five World Series (missing out only in 1924, 1925, and 1928). World championships in 1923, 1927, and 1928 highlighted Hoyt's career. Hoyt won 19 games in 1922 and 17 in 1923. After going 18-13 in 1924, he dropped to 11-14 with a 4.00 ERA the following year. He rebounded to a 16-12 mark in 1926, then compiled back-to-back 20-win seasons, the two best of his long career.

When people think about the 1927 New York Yankees, Hoyt's name is one of the last to come to mind. Babe Ruth, Lou Gehrig, and the other sluggers on the "Murderer's Row" team got most of the publicity. Hoyt, however, was the mound magician who kept the Yankees winning in that championship season. He led the American League in three categories: 22 wins (with just 7 losses), a .759 winning percentage, and a 2.63 ERA. Hoyt notched 23 complete games that year—a personal high. In the 1927 World Series, the Bronx Bombers topped their National League opposition, the Pittsburgh Pirates, in four quick games. In the Series opener, Hoyt spread out 11 Pittsburgh hits over 7.1 innings to gain a 5-4 win.

A second straight 20-plus-win season awaited Hoyt in 1928, along with a return trip to the World Series. Although Hoyt won 23 games in 1928, he was just 1 triumph behind Philadelphia's Lefty Grove and Yankee teammate George Pipgras, who shared the A.L. lead with 24 victories apiece. Hoyt was 2-1 with 8 saves as a reliever, and his save totals were the best in both leagues. The pinstriped American Leaguers steamrollered past the St. Louis Cardinals in four straight World Series games. Hoyt had half the Yankee victories. He opened the Series with a 4-1 victory, allowing just 3 hits in nine innings, one of them a Jim Bottomley homer. Hoyt returned for another complete-game win to clinch the Series for the Yanks in game four. While he was nicked for 11 hits and 3 runs over 9 innings, Hoyt was supported by 3 homers by Ruth and another by Gehrig.

Historians remember Hoyt first for his longevity and then for his 20-win contributions to the Yankees dynasty teams of 1927 and 1928. Hoyt won 237 games in his career in 3,763 innings pitched and registered 226 complete games and 26 shutouts. When Hoyt's 52 lifetime saves are added to his wins, it shows that the well-traveled hurler participated in 289 victories over two decades. Hoyt gained his biggest fame for his World Series achievements. In seven fall classics, Hoyt was 6-4 with 6 complete games and a sparkling 1.83 ERA.

A whole new generation of fans who never saw Hoyt on the mound got to know the Brooklyn native as a broadcaster for the Cincinnati Reds. He was a Redlegs announcer from 1942 to 1965, sharing his unique brand of humor and insight with fans for 23 years. Hoyt even wrote a few books on sports, including one about his playing days with Babe Ruth.

CAREER HIGHLIGHTS
WAITE CHARLES HOYT

Born: September 9, 1899 Brooklyn, NY **Died:** August 25, 1984
Height: 6'0" **Weight:** 180 lbs. **Batted:** Right **Threw:** Right
Pitcher: New York Giants, 1918, 1932; Boston Red Sox, 1919-20; New York Yankees, 1921-30; Detroit Tigers, 1930-31; Philadelphia Athletics, 1931; Brooklyn Dodgers, 1932, 1937-38; Pittsburgh Pirates, 1933-37.

★ Pitched 3 complete games and had a perfect 0.00 ERA in the '21 World Series
★ Led the A.L. with 22 wins in 1927
★ Ranks second in history with 11 World Series starts
★ Pitched the New York Yankees to six pennants in the 1920s
★ Pitched in seven World Series
★ Elected to the Hall of Fame in 1969

MAJOR LEAGUE TOTALS

G	IP	W	L	Pct.	SO	BB	ERA
674	3,763	237	182	.566	1,206	1,003	3.59

Waite Hoyt's best year as pitcher occurred in 1927 when he led his league with a 2.63 ERA, 22 wins, and a .759 winning percentage. Hoyt's off-the-field activities included a stint as a vaudeville singer and a part-time job as an undertaker.

KENT HRBEK

With a career-high .312 batting average and 25 home runs in 1988, first baseman Kent Hrbek continues to live up to his reputation as one of the Minnesota Twins heavy hitters. This comment may or may not be construed as a compliment. The tall left hand hitter made his debut with the Twins in 1981, weighing in at 215 pounds. By the top of the 1989 season, the agile, intelligent 28-year-old was tipping the scale at 250 pounds and drawing media comments that his biggest flaw was his inability to get up from the dinner table. Scouts have speculated that the star's weight gain has slowed his production by up to 20 RBI and 10 home runs per year and has cost countless baserunning opportunities. Because Hrbek is still haunted by chronic knee and shoulder woes, his weight is a very real concern, for his own health as well as that of the Twins.

If the projections about what a slimmed-down Hrbek could do are correct, he could quickly move from being one of the league's best first sackers to being the best, perhaps even matching the great Don Mattingly. Their stats are comparable: Mattingly has the edge in hitting against lefties and in home run percentage, but Hrbek fares better than his Big Apple counterpart on grass and during day games—which is too bad, since Hrbek spends the bulk of his season on astroturf in the closed-in confines of the Metrodome.

The Minneapolis native was selected as a 17th-round draft choice on June 16, 1978, after being discovered in high school by scout Angelo Guiliani. Growing up near the old Metropolitan Stadium, Hrbek was a Twins fan like other local youngsters. He got a chance to become a hometown hero with his selection by Minnesota. His 1979 season at Elizabethton was half given over to injuries, with "Herbie" appearing in only 17 games with a .208 average. It was one of only two times in his ten-year career that he would log fewer than 1,000 putouts. The second would be in 1988, when he netted only 842 putouts.

With 115 games in Wisconsin Rapids in 1980, Hrbek had more of a chance to strut his stuff. An early injury benched him for only three weeks, and he finished the season with 19 homers and a .267 batting mark. It was the only time in his professional career that Hrbek led the league in errors, with 20 miscues; he has never come close to such a high mark since.

His breakthrough year was in 1981 in Visalia. Hrbek led the California League in the two areas he is now best known for, batting at .379 and fielding at .989. He also led loop batters with a .630 slugging percentage, .453 on-base percentage, and 9 sacrifice flies. He was League Player of the Month in June, an All-Star selection, League MVP, and recipient of the Sherry Robertson award as the Twins Outstanding Farm Prospect. His reward was a prompt trip to the majors. He made his major league debut on August 24 of that same year, becoming the 15th native Minnesotan ever to play for the Twins. He homered in the twelfth inning of his first game and registered no errors in his first 24 games.

It looked like the start of a beautiful relationship between Hrbek and the Twins. On April 3, 1982, he christened the Twins' new Hubert H. Humphrey Metrodome with its first home run in an exhibition game against the Philadelphia Phillies. That one didn't go into the record books, but Herbie has made

up for that. He has clubbed over 90 total homers in his home park, more than any other player in the Dome's short history.

It was a very good year for Hrbek: A 23-game hitting streak soon became 40 out of 41 games. The streak included his first grand slam and an invitation to the All-Star game (making him the only rookie represented). He was named the team's top rookie and was second in American League Rookie of the Year balloting to Baltimore's Cal Ripken, Jr. Hrbek was the only unanimous choice on the 1982 Major League Rookie All-Star team. A vote among league managers named Hrbek the league's best hitting prospect.

Year after year the acclaim came in steady and sweet, rising like the numbers in Hrbek's season totals. In 1984 his 27 homers, career-high 107 RBI, and .307 average placed him second in the league MVP balloting to Detroit's Willie Hernandez. Three of his 21 homers in 1985 were grand slams, tying a team record. In 1986 he was the A.L. Player of the Month in June, later finishing the year with 29 homers and 91 RBI. His personal best of 34 homers came in Minnesota's 1987 world championship season. Hrbek fielded flawlessly for every postseason game, handling 108 total putouts. On October 24, 1987, his game-winning grand slam in the sixth game of the World Series tied two major league records with a single blow: most grand slams and most RBI in an inning for World Series play.

If his health holds out, Hrbek's dependable glove work and solid batsmanship should keep the Twins in pennant contention for many years to come.

CAREER HIGHLIGHTS
KENT ALAN HRBEK

Born: May 21, 1960   Minneapolis, MN
Height: 6'4"   **Weight:** 250 lbs.   **Bats:** Left   **Throws:** Right
First baseman: Minnesota Twins, 1981-1989.

- ★ Has hit 20 or more homers seven times
- ★ Hit a grand slam in the 1987 World Series
- ★ Only rookie named to the 1982 All-Star team
- ★ Drove in 90 or more runs five times
- ★ Compiled a 23-game hitting streak in '83
- ★ Has hit the most homers in the Metrodome

MAJOR LEAGUE TOTALS

G	AB	H	BA	2B	3B	HR	R	RBI	SB
1,156	4,178	1,212	.290	224	16	201	624	724	19

Kent Hrbek, the Minnesota Twins heavy hitter, has slammed over 90 home runs in the Metrodome—more than any other player in the stadium's short history. Hrbek's powerful bat and dependable glove should help the Twins for several seasons to come.

CARL HUBBELL

Despite Carl Hubbell's 16 successful seasons as a New York Giants pitcher, three trips to the World Series, and five consecutive 20-win seasons, the man nicknamed "King Carl" is best remembered for one exhibition game appearance.

That appearance was in the 1934 All-Star game, only the second interleague matchup ever played. Hubbell had been the leading winner in the National League the previous year with a 23-12 record, including league bests in innings pitched (308.2), ERA (1.66), and shutouts (10). As the National League starter, Hubbell was facing some of the American League's most potent bats. He began the game on shaky ground, yielding a single to Charlie Gehringer and a walk to Heinie Manush. With Babe Ruth coming to bat, it looked like curtains for the National Leaguers. However, Hubbell struck out The Sultan of Swat on three called strikes. Each strike was a wicked screwball, Hubbell's specialty pitch. The Babe's teammate Lou Gehrig followed, and he also struck out swinging. Muscleman Jimmie Foxx made the third out of the inning, fanning on three pitches.

After Frankie Frisch homered in the first to give the senior circuit a lead, Hubbell continued his dominance in the second inning. Back-to-back strikeouts of Al Simmons and Joe Cronin followed before Bill Dickey broke the string with a single. The man dubbed "The Meal Ticket" was relieved after three innings and the American League rallied for a win. The victory was overshadowed by Hubbell's performance. He whiffed five consecutive future Hall of Famers. Of the 13 batters he faced, Hubbell threw 27 strikes and 21 balls. Only 5 balls were hit into fair territory. At a time when it seemed as though the whole world was watching, Hubbell was at his best.

Reaching the majors hadn't been an easy task for Hubbell. After attending high school in Meeker, Oklahoma, Hubbell got his first baseball job pitching for Cushing of the Oklahoma State League in 1924. In 1925 he advanced to Oklahoma City, winning 17 games. The Detroit Tigers purchased Hubbell, but manager Ty Cobb was not impressed with the lanky lefty. He told Hubbell to stop trying to throw a screwball because he'd ruin his arm. The suggestion was well-founded because the pitch places undue stress on a pitcher's shoulder and elbow. Without giving him

a single inning of major league work, the Tigers dispatched Hubbell to Toronto. He stuck with his screwball, however. After Hubbell won 12 games with Beaumont of the Texas League in 1928, the Giants purchased his contract.

Hubbell never had a losing record in his 16 years with the Giants, winning in double figures in all but his last season. He went 10-6 with 8 complete games in his first year with New York. In 1929 Hubbell upped his record to 18-11. He kept winning: 17 games in 1930, 14 in 1931, and 18 in 1932. The National League named Hubbell its Most Valuable Player in 1933 after his 23-win season.

In the 1933 World Series, Hubbell hurled the Giants to a championship against the Washington Senators with 2 complete-game shutouts. He posted 20 scoreless innings in the Series, including one 11-inning whitewash. One of Hubbell's wins was an 18-inning complete game shutout against the Cardinals. In all that time, he didn't allow a single base on balls. He pitched

46 straight scoreless innings in 1933, a record that stood for 35 years.

Hubbell was never a great hitter; yet he did compile a lifetime mark of .191, which is respectable for any pitcher. He finished his career at the plate with 246 hits and 4 home runs. An illustration of Hubbell's dedication as a player can be judged by his work with the bat. In his 1928 rookie season, he batted left-handed. After only 5 hits, he adopted a right-handed approach. In 1931 and 1932, he had his best offensive years with identical averages of .241. Hubbell experimented with switch-hitting during that two-year span, then returned to the right side of the plate for the rest of his career.

Hubbell's pitching career included 253 wins and 154 losses. When his 33 saves are included in his final stats, his many contributions to the Giants become even more evident. He finished his career with 260 complete games and 36 shutouts, showing his durability as a starter. On the Giants all-time pitching list, Hubbell ranks second only to the immortal Christy Mathewson in wins, innings pitched (3,591), and complete games. He's third in shutouts and strikeouts (1,677), and fourth in appearances (535). Although he had a long career, manager Cobb was partially right about the screwball: Hubbell's arm became permanently misshapen from the unnatural delivery. In later years, he warned rookies to consider the consequences before adopting the pitch.

Hubbell was elected to the Hall of Fame in 1947. Following his retirement, he was director of the Giants minor league organization and was later director of player development for 35 years. From 1978 until his death, Hubbell served as a Giants scout.

CAREER HIGHLIGHTS
CARL OWEN HUBBELL

Born: June 22, 1903 Carthage, MO **Died:** November 21, 1988
Height: 6'0" **Weight:** 170 lbs. **Batted:** Both **Threw:** Left
Pitcher: New York Giants, 1928-43.

★ Won MVP awards in 1933 and 1936
★ Won three league ERA titles
★ Compiled five straight seasons of 20-plus wins

★ Pitched in three World Series
★ Elected to the Hall of Fame in 1947
★ Struck out five straight batters in the 1934 All-Star game

MAJOR LEAGUE TOTALS

G	IP	W	L	Pct.	SO	BB	ERA
535	3,591	253	154	.622	1,677	725	2.98

Though Carl Hubbell had a lengthy career as a pitcher, his dependency on the screwball—which was hurled with a clockwise snap of his left wrist—permanently twisted his left arm. His arm was so misshapen that the palm of his hand faced out.

CATFISH HUNTER

Very few pitchers in baseball have dominated their league to the extent that Jim "Catfish" Hunter ruled the American League through most of the 1970s. During the seven-year period from 1970 to 1976, Hunter averaged 21 victories a season. In that span, he led the league twice in wins and twice in winning percentage and placed among the leaders in both categories every year. Hunter began his career with the Kansas City Athletics in 1965, and three years later celebrated the club's move to Oakland by pitching a perfect game against the Minnesota Twins.

Hunter never had the benefit of minor league experience. He was signed by the Kansas City Athletics in 1964 for an estimated signing bonus of $75,000. Hunter was on the major league roster that first year but saw no action. Record books listed him as on the disabled list with Daytona Beach, but he was actually spending his time as a batting practice pitcher for the Athletics. Despite his 1968 perfect game, Hunter's first five seasons were quite ordinary. He posted unspectacular records: 8-8 in 1965, 9-11 in 1966, 13-17 in 1967, 13-13 in 1968, and 12-15 in 1969. Granted, he had little offensive support in those early years, but Hunter was learning big league pitching the hard way.

His first major success came in 1970, when he went 18-14. The following season, Hunter won 21 games and sparked the A's to their first Western Division title. Another 21-win season followed in 1972, when the A's won their first of three straight world championships. Hunter notched 2 complete-game victories in the World Series. In 1973 he registered his third straight season of 21 triumphs. The A's returned to the World Series via Hunter's 2 victories, the last being a pennant-clinching five-hitter against the O's. Hunter capped his Oakland career with a league-best 25-12 record in 1974, winning the Cy Young award. Despite Oakland's illustrious bullpen corps, Hunter completed 23 games.

Some of the biggest news Hunter ever made in baseball happened off the field. After Hunter's great 1974 performance, he battled with A's team owner Charlie Finley over the issue of his salary, claiming that Finley wasn't living up to the terms of the contract: he was deferring half of Hunter's annual $100,000 salary to the following year for tax purposes. Hunter sued Finley for breach of contract and won. The courtroom wrangling took more than three months and made Hunter a free agent. The historic legal decision was almost overshadowed by the frantic bidding for Hunter's services that ensued. For nearly two weeks, team representatives from far and wide flew to North Carolina to woo Hunter and his attorneys. Never before had clubs been so willing to offer high-priced multiyear contracts to a player. Eventually, free-spending New York Yankees team owner George Steinbrenner won out with a five-year contract for Hunter worth approximately $3.75 million.

Hunter provided immediate returns on the Yankees investment: He led the league with a 23-14 record, including a league-best 30 complete games and 328 innings pitched. His presence sparked the Bronx Bombers to three straight pennants, as well as world championships in 1977 and 1978.

Fans remember Hunter as a control artist who employed an assortment of breaking pitches. Although he allowed an above-average number of home runs and was never a power pitcher, Hunter relied on his wits and determination to compile a career record of 224 wins (including 42 shutouts) and 166 losses, with 2,012 strikeouts and a 3.26 ERA.

Hunter's aggressiveness shows in his batting record. Before Finley convinced the American League to adopt the designated hitter rule, Hunter was among the best-hitting pitchers in the league. He batted .196 with 2 homers in 1967, then kept his average above .200 for the next five years. His best year at the plate was 1971, when he batted .350 with 36 hits. He finished his eight-year batting career (pre-1973) with a .226 average and 6 home runs.

Hunter was elected to the Hall of Fame in 1987. The star hurler set the record straight about his nickname during the induction ceremonies. Legend had it that as a child he ran away from home one day and returned with two catfish. In reality, both the nickname and the story were dreamed up by team owner Finley to enhance Hunter's public image. Since his retirement, Hunter has been farming with his family in North Carolina.

Athletics owner Charlie Finley tried to spice up Jim Hunter's image with a colorful nickname—Catfish. But Hunter's pitching skills were enough to excite most baseball fans. He pitched five consecutive 20-win seasons and won the Cy Young award in 1974.

CAREER HIGHLIGHTS
JAMES AUGUSTUS HUNTER

Born: April 18, 1946 Hertford, NC
Height: 6'0" **Weight:** 190 lbs. **Batted:** Right **Threw:** Right
Pitcher: Kansas City Athletics, 1965-67; Oakland Athletics, 1968-74; New York Yankess, 1975-79.

- ★ Won the Cy Young award in 1974
- ★ Pitched in six World Series
- ★ Pitched in six League Championship Series
- ★ Posted five consecutive 20-win seasons
- ★ Hurled a perfect game in 1968
- ★ Elected to the Hall of Fame in 1987

MAJOR LEAGUE TOTALS

G	IP	W	L	Pct.	SO	BB	ERA
500	3,449	224	166	.574	2,012	954	3.26

MONTE IRVIN

Like other great black players of his era, Monte Irvin was a baseball superstar whose best years were spent in the now-defunct Negro Leagues. Irvin did eventually enjoy eight partial seasons in the major leagues and helped the New York Giants to two pennants, but when he was elected to the Hall of Fame in 1973, it was more for his sparkling career in the Negro Leagues than for his short but productive time in the majors.

Irvin started playing professional ball at age 17, and for the next decade he played summer ball in the Negro Leagues and winter ball in the Mexican Leagues. He developed into a power-hitting, slick-fielding, basestealing, triple-threat performer. Although accurate records were not kept for the Negro and Mexican Leagues, it is estimated that Irvin batted at about a .350 clip throughout the 1940s. One year he was named Most Valuable Player in the Mexican League after batting just 3 points shy of .400. The Mexican League offered an impressive income for black players in the 1940s, as well as the freedom to play in a society that was more free of racial discrimination.

Roy Campanella's autobiography, *It's Good to Be Alive*, explains how Monte Irvin almost became a Dodger. Campanella recommended to Dodger owner Branch Rickey that he sign Irvin and Larry Doby, both star players from the Newark Eagles of the Negro National League. The Dodgers chief scout signed Irvin when he was playing winter ball in Puerto Rico. Because the Newark team had folded, the Dodgers considered Irvin a free agent. The Newark team owner disagreed, insisting that Irvin was still under contract to his old team. When the Newark owner asked for $5,000 for the rights to Irvin, the Dodgers declined to pursue the gifted outfielder. The New York Giants paid the price and the rest is history.

Irvin was signed to a contract by the Giants and came up to the big leagues as a 30-year-old rookie in 1949. His first season was anything but an instant success: He hit only .224 with just 17 hits in 36 games. Irvin's sophomore campaign was much more impressive. Playing in 110 games, he divided his time between first base and the outfield and even tried one game at third base. His season totals were 15 homers, 66 RBI, and a .299 batting average.

By 1951, he was playing regularly beside Willie Mays in the Giants outfield and enjoying his best season in the majors. Leading the Giants to the National League pennant, the slugging outfielder batted .312 with a career-high 24 homers, a league-leading 121 RBI, and 12 stolen bases. In his first full season in left field, Irvin logged 10 assists and a sparkling .996 fielding percentage (making just 1 error all year). He went on to bat an amazing .458 in the 1951 World Series, when he stroked 11 hits in 24 at-bats. In the Series opener, he stole home and racked up 4 hits.

A fractured ankle during a spring training game in Denver caused Irvin to miss all but 46 games in 1952. He batted .310 for that abbreviated season, however. His mobility was hampered after that, although he continued to hit well. Irvin rebounded to a .329 average in 1953, with 21 homers and 97 RBI. Unfortunately, he reinjured the ankle in 1954, the year the Giants went on to win their second National League pennant in four years. He did appear in 135 games, tallying 19 homers, 64 RBI, and a .262 average. In New York's four-game World Series sweep of the Cleveland Indians that year Irvin had 2 hits and 2 RBI in nine plate appearances.

Although Irvin hit .253 in 51 games for the 1955 Giants, he was demoted to Minneapolis of the American Association. The Giants moved power hitter Whitey Lockman from first base to left field to replace Irvin. After batting .352 in the minors for the rest of the season, Irvin was picked up by the Chicago Cubs in 1956. At age 37, the Alabama native proved he could still hack it in the majors. He batted .271 with 15 homers and 50 RBI for the Cubs before retiring. It seems that the Cubs' last-place finish of 60-94 that year provided little encouragement for Irvin to continue his career.

Irvin's major league totals represent only a small part of his accomplishments in organized baseball. In eight years in the majors, Irvin batted .293 with 731 career hits, 97 doubles, 31 triples, 99 homers and 443 RBI.

Irvin's selection to the Hall of Fame in 1973 was special—he was chosen by The Special Committee on Negro Leagues. Previously only three Negro Leaguers (Josh Gibson, Satchel Paige, and Buck Leonard) had been appointed to Cooperstown. After his election, Irvin later served on that committee and helped other Negro League stars like Rube Foster, Judy Johnson, Oscar Charleston, and Martin Dihigo to gain recognition from the Hall of Fame.

Irvin became visible to a whole new generation of fans off the field. He worked as a representative of the Baseball Commissioner's office throughout the 1970s, often representing Commissioner Bowie Kuhn at special games and other public events. Irvin has been retired since 1983.

CAREER HIGHLIGHTS
MONTFORD IRVIN

Born: February 25, 1919   Columbia, AL
Height: 6'1" **Weight:** 195 lbs. **Batted:** Right **Threw:** Right
Outfielder: Negro Leagues, 1936-46; New York Giants, 1949-55; Chicago Cubs, 1956.

- ★ Led the league in RBI in 1951
- ★ Stole home in the 1951 World Series
- ★ Batted .299 or better for four straight seasons
- ★ Played in two World Series
- ★ Was a five-time Negro League All-Star
- ★ Elected to the Hall of Fame in 1973

MAJOR LEAGUE TOTALS

G	AB	H	BA	2B	3B	HR	R	RBI	SB
764	2,499	731	.293	97	31	99	366	443	28

While playing for the Newark Eagles of the Negro League, Monte Irvin was credited with two batting titles, averaging .396 in 1941 and .398 in 1946. His powerful bat helped his Eagles win the '46 black world championship over Satchel Paige's Kansas City Monarchs.

JOE JACKSON

The debate still rages over how the powerful slugger nicknamed "Shoeless Joe" should be remembered. Some fans prefer to remember Joseph Jefferson Jackson as a sweet-swinging hitter who was one of the greatest outfielders in the first 20 years of the American League's existence; others recall that he was one of eight men accused of purposely losing the 1919 World Series and banned from the majors for life after the 1920 season. For years, believers in Jackson's integrity have claimed that he did nothing wrong. His supporters feel Jackson should be allowed to take his rightful place in the Hall of Fame next to Ty Cobb and Rogers Hornsby, the only two hitters in baseball who compiled higher lifetime batting averages.

Jackson remains one of the most controversial and mysterious stars in baseball history. It all started when the Chicago White Sox won the 1919 American League pennant and faced the Cincinnati Reds in the World Series, then a nine-game affair. The powerful American League club was a heavy favorite to whip the Reds, but to the astonishment of many, the White Sox lost the fall classic five games to three. Some fans wondered aloud about the noticeably uninspired performances of several of the White Sox players. Over the course of the following season, it was revealed that the 1919 World Series had been rigged and that several members of the White Sox had accepted bribes to throw the Series. Supposedly, Jackson had accepted $5,000 from the mobsters who instigated the scheme but never got the $20,000 he was promised.

To clean up the sport, a quick investigation was conducted and eight members of the White Sox, including Jackson, were accused of participating in the fix and were banned from baseball for life. Even though a grand jury didn't find enough significant evidence to convict any of the accused players, baseball still banished the unfortunate eight.

Baseball legend has it that a little boy spotted Jackson leaving the courtroom after news of the World Series scandal broke. The disheartened youngster allegedly begged him, "Say it ain't so, Joe." The short reply from the fallen giant was, "Yes, kid, I'm afraid it is," though Jackson sometimes denied that the incident happened. The story of the World Series scandal was immortalized in the best-selling book, *Eight Men Out* by Eliot Asinof.

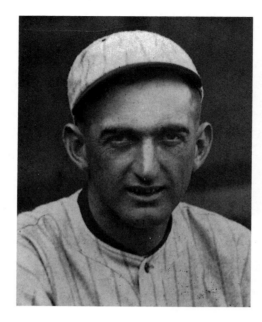

Jackson maintained his innocence until his death in 1951, and he had many supporters in his claim. The hard-hitting outfielder was the top batter in the Series and rapped out a dozen hits in 32 at-bats for a .375 average, making his offensive performance seem sincere. But skeptics often point out the two costly errors Jackson made in the field.

After being banned for life by baseball commissioner Judge Kenesaw Mountain Landis, Jackson returned home to South Carolina, where despite the controversy he remained a hero for the rest of his life. His supporters made continuous but unsuccessful attempts to convince the baseball establishment that Jackson belonged in the Hall of Fame.

Throughout his 13 seasons in the majors, played mostly for the Cleveland Indians and the White Sox, Jackson was consistently among the league's top hit-

ters. For a four-year stretch in his prime, he averaged better than .390. In 1911 he batted .408, only to lose the batting title to Cobb, who hit .420. The following season Jackson came back with a .395 average, but once again Cobb topped the .400 mark. Just 33 years old when he was banned, Jackson batted .382 in 1920, his final season, compiling a .356 lifetime average.

Jackson was an uneducated man for the most part. Instead of attending school, he worked in a cotton mill during his childhood. The Philadelphia Athletics discovered him playing on the mill's baseball team. Jackson agreed to play in Philadelphia, but he was naive to the ways of big-city life. Supposedly, Jackson could not read or write, which further isolated him from his surroundings. After just ten games in two years, the A's released the unhappy slugger. He fared better in Cleveland, where he stayed until early 1915, when the financially strapped team had to sell players as part of a housecleaning effort and to raise funds.

Ironically, Jackson and the White Sox did compete in one legitimate Series and won. In 1917 the White Sox beat the New York Giants in six Series games. Jackson had 7 hits, 4 runs, and 2 RBI for a .304 average in the fall classic.

It seems that Jackson made peace with himself after his expulsion from the major leagues. He played baseball for semipro teams under assumed names and then lived quietly in South Carolina. He remained financially comfortable through several earlier business investments. Jackson, like all of his "Black Sox" teammates, died without revealing many facts about the actual extent of gangster involvement in the Series.

CAREER HIGHLIGHTS
JOSEPH JEFFERSON JACKSON

Born: July 16, 1889 Brandon Mills, SC **Died:** December 5, 1951
Height: 6'1" **Weight:** 200 lbs. **Batted:** Left **Threw:** Right
Outfielder: Philadelphia Athletics, 1908-09; Cleveland Indians, 1910-15; Chicago White Sox, 1915-20.

* Batted .408 in 1911
* Compiled a .356 lifetime batting average
* Led the league in triples three times
* Batted over the .340 mark in eight seasons

MAJOR LEAGUE TOTALS

G	AB	H	BA	2B	3B	HR	R	RBI	SB
1,330	4,981	1,772	.356	307	168	54	873	785	202

Superstar Shoeless Joe Jackson played outlaw ball under an assumed name after his banishment from organized baseball for his role in the Black Sox scandal. Fans were occasionally able to recognize Jackson because of his smooth, near-perfect swing.

REGGIE JACKSON

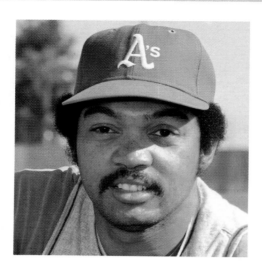

Reggie Jackson is not only a future Hall of Famer, but also one of the most memorable personalities to grace the junior circuit over the past two decades. One of only 14 players in major league history to top the 500-homer mark, he helped fill ballparks with fans from the day he arrived on the scene with the Kansas City Athletics

Jackson attended Arizona State University—a school noted for producing major leaguers—on a football scholarship. After Jackson disagreed with his college coach and quit football, he decided to pursue baseball. After he was named *The Sporting News* College Player of the Year in 1966, Jackson became a hot property in the June free-agent draft. The New York Mets passed on Jackson during the first round, but Kansas City Athletics owner Charlie O. Finley made Jackson his second choice in the first round. Jackson's signing bonus from the Athletics was estimated as high as $90,000.

The man who had spent his childhood years in Philadelphia spent just one and a half seasons in the A's minor league farm system. In 1966 Jackson played with Lewiston of the Northwest League for 12 games, then finished the year at Modesto of the California League with 21 homers, 60 RBI, and a .299 average. Jackson terrorized Southern League pitching while playing with Birmingham in 1967. He led the league in runs scored (84) and triples (17) while hitting .293 with 17 homers and 58 RBI. Jackson was called up for a 35-game trial at the end of the 1967 season but batted just .178.

Jackson's first full season came in 1968. He hit 29 homers and drove in 74 RBI but struck out a career-high 171 times. In 1969 Jackson belted personal bests of 47 homers and 118 RBI. Jackson powered the A's to their first of five straight American League West pennants in 1971, hitting 32 homers and driving in 80 runs. His first home run title came in 1973, when he socked 32 dingers and paced the American League with 117 RBI. In 1975, his final season with the A's, Jackson was first in the league with 36 homers.

Jackson was discarded by the A's team ownership when it was apparent that the gifted slugger would not be re-signing with Oakland. Jackson wanted to become a free agent, which meant the A's would get no compensation once he departed for more money. Team owner Finley traded Jackson, Ken Holtzman (also a free agent), and Bill

Van Bommel to the Baltimore Orioles for Don Baylor, Paul Mitchell, and Mike Torrez on April 2, 1976.

His Baltimore statistics (27 homers, 91 RBI, and a .277 average) weren't the usual numbers expected from Jackson, but his reputation as a premier slugger remained. Teams scrambled to sign the outspoken superstar, who constantly drew big headlines for his controversial comments.

The Yankees finally inked him to a five-year contract on November 29, 1976. The deal was estimated to be worth $3 million, the highest any free agent garnered that year. Supposedly the Montreal Expos offered even more money, but Jackson declined the offer. In his first four years with New York, his homer totals ranged from 29 to 41, while his RBI totals were 110, 97, 89, and 111. What gained Jackson everlasting fame was his stunning postseason performance, which earned him the nickname "Mr. October." He holds the major league record for playing in 11

League Championship Series and gaining 37 hits. In five World Series, he has the best slugging percentage in history (.755). Jackson is best remembered for hitting 3 home runs and notching 5 RBIs in the decisive seventh game of the 1977 World Series. Each homer, hit against three different Dodger hurlers, came on the first pitch. His World Series lifetime totals include 10 homers (fifth highest of all time), 24 RBI, and a .357 average.

Not all of the records Jackson set were that memorable. He set a major league record by striking out 2,597 times, including a record 18 seasons with 100 or more strikeouts. He also led the American League in errors four times (and tied for the lead once). Jackson accomplished many noteworthy and honorable feats, however: His 563 homers are sixth highest in history, and he tied an A.L. record with 16 seasons of 20 or more homers.

Following his release by the Angels after the 1986 season, Jackson signed a free-agent contract with his original team, the A's, for one final season in 1987. He hit .220 in 115 games, with just 15 homers and 43 RBI. Although he didn't make a significant contribution to the team as a player, his presence helped boost attendance.

Jackson started a new career as a baseball broadcaster before retiring as a player. During the 1970s he hosted a syndicated TV interview show titled *Greatest Sports Legends*. Recently, he has served as a color commentator on baseball postseason games for ABC-TV. Jackson will probably make headlines again in 1993, when he should be elected to the Hall of Fame during his first year of eligibility.

CAREER HIGHLIGHTS
REGINALD MARTINEZ JACKSON

Born: May 18, 1946   Wyncote, PA
Height: 6'0"   **Weight:** 200 lbs.   **Batted:** Left   **Threw:** Left
Outfielder: Kansas City Athletics, 1967; Oakland Athletics, 1968-75, 1987; Baltimore Orioles, 1976; New York Yankees, 1977-81; California Angels, 1982-86.

- ★ Voted A.L. MVP in 1973
- ★ Played in five World Series
- ★ Was the A.L. home run leader in 1973, 1975, 1980, and 1982
- ★ Drove in 100-plus runs six times
- ★ Appeared in 12 All-Star games
- ★ Sixth on the all-time home run list

MAJOR LEAGUE TOTALS

G	AB	H	BA	2B	3B	HR	R	RBI	SB
2,820	9,864	2,584	.262	463	49	563	1,551	1,702	228

Reggie Jackson earned his nickname, Mr. October, for his magnificent postseason performances. His World Series slugging percentage of .755 ranks highest for both leagues. His Series totals include 10 homers, 24 RBI, and a .357 batting average.

FERGIE JENKINS

Among the commodities that Canada exported to the United States in the early 1960s was one that made American baseball fans sit up and take notice. His name was Ferguson Jenkins, and his trade was pitching. The big hurler from Ontario proved to be a durable commodity—a rugged starting pitcher who lasted 19 years with four different teams.

The Philadelphia Phillies organization was the first to spot Jenkins' talent, signing him to a contract in 1962. He labored in the Philadelphia minor league system for three and a half years before getting a chance with the parent club. His first stunning season in the minors came in 1963 with Miami, when he went 12-5, and struck out 135 in 140 innings. In 1965 he won 15 games with Chattanooga and Arkansas. After going 8-6 in 32 games with Arkansas, Jenkins got his first call-up to the Phillies. The big Canadian fared quite well as a reliever. In seven games, he was 2-1 with 1 save and a 2.19 ERA. After just one game in 1966, the Phillies sent Jenkins packing. He was traded to the Chicago Cubs with outfielder Adolpho Phillips and first baseman/outfielder John Herrnstein in exchange for pitchers Bob Buhl and Larry Jackson on April 21.

The trade must have been arranged by Jenkins' fairy godmother. After finishing the 1966 season with a 6-8 record, Jenkins was suddenly transformed into a star pitcher. Manager Leo Durocher convinced him to try his hand as a starting pitcher, and the rest was history. Six straight 20-win seasons followed.

When Jenkins led the National League with a 24-13 record, 39 starts, 30 complete games, and 325 hits, he won that year's Cy Young award. The least number of starts he made during his first seven years in Chicago was 36. Furthermore, he liked to finish what he started. Jenkins logged at least 20 complete games every year except for 1973.

Unfortunately, neither the Cubs management nor the fans could tolerate any weakness in Jenkins' yearly successes. When his record slipped to 14-16 and just 7 complete games in 1973, Wrigley Field fans booed Jenkins with bloodthirsty delight. The troubled hurler decided he wanted a new environment in which he'd be more appreciated. He asked if he could be sent to a team a bit closer to his home in Canada. Instead, the Cubs shipped him in the opposite

direction and out of the National League entirely. He was traded to the Texas Rangers on October 25, 1973, for Bill Madlock and Vic Harris. At least Jenkins wouldn't be beating the Cubs on a regular basis.

Working for manager Billy Martin, Jenkins made a stunning debut in the A.L. In his first start, Jenkins scored a one-hit victory against the Oakland A's. He beat the pennant-winning Athletics five times that season. Jenkins ended the season with a 25-12 record, which was tops in the junior circuit. After winning 17 games the next season, Jenkins was traded to the Boston Red Sox for outfielder Juan Beniquez and two minor leaguers on November 17, 1975. He won 12 and 10 games in the next two seasons, before the Red Sox returned him to the Rangers in exchange for a minor leaguer prior to the 1978 season. In the next four seasons, Jenkins

would win 18, 16, 12, and 5 games.

In 1982 he became a free agent. The Cubs were under new ownership and they eagerly signed the veteran. He won 14 games in 1982 and claimed 6 victories in 1983 before calling it quits. During his farewell tour with the Cubbies, Jenkins got his 3,000th strikeout with the team in which his career had first blossomed.

After retiring at the end of 1983, Jenkins had a career record of 284 wins. His 3,192 strikeouts rank ninth in history. His Ks are even more impressive when viewed in conjunction with his low number of walks (997). Jenkins was a true workhorse in the majors, earning 267 complete games and 49 shutouts.

The veteran righthander was a difficult hitter when he played in the National League and had 148 lifetime hits with 13 home runs. Six of those homers came in 1971, when he batted a career high of .243. Jenkins could have achieved some offensive marks later in his career, if he hadn't been denied the opportunity due to the designated hitter rule in the A.L.

Jenkins finished fifth in the Hall of Fame balloting in 1989 with 234 votes. This was his first year of eligibility, and even baseball legends sometimes have to wait a year or so before getting their deserved recognition. Meanwhile, Jenkins at least has the pleasure of being a member of the Cubs Hall of Fame.

Jenkins is currently employed with the Rangers, serving as pitching coach for the Triple-A minor league team in Oklahoma City. Hopefully he can help build a contending pitching staff of the future for the Rangers.

CAREER HIGHLIGHTS
FERGUSON ARTHUR JENKINS

Born: December 13, 1943   Chatham, Ontario, Canada
Height: 6'5"   **Weight:** 200 lbs.   **Batted:** Right   **Threw:** Right
Pitcher: Philadelphia Phillies, 1965-66; Chicago Cubs, 1966-73, 1982-83; Texas Rangers, 1974-75, 1978-81; Boston Red Sox, 1976-77.

- ★ Led the league in wins twice
- ★ Topped the N.L. in strikeouts in 1969 with 273
- ★ Was first in the league in complete games four times
- ★ Won the Cy Young award in 1971
- ★ Has the ninth-highest strikeout total in history
- ★ Earned 49 career shutouts

MAJOR LEAGUE TOTALS

G	IP	W	L	Pct.	ERA	SO	BB
664	4,498	284	226	.557	3.34	3,192	997

Ferguson Jenkins played baseball for 19 years without pitching for a pennant-winning team. Yet he still managed to compile six straight 20-win seasons from 1967-72, cop the Cy Young award in 1971, and lead his league in wins twice.

TOMMY JOHN

Tommy John pitched his first professional season in 1961, at the age of 18, posting a record of 10 wins and 4 losses. In 1988, at the age of 45 and the oldest active player in the majors, he won 9 and lost 8. John may be one of the first players in history who appealed to two generations of fans.

John never won a Cy Young award nor was he knighted Most Valuable Player. He was never a splashy league leader in assorted pitching categories. Although he won 20 or more games three times in his long career, John wasn't known as a pitching superstar. But he became one of the 20 greatest winners in baseball history through his consistency. The man known as "TJ" has several pages worth of stats acquired through hard work and persistence. Even in the years when he enjoyed 20-win seasons, John struck out a high of just 124 batters. He defied the image of the power pitcher, instead using his experience to get the job done.

John's determination was evident through the numerous injuries he endured and recovered from through the years. The first disability occurred in August 1968. John's fourth year with the Chicago White Sox was his sixth in the American League. Normally known as a caring family man devoted to charitable causes and his religious faith, John got into a fight with Detroit Tiger Dick McAuliffe and came out of it with a broken collarbone. The incident abbreviated John's best major league season, which included a career-low ERA of 1.98 in 25 games. The scuffle also tore some left shoulder ligaments.

In 1972, after leading league pitchers with a perfect fielding average and recording his 1,000th strikeout, he was caught in a home plate collision that chipped a bone in his left elbow, requiring immediate surgery.

In 1973, with a decade of big league ball under his belt, John posted his 100th career win, leading the Los Angeles Dodgers with a 3.10 ERA and topping the league with his .696 winning percentage (by winning what then was a personal best of 16 games). In a major trade, the White Sox sent John and utility player Steve Huntz to the Dodgers in exchange for Dick Allen. John started out 1974 in fine shape, winning 13 and losing just 3. However, a routine pitch in Montreal on July 17 ruptured his left elbow ligament.

Rest did nothing to ease the pain, and surgery was decided upon. The left elbow was to be entirely reconstructed using ligaments from John's right forearm. Such an operation had never been performed on an athlete, and John was advised that he would never pitch again.

TJ, of course, did not play in 1975, but he was busy at home exercising, working out, and testing the limits of his reconstructed elbow. He was getting ready to stage what some would call one of the greatest comebacks in baseball history.

In 1976 he went 10-10 with a 3.09 ERA, 1 shutout, and a four-hitter. The National League Comeback Player of the Year award was his, as well as the annual Fred Hutchison award for competitive instinct, character, and desire.

The comeback shifted into high gear the following year, with John reaching the 20-win plateau for the first time in his career. He acquired 1 win and an 0.66 ERA during the National League Championship Series against the Philadelphia Phillies. John was 1-0 and uncharacteristically struck out 11 in 13.2 innings. The Yankees pounded John for 5 runs in his only Series start.

The next year, John won 17 games for the Blue Crew. His 220 innings were the most he had logged in six years. John got another N.L.C.S. win in 1978 against the Phillies on the way to another World Series, again versus the Yankees. This time John avenged his 1977 defeat with 1 win in two Series starts, but the New Yorkers squashed the Dodgers in six games.

Symbolic of his topsy-turvy career, John's free-agent acquisition by the Yankees in late 1978 put him on the losing side of the 1981 World Series against the Dodgers. This would be preceded by three impressive season records for the veteran lefty, however: a 21-9 record in 1979, a career-best mark of 22-9 in 1980, and a 9-8 mark in 1981 (which was blighted by one month on the disabled list when he cut his finger with a razor). The Indiana native had 2 wins in postseason, one against the A's in the American League Championship Series and one versus his former club in the Series. John started two games against the California club and also pitched in a separate relief appearance. His ERA in 13 innings was a sparkling 0.69.

John made the 1989 club as a non-roster player. The Yankees released John following the 1988 season, but owner George Steinbrenner had a change of heart and sought John's return in February. The team got a rubber-armed veteran, while John got a chance to shoot for the elusive 300-win mark. Unfortunately, that goal remained unattained by John as he retired during the 1989 season.

CAREER HIGHLIGHTS
THOMAS EDWARD JOHN

Born: May 22, 1943   Terre Haute, IN
Height: 6'3"   **Weight:** 203 lbs.   **Batted:** Right   **Threw:** Left
Pitcher: Cleveland Indians, 1963-64; Chicago White Sox, 1965-71; Los Angeles Dodgers, 1972-74, 1976-78; New York Yankees, 1979-82, 1986-89; California Angels, 1982-85; Oakland A's, 1985.

★ Three-time 20-game winner
★ Broke a modern record with his 26th big league season in 1989
★ Named to four All-Star teams
★ Tied a major league record with four wins in League Championship Series
★ Pitched in three World Series, winning two games

MAJOR LEAGUE TOTALS

G	IP	W	L	Pct.	SO	BB	ERA
760	4,706	288	231	.555	2,245	1,259	3.34

Tommy John underwent baseball history's first ligament transplant in 1974 when a ligament from his right forearm was used to replace the one he tore in his left elbow. Though advised he might not ever pitch again, John managed a 20-7 record in 1977.

BOB JOHNSON

In today's society, it is offensive to publicly refer to a player by his nationality. However, times were different in the 1930s. These types of nicknames provided a quick, easy way for sportswriters to assign quiet players with flashy character and personality. For instance, infielder Honus Wagner was called "The Flying Dutchman." Irish catcher Roger Bresnahan became "The Duke of Tralee," while Spanish-bred backstop Al Lopez was "Senor Al." Robert Lee Johnson, a hard-hitting outfielder with the Philadelphia Athletics during the 1930s, was known to the baseball world as "Indian Bob."

Johnson was proud of his Cherokee Indian heritage. When the editors for the 1933 edition of *Who's Who in Major League Baseball* asked players to list their nationalities, many who were sons of immigrants provided such answers as "English," "Scotch," or "Irish." Johnson responded on his questionnaire with "American." The publication pointed out this fact in its opening paragraph about Johnson, adding, "...he meant just that. He is one of the few original Americans playing major [league] baseball for, he says, 'I am a Cherokee Indian'." Johnson was preceded in the majors by brother Roy Johnson, who played outfield with the Detroit Tigers, Boston Braves, New York Yankees, and Boston Red Sox from 1929 through 1938.

Bob Johnson was born in Pryor, Oklahoma in 1906. His family moved to the Pacific Northwest during his youth. Johnson only went as far as the fifth grade in Oklahoma and did not go back to school when the family resettled in Tacoma, Washington. Though married at age 16, he didn't get his start in professional baseball until age 21. Johnson had played ball recreationally, but his first salaried position was with Wichita and Pueblo of the Western League. He hit 16 homers and .273 between the two teams in a combined 66 games. Then he moved on to Portland of the Pacific Coast League, where he spent the next three seasons.

In 1930, his first full season with the Beavers, Johnson hit .265 with 21 homers in 157 games. Johnson upped his hit total to 170 in 141 games in 1931, and his batting average soared to .337 with 22 home runs. In 1932 he hit 29 homers and batted .330. When in Portland, he developed the ability to play both the infield and the outfield. During his 13-year career in the major leagues, Johnson saw action at first

base, second base, third base, and the outfield (logging the most time at the latter spot).

At age 24 Johnson made his debut in left field for Connie Mack's Philadelphia Athletics. Because the team had disposed of previous starters Al Simmons and Mule Haas, Johnson found an immediate job opening. He responded with 23 home runs, 93 RBI, a .290 batting average, and 103 runs scored in his rookie season. His sophomore campaign included a career high of 34 homers with 92 RBI and a .307 average. A 26-game hitting streak and a single record-setting game in which he collected 6 hits were Johnson's season highlights.

After being a model of consistency in Philadelphia during the 1930s, Johnson was traded to the Washington Senators on March 21, 1943. There he went into the worst slump of his career, hitting just 7 homers and 63 RBI in 117 games. He was sold to the Boston Red Sox at season's end. In 1944 he staged a valiant comeback with a .324

average, 17 homers, 106 RBI, and 106 runs scored.

Following his 1945 season with the Red Sox, Johnson continued his career in the minor leagues until 1951, when he made an unsuccessful comeback at age 42 with a team in Tijuana, Mexico. He played with Milwaukee of the American Association in 1946, the Seattle Rainiers of the Pacific Coast League in 1947, and Tacoma of the Western Illinois League in 1949 (where he served as a player/manager).

Johnson's career totals include 288 home runs and a home run percentage of 4.2. His 2,051 hits rank higher than the hit totals of Hall of Famers Dave Bancroft, Earl Averill, Johnny Mize, Bobby Doerr, and Johnny Bench. Likewise, his 1,283 RBI rank above those of such notable players as Bill Dickey, Hank Greenberg, Gil Hodges, and Chuck Klein. Johnson was a seventime All-Star who once drove in 6 runs in one inning. His average never dipped below .265 in 13 full seasons of playing at least 117 games. During his first seven years with the Athletics, his average never fell below .290. He was also an excellent fielder.

Following the end of his baseball career, Johnson worked in a brewery and for the fire department in Glendale, California. He spent his final years back in his childhood home of Tacoma.

Bob Johnson probably does not have the name recognition that other Depression-era sluggers have because he played for such mediocre teams. Though Johnson hit over .300 for five seasons, it did little to help his last-place Philadelphia Athletics.

CAREER HIGHLIGHTS
ROBERT LEE JOHNSON

Born: November 26, 1906 Pryor, OK **Died:** July 6, 1982
Height: 6'0" **Weight:** 180 lbs. **Batted:** Right **Threw:** Right
Outfielder: Philadelphia Athletics, 1933-42; Washington Senators, 1943; Boston Red Sox, 1944-45.

* ★ Hit a minimum of 21 home runs in each of his first nine seasons
* ★ Batted over .300 five times
* ★ Drove in 100-plus runs eight times (including seven straight seasons)
* ★ Played on seven All-Star teams
* ★ Never played fewer than 117 games in a season

MAJOR LEAGUE TOTALS

G	AB	H	BA	2B	3B	HR	R	RBI	SB
1,863	6,920	2,051	.296	396	95	288	1,239	1,283	96

WALTER JOHNSON

In 1907 the Washington Senators signed 20-year-old Walter Johnson for the price of a $9 train ticket. Twenty years and 416 victories later, Johnson was still wearing a Senators uniform when he retired as the pitcher with the most wins in American League history. When the Hall of Fame was established in Cooperstown in 1936, Walter "The Big Train" Johnson was selected as one of the five original members. At 6-foot-1 and 200 pounds, it's easy to see how Johnson landed the nickname after he buzzed an opposing batter with one of his express fastballs.

Johnson played his entire career with the hapless Senators, a perennial second-division club that didn't win a pennant until Johnson was 37 years old. Despite that, he set many pitching records that stand to this day. He delivered the most scorching fastball of his era, and his 417 career triumphs are second only to the immortal Cy Young on the all-time list. Johnson's record of 110 shutouts will probably never be matched. A dozen times, he won 20 or more games per season—still the best in the American League. Ten of those seasons were consecutive which is yet another record. Two times he topped the 30-victory mark, and he finished his 21-year career with 3,506 strikeouts—among the best of all time. In the 1913 season he pitched 56 consecutive scoreless innings, a major league record that stood until it was broken by Don Drysdale in 1968 and then by Orel Hershiser in 1988. No American League hurler has ever threatened his accomplishment, though.

Earned run averages weren't recorded until 1913, and it almost seems as if the statistic was developed just to showcase Johnson's talents. Over the next seven seasons, he compiled ERAs of 1.14, 1.72, 1.55, 1.89, 2.28, 1.27, and 1.49. In September 1908 he shut out the New York Yankees (then called the Highlanders) three times in four days. During his career, he won 38 games by a score of 1-0, which is another major league record.

Because there were no All-Star games back in his day, Johnson had to wait 18 years to get a chance at some National League competition. In 1924 his wish came true when the Senators faced the New York Giants in the fall classic. In his first Series game, he pitched 12 innings and struck out 10 only to lose 4-3. After losing the fifth game 6-2, Johnson battled back. The

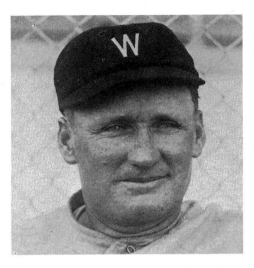

great veteran pitched the final four innings of a 12-inning battle, winning with four frames of shutout relief. The Senators finally won a world championship after a long drought. The Pittsburgh Pirates downed the defending champions in the 1925 World Series. Johnson lost the seventh game, but he had two postseason wins: a five-hit, ten-strikeout effort in the opener and a six-hit shut-out in the fourth game.

The son of Kansas farmers, Johnson did not fit the mold of the typical hard-living superstar of the 1920s. He was a quiet, small-town boy who had been transplanted into a different world. Drinking and smoking were out of the question for Johnson. Because he never swore or screamed at players, he was considered an unorthodox manager. He knew he possessed an awesome fastball, so he refused to throw at any batters. In fact, he seemed fearful of acci-

dentally hitting one, knowing that the results might be dire. The humble Johnson seemed truly surprised by the public's adoration, and he refused to believe that he was blessed with any special talents. "Ballplayers are born," he once told a reporter. "If they are cut out for baseball, if they have the desire and the ambition, they will make it. That's all there is to it."

Johnson's final season came in 1927. His final game was a loss against the Detroit Tigers on August 22, 1927, the same team that beat Johnson during his American League debut on August 2, 1907.

The Senators named Johnson their manager in 1929. His first club finished in fifth place with a 71-81 record. In 1930 the Senators improved to 94-60, a second-place mark only eight games behind the pennant-winning Philadelphia Athletics. His 1931 and 1932 clubs finished with respective totals of 92 and 93 wins, but both squads finished in third place. He was hired as a midseason replacement to manage Cleveland in 1933. Under his guidance, the Tribe finished at 49-51 in 100 games. The following season, he led the Indians to a third-place, 85-69 record. Impatient ownership replaced him in August 1935, when the club was in fifth place with a 46-48 record. His seven-year managing record in the majors totaled 530 wins and 432 losses for a .551 percentage.

Following his retirement as a manager, Johnson spent one season as a Senators radio announcer, then became a cattle rancher. A brain tumor took Johnson's life in 1946.

CAREER HIGHLIGHTS
WALTER PERRY JOHNSON

Born: November 6, 1887   Humboldt, KS   **Died:** December 10, 1946
Height: 6'1"   **Weight:** 200 lbs.   **Batted:** Right   **Threw:** Right
Pitcher: Washington Senators, 1907-27. Manager: Washington Senators, 1929-32; Cleveland Indians, 1933-35.

- ★ Ranks second on the list of winning pitchers with 416
- ★ Led the A.L. in wins six times
- ★ Holds the record for most career shutouts with 110
- ★ Pitched 56 consecutive scoreless innings in 1913
- ★ Pitched in two World Series
- ★ Won 12 strikeout titles, 8 of them consecutively

★ Elected to the Hall of Fame as a charter member in 1936

MAJOR LEAGUE TOTALS

G	IP	W	L	Pct.	SO	BB	ERA
802	5,925	417	279	.599	3,506	1,359	2.17

In a career filled with record-breaking statistics, Walter Johnson's banner year was probably 1913. His 36-7 record was the best in both leagues, and he led the A.L. in several categories. In the 346 innings he pitched, he walked only 38 batters.

JIM KAAT

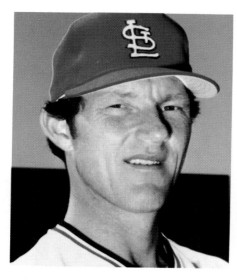

Jim Kaat pitched for almost 25 consecutive seasons. His career spanned four decades, stretching from 1959 through 1983. When Kaat made his big league debut, Ted Williams and Stan Musial were playing; by the time the big hurler retired, Wade Boggs and Don Mattingly were off the playground and into the majors.

Kaat traveled a long journey to get to the major leagues. It took three and a half seasons for Kaat to get firmly established. After he attended Hope College in Holland, Michigan, Kaat signed his first pro contract. He made his debut with Superior of the Nebraska State League in 1957. Although he won 5 and lost 6, Kaat struck out better than 1 batter per inning (95 in 73 frames). Upon advancing to Missoula, Montana in 1958, he improved his record to 16-9. Kaat was the Pioneer League leader in innings pitched (223), strikeouts (245), and ERA (2.99). In 1959 he was promoted to Chattanooga where he continued as a prosperous strikeout pitcher, gaining 132 Ks in 134 innings.

Kaat got a 1959 call-up to the Senators, but he was banged around in three appearances. In five innings he was nicked for 7 earned runs, for a 12.60 ERA. *Sport* magazine placed Kaat on a special rookie team it selected before the 1960 season. Despite the buildup, he suffered through a 1-5 record in 13 appearances, logging an ERA of 5.58. It was back to Charleston in 1960, where he finished the year with a 7-10 mark.

When Kaat finally reached the majors, his name did not immediately become a household word. In fact, the public usually mispronounced or misspelled his name. (It's pronounced "cat.") On one of his first baseball cards, the tall hurler suffered the indignity of having his name spelled "Katt." The company never corrected the error. Teammates who did pronounce his last name correctly gave him the inevitable nickname of "Kitty Cat." First baseman Earl Torgeson took one look at the towering pitcher and dubbed him "The Big Dutchman" for his size and ancestry.

It took Kaat some time to mature into a refined starting pitcher. He stayed for the full 1961 season with the Senators (who had now become the Minnesota Twins) but was saddled with a 9-17 record, including a 3.90 ERA in 36 games. He also had the dubious distinction of leading the American League in both wild pitches and hit batsmen in 1961 and 1962. However, he made substantial progress during the 1962 season and nurtured an 18-14 record and lowered his ERA to 3.14.

With Kaat on the mound, the Twins became contenders for the American League title. The 1962 club finished just five games out of first place, and the 1963 team won 91 games to finish third. After a losing record in 1964, the 1965 team won a record 102 games to win its first pennant. Kaat submitted a league-leading 42 starts and posted an 18-11 record. The Twins lost a seven-game World Series to the Los Angeles Dodgers.

Kaat enjoyed his greatest season in 1966. While the Twins wound up the season in second place, Kaat was named American League Pitcher of the Year by *The Sporting News* for his banner campaign. He won a league-leading 25 games and paced the junior circuit in starts (41), complete games (19), and innings pitched (304.2).

The Twins sold Kaat to the White Sox in mid-1973. He followed with 20-win seasons in 1974 and 1975. He rounded out his career with the Phillies, Yankees, and Cardinals before being released in July 1983.

One of Kaat's greatest accomplishments was winning 16 Gold Gloves for fielding excellence. His awards came in consecutive years from 1962 through 1977. Of Kaat's 283 career wins, 189 came while with the Minnesota franchise. He is the all-time leading winner for the Twins and also tops the team in a total of 14 pitching categories ranging from wins and innings pitched to categories like hit batsmen (89) and wild pitches (104). Kaat's total stats are even more impressive. His 898 games pitched are the eighth-best total in history. The tireless performer registered 180 complete games and 31 shutouts in his quarter-century of play. During his later years as a reliever, Kaat saved 18 games. While his wins don't add up to 300, his saves indicate that he contributed to more than 300 victories in his lifetime.

During his career Kaat led all active pitchers with 16 home runs. The hardworking lefty strove to be a good hitter as well as a pitcher. Opponents of the designated hitter rule should use Kaat's career to support their arguments. In 1972 Kaat batted .289.

Following his retirement he served as the 1984 pitching coach for the Cincinnati Reds. Kaat later became known to younger fans as a broadcaster, working for the cable TV network ESPN and the New York Yankees.

CAREER HIGHLIGHTS
JAMES LEE KAAT

Born: November 7, 1938 Zeeland, MI
Height: 6'4" **Weight:** 205 lbs. **Batted:** Left **Threw:** Left
Pitcher: Washington Senators, 1959-60; Minnesota Twins, 1961-73; Chicago White Sox, 1973-75; Philadelphia Phillies, 1976-79; New York Yankees, 1979-80; St. Louis Cardinals, 1980-83.

* Established a record for pitchers by playing in 25 straight seasons
* Compiled 283 lifetime wins
* Won 16 consecutive Gold Gloves
* Ranks eighth in all-time game appearances
* Won in double digits in 15 seasons
* Appeared in two World Series
* Led the A.L. with 25 wins in 1966

MAJOR LEAGUE TOTALS

G	IP	W	L	Pct.	SO	BB	ERA
898	4,528	283	237	.544	2,461	1,083	3.45

Jim Kaat pitched for a record 25 consecutive seasons, winning a total of 283 games. His longevity was the result of a difficult conditioning program, which ultimately helped his fielding as well as his pitching. Kaat won 16 straight Gold Glove awards.

AL KALINE

Without the benefit of a single game in the minor leagues, 18-year-old outfielder Al Kaline joined the Detroit Tigers on June 25, 1953, just a couple of weeks after graduating from Baltimore's Southern High School. Two years later Kaline exploded for a magnificent season that included a league-leading .340 batting average, 200 hits, 27 home runs, and 102 RBI. He became the youngest player in baseball history to win a batting title.

Kaline was serious concerning subjects he loved even as a child. The love of baseball came naturally, as his broom-maker father, his grandfather, and his uncles had all been catchers on semipro teams. He held fast to his desire to play baseball, even when a childhood disease necessitated the surgical removal of two inches of bone from his foot.

He carefully absorbed all his father taught him about pitching and posted a 10-0 record with his sandlot team at the age of 12. When told by high school coaches that he was too small to pitch, or indeed to play any infield position, he dug his spikes in and improved his high school batting average from a shining .333 in his freshman year to .488 upon graduation.

He joined so many extracurricular teams that he often played in three or four games on a given Sunday, changing uniforms in the car. Kaline once reminisced, just a mite regretfully, about his later childhood, recalling that there were no vacations or socializing "because I knew I wanted to be a ball-player."

His father and uncles drove him from game to game, and by the time he graduated, scouts from almost every team had expressed an interest in Kaline. But only one took the time to get to know the family, and so Ed Katalinas got 1952's hottest prospect for the Tigers. He sweetened the deal with a $30,000 bonus, which meant Kaline was required to spend his first two seasons with the parent club, as all bonus players did in those days.

Kaline made short work of his bonus money, and in characteristic fashion: what did not go for an operation to save his mother's eyesight was used to pay off the mortgage on his parents' house. This, he said in an interview, was in gratitude for his parents "doing everything they could to give me the time for baseball. I never had to take a paper route or work in a drugstore or anything. I just played ball." He contin-

ued to do just that for 21 more years.

Despite his early promise, Kaline's major league career was not always smooth. In 30 games with the Tigers in 1953 he posted a mediocre average of .250. Working through the winter swinging a weighted bat and squeezing baseballs (on the advice of the great Ted Williams), Kaline still only improved to a .276 average. His defensive ability, however, continued to attract attention. He'd go on to win 10 Gold Gloves for fielding excellence in his career.

No one was prepared for the burst of power that came in 1955. At the top of the season, Kaline clubbed 3 homers in a single game 2 of them in one inning. He ended the year just as brilliantly, with a .340 average, surpassing Mickey Mantle and Willie Mays in that category. With a circuit-pacing 321 total bases, Kaline was a sure thing for the All-Star team. Yet he called 1955 "the worst thing that happened to me."

Quiet by nature, Kaline cringed under the expectation that he would

be "another Ty Cobb, another Joe DiMaggio." This nervousness made him taciturn with the press and modest on the field. His statistics were steady but seldom spectacular, except when taken as a whole.

He joined the exclusive 3,000-hit club during the 1974 season, his last as a player. Kaline was the first in the American League to reach that milestone since Eddie Collins hit 3,000 a half-century earlier.

Nine times in his career Kaline batted over the .300 mark, and he was close on several other occasions, finishing with a .297 career mark. A consistent power hitter who hit 20 or more home runs in a dozen different seasons, Kaline finished his career with 399 home runs. Nagging injuries, including a fractured jaw (1959), broken collarbone (1962), broken hand (1967), and broken arm (1968), left him 1 shy of the 400-home-run plateau. Kaline played his entire 22-year career with the Tigers, and his easygoing style endeared him to Detroit baseball fans. Kaline was the best all-around right fielder in the American League during his career. He hit .379 in his only World Series, helping the Tigers defeat the St. Louis Cardinals in a seven-game fall classic.

Today the game is still part of his life, as the former star works for his beloved Tigers as an announcer (along with another Hall of Famer, George Kell).

Playing his entire career for the Detroit Tigers, slugger Al Kaline played in only one World Series. But he made that performance count with a .379 average and 8 RBI as the Tigers beat the Cardinals in seven games.

CAREER HIGHLIGHTS
ALBERT WILLIAM KALINE

Born: December 19, 1934   Baltimore, MD
Height: 6'1"   **Weight:** 175 lbs.   **Batted:** Right   **Threw:** Right
Outfielder: Detroit Tigers, 1953-74.

* Compiled 3,007 lifetime hits
* Batted .300 or better nine times
* Was youngest player ever to win a batting title
* Hit 399 home runs
* Hit .379 in the 1968 World Series
* Elected to the Hall of Fame in 1980

MAJOR LEAGUE TOTALS

G	AB	H	BA	2B	3B	HR	R	RBI	SB
2,834	10,116	3,007	.297	498	75	399	1,622	1,583	137

TIM KEEFE

Baseball teams of the 1800s seldom indulged in such practices as relief pitching. Pitchers made automatic commitments to hurl for a full nine innings, and many moundsmen had short careers simply because their arms couldn't stand the almost daily stress. The few pitchers who could overcome the frequent exhaustion and excel at their jobs over a long period were truly admirable.

Such was the case of Tim Keefe, a talented righthander who pitched in the major leagues from 1880 through 1893. Strength and wits were the hallmarks of his long, successful career in organized baseball. Logging more than 5,000 career innings kept Keefe busy. He relied on a striking change-of-pace pitch to complement his fastball and curve. His pinpoint control is evidenced by his strikeout/walk ratio. In 14 seasons Keefe fanned 2,527 batters but issued bases on balls to just 1,224 opponents.

Keefe began his career in a semipro league in 1879. He made his debut in the National League in 1880 with a team in Troy. His 6-6 record included 12 complete games and a league-leading 0.86 ERA.

Although Keefe won 36 games in his next two seasons with Troy, he had losing records both years as he suffered more than 20 losses. His first true success came the following year with the New York Metropolitans (the team that provided the name for today's New York Mets). Keefe's team was in the newly organized American Association, which was designed to compete with the resident National League starting in 1882. Cheaper admission, flashy silk uniforms, and liquor at games were just a few of the Association's selling points. However, the fledgling league wasn't very well stocked with players. Keefe wound up pitching an amazing 619 innings, with 68 complete games out of 68 games started. In 1883 he won 41 games. He won 37 more in 1884.

The New York Giants recruited Keefe in 1885. He responded with a league-leading ERA of 1.58 in his first season with his new team. In 1886 Keefe was the league leader in wins for the first time with a career-high of 42 triumphs. He also led the league in games (64), complete games (62), and innings pitched (540). Perhaps not surprisingly, the 478 hits he took were the second highest of his career, yet his ERA is estimated at only 2.53, not too shabby by any means.

Although 1887 seemed uneventful for "Sir Timothy," he was preparing for the last great crusade of his career. His 35 wins and .745 percentage in 1888 were league bests, as were his 333 strikeouts and 8 shutouts (the latter also a career best). Although the earlier years of his tenure show some guesswork in tabulating statistics, by 1888 his circuit-pacing 1.74 ERA was firmly substantiated. His 19 consecutive wins established a major league record, and his $4,500 paycheck established a new high for the Giants.

Only 32 years old in 1889, Keefe nonetheless began to show some signs of slowing down—not surprising considering the number of games he totted up annually. Maintaining winning seasons, he saw his ERA for the next two years rise to the 3.00 level and had his first of only 2 career saves. In 1890 he joined the ranks of the disgruntled who left established teams to form the idyllic Players' League, hopeful of restoring play and fair pay to the national pastime. After only one year the established leagues were ready to make peace, and Keefe happily finished the last three years of his career in the National League, where twice he pitched in the 4.00 range but once recaptured his form of old. In 1892, the year before he retired, Keefe won 19 games, lost 16, earned 2.36 runs per game, and got a relief win. Still posting winning numbers in his final year (with a 10-7 mark), Keefe ended by batting the third highest of his career with a .228 mark in 72 at-bats.

Upon retirement in 1893 Keefe had logged some impressive statistics for his 14 years in baseball. His 342 victories rank eighth highest in baseball history, while his 558 complete games rate third on the all-time list. Keefe tossed 39 career shutouts and failed to complete only 37 starts in his time in the majors. Playing during the dead-ball era didn't hinder Keefe as a hitter: He had 390 career hits to help his own cause, including 12 homers and a .187 lifetime average.

Keefe is also credited by baseball historians for another early contribution to the game. In 1888 Keefe designed a new uniform style for the Giants. The new togs were all-black, tight-fitting costumes with the "New York" team name emblazoned in big white letters on the front.

The Massachusetts native was one of the first players to go into coaching after his playing career ended. He managed teams at Tufts, Harvard, and Princeton universities. He also served as a National League umpire for two seasons.

CAREER HIGHLIGHTS
TIMOTHY JOHN KEEFE

Born: January 1, 1857 Cambridge, MA **Died:** April 23, 1933
Height: 5'10" **Weight:** 185 lbs. **Batted:** Right **Threw:** Right
Pitcher: Troy, NY, 1880-81; New York Metropolitans, 1883-84; New York Giants, 1885-89, 1891; New York (Players' League), 1890; Philadelphia Phillies, 1891-93.

* Led the N.L. in wins twice
* Has the eighth-highest win total in baseball history
* Pitched 619 innings and completed all 68 games he started in 1883
* Earned two strikeout titles
* Won 30 or more games for six straight years
* Elected to the Hall of Fame in 1964

MAJOR LEAGUE TOTALS

G	IP	W	L	Pct.	SO	BB	ERA
600	5,061	342	225	.603	2,527	1,224	2.62

Though it was standard practice for 19th century hurlers to pitch an entire game, Tim Keefe pitched both games of an Independence Day doubleheader in 1883. He won both contests—a one-hitter in the morning and a two-hitter that afternoon.

GEORGE KELL

For most of the late 1940s and early 1950s, the top third baseman in the American League was George Kell. Unlike many other Hall of Famers, Kell was not an immediate success in baseball. He started his professional career playing in the Brooklyn Dodgers farm system in the early 1940s, but he impressed no one and was released after two disappointing seasons. The young infielder was ready to quit the game when his new bride convinced him to give it one more try. Kell hooked on with Lancaster of the Inter-State League, and in two seasons there he tore up the league. In 1943 he batted .396, the highest average in organized baseball that year. Connie Mack brought him to the Philadelphia Athletics at the end of the season.

Kell struggled in the big leagues, turning in batting averages of .268 and .272. Convinced that Kell was never going to be a star, Mack traded him to the Detroit Tigers on May 18, 1946, for Barney McCosky. It was a move that Mack would later regret. When Kell finally agreed to try a lighter bat and a new hold on his lumber, his fortunes changed dramatically.

Once he mastered major league pitching, Kell proceeded to bat over .300 for nine of the next ten years. His best season at the plate came in 1949, when he batted .343 and edged out Ted Williams for the American League batting crown in one of the closest races in history. Kell had batted .3429 by season's end, while Williams finished at .3428. Both averages were rounded off to .343 for the record books, but Kell was awarded the title. Kell refused to sit out his final at-bat for the sake of winning the batting title. He was willing to bat one last time during his final game and risk dropping to second place, simply to be able to claim that he had rightfully earned the title. As it turned out, a teammate batted into a ninth-inning double play before Kell got his turn at the plate.

The following season Kell wound up with the short end of the baseball bat in the 1950 contest for best batting average, batting .340 with 8 homers and 101 RBI. Tommy Herr, a second baseman with the St. Louis Cardinals, was the only other player in the last 40 years to have 100-plus RBI without hitting at least 10 homers. Even without the benefit of the long ball, Kell still drove in runs by the handful. The Arkansas native was first in the junior circuit in doubles with 56 and hits with

218 (a personal best). This time, Williams' Red Sox teammate Billy Goodman was the batting champion. Goodman hit .354, but he had just 424 plate appearances, which was 217 fewer at-bats than Kell had.

In 1951 Kell was his usual successful self, hitting .319 and pacing the American League in hits (191) and doubles (36). Kell began the 1952 season with the Tigers but soon became part of one of the biggest trades of the year. Walt Dropo, Bill Wight, Fred Hatfield, Johnny Pesky, and Don Lenhardt were sent from the Boston Red Sox to Detroit in exchange for Kell, Dizzy Trout, Johnny Lipon, and Hoot Evers. Kell's average remained over .300 during the equivalent of two seasons he spent with the BoSox. While in Boston, Kell learned how to reach Fenway Park's short left field wall, known as "The Green Monster." As a result, his home runs climbed to a career-high total of 12. This was the only time he ever reached double figures in round-trippers.

One of the saddest parts of Kell's career is that he never reached a World Series in 15 major league seasons. While none of Kell's teams were hapless losers, they weren't the New York Yankees either. Because the Yankees dominated the American League during the 1940s and 50s, few other teams in the loop got the chance to experience postseason competition. Kell is on the Hall of Fame list of "bridesmaids," which includes Ernie Banks, Luke Appling, Billy Williams, Ralph Kiner, and Harmon Killebrew—all talented performers who never got into a single World Series game. Kell was not elected to the Hall of Fame until 1983, more than a quarter of a century after his retirement. Possibly, baseball writers overlooked Kell's talent because his time was divided among five different teams. More likely, he was passed over mainly because his quietly consistent major league play did not produce hordes of home runs.

After a seven-year stint as a Detroit Tigers scout Kell moved into the team's broadcast booth to announce Tigers games with another Hall of Famer, Tiger great Al Kaline. They were the first Hall of Fame duo to team up for baseball broadcasts. Brooks Robinson and Jim Palmer became the second when they paired up for the Orioles in 1989.

Though a consistent player and a sure-handed fielder, George Kell was not a power hitter. In 1950, for example, he racked up 100 RBI but hit less than 10 homers.

CAREER HIGHLIGHTS
GEORGE CLYDE KELL

Born: August 23, 1922   Swifton, AR
Height: 5'9"   **Weight:** 175 lbs.   **Batted:** Right   **Threw:** Right
Third baseman: Philadelphia Athletics, 1943-46; Detroit Tigers, 1946-52; Boston Red Sox, 1952-54; Chicago White Sox, 1954-56; Baltimore Orioles, 1956-57.

★ Compiled a .306 career batting average
★ Won the A.L. batting title in 1949
★ Drove in 101 runs in 1950, despite hitting just 8 homers

★ Batted over .300 nine times
★ Led the league in hits twice
★ Elected to the Hall of Fame in 1983

MAJOR LEAGUE TOTALS

G	AB	H	BA	2B	3B	HR	R	RBI	SB
1,795	6,702	2,054	.306	385	50	78	881	870	51

301

CHARLIE KELLER

Charlie Keller, a power-hitting outfielder with the New York Yankees, was the American League's shooting star of the 1940s. Playing beside Joe DiMaggio and Tommy Henrich, Keller showed promise of becoming one of the greatest Yankee sluggers in history until he was felled by back problems.

Keller attended the University of Maryland at College Park and earned his Bachelor of Science degree there. Because he was concerned about his education, Keller did not start his pro career until he was 20 years old. When he did arrive on the minor league scene, Keller was an instant success. He began his road to stardom in 1937 with a banner debut at Newark. Keller was named Minor League Player of the Year by *The Sporting News* for his heroic hitting. He led the league in batting average (.353), runs (120), and hits (189), while adding 13 home runs and 88 RBI. Buoyed by Keller's offense, the Bears finished first in the International League with a 109-43 record, later winning the Little World Series (the ultimate championship of various minor league titles) in seven games. In 1938 Keller surpassed his stunning first-season totals when he returned to Newark. In his second season Keller batted .365, pacing the circuit with 149 runs scored and 211 hits. Keller improved his totals to 22 round-trippers and 129 RBI in 150 games. Keller joined the majors as the Yankees' starting right fielder in 1939.

His first year was his best in terms of major league batting average. Keller batted .334 with 11 homers and 83 RBI, playing in 111 games. During the following season Keller's home run totals soared to 21, including 3 in a single game. He drove in 93 runs and scored 102 tallies himself. Keller led the junior circuit in walks (with 106) for the first of two seasons in 1940.

The Yankees got 33 home runs and a personal best of 122 RBI from Keller in 1941. In the World Series that year the Yankees whipped the Brooklyn Dodgers in five games. While most people remember the fourth game of the Series simply for the dropped third strike on Tommy Henrich that created the winning rally in the ninth inning, few realize that Keller's two-run double was the inning's big blow. In the Series he batted .389 with 7 hits, 5 runs scored, and 5 RBI.

The Maryland native's best postseason hitting was in the 1939 World Series versus the Cincinnati Reds. The mighty Bronx Bombers swept the Redlegs in four straight games. Keller provided the winning run in New York's opening 2-1 win against Paul Derringer. The rugged outfielder opened the ninth inning with a triple. The Reds countered with an intentional walk to DiMaggio, but Dickey ended the game by scoring Keller with a single. In the third game Keller had a pair of two-run homers and 3 runs scored to propel the Yankees to a 7-3 victory. In the decisive fourth game, Keller's hitting and baserunning made the difference in a 7-4 win. He hit a solo homer early in the game and then figured prominently in a three-run rally in the ninth. Keller reached first base safely when Reds shortstop Billy Myers bobbled his dribbler. With Keller on first and Frankie Crosetti (who led off the inning with a walk) on third, DiMaggio followed with a solid single to right field. When Reds right fielder Ival Goodman let the ball get past him, Keller chugged for home.

What followed was one of the strangest incidents of any Series. Goodman's throw appeared to beat Keller to the plate. However, Keller and Reds catcher Ernie "Schnozz" Lombardi collided and the ball rolled just a few feet away from Lombardi, who had toppled over in the collision. Lombardi, apparently stunned from the accident, didn't move as the ball rested only an arm's length away. DiMaggio spied the motionless catcher and flew around the bases for New York's seventh run. Reporters speculated that Keller might have kneed Lombardi as he approached the plate, but Lombardi denied this. Keller originally stated that he hadn't touched Lombardi when he crossed the plate. Whatever the facts of the matter, the play would keep Keller's name in the minds of fans for years.

Keller's career totals for 19 World Series games include 5 home runs, 18 RBI, 18 runs scored, and a total of 22 hits for a .306 average. His .611 slugging percentage is the eighth highest in Series history. His regular season statistics include 1,085 hits in 1,170 games for a .286 average. His total hits include 166 doubles, 72 triples, and 189 home runs. Keller's career slugging percentage is an impressive .518. Keller's lifetime statistics don't merit Hall of Fame consideration; however, he does deserve some consideration for his untapped potential. If back problems hadn't devastated his career, Keller could have been one of the greatest hitters of the 1940s.

Charlie Keller, Jr., tried to follow in the footsteps of his father by playing in the New York Yankees system. After winning one Eastern League batting title in 1961, however, he retired because of the same congenital back ailment that had plagued his father.

CAREER HIGHLIGHTS
CHARLES ERNEST KELLER

Born: September 16, 1916   Middletown, MD
Height: 5'10"   **Weight:** 185 lbs.   **Batted:** Left   **Threw:** Right
Outfielder: New York Yankees, 1939-49, 1952; Detroit Tigers, 1950-51.

* Had four seasons with 100-plus RBI
* Led the league twice in bases on balls
* Drew more than 100 walks per season five times
* Played in four World Series
* Had three seasons of 30-plus homers
* Drove in a career-high 122 runs in 1941

MAJOR LEAGUE TOTALS

G	AB	H	BA	2B	3B	HR	R	RBI	SB
1,170	3,790	1,085	.286	166	72	189	725	760	45

Charlie Keller was a competent player who came into his own during postseason play. In 19 World Series games, Keller blasted 5 homers, racked up 18 RBI, scored 18 runs, and made 22 hits. He hit .438 in the 1939 Series and .389 in the 1941 Series.

KING KELLY

A century ago America had a king. Michael Joseph Kelly was crowned king of baseball by his fans, and it was an appropriate title for a player who brought ability, politics, and slapstick to the show. Gymnastics and theatrics were often featured fare. Kelly would bend rules until they split and thrill the fans with his athletic der-ring-do.

He began his professional career at age 16, appropriately enough with the Troy Haymakers. Kelly surely made hay while the sun shone, because he learned to play every position. His skill at running, batting, and throwing at any position earned him the nickname "King of the Diamond."

By 1878 he was playing major league ball. In 1880 Kelly joined Cap Anson's Chicago White Stockings and played in the first of five championship seasons with the club.

He began work on the hallmarks of his style early on. He is credited with creating the base slide. As necessity is the mother of invention, Kelly created the slide to help him steal bases. Kelly also created the fine art of stealing bases—at least he claimed that he did. It really didn't matter to the fans, who asked only a chance to cheer his speed on the base paths, shouting "Slide, Kelly, Slide!" The battle cry became the title of a popular song of the era by J.W. Kelly (no relation) and was sung in music halls and in vaudeville theaters by songbird Maggie Cline. Strangely enough, King Kelly's name was mis-spelled in some versions of the song as "Slide Kely Slide." The colorful lyrics went, "If your batting doesn't fail ya, they will take ya to Australia. Slide, Kelly, on your belly. Slide, slide, slide." Kelly stole at least 50 bases annually for five successive years, including a personal best of 84 in 1887.

In 1887 the King was sold, despite his league-leading marks in doubles for two years and runs for three and his circuit-leading batting marks of .354 in 1884 and .388 in 1886. The Chicago fans were supposedly so incensed that they staged a boycott of their own stadium except during games when Kelly was a visitor.

The price on his head had been $10,000, a princely sum a century ago. Yet the King himself saw none of the money transacted from owner to owner. He was merely a puppet king, as many players were in that era. Kelly actually performed onstage on the vaudeville circuits and was known for his rousing rendition of "Casey at the Bat." Though he made money outside of baseball through his stage appearances and through the use of his picture on advertisements, he died in 1894 a penniless man. Only 36 years old, Kelly caught pneumonia supposedly giving his only suit to a tramp while on a boat to Boston to perform "Casey at the Bat" one more time.

In 1886 he marched in a revolution on his own kingdom, joining Fred Dunlap (who in 1886 had asked for half of his selling price to another team) and the Brotherhood of Professional Baseball Players labor union. Many members of the union had gone on strike protesting the blacklisting of non-compliant employees. The founder of the group, former baseball star and scholar John Montgomery Ward, blasted the contract practices as encouraging serfdom.

Official recognition as a labor union, which is difficult even today, was more of a backwater of red tape, distrust, and subterfuge a hundred years ago. Al Spalding, highly respected as one of the founders of the National League, led the fight against the players. He offered King Kelly $10,000 to turn traitor and abandon the cause.

Though probably tempted, Kelly responded as a true union man, and the fight for labor rights continued. Kelly and many other players joined forces to form the Players League. Kelly was elected manager of the Boston franchise, and in 1890 he batted .326, and stole up to 6 bases per game. His team won the new league's championship with a 81-48 record.

Kelly helped the Boston Red Stockings win championships in 1891 and 1892. He then played a few games with the New York Giants at the age of 35 before managing a minor league team until his death only one year after hanging up his spikes.

Cap Anson credited Kelly with inventing the hit-and-run play and claimed he was the first catcher to signal pitches to the mound and later to the infield. He was also the first catcher to block the plate for plays at home.

Kelly also claimed that he invented cutting bases (the art of not touching the base when the umpire isn't looking). Legend has it that Kelly once scored by going in a straight line from second to home, over the pitcher's mound, while the umpire was otherwise occupied. Whether true or not, almost anything was possible from the gent with the handlebar moustache, who was always dressed at the height of fashion —whether on the way to the ballpark or on a vaudeville stage.

CAREER HIGHLIGHTS
MICHAEL JOSEPH KELLY

Born: December 31, 1857 Troy, NY **Died:** November 8, 1894
Height: 5'10" **Weight:** 170 lbs. **Batted:** Right **Threw:** Right
Catcher, outfielder: Cincinnati Red Stockings, 1878-79; Chicago White Stockings, 1880-86; Boston Red Stockings (also known as the Beaneaters) 1887-89, 1891-92; Boston (Players' League), 1890; Cincinnati-Milwaukee (American Assoc.), 1891; Boston (American Assoc.), 1891; New York Giants, 1893. Manager: Boston (Players' League) 1890.

★ Compiled a .307 batting average   ★ Led the league twice in batting
★ Elected to the Hall of Fame in 1945

MAJOR LEAGUE TOTALS

G	AB	H	BA	2B	3B	HR	R	RBI	SB
1,455	5,894	1,813	.308	359	102	69	1,357	950	368

Mike "King" Kelly was as much a character as he was a player. Kelly would wait till the umpire was caught off guard and then cut from first base to third without going near second; or he would bypass third, going straight from second to home.

HARMON KILLEBREW

Of all the power hitters who have slugged their way into the American League record book, only one—Babe Ruth—blasted more home runs than Harmon Killebrew. In a fabulous 22-year career Killebrew totaled 573 home runs, ranking fifth on the all-time list. Among righthand American League hitters, Killebrew stands alone at the top. Playing nearly all of his career with the Washington Senators and the Minnesota Twins (when the Senators moved to the Midwest in 1961), Killebrew was one of the most popular players in baseball.

Killebrew was discovered by major league scouts when he was playing semipro baseball in his hometown of Payette, Idaho, in 1953. When the Senators sent their farm director, former player and manager Ossie Bluege, to watch the young phenom, Killebrew was batting .847 with about half of his hits being home runs. They signed the young slugger to a $12,000 bonus, and just after his 18th birthday in 1954, Killebrew was playing major league ball. He made the jump directly into the majors without previous minor league seasoning because of a rule that stated that young players signing for large bonuses had to be kept on the big league roster for two seasons before they could be sent to the minor leagues.

Killebrew's minor league seasoning came later. In his 1954 debut with Washington, the Senators used him as a second baseman. He hit .308 in his first nine games that year. In 1955 his average sank to .200 in 38 games. But, of his 16 hits, 4 were homers. After batting just .222 in his first 44 games in 1956, Killebrew was demoted to the minors for nearly two years.

The Idaho native finished the season with Charlotte of the Sally League in 1956. In 70 games he batted .325 with 15 homers and 63 RBI. Moving on to Chattanooga of the Southern League in 1957, Killebrew registered a league-leading 29 homers, 101 RBI, and a .279 average. The Senators brought him back up for nine games at the end of the season, and he hit a healthy .290 with 2 home runs.

After just 13 games in 1958, Killebrew was back in the minors, first with Indianapolis of the American Association, then with Chattanooga. Back in the Southern League, Killebrew clobbered 17 homers and 54 RBI in 86 games for a .308 average.

He returned to the majors to stay in 1959. His 42 home runs tied Cleveland

Indians star Rocky Colavito for the league lead, but his 7.7 home run percentage bested Colavito. Killebrew was third in the junior circuit with 105 RBI and second in total bases (282) and slugging percentage (.516). For the havoc he created for opposing pitchers, the slugger was dubbed " Killer."

In 1960 Killebrew's glovework was the only remaining problem in his overall performance. Although his defensive standing had improved each year, no one knew what position he'd be best suited for, and he shuttled between first and third base. Despite the juggling, he still produced 31 homers and 80 RBI in 124 games. Starting in 1961 Killebrew reeled off four straight seasons of homer barrages that ranged from 45 to 49 dingers a season. His long-ball wizardry was supreme in the American League. In 1961 he had 46 homers, an 8.7 homer percentage, and a .606 slugging percentage; in 1962 he slugged 48 homers, an 8.7 HR percentage, and a .545 slugging average (all-league highs); in 1963 he slugged 45 homers, had an

8.7 homer percentage and a .555 slugging average (again all league bests); and in 1964 he had a league-leading 49 homers, 8.5 homer percentage, and .548 slugging percentage.

After appearing in a seven-year low of 113 games in 1965, Killebrew's stats suffered. He clubbed his second of 3 career homers in that year's All-Star Game, however, and ended the year with 25 homers and 75 RBI. The Twins were bested by the Los Angeles Dodgers in the 1965 World Series. Killebrew batted .286 in the seven-game affair, with 1 homer and 2 RBI. In 1966 he blasted 44 round-trippers and 113 RBI in a full slate of 162 games, and his average climbed to .281, accelerated by fewer strikeouts. He led the league with 103 bases on balls while striking out just 98 times.

Killebrew had his most memorable season in 1969, when he won the League's MVP award and paced the Twins into the first divisional playoffs. He led the league with personal bests in home runs (49) and RBI (140). Once an easy strikeout, Killebrew drew 145 walks. His bases on balls for 1969 are the 12th highest in history.

Killebrew was elected to the Hall of Fame in 1984, becoming the first Twins player to gain the ultimate baseball honor. Since his retirement he has been a broadcaster.

Most of Harmon Killebrew's stats are not impressive; in some areas they're even mediocre. But only one A.L. player hit more homers than Killebrew, and that was Babe Ruth.

CAREER HIGHLIGHTS
HARMON CLAYTON KILLEBREW

Born: June 29, 1936   Payette, ID
Height: 6'0"   **Weight:** 195 lbs.   **Batted:** Right   **Threw:** Right
First baseman, third baseman, outfielder, designated hitter: Washington Senators, 1954-60; Minnesota Twins, 1961-74; Kansas City Royals, 1975.

- ★ Hit more than 40 home runs eight times
- ★ Led the A.L. in homers six times
- ★ Compiled 573 homers, first among A.L. righthand hitters
- ★ Voted the A.L. MVP in 1969
- ★ Appeared in the 1965 World Series
- ★ Elected to the Hall of Fame in 1984

MAJOR LEAGUE TOTALS

G	AB	H	BA	2B	3B	HR	R	RBI	SB
2,435	8,147	2,086	.256	290	24	573	1,283	1,584	19

RALPH KINER

When baseball fans look at the amazing statistics compiled by Ralph Kiner in just ten years, they have to wonder what the great slugger might have done if a back injury hadn't forced him to retire at age 32. In each of his first seven years in the majors, the 6-foot-2, 195-pound outfielder led the National League in home runs. Over a ten-year career he averaged 37 homers and 101 RBI per season. Twice he hit over 50 home runs, including a career high of 54 in 1949. In the category of home run percentage, Kiner ranks second only to Babe Ruth by averaging 7.1 home runs for every 100 major league at-bats. Kiner also led the league for seven straight years in that category. For two seasons, his home run percentage was over nine percent, meaning that Kiner hit a home run nearly once out of every ten at-bats.

Kiner played most of his career with the Pittsburgh Pirates, and he drew big crowds wherever he played. Although he was paid for his home runs, Kiner was not a bad hitter when it came to batting average. He batted over .300 on three occasions in his ten-year career, and he ended up with a respectable .279 lifetime mark. In addition to his amazing home run and RBI statistics, Kiner also averaged 97 runs scored and over 100 bases on balls per season over his big league career, which stretched from 1946 to 1955. He was truly the first of the modern era's super-sluggers, but because of his brief career, Kiner had to wait until 1975 before he was finally inducted into Cooperstown.

The Pirates saw Kiner's average drop to an all-time low of .244 in 1952. Desperate for any new faces that could help make the team a contender, the Pirates traded Kiner, pitcher Howard Pollet, outfielder/first baseman George Metkovich, and catcher Joe Garagiola (another player who would go on to a long career as a sportscaster) for catcher Toby Atwell, pitcher Bob Schultz, infielder George Freese, first baseman Preston Ward, outfielders Gene Hermanski and Bob Addis, and $100,000 on June 4, 1953.

Kiner played in 117 games with the Cubs that season, hitting .283. He finished the year with combined totals of 35 homers, 116 RBI, 100 runs scored, 100 bases on balls, and a .279 average. In 1954 Kiner hit .285 with 22 homers and 73 RBI in 117 games. Kiner again fetched big bucks in an off-season trade. The Cleveland Indians forked over $60,000, Sam Jones, and Gale Wade

to obtain the one-time home run king. Even though his abilities had faded somewhat, he could still excite the fans with his mighty swings. Kiner's accomplishments with the 1955 Indians were noticeable. He hit 18 homers and 54 RBI in 113 games. His homer percentage remained high at 5.6.

Looking at the Pirates all-time offensive records, Kiner's name pops up many times. While Willie Stargell was the greatest lefthand long-ball threat the Pirates ever had, Kiner has to be their greatest slugger from the right side. Some of his many team marks include most homers in one season (54); most grand slams (4 in 1949); most homers in a week (8 in 1947); most homers in a month (16 in September 1949); most consecutive homers (4, twice); most games in a season with 2 or more homers (10 in 1947); and most total bases in a doubleheader (19 in 1947).

One of the biggest disappointments in Kiner's exciting career was never appearing in a World Series. The closest Kiner ever came to postseason play was in 1955, when the Lopez-managed Cleveland Indians won 93 and lost 61, and the team wound up in second place, just three games behind the New York Yankees. Aside from that, Kiner knew what life on a losing team was like. The 1948 Pirates finished in fourth place with 83 wins. Kiner's other Pittsburgh teams had woeful records: a seventh-place finish in 1946 and 1947; sixth place in 1949; eighth in 1948 and 1950; and seventh again in 1951. The last Pirates team he spent a whole season with (in 1952) was one of the worst teams in history, winning just 42 games and losing 112.

Kiner was Pittsburgh's lone representative in four All-Star games. He was on the All-Star team from 1948 to 1952, starting two of the contests. His homer in the 1950 contest tied the game after nine innings, allowing the National Leaguers to win the contest in the 14th.

Fans who were never lucky enough to see Kiner play have been entertained by his continued involvement in baseball. After spending one year announcing games with the Chicago White Sox, Kiner joined the broadcasting staff of the newly organized New York Mets in 1962. He became one of the first famous former players to succeed in the medium. His presence in the broadcast booth was especially important during the Mets early years, when the shaky team might not have appealed to very many fans.

CAREER HIGHLIGHTS
RALPH McPHERRAN KINER

Born: October 27, 1922   Santa Rita, NM
Height: 6'2"   **Weight:** 195 lbs.   **Batted:** Right   **Threw:** Right
Outfielder: Pittsburgh Pirates, 1946-53; Chicago Cubs, 1953-54; Cleveland Indians, 1955.

★ Led the league in home runs in his first seven seasons

★ Twice hit over 50 home runs per season

★ Topped the league with 127 RBI in 1949

★ Averaged 100-plus walks per year in each of his ten seasons

★ Ranked first in league slugging percentage three times

★ Drove in 100 or more runs six times

★ Elected to the Hall of Fame in 1975

★ Led the league in walks three times

MAJOR LEAGUE TOTALS

G	AB	H	BA	2B	3B	HR	R	RBI	SB
1,472	5,205	1,451	.279	216	39	369	971	1,015	22

In addition to Ralph Kiner's other impressive statistics, he participated in five All-Star games, from 1948 to 1952. His All-Star batting average was .267, and 3 of his 4 hits were homers.

DAVE KINGMAN

ave Kingman moved around so much during his career that he may have needed to check the front of his uniform to remember what team he was playing on. In 1977, for example, he played for four clubs—the New York Mets, San Diego Padres, New York Yankees, and California Angels—and hit homers for all of them (tying a major league record).

Kingman was a member of seven different teams during his 16-year career and never spent more than three consecutive full seasons with the same club. No matter where he played, however, the big slugger hit a lot of home runs —442 in all. However, his career batting average of .236 is among the lowest of any player in baseball with such experience.

The tall first and third baseman made his major league debut with the San Francisco Giants during the 1971 season, after just two seasons in the Giants minor league system. He became a regular the following summer, batting just .225 but blasting 29 home runs with 83 RBI. As it turned out, this would be a typical season for "Kong" (so-named for his height and strength). His career at many locations was also typical of his entire life, for Kingman's family moved frequently when he was growing up.

Kong's prowess at the bat was established early. In California Little League he logged a streak of 15 home runs in as many games. As a high school pitcher he attracted offers from the Baltimore Orioles and the Oakland A's but turned them down to go to the University of Southern California, which he called "the best baseball school in the country."

He had all the markings of a Babe Ruth in the rough. During his freshman year at the university he pitched a 1.38 ERA, winning 11 and losing 4. At bat he tallied a .353 average with 8 homers and 26 RBI. This was in just 32 games.

Because of Kingman's value as a slugger, his coach took him off the pitching staff, for pitchers do not play every game. Kingman was unhappy at this turn of events but eventually adjusted to his new post in the outfield.

His success called him away from college just a few credits short of a marketing degree. Drafted by the San Francisco Giants in June 1970, he went immediately to the minors, where his 62 hits in 60 games advanced him despite poor fielding. Upon reaching the Triple-A Phoenix club, Kingman improved his average by some 70 points, climbing to a .295 mark. By July 1971 he was playing in the bigs. He finished his season with superlative stats—by almost disregarding an emergency appendectomy—and the Giants won the National League's Western Division, only to fall to the Pittsburgh Pirates in a four-game League Championship Series.

The next season Kingman led the Giants in many offensive categories but was never assigned a steady fielding position. This prolonged indecisiveness by the team led Kingman to seek his freedom in 1974. His wishes were granted, and he was sold to the New York Mets for $125,000. There he snapped back into form, belting 36 homers in 1975 and 37 in 1976. His 7.2 homer percentage led the league in 1975. While he was hitting balls out of the park by the dozen during those two years, National League pitchers frequently struck out Kingman. He whiffed 153 times in his Big Apple debut, then cut his strikeout total to 135 in 1976.

The free-agency bug with its high-salaried symptoms bit Kingman, so the Mets traded him to the Padres for Bobby Valentine and Paul Siebert in mid-1977. Three months later the A's got him on waivers but sold him to the Yankees in ten days. Kingman got into the middle of a frenzied pennant race with the Yankees but wound up back with the Mets, the team he had begun the season with.

A change of scenery and a five-year contract estimated at $1.4 million greeted free-agent Kingman when he arrived in Chicago in 1978. He modified his batting stance with the Cubs and pumped his batting average up to an unheard-of .266.

The Chicago press sang his praises after an incredible 1979 season with a league-leading 48 homers. The love affair ended in 1980 when Kingman dumped a bucket of ice water on a Chicago journalist. He added to his "bad boy" reputation with the press by harassing a California reporter for three years and then sending a live rat to her in the pressbox. Kingman's new employer in Oakland fined him $3,500 for the stunt.

Kingman had a dozen different seasons with 20 or more homers and seven years with 30 or more dingers. While his election to the Hall of Fame would be a longshot, Kingman remains one of the greatest sluggers of the 1970s.

CAREER HIGHLIGHTS
DAVID ARTHUR KINGMAN

Born: December 21, 1948 Pendleton, OR
Height: 6'6" **Weight:** 215 lbs. **Batted:** Right **Threw:** Right
First baseman, third baseman, outfielder, designated hitter: San Francisco Giants, 1971-74; New York Mets, 1975-77, 1981-83; San Diego Padres, 1977; California Angels, 1977; New York Yankees, 1977; Chicago Cubs, 1978-80; Oakland Athletics, 1984-86.

* Compiled 442 career homers
* Hit home runs with four different teams in 1977
* Led the N.L. in homers twice
* Hit for the cycle on April 16, 1972
* Named Comeback Player of the Year in 1984
* Named to three All-Star teams (1976, 1979, and 1980)

MAJOR LEAGUE TOTALS

G	AB	H	BA	2B	3B	HR	R	RBI	SB
1,941	6,677	1,575	.236	240	25	442	901	1,210	85

Despite his prowess with a bat, Dave Kingman played for seven different teams during his 16-year career. Part of the reason was undoubtedly his reputation as a difficult personality, particularly with the press.

CHUCK KLEIN

During the late 1920s and early 1930s Chuck Klein, the Philadelphia Phillies powerhouse outfielder, was the premier slugger in the National League.

Klein developed his massive muscles in a local steel mill and his batting skills on a local club team, where he was spotted by a pro scout and signed to a minor league contract with Evansville of the Three-I League. After just 102 games Klein appeared in his first major league box score with the Phillies in the middle of the 1928 season and responded with a .360 batting average and 11 home runs in 64 games.

In 1929 Klein celebrated his first full season in the majors by clubbing 43 home runs (then a National League record) with 145 RBI and a .356 batting average. His next year's totals were even more remarkable—a .386 batting mark with 40 homers and 170 RBI. Believe it or not, Klein didn't win the league title for run-scoring hits that year! Chicago Cubs hitter Hack Wilson did even better that season, driving in a major league record 190 runs. Klein did manage to break a major league record in the outfield, however. He chalked up 44 assists in one year, a 20th century mark that may stand forever.

In retrospect, it seems that Klein must have had a decent shot at baseball's triple crown in 1931. He led the league with 31 homers, 121 RBI, and an identical 121 runs scored; however, his .337 average ranked only third in the National League. Chick Hafey and Bill Terry tied for the league lead at .349, while Jim Bottomley was second at .347. Klein produced another solid all-around season in 1932. He banged a league-best 38 homers but was beaten out of the league RBI title by first baseman teammate Don Hurst. Hurst topped the league with 143 RBI, while Klein had 137. Klein's impressive .348 batting average was 20 points below league-leader Lefty O'Doul. Klein did amass 29 assists to best all National League right fielders.

Klein's final season of greatness came with the 1933 Phillies. He became the sixth man in National League history to win the triple crown. Klein bashed out 28 homers, 120 RBI, and a .368 average, all league-leading totals. Only Joe Medwick with the 1937 St. Louis Cardinals has won the honor since. Ironically, Klein's banner season provided little help to the Phillies, who finished with a seventh-place record of 60-92.

It seems amazing today that any team could bear to part with a slugger of Klein's caliber. However, the Philadelphia Phillies, like many other teams and businesses, were in grave financial trouble during the Depression era. So the Phils, on November 21, 1933, unloaded Klein to the Chicago Cubs in exchange for Mark Koenig, Harvey Hendrick, Ted Kleinhaus, and a much needed $65,000. While none of the three players proved to be godsends for the Phillies, Klein had two solid seasons with the Cubbies. In 1934 he batted .301 with 20 homers and 80 RBI. The following season Klein sparked the Cubs to the 1935 World Series with 21 homers, 73 RBI, and a .293 average. The Detroit Tigers beat their midwestern rivals in six Series games. Klein, however, was one of Chicago's bright spots. He had a score-tying single in the ninth inning of the third game, setting the stage for a 6-5 Cub victory. In Chicago's only other triumph, a 3-1 decision, Klein's two-run homer off

Detroit ace Eldon "Schoolboy" Rowe provided the winning difference.

The Phillies missed their star slugger and engineered a trade to reobtain Klein on May 21, 1936. The Phillies sent Ethan Allen and Curt Davis to the Cubs in exchange for Klein and Fabian Kowalik.

For all practical purposes, Klein's career ended after the 1940 season, when he was re-signed for a third stint in Philadelphia. It was the last season that Klein served as a starting outfielder, playing in 116 games. His skills had deteriorated, as evidenced by his 7 homers, 37 RBI, and .218 average. He became the Phillies chief pinch hitter in 1941. The job seemed a natural for the aging star who, only two seasons earlier, was the senior circuit's top pinch hitter with an 11-for-26 season. Klein batted miserably, getting just 4 pinch hits and ending the year at .123. Nevertheless, the Phillies knew that Klein's presence could help attendance, so he was made a player/coach from 1942 to 1944. He made only sporadic pinch-hitting appearances, but he was still a Phillie.

Klein ended his 17-year career with 300 homers, 1,201 RBI, and a .320 average. His lifetime slugging percentage was an impressive .523. Klein garnered 2,076 hits in his career, scoring 1,168 runs. Surprisingly, Klein differed from many contemporary home run specialists in that he never struck out more than 61 times in a season. He drew 601 bases on balls in his career, compared to just 521 strikeouts.

Klein ran a tavern in Philadelphia briefly after his career but soon moved back to his native Indianapolis. He died of a cerebral hemorrhage in 1958.

CAREER HIGHLIGHTS
CHARLES HERBERT KLEIN

Born: October 7, 1904 Indianapolis, IN **Died:** March 28, 1958
Height: 6'0" **Weight:** 185 lbs. **Batted:** Left **Threw:** Right
Outfielder: Philadelphia Phillies, 1928-33, 1936-39, 1940-44; Chicago Cubs, 1934-36; Pittsburgh Pirates, 1939.

* Won the N.L. MVP award in 1932
* Hit 20 or more homers eight times
* Drove in a career high of 170 runs in 1930

* Won the triple crown in 1933
* Elected to the Hall of Fame in 1980
* The last player to lead the N.L. in both home runs and stolen bases in 1932

MAJOR LEAGUE TOTALS

G	AB	H	BA	2B	3B	HR	R	RBI	SB
1,753	6,486	2,076	.320	398	74	300	1,168	1,201	79

In 1933 financial problems forced the Phillies to deal slugger Chuck Klein to the Chicago Cubs for Mark Koenig, Harvey Hendrick, Ted Kleinhaus, and $65,000. None of these players proved useful to the Phillies, while Klein had two good years with the Cubs.

TED KLUSZEWSKI

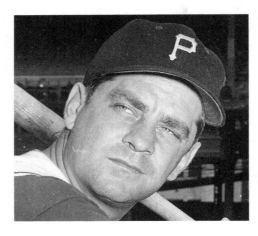

Ted Kluszewski was one of the greatest first basemen of the 1950s. He fielded well, he hit for respectable averages, and he displayed awesome long-ball power. When Cincinnati Reds fans think of an ideal first baseman from the team's past, they bring up the name of "Big Klu."

To call Kluszewski big was one of baseball's biggest understatements: He was 6-foot-2 and cast in solid muscle. The sight of the 225-pounder in the Cincinnati Reds old vest-style, sleeveless uniform top was unforgettable. Unlike other players, Kluszewski never wore the customary long-sleeved undershirt because it might constrict the movement of his huge biceps.

The Reds discovered Kluszewski at Indiana University, where he was attending on a football scholarship. They signed him in 1945 (for a reported signing bonus of $15,000) and he made his first appearance in a Reds uniform in late 1947, after just 205 games in the minors. During his official rookie season, Kluszewski played in 113 games, hitting .274 with 12 home runs and 57 RBI.

Fans considered the Illinois native a mystery. He looked physically capable of rewriting the league's home run records, yet he only exhibited modest power. On the other hand, he had a far better average than most power hitters of his day. In 1949 Kluszewski batted .309 with 8 homers and 68 RBI. The young first baseman learned how to pull the ball in 1950, and his 25 homers, 111 RBI, and .307 batting average reflected the change.

In 1951 his totals dipped to 13 homers, 77 RBI, and a .259 average. Kluszewski rebounded with a .320 average in 1952. His power was still partially untapped, as he socked just 16 dingers and knocked in 86 RBI. Kluszewski's best season as a Red came in 1954, when he led the loop with 49 homers and 141 RBI.

The Cincinnati Reds gave up on the injury-plagued Kluszewski and passed him on to the Pittsburgh Pirates late in 1957. The Pirates peddled Kluszewski to the Chicago White Sox for Harry "Suitcase" Simpson and a minor leaguer on August 25, 1959. The White Sox were in the middle of a fierce pennant race, and they knew that a veteran with a few homers left in his bat would be an inspiration to the rest of the team. After batting .262 in 60 games with the Pirates, Kluszewski batted .297 in 31 games with the team that would

be labeled the "Go-Go" White Sox. Everyone benefited from the arrangement. The former Red helped clinch a pennant for a team that had been searching for a league title for 40 years, and Kluszewski got his first and only chance to play in a World Series.

He made the most of his opportunity. Before a home crowd Kluszewski dazzled White Sox fans with his hitting in the Series opener. He clubbed 2 homers and chased in 5 runs as the White Sox pummeled the Dodgers 11-0. The Dodgers ultimately won the Series in six games, but Kluszewski, as Chicago's starting first baseman, fought the National Leaguers to the end. His two-run homer in the sixth game was the only serious threat to the Dodgers in the ChiSox's 9-3 defeat. For the Series, Kluszewski batted a team-leading .391. His 9 hits included 1 double and 3 homers, along with 10 RBI (no other Series participant had more than 6) and 5 runs scored.

He was released by the White Sox

after the 1960 season and signed on with the Los Angeles (later California) Angels for one last campaign. Often, veterans tarnish once-great careers by hanging on too long and submitting subpar statistics for their final years. Not Kluszewski. He appeared in 107 games, slugging 15 homers and 39 RBI for a .243 average.

The muscular slugger finished his career with 279 home runs and 1,028 RBI. Unfortunately, because he seldom had many men on base in front of him, many of Kluszewski's round-trippers were solo shots. Unlike most bulky batsmen, Kluszewski had few problems with strikeouts: He fanned only 365 times in 15 years. Conversely, Kluszewski drew 492 bases on balls. Pitchers walked Big Klu intentionally 25 times in 1955 and 22 more in 1956. His lifetime .298 batting average proves that he had all-around offensive talent, as evidenced by his total of seven seasons hitting .300-plus. Mediocre speed was one hindrance Kluszewski had to live with, and he stole just 20 bases during his entire career.

While many star hitters get stationed at first base to cover up their defensive shortcomings, Kluszewski led National League first sackers in fielding average for five years beginning in 1951. His league-best percentages for the five years were .997, .993, .995, .996, and .995.

At the conclusion of his playing career Kluszewski went back to the Reds, who employed him as a hitting instructor for 18 years in both the major and minor leagues. Kluszewski retired in 1986 after a serious heart attack.

CAREER HIGHLIGHTS
THEODORE BERNARD KLUSZEWSKI

Born: September 10, 1924 Argo, IL **Died:** March 29, 1988
Height: 6'2" **Weight:** 225 lbs. **Batted:** Left **Threw:** Left
First baseman: Cincinnati Reds, 1947-57; Pittsburgh Pirates, 1958-59; Chicago White Sox, 1959-60; Los Angeles Angels, 1961.

* Led the league in fielding for five straight years
* Hit more than 40 home runs in three consecutive years, from 1953-55
* Hit 3 homers in the 1959 World Series
* Led the league in home runs in 1954 with 49
* Was the N.L.'s starting first baseman in All-Star games from 1953-56
* Topped Cincinnati in RBI for seven straight years

MAJOR LEAGUE TOTALS

G	AB	H	BA	2B	3B	HR	R	RBI	SB
1,718	5,929	1,766	.298	290	29	279	848	1,028	20

During his 15 years in the majors, Ted Kluszewski hit over .300 seven times and slugged over 40 home runs in three consecutive seasons. Kluszewksi's career might have been extended if he could have served as a designated hitter.

SANDY KOUFAX

At the age of 36, when many pitchers are still going out to the mound every fifth day, Sandy Koufax was already in the Hall of Fame. Chronic arthritis kept him from becoming the greatest pitcher of all time, but for a period of six years in the 1960s, Koufax was the best hurler in baseball.

Koufax was born in Brooklyn, New York, on December 30, 1935. His father was a New York lawyer. Young Koufax spent a lot of his free time playing basketball, and he was a center and a leading scorer for his Lafayette High School team. When he played sandlot ball, he started out at first base. After graduation he accepted a basketball scholarship from the University of Cincinnati. He hadn't planned on becoming a pro basketball star; instead, he wanted to study architecture in college. Koufax also pitched for the college team. Despite pitching with great velocity, he suffered from control problems. The wild lefty tried out with the Pittsburgh Pirates, Boston Braves, and New York Giants before he auditioned with the Brooklyn team in 1954.

Koufax quit college in 1955 to join the Brooklyn Dodgers for a $25,000 bonus—signing with super-scout Al Campanis. Koufax later said that the Braves had offered more bonus money but didn't plan on inviting him to spring training. Koufax felt his hometown team could give him more coaching assistance. League rules said that "bonus babies" getting more than $6,000 had to remain on big league rosters for two years before going to the minors and Koufax knew he'd need some tutoring.

He was far from an instant success. In his first few seasons Koufax demonstrated a blazing fastball and a sharp-breaking curve but continually struggled with control problems. Over his first six years with the Dodgers, Koufax actually had a losing record (36-40) and an ERA of over 4.00. But in spring training of 1961, catcher Norm Sherry advised the hard-throwing southpaw to slow things down a bit, develop his natural curve ball, and concentrate on control. The advice paid off, and Koufax compiled an 18-13 season.

No one was able to help the talented pitcher at the plate, however. Koufax batted a puny .097 during his 12-year career. Of his 75 hits (with no home runs) 20 came during 1965, when he batted a career-high .177.

For the five-year period from 1962 through 1966, Koufax dominated the National League like no other pitcher before or since. For five straight years he led the league in ERA; for three seasons he led in wins and strikeouts; and three times he led in shutouts. In that five-year stretch the amazing hurler won three Cy Young awards and a Most Valuable Player award. Hall of Famer Willie Stargell said that trying to hit against Koufax was like trying to drink coffee with a fork. In both cases, the results were hard to swallow.

In 1963 Koufax went 25-5 with 11 shutouts, 306 strikeouts, and a 1.88 ERA, leading the league in every category. During the 1963 World Series versus the New York Yankees (which the Dodgers swept in four straight games), Koufax was at his best. In the opening game he set a new Series record with 15 strikeouts as the Dodgers marched to a 5-2 win. Pitching on three days rest, Koufax registered another complete-game victory to earn a 2-1 triumph and the Dodgers second World Series trophy in four seasons.

His 382 strikeouts in 1965 are still an N.L. record, as are his 4 no-hitters, one of them a perfect game. Koufax had a league-leading 26 victories against just 8 defeats in 1965, leading the league in ERA, innings pitched, and winning percentage. The Dodgers won the 1965 World Series against the Minnesota Twins in seven games. Koufax triumphed in the second game 5-1 with a six-inning effort. In game five it was classic Koufax all the way. He scattered 4 hits while striking out 10. Koufax clinched the series with a three-hit, ten-strikeout performance.

In 1966 Koufax pitched the Dodgers to their fourth pennant in eight years, leading the league with 27 wins, 317 strikeouts, and a 1.73 ERA. In the World Series Koufax lost his only start, a 6-0 decision in which the Dodgers managed only 4 hits and 6 errors (including a record 3 in one inning by outfielder Willie Davis). After the World Series, the 30-year-old Koufax announced his retirement, leaving the baseball world stunned. Before the season Koufax had agreed with star teammate Don Drysdale that they should hold out for bigger contracts. When Koufax got the pay raise he was seeking, some fans thought that would keep him in the game longer.

Five years later, in his first year of eligibility, Koufax became the youngest player ever elected to Cooperstown. As a Hall of Famer who spent his entire career with the Dodgers, Koufax remains extremely popular with fans today. He was an NBC-TV sports broadcaster for several years after his retirement and still serves the Dodgers today as a spring training coach.

CAREER HIGHLIGHTS
SANFORD KOUFAX

Born: December 30, 1935   Brooklyn , NY
Height: 6'2"   **Weight:** 210 lbs.   **Batted:** Right   **Threw:** Left
Pitcher: Brooklyn Dodgers, 1955-57; Los Angeles Dodgers, 1958-66.

* Selected the N.L. MVP in 1963
* Won three Cy Young awards (1963, 1965, and 1966)
* Established a league record with 382 strikeouts in 1965
* Elected to the Hall of Fame in 1972
* Pitched 4 no-hitters, including one perfect game
* Named *The Sporting News* Player of Year in 1965
* Set a modern southpaw record with 11 shutouts in 1963

MAJOR LEAGUE TOTALS

G	IP	W	L	Pct.	SO	BB	ERA
397	2,325	165	87	.655	2,396	817	2.76

Though Sandy Koufax's career was brief, he accomplished more than any other lefthand pitcher. From 1962-66, he won five ERA titles, pitched four no-hitters, won three Cy Young awards, and garnered one MVP nod. He retired in 1966 at age 30.

HARVEY KUENN

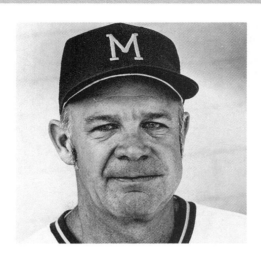

It wasn't until after a 15-year major league career—studded with honors such as Rookie of the Year and a batting title—that Harvey Kuenn became a hero on his home turf. In 1982 the native of West Allis, Wisconsin, a suburb of Milwaukee, managed his hometown Brewers to their first American League pennant in their 13-year history.

Dubbed "Harvey's Wallbangers" because of their offensive turnaround under his tutelage, Kuenn's Brewers were victorious in a five-game League Championship Series against the California Angels and battled the St. Louis Cardinals through seven tough World Series games before finally crumbling to the Cards. Despite the loss—and the loss of Kuenn the following year after he suffered numerous health problems—the Brewers were a team rejuvenated. They took Kuenn's message to heart, an axiom he had learned well himself: It was simply "Have fun."

Kuenn's fun-filled, 15-year playing career stretched from 1952 through 1966. He came up as a shortstop with the Detroit Tigers at the end of the 1952 season, batting .325 in 19 games. Still officially classified as a rookie the following season, the 22-year-old banged out a league-leading 209 hits for a .308 average that earned him the league's top rookie award. And so it continued. Each year Tiger fans could rely on their dependable shortstop to bat above .300 and be among the league leaders in both hits and doubles.

In his first two full seasons Kuenn kept his average above the .300 mark. His 200-plus hits each year were American League bests, as were his at-bats. In 1955 Kuenn slapped 38 doubles, the first of three times he would lead the league in two-base hits. Then in 1956 he hit .332 with a league-best 196 hits. His 12 home runs were a career high. Kuenn's average sank below .300 for the first and only time that decade when he swung for a .277 average in 1957. He bounced back in 1958 with a .319 average and a league high of 39 doubles.

Kuenn enjoyed his finest year in 1959, when he exploded for a .353 average with 198 hits and 42 doubles, leading the American League in all three categories. Despite those statistics, the reigning batting champion was traded to the Cleveland Indians for Rocky Colavito, the reigning home run champion. It was one of the most

talked-about and controversial trades of the century.

Kuenn batted .308 for the Indians in 1960, but after the season he was traded to the San Francisco Giants, where he remained for four years as an outfielder. In 1962 Kuenn batted .304 and came through with some timely hits to help the Giants to their first pennant in San Francisco. This would be Kuenn's only World Series as a player.

His last active years, 1966 and 1967, were split between two teams. Far from declining, Kuenn finished with a .296 batting average in his final campaign, his best mark in five years.

Over a 15-year career Kuenn was a steady, reliable performer who consistently hit around the .300 mark or better. He finished his career with 2,092 base hits, including 356 doubles. In past years Kuenn has received some Hall of Fame consideration but did not have enough spectacular seasons to warrant his election. Despite his inability to slug tons of home runs and his subpar glove

work, Kuenn remains a popular choice today with writers who vote for prospective members of the Hall. Kuenn received 115 votes for the 1989 election, ninth highest in the race.

His "unspectacular" career included Rookie of the Year honors, placement on *The Sporting News* All-Star Team, two years as a Milwaukee sports announcer, and the joy of guiding the Brewers to the biggest success of their first two decades.

Kuenn began his association with the Brewers in 1971, working as the team batting coach. Replacing Buck Rodgers in June 1982, Kuenn took the Brewers from a 23-24 record to the status of underdog pennant snatchers. The Brewers, in turn, helped Kuenn gain recognition as the American League Manager of the Year. His managerial record for 1982 was 72-43.

Sadly, another triumph was not to be. Poor health caused Kuenn to resign after leading the Brewers to a fifth-place 87-75 mark in 1983. Felled by illness in 1983 that included heart, intestinal, and circulatory problems, Kuenn lost a leg shortly before his untimely death in 1988 at the age of 57. Although he may never reach the Hall of Fame, the home-grown Kuenn will be forever remembered by the Badger State sports fans as the pride of Wisconsin.

Harvey Kuenn led his league in hits four times and batted over .300 nine times. Yet modern-day fans know him best as the manager of "Harvey's Wallbangers"— the Brewers team that won the pennant in 1982.

CAREER HIGHLIGHTS
HARVEY EDWARD KUENN, JR.

Born: December 4, 1930   West Allis, WI   **Died:** February 28, 1988
Height: 6'2"   **Weight:** 187 lbs.   **Batted:** Right   **Threw:** Right
Outfielder, shortstop, third baseman, first baseman: Detroit Tigers, 1952-59; Cleveland Indians, 1960; San Francisco Giants, 1961-65; Chicago Cubs, 1965-66; Philadelphia Phillies, 1966. Manager: Milwaukee Brewers, 1975, 1982-83.

* Named A.L. Rookie of the Year in 1953
* Topped the A.L. in hits four times
* Led the league with a .353 batting average in 1959
* Batted above .300 nine times
* Led the league in doubles three times
* Managed the Milwaukee Brewers to a 1982 A.L. pennant

MAJOR LEAGUE TOTALS

G	AB	H	BA	2B	3B	HR	R	RBI	SB
1,833	6,913	2,092	.303	356	56	87	951	671	68

319

NAP LAJOIE

There are many superstars in today's major leagues, but none of them have teams named after them. Imagine the fans in Boston calling the team the "Rogers" in honor of star pitcher Clemens, or the Yankees being called the "Dons" to salute first baseman Mattingly. At the turn of the century, the American League club in Cleveland was known to fans as the "Naps" in honor of player/manager Napoleon Lajoie, one of the sport's first superstars. It was there that the Rhode Island native spent the largest chunk of his 21-year major league career, becoming one of the greatest all-around players the game has ever known.

A consistent hitter and smooth second baseman, Lajoie's career stretched from 1896 to 1916 and included 3,242 hits and a .338 lifetime batting average. For ten seasons he batted over .350. With the Philadelphia Athletics in 1901, Lajoie hit an amazing .422, the highest mark ever recorded in the American League and only 2 points lower than Rogers Hornsby's major league record of .424.

Lajoie's first professional contract was signed on the back of an envelope with a semipro team in Fall River, Massachusetts. Later that year, when a Philadelphia Phillies scout bought the contract of a Fall River outfielder for $1,500, the Massachusetts team owner sweetened the deal by throwing in Lajoie for free. After his 39-game debut with the Phillies in 1896, Lajoie played his first full season in the majors in 1897. He divided his time between first base and the outfield, hitting .363 with a league-leading 10 homers (an impressive number in the dead-ball era).

Because he was still making only the salary limit of $2,400 after five stellar years with the Phillies, Lajoie jumped at the chance to join the Philadelphia Athletics in the newly formed American League. He won the American League's first triple crown in 1901, but the Phillies got a court injunction to stop him from playing in the new league. The Pennsylvania Supreme Court ruled that the injunction was valid only in Pennsylvania, making it possible for Lajoie to play in any other state. Connie Mack sent his short-lived star to Cleveland in mid-1902. Lajoie, who had stayed off the diamond for over two months awaiting the legal verdict, was free to continue his already glittering career.

Lajoie was involved in one of the most controversial sports stories of

1910. He had a banner season, leading the league in hits (227) and doubles (53). His average was .384, which was ruled to be less than 1 percentage point under Ty Cobb's .385. Since then, historians have discovered errors in the official scoring from that season, claiming that Lajoie actually batted .383 and that Cobb batted .382. Both players received automobiles as co-winners of the Chalmers award. It was the first of three batting crowns for Lajoie.

From 1905 to 1909, Lajoie managed the Cleveland Naps as well as played for them. As a manager, Lajoie was modestly successful. His 1905 debut as a manager produced a fifth-place club with a 76-87 record. In 1906 the team was third at 89-64. Lajoie's troops were 85-67 in 1907. In 1908 Cleveland finished just one and a half games out of first place with a 90-64 record. Lajoie resigned from his duty in mid-1909 after his club was 57-57.

When Lajoie left Cleveland after the 1914 season, the Naps became the Indians. Lajoie returned to the Philadelphia A's in 1916. The one major regret in Lajoie's career was that he never got to participate in a World Series. While Lajoie was pleased with the enthusiastic welcome from Philadelphia fans, he had to be disappointed that the A's couldn't repeat their league championship win of 1914 in the subsequent years.

Lajoie played in 1917 with Toronto of the International League and in 1918 with Indianapolis of the American Association before retiring. In 1917 Lajoie served as player/manager for Toronto, leading the team to a league pennant. At age 41, Lajoie proved he could still swing the bat, winning the International League batting title with a .380 average.

Even after he'd been retired for nearly a quarter of a century, Lajoie still made baseball history. On June 12, 1939, two years after Lajoie's induction into the Hall of Fame, all the greats of the game assembled in Cooperstown to celebrate baseball's centennial. One of the most famous pictures from that event shows Lajoie in a group photo posing with nine other early HOF inductees. It was a rare occasion to have so much baseball talent assembled in one place.

Following his retirement from the major leagues, Lajoie worked as a tire company representative and a plumbing supplier. Lajoie and his wife grew tired of the cold midwestern winters and resettled in Daytona Beach, Florida. He became an avid golfer and a supporter of Little League baseball. He died of pneumonia on February 7, 1959, at the age of 84.

CAREER HIGHLIGHTS
NAPOLEON LAJOIE

Born: September 5, 1874   Woonsocket, RI   **Died:** February 7, 1959
Height: 6'1"   **Weight:** 195 lbs.   **Batted:** Right   **Threw:** Right
Infielder: Philadelphia Phillies, 1896-1901; Philadelphia Athletics, 1901-02, 1915-16; Cleveland Naps (also known as the Blues and the Spiders), 1902-14. Manager: Cleveland Naps, 1905-09.

★ Set an A.L. record by batting .422 in 1901
★ Won three batting titles
★ Led the league in doubles five times

★ Was the A.L.'s first triple crown winner in 1901
★ Batted over .300 in 16 seasons
★ Elected to the Hall of Fame in 1937

MAJOR LEAGUE TOTALS

G	AB	H	BA	2B	3B	HR	R	RBI	SB
2,480	9,589	3,242	.338	657	163	83	1,502	1,599	381

*Already a star, Nap Lajoie jumped from the N.L. to the newly established A.L. in 1901.
His .426 average that year is still the highest ever achieved in that league. Lajoie was
shifted to Cleveland in 1902, where he played most of his career.*

TONY LAZZERI

If any player ever deserved a chance to play major league baseball, it was Tony Lazzeri. Lazzeri played in the majors for 14 years, spending most of that time as a second baseman for the New York Yankees. He toiled for four seasons in the minor leagues before getting his shot in the majors, but after the 1925 season, Lazzeri left no doubts about his diamond talents.

Lazzeri spent parts of 1922-24 with Salt Lake City of the Pacific Coast League. He developed a good reputation as a talented batsman. However, no one dreamed that the average-sized second baseman would accumulate such awesome statistics in a single season. Lazzeri set the baseball world abuzz when he hit 60 home runs and drove in 222 runs in a 197-game season. (Many of his homers were hit in Salt Lake City's small home park, however.) He batted .355, rapped out 252 total hits, and scored 202 runs. Lazzeri, blessed with average base-path speed, achieved a career-high 39 swipes.

Lazzeri, who had started working with his father in a San Francisco boiler factory at age 15, got his start in minor league ball in 1922. Initially, Lazzeri didn't hit breaking pitches well. He batted .248 in 135 games in Peoria in 1923, hitting 14 home runs. In 1924 with Lincoln of the Western League, Lazzeri belted 28 homers to complement his .329 batting average. During his final 85 games of the season with Salt Lake City, he hit 16 more homers, giving him a combined total of 44 for the year. Following his record-setting 1925 season, New York Yankees scout Bill Essick obtained Lazzeri from the team for $75,000.

Lazzeri became New York's starting second baseman in 1926. He batted .275 in his rookie season, hitting 18 homers and 114 RBI. His average rose to .309 in 1927, the year the Yankees became known as "Murderers' Row." The man nicknamed "Push-'Em-Up Tony" hit 18 homers and drove in 102 runs that year. In 1928 he played in just 116 games because of a separated shoulder.

A healthy Lazzeri rebounded in 1929 to hit a career high of .354. Besides 18 homers and 102 RBI, he rang up career highs in hits (193) and doubles (37). In 1930 Lazzeri hit .300-plus for his fourth consecutive year. Personal bests in runs scored (109) and RBI (121) highlighted this season.

Although he is most remembered for

striking out in the seventh game of the 1926 World Series (in the eighth inning with two out and the bases loaded, no less) against geriatric curveball pitcher Grover Cleveland Alexander, Lazzeri usually had considerable success in post-season play. His best average was a .400 mark in the 1937 fall classic against the Giants. He poked a leadoff triple in the fifth inning of the decisive fifth game and scored on a single by weak-hitting pitcher Lefty Gomez. In the 1932 World Series against the Cubs, Lazzeri homered twice in one game. He tied Lou Gehrig for the lead in RBI (with 7) during New York's six-game triumph over the crosstown Giants in the 1936 Series. Lazzeri's final Series was in 1938, when he was a pinch hitter for the Chicago Cubs (going hitless in just two at-bats). In seven Series his career totals include 32 games, 28 hits, 4 homers, 19 RBI, and a .262 average.

In 14 years Lazzeri hit a lifetime total of .292 but surpassed the .300 mark

five times. He had seven seasons of knocking in more than 100 runs. His total RBI count was 1,191, and his home runs numbered 178. While he never belted more than 18 homers in one year, Lazzeri topped double figures in four-baggers on ten occasions. He logged 148 lifetime steals over 14 years, surpassing 10 swipes in eight seasons. The only offensive league lead Lazzeri ever landed was in strikeouts, when he fanned 96 times in 1926.

While Lazzeri did hit for occasional power, he always kept the team's needs foremost in his actions. He contributed 116 sacrifice hits to the Yankees during his career, including 15 or more during his first five seasons. Lazzeri wound up with a lifetime on-base percentage of .374.

Although it will never show up in the record books, Lazzeri helped guarantee the future success of the Yankees even after he was no longer with the team. In 1936 Lazzeri befriended another young Italian from San Francisco who was just joining the club. The rookie's name was Joe DiMaggio.

Through 1943 Lazzeri was a player/manager in the minor leagues. Then he returned to his hometown of San Francisco and ran a tavern. He died at age 42 in 1946 from injuries suffered from an epileptic seizure.

Tony Lazzeri struck out in the eighth inning of the last game of the 1926 Series against veteran hurler Grover Alexander— who was pitching with a hangover. Sadly, Lazzeri is remembered more for that strikeout than for the rest of his career.

CAREER HIGHLIGHTS
ANTHONY MICHAEL LAZZERI

Born: December 6, 1903 San Francisco, CA **Died:** August 6, 1946
Height: 5'11" **Weight:** 170 lbs. **Batted:** Right **Threw:** Right
Infielder: New York Yankees, 1926-37; Chicago Cubs, 1938; Brooklyn Dodgers, 1939; New York Giants, 1939.

★ Drove in 100-plus runs seven times   ★ Batted .300 or better five times
★ Played in the first All-Star game   ★ Appeared in seven World Series
★ Hit a career-high .354 in 1929, tying for fourth in the league

MAJOR LEAGUE TOTALS

G	AB	H	BA	2B	3B	HR	R	RBI	SB
1,740	6,297	1,840	.292	334	115	178	986	1,191	148

BOB LEMON

Early in his career Bob Lemon was a versatile performer who played nearly every position except catcher. He didn't become a full-time pitcher in the major leagues until he was 25 years old. Then he developed into one of the best in baseball, winning 207 games in 12 years.

When Lemon came up to the Cleveland Indians to get some major league experience at the end of the 1941 and 1942 seasons, he was primarily a third baseman and saw no action at all on the mound. Then, like many other ballplayers of his era, Lemon's career was interrupted by three years of military service in World War II. While serving in the U.S. Navy, Lemon pitched for an armed forces team managed by Yankee catching great Bill Dickey. Word of his success as a hurler spread to Cleveland Indians owner Bill Veeck and team manager Lou Boudreau when Lemon returned from duty in 1946. Lemon wasn't fielding well at third base, and resident hot corner specialist Ken Keltner was returning from the Navy too. The Indians had tried Lemon in the outfield, but his hitting didn't justify keeping a starting position among the eight regulars. Starting out first in the bullpen and then as a starter, Lemon proved that his mound talent exceeded any expectations the team could have placed on "Lem" as a third baseman.

For a ten-year period from the late 1940s to the late 1950s, Lemon was one of the most dependable pitchers in the American League. During that time, he won 20 or more games on seven occasions. For three years he led the league in wins, and for five years he topped the junior circuit in complete games. Lemon's success was earned with huge investments of patience and effort. He toiled for five minor league seasons. Prior to his three-year hitch in the Navy, Lemon had hit over .300 in two different seasons in the minors.

The California native struggled to learn his new position as a pitcher for the Indians in 1946-47. Lemon was mostly used in the team's bullpen during his first year back from the war. He appeared in 32 games but in only 5 as a starter. Lemon went 4-5 but amassed a respectable 2.49 ERA. Control was a problem, as he walked 68 while striking out just 39 in 94 innings. In 1947 Lemon got part-time work in the starting rotation. He produced a snappier 11-5 record, 6 complete games, 3 saves, and a shutout.

His first major success came in 1948, the year the Indians rode their new pitcher's arm all the way to the world championship. Lemon won 20 and lost 14. His ERA was a respectable 2.82, and his strikeouts outnumbered his walks (147 to 129) for the first time in his career. He was first in the American League in shutouts (10), innings pitched (293.2), and complete games (20). On June 30, 1948, Lemon pitched a 2-0 no-hit win against the Tigers in Detroit. He was only the eighth Indians pitcher in history to hurl a hitless gem.

In the 1948 World Series, Lemon paced his team with 2 wins as the Tribe toppled the Boston Braves in six games. His first win was an eight-hitter in game two. Lemon's second victory was seven strong innings in the decisive sixth game, which eventually turned into a 4-3 Indians win. In the Series Lemon had a 1.65 ERA in 16.1 innings. Following the Series win, the Cleveland mayor presented him with keys to the city.

The big righthander was the American League's leading winner in 1950, 1954, and 1955. He won a career-high 23 games in each of the first two years, then was the top A.L. pitcher in 1955 with 18 victories. In his career Lemon received seven All-Star team invitations.

Lemon turned out to be one of the finest-hitting pitchers in the game's history. In 1946 and 1947 Lemon started a total of 14 games in the Indians outfield, and throughout his career the Indians used the multitalented Lemon as a pinch hitter. For his career Lemon chalked up 274 lifetime hits, 37 homers, 147 RBI, and a .232 batting average. In four different seasons Lemon had 5 or more homers. His career pinch-hitting average is .284, with 31 hits in 109 plate appearances.

Lemon managed for eight years in the majors, posting a career record of 432-401. When he took over the 1978 New York Yankees in midseason, he guided them from third place all the way to a six-game World Series win over the Dodgers. He was moved to general manager in 1979 to allow for the return of field manager Billy Martin. He returned to manage the Yanks for 42 games in 1981, and he skippered the Yanks to the World Series. He was the pilot for the Yanks for only 14 games in 1982 before turning the team over to Gene Michael. Lemon currently serves as a special assignment scout for the team.

CAREER HIGHLIGHTS
ROBERT GRANVILLE LEMON

Born: September 22, 1920   San Bernardino, CA
Height: 6'0" **Weight:** 180 lbs.   **Batted:** Left **Threw:** Right
Third baseman: Cleveland Indians, 1941-42. Pitcher: Cleveland Indians, 1946-58. Manager: Kansas City Royals, 1970-72; Chicago White Sox, 1977-78; New York Yankees, 1978-79, 1981-82.

★ Pitched a no-hitter in 1948 against the Detroit Tigers
★ Pitched in two World Series
★ Named to *The Sporting News* All-Star team three times

★ Won 20 or more games seven times in nine years
★ Elected to the Hall of Fame in 1976
★ Managed the 1978 world champion New York Yankees

MAJOR LEAGUE TOTALS

G	IP	W	L	Pct.	SO	BB	ERA
460	2,850	207	128	.618	1,277	1,251	3.23

In 1948 Bob Lemon spurred the Cleveland Indians on to their first pennant in 28 years.
He pitched a no-hitter that year plus 10 shutouts, in addition to winning 20 games. He
then pitched 2 more wins in the 1948 World Series.

CHET LEMON

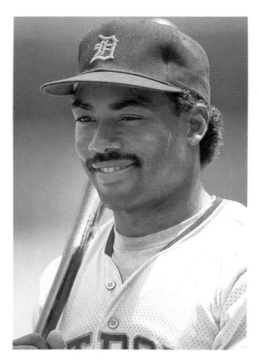

Chet Lemon, the 15-year veteran outfielder for the Detroit Tigers, is one of baseball's quiet stars, performing to a consistently high standard season after season without getting a great deal of attention from the media.

Lemon was a first-round draftee from Cerritos College in Norwalk, California, when the Oakland Athletics signed him in 1972. He played shortstop and third base in his first three seasons in the minor leagues. On June 15, 1975, Lemon was traded to the Chicago White Sox with Dave Hamilton in exchange for pitchers Skip Pitlock and Stan Bahnsen. While with the Denver Bears of the American Association, Lemon was converted into a center fielder. He came to the major leagues as the 1975 season drew to a close after finishing with a .307 average for Denver, which was the White Sox top minor league team.

His official rookie season in 1976 was strong and steady but unspectacular compared to some others. By his own standards, his .992 fielding average was a superlative effort, a mark he would match or surpass only twice over the next dozen years. His 353 putouts surpassed his annual average and gave some clue as to what lay ahead for the fielding demon.

In 1977, his second full year in Chicago, he set an American League record for putouts by an outfielder (512) but unfortunately missed another dozen because of errors. Still, his 524 accepted chances set another A.L. record and tied the A.L. mark for most years of 500 or more putouts. Lemon has surpassed the 400-putout mark four different times, most recently with 411 putouts in 1985 (his third consecutive 400-plus season). Such superior defensive stats have to be chalked up to outstanding baseball instincts rather than raw speed, for Lemon is not particularly fast: He has never stolen more than 13 bases in a season and has usually swiped fewer than 6 a year.

Lemon had back-to-back .300 seasons in 1978 and 1979. His 1978 mark might have been still higher if not for two weeks on the disabled list late in the season. In 1979 Lemon registered a number of personal highs as well as some league marks. His 556 plate appearances and 86 RBI were personal bests, as was his league-leading 44 doubles.

Lemon also began to suffer from a constant attack of inside pitches. Beginning in 1979 he was hit by more pitches per season than any other player for the next four seasons. How many balls got him that year? The same as in 1981—an unlucky 13. It increased to 15 in 1982 and to 20 in 1983. Despite all the lumps he suffered from being an easy target at the plate, none ever caused an injury that warranted any time out.

Following a .302 season in 1981, he was traded to the Detroit Tigers for outfielder Steve Kemp. Lemon was still with the Tigers at the end of the 1989 season, while Kemp is now just another name from baseball's past. During his Chicago years Lemon twice tallied errors in double digits. Under the guidance of Bengals coaches, he solidified his brilliant but erratic fielding. Only in 1988 did his errors for the team climb as high as 8, and the miscues stayed below 5 prior to that year. He still makes the occasional strong throw to the wrong base, but his 34 years have made him more conservative about mid day meetings with outfield walls.

Lemon's batting average has not prospered in Detroit, although he has continued to swing well for power. A little overanxious at times, Lemon is sometimes jammed by pitchers. He has adapted his stance to handle inside pitches.

The 1987 and 1988 seasons were atypical campaigns for Lemon—his 20 and 17 home runs fell toward the upper end of his career average. His .277 mark in 1987 was up 26 points over his 1986 total of .251 and hovered near his lifetime average, which stays between .275 and .280. His .264 posting in 1988 dropped his lifetime average just a bit.

Lemon seems to play well under pressure. His flawless fielding and near-.300 batting average in the 1984 World Series helped lead the Tigers to a Series victory over the San Diego Padres. The Tigers trampled the Padres four games to one. Ironically, Lemon's impressive Series performance came after an embarrassing showing in the A.L. playoffs between the Tigers and the Kansas City Royals. As the hard-luck player of the Championship Series, Lemon went 0-for-13.

Lemon and the Tigers hoped to repeat their World Series success in 1987, but the Tigers were defeated in the A.L. Championship Series by the Minnesota Twins despite Lemon's play-off contributions of 2 home runs and a .278 average.

CAREER HIGHLIGHTS
CHESTER EARL LEMON

Born: February 12, 1955   Jackson, MS
Height: 6'0"   **Weight:** 190 lbs.   **Bats:** Right   **Throws:** Right
Outfielder: Chicago White Sox, 1975-81; Detroit Tigers, 1982-89.

- ★ Batted .294 in the 1984 World Series
- ★ Has double figures in homers for 11 seasons
- ★ Played in two League Championship Series
- ★ Participated in three World Series
- ★ Established an A.L. record for chances accepted by an outfielder in 1977
- ★ Led the A.L. in being hit by pitches four times

MAJOR LEAGUE TOTALS

G	AB	H	BA	2B	3B	HR	R	RBI	SB
1,884	6,546	1,792	.274	380	57	210	934	852	55

Veteran outfielder Chet Lemon has been hit by more pitches than perhaps any other modern player. In 1981 he was struck by 13 pitches; in 1982 he was hit by 15; and in 1983 he was pelted at least 20 times. Fortunately, none resulted in serious injury.

MICKEY LOLICH

With 217 career wins, Mickey Lolich has compiled more lifetime victories than 16 of the 46 pitchers enshrined in the Baseball Hall of Fame. That, combined with the fact that he played for 13 straight seasons with the Detroit Tigers—winning 3 complete games for them in the 1968 World Series—makes Lolich an attractive candidate for membership among the Cooperstown elite.

The Portland native began major league life as a batboy for the Beavers of the Pacific Coast League. His father worked for the city Park Bureau, and Lolich was a practiced athlete by the time he reached high school.

By the age of 18, Lolich was attending Clark Junior College in Vancouver, Washington. His drilling of teammates during batting practice happened to catch the eye of a big league scout, and in 1958 Lolich signed a three-year contract with the Detroit Tigers, receiving a $30,000 bonus.

It took Lolich until 1963 to reach Detroit, and once there he posted an unspectacular 5-9 record in 33 games. He averaged 1 hit per inning during the 144 innings he pitched. But there was also a hint of promise as he threw 103 strikeouts, which was a healthy percentage for his time on the mound and a statistic he would maintain for some years to come.

Although he suffered typical rookie problems during his freshman year, Lolich had a fantastic second season, with 18 wins against 9 losses, 192 strikeouts, and 64 walks. His ERA dropped to 3.26, a comfortable range for the tall, thin hurler. He threw 6 shutouts in the 1964 season, a figure that also led the league when he achieved it again in 1967. He also had a .667 winning percentage his sophomore year.

In the 1968 World Series, Lolich became the first lefthand pitcher to win 3 complete games in one fall classic. He also had a 1.67 ERA to go along with his trio of triumphs, in addition to a .250 batting average, well above his career-high .197 of the previous season. He also hit the only homer of his career. Yet Lolich's magnificent Series performance was overshadowed by teammate Denny McLain's perfect regular season, when McLain became the most recent pitcher to win as many as 30 in a season.

During the decade spanning 1964 to 1974, Lolich won at least 14 games each season. In 1970 he topped the American League with 19 losses; the following year he did a complete turnaround by topping the league with 25 wins.

The 1971 season was the peak of his career. He struck out a league-high 308 batters and had 29 complete games, both league highs. His 376 innings were the most by a major leaguer in more than 50 years. In interviews Lolich has told reporters that he considered nine-inning performances his specialty. As evidenced by an occasionally high number of hits allowed, Lolich knew how to pace himself throughout a game. He'd remain focused on the final outcome of the game, scattering handfuls of hits without yielding large quantities of runs.

In 1975 he posted the second of two consecutive losing seasons, the third time in 13 years that he had done so. The Tigers decided not to gamble on the 35-year-old, a decision sadly borne out in the subsequent three seasons he logged with the New York Mets and the San Diego Padres. Lolich tried to retire after spending just one season with the Mets, but the Padres management lured him out of retirement by promising him that he could work with a young, enthusiastic team in California. Used more in relief after leaving the Tigers, Lolich in 1978 posted a career-best 1.54 ERA after an entire season's inactivity.

Still, 1979 was a disappointment, and Lolich retired for good after notching a personal-high ERA of 4.78. During his career he had averaged 7 strikeouts per nine-inning game and hurled 195 complete games and 41 shutouts. In 1971 and 1972 he won more than 20 games. His 2.50 ERA in 1972 was his best mark for a season of more than 20 games, which accounted for each year of his career, save one.

History should remember Lolich kindly. Because he faded from view quietly after signing with the Padres, fans underestimate his career achievements. However, record books now show that the rubber-armed lefty was an accomplished moundsman. His 41 career shutouts and 195 complete games are tributes to his hard-working dedication. Lolich was a brilliant control pitcher, as illustrated by his strikeout/walk ratio. Lolich whiffed 2,832 batters in his major league service, while issuing just 1,099 bases on balls. He even collected 11 saves to enhance his win total. Even though it may be several more years before he gets his due honors in Cooperstown, it's hard to believe that the baseball community can forever ignore the contributions of such a talented individual.

CAREER HIGHLIGHTS
MICHAEL STEPHEN LOLICH

Born: September 12, 1940 Portland, OR
Height: 6'1" **Weight:** 170 lbs. **Batted:** Both **Threw:** Right
Pitcher: Detroit Tigers, 1963-75; New York Mets, 1976; San Diego Padres, 1978-79.

★ Compiled 217 career wins
★ Led the league in four categories in 1971
★ Hit his only major league home run in 1968 in his first World Series at-bat
★ Was a 20-game winner twice
★ Posted 3 complete-game victories in the 1968 World Series
★ Earned 195 complete games in his career

MAJOR LEAGUE TOTALS

G	IP	W	L	Pct.	SO	BB	ERA
586	3,640	217	191	.532	2,832	1,099	3.44

Mickey Lolich played perfectly in the 1968 World Series between the Detroit Tigers and the St. Louis Cardinals. He pitched 3 complete games, had a 1.67 ERA, and belted the only home run of his major league career.

ERNIE LOMBARDI

Catcher Ernie Lombardi enjoyed an illustrious 17-year career that was long overlooked by Cooperstown. Not until 1986, nearly four decades after his retirement, was the hard-working backstop elected by the Veterans Committee into the Baseball Hall of Fame.

Lombardi was one of the best all-around receivers in the game, ranking with Gabby Hartnett as the best in his era. An exceptionally strong-hitting catcher, Lombardi compiled a very impressive .306 lifetime batting average, with 190 home runs. He won the National League batting title twice. In 1935 he hit a career-high .343 and three years later won the league's Most Valuable Player award after hitting a league-leading .342 with 19 home runs and 95 RBI.

Lombardi was a big man, and he compiled his lofty batting marks despite being one of the slowest runners on the field. He personified the typical catcher who's big but lethargic, and his 8 career stolen bases provide proof positive. It's easy to imagine how well a fleet-footed player could have done with Lombardi's batting talents. A .400 average could have been a solid possibility if Lombardi could have legged out more infield safeties. Also, the solid pull-hitter frequently faced a defensive shift, with all of the opposing infielders playing to the left of second. But Lombardi still managed to slash his way on base with amazing regularity. For ten seasons he batted over .300.

The California native began his pro career in 1927 with Odgen of the Utah-Idaho League and hit .398 in 50 games. He realized a dream when he played for his hometown Oakland Oaks of the Pacific Coast League later that year. In 1928 Lombardi batted .377 with Oakland. His average hovered at .366 in 1929, as his home run total grew from 8 the previous year to 24. The stocky catcher hit .370 with 22 homers in 1930, landing his first shot with the major leagues.

The Brooklyn Dodgers bought Lombardi from Oakland for $50,000 cash and players. However, with stalwart glove man Al Lopez monopolizing the Brooklyn backstop job, Lombardi was traded to the Cincinnati Reds on March 14, 1932.

Although Lombardi landed on a last-place team for the 1933 season, he made the most of his new starting assignment, hitting .283. He upped his marks to .305 with 9 homers and 62

RBI in 1934. In 1935 the Reds moved to sixth place in the National League, partially due to Lombardi's banner season of 12 homers, 64 RBI, and a .343 average (fourth highest in the league). The following season Lombardi logged an average of .333 with 12 homers and 68 RBI.

The Reds were in last place once again in 1937, despite Lombardi's 9 homers, 59 RBI, and .334 average. When Lombardi won his batting title and MVP award in 1938, the Reds finished fourth, just six games behind the pennant-winning Chicago Cubs.

Cincinnati finally put it all together in 1939, winning the National League pennant with a 92-57 record. Lombardi bashed a career-high 20 home runs to go with 85 RBI and a .287 average. That season he led N.L. catchers with 5.1 chances accepted per game. Cincinnati got swept four straight in the World Series by the New York Yankees, as Lombardi had just 3 hits and 2 RBI. In what has become known as the "snooze," Lombardi received a throw

home by an outfielder in game four and was bowled over by Yankee Charlie Keller, who scored. While Lombardi writhed on the ground with the ball an arm's length away, Joe DiMaggio flew around the bases and also scored, giving the Yanks a three-run lead and the Series. Lombardi led the 1940 Reds with a .319 average as the team avenged itself with a World Series triumph over the Detroit Tigers. Lombardi was second on the team with 14 homers and 74 RBI.

The Reds gave up on Lombardi after the 1941 season and sold him to the Boston Braves. Lombardi responded to his new surroundings by winning his second league batting title with a .330 performance (which included 11 home runs and 46 RBI). However, the Braves dumped the veteran backstop after one campaign, trading him to the New York Giants on April 27, 1943, for Connie Ryan and Hugh Poland. In New York Lombardi played three solid seasons, then became a competent backup catcher/pinch hitter in 1946 and 1947.

Lombardi was saddled with two nicknames during his career. A lesser-known moniker of Lombardi's was "Bocci," which is an Italian game similar to lawn bowling. Possibly someone compared Lombardi's body to a bocci ball. The second nickname was "Schnoz," in reference to Lombardi's large nose. The 1933 edition of Who's Who in Major League Baseball claims that the nasal nickname stuck when Lombardi was photographed in profile with comedian Jimmy Durante, another public figure who was known for his nose.

Lombardi died in 1977, nine years before his lifelong wish of induction to Cooperstown came true.

CAREER HIGHLIGHTS
ERNEST NATALI LOMBARDI

Born: April 6, 1908   Oakland, CA   **Died:** September 26, 1977
Height: 6'3"   **Weight:** 230 lbs.   **Batted:** Right   **Threw:** Right
Catcher: Brooklyn Dodgers, 1931; Cincinnati Reds, 1932-41; Boston Braves, 1942; New York Giants, 1943-47.

- ★ Selected as N.L. MVP in 1938
- ★ Batted over .300 on ten occasions
- ★ Was the only catcher ever to win two batting titles

- ★ Played in two World Series
- ★ Elected to the Hall of Fame in 1986
- ★ Never struck out more than 25 times in a single season

MAJOR LEAGUE TOTALS

G	AB	H	BA	2B	3B	HR	R	RBI	SB
1,853	5,855	1,792	.306	277	27	190	601	990	8

Though a solid .300 hitter throughout his career, Ernie Lombardi was one of the slowest runners in all of baseball. Historians speculate that if he had been quicker, he might have been a .400 hitter.

DAVEY LOPES

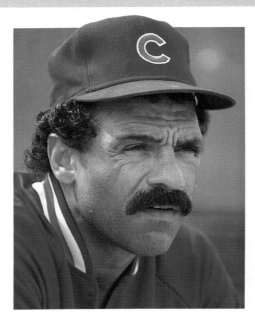

During his 10-year career in Los Angeles from 1972 to 1981, Davey Lopes stole his way into the hearts of baseball fans everywhere. With his daring baserunning and aggressive style of play, he became the most exciting player in the Dodger infield since Maury Wills starred for the Blue Crew in the 1960s.

Lopes played a total of 16 years in the majors and is best remembered for his many stolen bases. His lifetime total of 577 steals is the tenth-highest accumulation by any player in history. Besides being a stolen base terror, Lopes was a long-ball threat who used his speed when playing defense.

Lopes, who grew up in a family of 12, first gained prominence playing baseball at Iowa Wesleyan College in Mount Pleasant. There he was named to the NAIA All-America Team, both in baseball and basketball. The Los Angeles Dodgers signed Lopes as an outfielder, but after two minor league seasons as a flyhawker, Spokane manager Tommy Lasorda (the current Dodgers manager) advised the Rhode Island native to try second base. The results gave Lopes a new push toward the major leagues. After dividing his time between second and the outfield with Spokane in 1970 and 1971, Lopes became a starting second sacker with Triple-A Albuquerque in 1972. Although he committed 21 errors in 104 games, he achieved the highest marks of his short career in hits (126), home runs (11), RBI (53), and batting average (.317). His 48 steals led the Pacific Coast League.

After nearly five seasons in the minors, Lopes got his long-awaited chance to prove himself at the major league level. In 11 games near the season's end, Lopes batted just .214 and fielded adequately, but he stole 4 bases and displayed enough savvy to earn a full-time job with the Dodgers the next year. In 1973 Lopes joined with third baseman Ron Cey, shortstop Bill Russell, and first baseman Steve Garvey to form an infield foursome that would stay together for a record nine seasons.

In his rookie season Lopes hit .275 with 6 homers and 37 RBI. In his sophomore season he thumped 10 home runs and improved his stolen base totals from 36 in 1973 to 59 in 1974. In August at Wrigley Field, Lopes battered the Cubs for his biggest single outing as a leadoff hitter. He tallied 3 homers, a double, and a single for 15 total bases. In the same month, he had his first 5-steal game, tying another mark.

Lopes carved out his most memorable record in 1975. On his way to leading the National League with a career-high 77 steals (with a success rate of .865), Lopes swiped 38 bases in a row without getting thrown out. He began his streak against the Montreal Expos on June 10. Playing the Expos again on August 24, his streak ended when he tried a 12th-inning swipe against catcher Gary Carter. In the process Lopes had shattered a mark of 31 consecutive steals set in 1922 by Pittsburgh outfielder Max Carey.

Lopes won his second straight stolen base crown with 63 larcenies in 1976, even though he was on the disabled list for a month.

The 1977 season was Lopes' best effort at hitting for average, with a career-high .283 and 47 steals. Lopes helped the Dodgers win their first division title since 1974. Although he hit just .235 in the League Championship Series against Philadelphia, Lopes drove in the tying run and then scored the game-winner in the Dodgers third-game victory. The Dodgers lost the World Series to the New York Yankees in six games.

In 1978 Lopes won his first Gold Glove for fielding excellence and received his first All-Star game invitation. He ended his regular season with a .278 average, 17 homers, and 58 RBI (along with 45 steals). Lopes batted .389 in the N.L.C.S against Philadelphia, then was the Dodger star of the 1978 World Series, again won by New York in six games. He drove in 5 runs with a pair of homers in an 11-5 opening-game victory against the Yanks. He homered again in a losing seventh-game effort. His totals for the seven-game battle were 8 hits, 3 homers, 7 RBI, and 7 runs scored for a .308 average.

Through 1987 (when the Astros released him on November 12), his lifetime statistics included 1,812 games played and 1,671 hits for a .263 average. He had 232 doubles, 50 triples, 155 homers, and 614 RBI. His 557 stolen bases with the Dodgers rank him second on their all-time list.

If fans don't see Lopes back in baseball as a coach or manager soon, it may be because he's busy in a classroom. Unlike many players, who didn't plan for their post-athletic careers, Lopes earned a B.A. in education from Washburn University in 1969.

CAREER HIGHLIGHTS
DAVID EARL LOPES

Born: May 3, 1946   East Providence, RI
Height: 5'9"   **Weight:** 170 lbs.   **Batted:** Right   **Threw:** Right
Second baseman: Los Angeles Dodgers, 1972-81. Infielder, outfielder: Oakland A's, 1982-84; Chicago Cubs, 1984-86; Houston Astros, 1986-87.

* Has the tenth-highest stolen base total in history
* Led the N.L. in steals twice
* Played in six League Championship Series
* Set a new record in 1975 by successfully stealing 38 bases in a row
* Appeared in four World Series
* Ranks third in World Series steals with 10
* Played in four All-Star games

MAJOR LEAGUE TOTALS

G	AB	H	BA	2B	3B	HR	R	RBI	SB
1,812	6,354	1,671	.263	232	50	155	1,023	614	557

Though his statistics were never remarkable, Davey Lopes was a consistent player who used his speed to the best advantage. A basestealing threat for most of his career, Lopes snatched 38 bases in a row in 1975 without getting thrown out.

AL LOPEZ

Al Lopez won his place in the Hall of Fame in 1977 in recognition of a successful 41-year career that was divided evenly between playing and managing. As a catcher from 1928 through 1947, Lopez set a record for durability by catching in 1,918 games. Kansas City Royals catcher Bob Boone is the only man to break that mark so far. As a manager, Lopez was the only skipper who was able to stop the New York Yankees from grabbing every American League pennant in the 1950s. Between 1949 and 1964, the Yankees won the league title in every year but two. In 1954 the Cleveland Indians triumphed, and in 1959 the Chicago White Sox captured the crown. The manager of both clubs was Al Lopez.

Lopez, born in Tampa in 1908, was called "Pancho," "Chico" or "Lopee." Once he made the majors, he was known as "Senor Al" throughout his distinguished career. He had a strong reputation as a catcher, even as a teenager. When Walter Johnson came into town on a barnstorming tour, the 16-year-old Lopez was selected to catch "The Big Train" as a publicity gimmick. Playing with major leaguers, he turned in a sparkling performance. The next year he was playing professional ball with Tampa of the Florida State League.

Lopez had actually sworn off baseball at age 10, after getting hit in the face with a ball. He had been skipping school to play baseball but was caught after his playmates panicked and called an ambulance for their injured companion. Two years later he relented only when the regular catcher on the elementary school team was indisposed.

While attending George Washington Junior High School in Tampa, Lopez became the baseball team captain. His brother Emilio was an amateur catcher and inspired the younger Lopez to do the same. In his five-year minor league career, Lopez batted over .300 three times with a minor league high of 14 homers with the 1928 Macon team. The Brooklyn Dodgers purchased Lopez from the Atlanta franchise in 1929 for $10,000.

Lopez was tutored in the art of catching by Brooklyn manager "Uncle" Wilbert Robinson, once a top-notch major league backstop. As a rookie in 1930, Lopez caught in 126 games for the Dodgers. He hit .309 with 6 homers and 57 RBI. His 130 hits were a career best. Two seasons later, Lopez batted .301. He had one of his most productive years as a power hitter with 54 RBI. On December 12, 1935, Lopez was traded with Tony Cuccinello, Ray Benge, and Bobby Reis to the Boston Braves for Ed Brandt and Randy Moore.

The Braves were anxious to put Lopez's glove to use. He led the senior circuit in assists with 107 during his first year in Boston. Lopez became a second-string catcher under new manager Casey Stengel in 1938. The Braves posted their first winning record in three seasons (77-75), but Lopez played in just 71 games. He won his starting job back in 1939 and was second on the team in homers with 8, while Max West was first with 25. On June 14, 1940, the Pirates swapped catcher Ray Berres and $40,000 for Lopez. Lopez finished the season with a league-best fielding percentage of .992.

In his record-setting career, Lopez made his greatest contributions on defense. He was a durable and intelligent backstop who was among the best in baseball at handling pitchers. He also fared adequately as a hitter. He had a lifetime batting mark of .261.

His skill at handling pitchers served him well during his long career as a manager. He spent his first three years (1948-50) managing at Indianapolis of the American Association. Lopez landed the manager's spot in Cleveland in 1951, taking over for the extremely popular Lou Boudreau. Lopez delivered a pennant in four years. His 1954 club won a record 111 games, enough to take the American League championship by eight games over the always tough New York Yankees. The incredible year ended in disappointment as the New York Giants swept four straight World Series games from the Tribe.

Those pesky Yankees were constant foes of Lopez and his Indians. Cleveland won 93 games in 1951, 1952, and 1955; 92 games in 1953; and 88 in 1956. Yet those sterling team performances resulted in 5 second-place finishes behind the Bronx Bombers. When Lopez moved to Chicago to manage the White Sox, the same successful but frustrating results occurred—second-place finishes in 1957 and 1958 and in 1963-65. It was a different story in 1959, however. Lopez infused an aggressive running game into the team offense, and his club became known as the "Go-Go" White Sox. Chicago won the A.L. pennant, finished the season at 94-60, and battled with the Los Angeles Dodgers for six games before losing the World Series. Lopez was elected to the Hall of Fame in 1977.

CAREER HIGHLIGHTS
ALFONSO RAYMOND LOPEZ

Born: August 20, 1908   Tampa, FL
Height: 5'11"   **Weight:** 165 lbs.   **Batted:** Right   **Threw:** Right
Catcher: Brooklyn Dodgers, 1928, 1930; Boston Braves, 1936-40; Pittsburgh Pirates, 1940-46; Cleveland Indians, 1947. Manager: Cleveland Indians, 1951-56; Chicago White Sox, 1957-65, 1968-69.

- ★ Established a record by catching 1,918 games
- ★ Caught a record 12 seasons of 100 or more games
- ★ Tied a record with no passed balls in 1941
- ★ Caught 100-plus games for eight straight seasons
- ★ Managed the Cleveland Indians and the Chicago White Sox to pennants
- ★ Elected to the Hall of Fame in 1977

MAJOR LEAGUE TOTALS

G	AB	H	BA	2B	3B	HR	R	RBI	SB
1,950	5,916	1,547	.261	206	42	52	613	652	46

Al Lopez had a successful career first as a durable and reliable catcher and then as a popular and successful manager. From 1949 to 1964 Lopez was the only A.L. manager to lead a team other than the Yankees to a pennant.

GREG LUZINSKI

The "Bull" roamed the pastures of the Philadelphia outfield in the 1970s. That's what Phillies fans called outfielder Greg Luzinski, who used his massive size and strength to power in numerous home runs and clutch base hits.

The Phillies started Luzinski (originally a first baseman) with Huron in 1968. He hit .259 with 13 home runs and 43 RBI during his first 57 games. He was promoted to Raleigh-Durham of the Carolina League the following season, where he tallied 31 home runs, 92 RBI, and a .289 average. At Reading of the Eastern League in 1970, Luzinski got the attention of the Phillies in a big way. He socked 33 home runs and 120 RBI while batting .325.

Philadelphia gave Luzinski an eight-game audition at first base in late 1970. He went just 2-for-12 and was sentenced to one more year in the minor leagues. In 1971 with Eugene of the Pacific Coast League, Luzinski continued to display more power for each minor league level he advanced. With the Phillies Triple-A affiliate, Luzinski hit .312 with 36 home runs and 114 RBI. Philadelphia invited Luzinski back earlier in 1971, and he got to play in 28 games. His batting average climbed to .300 as he belted 3 dingers and drove in 15 runs.

The Phillies gave up on trying to convert Luzinski into a first sacker. Instead, he was installed full-time in the Philadelphia outfield. Due to his limited speed, Luzinski never became a Gold Glove player, but he handled his left field territory adequately. Besides, with fleet Garry Maddox flanking Luzinski, an antelope was always there to back up the Bull. In 1972 Luzinski played in 150 games, hitting .281, with 18 home runs and 68 RBI. During his sophomore season Luzinski improved to a .285 mark with 29 home runs and 97 RBI. Injuries held Luzinski's productivity to a minimum in 1974, as he played in just 85 games.

Luzinski staged a grand comeback in 1975. He played in a personal best of 161 games, and his statistics included 34 homers, a league-leading 120 RBI, and a .300 batting average.

In 1976 Luzinski had his first of five opportunities to play for a pennant-winning club. It's no coincidence that three of his best years came when the Phillies won three consecutive division pennants. His stats in 1976 included 21 homers, 95 RBI, and a .304 average. Luzinski's first League Championship Series was somewhat bittersweet. He hit Philadelphia's only postseason homer and batted .273 with 3 RBI, but the Reds swept the Phillies in three straight. Luzinski enjoyed his best season at the plate in 1977. He set career-highs in homers (39), RBI (130), and batting average (.309). The only league lead Luzinski obtained was in strikeouts with 140. In the 1977 League Championship, the Dodgers topped the Phillies in four games. Luzinski batted .286 and was responsible for the Phillies only win with a two-run homer in the first game, giving Philadelphia a 7-5 victory.

Prior to the start of the 1981 season, the Chicago White Sox purchased Luzinski from the Phillies. While the move was a shock for Phillies fans, the transaction brought Luzinski back to the town he was born in. He picked up a glove only briefly with Chicago, playing two games at first base. The rest of his career was spent as a full-time designated hitter.

Luzinski made the transition to a new league and team role rather easily. In the strike-shortened season, he collected 21 home runs, 62 RBI, and a .265 average. In 1982 Luzinski drove in 102 runs along with 18 homers, marking the fourth time he had passed the 100-RBI barrier. Luzinski was one of the league's top designated hitters in 1983, when he powered 32 home runs and 95 RBI.

Luzinski hung up his spikes after 1984, when he hit .238 with 13 round-trippers and 58 RBI. His final season was highlighted by 2 grand slams off the Minnesota Twins on June 8 and 9. While his average fell to its lowest since 1980, the burly slugger posted double-digit totals in home runs for the tenth consecutive year.

Luzinski played a total of 15 major league seasons, compiling 1,795 hits in 1,821 games for a .276 batting average. He chalked up 307 homers (for a 4.7 home run percentage) with 880 runs scored and 1,128 RBI. Being a free swinger meant that Luzinski had many "all or nothing" experiences at home plate—either homering or striking out. He didn't like drawing bases on balls, and only once did he reach 100 walks. However, he exceeded 100 strikeouts in 11 campaigns.

Because he spent two-thirds of his career with the Phillies, Luzinski ranks in the top ten in nine different all-time team offensive categories. Only Mike Schmidt, Del Ennis, and Chuck Klein have surpassed his 223 home runs for Philadelphia. Luzinski wound up on *The Sporting News* All-Star team three times, twice as a Phillies outfielder and once (in 1983) as designated hitter for the White Sox.

CAREER HIGHLIGHTS
GREGORY MICHAEL LUZINSKI

Born: November 22, 1950   Chicago, IL
Height: 6'1"   **Weight:** 220 lbs.   **Batted:** Right   **Threw:** Right
First baseman, outfielder: Philadelphia Phillies, 1970-80. Designated hitter: Chicago White Sox, 1981-84.

- ★ Led the N.L. with 120 RBI in 1975
- ★ Appeared in five League Championship Series
- ★ Hit 18 or more homers for nine straight years
- ★ Belted a career-high 39 homers in 1977
- ★ Participated in the 1980 World Series with the Phillies
- ★ Registered double-digit totals for homers in 12 out of 15 seasons

MAJOR LEAGUE TOTALS

G	AB	H	BA	2B	3B	HR	R	RBI	SB
1,821	6,505	1,795	.276	344	24	307	880	1,128	37

Greg Luzinski played with Philadelphia for the bulk of his career, participating in five A.L. Championship Series. In the 1976 A.L.C.S. he hit the Phillies only homer; in the 1977 A.L.C.S. he secured his team's only win with a two-run homer in the first game.

SPARKY LYLE

In 1977 relief champion Sparky Lyle became the first American League reliever—and only the second reliever in major league history—to receive the coveted Cy Young award.

Lyle discussed his classy career and his reputation as a ribald, irreverent guy in his autobiography, *The Bronx Zoo*. In his book, Lyle dusted home plate with some of baseball's most beloved heroes (Reggie Jackson, Jim Palmer, and George Steinbrenner, to name a few) and also allowed a peek beneath his own tough horsehide. He also chronicled the 1978 season when, as Graig Nettles put it, Lyle went from Cy Young to sayonara in a single year.

The trip to Cy Young had taken almost a full career. Sparky (nicknamed by his father to avoid the confusion of a namesake) grew up in Pennsylvania playing football and basketball at school because there was no baseball team. He progressed from backyard and sandlot baseball to American Legion teams, and it was there Baltimore scouts spotted the 19-year-old strikeout king. (He once fanned 31 in a 17-inning game.)

After a respectable year on the Orioles farm, the Red Sox drafted him, and Sparky progressed through three teams in 1965, winning 11, losing 9, and gaining a 3.25 ERA.

Late one night, Lyle had a vision—a mental image of how to throw a slider. He went out in the dead of night to practice against the wall of a tavern. Lyle had vowed to master the pitch because slugging champion Ted Williams had once confessed that he could never hit a slider. If it foiled Williams, it was good enough for everyone else.

Lyle's fastball had never been very speedy, but it didn't matter any more. His slider gave him a 2.30 ERA in his first big league call-up in 1967, advancing his Sox to the Series. By then Sparky had his first big league injury, and he sat out Boston's unsuccessful Series bid.

The next two seasons were good to him. After a 1970 slump he carved out 16 saves in 1971, with 6 wins and 4 losses.

It was a change in management, not poor performance by Sparky, that prompted his 1972 trade to New York. Lyle wanted more on-field time, but Red Sox management was busy grooming reliever Bill Lee. Meanwhile, Yankee manager Ralph Houk needed a reliever who was strong against both righties and lefties, and Lyle could fill the bill.

Houk got him by trading Danny Cater to the Red Sox, who desperately needed a first baseman.

Lyle felt needed in the Yankee bullpen and responded with a record-setting 35 saves, a 1.92 ERA (his lowest to date), 9 wins, and 5 losses. Houk was even understanding when Lyle purposely sat on the manager's birthday cake, not knowing whose it was.

Yankee owner George Steinbrenner was not so understanding when Lyle's performance was less than stellar the following year, although it was tidy at 27 saves and a 2.52 ERA. Salary negotiations lasted throughout the season, with Sparky appearing in 66 games (59 for the finish) with a career-low 1.66 ERA. Instead of the threatened pay cut, Lyle received a retroactive raise.

A slump in 1975 was followed by a another surge in 1976, with a league-leading 23 saves and a 2.26 ERA. The Yanks progressed to another unsuccessful World Series, although Sparky's two-game performance was nearly flawless.

History repeated itself to spectacular effect in 1977, with another great save total (26) and ERA (2.17), crowned this time with a successful Series. The Cy Young award was the frosting on the cake. Small wonder the Yankee's stadium organist—with tongue planted firmly in cheek—always played "Pomp and Circumstance" as Lyle took the mound.

Still, Lyle was 33 years old in 1977, and the Yankees began using him less and less, choosing instead to baptize newcomer Rich Gossage. Lyle argued that he was not given the opportunity to hit a seasonal stride and unhappily sought release. From 1978 to 1982, he finished with respectable saves (as high as 13 and as low as 2 in an average 55 games per season) and only once posted more losses than wins. His slowly growing ERA peaked at 4.62 in 1982. His professional days ended with work for three different teams—the Rangers, the Phillies, and the White Sox.

Despite his aggressive desire to be used fully by his teams, Lyle has said that he never aspired to being a starting pitcher. Coaches and teammates said he had the perfect disposition for a reliever. He had a fearless, take-no-prisoners personality that only intensified under pressure.

"Only today's game counts," he often said while playing, a philosophy that carries well beyond baseball. Combined with his outrageous sense of humor, this outlook on life sometimes got Sparky into hot spots too. His teams gave him numerous fines for various offenses, including showing up for spring training overweight.

CAREER HIGHLIGHTS
ALBERT WALTER LYLE

Born: July 22, 1944   DuBois, PA
Height: 6'1"   **Weight:** 182 lbs.   **Batted:** Left   **Threw:** Left
Pitcher: Boston Red Sox, 1967-71; New York Yankees, 1972-78; Texas Rangers, 1979-80; Philadelphia Phillies, 1980-82; Chicago White Sox, 1982.

★ Ranks fourth with 238 career saves
★ Set an A.L. record with 35 saves in one season
★ Pitched in 899 games without a single start

★ Appeared in two World Series
★ First A.L. reliever to win a Cy Young award (in 1977)
★ Ranks fourth with 99 relief victories

MAJOR LEAGUE TOTALS

G	IP	W	L	Pct.	SV	SO	BB	ERA
899	1,391	99	76	.566	238	873	481	2.88

When Sparky Lyle was nudged out of his reliever's job with the New York Yankees by Goose Gossage, he spilled the beans in his biography The Bronx Zoo. An insider's look at the 1970s Yankees, the book chronicles Lyle's highs and lows as a player.

FRED LYNN

Fred Lynn surprised everyone in 1988. The Baltimore Orioles, hoping to solve their losing woes by creating a quick youth movement, had swapped Lynn in late season to the Detroit Tigers for three rookies. However, wily Tigers manager Sparky Anderson is a master at getting the most mileage out of "middle-aged" players. Unlike the Orioles, Anderson wasn't willing to put Lynn out to pasture, and with this new-found support and a winning atmosphere as his inspiration, Lynn put together a fine season.

Lynn, who had belted 23 homers each year from 1983 through 1987, hit 25 with 56 RBI in 1988 (the most since 1969). His acquisition wasn't quite enough to push the Tigers to the pennant, however. The Red Sox, Lynn's first team, edged the Bengals by one game for the division title. The striking irony is that Lynn could only have been of limited help to his new club. Because Lynn's flight didn't arrive in Detroit on time when he first joined the team, he would not have been eligible for post-season play with the Tigers.

At age 37 at the top of the 1989 season, Lynn has lost a little off his batting average but nothing off his fielding or slugging. He has hit 20 homers or more for the last seven seasons in a row, one of only a handful of active major leaguers to do so.

Lynn's major league career actually got off to a quick start after only a year and a half in the minors. He had been a second-round pick in the free-agent draft of June 1973 and landed a $40,000 signing bonus. When he made his debut for the Boston Red Sox on September 15, 1974, as a pinch runner for Cecil Cooper, his speed was recognized as an asset to the team. Ten days later, in his first official start, he whacked a double and a homer.

Lynn charged into his rookie year with the same determination, leading the American League in runs (103) and doubles (a rookie record at 47). He also became the first rookie to snag the league lead in slugging percentage (.566). Lynn's baptism under fire continued. He earned Player of the Month acclaim for a June game in which he was responsible for 16 total bases and 10 RBI. At the end of the season, Lynn became the first player to be named Rookie of the Year and MVP in the same season. Hot postseason play resulted, with the lanky lefty helping the BoSox earn their first pennant in eight years. When the dust settled on the

seven-game battlefield, the Cincinnati Reds were victorious. But so was Lynn. He tied the Series record for the highest fielding average by an outfielder, a flawless 1.000 in 24 chances. His Series was also highlighted by a three-run homer in game six.

Injuries in 1976 and 1977 didn't stop the growth of Lynn's homer and batting average statistics. The first of three consecutive Gold Glove awards came in 1978, to be added to the one Lynn had received during his rookie season, along with a dozen other awards and tributes. Lynn's finest all-around year followed in 1979, with his .333 average and .673 slugging percentage topping the league. He achieved career highs in nine categories and a 27-game hitting streak. During the streak, Lynn batted .416 with 10

homers, 25 RBI, and an .820 slugging percentage.

Lynn ended his Boston career in 1980 in fine style, hitting for the cycle on May 13 and stealing 12 bases in 12 attempts. In December he embarked for Angels territory in exchange for pitcher Frank Tanana, Jim Dorsey, and outfielder Joe Rudi.

His first year with the Angels was not blessed, as two double plays resulted in two injuries to the same knee. He came back in 1982 to claim his first grand slam, take MVP honors, and crack a rib while making a spectacular catch.

More injuries in 1983 didn't stop the forward march of homers (22) or stop Lynn from setting two All-Star game records with a single blow—a grand slam (the game's first)—and the most RBI in one inning (4) on July 6, 1983.

Lynn's pinpoint aim and diverse throwing range caused him to platoon between right and center field in 1984, and although his fielding average began to drop, it stopped at a respectable .982. Three "sudden death" homers flew from his bat in 1985, two of them back-to-back, making his introduction to the Orioles as a free agent very sweet.

Laryngitis plus sprained wrists and ankles slowed Lynn down in 1986. Back spasms and a sore quadricep severely limited his playing time in 1987. He appeared in only 111 games, batting .253. Many fans may see Lynn as a high-mileage used car with worn parts; he has missed more than two full seasons' worth of games due to injuries throughout the years. However, injuries haven't quelled Lynn's enthusiasm for baseball. He should still have some high quality play left in him.

CAREER HIGHLIGHTS
FREDERIC MICHAEL LYNN

Born: February 3, 1952   Chicago, IL
Height: 6'1"   **Weight:** 185 lbs.   **Bats:** Left   **Throws:** Left
Outfielder: Boston Red Sox, 1974-80; California Angels, 1981-84; Baltimore Orioles, 1985-88; Detroit Tigers, 1988-89.

★ Named to the A.L. All-Star team nine straight years, from 1975-83

★ Set a major league mark for highest batting average (.611) in a League Championship Series in 1982.

★ Has hit 20-plus homers for ten seasons

★ Won both Rookie of the Year and A.L. MVP in 1975

★ Named to *The Sporting News* Gold Glove team in 1975 and 1978-80

★ Won the 1979 batting championship

MAJOR LEAGUE TOTALS

G	AB	H	BA	2B	3B	HR	R	RBI	SB
1,879	6,729	1,913	.284	385	42	300	1,045	1,088	70

The only player to win the MVP in his first year as a major leaguer, Fred Lynn started his career by leading his league in doubles and runs, belting 21 homers, averaging .331, and racking up 105 RBI.

TED LYONS

Ted Lyons stepped from the pitcher's mound at Baylor University to Chicago's Comiskey Park in 1923 and remained with the White Sox for his entire 21-year career. Had he played for a stronger team, Lyons might have joined the select circle of 300-game winners. But even with a team that consistently finished in the second division, Lyons won 260 games and election to the Hall of Fame.

Lyons was a star basketball player and second baseman in his high school days in Vinton, Louisiana. He originally thought of becoming a lawyer and headed to Baylor University in Waco, Texas, for an education in law. The first person to spot Lyons' talent was Harry Davis, a scout for Connie Mack's Philadelphia Athletics.

After three years with the collegiate club, Lyons was ready to accept any major league offers. Along came Chicago White Sox catcher Ray Schalk, who was visiting friends in Waco after attending spring training camp in nearby Marlin, Texas. Baseball reporters following Schalk suggested that he take a few pitches from one of the college boys. Baylor coach Frank Bridges introduced Schalk to star pitcher Lyons and the famous catcher warmed up the youngster. Schalk was impressed, and Lyons signed his first contract with White Sox owner Charlie Comiskey a week later. When school was out, Lyons headed north and joined the big league roster—without a single day of minor league experience.

Lyons got a baptism by fire that first year. When he joined the club in St. Louis, he was put to work immediately as a reliever. It was the first major league game Lyons had ever seen. He finished that first year with a 2-1 record. After winning 12 games in 1924, Lyons collected a league-leading 21 victories in 1925—quite an accomplishment on a team that finished with a mediocre 79-75 record.

The highlight of Lyons' 1926 season was a no-hitter. On August 21 Lyons spun the only no-hit effort in the majors that year, beating the Red Sox 6-0. The only baserunner came by way of a lead-off walk. Following a double play the rest of the batters were retired in order. Lyons finished the year at 18-16. In 1927 he bested the junior circuit in victories for the second time in his career. His record consisted of 22 wins versus just 14 losses. Lyons was the American League's hardest-working moundsman that season, toting league-best figures of

307.2 innings pitched and 30 complete games. While Lyons was dazzling the American League with his talent, the White Sox had precious little besides Lyons to rejoice about. The team wound up at 70-83, for a fifth-place standing behind the New York Yankees.

In 1928 Lyons won 15 games while earning a career-high 6 saves. In 27 starts he logged 21 complete games. Lyons' record dropped to 14-20 in 1929 and his ERA bulged at 4.10, but he bounced back in 1930 by winning 22 games. His 29 complete games and 297.2 innings pitched bested the league that year.

In spring training before the 1931 season, Lyons suffered shoulder damage that affected his delivery for the rest of his career. For the six years before the injury, Lyons had averaged 19 wins a season; for the six years afterward, he averaged 10 and never won more than 15 games again. To prolong his career (and to draw more weekend attendance) the White Sox used Lyons to start games only on Sundays. This strategy worked. Lyons won in double figures

during five of his last six seasons and had only one losing season record in that time. Always a tough competitor, Lyons enlisted in the Marine Corps after Pearl Harbor and saw action in the Pacific. After the war, at age 45, Lyons returned to Chicago to pitch five more games before being named manager in May 1946.

Unlike today's American League pitchers who never pick up a bat, Lyons even served as an occasional pinch hitter when needed by the Sox. He finished his career with a .233 batting average, including 364 hits (5 of them homers) and 149 RBI. He also logged one game in the outfield for the 1929 Chicago squad.

Even a wise old veteran like Lyons couldn't help the White Sox as a manager. He took over in mid-1946, and the Sox finished at 64-60 under his guidance. The next two seasons weren't as pleasant. The 1947 club dropped to sixth place with a 70-84 record. In 1948, Lyons' last as a skipper, the Sox landed in eighth place with a 51-101 outcome.

After coaching for the Tigers and Brooklyn Dodgers for the next four seasons, Lyons returned to the White Sox as a scout in 1955 (the same year he was elected to the Hall of Fame). He retired from baseball in 1966 and spent his final years in his native Louisiana. Lyons died on July 25, 1986, at the age of 85.

Ted Lyons spent his entire career with the Chicago White Sox, pitching 21 seasons and managing 3. Lyons enjoyed the devotion of the fans, who adored him for his tireless spirit.

CAREER HIGHLIGHTS
THEODORE AMAR LYONS

Born: December 28, 1900 Lake Charles, LA **Died:** July 25, 1986
Height: 5'11" **Weight:** 200 lbs. **Batted:** Right **Threw:** Right
Pitcher: Chicago White Sox, 1923-46. Manager: Chicago White Sox, 1946-48.

- ★ Pitched a no-hitter in 1926
- ★ Won 20-plus games three times
- ★ Ranks 33rd in career wins
- ★ Led the A.L. in wins twice
- ★ Had 17 double-figure winning seasons
- ★ Elected to the Hall of Fame in 1955

MAJOR LEAGUE TOTALS

G	IP	W	L	Pct.	SO	BB	ERA
594	4,162	260	230	.531	1,073	1,121	3.67

BILL MADLOCK

Though nicknamed "Mad Dog," Bill Madlock was actually one of the nicest baseball players of the past two decades. Madlock was first pursued by a major league team in 1969 after graduating from high school in Decatur, Illinois. The St. Louis Cardinals tried to make him a 14th-round draft pick, but Madlock refused, deciding instead to attend Southwestern Iowa Community College. In 1970 he signed a contract with the Senators and began his pro career. His first stop was at Geneva of the New York-Penn League in 1970. His first full season was spent with Pittsfield of the Eastern League in 1971, and he batted just .234. Madlock began the 1972 season there but soon advanced a step on the minor league staircase to Denver of the American Association. His finest minor league season came in 1973 with Spokane of the Pacific Coast League. In 123 games Madlock exploded for 22 home runs, 90 RBI, and a .338 average. He topped the league in total bases (268) and runs scored (119). A brief audition with Texas followed, and in 21 games Madlock hit .351.

One of the biggest challenges of Madlock's young career followed in 1974. On October 25, 1973, he was traded with utility man Vic Harris to the Chicago Cubs for pitcher Ferguson Jenkins. Jenkins was one of the winningest pitchers in Cubs history, so Chicago fans were naturally skeptical that Madlock would be fair compensation. Worse than that, he was being slated as the replacement for the ever-popular third baseman Ron Santo. Despite missing the entire month of May on the disabled list, Madlock submitted an outstanding effort of 9 homers, 54 RBI, and a .313 average in his first year as a Cub.

The following year Madlock had one of the single greatest offensive seasons in Cubs history. He became only the fifth Chicago player ever to win a National League batting title. Madlock went 6-for-6 in a game versus the Mets. He was co-MVP of the All-Star game for his tie-breaking single in the ninth inning that led the senior circuit to a 6-3 victory.

A second consecutive batting title came in 1976 as Madlock hit .339 with 15 homers and 84 RBI. The homer-hungry Cubs sent Madlock to the San Francisco Giants for Bobby Murcer and two other players on February 11, 1977.

The 1980 season was anything but memorable for Madlock. Although he had 10 homers and 53 RBI, he batted just .277. He was hobbled by a bad knee, and he missed 15 games and was fined $5,000 for hitting a home plate umpire with his glove. Following the season he had surgery on an injured thumb. During the strike-shortened 1981 season, Madlock gained his third batting title with a .341 mark. In 1982 he had his best power stats ever, amassing 19 homers and 95 RBI. Madlock became the 11th player in major league history to win four batting titles, with a league-best average of .323 in 1983. Assorted problems with his left leg caused him to miss more than 30 games that same year.

Being in a pennant race always seemed to bring out the best in Madlock. The Dodgers traded three promising rookies—Cecil Espy, R.J. Reynolds, and Sid Bream—to the Pirates for Madlock on August 31, 1985. Madlock sparked the Dodgers to a pennant by hitting .360 with 15 RBI in 34 late-season games. A 17-game hitting streak highlighted his Los Angeles debut. Although the Cardinals beat the Dodgers in a five-game N.L.C.S., Madlock batted .333 with 8 hits, 3 homers, and 7 RBI.

When the Dodgers cut him loose in 1987 he was hitting just .180 after 21 games. But after he signed with the Detroit Tigers, who were in the midst of a scramble for the American League pennant, his bat immediately came to life. Madlock batted .279 with 14 homers and 50 RBI for the Bengals. One of the highlights of his season was a three-homer game on June 28. Unfortunately, the Tigers were erased in the Championship Series by the Minnesota Twins. Madlock didn't find many takers in the off-season as a free agent, so he looked abroad for foreign aid. In 1988 Madlock played as a designated hitter in the Japanese League—one of 24 Americans competing in Japan. Madlock fared well, hitting .263 with 19 home runs and 61 RBI for the Lotte Orions.

While it seems that Madlock may be finished as a major leaguer, no one should count him out just yet. Players like Bob Horner have returned to the majors after stints in the Japanese League. Some things never change: There's always some team looking for an experienced batter with just one more hit in him. Bill Madlock may not be ready for retirement yet.

Though he won four batting titles and was a competent hitter, Bill Madlock was traded a great deal during his career. He played for six teams in all, logging the most time with the Pittsburgh Pirates.

CAREER HIGHLIGHTS
WILLIAM MADLOCK, Jr.

Born: January 12, 1951 Memphis, TN
Height: 5'11" **Weight:** 206 lbs. **Batted:** Right **Threw:** Right
Infielder: Texas Rangers, 1973; Chicago Cubs, 1974-76; San Francisco Giants, 1977-79; Pittsburgh Pirates, 1979-85; Los Angeles Dodgers, 1985-87; Detroit Tigers, 1987.

★ Won four batting titles
★ Socked 3 homers in one game in 1987
★ Hit .375 in the 1979 World Series
★ Batted .300 or better seven times
★ Batted a career-high .354 in 1975
★ Played in three World Series

MAJOR LEAGUE TOTALS

G	AB	H	BA	2B	3B	HR	R	RBI	SB
1,806	6,594	2,008	.305	348	34	163	920	860	174

MICKEY MANTLE

In these days of multiyear contracts and baby-faced players asking for instant wealth, it's hard to believe that one of the greatest players of the last 40 years cost the New York Yankees just $1,000. That was the signing bonus that bought the services of Mickey Mantle, an incredibly gifted high school boy from a small town in Oklahoma. Mantle's father was a onetime semipro player who loved the game and had spent years drilling his son on baseball fundamentals.

Yankees scout Tom Greenwade discovered Mantle by accident while driving through Oklahoma to recruit a young shortstop several towns away. Greenwade spotted Mantle en route and stayed to watch the star of the Baxter Springs Whiz Kids semipro team. The youngster was nicknamed "The Commerce Comet" because that was the town he hailed from. Mantle thrilled the scout by hitting 3 home runs—2 of them left-handed and one from the right side. Because Mantle was still in high school, Greenwade couldn't seal a deal on the spot. The Yankees got back to him after graduation, however, and gave him $500 to play the rest of the summer on a Class-D league team in Independence, Missouri.

Mantle struggled with playing shortstop during his initial minor league season. The result was a shocking 55 errors, which obscured his fine .383 average. It took special tutoring from ex-Yankee Tommy Henrich to turn Mantle into a first-class outfielder.

Mantle's first full season came with the 1952 Yankees. He exploded for 23 homers, 87 RBI, and a .311 batting average. Versus the Dodgers in the 1952 World Series, Mantle led New York's seven-game triumph with 10 hits for a .345 average. His seventh-game homer provided the go-ahead run in the Yanks 4-2 title win.

One of Mantle's greatest achievements was his triple crown in 1956. He topped the American League with 52 homers, 130 RBI, and a .353 average. Additionally, he led the junior circuit with a .705 slugging percentage and 132 runs scored. Mantle hit 3 homers in New York's World Series win over the Dodgers and won his first Most Valuable Player award (two more came in 1957 and 1962).

Mantle missed winning the MVP in 1961 by just four votes. He had clubbed 54 homers and 128 RBI, while batting .317 with league leads in home run percentage (10.5), runs scored (132), bases

on balls (126), and slugging percentage (.687). He was beaten out of both the MVP and the homer derby by teammate Roger Maris, who hit a single-season record of 61 homers. The baseball world was shocked, having assumed that Mantle was the only candidate to break Babe Ruth's single-season record of 60. Sportswriters dubbed the pair "the M & M boys." During Mantle's career he finished second in MVP balloting three times and wound up fifth on another occasion.

Playing in pain was an everyday reality for the Yankee slugger. The injuries started early. In the 1951 World Series Mantle, who was playing right field, tried to avoid colliding with center fielder Joe DiMaggio while chasing a fly ball from Willie Mays. In slowing up Mantle tripped on an uncapped drain, tearing cartilage in his knee. Three knee operations, pulled muscles, and other injuries

hampered Mantle throughout his career. Mantle's ailments began in high school, when he was diagnosed with osteomyelitis, a bone disease that causes pain and stiffness.

One of Mantle's biggest sources of pride must come from his World Series achievements. From a total of 12 World Series appearances, Mantle accumulated several records. He ranks first in history in the following categories: home runs (18), runs scored (42), RBI (40), bases on balls (43), and strikeouts (54). He places second in games (65), at-bats (230), and hits (59).

Mantle's long-ball feats reached everywhere during his career—he was the first person ever to hit a home run in the huge Houston Astrodome. The Astros inaugurated their new stadium on April 9, 1965, when Mantle slugged his homer during an exhibition game. In 1964 he tied a record by homering at least once in every American League park.

On June 8, 1969, two of the game's greatest players—center fielders DiMaggio and Mantle—stood together in Yankee Stadium to be honored in a special ceremony. Each man presented a plaque to the other, plaques that are now displayed in Monument Park in the stadium outfield. During the ceremony Mantle's uniform number (7) was retired. His plaque, in part, reads: "A magnificent Yankee .... The most popular player of his era .... In recognition of his true greatness in the Yankee tradition and for his unequaled courage."

The only tribute capable of topping this honor came in 1974, when hurler Whitey Ford, Mantle's faithful teammate and long-time friend, shared the spotlight when they were both inducted into the Hall of Fame.

CAREER HIGHLIGHTS
MICKEY CHARLES MANTLE

Born: October 20, 1931   Spavinaw, OK
Height: 5'11"   **Weight:** 195 lbs.   **Batted:** Both   **Threw:** Right
Outfielder, first baseman: New York Yankees, 1951-68.

- ★ Has the eighth-highest homer total in history (536)
- ★ Played in 12 World Series
- ★ Won the 1956 triple crown
- ★ Is first in World Series homers, RBI, and runs scored
- ★ Won three MVP awards
- ★ Elected to the Hall of Fame in 1974

MAJOR LEAGUE TOTALS

G	AB	H	BA	2B	3B	HR	R	RBI	SB
2,401	8,102	2,415	.298	344	72	536	1,677	1,509	153

Named after Mickey Cochrane, Mickey Mantle was the most powerful switch-hitter in baseball. He twice hit over 50 homers, led the A.L. in homers four times, and tied a record for belting a homer in every American League park.

HEINIE MANUSH

Heinie Manush had six talented brothers who also played pro baseball, but Heinie topped all with a 17-year career in the majors that paved the way to eventual membership in the Hall of Fame.

Manush journeyed west in his late teens to Salt Lake City, where he became an apprentice plumber and first baseman of the company baseball team. Manush grew weary of pipefitting, though his older brother was also in the business. His hitting feats captured the attention of local baseball scouts, and in 1921 the big slugger signed a minor league contract with Edmonton of the Western Canadian League. His solid .321 batting mark with a league-leading 9 home runs earned Manush a promotion to Omaha of the Western Association. There he batted even better: .376 with 20 home runs and 245 total hits. The next season he jumped into the major leagues as an outfielder with the Detroit Tigers, batting .334 with 103 hits in his rookie season. Manush later said that he benefited greatly from the hitting advice of veteran teammates Harry Heilmann and Ty Cobb. As "The Georgia Peach" slowed down, Manush got more playing time.

Although the Alabama native saw his average drop to .289 in his sophomore campaign, he hit 9 homers and 68 RBI. Manush batted .303 in 1925, then won his only batting title with a .378 mark in 1926. When his average dropped to .298 in 1927, Manush was traded to the St. Louis Browns with Lu Blue for Chick Galloway, Elam Vangilder, and Harry Rice on December 2, 1927.

In his first season with the Browns Manush was tops in the league in doubles (47) and hits (241). He drove in a career-high 108 RBI to complement his 13 homers. Manush kept his league lead in doubles in 1929 with 45, hitting .355. After 49 games with the 1930 Browns, General Crowder and Manush were traded to the Washington Senators for Goose Goslin on June 13. Manush was a prime reason why the Senators won the American League pennant in 1933. He hit .336 with league leads in triples (17) and hits (221). A 33-game hitting streak highlighted Manush's career. Although he had just 5 homers, Manush drove in 94 runs. In the World Series the New York Giants defeated the Senators in five games. Manush managed just 2 hits in the competition. He earned the dubious honor of becoming the first player to be ejected from a World Series game.

Manush was named to the All-Star team for the only time in his career in 1934. He earned the honor with a .349 average, 11 homers, and 89 RBI. Manush's slugging average was above .500 for the fifth time in his career.

Manush played with six teams and was among the top hitters for most of his career, which spanned baseball's golden years of the 1920s to the lean years of the Depression. Perhaps one of the reasons that Manush played for so many different teams was because several clubs experienced financial difficulties during the 1930s and were forced to sell their better players to those teams fortunate enough to escape financial disaster. Manush proved to be a tremendous asset for most of the clubs he played for.

The Alabama hitter compiled a lifetime batting average of .330 and hit over .300 for 11 of his 15 full major league seasons. In six seasons he batted over .340, and he scored 100 or more runs six times during his career. The big lefthander, checking in at 6-foot-1 and 200 pounds, won one batting title and was among the league leaders on several other occasions. More of a line-drive hitter than a home run hero, Manush banged more triples (160) than round-trippers (110) during his career.

Manush was involved in two of the closest battles for the batting crown in baseball history. In 1926 he robbed Babe Ruth of the triple crown by going 6-for-9 in a season-ending doubleheader to record a lofty .378 batting average to overtake Ruth for the batting title. Two years later, while with the St. Louis Browns, Manush duplicated his career-high .378 mark, only to lose the batting crown by 1 point to the Washington Senators' Goslin. Goslin won the batting title on the last day of the season, when he was playing Manush and the Browns.

On December 17, 1935, the Boston Red Sox gave Roy Johnson and Carl Reynolds to obtain Manush. He lasted there just one season and then served a brief stint with the Brooklyn Dodgers. Following a 10-game appearance with the Pirates in 1939, Manush played in the minor leagues until 1943. He later enjoyed some success as a manager in the minors, but spent the 1953 and 1954 seasons as a Washington Senators coach. Manush was elected to the Hall of Fame in 1964.

As a rookie for the Detroit Tigers, Heinie Manush played alongside Ty Cobb and Harry Heilmann, both of whom gave the young outfielder batting tips. Manush compiled a lifetime average of .330.

CAREER HIGHLIGHTS
HENRY EMMETT MANUSH

Born: July 20, 1901 Tuscumbia, AL **Died:** May 12, 1971
Height: 6'1" **Weight:** 200 lbs. **Batted:** Left **Threw:** Left
Outfielder: Detroit Tigers, 1923-27; St. Louis Browns, 1928-30; Washington Senators, 1930-35; Boston Red Sox, 1936; Brooklyn Dodgers, 1937-38; Pittsburgh Pirates, 1938-39.

- ★ Led the league in hits twice
- ★ Batted .300 or better for 11 seasons
- ★ Led the league in batting in 1926
- ★ Played in the 1933 World Series
- ★ Elected to the Hall of Fame in 1964

MAJOR LEAGUE TOTALS

G	AB	H	BA	2B	3B	HR	R	RBI	SB
2,008	7,654	2,524	.330	491	160	110	1,287	1,183	114

RABBIT MARANVILLE

Rabbit Maranville was a combination slick-fielding shortstop and diamond jester who fashioned a long, productive big league career that earned him an eventual spot in the Baseball Hall of Fame.

Maranville probably didn't look like a future Hall of Famer when he arrived in the majors with the Boston Braves in 1912. The 20-year-old infielder stood five feet five inches tall and weighed just 155 pounds. Though Maranville always claimed he gained the nickname "Rabbit" because he was so fast, others said it had more to do with his small size and large ears.

It was Maranville's glovework more than his hitting that made him one of the most respected shortstops in baseball for two decades. He collected 2,605 base hits during his long career but only once bettered .300. Upon retirement his lifetime average was .258. Of all the non-pitchers in the Hall of Fame, only two players—catcher Ray Schalk and home run slugger Harmon Killebrew—have lower career batting averages.

Despite his small size Maranville actually played catcher in high school in Springfield, Massachusetts. He began his pro career with nearby New Bedford in 1911. In 1912 Maranville was batting .283 with 128 hits and 29 stolen bases when he was obtained by the Boston Braves. The Braves gave up pitcher Bradley Hogg and $1,000 for Maranville. After 26 games that season, Maranville beat Frank O'Rourke out of the starting shortstop's job.

Maranville was the spark plug shortstop of the famous 1914 "Miracle Braves," a team that was mired in last place on July 4 but came back to capture the National League pennant and sweep the mighty Philadelphia Athletics in the World Series. That year Maranville batted only .246 with 4 home runs, but he paced his championship club with 78 RBI. At shortstop Maranville made a league-leading 65 errors; however, he was also first in chances per game (6.7), double plays (92), putouts (407), and assists (574). In the 1914 World Series Maranville batted .308 with 4 hits, 3 RBI, and 2 stolen bases.

After six seasons Maranville was traded from the Braves to the Pittsburgh Pirates. The Bucs gave up Billy Southworth, Fred Nicholson, Walter Barbare, and $15,000 to get the slick-fielding shortstop. Maranville logged four seasons with Pittsburgh. In 1921 he hit .294 in 153 games. The following season he played in a career-high 155 games, batting a career-high .295, with a league-leading 672 at-bats. In 1923 he led N.L. shortstops in fielding average, putouts, assists, and double plays. Offensively, his average remained respectable at .277. Pittsburgh missed the 1924 pennant by just three games, finishing at 90-63. Maranville moved to second base for a majority of the season. Even at his new position, he topped the league in fielding average, double plays, and assists. At bat Maranville hit .266 with 71 RBI (the second-highest total in his career).

Maranville got some managerial experience while he was playing for the Chicago Cubs in 1925. He piloted the team only briefly, winding up with a 23-30 record.

It looked as though Maranville's playing career was over when Brooklyn released him after only one season in August 1926. When no other team picked him up on waivers, Maranville went down to Rochester of the International League to prove that he could still play. The St. Louis Cardinals were impressed and gave him a second chance in the majors. He became the team's starting shortstop and helped the team to a pennant. Maranville hit .308 in the 1928 World Series. The Braves reacquired Maranville for the 1929 season, and he played his final six seasons back in Boston.

Although Maranville was a tough, hard-nosed competitor in the clutch, he was also known as a clown. He chased outfielders who robbed him of hits, mimicked umpires and managers, came to the plate with a coat and umbrella, and slid between the legs of umpires—which made him immensely popular with stadium crowds.

Off the field his reputation for mischief was even greater, and his stunts were more dangerous. Once he dove out of his hotel window into a shallow pool below. Another time he found himself locked out of his room and crawled along a narrow ledge outside the 12th floor and climbed in through the window. After the miracle 1914 season, Maranville joined several other players on a vaudeville tour.

In 2,670 games Maranville batted 10,078 times (13th highest in history). He had 2,605 hits, 177 triples (tying Stan Musial for 20th place on the all-time list), and 1,255 runs scored. He is among the all-time leaders in various fielding categories for shortstops. His 5,139 career putouts rank first for shortstops, while his 2,154 games at short rank fifth. Following the end of his major league career in 1935, he managed East Coast minor league teams for six seasons.

CAREER HIGHLIGHTS
WALTER JAMES VINCENT MARANVILLE

Born: November 11, 1891 Springfield, MA **Died:** January 5, 1954
Height: 5'5" **Weight:** 155 lbs. **Batted:** Right **Threw:** Right
Infielder: Boston Braves, 1912-20, 1929-33, 1935; Pittsburgh Pirates, 1921-24; Chicago Cubs, 1925; Brooklyn Dodgers, 1926; St. Louis Cardinals, 1927-28.
Manager: Chicago Cubs, 1925.

★ Collected 2,605 career hits
★ Led the N.L. in at-bats in 1922
★ Set an all-time record with 672 at-bats without a home run in 1922

★ Played for 23 major league seasons
★ Batted .308 in two World Series
★ Elected to the Hall of Fame in 1954

MAJOR LEAGUE TOTALS

G	AB	H	BA	2B	3B	HR	R	RBI	SB
2,670	10,078	2,605	.258	380	177	28	1,255	884	291

Fun-loving Rabbit Maranville once toured the vaudeville circuit with several other ballplayers. While demonstrating his basestealing technique to the audience, he slid off the stage into the orchestra pit and broke his leg.

JUAN MARICHAL

While Sandy Koufax was the game's top lefthand pitcher during the 1960s, Juan Marichal was the premier righthander. Spending all but two seasons of his 16-year career with the San Francisco Giants, Marichal compiled 243 lifetime wins, 2,303 strikeouts, and a 2.89 ERA.

Supposedly, Marichal got his start in the game playing with a homemade baseball. He dropped out of high school to play ball, first on an amateur level and later professionally in the Dominican Republic. The Giants discovered Marichal's talents and needed only a $500 bonus to sign him to a contract.

In 1958 Marichal made his pro debut with Michigan City of the Midwest League. He led the league in wins (21), innings pitched (245), and ERA (1.87). Marichal advanced to Springfield of the Eastern League in 1959 and again topped the league with 18 wins and 271 innings pitched, as well as 208 strikeouts and a 2.39 ERA. He needed only a half-season with Tacoma of the Pacific Coast League to earn a permanent promotion to the San Francisco roster. In Tacoma Marichal quickly won 11 out of 18 games to get the call-up.

In Marichal's first start in the majors, he pitched seven innings of no-hit ball, gave up a single in the eighth, and recorded a one-hit shutout over the Philadelphia Phillies. He finished the year with a fine 6-2 mark accompanied by a 2.66 ERA.

For the next 12 years, Marichal never had a losing season. He won more than 25 games three times in his career, and in six seasons he recorded more than 200 strikeouts. In 13 complete seasons in the majors, his ERA was under the 3.00 mark eight times. Twice he led the league in shutouts. Selected to play in ten All-Star games, he was named MVP in one of them and was the winning pitcher in two others. In 1963 he threw a no-hitter against the Houston Colt .45s. Marichal soon became known for his trademark high leg kick delivery and his huge assortment of pitches.

The man called "The Dominican Dandy" contributed 18 wins to San Francisco's 1962 pennant efforts but pitched only four innings in the World Series due to an injured finger. The next year Marichal was 25-8 with a league-leading 321.1 innings pitched. He won 21 games in 1964 and topped the league with 22 complete games.

Marichal was a consistent big winner for the Giants. Maybe that was why he

was always smiling, resulting in a second nickname of "Laughing Boy." In 1965 he collected 21 more victories. Although he won 25 games in 1966, Marichal narrowly missed the league lead due to Sandy Koufax's 27 triumphs. The weak-hitting Marichal had unusual success as a batter in 1966. He belted one of his 4 career homers and had 28 hits and a .250 average. He posted a career-high 26-9 season in 1968, along with a personal best of 30 complete games. During Marichal's final 20-win season in 1969, he hurled for a career-low ERA of 2.10 and a league-leading 8 shutouts.

After 12 winning seasons Marichal fell on hard times in 1972. His record sank to 6-16. In 1973 he still struggled with an 11-15 mark. Long-time Giants fans were shocked when Marichal was sold to the Boston Red Sox on December 7, 1973. The veteran righty spent one year in the American League, going 5-1 in 11 games. He was released

and then he hooked up with the Los Angeles Dodgers for just two games before retiring in early 1975.

Marichal retired with a career record of 243-142 for a .631 winning percentage. Highlights of Marichal's pitching career include 52 lifetime shutouts, 244 complete games, and a 2.89 ERA. Some of the many records he holds with the San Francisco Giants include most lifetime wins, most lifetime shutouts, most career complete games, most lifetime strikeouts, and most innings pitched in a career. He even ranks in the top six in eight different all-time Giants pitching categories, placing him in the company of New York Giants immortals Christy Mathewson and Carl Hubbell.

The only blemish on Marichal's record was an unfortunate episode in 1965, when he attacked Los Angeles Dodgers catcher John Roseboro with a baseball bat during an argument. Marichal thought Roseboro's return throw to the pitching mound was deliberately aimed to hit him as he stood in the batter's box. It was one of the most publicized fights in baseball history and resulted in Marichal being slapped with a nine-day suspension and a $1,750 fine, the severest penalty levied in the National League up to that time.

The incident may have delayed Marichal's election to the Baseball Hall of Fame, which finally came in 1983. Marichal denied the suggestion and said that he had become friends with Roseboro after retirement. Since his retirement Marichal has farmed in his native country. He has also served as a successful scout for the Oakland Athletics, signing several Latin American prospects.

CAREER HIGHLIGHTS
JUAN ANTONIO SANCHEZ MARICHAL

Born: October 20, 1937   Laguna Verde, Dominican Republic
Height: 6'0" **Weight:** 185 lbs.   **Batted:** Right   **Threw:** Right
Pitcher: San Francisco Giants, 1960-73; Boston Red Sox, 1974; Los Angeles Dodgers, 1975.

* Won 20 or more games six times
* Appeared in eight All-Star games
* Threw a no-hitter in 1963
* Led the N.L. in wins twice
* Won 25 or more games three times
* Elected to the Hall of Fame in 1983
* Pitched 300 or more innings per season four times

MAJOR LEAGUE TOTALS

G	IP	W	L	Pct.	SO	BB	ERA
471	3,506	243	142	.631	2,303	709	2.89

Juan Marichal began pitching for the San Francisco Giants in 1960 but did not have a losing season until 1972. Marichal averaged about 6 strikeouts per nine innings, while walking less than 2 batters.

ROGER MARIS

Everyone remembers Yankee slugger Roger Maris for his one season of glory, when he smashed a record-setting 61 home runs. However, Maris had a productive 12-year career in the major leagues—one that included participation on seven World Series teams.

Maris performed his amazing homer-hitting feat in 1961. Although he had established a reputation for powerful slugging in the minors, Maris didn't have the kind of record that would lead anyone to believe that he would have a shot at Babe Ruth's single-season mark of 60 home runs. Maris didn't even hit his first home run that year until the 11th game; but then he went on a tear. By the time home run number 25 was launched, Maris was on a pace to tie the record.

The shy slugger with the flat-top haircut was not prepared for the media hoopla that surrounded him the rest of the season. Adding to the stress was the fact that much of the baseball world seemed to be rooting against him, so great was the fans affection for the great Bambino. Baseball Commissioner Ford Frick increased the pressure by ruling that for Maris to be recognized as the single-season home run champ, he would have to break the record in 154 games, the same number Ruth played during the 1927 record-setting season. (The schedule was increased to 162 games in 1961.)

When that deadline passed, Maris was stuck on home run number 58. The record-breaking 61st homer came dramatically on the final day of the 1961 season. Maris slammed a fourth-inning home run off Boston's Tracy Stallard to win the game 1-0. The 34-year-old record was finally shattered, but Frick required that the feat be noted in the record books with an asterisk explaining that Maris had needed an additional eight games to establish the mark.

Although the Yankees whipped the Cincinnati Reds in five World Series games that year, the record-setting ordeal had sapped Maris' strength and spirit. He won the third game 3-2 with a ninth-inning homer off Bob Purkey, but he had just one other hit in the entire Series and batted only .105. The stress of dealing with the media and an angry public had tortured Maris throughout the year. His hair had even begun falling out due to the pressure.

Following his 1961 bonanza Maris was awarded a second Most Valuable Player award. He had earned his first MVP trophy the previous season by clubbing 39 home runs and recording a league-leading 112 RBI.

Maris hadn't begun his career with the New York Yankees. He grew up in Fargo, North Dakota, the son of a railroad worker who moved frequently. In Fargo Maris was a star in four sports. He was an excellent runner and shot putter and also played basketball. As a football halfback, he received a half-dozen college scholarship offers after leading the state in scoring his senior year. Instead he played American Legion baseball, winning MVP honors in a state tournament. He received tryouts from both the Cleveland Indians and the Chicago Cubs. Maris declined an immediate $15,000 bonus offer from the Tribe and tried to play football at the University of Oklahoma. After one week he changed his mind and accepted Cleveland's offer.

After one and a half seasons with the Indians beginning in 1957, Cleveland traded him to the Kansas City Athletics in early 1958. His combined homer total for the season was 28. In 1959 an appendectomy hampered Maris for the rest of the season. On December 11, 1959, the Yankees obtained Maris in a seven-player trade. He was the left-handed power they wanted to complement Mickey Mantle.

When the New York Yankees traded Maris to the St. Louis Cardinals on December 8, 1966, all the Yankees could get for their once-beloved slugger was a young unknown infielder named Charley Smith. Maris had batted a career low of .233 in 1966, and many fans thought he was washed up. He surprised the skeptics with two vital seasons that led the Redbirds to a 1967 world championship and a 1968 National League pennant.

In 1967 he batted .261 with 9 homers and 55 RBI in 125 games. In the outfield he made just 2 errors for a shining .991 fielding percentage. (Maris had won his only Gold Glove in 1960.) The Cardinals topped the Boston Red Sox in the 1967 World Series in a seven-game struggle. Maris paced the Cardinals attack with 10 hits (one a homer), a team-leading 7 RBI, and a .385 average.

Following his retirement Maris ran an Anheuser-Busch beer distribution franchise in Gainsville, Florida. The Yankees rewarded Maris by retiring his uniform number (9) before the first game of the 1985 season. Mickey Mantle was present at the emotional ceremony. Maris had been diagnosed with cancer in 1983 and battled the disease for two years before dying on December 14, 1985. He was 51 years old.

CAREER HIGHLIGHTS
ROGER EUGENE MARIS

Born: September 10, 1934 Hibbing, MN **Died:** December 14, 1985
Height: 6'0" **Weight:** 197 lbs. **Batted:** Left **Threw:** Right
Outfielder: Cleveland Indians, 1957-58; Kansas City Athletics, 1958-59; New York Yankees, 1960-66; St. Louis Cardinals, 1967-68.

- ★ Set a single-season record with 61 homers in 1961
- ★ Had five seasons of 25-plus homers
- ★ Topped the A.L. in RBI and slugging percentage in 1960

- ★ Led the A.L. with 142 RBI and 132 runs scored in 1961
- ★ Played on seven World Series teams
- ★ Won consecutive MVP awards in 1960 and 1961

MAJOR LEAGUE TOTALS

G	AB	H	BA	2B	3B	HR	R	RBI	SB
1,463	5,101	1,325	.260	195	42	275	826	851	21

After Roger Maris broke Babe Ruth's record of 60 homers in one season, the media hounded him with comparisons to the Yankee legend for much of his career. An anguished Maris responded, "I don't want to be Babe Ruth."

RUBE MARQUARD

When he was born in Cleveland in 1889, his birth certificate read Richard LeMarquis, but he was known to a whole generation of fans as Rube Marquard. Supposedly, the tall lefthander's last name was changed by a newspaperman for ease of pronunciation and spelling, and his nickname was provided by another writer who saw a resemblance to pitcher Rube Waddell.

Growing up in Cleveland was an ideal situation for a young boy wanting to take up baseball as a career. Serving as a batboy for barnstorming Cleveland players gave Marquard the chance to rub elbows with the big names in the sport. One of the players helped Marquard get a tryout with a club in Waterloo, Iowa, when he was only 16 years old. After pitching one game there, Marquard returned to Cleveland because Waterloo wanted him to play without a contract. The talented lefty worked in an ice cream factory until he landed a job with another team. His father strongly advised his son to get an education, and when young Marquard insisted on playing ball instead, the two were on terse terms for the next decade.

Marquard was pitching for Indianapolis in the American Association in 1908 and on his way to a 28-victory season when he attracted the attention of scouts from nearly every team in the majors. On September 5 Indianapolis sent Marquard to the mound against Columbus, announcing that the left-hander's contract would go to the highest bidder. When the bidding was completed, Marquard was a member of the New York Giants and Indianapolis was $11,000 richer for the transaction.

At the Polo Grounds in his first major league appearance, the nervous rookie gave up 4 base hits and 2 walks in five innings. The newspaper labeled Marquard "the $11,000 lemon" after his rocky start.

Marquard struggled with the Giants for two more seasons, winning only 5 games while losing 13 in 1909 and going 4-4 in 1910. Then he turned things around in 1911, winning 24 and losing just 7 for a sparkling percentage of .774, which was tops in the National League. It was the first of three consecutive seasons of more than 20 wins for Marquard and, not coincidentally, the first of three consecutive pennants for John McGraw's Giants. Marquard enjoyed his best season in 1912, when he won his first 19 starts in a row, a record that stands to this day. He fin-

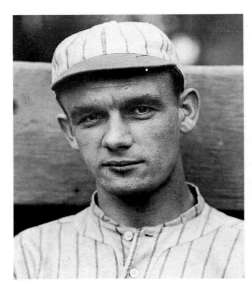

ished the season with a career-high, league-leading 26 victories. The following year Marquard continued to be one of the biggest winners of the 1913 season. He was 23-10 with a 2.50 ERA. Surprisingly, Marquard was one of the few players who never had any disagreements with the feisty manager. Of course, Marquard was also one of the few players willing to obey the team rules of no drinking, no smoking, and making curfew.

In 1915 Marquard spun a no-hitter against the Brooklyn Dodgers, but he wasn't winning at his usual pace. He had ended the 1914 season with a disappointing 12-22 record. The Giants were used to winning, so Marquard felt undue pressure to perform. Actually, Marquard became one of the few players in history to arrange his own trade. Manager McGraw allowed the 25-year-old hurler to arrange his own deal, and Marquard called up Dodgers manager

"Uncle" Wilbert Robinson, who jumped at the opportunity to pay the Giants $7,500 for the young veteran.

In his first full season in Brooklyn in 1916, Marquard rebounded to a 13-6 record with a 1.58 ERA, helping the Dodgers to a pennant. He was 19-12 the following season. The Ohio native slumped to a league-leading 18 losses in 1918. He earned 10 wins in 1920 and the Dodgers collected their second pennant in five years with Marquard's aid. Marquard was dispatched to the Cincinnati Red Stockings on December 15, 1920, for Dutch Reuther. Cincinnati traded Marquard to the Boston Braves for Larry Kopf and Jack Scott on February 18, 1922. After earning 2 victories in 26 games during the 1925 season, Marquard retired with 201 lifetime wins. His final stats include 197 complete games, 31 shutouts and 19 saves. As a hitter Marquard batted .200 or better five times. Lifetime, he had 198 hits and 1 home run.

In World Series play Marquard was 2-5 lifetime for five teams. Both of his wins came in the 1912 Series, when his Giants lost to the Boston Red Sox in seven games. His complete-game wins came in the third and sixth games, by respective scores of 2-1 and 5-2. Marquard finished the Series with an 0.50 ERA.

Following his retirement from the big leagues, Marquard managed and pitched part-time for four minor league teams through 1930. He even tried umpiring in the Eastern League for one year. He lived in Baltimore, Maryland, for nearly all of his last 50 years. Marquard was elected to the Hall of Fame in 1971 and died of cancer on June 1, 1980. He was 90 years old.

CAREER HIGHLIGHTS
RICHARD WILLIAM LeMARQUIS

Born: October 9, 1889 Cleveland, OH **Died:** June 1, 1980
Height: 6'3" **Weight:** 180 lbs. **Batted:** Both **Threw:** Left
Pitcher: New York Giants, 1908-15; Brooklyn Dodgers, 1915-20; Cincinnati Reds, 1921; Boston Braves, 1922-25.

- ★ Pitched in five World Series
- ★ Led the league with 26 wins in 1912
- ★ Established a record by winning his first 19 starts in 1912
- ★ Was a three-time 20-game winner
- ★ Topped the league in strikeouts in 1911
- ★ Elected to the Hall of Fame in 1971

MAJOR LEAGUE TOTALS

G	IP	W	L	Pct.	SO	BB	ERA
536	3,306	201	177	.532	1,593	858	3.08

Rube Marquard's best years came between 1911 and 1913 when he pitched for the New York Giants. Winning over 20 games in each of those seasons, Marquard was a major factor in the Giants' three straight pennant wins.

EDDIE MATHEWS

Eddie Mathews was the only member of the Braves who played with the franchise while it was based in Boston, Milwaukee, and Atlanta. He teamed with fellow Hall of Famer Hank Aaron to form one of the most awesome power-hitting combos in major league history. In 1967, in the twilight of his career, Mathews became just the seventh player in baseball history to hit 500 home runs. He finished his career with 512 round-trippers, tying him with Ernie Banks for 11th place on the all-time list and making him one of the most popular third sackers in history. As teammates, Mathews and Aaron had a shared total of 863 four-baggers, making them one of the most prolific long-ball twosomes of the 20th century.

During a 17-year major league career that stretched from 1952 to 1968, Mathews was one of the most consistent power hitters in the National League. For nine straight seasons, from 1953 to 1961, he socked over 30 home runs a year. The big third baseman, who was a favorite among Milwaukee fans, led the league in home runs twice. His 47 homers in 1953 established a record for third basemen that stood until Mike Schmidt broke it more than two decades later.

Mathews batted around .280 during his heyday and finished with a .271 mark. Born in Texarkana, Texas, he was one of the most feared batters in baseball. He hit 2 or more homers in a game on 49 occasions, ranking him sixth on the all-time list in that category.

The Braves discovered Mathews as a high school player in Santa Barbara, California. After graduation they signed him for a $6,000 bonus. Mathews began his pro career in 1949 in the North Carolina State League where he hit .353 with 17 home runs. Mathews spent his next two seasons in Atlanta (which was a Braves minor league affiliate at the time). In 1950 Mathews batted .286 with 32 homers and 106 RBI. After just 37 games with Atlanta in 1951, Mathews finished the season with Milwaukee (then an American Association minor league club). He came up to the major leagues in 1952, the Braves final season in Boston. That year Mathews became the first rookie ever to crack 3 home runs in one contest. He finished the season with 25 round-trippers.

During his sophomore season of 1953, Mathews won the league home run title with 47 dingers. He batted .302 with a career best of 135 RBI

while playing in all 154 games. Mathews led the senior circuit in bases on balls for the first of four seasons in 1955, earning 109 free passes. His season was highlighted by 41 homers and 101 RBI.

Milwaukee won its only world championship in 1957. Mathews contributed 32 homers, 94 RBI, and a .292 average to the effort. He batted only .227 in the World Series, with 5 hits, but his two-run homer in the ninth inning of the fourth game gave the Braves an important 7-5 win, evening the Series at two games apiece. The Braves made a return trip to the Series in 1958, only to lose to the Yanks. Mathews fueled the pennant drive with 31 homers and 77 RBI. In 1959 Mathews had a league-leading 46 homers, 114 RBI, and a .306 average.

Mathews was a prime reason why the Braves franchise was so successful during the 1950s. While the team won National League pennants only in 1957

and 1958, they finished in second place in 1953, 1956, 1959, and 1960. The 1956 squad lost the pennant by one game, while the 1959 team missed the pennant by two, losing a postseason playoff to the Los Angeles Dodgers.

Mathews was traded to Houston with Sandy Alomar and Arnie Umbach for Dave Nicholson and Bob Bruce on December 31, 1966. He played just 101 games with the Astros before getting dispatched to the Detroit Tigers. Mathews served there as a backup infielder but got to participate in the team's 1968 world championship during his final season. Mathews ended his career with a .271 average, 2,315 hits, 1,509 runs scored, and 1,453 RBI. He ranks behind only Aaron in nine all-time Braves offensive categories. His .517 career slugging percentage as a Brave is third best, behind Aaron and Wally Berger.

Following his retirement as a player Mathews became the Braves manager in late 1972, replacing Luman Harris for the final 50 games of the season. The team finished at 23-27 in fourth place under Mathews. In 1973 he piloted the Braves to a 76-85 record, good for fifth place in the Western Division. Mathews was replaced as Braves skipper in 1974, when the team had a 50-49 mark.

The Braves honored Mathews by retiring his uniform number (41) in 1967. The nine-time All-Star was only the second player in Braves history to receive the honor. Since then Aaron and pitcher Phil Niekro have been the only other team members to get such recognition. The Hall of Fame elected Mathews in 1978.

CAREER HIGHLIGHTS
EDWIN LEE MATHEWS

Born: October 13, 1931   Texarkana, TX
Height: 6'1"   **Weight:** 190 lbs.   **Batted:** Left   **Threw:** Right
Third baseman: Boston Braves, 1952; Milwaukee Braves, 1953-65; Atlanta Braves, 1966; Houston Astros, 1967; Detroit Tigers, 1967-68. Manager: Atlanta Braves, 1972-74.

- ★ Hit 512 homers in his career
- ★ Drove in 100 or more runs five times
- ★ Played in three World Series
- ★ Topped the 40-homer mark four times
- ★ Led the N.L. in walks four times
- ★ Elected to the Hall of Fame in 1978
- ★ Became the first rookie to hit 3 homers in one game

MAJOR LEAGUE TOTALS

G	AB	H	BA	2B	3B	HR	R	RBI	SB
2,391	8,537	2,315	.271	354	72	512	1,509	1,453	68

Eddie Mathews played most of his 17 seasons with the Braves, beginning with their last season in Boston and ending with their first year in Atlanta. He returned to the Braves to serve as manager from 1972 to 1974.

CHRISTY MATHEWSON

Christy Mathewson was the first pitcher elected to the Baseball Hall of Fame, becoming a charter member in 1936. During his illustrious 17-year career the man known as "Matty" compiled as many records on the mound as Ty Cobb and Babe Ruth did at the plate. Perhaps even more importantly, he was America's first real sports hero and did more to change baseball's rough image at the turn of the century than any other individual. Matty became a symbol of sportsmanship and a model of clean living. In fact, Mathewson was a man of such high morals that he even refused to pitch on Sunday.

Mathewson grew up in Pennsylvania and attended Bucknell College in 1898. He played three sports and soon drew the attention of pro scouts. With Taunton of the New England League in 1899, Mathewson got his first pro experience (winning 5 games). In 1900 Mathewson compiled a stunning 21-2 record with Norfolk of the Virginia League. He was traded to the Giants at the season's end for star pitcher Amos Rusie, who was at the end of his career. Rusie won only 1 game for the Reds.

Although Mathewson had a winless 0-2 record in five appearances in 1900, he soon established himself as a leading hurler in the senior circuit. In his rookie season of 1901 he compiled a 20-17 record with 36 complete games, 5 shutouts, and 221 strikeouts. He threw his first no-hitter that year, a 5-0 win against St. Louis on July 15.

Mathewson had what would be a rare losing season in 1902 (going 13-18). Still, Mathewson's 8 shutouts were tops in the National League. He rebounded in 1903 to register his first of four 30-win seasons. His 267 strikeouts led the league. He improved his sterling record to 33-12 in 1904. Mathewson didn't lead the league in victories until 1905, when his 31 wins (versus just 8 losses) paced the senior circuit. His .795 winning percentage, 1.27 ERA, 206 strikeouts, and 8 shutouts were other league highs that season. Mathewson earned the second no-hitter of his career on June 13, when he spun a 1-0 hitless gem against the Chicago Cubs.

Although Mathewson had a fine 1905 outing, his regular-season efforts were pale in comparison to his clutch performance in the World Series. Mathewson threw 3 complete-game shutouts to lead the Giants to a five-game Series victory over the Philadelphia Athletics. He beat Philadelphia ace Eddie Plank in the opener 3-0, allowing the A's just 4 hits. Matty pitched on only two days' rest in game three but yielded just 4 hits as his Giants coasted to a 9-0 victory. Two days later Mathewson secured the world championship for the Giants with a six-hitter. In 27 total innings Mathewson struck out 18 while walking just 1. He helped his own cause with 2 Series hits and a run scored.

While Mathewson won 22 games in 1906 and a league-leading 24 in 1907, the accomplishments seemed ordinary compared to Matty's past feats. But in 1908 the big Pennsylvanian was never better. He won a record 37 games, leading the league with a 1.43 ERA, 56 games, 44 games started, 34 complete games, 391 innings pitched, 259 strikeouts, and 11 shutouts.

The New York newsmen tagged Mathewson with his nickname. Writer (and ex-major leaguer) Sam Crane wrote, "Mathewson certainly is the Big Six of pitchers." The Big Six was the name of a famous fire engine in New York City.

Few fans may remember that Mathewson had a brother six years his junior who played very briefly in the major leagues. Henry Mathewson pitched in two games with the 1906 Giants, then pitched an inning in 1907. His lifetime record was 0-1.

Christy Mathewson's 372 career wins place him fourth on the all-time list. The big righty won 30 or more games four times, including three consecutive seasons. On 13 occasions Mathewson entered the 20-win circle. When Mathewson's 28 career saves are included in his lifetime totals, he had a hand in 400 wins.

His ERA was under 3.00 for 13 straight seasons and under 2.00 on five occasions. He topped the league in wins four times, in ERA five times, and in strikeouts five times. His 78 shutouts are the third-highest total in history. No one has ever matched his 4 World Series shutouts and 10 complete games. Mathewson was equally effective with a fastball or curve and frequently relied on his famous "fadeaway" pitch, a forerunner of the modern screwball.

Few pitchers of today could keep up with Mathewson's hitting, either. He finished his career with 362 hits, 7 homers, and a .215 average. In ten different seasons he batted .200 or better.

Mathewson moved to Cincinnati as player/manager in 1916, but near the end of the 1918 season (at the age of 37), he enlisted in the Army during World War I. Matty volunteered for chemical warfare service, and it's believed that his contact with nerve gas led to the tuberculosis that killed him in October 1925.

CAREER HIGHLIGHTS
CHRISTOPHER MATHEWSON

Born: August 12, 1880 Factoryville, PA **Died:** October 7, 1925
Height: 6'2" **Weight:** 195 lbs. **Batted:** Right **Threw:** Right
Pitcher: New York Giants, 1900-16; Cincinnati Reds, 1916. Manager: Cincinnati Reds, 1916-18.

- ★ Led the league in wins four times
- ★ Was 3-0 in the 1905 World Series
- ★ Established an N.L. 20th-century record with 37 wins in one season in 1908
- ★ Topped the league in strikeouts 5 times
- ★ Won 30 or more games four times
- ★ Elected to the Hall of Fame in 1936

MAJOR LEAGUE TOTALS

G	IP	W	L	Pct.	SO	BB	ERA
634	4,778	372	187	.665	2,502	838	2.13

In an era of hard-living, hard-drinking ballplayers, the great pitcher Christy Mathewson was a college man who sang in a glee club, belonged to a literary society, and served as a model of clean living.

GARY MATTHEWS

Even though Gary Matthews had a productive 17 years in major league baseball, he'll be best remembered for his contributions to the 1984 Chicago Cubs.

The power-hitting outfielder didn't have his best season with the '84 Cubs by any means. His 14 home runs, 82 RBI, and .291 average were surely respectable, but it was his team leadership that helped spark the Cubs to their first title since divisional play began in 1969. Matthews led the league with 103 bases on balls and 19 game-winning hits, both personal bests. He upped his average to .311 with 9 homers and 43 RBI after the All-Star break. He provided 7 home runs, 31 RBI, and 6 game-winning hits in the last two months of the season. Although he had just 3 hits in the five-game N.L.C.S. (which the Padres ultimately won), 2 of the hits were home runs. Both shots came in Chicago's 13-0 opening blowout of the Padres. Matthews wound up with a .200 batting average, including 5 RBI and 4 runs scored.

Matthews had been the Most Valuable Player in the 1983 N.L.C.S. between his Phillies and the Los Angeles Dodgers. During the 1983 season Matthews missed 30 games and finished with just 10 homers, 50 RBI, and a .258 average. However, he was reborn in postseason play. Matthews homered in the second, third, and fourth games of the League Series. His blast in game three highlighted a 3-for-5 effort as the Phils won by a 7-2 margin. Matthews' attractive postseason success made him a desirable player for the Cubs, who gave up Bill Campbell and Mike Diaz to get Matthews, outfielder Bobby Dernier, and pitcher Porfi Altamirano on March 27, 1984.

Matthews began as the Giants' top pick in the '68 draft and the 17th choice in that draft overall. Hitting .322 in 1969, he was named to the Midwest League's All-Star team. His batting dipped after that stellar debut to only .279 in 1970. Other improvements were in the making, however. In 1971 Matthews led his new Texas circuit in fielding with .984 (which was to remain his high mark until the incomplete, unflawed season of 1987), total bases (232), doubles (37), and RBI (86). He tied for the lead with 142 games and 10 sacrifice flies.

Still the Giants held out. The next year Matthews broke Dusty Rhodes' 1958 record by acquiring 108 RBI, 8 more than Rhodes. Hitting .313 in 136

games, he was called up in time to play 20 games with the Giants, slugging 4 homers and 14 RBI.

His .290 mark of the previous season rose to .300 during his official rookie year. He was only the fourth Giant ever to be named N.L. Rookie of the Year by both *The Sporting News* and the Baseball Writers Association of America.

Matthews kept up a steady offensive display for the Giants, which extended to keeping a cool head on the base paths, tempting pitchers with basestealing that almost always went to the two-digit mark. Still, when his time for free agency came in late 1976, the Atlanta Braves found a home for the mighty righty. Stealing a career-high 22 bases for the Braves, Matthews spent time on the disabled list with a bad shoulder. Even so, his 1977 marks (.283, 17 homers, and 64 RBI) nearly matched those of his 1978 season (.281, 18 homers, and 62 RBI).

In 1979 Matthews was finally named to an All-Star team. It took a .304 batting average and career highs in home runs (27) and hits (192). His hit production paced the league, as did his 34 doubles, and he enjoyed two different hitting streaks of 12 and 13 games each.

Management disputes with Matthews led the Braves to trade him for Phillies pitcher Bob Walk in 1980. Matthews ended the strike-shortened season with Player of the Month honors in September for his .330 batting average with 7 homers. His postseason play for the Phillies was brilliant in the 1983 pennant playoffs. He hit .429 in 14 at-bats. He fielded well during five games of Series play, but his average dropped to .250 in October.

Matthews was traded to the Chicago Cubs in 1984. After three acceptable but obviously declining years with the Cubs (including a nightmarish '85 season with arthroscopic knee surgery and a strained right quadricep), Matthews was traded in midseason 1987 for Mariners pitcher David Hartnett.

After that trade Matthews would end his career with a 45-game stint as a designated hitter. He batted just .235 in the experiment with 3 homers and 15 RBI. The Mariners made him a free agent on November 9, 1987. His decline seemed sudden. Just one year earlier Matthews had been a top hitter with the Cubs, clubbing 21 home runs and 46 RBI.

Matthews retired with 2,011 hits in 2,033 games. He hit 234 career homers with 978 RBI and batted .281. While his statistics don't merit election to the Hall of Fame, they do show that he was one of the most dependable players of the 1980s.

CAREER HIGHLIGHTS
GARY NATHANIEL MATTHEWS

Born: July 5, 1950   San Fernando, CA
Height: 6'3"   **Weight:** 205 lbs.   **Batted:** Right   **Threw:** Right
Outfielder: San Francisco Giants, 1972-76; Atlanta Braves, 1977-80; Philadelphia Phillies, 1981-83; Chicago Cubs, 1984-87; Seattle Mariners, 1987.

★ Played in the 1979 All-Star game

★ Hit in double figures for homers in 13 seasons

★ Collected a career-high 27 homers in 1979

★ Appeared in the 1983 World Series

★ Won the 1973 N.L. Rookie of the Year award

★ Batted .429 in the 1983 N.L. Championship Series

MAJOR LEAGUE TOTALS

G	AB	H	BA	2B	3B	HR	R	RBI	SB
2,033	7,147	2,011	.281	319	51	234	1,083	978	183

Though outfielder Gary Matthews' lifetime statistics will not get him into the Hall of Fame, Chicago Cubs fans will always remember him for the leadership he contributed to the pennant-winning 1984 Cubs team.

DON MATTINGLY

Not since the days of Mickey Mantle have the New York Yankees had a star shining so brightly as Don Mattingly. In the tradition of past Bronx Bombers like Lou Gehrig, Babe Ruth, and Joe DiMaggio, Mattingly has developed an amazing fan following after just six major league seasons. He has done it through consistent, high-quality play that rivals any big league first baseman of today.

For proof look at 1987 and 1988, viewed by most as a slump in the 28-year-old's career. His batting averages were .327 and .311 respectively. He notched 186 hits each year with 38 and 37 doubles. In 1987 Mattingly bashed 30 homers with 115 RBI; the next year, 18 dingers and 88 RBI. His fielding dropped from a league-leading percentage of .996 in 1987 to .993 in 1988, his second-worst percentage in the majors. In each season he tallied well over 1,200 putouts and 90-plus assists.

Most players dream of such "lousy" seasons. It is true, however, that these statistics pale in comparison with Mattingly's marks of 1984 to 1986, when "The Hit Man" came to the fore as the consummate all-around player.

Mattingly was signed by the Yankees in the 19th round of the June 5, 1979, free-agent draft, for a reported $22,000 bonus. Then 18 years old, he ended the season with flair for Oneonta of the New York-Penn League, claiming a .349 batting average as well as a bride.

Posted both in the outfield and at first base, Mattingly improved his marks in 1980 with Greensboro of the South Atlantic League. He was named the league Most Valuable Player. In 1981 Mattingly was named Yankees Minor League Player of the Year. For Nashville he batted .316 with 7 homers and 98 RBI. He proceeded to Triple-A ball in Columbus in 1982, becoming an All-Star outfielder in the International League. Then in September he arrived in the Big Apple: His debut consisted of seven games and a batting average that dropped from a minor league high of .315 to .167 in the majors.

Mattingly's official rookie season of 1983 began with much more promise: the James P. Dawson award as the top New York rookie at spring training and a place on the Yanks opening-day starting lineup. Still, he found himself back in Columbus in mid-April, where he continued to total top-notch stats until June 20, when he was called up for good to fill retiring Bobby Murcer's slot.

Four days later Mattingly muscled his first major league homer off wily left-hander John Tudor. That first year Mattingly even made an appearance at second base.

It's odd that Mattingly's rookie year passed with so little fanfare. Looking at his stats in 1984, it's hard to believe they belong to the same person. Mattingly's average zoomed 60 points from .283 in 1983 to a league-leading .343 the next season. His hits (207) and doubles (44) were also league highs. His defensive work prospered with a full season in the starting lineup. For the first of three consecutive seasons, *The Sporting News* named Mattingly American League Player of the Year.

There was no stopping the Indiana native after that. In 1985 he posted league highs in doubles (48), RBI (145), and fielding percentage (.995). *The Sporting News* named Mattingly the Major League Player of the Year in 1985, and he also earned the league's

MVP award. His 154 double plays tied for league best by a first sacker. It was the first year he played solely at first base, and he responded with a personal best of 35 homers.

For an encore Mattingly racked up another banner year for the 1986 Yankees. His batting average peaked at .352, with league highs in hits (238) and doubles (53). His 31 homers put him on the path of three straight seasons of 30-plus long balls. He led the league with 15 game-winning RBI (down from the previous year's 21), slugging percentage (.573), total bases (388), most sacrifice flies in a game (3), and most putouts and chances by a first baseman in nine innings (22). His doubles broke a team record set by Gehrig, while his hits erased the old team mark of 231 set by Hall of Famer Earle Combs. Gehrig, whose first-base position Mattingly plays so skillfully, is the only other Yankee to have produced 200 or more hits in three straight seasons. Gehrig did it in 1930-32; Mattingly did it in 1984-86.

Mattingly's rise to excellence was unhindered by arthroscopic knee surgery in 1985. A lack of speed forces Mattingly to get by on wits and determination. Mattingly has catlike quickness in the field, especially on 3-6-3 double plays.

Even in the years when he spent time on the disabled list, Mattingly was a record-setting performer. He had 2 doubles in an inning in 1987 and then hit homers in eight consecutive games that same year. He is a perennial Gold Glover, Silver Slugger, and All-Star—a truly amazing player. There is potential for many more phenomenal seasons to come.

CAREER HIGHLIGHTS
DONALD ARTHUR MATTINGLY

Born: April 20, 1961 Evansville, IN
Height: 6'0" **Weight:** 185 lbs. **Bats:** Left **Throws:** Left
Outfielder, first baseman: New York Yankees, 1982-89.

- ★ Was the A.L. batting champion in 1984
- ★ Voted A.L. MVP in 1985
- ★ Topped the A.L. with 145 RBI in 1985
- ★ Led the league in hits twice
- ★ Won four straight Gold Gloves
- ★ Hit a record 6 grand slams in 1987
- ★ Named to *The Sporting News* Silver Slugger team in 1985, 1986, and 1987

MAJOR LEAGUE TOTALS

G	AB	H	BA	2B	3B	HR	R	RBI	SB
1,015	4,022	1,300	.323	272	15	164	615	717	8

Baseball's golden boy during the mid-1980s, Don Mattingly won the American League batting title with a .343 mark in 1984 and MVP honors in 1985. In addition, he led the league in fielding percentage in 1987.

LEE MAY

It's easy to say that Lee May had a large impact during his 18 seasons in the major leagues from 1965 through 1982. In fact, the strapping slugger made an impact 354 times during his distinguished career. That's the number of home runs May belted for four different teams (the Cincinnati Reds, Houston Astros, Baltimore Orioles, and Kansas City Royals) during his tenure in the big leagues.

May started his career after he attended Miles College in Birmingham. He was discovered there by the Reds, who snared him with a $12,000 signing bonus. Despite the large bonus, May's road to the major leagues was a long one. He started with Tampa of the Florida State League in 1961, where he batted just .260 with no home runs in 26 games. Back in Tampa the following season May's average stayed the same, but his power production improved to 10 home runs and 65 RBI. Moving on to Rocky Mount of the Carolina League in 1963 May produced 18 homers, 80 RBI, and a .263 average.

In 1964 May played with Macon of the Southern League, where he had a .303 average with 25 home runs and a league-leading 110 RBI. After a banner year in 1965 with San Diego of the Pacific Coast League (34 home runs, 103 RBI, and a .321 average), May got a five-game tryout with the Reds. He went hitless in four pinch-hitting chances but scored a run.

May spent his sixth minor league season with Buffalo of the International League in 1966. There he hit .310 with 16 home runs and 78 RBI. He was called up late in the season for 25 games and batted .333 with 2 homers and 10 RBI. The Reds still had the talented Tony Perez as their starting first baseman; however, with a major juggling act, May was worked into the starting lineup starting in 1967. Perez moved from first base to third base, Tommy Helms moved from third base to second base, and second baseman Pete Rose moved to the outfield. For the next five years May owned the first base starting job in Cincinnati.

During a doubleheader on July 15, 1969, May had his greatest day ever at the plate. He belted 4 round-trippers and tallied 10 RBI. That season May clubbed 38 homers and accumulated a personal best of 110 RBI during a career high of 158 games played.

On November 29, 1971, May was involved in a seven-player swap between the Reds and the Houston Astros. May, second baseman Tommy Helms, and utility man Jimmy Stewart were sent to Houston in exchange for pitcher Jack Billingham, outfielders Ed Armbrister and Cesar Geronimo, and infielders Denis Menke and Joe Morgan. While the trade provided Cincinnati's foundation for "The Big Red Machine" that ruled the National League in the early 1970s, the trade was a tribute to May as well. The Astros, who play in the cavernous, homer-repelling Astrodome, were so anxious to obtain a quality power hitter like May that they were willing to part with a lot of talent to get him.

The Alabama native fared well in the long-ball department in the Astrodome, but it wasn't enough to guarantee a pennant for Houston. After three straight seasons of 30-plus homers with Cincinnati May got to prove himself with the Astros for three seasons. His homer totals were strong: 29 in 1972, 28 in 1973, and 24 in 1974. After leading the league with 145 strikeouts in 1972, he cut his Ks to 97 by 1974. During his final season with the Astros May joined a select group of hitters by smacking 2 homers in one inning.

The Baltimore Orioles gave up infielders Enos Cabell and Rob Andrews to obtain May and minor leaguer Jay Schlueter on December 3, 1974. With future Orioles first baseman Eddie Murray still a few years away, May was a welcome addition to a promising O's lineup.

May ended his sterling career by playing with the Kansas City Royals on a part-time basis in 1981 and 1982 before retiring. Unlike many stars, who retire after disastrous final seasons, May was a quality player until the end. During his 1982 finale with the Royals he hit .308 in 42 games, with 3 homers, 12 RBI, and 12 runs scored. He ended his career with 2,031 hits in 2,071 games, which included 340 doubles, 31 triples, and 1,244 RBI (in addition to his collection of home runs). May ranks high on the all-time homer list, but he's even higher on the career strikeout chart. May fanned 1,570 times in his career, the tenth-best (or worst) figure of all time. May's speed was limited, as evidenced by his 959 runs scored and 39 stolen bases. However, he compensated for any base-path shortcomings with his batting power. In 1971 May was a member of *The Sporting News* National League All-Star team.

Since his retirement Lee May has been active as a major league coach. Initially he served as a batting instructor for the Kansas City Royals. In 1989 he served as a Reds coach, working with old friends Perez, Helms, and Rose.

CAREER HIGHLIGHTS
LEE ANDREW MAY

Born: March 23, 1943 Birmingham, AL
Height: 6'3" **Weight:** 195 lbs. **Batted:** Right **Threw:** Right
First baseman, outfielder, designated hitter: Cincinnati Reds, 1965-71; Houston Astros, 1972-74; Baltimore Orioles, 1975-80; Kansas City Royals, 1981-82.

★ His 354 home runs rank 37th in history
★ Hit 19 or more homers for 12 straight seasons
★ Led the A.L. with 109 RBI in 1976
★ Belted double-digit homers in 13 straight seasons
★ Drove in 90 or more runs eight times
★ Batted .389 in the 1970 World Series

MAJOR LEAGUE TOTALS

G	AB	H	BA	2B	3B	HR	R	RBI	SB
2,071	7,609	2,031	.267	340	31	354	959	1,244	39

Slugger Lee May enjoyed his best day at the plate on July 15, 1969, when he belted 4 home runs and racked up 10 RBI. He went on to smash 38 home runs that season and drive in a personal best of 110 runs.

WILLIE MAYS

Willie Mays, "The Say Hey Kid," was a complete performer who astounded fans with his powerful home runs and delighted them with his speed on the base paths. His excellent glovework in center field matched his offensive abilities. He did it all with so much enthusiasm that he was one of the most popular major leaguers ever to put on a uniform.

The solid outfielder got his start in baseball in the now-defunct Negro Leagues, playing with the Birmingham Black Barons. As a 19-year-old, he was signed by the New York Giants organization (for a $6,000 bonus) and was called up to the big league club two years later. In his first season with Trenton he batted .353 in 81 games. Mays batted .435 with the Minneapolis Millers of the American Association before getting a permanent promotion to the Giants. Even though Mays was hitless in his first three starts, Giants manager Leo Durocher assured Mays that he'd remain the Giants starting center fielder for the rest of the season. With that vote of confidence, Mays ended up batting .274 with 20 home runs. During his banner debut he wound up as the National League Rookie of the Year, while helping the Giants to a league title. The Giants won the National League pennant against the Brooklyn Dodgers, thanks to Bobby Thomson's "shot heard 'round the world" homer. The rookie Mays was on deck when the historic blast was hit. With just one out as the difference, Mays could have decided the outcome of the game and the pennant.

Mays spent most of the 1952 and 1953 seasons in the U.S. Army, but he returned in 1954 to lead the Giants to another pennant. For his 41 home runs, 110 RBI, and league-leading .345 average, Mays was named the National League's Most Valuable Player.

Mays just kept getting better. He won another MVP award in 1965, when he walloped a league-leading (and career-high) 52 home runs. By the time he had finished his 22 major league seasons, he had accumulated 660 home runs, good enough for third on the all-time list. Only Hank Aaron and Babe Ruth have more. Mays slugged 20 or more homers for 17 seasons; in 11 years he hit over 30, and for 6 seasons he smashed 40 or more. He was named to a record 24 All-Star teams, won 11 Gold Glove awards, compiled 3,283 hits (becoming the tenth player to top the 3,000 mark), established numerous fielding records for outfielders, registered a .302 lifetime batting average, and was named Player of the Decade for the 1960s by *The Sporting News*.

As evidence of his all-around skills, Mays became the first player in major league history to compile 300 home runs and 300 stolen bases. He tallied 338 lifetime steals, including a career high of 40 in 1956. From 1956 through 1959 Mays was the senior circuit's champion basestealer. He stole 10 or more bases 11 times in his career. Many of his fielding plays are legendary, including his famous over-the-shoulder catch in the first game of the 1954 World Series to rob Cleveland's Vic Wertz of extra bases. Wertz's drive sailed 460 feet and two men were on base. Mays not only made the catch, he spun around and zipped the ball back into the infield quickly enough to keep the score tied at 2-2. While most outfielders caught fly balls above their heads, Mays liked to make basket-style catches around his waist.

Oddly enough, Mays never distinguished himself in postseason play. He batted .182 in the 1951 World Series versus the Yankees. When the Giants won the 1954 Series against the Cleveland Indians, Mays had only 4 hits. The Yankees beat the Giants again in the 1962 fall classic, with Mays compiling 7 hits for a .250 average. He finally belted his first postseason homer in the 1971 National League Championship Series versus Pittsburgh.

The San Francisco Giants shocked the baseball world by trading Mays to the New York Mets for pitcher Charlie Williams and $50,000 on May 11, 1972. Mays played in 69 games for the remainder of 1972, hitting .267. The trade was a nostalgic homecoming for Mays and fans. More than 20 years earlier Mays had starred in New York with the Giants. During his first Mets start against his former Giants team, Mays hit a game-winning homer. Mays was a part of the 1973 Mets team that won the National League pennant. Even though he couldn't hit anything like he did during his prime, his team leadership made an impact on the Mets. As one-time Cubs manager Charlie Grimm said of Mays years ago: "He can help a team just by riding on the bus with them." The veteran slugger was 1-for-3 in the National League Championship Series, and then he had 2 hits in seven World Series at-bats.

Mays received immediate induction into the Hall of Fame in 1979 by being named on 409 of the 432 ballots cast. He currently holds the title of special assistant to the president with the San Francisco Giants.

CAREER HIGHLIGHTS
WILLIE HOWARD MAYS

Born: May 6, 1931   Westfield, AL
Height: 5'11" **Weight:** 170 lbs. **Batted:** Right **Threw:** Right
Outfielder: New York Giants, 1951-57; San Francisco Giants, 1958-71; New York Mets, 1972-73.

- ★ Named the N.L. Rookie of the Year in 1951
- ★ Selected the N.L. MVP in 1954 and 1965
- ★ Hit 50-plus homers in a season twice
- ★ Played in four World Series
- ★ Named to 24 All-Star teams
- ★ Elected to the Hall of Fame in 1979
- ★ Hit 600 homers which ranks third on the all-time list

MAJOR LEAGUE TOTALS

G	AB	H	BA	2B	3B	HR	R	RBI	SB
2,992	10,881	3,283	.302	523	140	660	2,062	1,903	338

Willie Mays' remarkable talent for clubbing home runs and for fielding fast-flying balls to center field once prompted an announcer to say, "The only man who could have caught that ball just hit it."

BILL MAZEROSKI

The 1960 World Series between the New York Yankees and the Pittsburgh Pirates was one of the most unusual and exciting fall classics ever, and Bill Mazeroski was the hero whose effort would be remembered for years afterward.

The mighty Bronx Bombers exploded for 91 hits and 55 runs in the seven-game series; both records stand to this day. The Yankees had won three games by scores of 16-3, 10-0, and 12-0, while the Pirates had slipped by with scores of 6-4, 3-2, and 5-2. The final game was played in Pittsburgh on October 13, and the score was tied at 9-9 in the bottom of the ninth when second baseman Mazeroski hit a Ralph Terry offering over the left field wall for a home run, giving the Pirates a dramatic 10-9 triumph. The Pirates had been outscored by the Yankees 55-27 over seven games but still captured the world championship. Today one famous picture is chosen most often to represent that Series: It shows a grinning Mazeroski after his game-winning blast, waving to the crowd with one hand and holding his cap with the other as he trots around the bases. Ushers and jubilant fans are trailing behind him to home plate, where the rest of the team waits to greet him.

It was ironic that Mazeroski won the Series with his bat, because throughout his long career the scrappy competitor was more respected for his glovework than for his hitting. Mazeroski finished his distinguished career with just a .260 lifetime batting average but was the top-fielding second sacker in the league during his time.

Mazeroski played for 17 seasons in the big leagues, all of them with the Pirates. He began his pro career at age 17, straight out of high school in Ohio. His first season was as a shortstop for Williamsport of the Eastern League. There he hit .235 in 93 games. He began the 1955 season with the Hollywood Stars of the Pacific Coast League as a second baseman. After just 21 games (in which he fielded flawlessly), he was back with Williamsport. He upped his average to .293 back in the Eastern League, hitting 11 homers and 65 RBI. Mazeroski began the 1956 season with Hollywood, hitting .306 in 80 games before getting a permanent call-up to Pittsburgh.

In his 81-game debut with the Pirates Mazeroski hit .243. He replaced Johnny O'Brien (whose twin brother played on the same Pirates club) at sec-

ond base. During his first full season in 1957 "Maz" played in 148 games, hitting .283 with 8 homers and 54 RBI. He received his first All-Star invitation in 1958. His 19 homers, 68 RBI, and .275 average are three reasons why Mazeroski got the midseason invite. His fielding prowess began to show that season, as he led all National League second sackers in assists and chances.

Mazeroski had an off year in 1959, but he was in top form during the Pirates world championship season of 1960. The dauntless second baseman led the league in five defensive categories, including a sterling .989 fielding percentage. Offensively, Mazeroski chipped in with a .273 average, 11 homers, and 64 RBI. In the World Series Mazeroski batted .320 with 8 hits and a team-leading 5 RBI while fielding flawlessly. His two-run homer in the fourth inning provided the Bucs with a 6-4 victory in the Series opener.

From 1961 to 1968 his average danced between .251 and .271. He hit 10 or more homers in six campaigns (1958, 1960, 1961, 1962, 1964, and 1966), with a second-highest career effort of 16 dingers in 1966. That same year he had a career-best 82 RBI. Mazeroski's admirable career started winding down when Pirates rookie Dave Cash beat him out of his job in 1971. Mazeroski's team dedication was most evident in the final two years of his career, as he stuck around to help out as a backup infielder and pinch hitter. He appeared in the team's League Championship Series of 1970, 1971, and 1972 only in substitute roles, and he pinch-hit once in the 1971 Series against the Baltimore Orioles.

Mazeroski was an eight-time Gold Glove winner. He holds several major league records for second sackers, including most double plays in a single season (161 in 1966), most career double plays (1,706), most seasons with the league lead in assists (9), and most seasons leading the league in double plays (8). As a hitter, Mazeroski ended his career with 2,016 hits in 2,163 games, including 138 homers and 853 RBI. He leads the Pirates team today in games played at second base with 2,094. No second sacker before or since Mazeroski has played even 1,000 games there. He ranks fifth on the team in games played. Mazeroski's name appears in the top ten in nine different Pirates all-time offensive categories.

Following his retirement Mazeroski coached one year with the Pirates and two years as a minor league instructor for the Seattle Mariners. He now owns and operates a golf course and restaurant in Ohio. In 1987 the Pirates retired his uniform number (9).

CAREER HIGHLIGHTS
WILLIAM STANLEY MAZEROSKI

Born: September 5, 1936   Wheeling, WV
Height: 5'11"   **Weight:** 183 lbs.   **Batted:** Right   **Threw:** Right
Second baseman: Pittsburgh Pirates, 1956-72.

★ Won the 1960 World Series for Pittsburgh with a seventh-game homer

★ Won eight Gold Glove awards

★ Holds the all-time record for double plays by a second baseman (1,706)

★ Named *The Sporting News* Player of the Year in 1960

★ Was a seven-time All-Star

★ Is one of six Pirates to have played more than 2,000 games

★ Had his uniform number retired by the Pirates

MAJOR LEAGUE TOTALS

G	AB	H	BA	2B	3B	HR	R	RBI	SB
2,163	7,755	2,016	.260	294	62	138	769	853	27

Bill Mazeroski holds the record for most double plays by second sackers, with 1,706. He led the N.L. in double plays eight times, in assists nine times, and in putouts five times. He also won eight Gold Gloves.

WILLIE McCOVEY

It's obvious that a batter is feared and respected when he leads the league in intentional walks for four years in a row. Such was the case with Hall of Famer Willie McCovey, the National League's premier slugger in the late 1960s and the most popular San Francisco Giant ever.

Quiet McCovey was sometimes lost in the limelight of his flashier teammate, Willie Mays. At 6-foot-4 and 200 pounds, McCovey had the physical attributes to live up to his team's name.

McCovey's upbringing in a rough neighborhood in Mobile, Alabama, left him well prepared for any major league battles he would fight. Kids in his neighborhood either joined gangs or teams, McCovey once said. His team competed with ganglike ferocity, successfully taking on men's teams after the other boys' teams were licked. McCovey's athletic prowess gave him an incentive to do well in school, where he also played football and basketball. One of ten children, he became a good team player at a very early age.

His "team spirit" led him to drop out of school at the age of 16 in search of a salary to help out at home. Instead, a salary came looking for him: The New York Giants, alerted to McCovey's talent by a playground director, searched him out and bused him to Florida for a tryout. He sent his $500 signing bonus home to his mother.

Even before he got to his first assignment in Class-D ball, McCovey was tutored by Giants first baseman Bill White on how to put more wrist action into his swing. In his first pro season with Sandersville of the Georgia State League, he batted .313 with 19 homers and a league-leading RBI count of 113. He was tops among league first sackers with 897 putouts. In 1956 he was in Danville, Virginia, in the Carolina League. He again batted above .300 with 29 home runs and 89 RBI. McCovey moved to Phoenix of the Pacific Coast League in 1958, leading the league in putouts (1,171). In 1959 he peaked with a .372 batting average and a league-leading 29 home runs.

McCovey was promoted to San Francisco two-thirds of the way into the 1959 season. He hit safely in each of his first 4 at-bats. McCovey played 52 games in the bigs that year with a .354 average, hit 13 home runs, and drove in 38 RBI. He received National League Rookie of the Year honors for his efforts. In 1960 a slumping McCovey was sent down to Tacoma. After 17 games, he redeemed himself and was back in the majors to stay. When he returned to the Giants he was often benched when a lefthand pitcher opposed the Giants. He saw part-time duty as a first sacker and in the outfield starting in 1962.

The Giants won the National League pennant in 1962. McCovey hit a game-winning home run during the World Series versus the Yankees and nearly won the seventh game with a wicked line drive. However, his screaming shot was snagged by Yankee second baseman Bobby Richardson, squelching San Francisco's ninth-inning rally.

The next year McCovey led the National League with 44 home runs, while driving in 102 runs. Starting in 1965 McCovey was a full-time first baseman. Teammates Willie Kirkland and Leon Wagner had nicknamed him "Stretch" for the way he scooped low throws.

McCovey achieved his amazing success despite a string of injuries that started in the mid-1970s and hampered him for much of his career. He was traded to the San Diego Padres with Bernie Williams in exchange for pitcher Mike Caldwell on October 25, 1973. McCovey slugged 22 homers in his first season in San Diego, then belted 23 dingers in his second year as a Padre, playing in just 122 games. The Padres sold him to the Oakland Athletics in mid-1976, and he finished the season as a designated hitter. The Giants re-signed the famed slugger as a free agent prior to the 1977 season. McCovey won back his old position with the team and won National League Comeback Player of the Year recognition for his .280 average, 28 home runs, and 86 RBI. The beloved belter played three more seasons in San Francisco, retiring after the 1980 season.

The man known as "Big Mac" was inducted into the Hall of Fame in 1986, his first year of eligibility. He received 346 votes from the 425 voters of the Baseball Writer's Association of America and was the only nominee that year with the requisite percentage of votes.

Today he serves (along with Mays) as a special assistant to the general manager and vice president of the Giants. The Giants retired his uniform number (44), making him one of only eight Giants to receive such an honor.

The most popular player ever to wear a San Francisco Giants' uniform, Willie McCovey was a powerful home run hitter. He clubbed 521 home runs and tallied 1,555 RBI during his career.

CAREER HIGHLIGHTS
WILLIE LEE McCOVEY

Born: January 10, 1938   Mobile, AL
Height: 6'4"   **Weight:** 200 lbs.   **Batted:** Left   **Threw:** Left
First baseman, outfielder: San Francisco Giants, 1959-73; 1977-80; San Diego Padres, 1974-76; Oakland Athletics, 1976.

- ★ Named Rookie of the Year in 1959
- ★ Appeared in six All-Star games
- ★ Voted Comeback Player of the Year in 1977
- ★ Selected as the N.L. MVP in 1969
- ★ Elected to the Hall of Fame in 1986
- ★ Holds the N.L. record for grand slams (18)

MAJOR LEAGUE TOTALS

G	AB	H	BA	2B	3B	HR	R	RBI	SB
2,588	8,197	2,211	.270	353	46	521	1,229	1,555	26

DENNY McLAIN

Denny McLain, the only pitcher ever to win back-to-back Cy Young awards, was a nonconformist whose defiant lifestyle not only forced him out of baseball but also led to a federal prison term. Despite his personal problems, McLain's spectacular skill on the field makes him a favorite with baseball fans and historians.

His father was an insurance salesman, semipro ballplayer, and organist. He schooled his son in the last two pursuits, employing corporal punishment with a liberal hand. Likewise, McLain claimed he would beat up guys who chided him about time spent at the keyboard. Cruising through high school without "cracking a book," McLain signed with the White Sox immediately out of high school for a $17,000 bonus. His first professional game was a no-hitter.

McLain was unhappy in the small towns that hosted his minor league teams, and he often offended locals by bad-mouthing their towns. He also took days off without leave. A frustrated Chicago organization turned him loose on a somewhat insulting $8,000 waiver, which was picked up by the Detroit Tigers. Manager Chuck Dressen was able to soothe his bad boy with a new toy—a curve ball. After that McLain was devoted to his coach.

His debut with the Tigers was against the White Sox, and he played as though to avenge his own hard feelings, striking out 8 and slugging a home run for a 4-3 victory.

He spent half of the 1964 season on the farm, then was called up to Detroit for good in 1965. He had a record of 16-6 his first season. The next year he posted his first 20-win season, losing 14 and pitching 3 perfect innings as a starter in the All-Star game. By this time McLain had all the markings of a possible All-American baseball hero.

Unfortunately, manager Dressen died that year. Without his stabilizing influence, the hurler immediately and sharply declined in performance and offended Detroit fans with public statements about his teammates' ineptitude. He was later blamed for the Tigers' nip-and-tuck loss of the 1967 pennant, while he sat on the bench with broken toes. Fans believed his injury was the result of a clubhouse temper tantrum.

By 1968 coach Johnny Sain had won the loyalty of the difficult prodigy, teaching him a slider that led the Tigers to their first pennant in 23 years.

Blossoming under personal tutelage, McLain posted 31 wins, the one accomplishment that has kept his name alive in record books ever since. Six of these wins were shutouts; 28 outings were complete games. No pitcher had logged 30 wins since St. Louis Cardinal hurler Dizzy Dean in 1934.

The season ended with what sports writers called "the pitching duel of the century," with McLain and St. Louis star pitcher Bob Gibson squaring off in a heated fall classic.

McLain lost two Series games with a badly inflamed shoulder. After an injection from the doctor, he pitched a final full game six, battling on for a victory.

His last great season was in 1969. He repeated as Cy Young award winner in 1969 (sharing the honor with Baltimore's Mike Cuellar) when he collected a 24-9 record. Then his career took a drastic turn for the worse. In the 1970 season he was suspended for three months by Commissioner Bowie

Kuhn for his alleged participation in a bookmaking scheme three years earlier. McLain returned to work overweight and out of shape, and he was never able to regain his playing form.

McLain continued to reinforce his reputation as baseball's premier bad boy. He was suspended on two more occasions, once for carrying a gun and once for dumping a bucket of ice water on a reporter. McLain finished the 1970 season with a dismal 3-5 mark, and the following season he was sent to the Washington Senators. He was the foundation of a huge trade that also sent Don Wert, Norm McRae, and Elliott Maddox to the Senators in exchange for Joe Coleman, Ed Brinkman, Aurelio Rodriguez, and Jim Hannan.

The one-time Tiger great stumbled through a disastrous 10-22 season, leading the junior circuit in losses. He divided his final year between the Oakland Athletics and the Atlanta Braves, winning 4 games and losing 7. After the 1972 season McLain was out of baseball but not out of the headlines.

In 1984 he was convicted on federal charges of loansharking, bookmaking, extortion, and distribution of cocaine and was sentenced to 23 years in prison. In the summer of 1987 McLain's conviction was overturned on appeal because of a judicial error, and he was released on bail pending a possible retrial. In late 1988 a renewed guilty plea by McLain prompted a 12-year prison sentence that was reduced to a five-year probation period.

In spite of his bad boy image, he will always be remembered for his amazing 31 wins in 1968, a bright spot in a troubled life.

CAREER HIGHLIGHTS
DENNIS DALE McLAIN

Born: March 29, 1944   Chicago, IL
Height: 6'1"   **Weight:** 185 lbs.   **Batted:** Right   **Threw:** Right
Pitcher: Detroit Tigers, 1963-70; Washington Senators, 1971; Oakland Athletics, 1972; Atlanta Braves, 1972.

* Selected MVP in 1968
* Led the A.L. in games started twice
* The last pitcher to win 30 or more games in a season
* Pitched in the 1968 World Series
* Led the league in wins twice
* First in the A.L. in innings pitched twice

★ Won Cy Young awards in 1968 and 1969

MAJOR LEAGUE TOTALS

G	IP	W	L	Pct.	SO	BB	ERA
280	1,885	131	91	.590	1,282	548	3.39

Denny McLain's short but controversial career was highlighted by some amazing feats and statistics. The last pitcher to claim 30 victories in one season, McLain won consecutive Cy Young awards in the 1968 and 1969 seasons.

DAVE McNALLY

Dave McNally might be remembered by most fans as a talented lefthand starter with the Baltimore Orioles from 1962 to 1974 who helped the team to four World Series in a little over a decade. In retrospect, however, the biggest contribution he ever made to the game might have come when he was wearing a Montreal Expos uniform in 1975.

McNally was never successful with the Expos, winning 3 and losing 6 in 12 starts. His ERA was a whopping 5.26, and he seemed like only a ghost of his former star self. Unhappy with his performance, McNally retired from the game on June 8 of that year. However, McNally (along with Los Angeles Dodgers pitcher Andy Messersmith) challenged the validity of baseball's reserve clause. When McNally was traded with minor leaguer Bill Kirkpatrick and outfielder Rich Coggins to Montreal in exchange for outfielder Ken Singleton and pitcher Mike Torrez on December 4, 1974, McNally never signed a new contract with the Expos. The Expos renewed his contract and raised his salary to $125,000. However, at that time players were forever committed to a team. The Players Association filed a protest over McNally's contract situation. The courts ruled that McNally could not be bound to the Expos for more than the one-year renewal period in his contract. After that he'd be free to sign with anyone. Although this agreement was inconsequential to a man who was giving up the game to return to his car dealership in Billings, Montana, the decision had historic implications. Because of McNally's challenge, free agency was born. At age 32 McNally could have come out of retirement and landed a big-money pact as a free agent. He gave up a substantial chunk of his 1975 salary by leaving the Expos in midseason.

McNally was an $80,000 bonus baby who made the Orioles after just two minor league seasons. In his 1962 debut the 19-year-old lefty registered a two-hit shutout versus Kansas City for his first win. In his first six seasons with Baltimore McNally never won more than 13 games. Suddenly, in the next four seasons, McNally was a four-time 20-game winner. In 1968 his 22-10 season included a 1.95 ERA and a team record of 202 strikeouts. In September McNally started a streak of 17 straight wins that stretched into 1969. After winning 20 games in 1969 McNally tied with Minnesota's Jim Perry for the league lead in wins in 1970. McNally's 24-9 record was impressive, but Perry won the Cy Young award. McNally was 21-5 (with a league-leading winning percentage of .808) in 1971, when the Orioles had three other pitchers—Jim Palmer, Mike Cuellar, and Pat Dobson—with 20 wins each. (The 1920 Chicago White Sox were the last team to enjoy this distinction.)

The Montana native was a big influence on the many Orioles postseason teams. His impact was felt by the Los Angeles Dodgers in the 1966 World Series, which the O's swept in four straight games. After lasting less than three innings in his opening-game start, McNally clinched Baltimore's world championship with a 1-0 four-hit victory in the decisive fourth game. In 1969 McNally threw 11 shutout innings against the Minnesota Twins in the second game of the League Championship Series. In that stretch he struck out 10 batters and allowed just 3 hits. He also notched a win in the 1970 and 1971 A.L.C.S.

In 1970 McNally won 1 game against the Cincinnati Reds in the World Series. Although he threw a complete game, McNally is best remembered for his hitting in that game. Batting from the right side, McNally socked a grand slam to guarantee his victory, the only time a pitcher had turned the trick in postseason play. Although the Orioles lost the 1971 World Series to the Pittsburgh Pirates in seven games, McNally was on the mound for 2 of the O's victories.

McNally had every right to be proud of his lifetime stats, for they were some of the finest numbers posted in the late 1960s and early 70s. He won a total of 184 games while losing 119. His ERA was a tidy 3.24. He wound up with 120 complete games and 33 shutouts in 396 starts. Twice he tossed a one-hitter: in 1964 against the Washington Senators and in 1969 against the Minnesota Twins. McNally was not an incredible batsman, but he did have 97 career hits and 9 regular-season home runs. He ranks second on the all-time Orioles list in strikeouts (1,512), shutouts, innings pitched, and wins, trailing only Jim Palmer.

Although McNally's totals fall short of consideration for enshrinement with the Cooperstown elite, he was named to the Orioles Hall of Fame in 1978.

Dave McNally's major contribution to baseball history was not in terms of statistics or game accomplishments. Instead, he successfully challenged the validity of the reserve clause, which instigated the free agency system.

CAREER HIGHLIGHTS
DAVID ARTHUR McNALLY

Born: October 31, 1942   Billings, MT
Height: 5'11"   **Weight:** 185 lbs.   **Batted:** Right   **Threw:** Left
Pitcher: Baltimore Orioles, 1962-74; Montreal Expos, 1975.

★ Was a four-time 20-game winner
★ Led the A.L. with an .808 winning percentage in 1971
★ Appeared in four World Series, winning four games
★ Won 17 straight games in 1968-69
★ Pitched in five League Championship Series, winning three games
★ Hit a grand slam in a World Series, the only pitcher to do so

MAJOR LEAGUE TOTALS

G	IP	W	L	Pct.	SO	BB	ERA
424	2,729.1	184	119	.607	1,512	826	3.24

377

JOE MEDWICK

Joe "Ducky" Medwick was given his unflattering nickname because when he walked he waddled like a duck. Medwick was the last National Leaguer ever to earn the triple crown, an honor he acquired in 1937 with 31 homers, a .374 average, and 154 RBI.

Medwick grew up in New Jersey. In high school he was a runner on the track team, a forward on the basketball squad, a fullback in football, and a third baseman/first baseman/pitcher in the summer. Medwick recalled that he once struck out 22 high schoolers in a single nine-inning game. His career began in 1929 in the St. Louis Cardinals minor league system. "Jersey Joe," as he was also called, turned down a Notre Dame football scholarship to accept the Redbirds' offer.

Medwick was an instant success in the minor leagues. In 1930 with Scottsdale of the Middle Atlantic League he batted .419 with 22 homers. The next year, Medwick had 188 hits in 166 games with Houston. He was promoted to St. Louis following his 1932 season in Houston. In his last minor league season he hit .354 with 26 homers. Medwick did admit that his nickname was born in Houston, when the newspapers started calling him "Duckey Wuckey." He personally preferred to be called "Mickey."

By whatever name he was called, Medwick could certainly be called a success. In his 1932 major league debut he logged a batting average of .349 in 26 games. In the 14 full seasons of baseball that followed, he would only fall below .300 twice, each time being when he split a season between two teams.

His first under par season would not come for 11 years, however. In the meantime Medwick became a key character in the notorious "Gashouse Gang," the rowdy, irreverent group of Cardinals who blitzed the Tigers in the 1934 World Series. Before the war was over, Medwick had become the only player in Series history to be removed from a game by mob rule.

After he flashed his spikes in the direction of Tiger infielder Marv Owen while sliding into third base, Medwick was bombarded by angry Tigers fans flinging fruit, bottles, and debris as he tried to take his place in the outfield. Four times the game was stopped to clear the refuse; four times the heated outburst was repeated. Finally, baseball commissioner Judge Kenesaw Mountain Landis (famed for banning eight 1919 White Sox from major league ball)

removed Medwick from the field, both to protect him and to quell the fans so the game could continue. When it was over the Cardinals had whipped the Tigers in the seventh game 11-0. Medwick finished the Series with a .379 average, 1 home run, and 5 RBI.

Although Medwick distinguished himself with St. Louis for eight years by never batting below .300, the Brooklyn Dodgers lured the Cards into a trade for four players and $125,000. Cards pitcher Curt Davis was also part of the deal.

In one of his first appearances against his former teammates in 1940, Medwick was struck by a Bob Bowman beanball. After release from the hospital

for treatment of a concussion, teammates observed that Medwick was a changed man. Always volatile, aggressive, and fiercely determined in the past, he had somehow had that edge knocked out of him. His average remained high, except for his 1941 World Series play with the Dodgers (.235) and his final year as a player, when he hit just .211 in only 20 games. This 1948 mark is startling compared to his .307 of the previous year.

Medwick's medical woes went beyond the after-effects of a beanball concussion. Running became increasingly difficult after 1940. So Medwick's last two seasons were spent with the Cards in part as a pinch hitter, upholding until the end his proclaimed philosophy of "base hits and bucks."

Medwick ended his major league playing career with a .324 average, 2,471 hits, and 205 homers. He had 540 lifetime doubles, and 64 of them came in 1936, for the second-highest total in baseball history. Even though he spent a relatively short time with the Cardinals, he still ranks among the top ten in five Redbirds career offensive categories, including home runs, hits, runs, triples, and RBI.

Baseball stayed afloat in Ducky's heart even after the majors. Medwick was a minor league player/manager in the South for four years after 1948. In 1961 he began a four-year stint as an assistant coach at St. Louis University. In 1965 he embarked on a 10-year career as a St. Louis Cardinals farm coach, teaching hitting until his death in 1975. Medwick was elected to the Hall of Fame in 1968.

CAREER HIGHLIGHTS
JOSEPH MICHAEL MEDWICK

Born: November 24, 1911 Carteret, NJ **Died:** March 21, 1975
Height: 5'10" **Weight:** 187 lbs. **Batted:** Right **Threw:** Right
Outfielder: St. Louis Cardinals, 1932-40, 1947-48; Brooklyn Dodgers, 1940-43, 1946; New York Giants, 1943-45; Boston Braves, 1945.

* Selected N.L. MVP in 1937
* Played in two World Series
* Was the last N.L. player to win the triple crown in 1937
* Topped 200 hits four times
* Elected to the Hall of Fame in 1968
* Batted over .300 in 14 out of 17 seasons
* Set an N.L. record with 64 doubles in 1936

MAJOR LEAGUE TOTALS

G	AB	H	BA	2B	3B	HR	R	RBI	SB
1,984	7,635	2,471	.324	540	113	205	1,198	1,383	42

Joe Medwick earned acclaim as a member of the notorious Gashouse Gang, the St. Louis Cardinals 1934 pennant-winning team. In 1937 he became the last National League player to win the triple crown.

MINNIE MINOSO

Any baseball fan knows that it ain't over till it's over. And if Minnie Minoso, who will be 68 years old in 1990, has his way, his career as a beloved big league star isn't over yet.

Brought from the coaching bench back to the roster in 1980 by master showman Bill Veeck, Minoso became only the second player in major league history to appear in games over the space of five decades. (Nick Altrock was the first player to accomplish this feat.)

Minoso began his career in 1949, retired in 1964, and appeared in three games in 1976 and two in 1980. Although Veeck died in 1986, Minoso has since declared his determination to become the only major leaguer to appear professionally in six different decades. Even without Veeck, the White Sox are a good bet to continue Minoso's tradition of longevity because he remains one of the most popular and sought-after superstars of baseball's halcyon days.

Minoso's first season was with the Indians in 1951 at the none-too-tender age of 28. Much speculation concerns what his career statistics might have been if the big league color barrier had been broken sooner. He played in the Negro Leagues from 1946 to 1948. As it is, his statistics are comparable to those of Enos Slaughter.

In 1951 Minoso left his Indians after eight games and a whopping .429 batting average to finish the season with the Chicago White Sox, where in 134 games he batted an awesome .324. He finished the year with league highs in triples (14) and stolen bases (31). One reporter mused in print that Minoso's arrival got the team "off and running, but now, for the first time since 1920, they had a general idea of why and where."

Minoso's average remained above .300 for four of the six years he played in Chicago, and his RBI totals remained above 100 for three years, climbing to a career high of 116 in 1954. On December 4, 1957, the ChiSox traded Fred Hatfield and Minoso to the Cleveland Indians for outfielder Al Smith and pitcher Early Wynn. The deal helped the White Sox to a 1959 American League pennant. Minoso, meanwhile, hit a personal best of 24 home runs with the 1958 Indians. Chicago reacquired Minoso in a seven-player trade with Cleveland prior to the 1960 season. That year he led the league with 184 hits, while tallying 20 homers, 105 RBI, and a .311 average.

Minoso finished the first leg of his baseball career with two seasons on the St. Louis Cardinals roster and a 1963 campaign with the Washington Senators.

For 17 seasons Minoso had 1,963 hits in 1,835 games for a .298 average. His hits include 336 doubles, 83 triples, 186 home runs, 1,023 RBI, and 1,136 runs scored. Minoso claimed three straight stolen base titles in 1951 through 1953, with respective totals of 31, 22, and 25 swipes—ending his career with 205 pilfers. He earned the title "The Cuban Comet."

Although Minoso was never lucky enough to play on a World Series team, he did see action in three All-Star games. He'll always be remembered for snaring a line drive off the bat of Gil Hodges in the 1957 All-Star game, securing the 6-5 win for the American Leaguers.

Constant debate rages as to whether Minoso belongs in the Hall of Fame. In the 1989 balloting Minoso received 59 votes out of a possible 447, finishing 14th in the voting. Minoso's supporters argue that, like Slaughter, he didn't get started in the major leagues until he was in his late 20s because of baseball's color barrier. It's easy to speculate on the lost achievements in Minoso's career, considering that he was 28 years old during his first full season. With another five peak years in the majors from an earlier start, Minoso could have easily topped 3,000 hits and might have exceeded 300 home runs.

Minoso could be considered one of the greatest players of all time if his total stats in organized baseball were combined. That's because he played 10 years in the Mexican Leagues after he retired from the majors in 1964. He made White Sox history in 1976 when he made a brief three-game appearance as a designated hitter. At the age of 53 Minoso earned another spot in baseball history by collecting a hit in his fourth decade of play.

Minoso has been employed by the Chicago White Sox as a goodwill ambassador since his retirement. But watch your scorecards, folks. Smart bettors are prepared to see this baseball great in uniform just once more in 1990, if for only one more pinch-hitting appearance. Just because he's in his late 60s, don't believe for a second that Chicago's sweetheart would pass up a chance to leave a lasting mark on the game he loves. Then again, don't count out the year 2000 either.

CAREER HIGHLIGHTS
SATURNINO ORESTES ARMAS ARRIETA MINOSO

Born: November 23, 1922   Havana, Cuba
Height: 5'10"   **Weight:** 175 lbs.   **Batted:** Right   **Threw:** Right
Outfielder: Cleveland Indians, 1949-51, 1958-59; Chicago White Sox, 1952-57, 1960-61, 1964, 1976, 1980; St. Louis Cardinals, 1962; Washington Senators, 1963.

★ Batted over .300 eight times
★ Appeared on major league rosters in five different decades
★ Appeared in three All-Star games
★ Led the A.L. in stolen bases for three consecutive years

MAJOR LEAGUE TOTALS

G	AB	H	BA	2B	3B	HR	R	RBI	SB
1,835	6,579	1,963	.298	336	83	186	1,136	1,023	205

Minnie Minoso began his career in the Negro Leagues and did not get to play in the majors until he was 28 years old. Despite the late start he managed to accumulate 1,023 RBI, hit 336 doubles, and steal 205 bases.

JOHNNY MIZE

Johnny Mize was a fearsome slugger who led the league in home runs four times and was still able to hit for average. During his first four seasons in the majors with the St. Louis Cardinals, from 1936 to 1939, Mize averaged .346. In 1939 he led the league in home runs (28) and batting average (.349), and finished third in RBI (108). The next season he repeated as home run champ with 43, led the league in RBI with 137, and finished fifth in batting with a .314 mark. His homers set a single-season mark for the Cardinals, a mark that has not been threatened in nearly five decades. For much of his career Mize was among league leaders in home runs, batting average, and RBI.

Mize missed three seasons while serving in the U.S. Navy from 1943 to 1945, but he returned in 1946 to bat at a .337 clip with 22 home runs. The following season he batted .302 and again led the league with 51 home runs, 138 RBI and 137 runs scored.

Not just a slugging machine, Mize was also a great fielder whose skill at first base earned him the nickname "The Big Cat." He established a record for first sackers by playing 61 consecutive games without an error and once pulled off two unassisted double plays in the same contest. He split his 15-year career about evenly among the St. Louis Cardinals, New York Giants, and New York Yankees.

Growing up in a small Georgia community didn't make it easy to play a lot of baseball—simply because it was hard to get enough kids together to make a team. Mize recalled that he played more basketball because fewer youngsters were needed. The nearby Piedmont Academy provided the closest baseball action Mize and his buddies could see, and they often hung around the college practices. Mize was recruited to play for Piedmont part-time when he was still a sophomore in high school. Mize was signed to a pro contract by Frank Rickey, the brother of Branch Rickey (vice president of the St. Louis Cardinals). Mize made three stops before reaching the Cardinals in 1936: Greensboro in the Piedmont League, Elmira of the New York-Penn League, and Rochester in the International League. In his rookie season in St. Louis Mize hit 19 homers, 93 RBI, and a .329 average in 126 games. The 6-foot-2, 215 pounder went 7-for-15 as a pinch hitter and soon won the team's starting first baseman's job away from

Ripper Collins. In his sophomore season of 1937, Mize batted .364 with 25 home runs and 113 RBI. His slugging percentage climbed from .577 in his first year to .595 in 1937. Mize had three straight years of a .600-plus slugging percentage: .614 in 1938, .626 in 1939, and .636 in 1940. His lifetime slugging percentage of .562 is the eighth highest in baseball history.

The husky slugger who wore number 10 on his back had a noteworthy achievement in 1938. Unlike some lead-footed home run hitters, Mize had considerable speed early in his career. Proof of this is his league-leading total of 16 triples in 1938. Mize tripled 14 times in 1939 and had 13 in 1940.

The Giants sold Mize to the New York Yankees for $40,000 in August 1949. Mize wasn't physically capable of playing full-time; however, he still had the talent to serve well as a backup first baseman and pinch hitter. Mize spent four and a half seasons with the Yankees. During that time the team col-

lected five pennants and five world championships.

New York writer Dan Parker honored Mize's pinch-hitting achievements for the Yankees with this verse: "Your arm is gone; your legs likewise. But not your eyes, Mize, not your eyes."

After 15 seasons in the majors Mize finished his career with 359 homers, 1,337 RBI, 2,011 total hits, 1,118 runs scored, and a .312 average. In fact, Mize kept his average above .300 for his first nine seasons. He hit 19 or more homers for his first 11 seasons and homered in double figures in all but his final two seasons. Mize drove in 100 or more runs on eight occasions. Although he spent just six seasons with the Cardinals, Mize still holds the team's second-highest batting mark at .335. His 158 homers as a Redbird are the sixth-best on the team's all-time list, and his RBI total ranks tenth at 653. His career stats could have been much higher if he hadn't lost three prime years to military service.

Mize retired after the 1953 World Series. He served as a Giants scout in 1955 and coached for the Kansas City Athletics in 1961. Since his retirement Mize and his wife have owned and operated Florida orange groves.

After much lobbying by his devoted fans, the Veterans Committee elected Mize to the Hall of Fame in 1981.

Johnny Mize—a top slugger for the Giants and the Cardinals—won four home run titles and three RBI crowns. He also finished in the top three in certain offensive categories 54 times in his career.

CAREER HIGHLIGHTS
JOHN ROBERT MIZE

Born: January 7, 1913   Demorest, GA
Height: 6'2"   **Weight:** 215 lbs.   **Batted:** Left   **Threw:** Right
First baseman: St. Louis Cardinals, 1936-41; New York Giants, 1942-49; New York Yankees, 1949-53.

★ Hit 51 homers in 1947

★ Played in five straight World Series with the Yankees

★ Batted over .300 during his first nine seasons

★ Led the N.L. in batting in 1939

★ Has a .562 slugging percentage, eighth best in history

★ Topped the A.L. in pinch hits three seasons

★ Led the league in home runs four times

MAJOR LEAGUE TOTALS

G	AB	H	BA	2B	3B	HR	R	RBI	SB
1,884	6,443	2,011	.312	367	83	359	1,118	1,337	28

PAUL MOLITOR

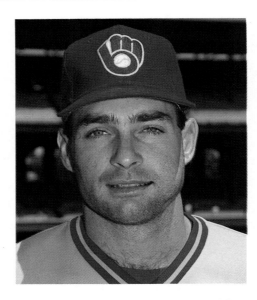

Scouts of the 1980s agree that Milwaukee Brewer third baseman/designated hitter Paul Molitor does just about everything well. He can hit the long ball, he's quick on the base paths, and he's good with a glove and at stretching out a single. Unfortunately, there's one other thing Molitor excels at: getting injured.

After just two years with the Brew Crew Molitor logged his first stint on the disabled list with a month out in 1980. He lost three months in 1981, then managed two complete seasons before being sidelined in May 1984 for surgery to replace his right elbow ligament. In 1985 he missed only two weeks. In 1986 and '87 he lost approximately two months each season.

It's small wonder that the Brewers, his home team since entering the game, considered letting Molitor get away at the end of 1988. By January of 1989, though, they changed their minds and signed him to a new contract. That, too, is no surprise. Molitor and teammate Robin Yount are perhaps Milwaukee's only legitimate superstars. Molitor cemented his claim to fame in August 1987 when he electrified baseball with his consecutive-game hitting streak.

Earlier in the month he set a Brewer team record at the 25-game mark. When the streak hit 30 the national press began to pay attention. By the time he hit 35, passing such Hall of Famers as Stan Musial, Rogers Hornsby, and Tris Speaker on the list of hitting streaks, the media was hanging on every one of his plate appearances, keeping up the pressure. Hitting safely in 39 consecutive games, Molitor finally ranked seventh on the all-time list. When he went 0-for-4 on August 26, no other American Leaguer had hit safely in more consecutive games since Joe DiMaggio's 56-game streak in 1941.

Molitor's hitting streak had raised his batting average to a league-leading .370 at the end of August, despite having been on the disabled list for a number of weeks early in the season. He wound up the season with a .353 average in 465 at-bats.

Molitor was named shortstop of The Sporting News College Baseball All-American team while attending the University of Minnesota. He was the third player selected in the 1977 draft, signing with the Brewers for a reported $100,000 bonus. He played only a single season of minor league ball, being named the Midwest League Most Valuable Player in 1977 when he hit .346. At age 21, playing at second base, shortstop, and third base for Milwaukee, he tallied 142 hits, 26 doubles, 401 assists, and 253 putouts, enough to snag The Sporting News Rookie of the Year award despite his 22 errors in the field.

In 1987 and 1988 the Brewers used Molitor at third base, and he enjoyed some of his best stats ever, with a to-date high of .353 in 1987 (pacing the circuit with 114 runs scored and 41 doubles), as well as a .972 fielding average, his best since 1981. The Sporting News named him to the American League All-Star team. He slugged another .300-plus year in 1988, earning his second consecutive Silver Slugger nod from The Sporting News and his third nomination to the A.L. All-Star team.

Fate was kind in 1982, keeping Molitor healthy for the Brewers nip-and-tuck bid for their first world championship. Many credit "Molitor the Ignitor" with the Brewers pennant, pointing out that when he suffers bad health, the team also suffers with a bad season.

Coming back from an injury layoff of almost a full season in 1981, Molitor entered 1982 in high gear, leading the circuit with 666 at-bats and 136 runs scored. He batted more than .300 for the third time in four years, clubbing a to-date high of 19 home runs. For the first time in his career he topped 40 stolen bases (with 41 swipes), a number he matched in 1983 and 1988 and surpassed in 1987 with a career high of 45 larcenies. During that year, 3 steals came on July 26, 1987, tying a major league record for most stolen bases in a single inning.

Molitor's team leadership showed early in 1982, as he hit 3 home runs in a single game on May 12, 1982. He led the league in double plays with 48.

His 2 home runs in 1982 postseason play tied the American League record for most homers in a five-game League Championship Series. Molitor's .316 average included 5 RBI and 4 runs scored. In the World Series he pushed even harder. Although he was denied any homers in the seven-game Series, he created and tied four Series records for most hits in a game (5 on October 12) and most at-bats in a nine-inning game (6).

Quite likely, Molitor will finish his career as a designated hitter in order to avoid future injuries. While the Brewers don't get their full value out of the Minnesota native when he works just as a DH, Molitor still has the experience and talent to help keep Milwaukee in pennant contention.

CAREER HIGHLIGHTS
PAUL LEO MOLITOR

Born: August 22, 1956   St. Paul, MN
Height: 6'0"   **Weight:** 185 lbs.   **Bats:** Right   **Throws:** Right
Infielder, outfielder, designated hitter: Milwaukee Brewers, 1978-89.

- ★ Batted .355 in the 1982 World Series
- ★ Hit .300-plus six times
- ★ Named The Sporting News A.L. Rookie of the Year in 1978
- ★ Named to three All-Star teams
- ★ Led the A.L. in runs scored twice
- ★ Set a World Series record with 5 hits in a game in 1982

MAJOR LEAGUE TOTALS

G	AB	H	BA	2B	3B	HR	R	RBI	SB
1,437	5,828	1,751	.300	310	60	119	989	581	344

Paul Molitor experienced two of his best seasons in 1987 and 1988 when the Milwaukee Brewers began to use him frequently at third base. Molitor remained at third for the 1989 season, batting .315 and tallying 84 runs.

JOE MORGAN

All-time great Pete Rose once admitted that speed on the base paths was not his strong suit. "I'm no Joe Morgan," he said, referring to his long-time teammate. Joe Morgan assessed his own talents by saying, "I hit for average. I'm not blessed with the great strength of a Pete Rose."

While it would be difficult to compare the careers of Morgan and Rose, it's apparent that both teammates built long careers using cool confidence and constant determination to tap into their full abilities. Sometimes two superstar elements on one team can cause undue friction; however, Morgan and Rose smoothly joined forces to spark "The Big Red Machine" of Cincinnati to three World Series appearances in five years during the early 1970s.

Morgan himself has always walked the balance beam of pride, proof of Dizzy Dean's famous quote, "If you can do it, you ain't braggin'." A self-confessed student of the game, Morgan always had ready analyses of his current playing habits and their effectiveness to relay to the press. He refined clubhouse chatter to an art, seeking to keep his teammates in high spirits.

Morgan had to work hard to have anything to brag about as a baseball player. At 5-foot-7 and 160 pounds, it was difficult for him to get scouts to seriously consider his worth to a team. His minor league fielding and baserunning were both under par, but his running improved when he stayed on a team long enough to analyze opposing pitchers. From the start of his pro career (in 1963 with Modesto, at the age of 19), Morgan was a patient hitter, a trait often ignored by scouts in view of his less-than-stellar batting average. His average improved greatly when Morgan learned to keep his back elbow high during his batting stance. A chicken-flap of his arm while at bat reminded him to raise the elbow; fans found the trademark ritual as amusing as opposing pitchers found it distracting.

After batting .332 with Durham of the Carolina League in 1963, Morgan got an eight-game audition with the Astros near the end of the season. He wound up with 6 hits in eight games for a .240 average. When he was sent down to San Antonio in 1964, he was named Texas League Most Valuable Player for his efforts, which included a league-leading 42 doubles, 12 home runs, 90 RBI, and a .319 batting average. Morgan led Texas League second sackers in fielding with a .967 average.

By 1965 "Little Joe" was the starting second baseman for the Astros (then called the Colt .45s). *The Sporting News* crowned him Rookie of the Year for his inaugural season of 14 homers, 40 RBI, a .271 average, 100 runs scored, and a league-leading 97 bases on balls. Within two years he had become a basestealing dynamo. He amassed 18 seasons of 11 or more annual stolen bases. By the time he finished his career, Morgan ranked seventh on the all-time steals list with 689 pilfers. His batting average was .285 in 1966 and .275 in 1967. Hitting in the cavernous Astrodome kept Morgan's homer tallies down. A possible four-bagger in any other stadium could wind up as a long fly ball in Houston.

Morgan began 1968 with a bang—or more exactly a crash. In a second base collision with an oncoming runner, Morgan was injured and required surgery. He saw action in only ten games that year. While he was on the disabled list, management dissected his play. The Astros decided that because of Morgan's average arm and difficulty in making double play pivots, he'd be best-suited for outfield duty. But meanwhile, Morgan had beefed up his defensive skills and ultimately kept his infield job.

On November 29, 1971, Morgan's career took a turn for the better when he was traded to Cincinnati in a massive eight-player deal. Reds second sacker Tommy Helms and Morgan traded starting jobs with one another. During the 1972 season Morgan set new career highs in virtually every offensive category, while the Reds won the pennant. The new Red batted .292 with 16 homers and 73 RBI, stole 58 bases, and led the league with 122 runs scored. He fielded surprisingly well, pacing the circuit with a .990 average. In the five-game N.L.C.S. against the Pittsburgh Pirates, Morgan hit .263 and paced the Reds with 2 homers and 5 runs scored.

Morgan won consecutive MVP awards in 1975 and 1976. He stole a career high of 67 bases in 1973 and again in 1975. In 1976 he set personal bests of 27 homers, 111 RBI, and a .320 batting average. He rejoined Houston as a free agent in 1980, then played the final four years of his career with the Giants, the Phillies, and the A's. He passed up a chance to manage the Astros in 1982, feeling he was still capable of playing.

Since his retirement Morgan has been active in private business in his hometown of Oakland, California. He also serves as a broadcaster for San Francisco Giants games.

CAREER HIGHLIGHTS
JOE LEONARD MORGAN

Born: September 19, 1943   Bonham, TX
Height: 5'7"   **Weight:** 160 lbs.   **Batted:** Left   **Threw:** Left
Second baseman: Houston Astros, 1963-71, 1980; Cincinnati Reds, 1972-79; San Francisco Giants, 1981-82; Philadelphia Phillies, 1983; Oakland A's, 1984.

★ Won back-to-back MVP awards in 1975 and 1976

★ Led the N.L. in walks four times

★ Has the third-highest walk total in history

★ Won five consecutive Gold Glove awards

★ Appeared in four World Series

★ Played in seven League Championship Series

MAJOR LEAGUE TOTALS

G	AB	H	BA	2B	3B	HR	R	RBI	SB
2,649	9,277	2,517	.271	449	96	268	1,650	1,133	689

Joe Morgan played more games at second base than any other player except Eddie Collins. A member of Cincinnati's Big Red Machine for much of his career, Morgan helped lead his team to three World Series.

JACK MORRIS

The pitcher with the most wins in the 1980s began the last season of the decade on a slippery slope. Detroit Tigers ace John Scott Morris, known to baseball fans everywhere as "Jack," suffered through 6 straight losses with nary a win to open the 1989 season. Ted Gray, who hurled with Detroit in 1953, was the last Bengal to endure such a fate. Thirty-four years old when he finally broke his curse with a win in May, Morris is hardly a senior citizen. Morris established—and still holds—the American League record for most consecutive starting assignments in a lifetime (336). In 1983 he led the league with 294 innings pitched, a mark he has approached again on numerous occasions. He averages a little more than seven innings per start and is quick enough off the mound to do his share of fielding.

The temperamental Tiger was signed in the fifth round of the free-agent draft of June 1976, which interrupted his studies at Brigham Young University in Utah. He managed to appear in 12 games for Montgomery that season, winning 2 and losing 3. His 6.25 ERA, 36 walks, and 18 strikeouts in 36 innings of work were nothing to write home about. Despite his problems Morris was promoted all the way to Triple-A Evansville in 1977. Pitching for the Triplets, Morris was 6-7 with a 3.60 ERA in 20 games. His strikeouts outnumbered his walks this time, 95 to 42.

Morris fared well enough to gain a seven-game trial with the Tigers in 1977 and a spot on the opening-day roster in 1978. After going 4-6 with an ERA near 4.00, he was demoted to Evansville to begin 1979. Morris returned to Detroit after just five games, posting a 17-7 record with a 3.27 ERA.

In 1981 he tied for the league lead with 14 wins in the strike-shortened season but gave up a league-leading 78 walks. His 3.05 ERA that year is the best he has managed so far in the majors. *The Sporting News* recognized Morris' efforts with election to their All-Star team and honors as American League Pitcher of the Year.

In 1983 Morris led the American League with 232 strikeouts as well as 18 wild pitches, the first of four years he would lead in the infamous category. These four seasons constitute a major league record for wild pitches, highlighted by another record in 1987 when Morris turned loose 27 errant offerings. Five of them escaped in a single game—another record.

Yet in the midst of these untamed moments, Morris hurled a no-hitter in the first week of the 1984 season against the Chicago White Sox. His spotless achievement paved the way for Detroit's 1984 world championship. On the heels of his first 20-win season in 1983 came a 19-11 performance. He added a masterful win in the American League Championship Series, in which he limited the Kansas City Royals to just 1 run and 5 hits over seven innings. The Tigers roared on to the World Series, where they devoured the San Diego Padres. Morris hurled a 3-2 complete-game victory in the Series opener, then hurled a five-hitter in game four to stake the team to a three-games-to-one lead. In 18 innings of work Morris had a 2.00 ERA with 13 strikeouts.

His best season to date was in 1986, when he was 21-8 with a career-high .724 win percentage and 223 strikeouts. At the end of the 1987 season Morris was only slightly off pace with an 18-11 record and 208 strikeouts. The Minnesota native, who considered sign-ing with the Twins in the mid-1980s before renewing his free-agent pact with the Tigers, slipped to a 15-13 season in 1988, his worst record since 1981. His ERA ballooned to a 3.94.

In 1988 his fastball still clocked in at more than 90 m.p.h. The slider, his bread-and-butter pitch, is almost as fast. And these are only two of the weapons in his arsenal, which also includes a split-fingered fastball, a forkball, and a straight change. His move to first base is one of the league's best, although critics say he doesn't use it enough, preferring to chase new batters off the doorstep rather than dust off yesterday's news.

Morris' stats show some sign of slowing, although he remains the only major league pitcher to have at least 15 wins per season throughout the 1980s (minus 1981's strike-marred season). Morris' competitive fires sometimes erupt into a hot temper, which has been aimed at assorted parties from teammates to management. Morris was the first to blast the Tigers for trading long-time infielder Tom Brookens to the Yankees in 1989. Morris can still make the sparks fly off the field; if he can still generate electricity as a Tiger starter the team can hold its perennial place as an Eastern Division contender.

Jack Morris' banner season occurred in 1986 when he won 21 games for his Tigers. He also struck out 223 batters, wound up with a .724 win percentage, and led the A.L. with 6 shutouts.

CAREER HIGHLIGHTS
JOHN SCOTT MORRIS

Born: May 16, 1955   St. Paul, MN
Height: 6'3"   **Weight:** 200 lbs.   **Bats:** Right   **Throws:** Right
Pitcher: Detroit Tigers, 1977-89.

- ★ Has won the most games of any active pitcher in the 1980s
- ★ Led the A.L. with 6 shutouts in 1986
- ★ Won 2 games in the 1984 World Series
- ★ Named *The Sporting News* A.L. Pitcher of the Year in 1981
- ★ Two-time 20-game winner
- ★ Pitched in four All-Star games

MAJOR LEAGUE TOTALS

G	IP	W	L	Pct.	SO	BB	ERA
370	2,623	177	118	.600	1,703	930	3.59

THURMAN MUNSON

Thurman Munson was in the prime of his outstanding career when he was tragically killed in a private plane accident in 1979 at the age of 32. It was an abrupt ending to a career that had definite Hall of Fame potential.

Munson joined the Yankees at the end of the 1969 season. The following year he won the starting position when he led the team with a .302 batting average and took home the trophy for American League Rookie of the Year. The determined backstop put together some great seasons. He won the league's Most Valuable Player award in 1976, when he batted .302 with 17 home runs and 105 RBI. The six-time All-Star hit a career best of .318 in 1975, one of five times he topped the .300 mark in 11 seasons.

Munson was a great defensive backstop who won three Gold Gloves in a row (1973 through 1975) and handled the Yankee staff with skill and precision. He had a strong arm, a sharp mind, and a take-charge attitude that inspired the rest of the club. Yankee owner George Steinbrenner named him team captain before the start of the 1976 season, an honor that had not been awarded since Lou Gehrig held the post in the 1930s.

In Munson's sophomore season of 1971, he tapered off to a .251 average, with 10 home runs and 42 RBI. In 1972 he lifted his average to .280. The following season Munson batted .301 with a career-high 20 homers and 74 RBI. He dipped to 13 homers, 60 RBI, and a .261 average in 1974, but he continued to be one of the league's defensive cornerstones. Munson highlighted his 1975 season with 12 home runs and 102 RBI.

Munson's regular season stats don't tell the full story of why he won the 1976 Most Valuable Player award. He became an offensive demon during postseason play. Starting with the American League Championship Series, he mauled Kansas City Royals pitching for 10 hits, 3 RBI, and a .435 batting average. When the Yankees won the five-game battle to advance to the World Series, they faced a superior Cincinnati Reds team. The Reds, however, found they had to play two opponents—the New York Yankees and Thurman Munson. The Yankees weren't such a problem, losing four straight games to "The Big Red Machine." Munson, however, was a different story. He had 9 hits to lead both teams (the entire Yankees club had just

30 hits combined). He batted .529 with 2 RBI and 2 runs scored. Munson may have really been the Yankees first "Mr. October."

In 1977 Munson tallied a .308 mark with 18 homers and 100 RBI. In the A.L.C.S. (again versus the Royals) Munson batted .286 with team highs in hits (6) and RBI (5). Also, he homered once and scored 3 runs. The Bronx Bombers were victors in a six-game World Series against the Los Angeles Dodgers. Munson's achievements included a .320 average, 8 hits, 1 homer, 3 RBI, and 4 runs scored.

In 1978, his last full season, Munson batted a decent .298 but saw his long hits decline to 6 homers and 71 RBI. For the third straight year the Yankees demolished the Royals in the League Championship Series. In game three an eighth-inning two-run homer by Munson gave the Yanks a 6-5 win. Replaying another scene from last season, the Yankees beat the Dodgers in a six-game Series. Again, Munson had 8 hits for a .320 average. He knocked in 7 runs and scored 5 others.

Munson was a devoted family man. At one time he even asked the Yankees to trade him to the Cleveland Indians so that he would be closer to his wife and three children in Canton, Ohio. Munson returned home every chance he could, and it was on one such visit, in August 1979, that his life ended. Munson, a licensed pilot, was practicing "touch-and-go" landings in a twin-engine jet he had purchased a month earlier. On an approach to the Akron-Canton airfield, he came down short of the runway and crashed. The plane was soon engulfed in flames. Two other passengers aboard were injured but lived.

The Yankees retired his uniform number (15) the night after his death. As a tribute to their great captain, the Yankees placed a plaque on the center field wall of Yankee Stadium. The entire Yankees team, complete with the players' wives, flew back to Canton for Munson's funeral. The city of New York, meanwhile, renamed part of a street running outside Yankee Stadium "Thurman Munson Way."

Although he may never be an official member of the Cooperstown elite, Munson is represented in the Hall of Fame. A re-creation of his locker, including his spikes and glove, has been preserved in a touching first-floor exhibit. Combined with a life-size statue of Babe Ruth waiting at the front door of the Hall, these two Yankee heroes have been preserved forever in the hearts of all true baseball fans.

Though Thurman Munson played less than ten full seasons in the majors, his total of 1,423 games exceeds those of other great catchers who played longer. Munson averaged 125 games per year.

CAREER HIGHLIGHTS
THURMAN LEE MUNSON

Born: June 7, 1947 Akron, OH **Died:** August 2, 1979
Height: 5'11" **Weight:** 190 lbs. **Batted:** Right **Threw:** Right
Catcher: New York Yankees, 1969-79.

★ Named A.L. Rookie of the Year in 1970   ★ Selected A.L. MVP in 1976
★ Won three consecutive Gold Gloves   ★ Batted over .300 five times
★ Played in three World Series

MAJOR LEAGUE TOTALS

G	AB	H	BA	2B	3B	HR	R	RBI	SB
1,423	5,344	1,558	.292	229	32	113	696	701	48

BOBBY MURCER

The New York Yankees thought they had a second Mickey Mantle when a young prospect named Bobby Murcer joined the team in 1965. The media even tagged him "the next Mantle." This was more than pure conjecture. In fact, the coincidences between the two men were fascinating.

Both men hailed from Oklahoma. Murcer and Mantle both began their pro careers as shortstops and later switched to outfield positions. The most vital relationship between the two men was power. When the Yankees saw that Murcer, like Mantle, had a penchant for long-ball power, the team (and all Yankee fans) immediately began hoping that Murcer could eventually assume the duties of the aging Mantle.

Yet Bobby Murcer never became a home run king. In fact, he never managed to lead the league in homers even once while hitting in cavernous Yankee Stadium. However, he was an offensive beacon on some of the worst teams in Yankees history during the 1960s. When fans of the once mighty Yankees had little else to look forward to, they knew they could count on Murcer for some power-hitting excitement.

Murcer was signed out of the University of Oklahoma in Norman. The Yanks gave him a reported $20,000 to sign a pro contract. In his first season with Johnson City in 1964, Murcer shuttled between second base and shortstop for 32 games, hitting .365 with 2 homers and 29 RBI. In Greensboro of the Carolina League in 1965, he batted .322 with 16 home runs and 90 RBI in 126 games. The Yankees called him up for an 11-game trial later that year. He batted .243 and hit his first home run that season. Surprisingly, the Yankees were using Murcer exclusively at shortstop then.

Shortstop Murcer was shuttled back to the minors for more seasoning at the start of the 1966 campaign. In Toledo of the International League, Murcer batted .266 with 15 homers and 62 RBI. Back with the Yankees to end the season, Murcer played in 21 games (again at shortstop), but he hit just .174. The Oklahoma native got a two-year vacation from his budding career when he was called for military service. He returned in 1969 to start his first full season with New York at age 23.

From 1969 through 1973, Murcer was a vital component in the Yankees offense. He clubbed no fewer than 22 home runs a season, while batting over .300 twice. In 1971 Murcer hit a career

high of .331 with 25 homers and 94 RBI. The next year he led the American League with 102 runs scored. He hit a personal best of 33 home runs and tallied a career-high 96 RBI.

The Yankees shocked die-hard fans by trading Murcer to the San Francisco Giants for Bobby Bonds on October 24, 1974. Murcer logged two impressive seasons by the Bay, batting .298 with 91 RBI the first year, then collecting 23 homers and 90 RBI in 1976. The Giants peddled Murcer to the Chicago Cubs with third baseman Steve Ontiveros and a minor leaguer in exchange for third baseman Bill Madlock and utility man Rob Sperring on February 11, 1977. His biggest success as a Cubbie came in 1977, a year highlighted by 27 round-trippers and 89 RBI.

Murcer didn't get a shot at postseason play until the twilight of his playing career, when he returned to the Yankees as a part-time player. In the 1980 American League Championship Series he went hitless in four plate appearances, starting one game. Things

were rosier in 1981. He had a single and a walk in three at-bats as a designated hitter in that A.L.C.S. Murcer was unsuccessful in three pinch-hitting assignments against the Los Angeles Dodgers in the 1981 World Series, but he finally knew what it felt like to play in a fall classic.

For his career Murcer accumulated 1,862 hits in 1,908 games for a .277 batting average. Of his many hits, 285 were doubles, 45 were triples, and 252 were home runs (for a home run percentage of 3.7). He drove in 1,043 lifetime runs and scored 972 on his own. Murcer acquired discipline at the plate early in his career after two seasons of 100-plus strikeouts. For his career he fanned 841 times, but he drew 862 bases on balls. He ranks 12th on the all-time Yankees list for home runs, while placing 17th for career RBI. It's intriguing to consider what Murcer's home run total might have been if he had played in a more homer-friendly park like Wrigley Field for his entire career. While the thought is just idle speculation, it's obvious that Murcer could have padded his final four-bagger totals substantially. Furthermore, if Murcer had been able to bypass his two-year military hitch, he would have added two peak years of competition to his final records.

Following his retirement in 1983 Murcer became an assistant vice president for the Yankees. Later he became a Yankees broadcaster.

Playing under the shadow of fellow Oklahoman Mickey Mantle, Bobby Murcer never matched Mantle's long-ball output. Still he managed to hit 20 or more homers seven times in his career.

CAREER HIGHLIGHTS
BOBBY RAY MURCER

Born: May 20, 1946   Oklahoma City, OK
Height: 5'11"   **Weight:** 170 lbs.   **Batted:** Left   **Threw:** Right
Outfielder, designated hitter: New York Yankees, 1965-74, 1979-83; San Francisco Giants, 1975-76; Chicago Cubs, 1977-79.

- ★ Led the A.L. in runs scored in 1972
- ★ Drove in 90 or more runs five times
- ★ Hit 20 or more home runs seven times
- ★ Appeared in the 1981 World Series
- ★ Played in two League Championship Series

MAJOR LEAGUE TOTALS

G	AB	H	BA	2B	3B	HR	R	RBI	SB
1,908	6,730	1,862	.277	285	45	252	972	1,043	127

DALE MURPHY

Despite a dismal 1988 season for outfielder Dale Murphy, the Atlanta Braves didn't trade the slugger, as many predicted they would. Murphy is perhaps the only superstar on one of baseball's losingest teams, and Atlanta needs a star to hitch its wagon to.

It's only fitting that Murphy be merited in terms other than money. His lineup of charitable endorsements and contributions is almost as lengthy as his major league stats, and such a personality is worth his weight in gold as a team representative. Murphy has to be one of baseball's finest 1980s ambassadors.

Selected by the Braves in the first round of the June 1974 free-agent draft, Murphy spent a year in the minors in 1974, then collected All-Star honors during his next three seasons in the Braves farm system. Murphy was in Atlanta to stay during his 18-game trial at the end of 1977. His .316 average was the highest he has ever hit in the majors.

His first full season in 1978 added 23 homers and 79 runs to his already promising stats. Platooned as a first sacker and catcher the following year, Murphy led the league with 20 errors but had an acceptable .978 fielding average as well as 21 round-trippers, 3 of them in a single game on May 18, 1979.

Murphy found his calling in 1980, when he earned All-Star honors in his first season as an outfielder. He finished third in the homer battle with 33, a competition that would be slowed by the strike of 1981. In 1981, for the first of two times, Murphy tied the major league record for most double plays by an outfielder (4), a feat he would repeat in 1985. Ironically, 1983 found him making history as the outfielder with the fewest double plays (0).

A very good fielder, Murphy's lack of double plays could well be attributed to a lack of opportunity. A perennial Gold Glove man, Murphy's eye is as fatal as his arm. This serves him well in the batter's box also. He hits forcefully to any field and can terrorize pitchers of any variety. Like any hitter, Murphy has his darker days—and he had them often in 1988, when his average sank to a career-low .226, despite 24 homers. But he makes up for lost time on the base paths, with above-average speed and larceny that reached a career high of 30 swipes in 1983.

That year saw him capture his second consecutive MVP award, making

him only the fourth player in history to be so honored. He led the league in slugging percentage (.540), RBI (121), and (for the second year) games played (162). He also matched his 1982 effort of 36 homers. *The Sporting News*, AP, and UPI showered Murphy with acclaim and kept it coming through 1986, when pitchers started walking the righthander on an all-too-regular basis.

The big-hearted Brave had a stellar season in 1985, earning the prestigious Lou Gehrig Memorial award as the player who best exemplified the spirit and character of the dedicated Hall of Famer. Murphy chairs and sits on committees for several medical foundations battling various diseases. He has been a public service spokesperson for causes ranging from the March of Dimes to American Legion Baseball to Georgia's public school system. Murphy is also the dedicated father of five boys.

Murphy's 1985 accolades included career-high statistics and a head-spinning amount of recognition, including April's Player of the Month, the N.L. All-Star team, and a Silver Slugger award. In April he had a .380 batting average, an .863 slugging percentage,

17 runs, and 8 doubles in only 19 games. Homering in four straight games for the second time in his career, Murphy matched Ron Cey's 1977 record for most April RBI with 29. He finished the year with a career-high 37 dingers, 185 hits, a 15-game hitting streak, and a healthy .300 average.

Dedication came to the fore when Murphy came off the bench in 1986 with day-old stitches in his hand to preserve a consecutive game streak dating from September 1981. It ended in September at 740, the seventh best in major league history.

Because he racked up such impressive totals in 1987 (a personal best of 44 homers, with 105 RBI and a .295 average) his 1988 season seems like a major letdown, both to Murphy and to baseball fans everywhere. Hopeful Braves fans are thankful that Murphy wasn't traded, pointing to the fact that his average has never decreased in two consecutive seasons.

Murphy has been one of the National League's most gifted outfielders of the 1980s. Playing the rest of his career with the Braves could put Murphy into a category with past superstars like Ernie Banks and Luke Appling, neither of whom ever got to prove himself in World Series play. Murphy's final and greatest challenge is to try to propel the sluggish Braves into the fall classic.

Perhaps the Atlanta Braves only superstar, slugger Dale Murphy has seen postseason play only once. In 1982 the Braves lost to the Cardinals in the N.L. Championship Series. Murphy had 3 hits in 11 at-bats for a .273 average.

CAREER HIGHLIGHTS
DALE BRYAN MURPHY

Born: March 12, 1956   Portland, OR
Height: 6'4"   **Weight:** 215 lbs.   **Bats:** Right   **Throws:** Right
Catcher, first baseman, outfielder: Atlanta Braves, 1976-89

★ Selected N.L. MVP in 1982 and 1983   ★ Led the league twice in homers and RBI
★ Named to seven All-Star teams   ★ Has driven in 100-plus runs five times

MAJOR LEAGUE TOTALS

G	AB	H	BA	2B	3B	HR	R	RBI	SB
1,829	6,749	1,820	.270	292	37	354	1,065	1,088	151

EDDIE MURRAY

Being number two isn't so bad when number one is Mickey Mantle. In a dozen years with the Baltimore Orioles, Eddie Murray chalked up switch-hitting statistics surpassed only by The Mick, including switch-hit home runs, lifetime game-winning RBI, and intentional bases on balls. In 1987 he became the first major leaguer ever to switch-hit homers in two consecutive games.

The bases on balls stat most clearly shows the high regard Murray commands from pitchers. A power player who has led the league in homers and RBI, Murphy learned over the years to temper his aggressive tendencies with the patience to wait for a good pitch.

Luckily, almost any pitch is a good one for Murray. A natural righthand batter, only the high inside and low outside corners from righthand pitchers are tough for him, and only extreme corner pitches from lefties throw him for a loop. Favoring the fastball, Murray averaged 27 homers annually after signing with the O's in 1977. His average has only once dipped below the .283 mark he posted in his rookie season, and five times it has sailed to .300 and beyond.

Standards of excellence were set early for Murray, who played on a high school team with future major leaguers Ozzie Smith, Darrell Jackson, Gary Alexander, and younger brother Rich Murray. Brothers Eddie and Rich followed three older brothers, Charles, Venice, and Leon, into the higher echelons of organized ball, and both surpassed their elders by making it to the majors. Even while on the diamond with his brother in high school, Murray was demonstrating the diversity that would make him a superstar in the future. He won 7 games pitching as a senior, and he was also a center on his school basketball team.

Nowadays Murray devotes his excess energies to charities, having twice been nominated for the Roberto Clemente humanitarian award. Murray has sponsored more than half a dozen medical, educational, and religious foundations. At age 33 he attends Cal State in the off-season, preparing for the day when he and baseball no longer need each other.

That day may be a long time coming. After 15 years of organized ball Murray continues to post excellent marks in both offensive and defensive play and has never yet experienced a subpar season. Perhaps the biggest surprise is that he spent four years in the minors,

despite leading O's farm clubs in homers and earning minor league All-Star honors on three occasions. Murray's minor league career began when he was 17 years old. At age 21, when he finally broke into the bigs, he did it with style, becoming the fourth Baltimore Oriole to capture American League Rookie of the Year honors.

A club leader in runs, hits, and RBI, Murray appeared in his first World Series in 1979. Establishing a trend he was to follow four years later when the O's again captured the A.L. pennant, Murray gave everything in postseason play. He batted .417 in the A.L.C.S. and reached base safely 10 times in 17 plate appearances. In the World Series Murray reached base 7 of his first 8 at-bats against the Pittsburgh Pirates, then went hitless for the remainder of the Series. However, he was errorless in the field, recording 60 putouts in seven games.

During his years as a first sacker with the O's he gained a reputation as a dazzling fielder. He's among the best at fielding bunts and gaining force-outs at

second base. Murray is a keen observer, ever alert for possible pickoff opportunities at first base.

From 1980 to 1983 Murray seemed to get hotter as the seasons progressed. He ended with long streaks of high averages and high hit ratios, tying league, team, and career highs in grand slams, home runs, runs, hits, and RBI. It all peaked in 1982 when Murray won his first Gold Glove. The veteran remained on a tear all season long. Hitting .441 with 5 homers and 17 RBI in only 18 games, Murray was April's Player of the Month. The season ended as propitiously as it had begun, with 25 homers and 87 RBI.

Murray was on a roll, as proved by Baltimore's five-game upset of the Phillies in the 1983 World Series. Now a two-time Gold Glove man, Murray's 2 homers in the final Series game made him a leading candidate for MVP. Cal Ripken, Jr. was able to nose him out by only 32 votes.

More Gold Gloves and a half-dozen Most Valuable Oriole awards accumulated, highlighted by an August afternoon in 1985 when Murray hit a solo homer, a three-run blast, and a grand slam, all in the same game.

Murray's 1986 stats are misleading due to his only stint on the disabled list. Despite a month on the sidelines, he led his club in batting (.305) for a record sixth time and ranked fourth in the league in on-base percentage. He had 30 homers and 91 RBI in 1987, then hit 28 and 84 in 1988. Murray has been one of the best first basemen in baseball for more than a decade. Despite impressive performances for the Orioles for almost 12 years, Murray was traded to the Los Angeles Dodgers after the 1988 season.

CAREER HIGHLIGHTS
EDDIE CLARENCE MURRAY

Born: February 24, 1956   Los Angeles, CA
Height: 6'2"   **Weight:** 200 lbs.   **Bats:** Both   **Throws:** Right
First baseman: Baltimore Orioles, 1977-88; Los Angeles Dodgers, 1989.

★ Was voted A.L. Rookie of the Year in 1977
★ Played in two World Series
★ Homered in double figures for 13 straight seasons
★ Led the A.L. in RBI with 78 in 1981
★ Seven-time A.L. All-Star
★ Has driven in 100-plus RBI five times

MAJOR LEAGUE TOTALS

G	AB	H	BA	2B	3B	HR	R	RBI	SB
1,980	7,439	2,168	.291	380	26	353	1,114	1,278	68

Most fans know that slugger Eddie Murray receives a multimillion dollar salary. Few realize, however, that he donates a sizable amount of his income to summer camps for inner-city kids in honor of his mother.

STAN MUSIAL

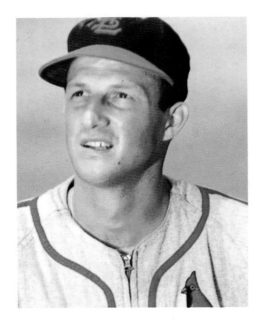

Stan Musial, a three-time Most Valuable Player and one of the greatest stars in National League history, might have given up before his illustrious career had ever begun if he hadn't been helped by a member of the 1919 "Black Sox" World Series team.

Dickie Kerr, a Chicago White Sox pitcher who won two 1919 World Series games despite the scandal, was Musial's minor league coach in Daytona Beach of the Florida State League. The St. Louis Cardinals had signed Musial as a lefthand pitcher. By August he had accomplished an impressive record of 18 wins and 5 losses. He was hitting just as well, exceeding a .300 clip. Manager Kerr used Musial as an outfielder between starts to keep his productive bat in the lineup. One day Musial attempted a diving catch in the outfield and injured his left shoulder so badly that his pitching career was permanently ended. Worse than that, Musial's throwing arm was so weakened that he seemed of little use in the outfield.

Because Musial had been married for just a year and his wife was expecting a baby, he had to think about his future employment. His minor league salary was only $100 a month and was paid only during the season. If he was unable to throw well, even his low-paying baseball job would be gone. Musial had passed up a college basketball scholarship at the University of Pittsburgh, and he now seemed destined to quit baseball to work in the steel mills of his native Pennsylvania. However, Musial's manager encouraged him not to quit and let him and his wife stay the rest of the season at the Kerr home to save money.

Thanks to Kerr's support, Musial continued with his baseball career. After advancing all the way to Triple-A Rochester in 1941, Musial continued to hit well. He was batting .326 in the International League when he got a late season call-up from St. Louis. With the Cardinals he registered a scorching .426 batting average in just 12 games. With such impressive hitting exploits, no one seemed to notice Musial's throwing difficulties.

Musial immediately had an enormous impact on the Cardinals. In his first four seasons with the Redbirds the team won four pennants and three World Series. Musial helped transform the Cardinals into one of the toughest teams of the 40s. In 1943 he won his first MVP award with a league-best .357 average. Following another batting title in 1946

(there'd be seven in all), Musial had an awesome campaign in 1948. He was league MVP, with league leads in every department except home runs. His .376 average was the highest since Bill Terry hit .401 in 1930. Musial nearly won his eighth batting title in 1962—at the age of 41. He batted a third-place .330, only 16 points behind batting leader Tommy Davis.

"Stan the Man," also known as "The Donora Greyhound" because of his quickness, retired after the 1963 season. He stole only 78 bases in his career, but he showed enormous agility in the field and impressive bursts of speed when legging out extra-base hits. At the plate Musial became one of the greatest batsmen in Cardinals history. He leads the team in the following all-time categories: games (3,026), at-bats

(10,972), runs (1,949), hits (3,630), total bases (6,134), bases on balls (1,599), doubles (725), triples (177), home runs (475), and RBI (1,951).

Even today his hits rank fourth on baseball's all-time list, trailing only Pete Rose, Ty Cobb, and Henry Aaron. He ranks third in baseball history in doubles behind Rose and Tris Speaker. Musial is sixth in runs and fifth in RBI. The 24-time All-Star had double-digit homer totals for every full season he played in the majors.

After setting what was then a National League record for consecutive games, Musial was sidelined after 895 straight appearances when he injured a shoulder swinging at a high, outside pitch. On May 13, 1958, Musial collected his 3,000th hit—a dramatic pinch-hit double—in Chicago's Wrigley Field. Musial remains as popular with fans today as he was with Cardinals supporters throughout the 1940s and 1950s. He was such a dignified performer both on and off the field that upon retirement, Commissioner Ford Frick referred to him as "baseball's perfect warrior, baseball's perfect knight."

Musial was elected to the Hall of Fame in 1969, his first year of eligibility. He now serves as vice president of the St. Louis Cardinals. Some of his other business ventures have included owning a restaurant and hotel in St. Louis, along with other real estate holdings. In tribute to the great player the Cardinals erected a life-size bronze monument of Musial outside Busch Stadium. The statue shows Musial in his coiled batting stance, the image fans have held of The Man throughout the last five decades.

CAREER HIGHLIGHTS
STANLEY FRANK MUSIAL

Born: November 21, 1920   Donora, PA
Height: 6'0"   **Weight:** 175 lbs.   **Batted:** Left   **Threw:** Left
First baseman, outfielder: St. Louis Cardinals, 1941-63.

- ★ Named the N.L. MVP in 1942, 1946, and 1948
- ★ Played in 24 All-Star games
- ★ Has the third-highest total doubles in history
- ★ Played in four World Series

- ★ Formerly held the N.L. record for most career hits
- ★ Won seven batting titles
- ★ Compiled a .331 lifetime batting average
- ★ Elected to the Hall of Fame in 1969

MAJOR LEAGUE TOTALS

G	AB	H	BA	2B	3B	HR	R	RBI	SB
3,026	10,972	3,630	.331	725	177	475	1,949	1,951	78

Stan Musial was not only a phenomenal player but a popular one as well. His career
spanned three decades, and as a 41-year-old grandfather in 1962, he could still hit .330.
He won his last batting title at the age of 36, with a .351 average.

GRAIG NETTLES

Graig Nettles has over 20 years of professional baseball under his belt. The lefthand pull hitter began his pro career at the age of 18, when he was selected in the fourth round of the free-agent draft by the Minnesota Twins in June 1966.

Nineteen homers the following season and a circuit-leading 34 double plays became Nettles' ticket to the majors. In only three games with the Twins, Nettles held his own with a .333 average. Most of 1968 was spent in Denver, however, until league-pacing marks of 12 triples and 20 double plays earned him a permanent call-up. In 22 Twins games near the season's end, he logged 5 homers (to add to the 22 dingers he hit in the minors earlier that year) and 50 putouts. The following year his time was divided between the outfield and third base; he played 96 games in the Twins first-place win in the brand-new Western Division of the American League. He was 1-for-1 in a pinch-hitting role during the first A.L. Championship Series, which was swept by the Baltimore Orioles.

On December 12, 1969, Nettles, pitcher Dean Chance, and Bob Miller were shipped to the Cleveland Indians in exchange for pitchers Luis Tiant and Stan Williams, and outfielder Ted Uhlaender. Statistically speaking, Nettles' three years with Cleveland were some of his best, although emotionally they could not compare with his six pennant races and five World Series to come.

Although his 1969 fielding average of .985 was his career high, Nettles led the league in 1970 with his .967 mark, acquired at third base and in the outfield. Playing exclusively at third in 1971, Nettles led in putouts (159), total chances (507), double plays (54), and assists (412), and he notched 28 homers. His marks in assists and double plays established major league records. In 1972 he repeated his lead in assists (358) while adding a league-high 21 errors for the only dark record of his career.

Nettles became part of a two-for-four trade in 1972. He and catcher Jerry Moses went to New York, while John Ellis, Jerry Kenney, Charlie Spikes, and Rusty Torres journeyed to Cleveland.

With the Yankees, Nettles led in assists for the third consecutive season with 410 in 1973, earning a pace-setting 553 chances. He continued hitting for power, smacking 22 dingers and 81 RBI. The following year included a bit of shortstop play. However, he remained first in the league in chances (545) and putouts (147).

Nettles was the second team member of the 1970s New York Yankees to write a kiss-and-tell account of their playing days. Once quoted as saying that his childhood ambitions were to join the circus and to play professional ball, Nettles claimed that with the Yankees, he hit two birds with one stone.

The three-ring circus began in 1976, with the Bronx Bombers making the first of three successive grabs for the world championship. Despite Nettles' league-best 32 homers that year (plus 3 during the Series), the first bid against the Cincinnati Reds was not victorious. In the next two years, however, the Yankees beat the Dodgers in the Series, winning in six games each time.

In 1981 Los Angeles had one more chance against the Yanks in postseason play, and perhaps it's only fair that they were the winners this time. A competitor until the end, Nettles outdid himself with a .400 batting average in the three games he played.

Traded to the San Diego Padres at the end of 1983, Nettles logged three years with this National League club, concluding 17 consecutive seasons of 15 or more homers per season. His presence helped solidify the Padres and show them the way to their first National League pennant. Things started winding down for the slugger in 1987. His fielding average, batting average, games played, and number of homers were all down.

In 1988, Nettles was active in 80 games for the Expos. He had just 16 hits, but still managed to convert them into 14 RBI. His 1 homer drove his career total to 390. Unfortunately his average was a meager .172. Nettles was considered unofficially retired after that season when the Expos did not pick up his option.

Whether the long and illustrious career of Graig Nettles is really over is open to debate however. His brother Jim Nettles (a long-time major league outfielder, now an A's minor league coach) wasn't sure about Graig's plans before the season began. "He wasn't going to play last year, but...," Jim said about his brother's one-year hitch with the 1988 Montreal Expos. Jim Nettles seemed to hint that Graig's love for the game could compel him to try to prolong his career.

CAREER HIGHLIGHTS
GRAIG NETTLES

Born: August 20, 1944   San Diego, CA
Height: 6'0"   **Weight:** 189 lbs.   **Batted:** Left   **Threw:** Right
Third baseman: Minnesota Twins, 1967-69; Cleveland Indians, 1970-72; New York Yankees, 1973-83; San Diego Padres, 1984-86; Atlanta Braves, 1987; Montreal Expos, 1988.

* Led the A.L. in homers in 1976
* Hit 20 or more homers for 11 years
* Led A.L. third basemen in assists six times
* Established N.L. records for most assists and double plays by a third baseman in a season
* Named to the All-Star team six times
* Appeared in five World Series
* Played in seven League Championship Series
* Established an A.L. record for most homers by a third baseman, accumulating 319 by 1985

MAJOR LEAGUE TOTALS

G	AB	H	BA	2B	3B	HR	R	RBI	SB
2,700	8,986	2,225	.248	328	28	390	1,193	1,314	32

Graig Nettles not only won two Gold Glove awards but also led A.L. third sackers in assists six times during his career. A power hitter as well, Nettles led the A.L. in homers in 1976, with 32.

HAL NEWHOUSER

If Hal Newhouser had been able to perform during his entire career the way he pitched in the mid-1940s, his plaque would be displayed in Cooperstown alongside those of the other great hurlers of his era. Newhouser pitched for 17 seasons in the majors from 1939 to 1955, but a dismal six years at the start of his career and problems with bursitis at the end prevented him from achieving the consistency required for real greatness.

From 1944 to 1948, however, Newhouser compiled a win-loss record of 118-56, averaging just under 24 victories a season. He led the league in wins four years, and twice recorded the best ERA. Newhouser so dominated the circuit that he won the Most Valuable Player award in both 1944 and 1945. The man known as "Prince Hal" became the league's only pitcher to take the award twice. Only Philadelphia Athletics first baseman Jimmie Foxx had won the honor in consecutive years before Newhouser.

Newhouser's 1945 season was especially awesome. He led the league in starts (36), complete games (29), wins (25), strikeouts (212), shutouts (8), ERA (1.81), and winning percentage (.735), to take his Detroit Tigers to the World Series, where they beat the Chicago Cubs in seven games. Newhouser won 2 games, including the decisive seventh game, and lost 1 versus the Cubs. The durable lefty logged 3 complete-game performances and posted a record 22 strikeouts while walking just 4. Newhouser would not see postseason play again with the Tigers.

Newhouser's career totals of 207 wins and 150 losses compare favorably with the records of many Hall of Fame pitchers. In fact, ten pitchers enshrined in Cooperstown won fewer games. He's the only two-time MVP winner not elected to the HOF. Critics point out that the big southpaw earned his success during the war years, when over half of the regular major leaguers were gone from the game. (Newhouser wanted to serve in the military, but was classified 4-F because of a heart ailment). Yet he remained the top pitcher in the league in 1946, when the big sluggers and hard hitters returned from the military. That year he led the circuit in both wins (26) and ERA (1.94). Two years later he topped the league in wins for a fourth time with 21. His 170 wins for the decade surpassed all other American League pitchers.

Newhouser grew up in Detroit and began his career as a 17-year-old high school graduate. All the Tigers needed to sign the hurler was a $400 bonus and a $150 monthly salary. His ascent to the major leagues took less than two seasons. He began with Alexandria, winning 8 and losing 4. Most impressively, Newhouser whiffed 107 batters in 96 innings. His ERA was a tidy 2.34.

The Tigers advanced Newhouser to Beaumont of the Texas League, where he slipped to a 5-14 record and a 3.83 ERA. Nevertheless, the Tigers gave Newhouser a one-game shot in the majors at season's end. In five innings pitched he wound up allowing 3 runs on 3 hits for his first American League loss. Although he didn't return to the minors for more polishing, Newhouser learned slowly through his major league experiences. Many lessons were disappointing, and Newhouser didn't have a winning season until 1944. He never won more than 9 games in one season, and had a shocking 8-17 record in 1943 with a league-leading 111 bases on balls. But once he turned his luck around he became one of the American League's toughest moundsmen.

Cleveland finally got its wish to sign Newhouser when Detroit released the veteran lefty on July 22, 1953. He was signed in April 1954. Newhouser showed that he wasn't washed up, posting a 7-2 record for the Tribe in 26 appearances (with only one start). His ERA was only 2.49, his lowest in years. Newhouser had one uneventful outing in the 1954 World Series. The Indians had won a record 111 games that year but got swept in four straight games by the New York Giants. Newhouser went in as a reliever in the fateful fourth game. After giving up 1 walk and 1 hit, Indians manager Al Lopez yanked the veteran. Following just two games in 1955 Newhouser retired.

Newhouser was named to five All-Star teams from 1943 to 1948. In 10.2 total innings he had no wins or losses, but struck out 8 and walked just 3 while giving up 2 earned runs (both scored in 1944). Newhouser started the 1947 midseason classic but is remembered more for his efforts in the 1946 All-Star game. The American League jumped out to a 3-0 lead behind the pitching of Bob Feller. After three innings Newhouser relieved for the next three frames. His work was even sharper than Feller's. He set down 8 straight National Leaguers before giving up just one single to "Peanuts" Lowrey. His shutout relief included 4 strikeouts. By the time he left the game his American League teammates had staked out a 6-0 lead and would go on to a 12-0 slaughter.

Following his retirement Newhouser became a banker in Pontiac, Michigan. He scouted in the 1950s for the Baltimore Orioles and in the early 60s for the Indians. He is currently retained as a scout for the Houston Astros.

CAREER HIGHLIGHTS
HAROLD NEWHOUSER

Born: May 20, 1921   Detroit, MI
Height: 6'2"   **Weight:** 180 lbs.   **Batted:** Left   **Threw:** Left
Pitcher: Detroit Tigers, 1939-53; Cleveland Indians, 1954-55.

- ★ Led the league in wins four times
- ★ Won back-to-back A.L. MVP awards in 1944 and 1945
- ★ Topped the A.L. in complete games in 1945 and 1947
- ★ Earned two A.L. strikeout crowns
- ★ Named Player of Year by *The Sporting News* in 1945
- ★ Pitched in two World Series, winning 2 games

MAJOR LEAGUE TOTALS

G	IP	W	L	Pct.	SO	BB	ERA
488	2,993	207	150	.580	1,796	1,249	3.06

Ted Williams referred to Hal Newhouser as one of the three best pitchers he had ever faced. Newhouser won two consecutive MVP awards in 1944 and 1945 and led the A.L. in victories four times.

KID NICHOLS

Beneath his youthful countenance Charles "Kid" Nichols had nerves of steel and an arm to match. His 15-year career, averaging well over 300 innings annually, defies reasonable expectations even for today's pitchers who have modern medicine at their disposal. Yet Nichols hurled seven seasons of 30 or more wins in the 1890s, appearing in an average of 40 games per year, without a team trainer or a star reliever ready to jump in after only 100 pitches.

The Boston Beaneaters introduced the Kid to the baseball world in 1890, when he was just 20 years old. The Wisconsin native was anything but a slow starter as he reeled off 27 victories against 19 losses. Nichols started 47 games, and completed all of them. He was first in the league with 7 shutouts and notched a spiffy 2.21 ERA. His winning percentage even surpassed that of his team. This would be par for the course for his entire career. By the end of his first nine seasons he had led his Boston team to five championships. An overhand, righthand thrower with pinpoint control, Nichols led the league in shutouts twice more and compiled 48 no-run games in his career.

As might be expected from such an active pitcher, ERA was not one of Nichols' strongest suits (although ERA wasn't kept as a statistic at the time). Even so, he went over 4.00 only once in a regular season, as his lifetime ERA of 2.95 demonstrates. More indicative of his talents are his impressive totals in strikeouts (222 and 240 in his first two years, dipping below 100 only three times in 14 full seasons), and in walks, which never exceeded 90 in his last seven years.

In 1896 Nichols started a three-year streak of league-leading wins, although none touched his 1892 achievement of 35 victories. In his first five seasons he pitched well over 400 annual innings; in his first ten campaigns he never won fewer than 20 games.

Although only in his early 30s, Nichols made a drastic career change. He curbed his playing aims and decided to concentrate on a future in managing. After 12 admirable seasons with Boston he bought part-interest in Kansas City's Western Association club. As the player/manager he pitched 48 victories over the next two seasons. Because this service wasn't with a major league club, Nichols' many wins in Kansas City aren't counted in his lifetime totals. Having proven himself by bouncing

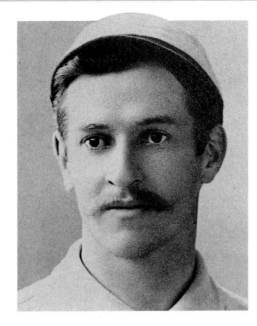

back from his 20-15 season in 1901 while still with Boston, Nichols went on to get a player/manager position with the St. Louis Cardinals in 1904. As the Cardinals skipper Nichols won just 94 out of 202 games in two seasons. He helped his own cause in 1904 by winning 21 decisions at age 35. Even then he went the distance in a 17-inning game, striking out 15 Brooklyn batters.

Nichols had passed the 300-win mark when he was just 30 years old. As of 1989 his 362 wins put him seventh on the all-time list. His 533 complete games ranks fourth, his 5,061 innings pitched ranks tenth, and his .636 winning percentage is the 19th-best in history. These marks have held up for the greater part of a century. The Kid, it seems, has aged very well.

On the Braves all-time list Nichols is considered the most accomplished

righthander in the team's history (Warren Spahn holds the honors from the left side). Only Spahn and Nichols achieved more than 300 victories in a Braves uniform. Nichols ranks fourth on the Braves all-time list in games pitched with 543. He's second (behind Spahn) in shutouts with 44 and in innings pitched with 4,570; he's third (behind Phil Niekro and Spahn) in strikeouts with 1,684. He was the perennial wins leader on the Braves club every year. Long before the Braves had relievers like Bruce Sutter or Gene Garber, Nichols was subbing in the bullpen between starts.

Nichols accepted the inevitable decline of his physical abilities with good grace. After 4 appearances in 1906 earned him a 9.82 ERA and 1 loss, Nichols turned his enterprising skills to the motion picture and real estate industries. He also managed one of the largest bowling alleys in the state of Missouri, becoming a bowling champion himself at the age of 64. Coaching a small town college baseball team, Kid Nichols remained young at heart until his death at age 83 in 1953. Happily, Nichols was still enjoying an active life when the Baseball Hall of Fame honored him in 1949.

Kid Nichols, one of those colorful 19th-century hurlers, actually pitched with no windup. Known for his control and speed, the Kid enjoyed seven straight seasons with 30 or more wins, which is still a record.

CAREER HIGHLIGHTS
CHARLES AUGUSTUS NICHOLS

Born: September 14, 1869 Madison, WI **Died:** April 11, 1953
Height: 5'10" **Weight:** 175 lbs. **Batted:** Both **Threw:** Right
Pitcher: Boston Beaneaters, (later Braves) 1890-1901; St. Louis Cardinals, 1904-05; Philadelphia Phillies, 1905-06. Manager: St. Louis Cardinals, 1904-05.

- ★ Led the N.L. in shutouts three times
- ★ Ranks sixth on the all-time pitching list with 362 wins
- ★ Elected to the Hall of Fame in 1949
- ★ Posted double-digit wins in *every* full season
- ★ Recognized by most historians as the best pitcher of the 19th century

MAJOR LEAGUE TOTALS

G	IP	W	L	Pct.	SO	BB	ERA
621	5,061	362	207	.636	1,868	1,268	2.95

JOE NIEKRO

For years Joe Niekro suffered the traditional fate of younger brothers, trying hard to keep up but not getting a lot of recognition. Niekro, whose brother Phil is a sure bet for the Hall of Fame, has always been compared to his older sibling. After all both Niekros pitched past age 40, and both made their living by throwing knuckleballs as their "out" pitches. Joe Niekro finally got his first advantage over his big brother in 1987. Phil toiled for 24 years dreaming of a World Series appearance, but never got his wish; Joe has a World Series ring on his finger. Joe was a member of the 1987 world championship Minnesota Twins. Although his two innings of scoreless relief against the St. Louis Cardinals wasn't the turning point in the seven-game matchup, it was a symbolic victory for the hardworking hurler who was always known as "the other Niekro."

Joe Niekro began his professional career in 1966. He declined the interest of the Cleveland Indians, who chose him in the seventh round of the January free-agent draft. He signed with the Chicago Cubs as a third-round selection in the June draft. With only a half-season's worth of minor league experience (in Caldwell, Quincy, and Dallas-Fort Worth), Niekro made the Cubs opening-day roster in 1967. He submitted a respectable rookie season performance of 10 wins, 7 losses, and a 3.34 ERA in 36 games. Niekro had 7 complete games and 2 shutouts to his credit that year. During his sophomore season Niekro was 14-10 with 2 saves.

After just four games with the 1969 Cubs, Niekro was traded to the San Diego Padres with Gary Ross and Francisco Libran for pitcher Dick Selma on April 24. Niekro suffered through an 8-17 season with the struggling expansion team.

The Padres shipped Niekro to the Detroit Tigers for Pat Dobson and infielder Dave Campbell on December 4. Niekro was 12-13 and 6-7 for the Bengals in 1970 and 1971. After a demotion to the team's Triple-A minor league affiliate in Toledo (where he pitched a seven-inning perfect-game win), Niekro was 3-2 with 1 save in just 18 appearances with the 1972 Tigers. Banished to the minors again in 1973, Niekro was rescued by the Atlanta Braves from minor league oblivion.

While Niekro's years with the Braves weren't filled with success, he did spend two seasons with his brother Phil, a Brave since 1964.

The Houston Astros got one of the best deals in baseball history when they purchased Niekro on April 5, 1975. For seven seasons Niekro had 13 or more victories. His first success on the comeback trail came in 1977, when he was 13-8 with 5 saves. After a 14-14 season in 1978, Niekro was 21-11 in 1979. He tied for the league lead in wins and shutouts (5) and finished second in the Cy Young award balloting to Bruce Sutter. His 21 victories set an Astros record. The following season Niekro registered another fine showing, winning 20 and losing 12. The Astros won their first divisional pennant that year. After winning 17, 15, and 16 games from 1982-1984, Niekro suddenly ranked in 14 Astros career pitching categories.

The Niekro brothers were reunited in 1985 with the New York Yankees, when the Astros traded Joe to the Yanks in exchange for pitcher Jim Deshaies and two minor leaguers on September 15. Joe won 2 late-season games, but the Yankees fell short of the Eastern Division pennant they pursued. Both brothers signed free-agent contracts to stay with the club the next year. In 1985 Phil won 16 games for New York, while Joe won 2 for the Yankees. Phil was released at season's end, and Joe was traded to the Minnesota Twins for catcher Mark Salas and cash on June 7, 1987. His 4-9 record wasn't a big lift to the Twins, but it helped them win the Western Division pennant away from the Oakland A's.

Perhaps Niekro's 1987 record would have been brighter if he hadn't been slapped with a ten-day suspension for doctoring baseballs. While he was pitching against the Angels in California on August 3, the umpires discovered some nicked-up balls in play. As the umps approached the mound and ordered him to surrender the contents of his pockets, Niekro tried to toss an emery board and a piece of sandpaper out of sight. Although Niekro denied the charge, the umps ruled that he had been illegally scuffing baseballs to gain an unfair advantage over hitters.

Niekro retired after making just two starts for the 1988 Twins. Although he was 1-1, he compiled a whopping 10.03 ERA by giving up 13 runs in 12 innings. His lifetime totals include 221 wins, 204 losses, and 1,747 strikeouts.

Always playing in the shadow of his older brother, Joe Niekro had one accomplishment over brother Phil. Joe got to pitch in a World Series game while on the Twins roster in 1987.

CAREER HIGHLIGHTS
JOSEPH FRANKLIN NIEKRO

Born: November 7, 1944   Martins Ferry, OH
Height: 6'1"   **Weight:** 195 lbs.   **Batted:** Right   **Threw:** Right
Pitcher: Chicago Cubs, 1967-69; San Diego Padres, 1969; Detroit Tigers, 1970-72; Atlanta Braves, 1973-74; Houston Astros, 1975-85; New York Yankees, 1985-87; Minnesota Twins, 1987-88.

- ★ Appeared in the 1987 World Series
- ★ Winningest pitcher in Astros history
- ★ Pitched 10 scoreless innings in the 1980 N.L. Championship Series
- ★ Won 20 games two times
- ★ Won in double figures ten times
- ★ Played on the 1979 All-Star team

MAJOR LEAGUE TOTALS

G	IP	W	L	Pct.	SO	BB	ERA
702	3,585	221	204	.520	1,747	1,262	3.59

PHIL NIEKRO

Phil Niekro and Hoyt Wilhelm have several things in common: Both major league pitchers used the knuckleball to build long careers in baseball, and both men pitched in the majors well after their 45th birthday, a practice seldom seen. Wilhelm is already a member of the Baseball Hall of Fame. In 1993, when Niekro becomes eligible for election to the Hall, perhaps they will share another bond.

Niekro retired after a remarkable 24-year career in the major leagues. As of 1987, he was the last active player from the days of the Milwaukee Braves. He hung up his glove at age 48, ending a career that began with the 1964 Braves.

Niekro's minor league experience must have raised doubts about the possibility of his ever reaching the majors. He started with Wellsville of the New York-Penn League in 1959, winding up the season in the Nebraska State League with a combined 9-2 record and a league-leading 23 appearances in Nebraska. Stops in Jacksonville and Louisville of the American Association followed in 1960. In 1961 he appeared in 51 games with Austin of the Texas League. Back with Louisville in 1962 Niekro hurled in 49 games, going 9-6. Although he was on the Denver (Pacific Coast League) roster in 1963, Niekro missed the entire season due to military service. He began the 1964 season in the majors with Milwaukee, but he was demoted to Denver after compiling no win-loss record and a 4.80 ERA in his debut. With Denver, Niekro won a career high of 11 games, striking out 119 in 172 innings. He was in the majors to stay starting in 1965.

In his long career Niekro pitched one no-hitter (against the San Diego Padres on August 5, 1973) and led the National League in wins on two occasions, with 20 in 1974 and 21 in 1979. Phil lost 20 games twice in his career, but as many baseball experts say, a pitcher has to be pretty good to have the opportunity to lose 20 games. A five-time All-Star, Niekro and brother Joe (who is five years younger) together have won more than 500 games. Their 539 combined victories make them the winningest pair of brothers in major league history, ranking 10 wins above Gaylord and Jim Perry.

The knuckleballer became the 18th player in baseball history to win 300 games, which occurred on the final day of the 1985 season with an 8-0 shutout over the Blue Jays. It was his only shutout of the season and his seventh complete game as he compiled a 16-12 record for the 1985 New York Yankees. Although Niekro had been a hurler for the Braves' first 18 seasons in Atlanta, it was the Yankees who had the most faith (and the most money) for the veteran. Niekro became the oldest pitcher ever to toss a shutout, eclipsing the mark of the legendary Satchel Paige.

While Niekro lasted so long because of his knuckleball, sometimes his unpredictable knuckler looked to be his undoing. He once tied a record with 6 wild pitches in a game. Niekro holds the dubious record of most lifetime wild pitches with 229.

Just before he was traded by the struggling Cleveland Indians to the Toronto Blue Jays for outfielder Darryl Landrum and pitcher Don Gordon on August 9, 1987, Niekro alluded to the fact that he wanted to be with a contender, saying, "Nobody wants to finish their career 25 games out of first place." Niekro got his wish, but neither he nor the Blue Jays got what they wanted—a place in the World Series. Toronto had picked Niekro up for help in their pennant chase. But the Jays faded near the finish, and Niekro was released on August 31 after three games (going 0-2).

Niekro never got to participate in a single World Series game during his career, although he did pitch in both the 1969 National League Championship Series versus the New York "Miracle" Mets and the 1982 N.L.C.S. versus St. Louis.

Probably one of the biggest regrets Atlanta Braves owner Ted Turner ever had was letting Niekro leave the team. Fans grilled the TV mogul constantly about the blunder. He apologized publicly for the move, and even talked about having a statue of Niekro placed in front of Atlanta's Fulton County Stadium. Long before his retirement the Braves retired Niekro's uniform number (35), giving him an honor afforded to only four Braves in history.

Turner couldn't be faulted for thinking logically, however. He simply saw the 44-year-old Niekro as a very used car, a machine that still ran but was going to wear out quickly. Or so he thought. Turner did his best to make amends by signing Niekro on September 23 for one final week in a Braves uniform. With the Braves hopelessly out of the pennant race again, Turner had nothing to lose. He pitched the first three innings of a game, giving up 5 runs before making the final exit of his major league career. Braves fans were grateful to see one of their first heroes come back to the fold before his retirement.

CAREER HIGHLIGHTS
PHILIP HENRY NIEKRO

Born: April 1, 1939   Blaine, OH
Height: 6'1"   **Weight:** 180 lbs.   **Batted:** Right   **Threw:** Right
Pitcher: Milwaukee Braves, 1964-65; Atlanta Braves, 1966-83, 1987; New York Yankees, 1984-85; Cleveland Indians, 1986-87; Toronto Blue Jays, 1987.

★ Led the N.L. in ERA with 1.87 in 1967

★ Had three 20-win seasons

★ Belongs to the 3,000-strikeout club and the 300-win club

★ Topped the N.L. in wins in 1974 and 1979

★ Named to five All-Star teams

★ Pitched a no-hitter against the San Diego Padres on August 5, 1973

MAJOR LEAGUE TOTALS

G	IP	W	L	Pct.	SO	BB	ERA
864	5,404	318	274	.537	3,342	1,809	3.35

Famous for his knuckleball, Phil Niekro pitched in the majors for 24 years, finally reaching 300 wins on the last day of the 1985 season. Niekro also saved 30 games, which is a rarity for a modern-day starter.

TONY OLIVA

It's a shame that the American League's designated hitter rule wasn't adopted a decade earlier. Or that Pedro Oliva couldn't have started his career ten years later.

This is one of baseball's most fascinating "what-ifs." Oliva, forever known to the baseball world as Tony, had a stellar career as a member of the Minnesota Twins from 1962 to 1976. In that time span he played in just 11 full seasons. Oliva was one of the most gifted hitters ever to grace the Minnesota roster; the trouble was that his knees wore out after only a few years in the Twins outfield. His career was prolonged for four seasons by the newly adopted designated hitter rule in 1973, but the change came along a bit too late for Oliva, who endured five knee operations in his career. However, it's intriguing to speculate on whether his health could have been preserved if he had been a designated hitter from the beginning.

As it was Oliva made the most of the seasons in which he enjoyed good health. Oliva graduated from Herraduda High School in Cuba and was one of the last players from that country to make it to the major leagues. He grew up in a family of ten children. He has two brothers who pitched and played outfield for the Cuban National Team. (In fact, he used his brother Tony's passport to leave Cuba and has used the name Tony ever since.) Before getting his starting job with the Twins, he distinguished himself in three minor league seasons. In 1961 with Wytheville Oliva batted .410 with 10 home runs and 81 RBI. He earned a silver Louisville Slugger for having the highest batting average in organized baseball that season. In 1962 with Charlotte Oliva batted .350 but missed winning the league title by less than 1 percentage point. In a brief nine-game debut with the Twins that year, Oliva hit a blistering .444.

Oliva burst onto the major league scene in 1964 and enjoyed one of the best rookie seasons ever recorded. Playing 161 games in right field for the Twins, Oliva led the league in batting average (.323), hits (217), runs scored (109), and doubles (43). This was the only time in the 20th century that a rookie had led his league in batting, while his total hits set an A.L. record for rookies. He clubbed 32 home runs and 94 RBI, finishing among the league leaders in virtually every offensive category. One of his most memorable homers that year was a grand slam

against the Los Angeles Angels on May 7, 1964. It was one of 3 four-run homers he would clobber in his time with the Twins. Oliva won the American League Rookie of the Year award but lost the MVP trophy to Oriole third baseman Brooks Robinson. Twin Cities baseball writers voted Oliva the team's outstanding rookie, and he won the Rookie of the Year award from *The Sporting News*. He also received the honor of starting in the All-Star game during his rookie season. Oliva would be an eight-time All-Star during his American League career.

The Twins won their first American League pennant in 1965, thanks in part to Oliva's second straight batting championship, a .321 effort. He paced the league with 185 hits, while slugging 16 homers and 98 RBI. He had only 5 hits in the team's seven-game World Series loss to the Los Angeles Dodgers. He was named American League Player of the Year by *The Sporting News*.

In 1969 and 1970 Oliva sparked the Twins to division titles by leading the league in hits both years. In both sea-

sons he batted above .300 and drove in 100-plus runs. He had a .440 cumulative average for the two unsuccessful A.L. Championship Series.

The master batsman holds a high place in Twins history. He ranks first or near the top of several all-time offensive lists for the team. Oliva led the team in batting average in six seasons and in RBI for three more years. Single-season marks set by Oliva include 84 extra-base hits in 1964, 374 total bases in 1964, and 9 consecutive hits in 1967. He holds a lifetime .304 batting average with 1,917 hits—both second in team history only to Rod Carew. His 220 home runs rank only behind Harmon Killebrew. Oliva is the all-time doubles champion for the Twins, with 329 two-base raps (including four league-leading seasons in that category). Five league-leads in total hits (including two years over the 200 mark), three batting titles, and one first in slugging percentage (.546 in 1971) are other highlights in Oliva's brief but glorious career.

Oliva retired as a player in 1976 after hitting .211 in 76 games. He served as a player/coach that season and found his future calling. He coached for the Twins in 1977 and 1978, then became a minor league instructor for the team from 1979 to 1984. Having coached first base for Minnesota in the past, he became the club's hitting instructor in 1986, a position he still held as of the 1989 season.

The Baseball Hall of Fame should be summoning Oliva soon. In the 1989 balloting he was seventh with 135 votes, drawing 30 percent of the total votes available. He fell 201 votes short, but he should be recognized by Cooperstown for his outstanding achievements in the near future.

CAREER HIGHLIGHTS
PEDRO OLIVA

Born: July 20, 1940   Pinar Del Rio, Cuba
Height: 6'1"   **Weight:** 175 lbs.   **Batted:** Left   **Threw:** Right
Outfielder, designated hitter: Minnesota Twins, 1962-76.

★ Won three A.L. batting titles
★ Led the A.L. in hits five times
★ Batted .440 lifetime for two A.L. Championship Series

★ Named A.L. Rookie of the Year in 1964
★ Played in the 1965 World Series
★ Named to eight All-Star teams

MAJOR LEAGUE TOTALS

G	AB	H	BA	2B	3B	HR	R	RBI	SB
1,676	6,301	1,917	.304	329	48	220	870	947	86

Fans often speculate on how great Tony Oliva's career might have been if his knee hadn't given out, but Oliva managed to have a significant career regardless, batting .304 lifetime and clubbing 220 homers.

AL OLIVER

Performing with quiet consistency over a productive career spanning 18 seasons in the major leagues, Al Oliver assembled a .303 lifetime batting average. With 2,743 career base hits, Oliver probably retired about two seasons short of the magic 3,000-hit mark that would have guaranteed him a plaque in Cooperstown, but his many great seasons both at the plate and in the field will be remembered by baseball fans for years to come.

Oliver's other career statistics compare favorably with the totals of many Hall of Famers. Just take a look at his 529 doubles, 77 triples, 219 home runs, and 1,326 RBI. In fact he played two fewer seasons than the great Reggie Jackson yet achieved a batting mark 40 points higher and had 233 more hits overall. Oliver was the center fielder for the Pittsburgh Pirates of the early 1970s, a team that won five division titles and one world championship. The seven-time All-Star batted over .300 for 11 seasons during his career, including a league-leading .331 in 1982, his first season with the Montreal Expos.

Oddly enough this dedicated player was 35 years old before he notched his first league lead. After 14 full seasons in the majors Oliver exploded in 1982 with league-high hits (204), doubles (43), RBI (109), and batting average (.331). The following year he led only in doubles (38) yet batted .300 with 184 hits and 84 RBI. These high marks in his career came close to his retirement at the end of the 1985 season. Splitting 1984 between the San Francisco Giants and the Philadelphia Phillies, Oliver carried on business as usual, with a .301 average and 26 two-base hits.

He began as a lefthand high school catcher, rejecting a Kent State University basketball scholarship for a $5,000 signing bonus and a chance to play with the Pittsburgh Pirates. A knee injury kept him on the bench for the entire 1964 season.

By 1965 he was in good health, playing with Gastonia of the Western Carolina League. By this time he had been transferred to first base and showed considerable promise both at the plate and in the field. Gastonia fans called him "Mr. Scoop" because of the fine way he handled low throws from infielders. He led the league that year with 515 at-bats and 159 runs scored in 123 games. He hit .309 with 10 home runs and 71 RBI. For the next three years he didn't match his Gastonia performance, although his batting average was close to .300 on two occasions.

During the 1966 campaign with Raleigh he batted .299 with 10 home runs and 57 RBI. He split the 1967 season between Macon and Raleigh. Oliver hit just .222 with 4 RBI in 38 games for Macon, possibly because he was making his first-ever attempt to play the outfield when not patrolling first base. However, back in Raleigh he hit .297 with 2 homers and 15 RBI in 40 games. Oliver progressed to Columbus of the International League in 1968, where he hit .315 with 14 home runs and 74 RBI in 132 games. Pittsburgh finally took notice and called him up for four games; he batted .125 with just 1 hit.

Oliver became the Pirates starting first baseman in 1969 when resident first sacker Donn Clendenon was dispatched to the Mets in a trade. In his first full season with the Bucs, Oliver hit .285 with 17 home runs and 70 RBI. It was the first of nine quality seasons he would spend in a Pittsburgh uniform.

The smooth-hitting veteran ended his distinguished career with a flourish in 1985. Although he played with four different teams during his last two seasons, his final 61 games were with the Toronto Blue Jays. His acquisition in midseason helped guarantee the Canadian team a much desired pennant. In the 1985 American League Championship Series, he batted .375, knocked in 3 runs, and provided 2 game-winning hits. Postseason play was nothing new to Oliver. He had appeared in five previous League Championship Series and had been a member of the 1971 world championship Pirates.

Oliver didn't go totally unrecognized during his career. He was a member of *The Sporting News* 1975 All-Star team and received the honor again in 1982 (this time as a first baseman). With Steve Garvey pulling down constant honors as the league's top first baseman, Oliver and many others got overlooked regularly. Oliver was a member of the first three Silver Slugger teams in 1980 through 1982 and was named to a different position each time: He was cited as an outfielder with the Texas Rangers in 1980, as a designated hitter with the Rangers in 1981, and as a first baseman with the Expos in 1982.

In 1974 Oliver won the Roberto Clemente award as the Pirate who best exemplified the late Clemente's standard of excellence. He was only the second person to receive the award, following Hall of Famer Willie Stargell, who had captured the honor twice.

CAREER HIGHLIGHTS
ALBERT OLIVER

Born: October 14, 1946   Portsmouth, OH

Height: 6'0"   **Weight:** 195 lbs.   **Batted:** Left   **Threw:** Left

Outfielder, first baseman, designated hitter: Pittsburgh Pirates, 1968-77; Texas Rangers, 1978-81; Montreal Expos, 1982-83; San Francisco Giants, 1984; Philadelphia Phillies, 1984; Los Angeles Dodgers, 1985; Toronto Blue Jays, 1985.

★ Led the league in hits, doubles, and RBI in 1982

★ Batted .300 or better 11 times

★ Played in six League Championship Series

★ Earned double-digit totals for homers 13 times

★ Won the N.L. batting title in 1982

★ Appeared in the 1971 World Series

MAJOR LEAGUE TOTALS

G	AB	H	BA	2B	3B	HR	R	RBI	SB
2,368	9,049	2,743	.303	529	77	219	1,189	1,326	84

Al Oliver had been in the majors for 14 full seasons before he exploded in 1982 with league leads in hits, doubles, and RBI. He also won the N.L. batting title that year with a .331 average.

AMOS OTIS

Amos Otis was a star when the fledgling Kansas City Royals needed one badly. Long before George Brett or Willie Wilson came along, Otis was the cornerstone of both the Royals offense and defense. The one-time third baseman then became a fixture in the Kansas City outfield for 13 seasons.

Otis began his involvement with sports during his youth at Williamson High School in Mobile, Alabama, where he starred in football and basketball, but baseball was his future calling. He signed his first pro contract with the Boston Red Sox in 1965 but was drafted by the New York Mets in 1966. He spent his first full season in the minors with Oneonta in 1966, where he hit .270 in 116 games while playing first base, third base, and the outfield. He was promoted to Jacksonville in 1967 and racked up a .268 average with 29 stolen bases. The Mets moved him around the infield, at each of the bases, and in the outfield. New York brought Otis up for 19 games, but he hit just .220.

The next year he upped his average to .286 in Jacksonville, hitting 15 homers and 70 RBI. In 1969 Otis started the season at Tidewater, the Mets Triple-A affiliate. He hit .327, the best ever in his young pro career, with 10 homers. Called up to the Mets again, Otis hit just .151 in 48 games. The Mets went on to a world championship, but Otis wasn't included on the postseason roster. Instead, he was traded with pitcher Bob Johnson to the Kansas City Royals for third baseman Joe Foy.

Otis was installed immediately as the Royals starting center fielder. He responded with admirable first-season totals of .284 with 11 homers, 58 RBI, and 33 stolen bases. Not only did he adjust well to his first full season as a starter, he made a smooth conversion to another league.

Otis was first in the American League with 52 stolen bases in 1971. On September 7 versus Milwaukee, Otis stole 5 bases, a feat that hadn't been matched in the majors in 44 seasons. Otis wasn't baseball's most prolific basestealer, but he was one of the most successful. He collected double-digit steals in 12 seasons and was above 30 pilfers five times. He swiped 341 bases out of 430 attempts in his career, giving him a success rate of 79.3 percent. The Alabama native hit a career-high .301 that year and belted 15 home runs. During his time with the Royals, Otis would be a five-time All-Star and three-time Gold Glove winner (in 1971, 1973, and 1974). Otis was named to *The Sporting News* All-Star team during those same years.

Otis had a fast start in 1972 but was shaken after smashing into an outfield wall just two days before the All-Star game. He was slowed for the second half of the season and wound up with just 11 homers and 54 RBI. Against the Angels in 1972, Otis stole home against Nolan Ryan to give the Royals a 1-0 win. The straight steal came on a 3-2 count. The talented center fielder progressed to 26 home runs, 93 RBI, and a .300 average in 1973.

Otis played in just 107 games in 1980. Working out on his own during the spring, he was hit by a pitch from a batting practice machine and suffered a ruptured tendon in his finger. Although the Royals were defeated in the 1980 World Series after a six-game battle with the Philadelphia Phillies, Otis returned and hit with gusto throughout the Series. His 11 hits and .478 average topped all regulars from both teams.

Otis hit 3 homers and drove in 7 runs. His one Series failure came in the fifth game. Reliever Tug McGraw struck out Otis with two outs and the bases loaded in the ninth inning, giving the Phillies a 4-3 win. He played in four League Championship Series, hitting .429 and .333 in his final two A.L.C.S. appearances.

Otis played out his option with Kansas City following the 1983 season and signed a free-agent contract with the Pittsburgh Pirates in 1984. His last season consisted of just 40 games and a .165 batting average.

For his career with the Royals, Otis batted .280 with 193 home runs, 992 RBI, and 1,977 hits. He ranks among the top five in nearly every all-time batting category in Royals' history. Otis and pitcher Steve Busby were the first two players elected to the Royals Hall of Fame in 1986.

The San Diego Padres have employed Otis for four seasons as a coach. After instructing in the minors for two years, Otis took his current job as batting coach with San Diego in 1988. He is a chief assistant to manager Jack McKeon, who had managed Otis for several seasons at Kansas City.

Amos Otis, the cornerstone of the Royals during the 1970s, remains an underrated player. Otis was an excellent baserunner in his day, leading the A.L. in stolen bases in 1971 with 52. He was also a good fielder, going 165 games without an error.

CAREER HIGHLIGHTS
AMOS JOSEPH OTIS

Born: April 26, 1947   Mobile, AL
Height: 5'11"   **Weight:** 165 lbs.   **Batted:** Right   **Threw:** Right
Outfielder: New York Mets, 1967-69; Kansas City Royals, 1970-83; Pittsburgh Pirates, 1984.

* Was a five-time A.L. All-Star
* Led the A.L. in doubles twice
* Batted .478 in the 1980 World Series
* Won three Gold Glove awards
* Stole a league-leading 52 bases in 1971
* Elected to the Kansas City Royals Hall of Fame

MAJOR LEAGUE TOTALS

G	AB	H	BA	2B	3B	HR	R	RBI	SB
1,998	7,299	2,020	.277	374	66	193	1,092	1,007	341

MEL OTT

Mel Ott was one of the most powerful home run sluggers in all of baseball, and was also one of the youngest. He was just 16 in 1925 when he signed a contract with John McGraw's mighty New York Giants, the team he played for during his entire 22-year major league career.

"Master Melvin" never played a single game in the minors. Ott had been a catcher in high school in New Orleans, but when the great Giants right fielder Ross Youngs became ill, McGraw needed a quick successor. He chose Ott. Because Youngs was a fine-fielding fan favorite, the 17-year-old rookie had a big challenge in front of him.

He responded in fine fashion. McGraw was so impressed with the youngster's raw talent that he refused to let Ott develop in the farm system, fearing that a minor league manager might ruin his naturally perfect batting stance or change his distinctive style of striding into a pitch with his right foot raised. In the batter's box Ott looked as though he was winding up before hitting a pitch. McGraw worked slowly with the young slugger for several years, only occasionally inserting him into the lineup. In 1927 the youngster from Louisiana was first in the National League with 46 pinch-hitting at-bats.

Ott became a full-time Giant right fielder soon after that. In 1929, at just 20 years old, the lefthand slugger exploded with 42 home runs, 151 RBI, and a .328 batting average. He showed remarkable discipline at the plate by drawing a league-leading 113 bases on balls (the first of ten seasons in which he'd earn 100 or more walks). Soon the talented young pull hitter mastered the short distance needed to reach the right field stands in the Polo Grounds.

It was the first of eight years that Ott would hit 30 or more home runs—six times leading the league. Ott could also hit for average, compiling an impressive .304 lifetime mark, including 11 seasons over .300. In 1930 his power totals dipped to 25 homers and 119 RBI, but he hit a career-high .349 in 1930.

From 1934 to 1938 Ott was unbeatable. During those years he was the National League's leading home run hitter four times (with totals ranging from 31 to 36) and twice he registered a career-high 135 RBI. In 1942 he paced the National League with 30 homers, 118 runs scored, and 109 walks.

Ott is most remembered for his fine play in right field. However, he was a team-spirited player who would fill in at third base whenever he was needed. He logged 256 games there throughout the years, including 113 games in 1938, when he was the Giants starting third sacker.

At the time of Ott's retirement, his 511 career home runs trailed only Babe Ruth and Jimmie Foxx. Now he ranks 14th on the all-time list. On the Giants' all-time list he's the career leader in RBI with 1,860 and ranks second only to Willie Mays in the following categories: games (2,730), at-bats (9,456), runs (1,859), hits (2,876), doubles (488), home runs (511), total bases (5,041), and extra-base hits (1,071). His bases on balls record is the sixth-best total in major league history.

The 11-time All-Star appeared in his first World Series in 1933. Ott helped his Giants beat the Washington Senators by batting .389 and slugging 2 home runs in the five-game fall classic.

Master Melvin served as a Giants manager from 1942 to 1948. Still active as a player, he took over for Bill Terry. Ott was only the third Giant manager in New York since John McGraw took over the team leadership in mid-1902. He skippered the 1942 Giants to a third-place finish of 85-67. After two losing seasons the 1945 Giants finished at 78-74, landing in fifth place. His 1946 squad lost 93 games, but the 1947 team was fourth at 81-73. When he was relieved of his duties in 1948, the Giants were in fourth place at 37-38. His career managing record consisted of 464 wins and 530 losses.

In July 1948 Ott was moved up to the front office to make room for new manager Leo Durocher, who had previously piloted the archrival Brooklyn Dodgers. Ott managed the Oakland Oaks of the Pacific Coast League in 1951 and 1952. The soft-spoken Ott was elected to the Hall of Fame in 1951. He was an announcer for the Detroit Tigers before being killed in a car accident in November 1958. He was 49 years old. Ott, known as number 4 during his days with New York, is one of only eight Giants in history whose uniform numbers have been retired.

Slugger Mel Ott spent his entire career with the New York Giants, serving as both a player and a manager. Leo Durocher replaced the gentle Giant as manager in 1948. Durocher was referring to Ott when he said, "Nice guys finish last."

CAREER HIGHLIGHTS
MELVIN THOMAS OTT

Born: March 2, 1909 Gretna, LA **Died:** November 21, 1958
Height: 5'9" **Weight:** 170 lbs. **Batted:** Left **Threw:** Right
Outfielder: New York Giants, 1926-47. Manager: New York Giants, 1942-48.

- ★ Led the N.L. in home runs six times
- ★ Played in three World Series
- ★ Batted .300 or better ten times
- ★ Drove in 100 or more runs nine times
- ★ Hit 30 or more homers eight times
- ★ Elected to the Hall of Fame in 1951

MAJOR LEAGUE TOTALS

G	AB	H	BA	2B	3B	HR	R	RBI	SB
2,730	9,456	2,876	.304	488	72	511	1,859	1,860	89

SATCHEL PAIGE

Although no one was ever really certain about his age, it's generally assumed that Leroy "Satchel" Paige was 42 years old when he came to the Cleveland Indians as a major league rookie pitcher in 1948. Paige started just 26 games in the majors and ended his brief career with a losing record, but he is considered one of the greatest pitchers who ever lived. Paige was elected to the Hall of Fame in 1971, not for his accomplishments in the major leagues, but for his achievements in the Negro Leagues.

Some say Paige acquired his unusual nickname as a youngster working as a porter at the train station in Mobile, Alabama. Others claim he was called "Satchelfoot" in joking tribute to his big feet. He first played baseball with his hometown semipro team and assorted other teams before advancing to the National Negro League, pitching for the Birmingham Black Barons, Nashville Elite Giants, New Orleans Pelicans, and Pittsburgh Crawfords. He pitched year-round, alternating between the Negro Leagues in summer and winter ball in Latin America. He also played in exhibition games against major leaguers when time permitted. During one of these exhibitions in 1937, he faced Joe DiMaggio, who called him the best pitcher he had ever faced.

No complete records exist from the Negro Leagues, but snippets of Paige's greatness have survived. In 1933 with the Crawfords, Paige was 31-4 with 21 straight wins and a streak of 62 straight scoreless innings. In 1946 Paige yielded just 2 runs in 93 innings with the Kansas City Monarchs, throwing 64 consecutive scoreless innings.

Even records of Paige's actual birth are sketchy. Paige claimed he didn't know his true age. Official team records said that Paige was born July 7, 1906. Some said he was born in 1899; others claimed 1904. The reason Paige's age evoked so much curiosity was because of his never-ending success. He had a youthful face, and his performance often outstripped pitchers half his age.

By the time Jackie Robinson tore down baseball's color barrier in 1946, it seemed that Paige was too old for major league duty. But in July 1948, when the Indians needed extra pitching for their pennant race, Veeck signed Paige, who helped the Tribe win their pennant. Paige contributed 6 wins (with just 1 loss) and a save to go along with his 2.48 ERA.

Veeck remembered going to Negro

League games as a youngster to watch Paige pitch. Veeck later said that he didn't want to sign Paige as the first black in the American League simply because he might be accused of bringing in Paige as a promotional gimmick. After all, Paige was of retirement age for most major leaguers, not the age in which baseball careers start. The Indians signed outfielder Larry Doby before they recruited "Ol' Satch." Paige was the seventh black in major league history. Sellout crowds greeted Paige wherever he pitched that first season. News of Paige pitching his first major league start against the Chicago White Sox brought a night game attendance record of 51,013 to Comiskey Park on August 13, 1948. Paige came through with a five-hit shutout against the ChiSox, winning the game 5-0. The veteran moundsman was once known as a fireballer in the Negro Leagues. As he grew older, though, he relied on a variety of pitches and deliveries, including a submarine motion and a "hesitation" pitch.

Fans also loved him for his easygoing observations and his unique brand of baseball wisdom. When someone asked him how he had become such a gifted pitcher, he replied, "Just take the ball and throw it where you want to. Throw strikes. Home plate don't move."

After two seasons with Cleveland, Paige joined the St. Louis Browns for three seasons. When Veeck took control of the Browns, he signed Paige again. In 23 relief appearances in 1951, Paige won 3 games and lost 4 while registering 5 saves. The 6-foot-3, 180-pound hurler had his best success in the majors with the 1952 Browns. Paige's record was 12-10 with a 3.07 ERA. He saved 10 games and paced American League relievers with 8 victories in relief. He was the team's only All-Star representative. Manager Casey Stengel had promised Paige a chance to pitch the sixth inning, but the game was rained out after five frames. The Browns released Paige after 1953 when his record dipped to 3-9 with 11 saves.

Paige continued his active career well into his 50s, pitching with minor league clubs in Miami and Portland before the Kansas City Athletics brought him back for one last hurrah in 1965. The 59-year-old Paige took the mound for three final innings and shut out the Boston Red Sox.

Paige returned briefly to the major league scene in 1968, when the Atlanta Braves hired him as a pitching coach so he could log the needed time in the big leagues to qualify for a pension.

CAREER HIGHLIGHTS
LEROY ROBERT PAIGE

Born: July 7, 1906   Mobile, AL   **Died:** June 8, 1982
Height: 6'3"   **Weight:** 180 lbs.   **Batted:** Right   **Threw:** Right
Pitcher: Negro Leagues, 1924-48; Cleveland Indians, 1948-49; St. Louis Browns, 1951-53; Kansas City Athletics, 1965.

★ Was the most celebrated player in the Negro Leagues

★ Became the oldest rookie in major league history in 1948

★ Played professional and semipro baseball for more than four decades

★ Won 3 games in the 1942 Negro League World Series

★ Became the first black player to pitch in the World Series (in 1948)

★ Elected to the Hall of Fame in 1971

MAJOR LEAGUE TOTALS

G	IP	W	L	Pct.	SO	BB	ERA
179	476	28	31	.475	290	183	3.29

Satchel Paige did not pitch in the majors until he was well over 40 years old. Paige pitched a shutout for his second start in the big leagues and drew over 200,000 fans to the ball park in his first three starts.

JIM PALMER

Jim Palmer gained overnight acclaim in 1966, when at the tender age of 20 he pitched the final game of a World Series shutout against the great Sandy Koufax. Palmer gained even more exposure ten years later when he stripped down to his briefs for a national advertising campaign for Jockey underwear. He still represents the company at age 44.

Whether pitching shorts or pitching fastballs, Palmer has a style all his own. Widely proclaimed a "thinking pitcher," Palmer posted low walk ratios each season, tantalizing batters to protect the plate. He employed psychology when the count was up, the same psychology that makes him such a hit with fans.

Although proud of his many 20-win seasons—all eight of them—he says his best accomplishment was being part of a winning team. Like teammate Brooks Robinson, Palmer was a loyal and steadfast player. Trained on the Orioles farm system, Palmer spent two whole decades with the Birds, requiring only one season in the minors before receiving his major league call-up. Like Robinson, Palmer handled fielding chores with ease. The graceful pitcher earned four Gold Gloves in his career.

Palmer spent a total of three years in the minors—two of them following his brilliant rookie season. After the thrill of the World Series had waned, Palmer revealed in a press interview that he had pitched his shutout with an injured arm. Amazingly, surgery did not follow until after a bad start in 1967 and months in the Orioles farm system.

He came back with a vengeance in 1969, with 16 wins that were only a warmup for his next four campaigns of 20-plus triumphs. After another year of injury in 1974, Palmer came back with four 20-win seasons.

True to form, Palmer waxes philosophical about his two lost years, when both he and his team wondered if he had ruined his chance for success. The injury, he said, made him appreciate his talent, and he became determined to protect and use it. He couldn't have had a better career, he claims, because of the fine team it was his good fortune to have worked with.

Palmer appeared in six American League Championship Series and as many World Series. He finished his last fall classic as he did his first. In 1983 Palmer won his last Series game (and his final career win) with two perfect innings of relief against the Philadelphia Phillies. Palmer is, to date, the only pitcher to have won Series games in three consecutive decades.

Palmer is one of only four players to receive three Cy Young awards. Never in his lengthy major league career did he give up a grand slam home run. Digging into the record books, evidence of only one four-run homer hit against him is found, a shot surrendered while pitching in the minors. While rehabilitating in Rochester, Palmer was nicked by Johnny Bench for a grand slam, the only time the smooth righthander would yield such a blast.

Baltimore pitching records read like a copy of Palmer's lifetime stats. He leads the team in numerous career categories: wins (268), losses (152), games pitched (558), innings (3,948), shutouts (53), complete games (211), strikeouts (2,212), and walks (1,311). His 2.8568 ERA is fourth on the all-time list of major league pitchers with 3,000 or more innings (active since the end of the dead-ball era). Palmer's regular-season ERA stayed well below 3.00 for half of his career; his ERA for postseason play is 1.84 for A.L.C.S. games (including two 1.00 marks and one 1.84), and 3.20 for the Series (with two perfect marks). He pitched four pennant-clinching wins for the O's over the years. Although he had just one no-hitter (in 1969), he threw a grand total of 59 games in his career in which he allowed 4 hits or less.

With his glamour-boy features and polished demeanor (attributes of a privileged childhood), Palmer was never dubbed with a nickname that went outside the dugout. Teammates called him "Reginald" in joking reference to his tony upbringing. Later he received the surname "Cakes" in honor of his underwear endorsements.

Since his retirement Palmer has continued his active campaigning for the Cystic Fibrosis Foundation and has embarked on a career as a sports broadcaster, working in tandem with longtime teammate Brooks Robinson. Palmer did play-by-play for the first time in 1989.

Palmer is aware of the need for restraint in play-by-play commentary, a restraint he sometimes failed to display in his famed verbal battles with Orioles manager Earl Weaver. Palmer has hinted that someday he may walk a mile in Weaver's shoes—managing the new Orioles the way he wanted Weaver to manage the old.

A loyal team player, Jim Palmer pitched for the Orioles for his entire career. The hurling ace won 20 or more games in eight of his 20 seasons and helped his team bring six pennants to Baltimore.

CAREER HIGHLIGHTS
DAVID GENE PARKER

Born: June 9, 1951   Cincinnati, OH
Height: 6'5"   **Weight:** 225 lbs.   **Bats:** Left   **Throws:** Right
Outfielder: Pittsburgh Pirates, 1973-83; Cincinnati Reds, 1984-87. Designated hitter, outfielder: Oakland A's, 1988-89.

- ★ Voted the N.L. MVP in 1978
- ★ Participated in six All-Star games
- ★ Was the N.L. batting champion in 1977 and 1978
- ★ Topped the N.L. with 125 RBI in 1985
- ★ Appeared in four World Series
- ★ Played in six League Championship Series

MAJOR LEAGUE TOTALS

G	AB	H	BA	2B	3B	HR	R	RBI	SB
2,177	8,246	2,416	.293	470	70	307	1,154	1,342	147

DAVE PARKER

The legendary Dave "The Cobra" Parker has always had the tools to be a great player. He got the serpentine moniker by virtue of his quick-striking bat, which he releases from a deadly coiled stance. Tragically, drug problems have gotten in his way, and he has had to overcome many obstacles to earn the numerous honors that baseball has bestowed on him.

A native of Cincinnati, Parker was picked in the 14th round of the 1970 draft by the Pittsburgh Pirates. He broke into pro ball with their Bradenton farm club that season, batting .314 with 6 home runs and 41 RBI in just 61 contests. That year he even tried pitching in one game but abandoned the experiment after yielding 2 runs in four innings. His major league debut came three seasons later when the Bucs recalled him from the Charleston Triple-A team in the International League. He was stationed there after being named the Carolina League's MVP in 1972 for topping loop competition in nine different hitting categories. He batted .288 in 54 contests in his first big league season in 1973—good for a rookie, but nothing compared to what Parker would accomplish later.

He kept his audience in suspense for one more year, nursing injuries that limited him to only 73 games in 1974. In 1975 he posted his first of five consecutive .300-plus major league seasons with 25 home runs. In 1976 he marked his first of four consecutive years of leading the league in errors.

Even Parker's detractors agree that his high error ratio is part and parcel of his greatest asset: he puts his heart and soul into every putout, every at-bat, and sometimes enthusiasm leads to error.

It also leads to success, which Parker enjoyed tenfold in the late 1970s. The lefthand hitter carried the 1977 Bucs with league leads in hits (215), doubles (44), and batting average (.338); as a righthand outfielder he led the league in putouts (389) and assists (a career high of 26). He handled more chances (430) and made more double plays (9) than any outfielder in the senior circuit and was named to his first of six N.L. All-Star teams. The batting title was his again in 1978 (with a .334 average), along with the National League Most Valuable Player award.

By 1979 Parker had already sojourned twice to the National League Championship Series with Pittsburgh, never living up to his seasonal success while batting in postseason play. He

had just 1 hit in 8 at-bats in the 1974 N.L.C.S., then went hitless in 10 plate appearances in the 1975 playoffs. All that changed in 1979, when Parker's .333 average in three games led the Pirates to the World Series. With the Sister Sledge hit "We Are Family" as inspiration, Parker danced to the tune of a .345 batting average and 13 putouts as the Pirates downed the Baltimore Orioles in seven Series games.

Nevertheless, this was Parker's toughest year in his relationship with the fans. A $5 million contract over five years made him baseball's highest-paid player at the time, provoking the indignation of media and fans. Time on the disabled list in 1981 and 1982 worsened the criticism, and his 1983 free agency to his hometown of Cincinnati came not a moment too soon.

Parker had his best season ever at age 34 in 1985, smashing 35 home runs with 125 RBI and registering a .312 batting average (his first over .300 in five years). Some attribute the fact that he was bypassed for Most Valuable

Player recognition that year to his earlier admission of drug abuse.

Parker accomplished another milestone in 1986 when he drove in his 1,000th RBI. Bill James, in his *Baseball Abstract*, rated Parker as the National League's second-best right fielder—behind only Tony Gwynn at the end of the 1987 season. However, on December 8, 1987, Parker was traded to the Oakland A's for pitchers Tim Birtsas and Jose Rijo. Parker played outfield, first base, and designated hitter in his first season with the A's. On the disabled list for about six weeks, Parker got into only 101 games. Even in his short season he hit .257 with 12 homers and 55 RBI. His leadership helped bring the A's an American League pennant. In their four-game sweep of the American League Championship Series, Parker hit .250. He had just 3 hits during the Dodgers' five-game pummeling of Oakland in the World Series.

In his 11 seasons as a Pirate, Parker established himself in the top ten of several all-time Pittsburgh offensive categories. Parker's long career, his .295 lifetime batting average, and his extra-base hitting potential should make him a candidate for the Hall of Fame someday. At 38, Parker had a fine 1989 season with Oakland. He hit 22 dingers and 97 RBI.

Dave Parker's career was born again when he joined the Cincinnati Reds for the 1984 season. The following year Parker enjoyed one of his best seasons, clubbing 35 home runs with 125 RBI for a .312 average.

CAREER HIGHLIGHTS
DAVID GENE PARKER

Born: June 9, 1951 Cincinnati, OH
Height: 6'5" **Weight:** 225 lbs. **Bats:** Left **Throws:** Right
Outfielder: Pittsburgh Pirates, 1973-83; Cincinnati Reds, 1984-87. Designated hitter, outfielder: Oakland A's, 1988-89.

* Voted the N.L. MVP in 1978
* Participated in six All-Star games
* Was the N.L. batting champion in 1977 and 1978
* Topped the N.L. with 125 RBI in 1985
* Appeared in three World Series
* Played in five League Championship Series

MAJOR LEAGUE TOTALS

G	AB	H	BA	2B	3B	HR	R	RBI	SB
2,033	7,693	2,270	.295	443	70	285	1,098	1,245	147

LANCE PARRISH

Catcher Lance Parrish broke out of a National League twilight zone in 1989, ending two years of professional and personal misery with the Philadelphia Phillies. Although Parrish is an easterner by birth and developed as a player with the Detroit Tigers, he grew up in California and graduated from California's Walnut High. He turned down a football scholarship to UCLA to play pro baseball. So going to the Angels for the 1989 season is a real homecoming for the big slugger.

At age 30 Parrish left Detroit, a town that loved him, because the lure of free agency beckoned. Suprisingly, few teams wanted any connection with Parrish or any other free agents. Parrish and his agents charged that the owners had conspired not to sign free agents. Eventually, harboring much ill will toward the Tigers, Parrish took a contract offer from the Phillies that was supposedly smaller than what he would have made by staying in Detroit.

A slow start with Philadelphia set the tone for Parrish's two-year stay in the National League. He was performing adequately, but he was just a shadow of his former All-Star American League days. Though still fielding competently and hitting home runs in double digits in 1988, Parrish posted his worst batting average in a decade at .215. His 1987 totals were slightly better, with a .245 batting mark, 17 home runs, and 67 RBI in 130 games.

The Phillies knew that Parrish was unhappy both with his new team (which struggled to earn even a .500 winning percentage) and his new league. So Philadelphia granted his wish and traded him close to home and to the league where his career had been at its brightest. Due to his eagerness to get to California, all the Angels needed to offer the Phillies in trade was minor league pitcher David Holdridge on October 3, 1988. Although Parrish's 1989 numbers are not fantastic, he seems to be fitting into the Angels team well. His mere presence on the team seems to have boosted the Angels' spirits, and as one of the team leaders in home runs, he helped his team mount an unsuccessful but valiant effort to take the Western Division title away from the Oakland A's. Most importantly, Parrish seemed in good health. After missing more than 100 games in the last three seasons due to back ailments, the 33-year-old seemed ready for action again.

Parrish spent ten years with Detroit, which explains the city's affection for

him. Drafted in the first round of the 1974 free-agent draft, Parrish logged 68 games that year with Bristol as a third baseman/outfielder. In 1975 he started catching in the Florida League. His fielding average jumped for joy. In 1976 he led the Southern League in fielding percentage (.984), assists (79), and putouts (600). It wasn't until he repeated—and bettered—these leads the following year with Triple-A Evansville (with a .987 fielding average, 82 assists, and 722 putouts) that Parrish finally found himself in Tiger Town.

Parrish performed in only 12 games with Detroit in 1977, but he made the most of them with flawless fielding, 76 putouts, and 3 home runs (for a combined season total of 28, a mark he wouldn't pass for five years).

Soon he became the team's most dependable backstop in recent years, gaining comparisons to the 1960s-era receiver Bill Freehan. From 1979 through 1985 Parrish caught over 130 games six times. He earned five Gold Gloves and proved to be a steady influ-

ence in guiding Tiger pitching staffs. In the 1982 All-Star game he set a record by throwing out three of four National League basestealers. He received Tiger of the Year honors from the local media in Detroit in 1982. From 1983 through 1985 Parrish had his greatest years as a hitter: 27 homers and a career high of 114 RBI in 1983, followed by a personal best of 33 homers and 98 RBI in 1984. In 1985 Parrish had 98 more RBI to go with 28 round-trippers.

During the 1984 season the Tigers stormed to their first world championship since 1968. Manager Sparky Anderson coined the saying, "Bless you, Boys!" as Parrish and his teammates pulled off one miracle after another. As the Tigers derailed the Kansas City Royals in three straight American League Championship games, Parrish was there with an opening-game home run. A highlight of his World Series (during which he hit .278) was a home run off ace Padres reliever Rich Gossage in the seventh inning of the fifth game.

Having Parrish play for the Angels instead of against them will benefit the California club. During his years with the Tigers, Parrish had feasted on California pitching, hitting .320 with 19 home runs and 56 RBI. If Parrish can avoid the kind of lower back injury that plagued him two seasons earlier, his future as an Angel looks angelic. His throwing arm remains one of the deadliest guns in the American League.

Lance Parrish, recently acquired by the California Angels, has been a dependable backstop for over 12 years. The winner of three Gold Gloves, Parrish has been a steady if not spectacular home run hitter.

CAREER HIGHLIGHTS
LANCE MICHAEL PARRISH

Born: June 15, 1956   Clairton, PA
Height: 6'3"   **Weight:** 210 lbs.   **Bats:** Right   **Throws:** Right
Catcher: Detroit Tigers, 1977-86; Philadelphia Phillies, 1987-88; California Angels, 1989.

★ Won the Gold Glove award three times
★ Batted .278 in the 1984 World Series
★ Hit at least 10 homers in every major league season

★ Named to seven All-Star teams
★ Drove in 6 runs in a game twice
★ Won four Silver Slugger awards

MAJOR LEAGUE TOTALS

G	AB	H	BA	2B	3B	HR	R	RBI	SB
1,523	5,596	1,431	.256	251	26	261	711	877	23

LARRY PARRISH

Because he toiled in relative obscurity on the rosters of second-division teams for virtually all of his 15-year career, Larry Parrish (no relation to Lance) has never achieved the respect his statistics deserve, except among his fellow professionals.

Parrish was attending junior college in his native Florida when he was signed by the Montreal Expos as a free agent in 1972. Playing the outfield in his first season of pro ball, he hit only .260, with little power. The following year, playing with West Palm Beach, things began to click for him. He was shifted to the left side of the infield, where he led Florida State League third basemen in putouts and assists. He paced the circuit with 9 sacrifice flies and a .925 fielding average. All this plus his .293 batting average made Parrish the league's Most Valuable Player. Montreal called up Parrish in September 1974, ignoring his 31 errors with Quebec City and relying on the strength of his 108 putouts and 277 assists that season. He was invited to stay for opening day in 1975.

Although he began that first full major league season playing shortstop, second base, and third base, in the next four seasons Parrish played a steady third base and tried to improve his batting average. In 1976 he tied for the National League lead in double plays by a third baseman with 35. But his best season came in 1979, when he doubled his 1978 home run output from 15 to 30 and hit .307, his only .300-plus season to date. The following year he spent a month on the disabled list, immediately dropping to 15 homers and shaving more than 50 points off his batting average. After losing another 10 points off his average in 1981 (.244), he was traded with first baseman Dave Hostetler to the Texas Rangers on March 31, 1982, in exchange for Al Oliver. Tim Wallach replaced Parrish as the Expos third baseman.

Parrish brought to the Rangers a big swing and a fondness for fastballs. A guess hitter not good at taking walks, Parrish worked with the Rangers to keep his eye on the ball. He achieved some of his best fielding in Texas, making the most of his accurate throwing arm and overcoming his average release on throws. Many of Parrish's duties were in the outfield from then on.

Playing through all of 1984 and part of 1985 with a damaged knee, Parrish was finally forced to have arthroscopic surgery in July 1985. He was out of the

game until September, completing just 94 games that season with a .992 fielding percentage. Had it not been for the surgery, he could have logged five consecutive seasons of 20 or more home runs; as it is, he posted 26 in 1983, 22 in 1984, 28 in 1986, and a personal best of 32 in 1987. A consistent power hitter, only once in 15 years did he have a single-digit season in homers; he has averaged 18 homers a year.

He tied a major league record by hitting 3 grand slams in a month in July 1982. Four times he has hit 3 homers in a single game: in 1977, 1978, 1980, and 1985.

Parrish flourished with the Rangers. His batting average floated between .249 and .285, and he hit 17 to 32 home runs a season. The improvement may have been related to the Rangers'

conversion of Parrish to an outfielder during his first four years there. When he became a designated hitter and third baseman in 1986, he was able to maintain his new, higher standards. Batting .268 with 32 home runs and 100 RBI in 1987, Parrish again proved himself to be a star-caliber player performing in the anonymity of a so-so team. His 1988 release by the Rangers seemed puzzling, considering his 32 homers and 100 RBI just one season earlier. He played just 68 games in Texas before the team cut the Floridian adrift. The Boston Red Sox, in the midst of a pennant scramble, threw Parrish a lifeline and signed him just one week after the Rangers had released him in July.

Parrish socked 14 homers and 52 RBI for the year but was hitless in six plate appearances during Boston's humbling four-game loss to the Oakland Athletics in the 1988 American League Championship Series. The Red Sox let the veteran slugger go on October 28, 1988. The 35-year-old Parrish headed overseas to play professional baseball in Japan.

If he can prove in Japan that his legs are still sturdy and his bat can still handle tough breaking pitches, he could reappear in the big leagues.

Power hitter Larry Parrish tied a major league record in July 1982 by belting 3 grand slams in a month. Four times during his career he has smacked 3 home runs in one game—in 1977, 1978, 1980, and 1985. His career high of 32 homers came in 1987.

CAREER HIGHLIGHTS
LARRY ALTON PARRISH

Born: November 10, 1953   Winter Haven, FL
Height: 6'3"   **Weight:** 215 lbs.   **Bats:** Right   **Throws:** Right
Infielder: Montreal Expos, 1974-81. Infielder, outfielder, designated hitter, third baseman: Texas Rangers, 1982-88; Boston Red Sox, 1988.

* ★ Hit 3 home runs in four different games
* ★ Drove in 90 or more runs three times
* ★ Hit in double figures for home runs in 13 seasons
* ★ Played in two League Championship Series
* ★ Had a career-high 32 homers in 1987
* ★ Named to two All-Star teams

MAJOR LEAGUE TOTALS

G	AB	H	BA	2B	3B	HR	R	RBI	SB
1,891	6,792	1,789	.263	360	33	256	850	992	30

HERB PENNOCK

Hall of Fame pitcher Herb Pennock recorded 240 victories during his career. Many fans still insist that Pennock was the smartest pitcher who ever put on a uniform. A model of precision, he had an easy, graceful motion. He never overpowered batters with blinding speed or wicked curve balls but fooled them by calmly analyzing each situation before winding up.

Pennock attended exclusive East Coast prep schools, where he demonstrated his skills as a standout athlete. At 18 he chose baseball over college when he signed a contract with Connie Mack's Philadelphia Athletics in 1912.

Pennock went straight to the big leagues but won only 1 game in 1912 and 2 games the following year. Mack let Pennock see a little more action in 1914, and the young lefthander responded with an 11-4 record and a 2.79 ERA as the A's won the American League pennant for the second year in a row. But after the A's lost the World Series to the Boston Braves in four straight games, a disgusted Connie Mack revamped his entire ball club, and Pennock was picked up on waivers by the Boston Red Sox on June 13, 1915.

Pennock remained in Boston for six seasons with moderate success, winning 16 games in both 1919 and 1920. (He took a year off in 1918 to serve in the U.S. Navy.) Pennock was traded to the New York Yankees on January 23, 1923, for Camp Skinner, Norm McMillan, George Murray, and $50,000. The Yankees, who had purchased a young lefthander named Babe Ruth from the Red Sox just three years earlier, found Boston a veritable bargain basement of talent. Wealthy teams like the Yankees found that they could bail out needy franchises by buying up their talented players.

It was in New York that Pennock blossomed into a Hall of Fame pitcher. The Yankees weren't expecting nearly this much success out of the ten-year veteran, knowing that he had been active since 1912. His first season there the Yankees captured the American League title and Pennock went 19-6, leading the league with a winning percentage of .760. In the 1923 World Series against the New York Giants Pennock helped his team win the competition in six games. In game two he scattered 9 hits over nine innings for a 4-2 triumph. When pitcher teammate Urban Shocker got into trouble after going 7.2 innings in the fourth game, Pennock came in to finish the game

and earn the save. A worn-out Pennock started the sixth game just two days later. The lanky lefty lasted seven innings, long enough to earn the victory in the Yankees' 6-4 triumph. The control master was touched for 19 hits in three appearances, but he struck out 8 and walked only 1 in his 17.1 innings of work.

Following his surprising success Pennock elicited more attention by winning 21 games and losing just 9 (along with 3 saves) in 1924. The shrewd control artist displayed some heat that season by fanning 101 batters, the highest K total he ever achieved. In 1925 Pennock's record sank to 16-17. However, he proved to be one of New York's most durable throwers that year, appearing in a personal best of 47 games. His 277 innings were tops in the junior circuit.

Pennock won a career-high 23 games in 1926. The mighty Yankees regained their American League pennant and faced the St. Louis Cardinals in the World Series. The Redbirds edged the Yanks in seven tough games, despite Pennock's strong efforts. Pennock won the opening game 2-1, allowing just 3 hits over nine innings. In the fifth game he threw ten innings of seven-hit ball to gain a 3-2 victory, giving the Yanks a three-games-to-two edge. The Cardinals rallied for wins in the sixth and seventh games. Pennock even threw the final three innings of the seventh game, holding the Cards scoreless. It was to no avail, though, as starter Waite Hoyt had already been nicked for three fourth-inning tallies.

Pennock was a key participant in the 1927 "Murderers' Row" Yankees team. While Ruth, Gehrig, and friends were clubbing record numbers of homers, Pennock and Hoyt were big winners on the team as well. The overmatched Pittsburgh Pirates lost four straight games to the fabulous Yankees. Pennock's victory in the third game had to be the highlight of the Series. He put down the first 22 Pirate batters in order and had a perfect game going into the eighth inning before Pie Traynor broke it up with a single. Pennock eventually won the game 8-1, giving up 3 hits.

Known as "The Squire of Kennett Square" because he owned a farm in his Pennsylvania hometown, Pennock worked as a Boston Red Sox coach from 1936 to 1944. For the last four years of his life he was general manager of the Philadelphia Phillies. Pennock was elected to the Hall of Fame in 1948, the year of his death.

CAREER HIGHLIGHTS
HERBERT JEFFERIS PENNOCK

Born: February 19, 1894 Kennett Square, PA **Died:** January 30, 1948
Height: 6'0" **Weight:** 160 lbs. **Batted:** Both **Threw:** Left
Pitcher: Philadelphia Athletics, 1912-15; Boston Red Sox, 1915-22, 1934; New York Yankees, 1923-33.

* Earned 33 career saves
* Compiled a perfect 5-0 record in World Series play
* Had a league-leading .760 winning percentage in 1923

* Elected to the Hall of Fame in 1948
* Led the league in innings pitched in 1925
* Logged 247 complete games in his career

MAJOR LEAGUE TOTALS

G	IP	W	L	Pct.	SO	BB	ERA
617	3,571	240	162	.597	1,227	916	3.60

Pitcher Herb Pennock spent his most successful years, 1923-33, with the New York Yankees. His record was 21-9 in 1924 and 23-11 in 1926. He also had two other seasons with 19 wins.

TONY PEREZ

Pete Rose and Joe Morgan provided the punch, while Johnny Bench and Tony Perez provided the power, as the Big Red Machine brought four pennants and two world championships to Cincinnati in the 1970s.

The big, strong first baseman started and finished his 23-year career with the Reds. In between he played with the Montreal Expos, the Boston Red Sox, and the Philadelphia Phillies. By the time he retired after the 1986 season, Perez had amassed some amazing statistics—a .279 lifetime batting average, 2,732 base hits, 379 home runs, 505 doubles, and 1,652 runs batted in.

Perez started his pro career in the Cincinnati Reds organization in 1960. The 18-year-old Cuban native was slated to be the team's second baseman, but when a young second baseman named Pete Rose was added to the team, Perez had to move over to third base. It was the first of five seasons Perez had to endure in the minors before getting a full-time job on the Cincinnati roster. In 1963 future Reds first baseman (and current Reds coach) Lee May gave Perez a lasting nickname: He called Perez "Doggie" because of the fierce, canine look he'd acquire when hitting. If Perez had been a 1980s rookie his teammates might have called him "Pit Bull" for the way he attacked opposing pitchers.

In 1961 with Geneva, Perez won the New York-Penn League batting crown with a .348 average. He also led the league with 160 hits and 132 RBI. Perez quickly adapted to the rigors of the hot corner, and he led loop third sackers in putouts and assists. Perez spent 1962 with Rocky Mount of the Carolina League, where he batted .292 with 18 home runs and 74 RBI. Another promotion to Macon of the Sally League in 1963 produced 11 homers, 48 RBI, and a .309 average in 69 games. Perez capped his minor league success with a triumphant effort with San Diego of the Pacific Coast League in 1964. He was at his best with 34 round-trippers, 107 RBI, and a .309 batting average.

Perez got an early lesson with Geneva in 1960 about the need to play more than one position. In his upcoming 23 years in the major leagues, Perez would split his time between first and third base. Stationed at first base during his rookie season of 1965, Perez hit .260 with 12 home runs and 47 RBI. In his sophomore season he had just 4

homers and 39 RBI. Good fortune smiled on Perez before the 1967 season began. He got a shot at third base, which was made available due to complex lineup juggling. Rose moved from second base out to left field. Third baseman Tommy Helms (also a current Reds coach) took over at second, leaving the hot corner open for Perez. Perez responded with his best season to date, hitting team highs of 26 home runs and 102 RBI.

When Perez registered personal bests of 40 home runs, 129 RBI, and a .317 batting average in 1970, he helped spark the Reds to their first division title and an appearance in the newly created National League Championship Series. He batted .333 in the N.L.C.S. but got just 1 hit in 18 plate appearances versus the Baltimore Orioles in the World Series. Fortunately, Perez would be

returning to the fall classic four more times before his career ended. In the 1972 World Series against the Oakland A's Perez batted .435 with 10 hits. He was a hero in the 1975 Series as the Reds won their first Series in three tries during the previous five years. Perez went 0-for-15 to start the Series against the Boston Red Sox, but he boomed 2 homers and 4 RBI to get Cincinnati a 6-2 win and a three-games-to-two advantage.

In the 1976 Series Perez batted .313 with 5 hits to help the Reds sweep four straight games from the New York Yankees. In 1977 the Reds traded Perez to the Montreal Expos. He stayed in Canada for three seasons, then spent the next three years with the Boston Red Sox. His final season of greatness came in 1980 with the BoSox, when he hit 25 round-trippers and 105 RBI.

After Perez retired as a player he became a coach for the Reds under manager Pete Rose. The two are only a year apart in age and had been teammates for many years, not only with the Reds but with the 1983 Philadelphia Phillies "Wheeze Kids" team. The Philadelphia club got its nickname (a take-off on the 1950 Phillies "Whiz Kids") because of its elderly lineup. Perez was 40, Rose was 41, Joe Morgan was 39, and more than half of the team members were over age 30 that year.

Throughout his long career Perez was a steady, dependable performer who topped the .300 mark several times in batting, compiled more than 100 RBI in seven different seasons, and clubbed 20 or more home runs in nine different campaigns. He will be eligible for Hall of Fame election in 1992.

CAREER HIGHLIGHTS
ATANACIO RIGAL PEREZ

Born: May 14, 1942   Camaguey, Cuba
Height: 6'2"   **Weight:** 175 lbs.   **Batted:** Right   **Threw:** Right
First baseman, third baseman: Cincinnati Reds, 1964-76, 1984-86; Montreal Expos, 1977-79; Boston Red Sox, 1980-82; Philadelphia Phillies, 1983.

- ★ Notched 19 or more homers 11 times
- ★ Knocked in 100 or more runs in seven seasons
- ★ Played in five World Series
- ★ Had career highs in homers (40) and RBI (129) in 1970
- ★ Appeared in six League Championship Series

MAJOR LEAGUE TOTALS

G	AB	H	BA	2B	3B	HR	R	RBI	SB
2,777	9,778	2,732	.279	505	79	379	1,272	1,652	49

As a member of Cincinnati's Big Red Machine, infielder Tony Perez helped the Reds get into four World Series. In the '72 Series, he batted .435; in the '75 Series, he hit 2 homers and racked up 4 RBI to win the fifth game.

GAYLORD PERRY

aylord Perry has claimed that in the latter part of his career he never threw any illegal pitches. What the once infamous spitballer did do was "leave a lot of evidence lying around." Such as shaking an opponent's hand before the game and leaving it full of grease. Or spending a lot of time fussing on the mound before finally releasing the ball. Perry was a master of psychological warfare, creating so much fear of his dreaded spitball that his sinker became much harder to hit. Regardless of which pitches he threw, Perry was successful for 22 major league seasons, notching 314 career wins (the 14th-highest total in history).

This isn't really surprising from a man who mastered spitball sleight-of-hand early in his career while with the San Francisco Giants. His notoriety as a greaser helped bring about the more stringent rules developed after 1973. In 1974 Perry published an autobiographical confession entitled *Me and the Spitter*. In his memoir he claims to have tried every rub-on substance known to man except "salt and pepper and chocolate toppin'."

After brief appearances during two previous seasons Perry logged his first full season with the San Francisco Giants in 1964. His ERA plummeted to 2.75 and he won 12 games. He slumped in 1965 despite notching a win in the All-Star game, before coming back in 1966 with a more even temper, a new warm-up regimen (a game of pepper), and a brand new pitch to add to his repertoire of fastball, curve, and slow slider. He called it a fast slider; his opponents called it a spitball. Perry took the comment as a compliment. To a ballplayer, he said, a spitballer is an artist.

He earned his first 20-win season in 1966, then fell to 15-17 in 1967. National League pitching rules were changed, disallowing the wetting of a pitcher's fingers, even if he appeared to dry them. Perry switched from spitballs to greaseballs, stashing some goo on the brim of his cap. His victories climbed from 16 in 1968 to 19 in 1969. Both years his ERA stayed under 2.50. The highlight of his 1968 season was a no-hitter against the St. Louis Cardinals.

In 1970 he joined his major league brother, Jim, to set a few of the game's most interesting records. With Gaylord leading the National League with 23 victories and Jim pitching an American League high of 24 wins with the

Minnesota Twins, they became the first brothers to win 20-plus games each in the same major league season. That year they also played against one another in the All-Star game, another baseball first. They nearly cornered both Cy Young awards that year. Jim won the A.L. Cy Young, but Gaylord was nosed out by Bob Gibson.

Gaylord Perry would later go on to become the first pitcher ever to receive the coveted Cy Young in both leagues: in 1972 with the A.L. Cleveland Indians and in 1978 with the N.L. San Diego Padres. Perhaps it was only fair that Jim be recognized first: The older brother had signed a contract the same year as Gaylord. But Jim got an estimated bonus of $4,000, while Gaylord is said to have raked in about $60,000.

In 1974 and 1975 the brothers pitched side-by-side on the Cleveland Indians together compiling 38 wins. It

ended when Gaylord and then-manager Frank Robinson proved to have incompatible personalities. At year's end, with 17 years of service under his belt and his brother now with the Texas Rangers, Jim retired.

Gaylord, meanwhile, continued serving one- and two-year stints with various clubs for the next seven years, enabling him to assemble some big numbers for his lifetime statistics. The New York Yankees, the Atlanta Braves, the Seattle Mariners, and the Kansas City Royals hosted Perry during the twilight years of his career. Perry brought fame to an unknown Mariners team in the early 80s, gaining his 300th career win with the struggling franchise. Perry's career numbers include 3,543 strikeouts (the fifth highest in history) and 5,352 innings pitched (fifth on the all-time list). The durable hurler collected 53 shutouts and 303 complete games in his 22 major league seasons.

The last two years of his career were dotted with suspense. Umpires became more zealous than ever with the crafty veteran, giving him frequent on-field security searches for illegal substances. Just before retiring he introduced a "puff ball," a pitch that gave off clouds of rosin on its way to the batter.

After his retirement Perry tried to make a career for himself as a peanut farmer. Recently he has served as a college baseball coach in his native North Carolina. His name will become nationally known again soon, when his expected election to the Baseball Hall of Fame becomes a reality.

CAREER HIGHLIGHTS
GAYLORD JACKSON PERRY

Born: September 15, 1938   Williamston, NC
Height: 6'4"   **Weight:** 205 lbs.   **Batted:** Right   **Threw:** Right
Pitcher: San Francisco Giants, 1962-71; Cleveland Indians, 1972-75; Texas Rangers, 1975-77, 1980; San Diego Padres, 1978-79; New York Yankees, 1980; Atlanta Braves, 1981; Seattle Mariners, 1982-83; Kansas City Royals, 1983.

★ Was the only pitcher to win a Cy Young award in both leagues in 1972 and 1978

★ Led the N.L. in wins twice and the A.L. once

★ Led the N.L. in innings pitched twice

★ Compiled 314 career wins and 3,534 strikeouts

★ Ranks fifth in history with 5,352 innings pitched

★ Won 20 or more games five times

★ Pitched a no-hitter against the Cardinals in 1968

MAJOR LEAGUE TOTALS

G	IP	W	L	Pct.	SO	BB	ERA
777	5,352	314	265	.542	3,534	1,379	3.10

Gaylord Perry, notorious for his use of the spitball, claimed to have offered his services as a spokesperson to the makers of Vaseline petroleum jelly. The company refused, however, stating their product was for babies.

RICO PETROCELLI

Rico Petrocelli is, it seems, something of a reluctant star, and always was. When questioned about his early years in the game, he is apt to comment on the hotels and food encountered on the road, the methods of team transportation, and the length of the trips. With a little encouragement he'll talk about the game.

Actually, there isn't much need for the dynamic shortstop to reflect on his accomplishments because he said it all on the diamond without uttering a word. He was a prolific power hitter who in 1969 posted single-season career highs in doubles (32), home runs (40), and batting average (.297). He was a valued utility player during his later years, roaming three infield positions, pausing at short, and also serving as a designated hitter. Petrocelli was an exceptional clutch hitter, as proven by his World Series and American League Championship Series performances.

The self-professed homebody from Brooklyn began playing pro ball at the age of 19, signing with the Boston Red Sox for a reported $40,000 bonus. His first set of marks with Winston-Salem were passing grades, certainly in the B to B+ range with a .277 average, 30 doubles, and 17 home runs. Learning the ropes around shortstop didn't come easy for Petrocelli, who had a first-season fielding average of .923.

He studied hard the following season at Reading, Pennyslvania. There he led the league with 266 putouts and 464 assists (a personal minor league high). His 42 errors were offset by 23 doubles and 19 home runs. On the strength of his second minor league season he was called up to the Boston Red Sox for one game in 1963. Although the 20-year-old shortstop logged a big league double and 3 putouts, his memories of that fast-paced year are primarily of bad field lighting and crummy hotels. Yet he held that hardships were good for young players, weeding out those who did not have a pervasive love of the game.

His last minor league year was spent in comparative luxury, with the Seattle Rainiers of the Pacific Coast League. Petrocelli was pleased with the promotion because it meant he was one step closer to the big leagues. He was also delighted with Triple-A because Seattle flew its players to most road game locations, including Hawaii. Petrocelli's offense receded somewhat in 1964, but his defense suddenly blossomed. His 29 errors were his lowest ever; his .956 fielding average was his highest. The following year he was called up to Boston for good, where his marks continued to improve.

It is true that Petrocelli never in 13 years of big league service batted as high as .300 (although he came within 3 points in 1969). Yet the Brooklyn native made sure his team wasn't cheated in the tradeoff between power and average. In 1969 he slammed 40 home runs, a new record for American League shortstops.

Although 1965 was his rookie season, Petrocelli once said that he really became a major leaguer in 1967, when—on a winning team for the first time—he realized that the pennant was the ultimate goal. His spirit renewed, he paced the BoSox to contending position with 75 RBI in 1972 and 76 RBI in 1974. He appeared in his first World Series in 1967, smacking 2 homers. In 1975 he bested that effort with a .308 batting average and 4 RBI with a single homer in the four-game League Championship Series. Both of Petrocelli's World Series appearances were destined to end in defeat, yet both went down to the seventh-game wire.

It was this kind of down-to-the-wire effort in 1967 that produced Petrocelli's most prized baseball memory. He scored the sixth game's first run with a solo homer and slugged another one in the fourth inning to pace his team to victory.

His worst baseball memory is an odd footnote in the saga of the beloved shortstop, who began a seven-year stint at third base when Luis Aparicio was acquired in 1970. About this time an airline attendant accused Petrocelli of sexual harassment, a charge that brought many teammates to the aid of the accused family man and that was eventually disproved in court.

Petrocelli has said that the experience shattered his faith in human nature. Yet he has nothing but praise for the Red Sox organization, despite his many threats to quit before his final year in 1976, simply to avoid travel and long stays away from his family.

Following his retirement Petrocelli served as a coach in the Red Sox minor league system. He's remembered as one of the greatest all-around Boston shortstops since Joe Cronin.

On the Boston roster for his entire major league career, Rico Petrocelli was a consistent and dedicated player, if not a spectacular one. Petrocelli's biggest claim to fame is the A.L. record he set in 1969 for the most home runs by a shortstop in a single season, with 40.

CAREER HIGHLIGHTS
AMERICO PETROCELLI

Born: June 27, 1943   Brooklyn, NY
Height: 6'0"   **Weight:** 175 lbs.   **Batted:** Right   **Threw:** Right
Shortstop, third baseman: Boston Red Sox, 1963, 1965-76.

* Hit in double figures for homers in ten straight seasons
* Set the A.L. record for single-season homers by a shortstop with 40 in 1969
* Drove in a career-high 103 runs in 1970
* Hit two homers in the 1967 World Series
* Batted .308 in the 1975 World Series

MAJOR LEAGUE TOTALS

G	AB	H	BA	2B	3B	HR	R	RBI	SB
1,553	5,390	1,352	.251	237	22	210	653	773	10

VADA PINSON

Vada Pinson has the unique distinction of having compiled more base hits than any other eligible player who is not yet enshrined in the Hall of Fame. An outfielder who played most of his career with the Cincinnati Reds in the 1950s and 1960s, he stroked a total of 2,757 base hits during his 18 years in the major leagues.

Pinson needed just two years in the minor leagues to earn his first shot at the big leagues. He began his pro career as a first baseman in 1957 in Wausau, Wisconsin. He hit a modest .278 with 2 home runs in 75 games. Advancing to Visalia of the California League in 1958, Pinson started switching to the outfield, where he would eventually gain his fame. He led league outfielders with 30 assists, while pacing the loop in four offensive categories: hits (209), doubles (40), triples (20), and runs scored (165). The Reds brought Pinson up for a substantial outfield audition near the end of the season. He hit .271 with 1 homer and 8 RBI and played errorless baseball in 27 games.

It's easy to see why stardom was predicted for Pinson in the early 1960s. After his first five years with Cincinnati, he had accumulated 985 base hits. That total surpassed the first five-year achievements of Stan Musial (975), Willie Mays (954), Hank Aaron (914), and Frank Robinson (818). Pinson had to cope with constant comparisons to Robinson, his long-time teammate and outfield partner in Cincinnati. Both grew up in Oakland, and they were high school teammates at McClymonds High School. Another famous outfielder, Curt Flood, also attended the Oakland high school. Pinson and Flood were united in the majors for one season when the Reds traded Pinson to the St. Louis Cardinals on October 11, 1968, in exchange for outfielder Bobby Tolan and reliever Wayne Granger. With Flood, Pinson, and Lou Brock, the Cardinals had one of the speediest outfields of the 1960s.

Pinson was a disappointment with the Redbirds, hitting just .255 with 10 homers and 70 RBI. He was traded after one season to the Cleveland Indians on November 21, 1969, for outfielder Jose Cardenal. He hit a personal best of 24 home runs in 1970 during his first American League season. In 1971 he stole 25 bases, his highest total since 1967. The Indians sent Pinson to the California Angels with Frank Baker and Alan Foster on October 5, 1971, in exchange for Alex

Johnson and Gerry Moses. In two years with the Angels Pinson tallied averages of .275 and .260. On February 23, 1974, the Kansas City Royals picked up Pinson from the Angels in exchange for cash and a minor leaguer. He batted .276 in 1974 but retired after the 1975 season when his average fell to an all-time low of .223. Pinson played just 103 games in his final season, which was the least action he had ever seen in 18 major league seasons.

In 1961 Pinson had an incredible season to help the Reds to the National League pennant. He batted .343 with a league-leading 208 hits, 16 homers, and 87 RBI to spark the pennant run. Pinson won his only Gold Glove that year as well.

Many of Pinson's career statistics are of Cooperstown caliber. He has a lifetime .286 batting mark, 485 doubles, 127 triples, 256 homers, 1,170 RBI, and 1,366 runs scored. The fleet-footed center fielder swiped 305 bases in his

career. Although he had nine seasons of 20 or more steals, he never topped 32 pilfers in a single season. He was one of the fastest men in the majors, but his speed was never used to its greatest potential. He batted over .300 four times during his career. Pinson had seven seasons of 20 or more home runs, six of them with the Reds in the National League. Pinson was a solid performer who consistently ranked among the best at his position. He played in 505 consecutive games for the Reds from 1958 to 1962.

Pinson apparently didn't have enough spectacular seasons to impress the baseball writers who determine Hall of Fame selection, a situation similar to that of Richie Ashburn. Both were dependable center fielders who have gone largely unappreciated because they played their careers in the shadow of such great power-hitting center fielders as Willie Mays, Duke Snider, and Mickey Mantle. Pinson is unfairly judged in relation to the star trio, simply because he never had enough World Series exposure. Even mediocre players are remembered more favorably if they are lucky enough to play with perennial pennant winners.

After retirement Pinson served as a minor league hitting instructor for the Seattle Mariners. He has been with the Detroit Tigers since 1985 and is a coach for the 1989 Bengals. His knowledge of the game and leadership qualities have made him an ideal candidate for a future managerial job in the majors, a fact that many teams are aware of. If he does land a position as a team skipper, he would be only the fourth black in history to manage a major league team.

CAREER HIGHLIGHTS
VADA EDWARD PINSON, JR.

Born: August 8, 1936   Memphis, TN
Height: 5'11"   **Weight:** 170 lbs.   **Batted:** Left   **Threw:** Left
Outfielder: Cincinnati Reds, 1958-68; St. Louis Cardinals, 1969; Cleveland Indians, 1970-71; California Angels, 1972-73; Kansas City Royals, 1974-75.

* Led the league twice in hits
* Played in 505 consecutive games
* Paced the N.L. in doubles in 1959 and 1960

* Led the N.L. in triples twice
* Played in the 1961 World Series
* Had seven seasons with 20 or more homers

MAJOR LEAGUE TOTALS

G	AB	H	BA	2B	3B	HR	R	RBI	SB
2,469	9,645	2,757	.286	485	127	256	1,366	1,170	305

Vada Pinson's lifetime stats are of Hall of Fame caliber. He averaged .286 during his career, hit 256 home runs and 127 triples, and racked up 1,170 RBI. Most impressive is his base hit total of 2,757.

EDDIE PLANK

ightseers who visited Pennsylvania's famous Gettysburg Civil War Battleground at the turn of the century may have been guided around the historic grounds by Eddie Plank, a young man who would soon be making history himself in the baseball record books. Plank went on to enjoy a 17-year career in the major leagues, winning 326 games on his way to a spot in the Baseball Hall of Fame.

Born on a Gettysburg farm in 1875, Plank never wandered far from home. At Gettysburg College the baseball coach (former major league pitcher Frank Foreman) noticed Plank's athletic talents and convinced him to try the game. The lefthand hurler was 22 years old, but with his amazing natural ability and careful coaching, he quickly mastered the three-quarter pitching motion as well as the sidearm delivery. Four years later (after his college graduation) Plank went directly to Connie Mack's Philadelphia Athletics. During his long career with the American League club Plank would be known as one of the greatest hurlers of his day, helping the A's to six pennants. Fans would call him "Gettysburg Eddie," in tribute to his hometown and to the real battles he fought on the mound.

Despite his competitive fervor, Plank's biggest aid as a pitcher was psychological warfare. He was a fidgety hurler, one who seemed to take forever between offerings. Plank would adjust his cap, tug at his pants, and fiddle with his stance on the mound. Umpires would become irate over Plank's delays, but the hurler knew what he was doing. His purposeful dawdling threw hitters off stride and worked to his advantage. Plank didn't have a blazing fastball to rely on. It was timing and an impressive assortment of pitches including many sharp-breaking curves that kept him in business for 17 seasons.

Incredibly, Plank never once led his league in wins, although he was a 20-game winner for almost half his career. He did top the American League in winning percentage in 1906 with a .760 mark (going 19-6). Mack picked specific situations for using his 5-foot-11, 175-pound lefty. Although it seems hard to fathom today, Plank was kept on the bench during the 1910 World Series, even after logging a 16-10 record with a 2.02 ERA during the regular season. Mack, who apparently wasn't a big believer in pitching rotations, used only Jack Coombs and Chief Bender in winning the five-game Series.

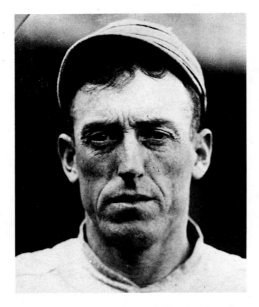

The Athletics released Plank after the 1914 season, when his record fell to 15-7. His ERA had zoomed to 2.87, still a respectable figure but the highest average he had accumulated in the past 11 seasons. He hooked up with the St. Louis Terriers of the newly formed Federal League. Plank was one of the league's finest pitchers, collecting 21 wins, 11 losses, 3 saves, and a 2.08 ERA. His team finished less than one game out of first place. The major leagues threatened all Federal League players with a possible lifetime ban if they played with the outlaw teams. Plank knew that his career was nearing its end, so he wasn't concerned about the ultimatum. When the Federal League folded after just one season, the other leagues relented and anxiously signed the out-of-work players. The St. Louis Browns discovered Plank. Even though he had passed his 40th birthday,

he proved he could still be effective. He was 16-15 in 1916 and was 5-6 in his final season, with an ERA of 1.79.

For 8 of his 17 seasons Plank won 20 or more games, and two other years he won 19. He twice won 26 games in a season, and he finished his career with 326 wins, compiling 69 shutouts and 193 losses for a .628 winning percentage to go along with his 2.35 ERA. His shutouts and complete games (410) are records for lefthanders, while his victory total is third behind tireless southpaw Warren Spahn's 363 triumphs and Steve Carlton's 329 wins. Plank's postseason success wasn't so great. He was 2-5 in four World Series, although his ERA was only 1.32, the tenth lowest in history. Plank went the distance in all but one of his Series starts. Even though he compiled an impressive lifetime ERA of just 2.35, Plank never did pace the league in that department.

Following his retirement Plank farmed and worked as an auto dealer. He died in Gettysburg in 1926 at the age of 50. He was elected to the Hall of Fame 20 years later.

Despite pitcher Eddie Plank's impressive achievements, including winning 20 or more games eight times during his career, he never led his league in wins, strikeouts, or ERA. He did, however, strike out 2,246 batters in the majors and pitch 69 shutouts.

CAREER HIGHLIGHTS
EDWARD STEWART PLANK

Born: August 31, 1875 Gettysburg, PA **Died:** February 24, 1926
Height: 5'11" **Weight:** 175 lbs. **Batted:** Left **Threw:** Left
Pitcher: Philadelphia Athletics, 1901-14; St. Louis Minors (also known as the Terriers), 1915; St. Louis Browns, 1916-17.

★ Won 20 or more games eight times
★ Has 69 career shutouts, fifth highest in history
★ Pitched in four World Series
★ Registered 410 complete games in his lifetime

★ Elected to the Hall of Fame in 1946

MAJOR LEAGUE TOTALS

G	IP	W	L	Pct.	SO	BB	ERA
622	4,497	326	193	.628	2,246	1,072	2.35

BOOG POWELL

When Baltimore Orioles fans of the 60s or early 70s wanted a quick home run for the team, chants of "Boog! Boog!" would ring out. The fans weren't booing. They just wanted the trustworthy hitting of John Wesley Powell for a quick fix.

Powell's nickname can be traced to his father, who called him "Booger" due to all the trouble his young son got into. Young Powell used his 6-foot-4, 230-pound frame to his best advantage in high school sports. Powell declined several college football scholarship offers because he wanted to play major league baseball. His decision netted him an estimated signing bonus of $35,000 from the Orioles, who inked him to a pact in 1958.

He began his career in the Orioles farm system in 1959 at Bluefield of the Appalachian League. In his debut he hit 14 homers, 59 RBI, and a .351 average. A 1960 promotion sent Powell to the Fox Cities for work. In 136 games Powell posted a .312 average with 13 round-trippers and 100 RBI. It took just one more season in the minors to prove that Powell was ready for big league action. With the Rochester Red Wings in 1961 Powell was the International League's home run champion with 32. His 92 RBI and .321 were other highlights of his season.

For the next three years Powell was a full-time outfielder for Baltimore. Powell remained in left field while Jim Gentile or Norm Siebern manned first base, even though first seemed like Powell's natural position. Starting with his first full season of 1962, Powell immediately became Baltimore's resident long-ball specialist, hitting 15 homers with 53 RBI in 124 games. The following year Powell's totals climbed to 25 homers and 82 RBI. By 1964 Powell had become a pitcher's nightmare. He belted 39 home runs (second in the league behind Harmon Killebrew's 49 homers) and 99 RBI with a .290 batting average.

The next year Powell beat Siebern out of a starting job at first base. He slumped to 17 homers and 72 RBI but showed fine defensive skills as an infielder. Powell rebounded to hit .287 with 34 home runs and 109 RBI in 1966, the year the Orioles won their first world championship. As the O's swept the favored Los Angeles Dodgers in four straight World Series games, Powell earned a team-leading postseason average of .357.

In 1969 Powell hammered 37 homers, a personal best of 121 RBI, and a career-high .304 average. Baltimore played in the first-ever League Championship Series, with Powell batting .385. His first-game homer in the ninth inning tied the score with the Twins and set the stage for a 12th-inning win.

Powell was named the A.L. Most Valuable Player in 1970. During the regular season he had 35 homers, 114 RBI, and a .297 average. He batted .429 in the A.L.C.S. and hit .294 with 2 home runs, 6 runs scored, and 5 RBI in the World Series victory over Cincinnati.

An era ended when the Orioles traded Powell and pitcher Don Hood to the Cleveland Indians for catcher Dave Duncan and a minor leaguer on February 25, 1975. Powell lasted just two seasons with the Tribe, but he helped sell lots of tickets and provided a mediocre team with some much needed power. Despite hitting only 11 and 12 homers in his two previous seasons, Powell staged a marvelous comeback in 1975. He bashed 27 home runs and tallied 86 RBI while hitting .297. After his release he caught on with the Los Angeles Dodgers for a final season in 1977. Used almost exclusively as a pinch hitter, Powell had 10 hits in 41 plate appearances with no home runs.

Powell's lifetime statistics include 1,776 hits in 2,042 games for a .266 average. He registered 270 doubles, 11 triples (he was a slow baserunner), and 339 home runs. Even though he whiffed 1,226 times in his career, Powell only topped 100 Ks during one season. Powell was patient enough to take bases on balls when he could get them. During his final season as a Dodger pinch hitter he made the late-inning walk his trademark. Pitchers still fearsome of Powell's reputation for power would pitch quite carefully.

He was a member of the 1968 American League All-Star team, then became an elected starter in both 1969 and 1970. In 1971 Powell declined an All-Star invitation due to an injury.

Powell earned a lasting place in the Orioles record books during his stay in Baltimore. He led the Birds in home runs during five seasons and in RBI for four. On July 6, 1966, Powell set an Orioles record with 11 RBI in a doubleheader versus the A's. Three times during his career Powell registered 3 homers in one game. Powell is second in hits on the Orioles all-time list. He is only one of two O's ever to top 300 homers, the other being long-ball leader Eddie Murray.

Upon his retirement from baseball Powell returned to his native state of Florida. In 1979 Powell was named to the Baltimore Orioles Hall of Fame.

CAREER HIGHLIGHTS
JOHN WESLEY POWELL

Born: August 17, 1941   Lakeland, FL
Height: 6'4"   **Weight:** 230 lbs.   **Batted:** Left   **Threw:** Right
First baseman, outfielder: Baltimore Orioles, 1961-74; Cleveland Indians, 1975-76; Los Angeles Dodgers, 1977.

* Won the A.L. MVP award in 1970
* Led the A.L. with a .606 slugging percentage in 1964
* Clubbed 30 or more home runs four times
* Hit 20 or more home runs nine times
* Batted .306 in five League Championship Series
* Appeared in four World Series

MAJOR LEAGUE TOTALS

G	AB	H	BA	2B	3B	HR	R	RBI	SB
2,042	6,681	1,776	.266	270	11	339	889	1,187	20

Boog Powell's lifetime statistics include a home run percentage of 5.1 and a slugging percentage of .462. His home run total of 339 ranks above Rogers Hornsby, Hank Greenberg, and Al Simmons.

KIRBY PUCKETT

After only five years in the majors, outfielder Kirby Puckett had played in four All-Star games and one World Series cliffhanger and had worked hard enough to lead the 1988 American League in both offensive and defensive categories. His 234 hits and 450 putouts were the most obvious fruits of his labors; his stellar batting average of .356 was, unfortunately, eclipsed by Wade Boggs' effort, which was superior by an amazing 10 points.

Puckett showed no sign of discouragement at the top of 1989, however, as he scrambled to acquire the needed hits to top Joe "Ducky" Medwick's record for most hits by a player in his first five major league seasons (1,064). He has become one of only four players in history to get 1,000 hits in his first five seasons. Medwick, Paul Waner, and Earle Combs—all Hall of Famers—are the other players to match the 1,000-hit feat. Not only did Puckett break records in 1989, he also won the A.L. batting crown with a .339 average.

Puckett was the third player chosen in the free-agent draft of June 1982. A 21-year-old rookie that year, Puckett paced the Appalachian League in batting average (.386) and five other offensive categories, as well as outfield assists, putouts, and chances accepted. *Baseball America* crowned him the league's player of the year, and other first-year titles affirmed the ability scout Ellsworth Brown had seen in the Twins future star. With Visalia in the California League in 1983, Puckett kept succeeding. He batted .314 with 9 homers and 97 RBI. He was first in the league in at-bats, double plays, and assists (22). After just 21 games at Toledo in 1984 (skipping the Double-A minor league level) Puckett got his permanent promotion to the Twins outfield.

Puckett made his major league debut with the Minnesota Twins on May 8, 1984, with a single. He became only the ninth player in major league history to get 4 hits in his first nine-inning game. He posted a .296 batting average his first season, although he went 128 games without a home run. The Chicago native did have 165 hits, driving in 31 runs. Puckett displayed a strong throwing arm, tallying a league-high 16 assists.

In 1985 Puckett's batting average dipped to .288, and he had just 4 home runs (his first ever was off Seattle's Matt Young on April 22 at home). He drove in 74 runs and set a Twins' record with 691 at-bats (which led the major leagues also). His 199 hits just missed the 200-hit mark, a barrier he has broken three times going into 1989. He played in 161 games, tying a league high for A.L. outfielders. Puckett paced outfielders in putouts (465) and total chances (492).

Puckett's weight increased after his first season with the Twins. This may be the only possible explanation as to why he suddenly found the key to long-ball hitting. The same man who went without a single homer in 557 at-bats just two years earlier became one of the league's resident home run threats in 1986. His unprecedented 31 round-trippers amazed the baseball world.

The whole baseball world finally began to notice Puckett's many talents. Along with the homers, he tallied 96 RBI (77 as a leadoff hitter), 223 hits, and a .328 average. Puckett was voted the junior circuit's starting center fielder in the All-Star game. The Twins named him the team MVP, he was voted onto the Silver Slugger team, and he won Player of the Month honors for April. Puckett won his first of a string of Gold Gloves beginning in 1986. His season was highlighted by an August 1 game in which he hit for the cycle versus Oakland.

Puckett was a key member of the underdog team of 1987 that landed a world championship. He batted .332 with 28 homers, 99 RBI, and 207 total hits that season. A repeat All-Star, Puckett set an A.L. record and tied a major league mark with 10 hits in two consecutive games on August 29-30 versus the Brewers. Although he hit just .208 in the A.L. Championship Series versus the Detroit Tigers, Puckett had a fourth-game homer and 3 RBI for the event. Puckett was a star in the seven-game World Series against the Cardinals. He led the upstart Twins with 10 hits and a .357 average. He tied a pair of Series records by reaching base 5 times and scoring 4 runs in the Twins 11-5 win in the sixth game.

In 1988 Puckett drove in a career-high 121 runs. He led the majors in total bases, singles, multihit games (a club record of 73), outfield putouts, and total chances. Another All-Star appearance and his third consecutive Silver Slugger and Gold Glove followed. Rod Carew was the only other Twin in history to hit .300, get 200 hits, score 100 runs, and drive in 100.

As long as he continues playing injury-free, it looks as though Puckett is in the express lane headed for 3,000 hits. While he doesn't look like a typical superslugger, the Twins star has the potential to be a future triple crown winner.

CAREER HIGHLIGHTS
KIRBY PUCKETT

Born: March 14, 1961   Chicago, IL
Height: 5'8"   **Weight:** 178 lbs.   **Bats:** Right   **Throws:** Right
Outfielder: Minnesota Twins, 1984-89.

★ Hit a career-high .356 in 1988
★ Earned his 1,000th big league hit in 1988
★ Batted .357 in the 1988 World Series
★ Played in All-Star games from 1986 through 1989

★ Topped 200 hits in the last four seasons

MAJOR LEAGUE TOTALS

G	AB	H	BA	2B	3B	HR	R	RBI	SB
924	3,844	1,243	.323	197	38	96	542	506	84

Kirby Puckett was the ninth player in major league history to rap 4 hits in his first nine inning game, back on May 8, 1984. In 1988 he became one of only four players to top 1,000 hits in his first five seasons of play.

DAN QUISENBERRY

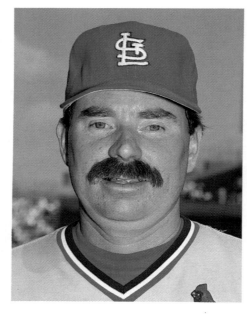

Dan Quisenberry could be called "the man from down under." After getting a tired arm in college pitching a record 194 innings, Quisenberry became a traditional sidearm-style pitcher. After working with Pittsburgh's Kent Tekulve during spring training in 1980 he adopted the submarine motion he still uses today. The underhand delivery made him one of the greatest A.L. relievers in history.

Despite his successful career at the University of California at La Verne (where he made the National Association of Intercollegiate Athletics All-American team), Quisenberry was not drafted by any major league teams. He was signed as a free agent by the Kansas City Royals in 1975. Beginning his pro career at the relatively advanced age of 22, Quisenberry's first minor league stop was in Waterloo, Iowa. That year he got the only start of his lengthy pro career, and he earned a complete-game victory. He split the 1976 season between Waterloo and Jacksonville, Kansas City's Double-A franchise. Finishing in Waterloo he had 11 saves, 2 wins, and an 0.64 ERA. He pitched with Jacksonville for two more years, then advanced to Omaha in 1979. After just 26 games he earned a permanent place in the Royals bullpen. He closed out his minor league career with 14 wins, 42 saves, and a 2.02 ERA.

Following his July 7 call-up to Kansas City, Quisenberry earned 3 wins, 2 losses, 5 saves, and a 3.15 ERA in his major league rookie season. His herky-jerky motion and ever-sharp control were the keys to his mastery of opposing hitters. In his sophomore campaign of 1980, Quisenberry was the Rolaids Fireman of the Year. He tied Rich Gossage for the league lead in saves with 33. The man nicknamed "Quiz" converted all but 8 save opportunities. He earned a career-high 12 victories, and he led the league in appearances (75).

The Royals whipped the Yankees in three straight games in the A.L.C.S., thanks to a win and a save by their ace reliever. Quisenberry hurled the final 3.2 innings of the third game to clinch the American League pennant. In the 1980 World Series Philadelphia beat the Royals in six games. Quisenberry tied a record by appearing in all six games. While he had 1 win and 1 save, he also suffered 2 losses.

In 1981 Quisenberry logged a career-best 1.74 ERA and led the Royals with 18 saves and 40 games pitched. The Royals won half of the Western Division pennant. Due to the split season forced by the players' strike, the Royals were beaten out of the A.L.C.S. by a three-game divisional playoff against the A's.

Quisenberry earned his second Fireman of the Year award in 1982. He paced the junior circuit in games finished (68) and saves (35). He had 9 wins and a 2.56 ERA in 137 innings, yielding only 12 walks all season. His 1983 season was the stuff that relievers dream about. Quisenberry earned 45 saves in 54 opportunities, breaking John Hiller's 1973 record of 38 saves. His ERA was a sparkling 1.94, and his 69 games pitched topped the American League. He finished second in the Cy Young award balloting that year.

In 1984 Quisenberry became the first reliever in history to have back-to-back seasons of 40 or more saves—with a league-best 44. Quiz pitched 129.1 innings in a total of 72 games, allowing just 12 walks and striking out 41. The Royals streaked to a world championship in 1985, thanks to Quisenberry's league-best 37 saves and career-high 84 appearances. He reached the 200-save milestone in 1985, becoming only the sixth pitcher in history to do so. Quisenberry made four appearances in the A.L. Championship Series against Toronto and against the Cardinals in the World Series. He saved a game against the Blue Jays and won the sixth game of the Series against St. Louis. Quisenberry also won his fifth Fireman of the Year award.

After 20 appearances in 1988 Quisenberry was released by the Royals on July 4. He was snatched up by the cross-state Cardinals just ten days later. The veteran reliever went 2-0 in 33 games in St. Louis in 1988. After 9½ seasons in the American League Quisenberry had his first major league at-bat with the Cardinals in 1988. Fortunately he walked. Quisenberry's stats improved in 1989 and his ERA was back down in the low 2.40s.

Through the 1988 season Quisenberry had a 53-44 record and 2.70 ERA. His strikeout-to-walk ratio was 340 to 145 in 957 innings and his 238 saves ranked fourth (tied with Sparky Lyle at the end of 1988) on the all-time list. He is the sixth pitcher in history to gain 200-plus saves. When Quisenberry's wins and saves are combined, he has participated in 283 victories.

Quisenberry might not be the feared bullpen stopper that he was during his glory days with the Royals, but his years of experience and on-the-field determination still make him a valued member of any pitching staff.

CAREER HIGHLIGHTS
DANIEL RAYMOND QUISENBERRY

Born: February 7, 1953 Santa Monica, CA
Height: 6'2" **Weight:** 170 lbs. **Bats:** Right **Throws:** Right
Pitcher: Kansas City Royals, 1979-88; St. Louis Cardinals, 1988-89.

★ Set an A.L. record with 238 career saves ★ Led the A.L. in appearances three times
★ Was first in the A.L. in games finished three times ★ Named *The Sporting News* Fireman of the Year five times
★ Appeared in two World Series

MAJOR LEAGUE TOTALS

G	IP	W	L	Pct.	SV	SO	BB	ERA
669	1,035	56	45	.554	244	377	159	2.70

Dan Quisenberry was the first reliever in baseball history to have consecutive seasons of 40 or more saves, back in 1983-84. Quisenberry reached the 200-save mark in 1985, becoming only the sixth pitcher to do so.

TIM RAINES

The failure of any team to sign Tim Raines as a free agent following the 1986 season is probably the players union's greatest proof that the owners conspired to destroy the free-agency system. Could there really have been 25 other teams that couldn't use a switch-hitting leadoff batter who led his team in 1987 with a .330 batting average, hit 18 home runs, and stole 50 bases—even while sitting out the month of April? For that matter, the Montreal Expos management must regret forcing Raines into free agency. As the 1987 season waned and the Expos faded behind the St. Louis Cardinals in the pennant race, the Montreal team's ownership must have wondered how many of the lost April games might have gone into the win column if Raines had been on board.

Raines was not selected by the Expos until the fifth round of the free-agent draft in June 1977. In his first three minor league seasons, he batted between .280 and .290 and had no power. The Expos tried to make a second baseman or a shortstop out of him, but he was consistently at or near the top in errors in the league—although his natural speed and range put him near the top in putouts, assists, and chances accepted.

Fans might wonder what took the Expos so long to give Raines his first major league shot in 1979. After all he had had a good season with Memphis of the Southern League. In 145 games (tying for the league lead) Raines topped the league with 104 runs scored and batted .290. He made 23 errors at second, but he was first in putouts (341) and assists (413). When he was called up in 1979 to Montreal, he never got the chance to bat; he was used exclusively as a pinch runner. Raines swiped 2 bases and scored 3 runs.

He began the 1980 season with the Denver Bears of the American Association, Montreal's Triple-A affiliate. He was named the Minor League Player of Year as he led his league with a .354 average, 11 triples, and 77 stolen bases. He again received a September call-up to the Expos, but he hit a dismal .050 in 15 games. He was flawless in the field, however. The Expos stuck with Raines in 1981, although he was shifted primarily to outfield assignments. He hit .304 in his rookie season and paced the circuit with 71 stolen bases in the strike-shortened year.

Without a doubt, the energy of this 5-foot-8, 160-pound spark plug helped propel the Expos to the five-game 1981 National League Championship Series, where he rapped out 5 hits and fielded flawlessly. Although the Expos never made it to the World Series, Raines was crowned National League Rookie of the Year by *The Sporting News*.

Since then, Raines has been showered with honors by the publication. He won their Gold Shoe award in 1984, earned their Silver Slugger in 1986, and was a member of their All-Star teams in 1983 and 1986.

After two seasons of sub-.300 batting (although his 133 runs scored led the league in 1983 and his fielding was still improving), he began hitting over .300 consistently after the 1984 season. He led the league in stolen bases every year from 1981 to 1984 with totals ranging from 71 to 90. In 1982 he began a six-year streak of whacking 30 or more doubles per year, leading the league with a career-high 38 in 1984. It was the second straight year Raines landed on the All-Star team, an honor he received every year through 1987, for a total of seven consecutive years.

In 1986 his .334 average was a league best. In 1987 he was third in batting, topped the league in runs scored, and slugged a career-high 18 home runs. He also posted a major league high of 26 intentional walks for a switch-hitter. That same year he hit for the cycle on August 16.

Although 1988 was a relatively quiet year for the 29-year-old slugger, he did switch-hit homers in a single game and increase his lifetime stealing percentage to an all-time high .870.

Only twice in his career has "Rock" (as he likes to be called) served time on the injured list. He was disabled once during his tenure with the Expos in 1988. He finally had surgery on his left shoulder late that season, although the pain kept him down to 109 games and a .270 batting average.

The 1989 season found Raines back in the Montreal lineup, leading his team in a four-way battle with the Mets, the Cardinals, and the Cubs for first place in the N.L. Eastern Division. Montreal fell from glory the last month of the season, but don't count them out next year. With a healthy Raines on board, the Expos can expect to be in contention for many seasons to come.

Tim Raines' amazing speed and switch-hitting capabilities make him one of the best players of the 1980s. Despite the fact that Raines missed spring training in 1987, he still batted .330.

CAREER HIGHLIGHTS
TIMOTHY RAINES

Born: September 16, 1959   Sanford, FL
Height: 5'8"   **Weight:** 160 lbs.   **Bats:** Both   **Throws:** Right
Second baseman, outfielder: Montreal Expos, 1979-89.

- ★ Holds the major league career record for highest stolen base percentage (.870)
- ★ Won the 1986 batting title with a .334 mark
- ★ Led the N.L. in steals four times
- ★ Set a new rookie record with 71 steals in 1981
- ★ Represented the N.L. on seven All-Star teams
- ★ Batted over .300 five times
- ★ Nominated for the 1986 Silver Slugger team

MAJOR LEAGUE TOTALS

G	AB	H	BA	2B	3B	HR	R	RBI	SB
1,275	4,848	1,467	.303	262	76	87	869	490	585

WILLIE RANDOLPH

Despite a successful 13-year career with the New York Yankees as one of the most durable, dependable second basemen in team history, Willie Randolph may spend the remainder of his career being compared to former Dodger Steve Sax.

That's because in the fall of 1988 these two players swapped teams. Sax, after nearly a decade in Los Angeles, played out his option and signed a free-agent contract with the New York Yankees. This move made the veteran Randolph expendable, so free-agent Randolph found a team in need of a middle infielder and took Sax's place with the Dodgers.

The Yankees saw the 29-year-old Sax as a younger, better hitter than Randolph, although both men have been All-Stars and Silver Slugger award winners. The Dodgers signed the 35-year-old Randolph on December 10, 1988, to plug the defensive hole that had been gaping in the middle of the Dodger infield since Davey Lopes left the position. Despite various 1988 injuries, Randolph posted a major league career-high .988 fielding percentage in 1988. Both Randolph and Sax have led their respective leagues in errors before, but Randolph usually keeps his gaffes in the low teens. While Sax's stats reflect high highs and low lows, Randolph shows the ability to play with a steady head and accurate arm. His years of dedicated infield leadership were apparent when he and Ron Guidry were named the eighth and ninth Yankee team captains in history.

Randolph draws lots of walks each year, showing that he has analyzed his strengths as a player. His .274 lifetime batting average going into the 1989 season has been marred by a career-low .230 mark in 1988. Randolph's major league averages have held steady near .280 most of his career, peaking at .305 in 1987 (with a career-high 67 RBI). Not a long-ball hitter, Randolph is patient and keeps alert for opportunities on the base paths. What Randolph lacks in natural ability at second base is more than made up for by his intelligence and determination.

At age 18 in 1972 Randolph was one of the most sought-after infield prospects in baseball: He could hit, get on base, and steal equally well. Signed by the Pirates in the seventh round of the free-agent draft in June 1972, Randolph batted .317 in his first pro year and led the International League with 90 walks the next. He topped the

league in 1974 with 110 walks, and in 1975 he was leading the league with a .339 average before being called up to finish the season as a Pirate.

Because Rennie Stennett seemed to have the starting second baseman's job secured in Pittsburgh at that time, Randolph was dealt with Ken Brett and Doc Ellis to the New York Yankees for pitcher Doc Medich on December 11, 1975. Having grown up in Brooklyn, Randolph was familiar with the turf. He had played stickball in the streets with his three younger brothers and little sister. He had begun playing baseball at Tilden High School.

Randolph and New York were good for each other. Randolph was recognized by the Yankees with the James P. Dawson award as the outstanding rookie of the year. He nearly broke a rookie team record with 37 steals. Since then he has averaged 10 swipes per year.

His stats have stayed at team-leading levels, despite stints on the disabled list

in 1978, 1983, 1987, and 1988. Five times he has been selected for the American League All-Star team, appearing in all but one game (due to injuries). Randolph registered a full nine innings in his first All-Star game, and he set a new record for second basemen with 6 assists. In three World Series he has logged 39 assists and 36 putouts and maintained a flawless fielding percentage.

In 1977 Randolph batted .274 with 4 homers and 40 RBI. He hit .305 with runners on base. He was a defensive stalwart for the Yanks, finishing second in the league in double plays, total chances accepted, and putouts. Randolph hit .278 in the American League Championship Series but had just 4 hits in a losing effort against the Dodgers in the World Series.

Sadly, Randolph missed out on a world championship in 1978. Running out an infield single on September 29 of that year, he pulled his left hamstring muscle and had to sit out both the Championship Series and the World Series. It was little consolation, but Randolph was named to both the AP and UPI All-Star teams that year for hitting .279 with 3 homers and 42 RBI. In 1979 Randolph managed to avoid injuries and played in a career-high 153 games. He tied for third in the American League in triples with 13, the most hit by a Yankee since Tommy Heinrich had 13 three-baggers in 1948.

Randolph will always be remembered as one of the hardest-working second sackers in Bronx history. And with his .282 average and his errors kept in single digits in 1989, he is making a name for himself as a dependable, hardworking player with the Dodgers.

CAREER HIGHLIGHTS
WILLIE LARRY RANDOLPH

Born: July 6, 1954   Holly Hill, SC
Height: 5'11"   **Weight:** 165 lbs.   **Bats:** Right   **Throws:** Right
Second baseman: Pittsburgh Pirates, 1975; New York Yankees, 1976-88; Los Angeles Dodgers, 1989.

- ★ Named to six All-Star teams
- ★ Hit two homers in 1981 World Series
- ★ Second on the Yankee list in all-time stolen bases
- ★ Played in five Championship Series
- ★ Served as the N.Y. Yankees co-captain
- ★ First among Yankee second basemen in lifetime games played

MAJOR LEAGUE TOTALS

G	AB	H	BA	2B	3B	HR	R	RBI	SB
1,869	6,904	1,896	.275	278	58	50	1,098	588	259

Willie Randolph has played most of his career for the New York Yankees, but he was
acquired by Los Angeles for the 1989 season. Randolph helped the Yankees to five titles
in six years, and the Dodgers hope he can do the same for them.

JEFF REARDON

Relief artist Jeff Reardon, the National League's 1985 Fireman of the Year, joined the Minnesota Twins in 1987 and helped stop the team's world championship dreams from going up in smoke. His perfect ERA in almost five innings of Series play helped rally the Twins to a seven-game World Series victory over the St. Louis Cardinals. His year-long efforts earned him the team's Most Valuable Player award, and while he shared the A.L. Fireman of the Year award with New York's Dave Righetti, Reardon received more votes (37) than any other pitcher in the league's MVP balloting.

His ERA, steadily gaining weight since 1984, finally broke the scale with a 4.48 in 1987. But the end of the 1988 campaign found him with a trim 2.47 and a new peak of 42 saves to his credit. Yet acclaim eluded him in 1987, and he stayed in the shadow of the A's Dennis Eckersley, who posted 45 saves with a 2.35 ERA.

Reardon made his minor league debut at the age of 22 in the Mets Carolina League franchise. In 1977, his first year out, he led the league in shutouts with 3. He led the 1978 Texas League in wins (17) and winning percentage (.810). In 1979 he saw his first action as a swing man, earning a .209 ERA in 30 games in Triple-A Tidewater and a smashing 1.71 ERA in 18 games in New York. His first big league win came two days after his debut.

Mixed reviews came in Reardon's sophomore year. He had a 2.62 ERA and was battling a spindly .533 winning percentage. He notched 101 strikeouts in 110 innings but carved out only 8 wins against 7 losses.

On May 21, 1981, the righthander was traded to Montreal with outfielder Dan Norman for outfielder Ellis Valentine. It is a trade New York may have regretted. The trade came in the middle of Reardon's streak of 94 consecutive appearances without a loss—a string that was not to end until July 10, 1982, with Reardon attaining a 7-0 streak record with 24 saves.

Reardon's maniacal fastball is now very slightly tamed. At long last, however, it is working in tandem with his hard-won curve, a pitch he did not quite perfect until 1986. With a history of arm and back problems (the reason it took him so long to master the curve), Reardon is becoming strictly a ninth-inning man. He calibrates the competition with care; his ailments make fielding a problem he wants to avoid.

In 43 games in 1981 he saved 8, won 3, and lost none. His 2.06 ERA earned him the New England Player of the Year title in 1982, the same year he notched his first in a series of seven seasons (as of early 1989) in which he saved 20 or more games. He is the only major leaguer to have compiled this statistic and is one of only three players—including Dan Quisenberry and Lee Smith—to get 30 or more saves for four straight seasons. He leads all current relievers in wins-plus-saves over the last three seasons, and his 49 percent share in his team's wins is second only to Steve Bedrosian's 50 percent with Philadelphia.

Reardon came to the Twins in 1987; he was traded with catcher Tom Nieto for catcher Jeff Reed and pitchers Neal Heaton, Al Cardwood, and Yorkis Perez. The Twins needed saving, and Reardon was the ideal choice. He set a new save record in less than two years.

Leading Twins pitchers in 1989 with 65 appearances, Reardon has carved quietly at league records. He currently leads the majors with 207 saves over the last six seasons—fifth on the all-time list and fourth on the active list. Having never started a game in the majors, he ranks third in Rolaids Relief points (a measure of wins plus saves) for all-time, second in the league, and first for the Twins. In 1985 he was the Rolaids Relief Man of the Year; he also held the monthly honor in August of 1988. His conversion percentage for saves from 1984-88 was 80 percent. Without Reardon the Twins would have been watching the World Series on TV; he saved games four and five of their American League Championship Series. He repeated his performance at the Series, when he was brought into the seventh game to secure the championship.

Such hair-breadth escapes are what keeps relievers and their teams alive. The only problem is that after the fire is out, the fans often forget about the fireman who doused the flames. But the team doesn't forget, and the Twins are hanging onto Reardon because they may get caught in more run-scoring infernos in the coming seasons.

As a relief pitcher for the Minnesota Twins, Jeff Reardon earned his keep in the 1987 American League Championship Series when he saved games four and five against the Tigers. The Twins went on to win the Series against the Cardinals, 4-3.

CAREER HIGHLIGHTS
JEFFREY JAMES REARDON

Born: October 1, 1955 Dalton, MA
Height: 6'0" **Weight:** 190 lbs. **Bats:** Right **Throws:** Right
Pitcher: New York Mets, 1979-81; Montreal Expos, 1981-86; Minnesota Twins, 1987-89.

- ★ Earned 40-plus saves in 1985 and 1988
- ★ Tied an A.L. record with two saves in the 1987 A.L. Championship Series
- ★ Threw 4.2 shutout innings in four 1987 World Series games
- ★ Pitched in the 1985 All-Star game
- ★ Named the A.L. Co-Fireman of the Year in 1987
- ★ Named the N.L. Fireman of the Year in 1985

MAJOR LEAGUE TOTALS

G	IP	W	L	Pct.	SV	SO	BB	ERA
647	892	57	62	.479	266	722	301	3.03

PEE WEE REESE

Harold "Pee Wee" Reese didn't get his nickname because of his size; he got it because he was so good at shooting marbles. It was a nickname he had earned as a 12-year-old marbles champion in Kentucky, but it stuck with him throughout his baseball career.

Every fan of baseball who followed the game in the 1940s and 1950s is familiar with the brilliant career of the scrappy shortstop who was the captain of the Brooklyn Dodgers team that won seven pennants between 1941 and 1956. And most fans feel that a tremendous injustice was finally corrected when Reese was elected to the Baseball Hall of Fame by the Veterans Committee in 1984.

Although Reese was athletic in high school, at graduation he weighed just 110 pounds. His future in professional sports seemed limited because of his small size, and he became a cable splicer for a Louisville telephone company, playing ball only on weekends. The Louisville Colonels, the local minor league team, discovered Reese playing in a church league and signed him to his first pro contract. Later Reese would acquire "The Little Colonel" as a nickname, partially due to his first team, but also because of his quiet brand of leadership. The Boston Red Sox purchased the entire American Association franchise, mostly to obtain the services of Reese. Although he hit well and stole a league-leading 35 bases that season, the Red Sox sold him to the Dodgers for $150,000.

Except for that short stint as a Red Soxer, Reese played his entire 16-year major league career with the Dodgers: 15 seasons in Brooklyn and one in Los Angeles. He batted over .300 only once in his career (.309 in 1954), but he was a dependable clutch hitter who consistently batted in the .270s or .280s. He was a constant threat on the base paths, as evidenced by his 232 career steals. Reese led the senior circuit in stolen bases in 1952, when he pilfered a career-high 30 bases.

Reese was also a valuable asset to the Dodgers off the field. He was photographed with newly arrived Jackie Robinson as the pair shook hands, and newspapers across the country gave the photo prominent play. Fans everywhere knew that Reese was the leader of the Dodger players, and if Robinson had Reese's backing, the whole team would stand behind him. Reese's support was more than just a token gesture; he teamed with Robinson (who played sec-

ond base) to form one of the National League's toughest double-play combinations. Reese's Hall of Fame plaque refers to how he helped ease acceptance of Jackie Robinson.

Reese was also a main figure at Roy Campanella Night in 1959. The Dodgers honored Campanella, who was seriously injured in a car accident, with a special ceremony and an exhibition game against the Yankees on May 7, 1959. Reese put his cap on Campanella's head and pushed his long-time teammate's wheelchair onto the field. They remained together throughout the ceremonies, in front of a major league record crowd of 93,103. The lights of the L.A. Coliseum were turned off, and the fans held up matches to create the effect of a lit birthday cake for Campy. In 1955 the Dodgers had celebrated Reese's birthday in the same fashion in Brooklyn: and Campanella had stood with his team captain throughout the ceremony while the fans held their matches aloft.

Even though his batting averages

may seem modest by today's standards, Reese was one of the greatest offensive players in Brooklyn Dodgers history. His 231 lifetime stolen bases were a team record, as are his 1,317 runs scored. His 2,107 games in a Brooklyn uniform rank behind only Zach Wheat's 2,322 games. He rates second in at-bats (7,911), second in hits (2,137), third in doubles (332), fifth in triples (78), eighth in home runs (122), and fifth in RBI (868). He led Brooklyn in seven World Series appearances, batting .272 with 46 hits (7 for extra bases) and 16 RBI. Those totals are for Brooklyn and don't include the 1958 season he played in Los Angeles, serving as a pinch hitter and backup infielder in 59 games. He hit just .224 that year, but by including Brooklyn's greatest shortstop in the opening-day lineup in the team's first game as Californians, the Dodgers indicated that they would not be forsaking tradition.

Following his retirement as a player, Reese coached the Dodgers for one year. He served as a baseball broadcaster for NBC-TV, later working for the Cincinnati Reds in the same capacity. Back in Kentucky he opened a bowling alley, became active in banking, and served as a representative for the Hillerich and Bradsby Company, the manufacturer of Louisville Slugger bats.

Pee Wee Reese was not only a talented basestealer who topped the N.L. in stolen bases in 1952, but also an inspired leader who served as captain of the Brooklyn Dodgers. His team won seven pennants between 1941 and 1956.

CAREER HIGHLIGHTS
HAROLD HENRY REESE

Born: July 23, 1918 Ekron, KY
Height: 5'10" **Weight:** 160 lbs. **Batted:** Right **Threw:** Right
Shortstop: Brooklyn Dodgers, 1940-42, 1946-57; Los Angeles Dodgers, 1958.

★ Was the captain of the Brooklyn Dodgers ★ Played in seven World Series
★ Led the league in walks in 1947 ★ First in the N.L. in runs in 1949
★ Topped the N.L. in stolen bases in 1952 ★ Elected to the Hall of Fame in 1984

MAJOR LEAGUE TOTALS

G	AB	H	BA	2B	3B	HR	R	RBI	SB
2,166	8,058	2,170	.269	330	80	126	1,338	885	232

RICK REUSCHEL

In 1985 pitcher Rick Reuschel, then 36 years old, was voted the National League's Comeback Player of the Year. Since then Reuschel has kept coming back, with even more games, more wins, and more Gold Gloves than during his younger glory days with the Chicago Cubs.

In 1970 Reuschel started fashioning a competent, consistent career. His statistics are seldom extraordinary, but they are always above average. He won 20 games once and has come close on two occasions. The last time was in 1988, when, a year shy of his 40th birthday, Reuschel posted a record of 19 wins and 11 losses for the San Francisco Giants.

Some are surprised he survived in baseball past his 30th birthday. In June of 1981 the Chicago Cubs traded their one-time star pitcher to the New York Yankees for hurlers Doug Bird, Mike Griffin, and $400,000. In 1980 he had yielded a circuit-leading 281 hits, the third time in his career that he led the league in that dubious category. It was an indication of his impending shoulder problems. Following half of a season with the Yankees (going 4-4 with a start in the fourth game of the World Series), Reuschel was felled by what looked like a career-ending injury. He was placed on the disabled list on March 23, 1982. He needed rotator cuff surgery. Reuschel was out of commission for the entire 1982 season. The Yankees placed Reuschel on a rehabilitation assignment with their Triple-A Columbus team in 1983, but he was released after four appearances—a major league orphan. The best the Cubs could offer their former ace was a Class-A minor league contract and a challenge to work his way back to the major leagues.

Reuschel pitched 13 games for the Class-A Quad Cities Cubs. He beat the odds and was recalled by Chicago. On September 11, 1983, he made his first major league start in nearly two years (his last big league game had been in the 1981 World Series).

This wasn't the full story of his comeback. He didn't start the 1984 season until the third week in April due to a sore shoulder. The shoulder also kept him sidelined from August 23 to September 1 and he was 5-5 in his short season. Chicago gave up on Reuschel and released him and his gimpy shoulder at season's end. All that was available for Reuschel was a job in the minors, this time with Triple-A

Hawaii, the Pirates top minor league team. There Reuschel was 6-2. The Pirates recalled him on May 21, 1985, and the Illinois native went 14-8. Far from fragile, Reuschel showed his stamina with 9 complete games (more than the rest of the staff combined), 1 shutout, and 1 save; he tallied a career-low ERA of 2.27. At Pittsburgh, Reuschel set a team record with 13 wins in Three Rivers Stadium. On the mound he showed amazing agility for a man of his size. He handled 64 chances without a single error, winning his first Gold Glove. His death-defying sinker emerged intact, and somehow his fastball was even faster. His successful comeback was honored with the Roberto Clemente and Fred Hutchison awards.

In 1986 he started his 400th career game with the Pirates. Despite 2 shutouts it was not a stellar season; he finished with a 9-16 record. Reuschel quickly remedied that in 1987 when he gained 13 wins against 9 losses with a 3.09 ERA. The Giants were battling their way to a Western Division pen-

nant, but their pitching staff was suffering through a midseason slump. The addition of Reuschel, by way of an August 21 trade, gave the team the pitching insurance they needed to stay in first place.

Reuschel exercised great control in 1987, and he led the league with only 78 walks, which is an average of 1.7 per nine innings. In 1988 he was down to 1.5. During the 1987 season he recorded a personal best with 12 complete games and matched his previous high of 4 shutouts. Reuschel demonstrated his regained health by hurling 227 innings, his best total in the last seven seasons. Upon his August arrival in San Francisco, he took the heat off the Giants bullpen immediately with three straight complete games.

In 1988 Reuschel just missed the 20-win plateau with a 19-11 season and a 3.12 ERA. His 36 starts tied him with Tom Browning of the Cincinnati Reds for the busiest league hurler. He had the fourth-highest number of wins in the league, behind Orel Hershiser, Danny Jackson, and David Cone.

In 1989 Reuschel again emerged as the Giants' workhorse. He finished the season at 17-8 with a 2.94 ERA. The crafty righthander sailed past his 200th career win and is only 38 strikeouts short of his 2,000th. Not only did he prove his worth to his team, he proved it to the whole baseball world as he helped lead his team to the N.L. Western division title. Baseball may never remember Reuschel as a pitching immortal, but his dogged determination in twice battling back from serious shoulder injuries to succeed in the major leagues makes him one of the game's greatest competitors.

CAREER HIGHLIGHTS
RICKEY EUGENE REUSCHEL

Born: May 16, 1949   Quincy, IL
Height: 6'3"   **Weight:** 215 lbs.   **Bats:** Right   **Throws:** Right
Pitcher: Chicago Cubs, 1972-81, 1983-84; New York Yankees, 1981; Pittsburgh Pirates, 1985-87; San Francisco Giants, 1987-89.

* ★ Won 20 games in 1977
* ★ Has won 10 or more games for 14 seasons
* ★ Named Comeback Player of the Year in 1985
* ★ Won the Gold Glove award twice
* ★ Appeared in two World Series
* ★ Helped secure the N.L. pennant for the 1987 Giants

MAJOR LEAGUE TOTALS

G	IP	W	L	Pct.	SO	BB	ERA
538	3,452	211	183	536	1,962	897	3.36

A sore arm almost ended Rick Reuschel's career in the early 1980s. But the determined hurler made a successful comeback in 1985 with the Pirates, with a 14-8 record. His comeback was complete in 1988 when he won 19 games for the Giants.

JERRY REUSS

When Jerry Reuss won his 200th career game in 1988, some historians pointed out that the 6-foot-5, 227-pound hurler had never been a 20-game winner. Instead he reached the elusive milestone of 200 wins by aiming for victory one win at a time.

To still be pitching in the majors at 40 years old, especially after Reuss's past arm problems, is a true accomplishment. With the 1988 ChiSox Reuss turned up with a sparkling 13-9 mark in 29 starts. His .591 winning percentage was his best in six years and his 3.44 ERA was his best in four. Named Comeback Player of the Year for an outstanding performance in 1980, fans are wondering if Reuss can recover his old form or whether his career is at an end. His 1989 stats don't bode well. Traded to Milwaukee in 1989, he finished the season at 9-9 and with a 5.13 ERA.

Good things come to those who wait, and Reuss has been around baseball long enough to deserve at least a couple of comebacks. He began as an 18-year-old second-round draft choice for the St. Louis Cardinals in 1967, receiving a reported $30,000 bonus to sign. The parent club was patient with its new adopted child, testing him with three different minor league teams in 1967 to see where he could learn the most. In nine games with Cedar Rapids he posted a sound 1.86 ERA; in one unlucky inning with Tulsa the result was a laughable 54.00.

After spending 1968 in Arkansas, Reuss returned to Tulsa a hero the next season; he lead the league with 186 innings, 13 wins, 112 runs, and 151 strikeouts. It earned him a one-day call-up to the city, but it wasn't until the middle of the 1970 season that Reuss arrived in the majors to stay.

In the 20 games that Reuss appeared in that year, he won 7 and lost 8, with a 4.11 ERA. After a 14-14 1971 season, where he once went eight innings before allowing just 1 hit, Reuss was traded to the Houston Astros.

Two seasons with Houston produced Reuss's first winning major league mark (16-13) and his lowest major league ERA to date (3.74). Although he led the Nationals with 117 walks, his 177 Ks were a personal all-time best. Since then his walks have traveled steadily downhill.

At the end of 1973 the Pittsburgh Pirates let catcher Milt May go in exchange for the gangly lefty, and there Reuss prospered. In five seasons he

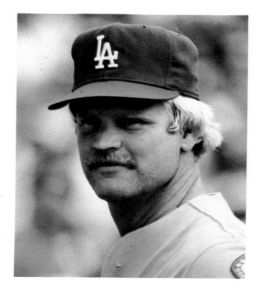

went 42-16 pitching at home in Three Rivers Stadium. A 16-11 season in 1974 ended with a ten-inning appearance in the National League Championship Series, where Reuss walked a record-setting 8 batters. But he still posted his lowest ERA (3.72) of his five championship appearances.

Six shutouts the following year erased the disgrace, and Reuss won his first of two berths on the All-Star team. Starting off the game Reuss delivered three flawless innings of work; he would add one more perfect inning to his All-Star record in 1980, sweetening the pot by being credited with the win.

Before leaving the Pirates Reuss proved his worth. In 1977 he logged his 1,000th career strikeout and enjoyed a 21-inning streak without allowing an earned run.

Reuss hoped to become a starter when he became a Dodger in 1979 (he was exchanged for pitcher Rick Rhoden), and after two months he found a spot on the starting rotation. His dismal 7-14 record was miraculously overshadowed when Reuss enjoyed two of his most graceful seasons in 1980 and 1981. In 1980 he led the Nationals with 6 shutout games; in June he pitched a no-hitter, the only one of his career to date. His 1980 ERA was 2.52, followed by 2.29 in 1981, the lowest marks of his career.

His movement out of the bullpen came when another starting pitcher was ill and Reuss filled in. The Dodgers never seemed to regret their choice, for he stayed in L.A. for many years, fashioning few losing seasons and chiseling away at a sound ERA.

After disability layoffs in 1984 and 1986, Reuss spent 1987 going from team to team as part of the bizarre spring ritual that even a steady, stout-hearted professional finds himself in when his career is in its twilight.

Reuss does not intend to go gently into that dark night. With the ChiSox in 1988 Reuss's winning season backed a 3.44 ERA and his highest number of strikeouts since 1985. His bread and butter is the pinpoint control he has developed after 19 years in professional ball. Shoulder surgery in 1985 has hampered his delivery just a little and has affected his fielding, also. Overall, however, Reuss shows no signs of quitting, and he looks to be a good bet in the starting rotation for some time to come.

CAREER HIGHLIGHTS
JERRY REUSS

Born: June 19, 1949   St. Louis, MO
Height: 6'5"   **Weight:** 200 lbs.   **Bats:** Left   **Throws:** Left
Pitcher: St. Louis Cardinals, 1969-71; Houston Astros, 1972-73; Pittsburgh Pirates, 1974-78; Los Angeles Dodgers, 1979-87; Cincinnati Reds, 1987; California Angels, 1987; Chicago White Sox, 1988-89; Milwaukee Brewers, 1989.

- ★ Led the N.L. in shutouts in 1980
- ★ Won the 1980 All-Star game
- ★ Threw a no-hitter versus San Francisco in 1980
- ★ Went 1-1 in the 1981 World Series
- ★ Played in five N.L. Championship Series
- ★ Named Comeback Player of the Year in 1980

★ Became the second pitcher in history to win 200 games without ever winning 20 games in a season

MAJOR LEAGUE TOTALS

G	IP	W	L	Pct.	SO	BB	ERA
624	3,660	220	191	.535	1,906	1,124	3.64

Yielding just slightly less than 2 walks per nine innings, pitcher Jerry Reuss has perfected a slow curve and a change-up to draw attention away from his rather sluggish fastball.

ALLIE REYNOLDS

Because Allie Reynolds had been a javelin champion at school, he said he was later "expected to be a strikeout pitcher." He more than lived up to those expectations. "Superchief" (his nickname was due to his Creek Indian heritage) helped the New York Yankees railroad their way to many World Series contests.

Reynolds first signed with the Cleveland Indians in 1939. The 24-year-old's father was a minister and had hoped his son would be called to the church. Allie, an all-around athlete, attended Oklahoma A&M on a track scholarship and was much admired on the gridiron. He finally found his calling in what some dub "the church of base-ball."

He acquired his college degree with honors in 1939. Reynolds immediately began work on another four-year degree, for he needed that much time to graduate from the Cleveland farm system. They didn't seem to know quite what to do with this talented newcomer, trying him in the outfield, behind the plate, and finally on the mound. He had a grand finale season in the minors with 18 wins, 7 losses, and league leads in strikeouts (193) and ERA (1.56).

Reynolds added to this stellar season with a late-season call-up to the bigs. Cleveland desperately needed some consistent pitching at this time and called on the hot hurler to help them out. He had only five innings of relief to prove himself, and he yielded not a run. Reynolds was already 28 years old by the time he reached the majors, and historians often speculate on what his lifetime stats would have been if he had been called up a little earlier.

In 1943 the newborn Indian—at age 28—led the American League with 151 strikeouts, living up to the expectations held for him. His pitching seemed to suffer throughout 1945. Despite his 18-12 record, he issued a league-high 130 walks (against just 112 strikeouts). Although the 1946 season brought Allie a winning streak of six games and much acclaim, because of the team's infield weakness he was traded to the Yankees for Joe Gordon and Eddie Bockman.

The newly recruited Yankee had one of his best seasons the following year, posting 19 wins against 8 losses for a .704 winning percentage and pacing the Yanks to a pennant and a World Series title.

At this time arm problems, which had long troubled Reynolds, began to affect his once solid performance. Bone chips in his pitching elbow were a recurring nightmare. Although Reynolds won 17 games in 1949, fans claimed the Yankees best pitcher was "Reynolds-Page" because reliever Joe Page had to finish many of Allie's games. But he silenced the critics with a breathtaking World Series performance in game one against the Brooklyn Dodgers, allowing only 2 hits and fanning 9 that year. His Yanks were victorious 1-0, courtesy of a Tommy Henrich home run. The Yankees eventually defeated Brooklyn in that Series four games to one.

Reynolds' total wins in six World Series was 7, placing him with Red Ruffing and Whitey Ford as the most successful postseason pitchers. In World Series play Reynolds also batted .308 (going 8-for-26).

In 1951 Reynolds earned every pitch-er's dream—a no-hitter. Then Reynolds pitched another in the same season. Although Reynolds didn't have a fantas-tic start to his season, he spun his first no-hit gem on July 12, 1951. In the seventh inning he defied tradition and talked about his possible prize with Yogi Berra. "I'm not going to throw any fast-balls," he vowed. It took only two weeks for history to repeat itself, and Reynolds was the co-owner of a single-season no-hitter record. Reynolds was the 1951 Player of the Year and received the Sid Mercer Memorial award and the Hickok award. Reynolds retired three years later, serving as the chairman of an Oklahoma oil drilling company.

Taking into account his late start in the majors, Reynolds' stats seem even more admirable today. Despite all the ob-stacles facing him, he wound up with 182 wins and 49 saves, giving him a hand in 231 total victories during his career. He ranks in the top 20 in eight different all-time pitching categories among Yankee hurlers. Reynolds de-serves a footnote in baseball history for being one of the last pitchers to pull dou-ble duty as both a starter and a reliever. Casey Stengel was the last manager to expect his ace hurlers to also work as relievers, and he used Reynolds this way with great success. In his biography, Stengel cited Reynolds over Whitey Ford as the greatest pitcher that he had ever managed, specifically because Reynolds could both start and relieve.

Allie Reynolds, who served as both a starter and a reliever for the New York Yankees, faced the Yankees' crosstown rivals—the Brooklyn Dodgers—in four World Series. The Yanks beat the Dodgers each time.

CAREER HIGHLIGHTS
ALLIE PIERCE REYNOLDS

Born: February 10, 1915 Bethany, OK
Height: 6'0" **Weight:** 195 lbs. **Batted:** Right **Threw:** Right
Pitcher: Cleveland Indians, 1942-46; New York Yankees, 1947-54.

★ Won two A.L. strikeout titles
★ Threw two no-hitters in 1951
★ Posted a league-leading 2.07 ERA in 1952

★ Topped the A.L. in shutouts twice
★ Earned 49 career saves
★ Ranks second in history with 7 World Series wins

MAJOR LEAGUE TOTALS

G	IP	W	L	Pct.	SO	BB	ERA
434	2,492	182	107	.630	1,423	1,261	3.30

JIM RICE

After the 1988 season ended with the Boston Red Sox losing four straight A.L. Championship Series games to the Oakland Athletics, Jim Rice's future came into question. The Red Sox displayed a stable of young sluggers—including Mike Greenwell and Ellis Burks—in the 1988 campaign. Rice, now a designated hitter, showed signs of slowing down. In 1988 he hit just .264 with 15 home runs and 72 RBI in 135 games. But in the first month of 1989, just when fans were ready to drive the final nail into Rice's coffin, he showed that he wasn't finished yet. Rice was hitting .291 with 3 homers and 16 RBI through April 30, and his RBI totals were fifth highest in the league. Unfortunately Rice's numbers did not stay that high; the perennial .300 slugger hit only .234, finishing the season with only 28 RBI.

At age 36 when the 1989 season began, Rice was beginning his 16th major league campaign. The South Carolina native won ten sports letters in high school; he played baseball, football, basketball, and track (which is surprising considering his average speed). He did run quickly through the Red Sox farm system after being the Red Sox's first pick in the 1971 free-agent draft. He earned a $45,000 signing bonus before beginning his pro career with Williamsport. After a so-so debut year he advanced to Winter Haven in 1972, where he led the Florida State League in runs (80) and hits (143), and was named to the FSL All-Star team. Playing for two teams in 1973—Bristol and Pawtucket—he notched averages of .317 and .378, upping his home run production to 31 in the season, compared to 17 dingers the year before. In 1974 he started out with Triple-A Pawtucket and was named the International League Most Valuable Player and the Minor League Player of the Year with his triple crown win. His circuit-leading marks of .337, 25 home runs, and 93 RBI gained him a major league call-up. He finished 1974 with 24 games in Boston.

Two rookie stars, Rice and teammate Fred Lynn, bloomed side by side in the Red Sox outfield in 1975. Although Rice's season statistics were more than adequate with a .309 average, 22 home runs, 102 RBI, and flawless fielding in 144 games, he was nosed out of league MVP honors and the league Rookie of the Year award by teammate Lynn. During the last week of the regular season, Detroit hurler Vern Ruhle broke

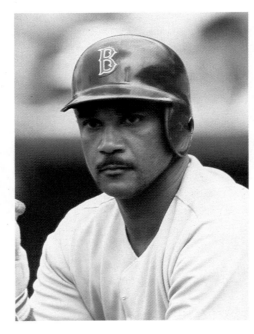

Rice's hand with a hard-thrown pitch. The injury kept Rice from making even a single appearance in the League Championship Series against the Oakland Athletics or in the seven-game World Series against the Cincinnati Reds. Lynn, meanwhile, was an active participant in both, giving him a slight edge on baseball writer's ballots.

Rice performed suitably in his sophomore season of 1976; he posted respectable marks of .282, 25 homers, and 82 RBI, but they were a far cry from 1975. In 1977 Rice had his best season yet. He paced the circuit with 39 home runs, his batting average soared to .320 (a level he bettered the next two years), and his RBI total jumped to 114. Rice led the league with a .593 slugging percentage, 382 total bases, and 83 extra-base hits. He won the A.L. Designated Hitter award.

The Boston boomer had what has been called his finest performance ever in 1978. He topped the league in six categories: games, at-bats, hits, triples, home runs (a career-best 46), and RBI (139, also a personal milestone). He again led in total bases with 406 and in slugging percentage with a .600 mark. In 1979 Rice hit a best-ever .325, marked his third straight year of 39 or more homers, and was first in total bases with 369 (tying Ted Williams and Ty Cobb for the lead for three straight seasons).

Rice has had 20 or more homers in 11 seasons. In 1983 he won his third home run title with 39 blasts, while tying the league RBI lead with 126. He surpassed the .300 mark seven times, the highest being a .325 average in 1979. His 110 RBI kept his total above the 100 mark for the fourth straight year in 1986. Rice got a second chance at World Series play in 1986. The Mets won the Series in seven games, but Rice batted .333, earning 9 hits and scoring 6 runs.

Going into the 1989 season, Rice was the only active player with more than 300 home runs and a lifetime .300 batting average. Already Rice has hammered out solid third-place standings on many all-time Red Sox record lists, including career home runs, at-bats, RBI, games, and hits. He is third only to the offensive heroics of former Red Sox outfielders Ted Williams and Carl Yastrzemski, who occupy the two top spots in the hitting departments. But Rice has bypassed the two previous BoSox greats in one category: triples. Yaz earned just 59 career three-baggers, while Williams had 71. Rice had 79 career three-base hits by the 1989 season's end.

CAREER HIGHLIGHTS
JAMES EDWARD RICE

Born: March 8, 1953   Anderson, SC
Height: 6'2"   **Weight:** 200 lbs.   **Bats:** Right   **Throws:** Right
Outfielder, designated hitter: Boston Red Sox, 1974-89.

- ★ Named A.L. MVP in 1978
- ★ Named to eight All-Star teams
- ★ Topped the A.L. in homers three times
- ★ Led the A.L. in RBI in 1978 and 1983
- ★ Batted .333 in the 1986 World Series
- ★ Appeared in two A.L. Championship Series

MAJOR LEAGUE TOTALS

G	AB	H	BA	2B	3B	HR	R	RBI	SB
2,089	8,225	2,452	.298	373	79	382	1,249	1,451	58

*Jim Rice's banner year came in 1978, when his Boston Red Sox were embroiled in a hot
pennant race with the Yankees. Though the Yanks won the flag, Rice was named MVP
over New York's Ron Guidry. Rice led the A.L. with 42 homers and 213 hits.*

SAM RICE

Sam Rice was 44 when he retired from the game in 1934, just 13 hits shy of the magic 3,000 mark. Had he reached the coveted goal Rice no doubt would have been ushered into the Hall of Fame sooner. As it was Rice had to wait almost 30 years and was in his 70s before he finally received the call from Cooperstown.

Rice was a hardworking individual before he began his baseball career. After getting his education at an Illinois country school, he held many jobs: a whiskey bottler, a railroad yard worker, and a farm laborer.

Rice did not arrive on the major league scene until he was 25 years old, and then he appeared in only four games at the end of the Washington Senators' 1915 season. He had been introduced to the game while serving in the U.S. Navy. Stationed aboard the U.S.S. *New Hampshire*, Rice made the ship's team as a pitcher. They played their games at their winter base in Guantanamo, near Cuba. Due to his pitching success in the Navy, he pitched for Petersburg while on furlough and won 5 straight games.

Rice got his release from the military in 1914 and began his baseball career that year. He played two seasons with Petersburg of the Virginia League before he was obtained by the Senators. Rice worked as a pitcher during his first two pro seasons with Petersburg. In his first year he won 9 and lost just 2. His pitching record slumped to 11-12 in 1915, but he still struck out 133 (in 233 innings) while walking just 43. His first four games with the Senators came on the mound. When the Indiana native's signing was announced, Senators owner Clark Griffith forgot Rice's first name and without hesitation called him Sam, the name Rice used the rest of his life. Other players sometimes called Rice "Baseball's Man O'War," partly because he served in the military and also because he had the speed of a racehorse. He played all but one of his 20 major league seasons in a Senator uniform.

Rice batted over .300 for 15 of his 20 big league seasons on his way to a career batting mark of .322. Six times he compiled over 200 hits in a season, and twice he led the league in that stat. A smart and speedy baserunner, Rice swiped 351 sacks, including a career-high, league-leading 63 stolen bases in 1920. For eight consecutive seasons Rice stole at least 20 bases.

Rice was involved in one of the most controversial fielding plays in World Series history. In the third game of the 1925 fall classic, with two out in the eighth inning and the Senators leading Pittsburgh 4-3, Pirate Earl Smith stepped up to the plate and launched a rocket to deep right center. Rice raced over from his right field position, lunged at the ball, and toppled into some temporary bleachers. A few seconds later Rice emerged displaying the ball in his glove, and the second-base umpire ruled it the final out of the inning. Whether Rice actually caught the ball was debated by a generation of baseball fans. For years the only comment Rice would offer was, "The umpire said I caught it." After his death the Hall of Fame produced a letter that Rice had sent with instructions that it not be opened until he died. Inside, Rice assured a still-wondering public that he had indeed caught the ball!

Besides his dramatic catch, Rice bat-ted .364 in the seven-game battle (which was eventually won by the Pirates). Rice started the Series with a two-run single, which proved to be the game-winning hit in Washington's 4-1 opening win. Rice had a total of 12 hits, all singles, to tally a .364 batting average. He scored 5 runs and drove in 3 others.

His career batting average doesn't reflect his discipline at the plate. In a total of 9,269 at-bats, Rice struck out just 275 times while drawing 709 bases on balls. In today's atmosphere of record-crazy players, it's hard to believe that Rice didn't try playing just one more season in order to reach the 3,000-hit plateau. However, not everyone attached such meaning to arbitrary milestones back then. Winning (and getting paid correspondingly) were the goals. Even if Rice didn't top the 3,000-hit mark in the record books, he surpassed the total in spirit since he did accumulate 19 hits in three World Series appearances.

During his long baseball career Rice was responsible with his money. He told reporters that he was proud he wouldn't be forced to play minor league ball after his career was over simply to make a living. He retired and became a farmer in Maryland. He died at age 84 in 1974.

Sam Rice batted .322 lifetime, topped .300 14 times during his career, stole 351 bases, played on all three of the Washington Senators pennant-winning teams, and was just 13 hits short of the 3,000 mark when he retired.

BOBBY RICHARDSON

If Yankee second baseman Bobby Richardson had hit during the regular season the way he did in his seven World Series, he might have won a few batting titles. As it turned out, the rugged competitor always seemed to save his best efforts for postseason play.

Richardson was generally regarded as a light-hitting second baseman who earned his pay with his glove rather than his bat. Surrounded by such powerhouses as Mickey Mantle, Roger Maris, Yogi Berra, and Bill Skowron, Richardson wasn't expected to contribute much at the plate.

Surprisingly, each time the hustling second sacker made it to the fall classic, he forgot his reputation for being merely a good-fielding, light-hitting performer. In his seven World Series Richardson batted .305 with 40 hits in 131 at bats. In the 1960 Series Richardson batted .367 and drove in a record 12 runs to become the first player ever from a losing team to capture the World Series MVP award. His mark of 12 RBI that year in the Series is a record that has never been equaled. In the 1961 postseason matchup Richardson set another World Series record when he smacked 13 base hits for an amazing .406 Series average.

Richardson was brought to New York for his first taste of major league ball at the end of the 1955 campaign, and he stayed in Yankee pinstripes for his 12-season major league career. The young infielder played in a few games at the end of the 1956 season and then appeared in 97 games with the Yankees in 1957, hitting .256. The following year Richardson became the Bronx Bombers regular second baseman.

The South Carolina native became a backup to starting second baseman Gil McDougald in 1958. He became a starter again in 1959 and responded with his first .300 season in the majors (.301). He hit his first 2 big league homers and knocked in 33 runs.

In 1960 the sturdy second baseman was playing only adequately during the regular season, hitting .252 with 1 home run and 26 RBI. Based on his average showing, few people would have guessed that he would become the slugging star of the 1960 Series. Richardson made steady gains in his hitting in 1961, increasing his totals to 3 home runs, 49 RBI, and a .261 average. Richardson's finest regular-season effort came in 1962. He finished second in the MVP voting only to Mickey Mantle. Richardson attained career

bests in average (.302), hits (a league-leading 209), homers (8), RBI (59), and runs scored (99). Ironically, his best season ever would be tarnished by his World Series struggles. After starring in the 1960 and 1961 matchups, Richardson batted only .148 versus the San Francisco Giants, earning only 4 singles. He compensated for his hitting slump by making a dramatic catch in the ninth inning of the seventh game. With two runners on and two out in the bottom of the ninth, Willie McCovey lined a shot off Yankee pitcher Bill Terry. Richardson successfully speared the liner, saving both the victory and the world championship.

Richardson came up to the Yankees at the same time as shortstop Tony Kubek, now a TV sportscaster. The pair formed a formidable double-play combination. The media dubbed them "the milkshake twins" because of their clean living. The pair roomed together for years and agreed not to retire at the same time in order to make the transi-

tion less stressful for the Yankees. When Kubek had to retire at the end of the 1965 season due to injuries, Richardson agreed to wait one more season.

Throughout his career Richardson was a durable, consistent foundation for the Yankees. For six straight seasons, from 1961 to 1966, the steady second baseman had more than 600 at-bats, leading the league three times in that category. Richardson's numerous plate appearances tied an American League record for three-year spans, while his 692 at-bats during 1962 set a new junior circuit mark. His lifetime stats include a .266 average, 1,432 hits, 196 doubles, 37 triples, and 34 homers. In the field Richardson led the league in double plays in 1961, 1962, 1963, and 1965. He won a string of five straight Gold Gloves for fielding excellence, from 1961 to 1965.

Richardson, a member of the Fellowship of Christian Athletes, used his biography (published in 1965) to speak out against the drinking, gambling, and promiscuity in which some players indulge. When Richardson nearly left baseball after the 1958 season (in which he hit .247 in 73 games), manager Ralph Houk convinced Richardson not to quit, saying that he could serve as a role model to the public. For years after Richardson remained anxious to quit baseball; he wanted to become actively involved in some form of social service that would reflect his religious dedication. Richardson announced his retirement publicly on September 17, 1966, during "Bobby Richardson Day" at Yankee Stadium.

Richardson's knowledge of baseball and his devotion to Christianity finally meshed when he was named head coach at a small Christian college.

CAREER HIGHLIGHTS
ROBERT CLINTON RICHARDSON

Born: August 19, 1935 Sumter, SC
Height: 5'9" **Weight:** 170 lbs. **Batted:** Right **Threw:** Right
Second baseman: New York Yankees, 1955-66.

- ★ Led the A.L. in hits in 1962
- ★ Was named the World Series MVP in 1960
- ★ Appeared in seven World Series
- ★ Set a record with 13 base hits in the 1964 World Series

★ Topped the A.L. in at-bats for three straight years

MAJOR LEAGUE TOTALS

G	AB	H	BA	2B	3B	HR	R	RBI	SB
1,412	5,386	1,432	.266	196	37	34	643	390	73

In the mold of Cy Young, second baseman Bobby Richardson was a clean-living player who neither smoked nor drank. In a 1965 biography, Richardson spoke out against those players who gambled and indulged in promiscuous activity.

DAVE RIGHETTI

Imagine the uproar that would ensue if wiz pitcher Orel Hershiser, the baby-faced 30-year-old hero of the '88 World Series, was slapped into the bullpen in 1989. The turmoil you might imagine was a reality in 1984, when Yankee management yanked 26-year-old Dave Righetti, fresh from his first no-hitter, out of the starting lineup and put him in relief.

Two months younger than Hershiser and as childlike in countenance, Righetti has proven himself a phenomenal player. In his first year in relief he registered 31 saves from 40 save situations. At that time only two Yankees (Sparky Lyle and Goose Gossage) had ever done better. The lanky Yankee accomplished this despite a two-week layoff resulting from a cut on his all-important left hand.

He continued setting records the following year; his 74 appearances were the most ever by a Yankee reliever. In his first seven outings that year he didn't allow a single run, and he logged 4 saves. In August he enjoyed a streak of 13 innings without an earned run and was subsequently named the American League Pitcher of the Month. His August 1985 statistics showed a 4-0 record with 5 saves, a 1.17 ERA, 11 out of 16 games finished, and 22 strikeouts. Finishing 81 percent of the games he showed in that season, Righetti recorded saves in his final four 1985 appearances.

His third year in the bullpen was 1986. Still, it could hardly have been beginner's luck that propelled "Rags" to his record-shattering 46 saves, surpassing the 45 mark previously set by Dan Quisenberry and Bruce Sutter. Righetti snapped the record by finishing up both games of a double header, capping an end-of-the-season streak in which he was successful in 29 out of 30 save opportunities. Adding in Righetti's 8 wins that season, he was personally responsible for 60 percent of the Yankees wins in 1986. He notched an .811 winning percentage, a 2.45 ERA, and was A.L. Fireman of the Year and Rolaids Relief Man of the Year. These awards would come home to him the following year, too.

In 1988 he became the Bronx Bombers all-time saves leader with his 151 rescues. He left behind Goose Gossage's 150, established, like Righetti's, over a five-year period. Righetti finished the season with 163 career saves, second only to the Twins Jeff Reardon, the co-winner of the 1987 Fireman award.

The six years he has spent in relief represent half of his professional career and two-thirds of his time in the majors. Righetti had been in the bigs less than three seasons before being assigned to the bullpen.

Baseball—and pinstripes—were in his blood from the start. His father, Leo, was a shortstop in the Yankees minor league system. His brother Steve played for Texas. Righetti grew up in California, where baseball was never out of season, and he was surrounded by playmates who would also become major league players, including Dave Steib and Carney Lansford.

In 1977 Righetti, like his brother, was selected by Texas in the first round of the 1977 draft. In his first minor league season he boasted an excellent 11 wins and 3 losses. In 1978 he struck out 21 hitters in a single game; he then retired on the disabled list for the last two months of the season. At that time he and four other players went to New York while five cash-carrying Yankees made their way south. One of the Yanks traded was Sparky Lyle, whose records have beckoned to be broken since Righetti became a reliever.

Due primarily to chronic injuries, Righetti didn't return to New York until the end of the '81 season, when his 8-4 record earned him the American League Rookie of the Year award. His 2.06 ERA missed the crown by only 1.2 innings, but Righetti's reward was accompanying his team deep in post-season play. He started and won game two of the division series versus Milwaukee and won the clinching game of the American League Championship in Oakland. He appeared in two innings of game three in the World Series, where he garnered a no-decision.

Plagued by the sophomore jinx in 1982, Righetti mustered a team-leading 163 Ks and an 11-10 record, but he had no other distinguishing marks. In 1983 he grabbed the attention of the baseball world when he hurled the Yankees' first no-hitter in 22 years; he was only 25 years old. Proving his no-hitter was no fluke, Righetti finished the season with a 14-8 record and career-highs in strikeouts (169) and innings (217). He struck out 7 or more batters on a dozen different occasions and once whiffed as many as 11. One week before he made sports-page headlines with his no-hitter, he had worked back-to-back shutouts.

Whether he starts or relieves, a healthy Righetti is one of the toughest pitchers in baseball.

CAREER HIGHLIGHTS
DAVID ALLAN RIGHETTI

Born: November 28, 1958   San Jose, CA
Height: 6'2"   **Weight:** 170 lbs.   **Bats:** Left   **Throws:** Left
Pitcher: New York Yankees, 1979, 1981-89.

★ Pitched a no-hitter against the Boston Red Sox on July 4, 1983

★ Appeared in the 1981 World Series against the L.A. Dodgers

★ Named to A.L. All-Star team in 1986

★ Named *The Sporting News* A.L. Relief Pitcher of the Year in 1986

★ Set a major league single-season save record with 46 in 1986

★ Ranks 16th in all-time saves

MAJOR LEAGUE TOTALS

G	IP	W	L	Pct.	SV	SO	BB	ERA
414	1,014	71	54	.568	163	846	421	3.10

Relief pitcher Dave Righetti was born into a baseball family. His father, Leo, played shortstop in the New York Yankees minor league system, while brother Steve played briefly for the Texas Rangers.

CAL RIPKEN

The truth is that most shortstops are not especially tall. Take star shortstop Ozzie Smith, who stands 5-foot-10; or Red Sox shortstop Jody Reed, who's an agile 5-foot-9. But then throw into the pool Cal Ripken, Jr.—at 6-foot-4 and 200 pounds he is the tallest full-time shortstop in major league history—and he's bound to make a ripple. The waves he produces cover the entire field, for the nine-year veteran is an all-around player, as respected for his bat as he is for his glove.

This six-time All-Star "slumped" to 23 homers, 81 RBI, and a .264 average in 1988, but against southpaws he hit .316. While those stats seem impressive, they were only a shadow of Ripken's past accomplishments. His 1988 productivity was obscured by the Orioles all-time-worst record of 54-107. However, Ripken continued his consecutive-game streak going through the year, playing in every one of the Orioles 161 games. As usual, Ripken was in the lineup for all of 1989, continuing his consecutive-game streak. With his constant perseverance, he helped the Orioles come within two games of capturing the A.L. East division title.

Ripken's consecutive-game streak began on May 30, 1982, and includes eight full seasons of games played going into 1989. Ripken passed Steve Garvey (who is third on the consecutive-games list with 1,207) by the end of the season. Even more incredible is Ripken's consecutive-innings streak. He had played 8,243 frames before sitting out the last two innings of a September 14, 1987, blowout against the Toronto Blue Jays. The O's were leading 18-3 and didn't need to risk Ripken to clinch the win.

Ripken had his second straight .300-plus season in 1984. His .304 mark was accented by 195 hits, 103 runs scored, 27 homers, and 86 RBI. While Ripken has never been known for his fielding wizardry, he set a new mark for American League assists with 583.

In 1985 Ripken scored career highs in both RBI (110) and runs scored (116). Although he hit just .282, Ripken batted .321 with runners in scoring position. He was the league's leading shortstop in putouts and double plays.

Picked by the Orioles in the second round of the June 1978 draft, Ripken made his debut at Bluefield in the Class-A Appalachian League. The next year he moved up to Miami and then to Double-A ball at Charlotte. The year 1981 was his first in Triple-A baseball and also his last. After batting .288 with the Red Wings, he was called up to Baltimore for a 17-game stint with the Orioles.

In 1982, his first full season as a big leaguer, he clubbed 29 home runs and chalked up 93 RBI, an accomplishment that helped him secure the American League Rookie of the Year award. He started the year as the club's top third baseman, playing that position for 72 games. The following year he was selected as the American League Most Valuable Player after leading Baltimore to the 1983 World Series. His league-leading 211 hits and 47 doubles, combined with a .318 batting average, 27 homers, and 102 RBI, made him a strong offensive force. In post season play that year he hit an even .400 in the American League Championship Series but managed only a .167 batting mark and 1 RBI in the World Series.

Each year fans speculate on Ripken's future. Because his tremendous hitting ability outweighs his respectable defensive work, the possibility of Ripken finishing his career at third base has been suggested. With a less stressful position Ripken might prolong his career (and his consecutive-game streak) and he could concentrate more on what he does best—knocking in runs. He's a thoughtful hitter who handles a variety of pitches well. For now though, he's doing just fine at shortstop. Ripken has analyzed how various hitters react to different Oriole pitchers, so he knows where to position himself for each batter.

Beside him at second base is brother Billy Ripken. Only four brother combinations in history have been keystone combinations for one team. While 16 other families have had three or more members in major league baseball, having three on one team at the same time is unique. That third is Cal Ripken, Sr., the Orioles third-base coach.

Already Ripken is showing up in the top-ten listings in several all-time Orioles offensive categories. He's one of only three active major leaguers with 20 or more homers in each of the past eight seasons. Ernie Banks is the only other shortstop in history with such a streak. With another decade of major league play under his belt, Ripken will carve a lasting niche in both Baltimore and major league history. He'll be remembered as one of the biggest, hardest-hitting shortstops baseball has ever seen.

CAREER HIGHLIGHTS
CALVIN EDWARD RIPKEN Jr.

Born: August 24, 1960   Havre de Grace, MD
Height: 6'4"   **Weight:** 200 lbs.   **Bats:** Right   **Throws:** Right
Third baseman, shortstop: Baltimore Orioles, 1981-89.

★ Was the A.L. MVP in 1983

★ Won the A.L. Rookie of the Year award in 1982

★ Batted .400 in the 1983 A.L. Championship Series

★ Topped the league with 47 doubles and 121 runs scored in 1983

★ Played in seven All-Star games

★ Led the A.L. with 211 hits in 1983

★ Holds the A.L. record for most season assists by a shortstop (583 in 1984)

★ Played a record 8,243 consecutive innings

MAJOR LEAGUE TOTALS

G	AB	H	BA	2B	3B	HR	R	RBI	SB
1,315	5,055	1,402	.277	266	24	204	793	744	19

Originally a third baseman, Cal Ripken switched to shortstop in 1982. That year he batted only .264, but he racked up 93 RBI and belted 28 round-trippers to garner the A.L. Rookie of the Year award.

PHIL RIZZUTO

Anchoring the infield for nine pennant-winning seasons for the New York Yankees during the 1940s and 1950s, Phil Rizzuto is one of the most popular Yankees of all time. After his 1956 retirement he immediately began anchoring Yankee radio and television broadcasts. Combining his stellar playing days with his enthusiastic announcing, "Scooter" will celebrate his golden anniversary with the Yankees during the 1990 season. Fifty years with the same team? As Rizzuto himself would say, "Holy Cow!"

Rizzuto's role during his playing days was similar to that of the great Dodgers shortstop Pee Wee Reese. Both were excellent fielders who played with fiery enthusiasm, but neither was depended upon for his bat because both were surrounded by great sluggers (although they provided plenty of punch with their timely clutch hitting), and both made intangible contributions that don't show up in the record books.

During his initial major league tryout at the age of 19, Rizzuto was dismissed by Brooklyn Dodgers manager Casey Stengel who told him, "Go find a shoebox!" The crack was in reference to Rizzuto's modest height of 5-foot-6. Stengel would later become manager of the Yankees and would coach Rizzuto through his best season ever.

Obviously Rizzuto didn't accept Stengel's dismissal, and his first minor league season in 1937 was nothing to look down on. In 67 games he hit .310 and fielded at a .933 clip. The next year he was teamed with second baseman Gerry Priddy, and the keystone combo became almost a permanent fixture, with both advancing to the Yankees in 1941. Before that Scooter (dubbed for his swiftness in covering second) logged .300-plus batting marks every season and in 1940 led his league with 35 stolen bases and was crowned Minor League Player of the Year by *The Sporting News.*

"The Heavenly Twins," as Rizzuto and Priddy were known, were expected to save the Yankees from "a fate worse than death—third place," quipped a beat reporter. But both youngsters hit an immediate slump and were benched before the end of the season. Even so, Rizzuto registered 133 games, batted .307, fielded .957, and led the American League with the most double plays. Rizzuto was released from his banishment in time to appear in five World Series games, notching 2 hits and 12 putouts.

In the 1942 regular season Rizzuto batted a decent .284, and his fielding improved to a .962 percentage. Although the Cardinals beat the Yankees in that year's World Series, Rizzuto was the unlikely offensive hero in postseason play for the Yankees. He batted .381 with 8 hits and 2 stolen bases. Rizzuto led the league in double plays and putouts that year (342), and he tied a major league record by keystoning 5 double plays in a single game on August 14, 1942. Rizzuto's fielding was a key to New York's continued success. Yankee hurler Vic Raschi hailed the dependable shortstop by saying, "My best pitch is anything the batter grounds, lines, or pops up in the direction of Rizzuto."

Like so many players of his generation, Rizzuto lost three prime seasons to the military during World War II. After one year he came down with malaria and was assigned to manage a Navy League team. In 1944 he played third base for the Army-Navy World Series.

He was discharged the following year as a chief specialist.

Rizzuto was back in civvies and Yankee pinstripes in 1946. His 1947 World Series performance was a glittering return to baseball. Rizzuto batted .308 (with 8 hits), while playing errorless ball over seven games.

In 1949 Rizzuto finished second in the MVP balloting. The often injured Yankee appeared in 153 games, batting .275 and notching a league-leading fielding percentage of .971. He left no doubt about his qualifications in 1950, with a career-high batting average of .324, the second and final time he would pass the .300 mark. He registered career highs in hits (200), doubles (36), home runs (7), runs (125), and bases on balls (92). Baseball writers gave him 16 out of 23 first-place ballots in that year's MVP race. In the 1951 World Series the Yankees needed six games to defeat the New York Giants. Rizzuto batted .320 in the matchup. His influence led the Yanks to ten pennants and eight world championships. His totals (in nine Series) include a .246 average with 45 hits, 21 runs scored, 30 bases on balls, and 10 stolen bases (the third-highest total in history).

Perhaps the greatest tribute ever paid to Rizzuto came from his Yankee teammates when his uniform number (10) was retired in 1985. Only 12 Yankee players have had their uniform numbers retired. In the August ceremony a plaque honoring Rizzuto was added to Monument Park in the Yankee Stadium outfield. The plaque, which details his accomplishments as a Yankee, reads in part: "A man's size is measured by his heart." Nothing could be a better description of Phil Rizzuto, who has always been a giant in the eyes of his adoring fans.

CAREER HIGHLIGHTS
PHILIP FRANCIS RIZZUTO

Born: September 25, 1917 Brooklyn, NY
Height: 5'6" **Weight:** 150 lbs. **Batted:** Right **Threw:** Right
Shortstop: New York Yankees, 1941-56.

★ Named the A.L. MVP in 1950
★ Played shortstop for nine pennant-winning Yankee teams
★ Appeared in five All-Star games
★ Led the A.L. in sacrifice hits five times

MAJOR LEAGUE TOTALS

G	AB	H	BA	2B	3B	HR	R	RBI	SB
1,661	5,816	1,588	.273	239	62	38	877	562	149

Phil Rizutto played shortstop for nine pennant-winning Yankee teams during his career.
He experienced banner years in 1949 and 1950 when he led A.L. shortstops in fielding
and scored over 100 runs both seasons. In 1950 he was named league MVP.

ROBIN ROBERTS

obin Roberts, the resident pitcher on the 1950 Philadelphia Phillies "Whiz Kids," was known as a control pitcher. In his baseball career Roberts yielded fewer than 2 walks for every nine innings on the average.

This probably came as no surprise to his family, for Robbie had taken charge of situations from a very early age. He was a whiz kid in elementary school, with honors in math and speech. Although his father often took the children to professional baseball games, Roberts didn't take much interest in the sport until his junior year in high school.

When he finally took notice of athletics, coaches took notice of him because he dedicated himself on the field the way he did in the classroom. He played basketball and football as well as spending considerable time on the baseball team.

After graduating in 1944, Roberts became an Air Force Cadet. He played basketball for the service team, and he was offered an athletic scholarship. He accepted and began work on a physical education degree as soon as his duty was over.

By 1948 he had received his bachelor's degree and had established himself as the premier pitcher on Michigan State's baseball team. In his debut on the mound he lost by a disheartening 9-1 margin. In his follow-up game—against a Naval Training team with a nasty reputation—he hurled a no-hitter, shutting out his foes. He pitched another perfect game before school was out, against a Michigan team coached by Ray Fisher, a former major league pitcher. Fisher drafted Roberts in 1946 for two summers with a collegiate team of aspiring pros.

Small wonder scouts had been on Roberts' tail since 1946; five clubs had offered him contracts. The Philadelphia Phillies signed him in 1947 for a $25,000 bonus and waited for him until 1948. He spent two profitable months in the minors before joining the Phillies in June. His first game was not a victory. He finished the season by winning 9 and losing 7 while notching a 3.18 ERA in 20 games.

The next year was a year of adjustment. Roberts was rushing his delivery, a flaw that coach Benny Bengough worked to correct. Roberts was an apt pupil, and his ERA fell in 1950 to 3.02, staying in the nether regions until 1956. Roberts also coached himself. While Bengough worked on his windup, Robbie kept a diary on opposing bat-

ters, studying their quirks. With this ammunition Roberts had a phenomenal 1950 campaign.

He posted 20 wins for the first of six consecutive seasons, with 146 strikeouts and just 77 walks. On the last day of the season the moundsman clinched the pennant for the Phillies, allowing only 5 hits and 1 run in a ten-inning game versus the Brooklyn Dodgers.

The resulting World Series was a disappointment for Roberts and the cinderella Phillies team that had surprised teams all year long. The New York Yankees shocked the Phils with four straight World Series wins. Roberts pitched brilliantly in the second game of the Series, holding the Yankees to just 1 run in nine innings. However, Yankee hurler Allie Reynolds had done the same. The game was decided unfavorably in the 10th inning when Joe DiMaggio clipped Roberts for a game-winning solo home run. Roberts' seven-hit effort had gone to waste.

There were more high moments to come to erase Roberts' Series nightmare. In 1952 he had his best season ever, leading the league with 28 wins, an .800 winning percentage, and a career-low 2.59 ERA. Although he also led for the first time in hits allowed (with 292), many factors influenced this number, including team support, the high number of innings Roberts pitched (pacing the circuit in this category for six years), and his stunningly low ratio of walks per game (just 1.7 free passes per nine innings during his career).

By the age of 35, the long, grueling years were catching up with Roberts. His 1-0 record in 1961 ended his 14 years with the Phillies. He went on to enjoy three good years with the Orioles, winning in double figures each year. Arm trouble in 1966 squelched his hopes for a true comeback with either Houston or the Chicago Cubs, who had each picked him up for short stints near the end of his career.

Roberts, however, is never a person to lose control, even if his arm appears to. Upon retiring in 1968 he returned to his Philadelphia home to work in investment and brokering. By the 1980s he was coaching baseball at the University of South Florida. In 1985 he served as coordinator of minor league instruction for the Phillies.

Roberts could be considered the greatest Phillies righthander of all time. Steve Carlton holds the distinction from the left side. Roberts and Carlton share nearly all of the Phillies all-time records, and in 1983 local fans elected both hurlers as starters on the "Greatest Phillies Team Ever."

CAREER HIGHLIGHTS
ROBIN EVAN ROBERTS

Born: September 30, 1926   Springfield, IL
Height: 6'0"   **Weight:** 190 lbs.   **Batted:** Both   **Threw:** Right
Pitcher: Philadelphia Phillies, 1948-61; Baltimore Orioles, 1962-65; Houston Astros, 1965-66; Chicago Cubs, 1966.

* Compiled 286 career wins
* Pitched in five All-Star games
* Won 20 or more games in six consecutive seasons
* Was *The Sporting News* Pitcher of the Year in 1952 and 1955

* Appeared in the 1950 World Series
* Elected to the Hall of Fame in 1976
* Holds the career record for surrendering most home runs (505)
* Won 28 games in 1952, the most for any N.L. pitcher since 1934

MAJOR LEAGUE TOTALS

G	IP	W	L	Pct.	SO	BB	ERA
676	4,689	286	245	.539	2,357	902	3.40

Robin Roberts and Steve Carlton share most of the Phillies' team records for pitchers.
Roberts retired just shy of the 300-win mark, but he was victorious in 20-plus games for
six straight seasons and topped the N.L. with 28 wins in 1952.

BROOKS ROBINSON

Third baseman Brooks Robinson gave the best years of his life to the Baltimore Orioles and continues to do so today. The 1989 season found Robinson where he has been for the last dozen years since his retirement as a player: in the press box. High behind home plate in Memorial Stadium, Robinson provides color commentary for Orioles television. There is no one better suited for the position, for Robinson participated in all but one year of the Orioles' history.

In 1954 the St. Louis Browns traveled east and became the Baltimore Orioles. The next year Robinson entered the fold; and there he remained, endearing himself to fans who turned out in record numbers for his final game in 1975. His faithful following saw him only sporadically during his first three years, as he traveled between the O's and their farm system teams. In 1958 he became the Birds permanent third sacker. He started every opening-day game in that position for 20 years.

Only Carl Yastrzemski and Ty Cobb have played more games for the American League than Robinson, who notched 2,896 games. Only Yaz, Hank Aaron, and Stan Musial played more games with one franchise. And only seven other players have appeared in more total games, with Pete Rose's 3,562 games at the top of the list.

There is more to Robinson than mere longevity, however. There is the skill that kept him so long in the game and that keeps him foremost in people's minds when they define what an ideal third sacker should be.

Of all major league third basemen, Robinson holds the record for highest lifetime fielding percentage (.971), and he led the A.L. for 11 consecutive years in that category. He also holds the record for most chances accepted (8,902), most putouts (2,697), most double plays (618), most assists (6,205), and most circuit-leading seasons in assists (8).

Robinson enjoyed his finest season in 1964 when he captured the Most Valuable Player award, batting .317 with 28 home runs and a league-leading 118 RBI. It was a tremendous season at the plate for a man who was best known for his defensive skills.

In his 23-year career Robinson hit 17 or more homers 9 times and 11 or more 11 times, and he hit double-digit totals in home runs until 1971. He holds the record for most lifetime homers in Memorial Stadium (including

4 grand slams), as well as club records for hits, doubles, triples, runs, RBI, and total bases. Looking over his lifetime statistics, single digits are hard to find year by year; even in the difficult category of triples Robinson posted above-average marks, with 9 in both 1960 and 1962.

Robinson had been in baseball a decade before his first trip to the Series. In 1966 the Arkansas native stepped up to the plate for his first Series at-bat in the first inning. Fellow Oriole Frank Robinson had just belted a two-run homer off Don Drysdale. It was a tough act to follow, but Brooks did the best he could; he hit a solo homer that brought the house down and paced the O's to their four-game sweep of the Dodgers.

Baltimore was back in the Series in 1969, 1970, and 1971 against the New York Mets, Cincinnati Reds, and Pittsburgh Pirates. Then Baltimore bat-

tled Oakland unsuccessfully for the pennant in 1973 and 1974. Robinson was in all of the Orioles first 39 postseason games, batting .348 in the League Championships and .263 for the World Series. This included his spectacular World Series MVP season of 1970, when he went 9-for-21 (a .429 average), tied the record for most hits in a five-game Series (9), handled 23 of 24 chances not only flawlessly but brilliantly, and was at long last given a nickname. He was called "Hoover," because he cleaned up the field like a vacuum; he also cleared a permanent path in the hearts of Baltimore fans.

The last home run of his career further secured that spot on April 19, 1977, at Memorial Stadium. In an extra-inning game, the O's trailed 5-3. With one out, Robinson, in for Larry Harlow, worked pitcher Dave LaRoche to a full count with two runners on base. After a number of fouls, Brooks sent the ball into the left field stands for a game-winning three-run homer. In the ultimate sacrifice for his team, he retired in midseason to make room on the roster for catcher Rick Dempsey, who was back from the disabled list. He finished the season as a team coach.

That year he began devoting time to his own business, Shapiro, Robinson and Associates, a company that provides professional athletes with counseling and support in their professional, financial, and private matters.

Robinson was voted into the Hall of Fame during his first year of eligibility, the ultimate honor for retired stars. His uniform number (5) has been retired by the Orioles, making him one of only five O's in history to receive the honor.

CAREER HIGHLIGHTS
BROOKS CALBERT ROBINSON

Born: May 18, 1937   Little Rock, AR
Height: 6'1"   **Weight:** 180 lbs.   **Batted:** Right   **Threw:** Right
Third baseman: Baltimore Orioles, 1955-77.

* Selected the A.L. MVP in 1964
* Played in four World Series
* Established numerous career fielding records for third basemen
* Holds the record for most career hits by a third baseman (2,848)

* Named the 1970 World Series MVP
* Elected to the Hall of Fame in 1983
* Appeared in 18 consecutive All-Star games
* Holds the record for most games played at third base (2,870)

MAJOR LEAGUE TOTALS

G	AB	H	BA	2B	3B	HR	R	RBI	SB
2,896	10,654	2,848	.267	482	68	268	1,232	1,357	28

Brooks Robinson was an amazing fielder for any era. He won 16 straight Gold Glove awards and led A.L. third basemen in fielding average ten times. He also holds the record for most career hits by a third sacker, with 2,848.

FRANK ROBINSON

The career of Frank Robinson is a study in contrasts. The player who set an all-time record for rookies by getting hit with 20 pitches went on to garner two Most Valuable Player awards, one from each major league. He is the only player in history to be so recognized.

He also snared numerous home run records, holding his own with the likes of Hank Aaron and Babe Ruth. Only Aaron, Ruth, and Willie Mays hit more career homers. He not only played, but played well, for 21 astonishing years. Then at age 53 a blot threatened his heretofore unblemished career. Hired in midseason as manager for a team dear to his heart, the Baltimore Orioles, Robinson found himself trapped in the club's downward slump; a losing streak of 21 consecutive debits marred the opening of the O's 1988 season.

Team management held on to "Frank Robby," at least for 1989. As in his previous managerial stints with the Cleveland Indians (1975-77) and the San Francisco Giants (1981-84), Robinson brought in staff that he had known, had worked with, and had played with for years. The strategy worked for the 1989 Os, who battled Toronto for the A.L. Eastern division title. Toronto won but it came down to the last two games of the season.

Before that Robinson took an even more direct approach; he led the Indians to victory as a player/manager. He immediately set to rest any doubts about his age in 1975 (39 on opening day) or his ego. His debut at-bat with the Tribe produced an upset homer that fans still talk about. This game-winning homer in Municipal Stadium was dramatic. Yet it was part of only one of Robinson's many records, that of hitting homers in more major league parks than any other player. His total stands at 33; Aaron is a step behind at 32.

In his minor league debut year (1953), he boasted a .348 average, with 94 hits in 72 games. He led the Sally League in runs the following year with 112, averaging .336 and more than doubling his putouts to 258. One more year in the minors and the 20-year-old was off to Cincinnati, where he led the senior circuit in runs and was dubbed Rookie of the Year. He was nominated to his first of a dozen All-Star teams. He also tied the league record for most homers by a rookie (38), originally set by Brave Wally Berger.

A Gold Glove came two years later, and 1960 started a three-year run of

league-leading slugging stats for Robinson. Flawless fielding in the 1961 World Series capped an MVP-winning season in the National League.

Although the Reds' Series bid was unsuccessful, Robinson gave one of his best performances the following year. Notching a career-high batting average (.342) and fielding average (.994), Robinson also carried highs with 51 doubles and 134 runs. Of his 208 hits 39 were homers, and he had 136 RBI.

There was no drastic fallout in Robinson's performance as he neared his 30th birthday. In anticipation, however, the Reds traded Robinson to the Orioles in late 1965 for outfielder Dick Simpson and pitchers Milt Pappas and Jack Baldschun. The trade was, to put it mildly, a mistake.

The Orioles exploded in 1966 with Robinson at the fore. Leading the league in four offensive categories, he

slammed 49 homers with 122 RBI and a .316 average. Robinson would have his second MVP award, baseball's coveted triple crown, and a sports car awarded to him for his 2 homers in Baltimore's glorious World Series sweep.

A second-base collision with Al Weis hindered Robinson for the next 18 months, inflicting him with double vision. Despite the injury Robinson swatted 30 homers that year; not bad for a disabled player.

A string of trades began in 1971 for the aging outfielder. His batting average was slipping, though he bashed up to 20 homers yearly until 1975. It was one year with the Dodgers and one with the Angels before he finally settled with Cleveland for two and a half years. He became the first black manager in major league history and was a rallying force for the team for two years. In 1976 he played in 36 games, fielded errorlessly, and hit his final 3 homers. His 586 career round-trippers rank fourth in major league history.

Robinson had totted up a remarkable set of accomplishments when he was elected to the Hall of Fame in 1982. He collected 2,943 career hits, just 57 shy of the elusive 3,000-hit plateau. He drove in 1,812 runs and his 1,829 runs scored rank tenth on the all-time list. He scored 100-plus runs in six different campaigns, leading his league on three occasions. The master batsman also knocked in 100 or more runs in six seasons. In his career Robinson played on five World Series teams.

CAREER HIGHLIGHTS
FRANK ROBINSON

Born: August 31, 1935 Beaumont, TX
Height: 6'1" **Weight:** 183 lbs. **Batted:** Right **Threw:** Right
Outfielder, designated hitter, first baseman: Cincinnati Reds, 1956-65; Baltimore Orioles, 1966-71; Los Angeles Dodgers, 1972; California Angels, 1973-74; Cleveland Indians, 1974-76. Manager: Cleveland Indians, 1975-77; San Francisco Giants, 1981-84; Baltimore Orioles, 1988-89.

- ★ Won the N.L. MVP award in 1961
- ★ Won the N.L. Rookie of the Year award in 1956
- ★ Won the 1966 A.L. MVP award, becoming the first player to win the award in both leagues
- ★ Won the triple crown in 1966
- ★ Became the first black manager in the major leagues in 1975
- ★ Elected to the Hall of Fame in 1982

MAJOR LEAGUE TOTALS

G	AB	H	BA	2B	3B	HR	R	RBI	SB
2,808	10,006	2,943	.294	528	72	586	1,829	1,812	204

Frank Robinson played on five World Series teams during his amazing 21-year career, belting 8 home runs in the process for the third-best homer percentage in Series history, with 8.7.

JACKIE ROBINSON

Sometimes it takes many years to right a wrong—if, indeed, it can ever be righted at all. Such is the case with Jackie Robinson, the first player to break the color barrier that segregated major league baseball for more than 50 years.

Robinson has often been described as "docile," "quiet," "unassuming," and "meek." But this was only a veneer Robinson wore to shield himself during his tumultuous rookie season with the Brooklyn Dodgers in 1947. By the end of the season Robinson allowed himself to react with righteous, dignified anger at the unjustified sleights that came his way. It is difficult to imagine how he drew the strength to not fight.

Growing up in a large, single-parent family, Robinson excelled early at all sports and learned to make his own way in life. His college education at UCLA was left incomplete because of financial pressures. His enlistment in the U.S. Army, in which he progressed to second lieutenant in two years, was cut short due to a court-martial sparked by Robinson's objections to racial discrimination. He was honorably discharged.

The Negro Leagues were known for extremely poor playing conditions. Robinson was discouraged and ready to give up on baseball when he received a call from Brooklyn general manager Branch Rickey. Robinson assumed he was being scouted for the Brooklyn Browns, a black team. He was not.

Rickey's tightrope walk between humanitarian and business motives has been much explored by writers. Rickey's own words make it clear that he knew what indignities major league baseball's first black player would suffer. And Rickey has been accused of breaking the color barrier simply to gain access to more and better athletes.

He hand-picked this all-important ambassador, swearing him to keep his temper for exactly three years. Although Rickey was satisfied that the bargain was kept, Robinson had been peeking from behind his mask from the start. At the end of his rookie season—where he was National League Rookie of the Year with 12 homers, a league-leading 29 steals, and a .297 average—Robinson had his first on-field argument, with St. Louis catcher Joe Garagiola, who had stepped on Robinson's foot. Garagiola claimed it was an accident, yet Robinson cannot be faulted for his disbelief. After all it was the Cardinals who had threatened a

strike earlier that year rather than share the field with a black man. Ford Frick, then National League president, had responded to St. Louis: "I do not care if half the league strikes . . . I don't care if it wrecks the National League for five years. This is the United States of America, and one citizen has as much right to play as another."

The Garagiola altercation ended without coming to blows, though in later years Robinson wouldn't shy away from that either. By 1951 he was comfortable shouting the lewd and not-so-witty insults players so often exchange. Robinson-the-rookie only brushed himself off when beaned, but Robinson-the-veteran would respond by plowing down an offending opponent in a slide.

The Georgia native's on-the-field impact on the Dodgers was obvious. The team earned six National League pennants (and a 1955 world championship). Because he was in postseason competition so often, Robinson was on display for the whole country to judge.

Robinson died in 1972 believing he had never made it in a white man's

world. It must have been heartbreakingly difficult for Robinson to distinguish true admiration from reverse discrimination; to gauge if he (a rookie at age 27) was equal to rookies 10 years his junior; to judge whether curbing his instinct to fight back was justified when the war went on for so long. His teammate Pee Wee Reese made front pages across the nation when he was photographed with his arm around Robinson. Because Reese was from the south, this action had extra meaning. "I don't know any other ballplayer who could have done what he did," said Reese, "to be able to hit with everybody yelling at him. He had to block all that out, block out everything but the ball . . . to do what he did has got to be the most tremendous thing I've ever seen in sports." Another black superstar, Willie Mays, described the Dodger great's impact on him in other terms. "Every time I look at my pocketbook," Mays has said, "I see Jackie Robinson."

During his career Robinson was a well-known celebrity; he even performed as himself in the movie biography of his life, *The Jackie Robinson Story*. On the 40th anniversary of Robinson's historic debut in the majors, teams across the nation celebrated the milestone. The United States Post Office has honored Robinson as well, by making him the subject of a commemorative postage stamp.

Jackie Robinson played big league ball for only ten years, but his contribution as the first black player in the majors makes him one of the most pivotal men in the game's history.

CAREER HIGHLIGHTS
JACK ROOSEVELT ROBINSON

Born: January 31, 1919 Cairo, GA **Died:** October 24, 1972
Height: 5'11" **Weight:** 195 lbs. **Batted:** Right **Threw:** Right
Infielder: Brooklyn Dodgers, 1947-56.

* Selected as the N.L. MVP in 1949
* Named N.L. Rookie of the Year in 1947
* Was the first black player in the major leagues since 1884
* Led the N.L. in stolen bases twice
* Elected to the Hall of Fame in 1962
* Won the 1949 batting title with a .342 average

MAJOR LEAGUE TOTALS

G	AB	H	BA	2B	3B	HR	R	RBI	SB
1,382	4,877	1,518	.311	273	54	137	947	734	197

PETE ROSE

The talent scout who persuaded the 1960 Cincinnati Reds to sign 18-year-old Peter Rose did so by arguing that the men in Rose's family were late bloomers. He was right, but that's no surprise; the scout was Buddy Bloebaum, Rose's uncle.

Pete's dedication to sports, fired by his father's enthusiasm, resulted in an extra year in high school—it seems he spent more time on the playing field than in the classroom. A scrawny 5-foot-11 and 140 pounds at graduation, Rose was, surprisingly, offered a football scholarship. He turned it down with the hope of pursuing a baseball career, though interest from teams was slim.

The Reds put Rose in their farm system, where he did little in his first year to distinguish himself. Hitting .277, he led his league with 36 errors at second base and notched a career-low fielding mark of .916. He spent the off-season pumping iron, trying to beef up his youthful frame. His next two years in the minors were highlighted by a .330 batting average, improved fielding (.966), and circuit leads in runs, hits, and triples (a career high of 30 in 1961).

Rose was looking good and the Reds knew it. Still, they had talented veteran Don Blasingame at second base. Cincinnati had all but packed Rose off to their San Diego minor league affiliate, but then Blasingame was injured during spring training.

Rose started the 1963 season as the Reds second baseman. His enthusiasm immediately endeared him to fans and players alike. Taking a base on balls, Rose would dash to first base as if he had a traffic cop on his tail. That is why Whitey Ford dubbed him "Charley Hustle." Cincinnati closed the season flirting with the pennant, and Rose was 1963's N.L. Rookie of the Year.

A sophomore slump hit the future star in a big way: Rose's batting average was only .269 while his fielding suffered at .979 as he struggled to make double plays. He spent the next season playing Venezuelan winter ball, but in 1965 he was back with the Reds, leading the league in hits (209) and putouts (382). He was named to his first of 17 All-Star teams, appearing in a consecutive ten from 1973 to 1982. He also hit a hefty .312, the first of 15 times he would top the .300 barrier in his major league career.

In 1967 the Reds started playing their leadoff man in the outfield, and his fielding average immediately improved.

Rose would post his first of five leads in that category starting in 1970. His already prolific hitting also improved, with back-to-back batting titles—in 1968 with .335 and in 1969 with .348 (his personal best).

Backed by the outstanding "Big Red Machine," Rose found himself starting in four World Series over a seven-year period. In 1975 and 1976 the Reds were triumphant, with Rose fielding flawlessly in both seven-game battles. His average climbed to .370 in the 1976 Series. It was an incredible streak that Rose would stretch even further in 1980 and 1983 when he paced the Philadelphia Phillies to two World Series.

A free agent after the 1978 season, Rose signed a four-year pact worth over $3.2 million with the Phillies. The Phillies asked the TV station broadcasting their games to increase their broadcast rights payments because Rose would mean extra advertising income for the station. Rose had amassed a 44-game hitting streak in 1977, which made his value even sweeter. The veteran chose the Phils over strong offers from the Cardinals, Pirates, and Braves. He spent five prosperous years in Philly. Even at age 40 he slid head-first, symbolizing an impetuousness that writers likened to Peter Pan's refusal to grow up.

Rose did grow up though—just a little—by returning to the Reds as a player/manager in 1984. There he inspired his players with his own reckless brand of competition. "Everything I am, I owe to the game," he has said. By the time Rose decided to stick strictly to managing in 1986, he had nuked Ty Cobb's long-standing record of 4,191 career hits with a new record of 4,256.

Rose's headline-grabbing career as a player and manager came to a thundering halt in August 1989 when baseball commissioner A. Bartlett Giamatti banned him from the game for life. Evidence suggested that Rose had bet on baseball games while a manager and player/manager, though nothing was ever proven in court. Giamatti noted that Rose could apply for re-admission to baseball after one year. Giamatti died of a heart attack ten days after his announcement about Rose.

CAREER HIGHLIGHTS
PETER EDWARD ROSE

Born: April 14, 1941   Cincinnati, OH
Height: 5'11"   **Weight:** 192 lbs.   **Batted:** Both   **Threw:** Right
Second baseman, outfielder, third baseman, first baseman: Cincinnati Reds, 1963-78, 1984-86; Philadelphia Phillies, 1979-83; Montreal Expos, 1984. Manager: Cincinnati Reds, 1984-89.

* Holds major league records for career hits and at-bats
* Played in 16 All-Star games
* Has a .381 mark for seven N.L. Championship Series with the Reds
* Named as Player of the Decade for the 70s by *The Sporting News*
* Won the N.L. Rookie of the Year award in 1963
* Won three batting titles
* Made 200 or more hits for ten seasons
* Was the only major league player to be a regular at four different positions
* Won the N.L. MVP award in 1973

MAJOR LEAGUE TOTALS

G	AB	H	BA	2B	3B	HR	R	RBI	SB
3,562	14,053	4,256	.303	746	135	160	2,165	1,314	198

Pete Rose's dauntless enthusiasm for baseball throughout his career will undoubtedly be overshadowed by his permanent suspension from the game in 1989. Yet, Rose surpassed Ty Cobb's record for career hits, and no one can take that away from him.

EDD ROUSH

The full truth may never be known about the 1919 "Black Sox" World Series scandal, in which several members of the Chicago White Sox were bribed by members of organized crime to lose the postseason competition against the Cincinnati Reds. The last surviving member from this dark day in sports history, Cincinnati Reds outfielder Edd Roush, died in 1988 at age 94.

Roush wasn't involved in the Series betting scandal. But after he retired he admitted that he was worried initially that gangsters may have bribed players from both teams. He said that numerous players had been approached by shady characters, and that no one really knew the full extent of player involvement in the scandal. Roush, who hit just .214 in what would be his only fall classic, said he regretted the scandal because it deprived him and his Reds teammates from proving that they could beat the much-favored White Sox in a fair contest.

Despite the tainted World Series championship, Roush's career was filled with accomplishments that would make him one of baseball's most exciting and memorable personalities. The perennial .300 hitter gained his fame while swinging a 48-ounce bat, the largest stick in major league history. Roush was no musclebound slugger either. At 5-foot-11 and 170 pounds, the thin flyhawker simply met the ball square with his thick-handled lumber. As a result he became a dangerous spray hitter who could direct the ball to any field. Roush played the first eight years of his career in the dead-ball era and he often claimed that he saw no use in trying to swing for the fences when he could be successful as a contact hitter.

Roush was the son of a noted semipro player who played during the late 1800s. Unlike some parents who wanted their sons to avoid what they considered a wild lifestyle in professional sports, Roush's father encouraged his son's potential on the diamond.

The young athlete began playing for a local amateur team in Oakland City, Indiana. As a youth Roush could throw with either hand (depending on what type of glove was available), but he favored his left when he began playing ball seriously. Roush joined a rival town's team when he found out that only some local players got paid. After being discovered by a pro scout, he signed his first contract with Evansville in 1912. Less than a year later he was

playing for the Chicago White Sox.

Because Roush had only 1 hit in 10 at-bats that year, the Sox sent him down to a minor league club in Lincoln, Nebraska. The next year the feisty outfielder jumped ship and signed with the outlaw Federal League, which was raiding all other teams for players. There he distinguished himself by hitting .325 and .298. The New York Giants obtained Roush at the start of the 1916 season but quickly traded him to the Cincinnati Reds with Bill McKechnie and immortal pitcher Christy Mathewson for Wade Killefer and Buck Herzog. Mathewson then became Roush's first manager on the Reds.

In ten full seasons in Cincinnati, Roush enjoyed some of his most productive years as a player. Unlike many players, who gained success through constant hard work, Roush relied more on natural talent. He'd stage yearly contract holdouts partially to gain more money but also to avoid attending spring training. He'd jokingly claim that

he got his spring training hunting and fishing near his Indiana home. Roush sat out the entire 1930 campaign to avoid taking a $7,000 pay cut. But when Roush did play he accumulated some impressive statistics. In 1917, his first full year with the Reds, Roush won the batting title with a .341 mark. Surprisingly, his lowest average during his decade in Cincinnati was in 1919, when he earned his second batting crown with a .321 average. His average never dropped below .300 while in the Reds outfield.

Roush retired with a .323 average, highlighted by 2,376 hits, 1,099 runs scored, and 268 career stolen bases. He retired in Florida and was a yearly visitor to spring training games in Bradenton. In fact he was attending a Pirates spring training game when he became ill immediately before his death.

Despite his occasionally cynical attitude about baseball being nothing more than a business, Roush derived constant pleasure from being able to meet old friends during the preseason and reflect on his career. It was ironic that Roush avidly attended spring training games each year, considering that he detested participating in the preseason workouts as a player. Up until his final days, Roush enjoyed being close to the game he loved. Roush was elected to the Hall of Fame in 1962.

Edd Roush supposedly swung the heaviest bat in the league during his day—a 48-ounce club that helped him to win two batting titles and hit over .300 in 13 seasons.

CAREER HIGHLIGHTS
EDD J. ROUSH

Born: May 8, 1893 Oakland City, IN **Died:** March 21, 1988
Height: 5'11" **Weight:** 170 lbs. **Batted:** Left **Threw:** Left
Outfielder: Chicago White Sox, 1913; Indianapolis Hoosiers (Federal League), 1914; Newark Peppers (Federal League), 1915; New York Giants, 1916, 1927-29; Cincinnati Reds, 1916-26, 1931.

★ Won two batting titles
★ Had 10 or more triples in 11 seasons
★ Appeared in the 1919 "Black Sox" World Series for the Cincinnati Reds

★ Batted over .300 on 13 occasions
★ Elected to the Hall of Fame in 1962
★ Struck out just 260 times in an 18-year career

MAJOR LEAGUE TOTALS

G	AB	H	BA	2B	3B	HR	R	RBI	SB
1,967	7,363	2,376	.323	339	183	67	1,099	981	268

RED RUFFING

Fifteen-year-old Red Ruffing thought he had played his last baseball game when in the summer of 1919 he lost four toes on his left foot in a mining accident. The youngster was forced to try a new position, and some 40 years later, when Ruffing was inducted into the Hall of Fame, his plaque would read pitcher instead of outfielder.

Immediately after the accident he was trying to accept the sad reality that he would never become a major league outfielder. But when the company pitcher went down with an ailing arm, Ruffing's teammates convinced him to take a shot at pitching. The hard-throwing righthander turned out to be a natural. He quickly advanced from semipro ball to the minor leagues, and by 1924 he was wearing a Red Sox uniform.

In his six seasons with Boston, Ruffing never had a winning record and, in fact, twice led the league in losses. When he won 10 and lost 25 in 1928, few people would have believed he was a future Hall of Famer. He floundered again in 1929, pacing the American League with 22 losses. The Red Sox, a perennial last-place team, gave Ruffing few leads to work with. After losing his first three decisions in the 1930 season, he was dealt to the New York Yankees for outfielder Cedric Durst and $50,000. With all those booming bats behind him, he developed into an instant winner. During his 34-game debut with the Bronx Bombers in 1930 Ruffing was 15-5.

Ruffing won 16 games in 1931 and improved his mark to 18-7 in 1932. He dropped his ERA from 4.41 to 3.09 and struck out a league-leading 190 batters. That season the Yankees trampled the Chicago Cubs in four straight World Series games.

In 15 years with the Yankees, Ruffing failed to record a winning record for only one season. In 11 years he won more than 15 games a season, including four straight seasons when he won 20 or more (from 1936 through 1939). His 21 victories in 1938 were an American League high, as was his .750 winning percentage. Ruffing was also tops in the American League in shutouts in 1938 and 1939.

Ruffing was considered one of the best-hitting pitchers of his era. On days when he wasn't hurling, Ruffing was frequently used as a pinch hitter. Despite his handicap he compiled a respectable .269 lifetime batting average. His greatest season at the plate came in 1930, when he put together a .364 mark by slashing out 40 hits in 110 at-bats.

He pitched in seven World Series while with the Yankees, registering a stunning 7-2 mark, with a 2.63 ERA. His presence helped bring six world championships to the Yankees during his career. In total World Series play he ranks fourth on the all-time list in complete games (7), games started (10), and strikeouts (61). His 85.2 innings are the fourth-highest total ever accumulated in World Series competition. In his final World Series in 1942 Ruffing almost made baseball history when he came within four outs of pitching a no-hitter against the St. Louis Cardinals. He posted 1-0 records in 1932, 1937, 1939, and 1941. His only losses came in 1936, when he finished at 0-1, and in 1942, when he finished with a 1-1 mark. Ruffing's loss in 1942 came in the fifth game of the 1942 Series, when the Cardinals beat the pinstriped American Leaguers. The Cards got 9 hits off Ruffing, but they victimized the Yankee hurler primarily through a solo homer by Enos Slaughter and a two-run shot by Whitey Kurowski.

Ruffing missed the 1943 and 1944 seasons while he was serving in the armed forces. Most historians feel that Ruffing could have won the 27 games he needed to reach the 300-win plateau if he could have played those two seasons. He resumed his career in 1945 and pitched to a 7-3 record. In 1947 he was released, and he hooked up with the Chicago White Sox, where he served as a pitcher and pinch hitter one more year before retiring.

Ruffing had few pitching contemporaries who could match his offensive output. At the plate he had eight .300-plus seasons. His lifetime hitting totals include 521 hits for a .269 average. He wasn't just a singles hitter either. Ruffing had 98 career doubles, 13 triples, and 36 homers, along with 273 RBI and 207 runs scored. Despite his injured foot he played in three games as an outfielder during his long career.

Ruffing remains one of the greatest Yankee pitchers in history. His 261 complete games are a Yankees high. He's second on the all-time list behind Whitey Ford in wins (231), innings pitched (3,169), strikeouts (1,526), and games (426). He's tied with Mel Stottlemyre for second in career shutouts (with 40).

Ruffing spent many years after his retirement working as a scout for the White Sox, Cleveland Indians, and New York Mets. The Hall of Fame enshrined Ruffing in 1967. He died on February 17, 1986, at age 81.

CAREER HIGHLIGHTS
CHARLES HERBERT RUFFING

Born: May 3, 1904 Granville, IL **Died:** February 17, 1986
Height: 6'1" **Weight:** 205 lbs. **Batted:** Right **Threw:** Right
Pitcher: Boston Red Sox, 1924-30; New York Yankees, 1930-46; Chicago White Sox, 1947.

- ★ Compiled 273 career wins
- ★ Had four straight 20-win seasons
- ★ First in the A.L. in complete games in 1928
- ★ Led the league in wins in 1938
- ★ Won 7 World Series games
- ★ Has the highest career ERA of any pitcher in the Hall of Fame

★ Elected to the Hall of Fame in 1967

MAJOR LEAGUE TOTALS

G	IP	W	L	Pct.	SO	BB	ERA
624	4,342	273	225	.548	1,987	1,541	3.80

Though fastball hurler Red Ruffing got off to a mediocre start with the Boston Red Sox, he improved a great deal after he was traded to the Yankees. With the Yanks, he had four straight seasons of 20 or more wins.

BILL RUSSELL

When most people talk about Bill Russell, they automatically recall the famous basketball star who played center for the Boston Celtics in the 1960s. Well, another Bill Russell (no relation) is fondly remembered by Los Angeles Dodgers fans. His name recalls thoughts of a dependable-hitting, slick-fielding shortstop who amassed 18 successful seasons in the National League from 1969 to 1986.

Russell's long association with the Dodgers began in 1966. He was a ninth-round selection in the June 1966 free-agent draft. The Kansas native was a high school basketball player, but baseball was to be Russell's future calling. He batted .356 during his pro debut with Ogden in 1966. In 1967 Russell advanced to Dubuque of the Midwest League, where his average plummeted to .221. He still managed to climb the Dodgers minor league ladder another rung with a 1968 promotion to Bakersfield. Russell pumped his average up to .280, and he hit an unprecedented 17 home runs in 115 games.

The Dodgers brought Russell up for the 1969 season. While Los Angeles intended to use him as a center fielder, he just didn't have the long-ball productivity flyhawkers usually produce. During his rookie season Russell batted .226 with 5 home runs and 15 RBI in 98 games. The Dodgers sent him down to Spokane to start the 1970 season in hopes of sharpening his batting eye.

The move paid off. In 55 games with Spokane Russell hit .363 with 3 home runs and 30 RBI. The Dodgers recalled Russell in midseason and used him in 81 games. This time his average improved to .259. In the 1970 Arizona Instructional League, coach Monty Basgall helped convert Russell from an outfielder into an infielder. The conversion was tested in 1971 when Russell played 41 games at second, 40 in the outfield, and 6 at shortstop. In a total of 91 appearances, Russell hit .227. However, his fielding was good enough to make him the Dodger starting shortstop on opening day in 1973.

Russell was a fixture at the position every opening day through 1984 (excluding his injury-filled campaign of 1980). In 1972 Russell played in 129 games, 121 at shortstop. Although he led the league with 34 errors during his first season while learning the tricks of the trade, Russell also topped N.L. shortstops with 5.5 chances accepted per game. At the plate Russell hit .272 with 4 homers and 34 RBI. A gritty competitor, Russell showed constant growth as a middle infielder. He played in all 162 games in 1973 and led the league with 560 assists. Having the throwing arm of an outfielder was an advantage, Russell found. His offense continued to flourish with 4 homers, 56 RBI, and a .275 average. Russell was rewarded with his first All-Star appearance that season.

In 1974 the Dodgers won the Western Division. The long-running infield combo of Ron Cey at third, Russell at short, Davey Lopes at second, and Steve Garvey at first was launched. Russell set a career high 65 RBI (which he'd tie two seasons later), while hitting .269. In postseason play Russell hit with new-found fervor. Russell raked Reds pitching for 7 hits and a .389 batting average in the National League Championship Series.

A broken left hand and an injured knee limited Russell's 1975 season to 84 games. He returned in top form in 1976, hitting .274 with 5 homers and 65 RBI. When the Dodgers went to the 1977 World Series to face the Yankees, Russell played a large role in the team's success. He batted .278 during the regular season and led N.L. shortstops with 102 double plays.

Another National League pennant and another World Series loss to New York faced Russell's Dodgers in 1978. Russell had a career-high 179 hits (second highest on the Dodgers), and he hit .286. He was the hero in the fourth game of the N.L.C.S. against the Phillies with a tenth-inning single. His hit gave the Dodgers a 6-5 win and a trip to the World Series. Russell wound up with a .412 N.L.C.S. average. In the World Series Russell was 11-for-26 against the Yanks for a Dodger-best mark of .423.

A quick start in 1980 got Russell voted the starting shortstop for the N.L. All-Stars. He batted .291 at the midseason break but faltered due first to a bruised foot, then an injured wrist, and finally a broken right index finger.

Since his retirement in 1986 Russell has remained with the Dodgers as a coach. He continued an era by taking over for coach Basgall (Russell's tutor at shortstop), who was retiring. Like players, coaches usually work their way up from the minors to the majors, but Russell was recruited immediately as one of manager Tommy Lasorda's top aides.

Even though he wasn't playing, Russell contributed to the Dodgers' 1988 world championship through his coaching assistance. Following the World Series Russell got his first managerial experience with the Licey team in Santo Domingo, Dominican Republic. Because of his many years as a player and his savvy baseball intellect, Russell may find his second calling as a big league manager someday soon.

CAREER HIGHLIGHTS
WILLIAM ELLIS RUSSELL

Born: October 21, 1948 Pittsburg, KS
Height: 6'0" **Weight:** 175 lbs. **Batted:** Right **Threw:** Right
Outfielder, shortstop: Los Angeles Dodgers, 1969-86.

★ Played in four World Series
★ Has the highest total of career games played for the Los Angeles Dodgers
★ Appeared in three All-Star games
★ Ranks in the top ten on ten different Dodger all-time offense lists
★ Averaged .337 in five N.L. Championship Series

MAJOR LEAGUE TOTALS

G	AB	H	BA	2B	3B	HR	R	RBI	SB
2,181	7,318	1,926	.263	293	57	46	796	627	167

Bill Russell became the Dodgers starting shortstop on opening day of the 1973 season, inheriting the job from Dodger legend Maury Wills. Russell played in four World Series for the Blue Crew as well as in five N.L. Championship Series.

BABE RUTH

Probably more words have been written about George Herman Ruth than about any other baseball player. Author Paul Gallico even described Ruth as "God himself." "Babe" and "Bambino" are strangely diminutive names for this god, this "Sultan of Swat," a player who was bigger than life both on and off the field.

Ruth was born to working class parents in 1895. Ruth claimed that he started chewing tobacco at the age of seven and was downing whiskey by the time he was ten. Even before these vices surfaced, Ruth was sent to a home for wayward boys.

Introduced during his career to President Harding, the Babe gamely opened with, "Hot as hell, ain't it, Prez?" Some years later, when the southpaw slugger was earning more than the nation's chief executive (then Herbert Hoover) Ruth reasoned, "Why not? I had a better year than he did."

His on-field prowess matched his off-the-field flamboyance. In 1927 he established a new all-time record by smashing 60 home runs (breaking his own mark of 59). Whenever he whiffed, Babe made a great show of examining his bat, staring at it in disbelief as if it were somehow to blame.

The adoration of the crowds was returned tenfold by Ruth; he signed autographs willingly, offered strangers draws off his soda, and surreptitiously visited ailing children who idolized him. But this charm could change instantly into rabid anger, with Ruth flying into the bleachers on the heels of a heckler.

In the world of baseball, work is play. Ruth played twice as hard off the field and was infamous for his drinking and womanizing. Some of his self-indulgence, however, showed a more boyish side of the Babe. One hot afternoon in 1925 the Bambino, at the age of 30, collapsed and was hospitalized after eating a dozen hot dogs and drinking as many soda pops.

No matter what Ruth did, he gave it all he had and more. Starting out as a catcher on his boyhood teams, he switched to pitching because teammates complained about the force of his throws. By age 19 the lefthander had his option picked up by the Baltimore Orioles, who gave him his famous nickname. He was sold in 1914 to the Red Sox, where he logged a 2-1 record in just four games.

The Bambino was burning by 1915. His 18-8 record sparked the BoSox to the Series, where Ruth's flawless fielding and .064 ERA in 14 innings led to an ultimate five-game Boston triumph. After 20-plus wins in both 1916 and 1917 the Bambino repeated his performance in the 1918 Series, besting his 14-inning one-hitter with an almost 30-inning shutout streak.

The next year was his last real year of pitching, although he pitched an occasional game—never losing after 1919—and compiled a lifetime winning percentage of .671 with a 2.28 ERA.

From 1914 to 1919 not only had Ruth been a successful pitcher, he had been a successful lefty in Boston's Fenway Park. With its short left field wall known as the "Green Monster," righthanders have been known to make mincemeat out of southpaws brave enough to pitch in the explosive ballpark. Ruth, however, posted an incredible .764 winning percentage during those six years.

Red Sox owner Harry Frazee began selling off players to help finance his theatrical productions. Despite the fact that Ruth had helped the Red Sox win four world championships (from 1912 to 1918), all it took was money, and lots of it, for the Yankees to get Ruth. Colonel Jacob Ruppert gave up $100,000 and a $300,000 loan to the Red Sox owner, and Ruth was a Yankee. Ruth didn't want to leave his old team at first; he was happy in Boston, where he had a nearby farm. But when the Yankees offered him a $40,000 two-year contract, he suddenly became more committed to the boys in pinstripes.

Long after his retirement, Ruth was still a popular American hero. In 1948, the year of his death from cancer, a biographical movie called *The Babe Ruth Story* with William Bendix was made. Ruth's name was a synonym for the term baseball superstar. Besides being inducted as a charter member of the Hall of Fame in 1936, Ruth was honored in nearly every way imaginable, by speeches, songs, and the written word. A striking tribute to Ruth was written on a monument in the New York Yankees outfield in 1949. It simply reads: "George Herman 'Babe' Ruth. A Great Ball Player. A Great Man. A Great American."

CAREER HIGHLIGHTS
GEORGE HERMAN RUTH

Born: February 6, 1895 Baltimore, MD **Died:** August 16, 1948
Height: 6'2" **Weight:** 215 lbs. **Batted:** Left **Threw:** Left
Pitcher, outfielder: Boston Red Sox, 1914-19. Outfielder: New York Yankees, 1920-34; Boston Braves, 1935.

- ★ Collected a record 2,056 walks
- ★ Hit 714 home runs, a record that stood for 40 years
- ★ Compiled a lifetime .342 batting average and .690 slugging percentage
- ★ Led the league in home runs 12 times
- ★ Won 94 games as a pitcher, with a 2.28 ERA
- ★ Pitched 29.2 consecutive scoreless innings in World Series competition, a record that held until 1961

- ★ Hit better than .300 in 17 seasons
- ★ Hit 60 homers in 1927, a record that stood until 1961
- ★ Collected 2,211 RBI, second best in major league history
- ★ Posted a record 457 total bases in 1921
- ★ Had a record .847 slugging percentage in 1920
- ★ Elected to the Hall of Fame as a charter member in 1936

MAJOR LEAGUE TOTALS

G	AB	H	BA	2B	3B	HR	R	RBI	SB
2,503	8,399	2,873	.342	506	136	714	2,174	2,211	123

Babe Ruth is more than just baseball's greatest player, he is intrinsically wrapped up in the game's mythology. His public image as the player so powerful that he could call his home run shots will outlast even the game itself.

NOLAN RYAN

In 1989 Nolan Ryan quickly silenced the skeptics. The 42-year-old hurler was signed as a free agent by the Texas Rangers in the off-season. Some fans wondered how effective Ryan could remain after throwing thousands of fastballs during the last 22 seasons in the majors. Only one month into the 1989 season "The Ryan Express" had flirted with not one but two no-hitters.

In one game in early April Ryan struck out 13 of the first 19 batters he faced, finishing the game with 15 Ks. It wasn't until the 8th inning that Brewer utility infielder Terry Francona singled. Later that month Ryan reached the ninth inning of a no-hit bid against the Toronto Blue Jays before being touched for a safety by Nelson Liriano. In his first 1989 one-hitter the 22-year veteran threw 134 pitches—95 fastballs, 11 big-breaking curves, and 28 offerings of his newly acquired change-up that fades low and away. After 20 years of averaging 200 innings a season, Ryan still hurls a fastball that nips 100 m.p.h.

There's no question of making Ryan a reliever. In 1989 he started 32 games, winning 16 and losing 10. His 301 strikeouts led the league, as did his 228 the previous year. The 1987 campaign also saw Ryan celebrate his 40th birthday by taking top honors in the league ERA department with 2.76, the lowest since his career-best 1.69 in 1981. His 1989 strikeout-to-walks ratio was a healthy 301/98, proving that old dogs can learn new tricks and learn them well. More than a decade ago Ryan posted six seasons of pacing the circuit in both strikeouts and walks. With great effort he has held his walks to two digits every year since 1983.

Ryan is 11 games shy of claiming 300 wins, a milestone he hungers for. He already owns the title of Baseball Strikeout King and surpassed 5,000 Ks in 1989. Meanwhile the league strikeout titles keep coming. His loop-leading Ks in 1989 marked the tenth time he has achieved the feat. Not bad for a thrower who admits that for the first few years he "hadn't the slightest idea where the ball was going."

The New York Mets signed Ryan in 1965 after selecting him in the fifth round of the draft. He first appeared in the major leagues for a three-game stint in 1966, and he returned to the majors permanently in 1968. The following year he was a key member of the "Miracle Mets" of 1969, concluding the season with 6 wins and 3 losses in 25 outings. He set a National League Championship Series record for most strikeouts by a reliever in his one playoff outing that year, fanning 7 Atlanta Braves and notching a win with a 2.57 ERA. Striking out 3 Orioles in a no-decision Series appearance, Ryan concluded his sophomore season with a world championship ring.

Ryan was traded to the Angels in 1971 for Jim Fregosi but did not experience his first winning season for California until 1972, when he won 19 games against 16 losses in 39 outings. He struck out a league-leading 329 batters that year. In 1973 he set a record for most strikeouts by a pitcher in a single season with 383 and collected his first of two 20-win seasons. In 1977 he was the American League Pitcher of the Year. Ryan remained with the Angels until 1979, when he declared himself a free agent. He signed with the Houston Astros to be close to his home in Alvin, Texas. He grew up there and now raises his three children there. He claims that in the off-season he never thinks about the game, only about ranching, his wife Ruth, and his kids. During the season it's another story.

Ryan thrived at the Astrodome, and some believe that the perfectly controlled climate there prolonged his career. In 18 of the past 19 seasons he has posted wins in double figures, including seven straight campaigns with Houston. Unfortunately, he ran into a streak of bad luck in 1987 and concluded the season with 8 wins and 16 losses. He still managed to accumulate more than 200 strikeouts (270 to be exact) and led the league in ERA.

Ryan's critics often point to his relatively low career winning percentage— .519 at the end of the 1988 season. Another debit often mentioned is Ryan's rather poor fielding. By the end of 1987 Ryan had almost reached the all-time career record for errors.

But it's easy to ignore any possible shortcomings given Ryan's many accomplishments. Ryan is the only pitcher to have three straight seasons with 300 or more strikeouts (from 1972 to 1974), and he is the only hurler to have notched five no-hit games. His fifth no-hitter, which came on September 26, 1981, was extra-special. "The fact that this one came in a pennant race, on national TV, and in front of my mom makes it that much more significant. I never think about a no-hitter until after seven innings. I've been there and lost them too often to think about it before then. It's the one thing I wanted to do since I got the fourth one," Ryan said.

CAREER HIGHLIGHTS
LYNN NOLAN RYAN

Born: January 31, 1947   Refugio, TX
Height: 6'2"   **Weight:** 170 lbs.   **Bats:** Right   **Throws:** Right
Pitcher: New York Mets, 1968-71; California Angels, 1972-79; Houston Astros, 1980-88; Texas Rangers, 1989.

★ Posted two 20-win seasons
★ Became the all-time strikeout king in 1985
★ The only pitcher ever to lead the league in Ks after age 40
★ Has five no-hitters

★ Named to eight All-Star teams
★ Won his tenth strikeout title in 1989
★ Has struck out more than 300 batters seven times
★ Fanned a record 383 batters in 1973

MAJOR LEAGUE TOTALS

G	IP	W	L	Pct.	SO	BB	ERA
710	4,786	289	263	.524	5,076	2,540	3.15

Nolan Ryan is the only hurler in baseball history to have three straight seasons of 300-plus strikeouts, and he is the only one to pitch five no-hitters. Still pitching after 22 seasons in the majors, Ryan has never won a Cy Young award.

RYNE SANDBERG

In one of the great baseball ironies, Bill Giles, president of the Philadelphia Phillies, was so eager to trade Larry Bowa to the Chicago Cubs after the 1981 season that he threw in Ryne Sandberg. In return, the Phillies received the less-than-immortal Ivan DeJesus. Sandberg, believed to be the best second baseman in the National League today, wound up in a deal that was mainly designed to get rid of Bowa, who had personality conflicts with Giles. Cubs general manager Dallas Green, a former Phillies field manager, was aware of Sandberg's potential and knew what kind of deal he was swinging.

Signed by the Phillies in 1978 for an estimated bonus of $30,000, Sandberg did quite well offensively in their farm system. He had starred in three sports in high school and signed his first major league contract only four days after agreeing to attend Washington State University on a football scholarship. It took Sandberg four years to climb Philadelphia's minor league ladder. He played shortstop with the Phillies organization primarily because Juan Samuel was projected as their future second baseman. He had several fine seasons in the minors—most notably his 1980 season at Spartanburg, when he led the Western Carolina League shortstops in assists and fielding percentage. As a hitter, Sandberg's best season in the minors was in 1982, when he held a Double-A rating. He batted .310 with 11 homers and 79 RBI that year.

Since then Sandberg has been a beacon in the Cubs infield. With only eight seasons in the majors, he has barely had time for a slump. Injuries limited Sandberg to only 132 games in 1987—affecting his power statistics as well. He did manage to reach a career milestone when he passed the 1,000 mark in base hits.

Wrigley Field has been ideally suited to Sandberg's power. In 1985 he became the third player in major league history to smash 25 or more home runs and to steal 50 or more bases in a single season. The 26 homers he hit that year were the most hit by a Cubbie second baseman since Rogers Hornsby smashed 39 in 1929. His 54 stolen bases were the most by a Cubs player since Frank Chance stole 57 in 1906. Of the numerous homers he has hit since he became a slugging second sacker, most have been launched into orbit from Wrigley Field.

In his 1982 debut with the Cubs,

Sandberg played 140 games at third base. He hit .271 and scored 103 runs—a new record for Cubs rookies. Changed to second base in the last month of the season, he quickly adapted to his new position. In 1983 Sandberg became the first player in National League history to win a Gold Glove in his first season at a new position. His glovework was consistent throughout the season, and his .986 fielding average was tops in the senior circuit. On June 12 he tied a major league record with 12 assists in one game.

During the 1984 season, when the Cubs got into the National League Championship Series for the first time, Sandberg proved to be a valuable asset. He clubbed 19 home runs that year, batted .314, scored a league-leading 114 runs, and hit a league high of 19 triples. For his efforts he was named the National League's Most Valuable Player.

The Cubs did not make it to the World Series—they were defeated by the San Diego Padres in the playoffs. In this matchup, Sandberg had 7 hits and a .368 batting average.

In 1985 Sandberg registered a .305 average in 153 games. An 18-game hitting streak, a third straight Gold Glove, and membership on *The Sporting News* Silver Slugger team highlighted his season.

This Washington native's average dropped to .284 in 1986, but he batted .404 with runners on third base. His power totals included 14 homers and 76 RBI. Sandberg continued his fielding dominance in the league with his fourth straight Gold Glove. He tied a major league record by making just 5 errors all season long. He also ranked first in the league in assists. In 1987 Sandberg injured his ankle while trying to avoid a first base collision with Jack Clark. This was the first time in six seasons that he didn't surpass the 150-game mark. With a healthy ankle, he quite likely would have become the first Cubs player in history to steal 30-plus bases in six consecutive seasons. He did hit .264 with 19 homers and 69 RBI. Sandberg became the first Cub since Ron Santo to win five straight Gold Gloves with his 1987 award.

In 1989 Sandberg led the Cubs with 30 homers on their way to an N.L. Division title. Sandberg could be one of the National League's star second sackers for at least another decade. Already he's challenging Johnny Evers' reputation as the greatest Cub second baseman ever. In a few more years, he may be called one of the greatest in baseball history.

CAREER HIGHLIGHTS
RYNE DEE SANDBERG

Born: September 18, 1959 Spokane, WA
Height: 6'1" **Weight:** 175 lbs. **Bats:** Right **Throws:** Right
Shortstop: Philadelphia Phillies, 1981. Second baseman: Chicago Cubs, 1982-89.

★ Played in six consecutive All-Star games
★ Named the N.L. MVP in 1984
★ Batted .400 in the 1989 N.L.C.S.
★ Collected a career high of 54 stolen bases in 1985
★ Batted .368 in the 1984 N.L.C.S.
★ Chosen for three Silver Slugger teams

★ Established the N.L. record for highest season fielding average (.994 in 1986) for second baseman

MAJOR LEAGUE TOTALS

G	AB	H	BA	2B	3B	HR	R	RBI	SB
1,234	4,893	1,395	.285	226	54	139	756	549	250

Ryne Sandberg, the star second sacker for the Chicago Cubs, batted .290 during the 1989 season and belted 30 homers to help his team get into the N.L. Championship Series. Unfortunately the Cubs lost the N.L.C.S. to the San Francisco Giants.

RON SANTO

While American League fans still rave about Brooks Robinson as the all-around talented third baseman of the 1960s, enthusiasts in the National League will avidly dispute the claim that Robinson was the only gifted hot corner guardian of the decade. These rebuttals are usually backed up with two words: Ron Santo.

From 1960 to 1973 Santo stalked the left side of Wrigley Field's infield. In that time Santo created such an assortment of offensive and defensive statistics that it made him worthy of Hall of Fame membership.

The Cubs gave Santo his first chance in mid-1960 after less than two full seasons of minor league ball. Santo batted .327 with 11 homers and 87 RBI against San Antonio in 1959. He was called up from Houston after just 71 games.

The seven-time All-Star came into his own as a hitter in 1963. In 162 games Santo batted .297 with 25 homers and 99 RBI. In 1964 he hit 30 dingers with 96 RBI while batting a personal best of .313. He reeled off four straight seasons of 30 or more homers through 1967. Meanwhile, his RBI totals didn't drop below 90 until 1971. Santo drove in more than 100 runs four times—his high mark was 123 in 1969. This Washington native never led in any major hitting departments (aside from his loop-best 13 triples in 1964). However, he always ranked in the top five of several categories each year.

Santo was a victim of the Cubs youth movement following the 1973 season. Even though he had respectable success that year with 20 home runs, 77 RBI, and a .267 average in 149 games, Santo was traded to the crosstown White Sox. He ended his career there after just one season. The 1974 White Sox management futilely tried to make Santo into a second baseman; then they tried him in all four infield spots and as a designated hitter. The utility man role hindered Santo's hitting. He batted just .221 before retiring.

Today this smooth slugger ranks in the top ten in virtually every all-time batting category for the Cubs—excluding triples and batting average. Including his one American League season, Santo had 2,254 hits in 2,243 games for a .277 batting average. His extra-base hits include 365 doubles, 67 triples, and 342 homers. Santo scored 1,138 runs in his career and drove in 1,331 others. His one unsatisfied goal was to play in a World Series—a frustration that other

Cubs stars of the 1960s, such as Billy Williams and Ernie Banks, shared.

Defensively, Santo was one of the finest glove men of the 1960s. Philadelphia Phillies third sacker Mike Schmidt was the first fielder in the senior circuit who compared with Santo in defensive grace—he quickly moved up to the top ten in several major league defensive categories. In his statistical journeys, Schmidt usually found Santo's name waiting near the top of each list.

Santo's fielding marks and rankings include the following: games played, 2,181 (fifth); putouts, 1,955 (13th); assists per game, 2.2 (12th); total chances, 6,853 (third); and double plays, 395 (sixth). Santo won five Gold Gloves from 1964 to 1968.

Santo enjoyed a long-time love affair with the city of Chicago. In 1973 the owners and players signed a new contract that allowed players with ten years of major league experience (with the last five coming from the same club) to have the right of approval for any trade they might be involved in. Santo was the first player in the majors to take

advantage of this new rule. The Cubs wanted to trade Santo to the California Angels, but Santo declined, demanding that he stay in Chicago if he was traded. Knowing that no competition existed from other teams as potential traders, the White Sox were able to obtain Santo for pitchers Steve Stone and Ken Frailing, catcher Steve Swisher, and a minor leaguer on December 11, 1973.

While it never showed up in the statistics, Santo was one of baseball's most courageous players. Aside from his flashy fielding and constant clutch hitting, Santo coped with another continual challenge—his battle with diabetes. Santo never said much about his physical well-being, but his quiet courage in the face of the affliction was an inspiration to all Americans.

Following his retirement Santo became an oil company executive. Before that he had been involved with his own pizzeria. Cubs fans everywhere have been waiting for the last decade to see this hardworking third sacker elected to the Hall of Fame. Santo has been overlooked in large part because he never played with a pennant-winning club during his career. Only 75 ballots out of 427 included votes for Santo. If he isn't voted into the Hall within five years, his name will be forwarded to the Veterans Committee. There the wait for his deserved recognition could last forever.

Third baseman Ron Santo played 14 seasons for the Cubs before moving across town to help the White Sox. The Hall of Fame candidate belted 20-plus homers 11 times in his career and won 5 Gold Gloves.

CAREER HIGHLIGHTS
RONALD EDWARD SANTO

Born: February 25, 1940   Seattle, WA
Height: 6'0"   **Weight:** 190 lbs.   **Batted:** Right   **Threw:** Right
Third baseman: Chicago Cubs, 1960-73; Chicago White Sox, 1974.

- ★ Drove in 98 or more runs seven times
- ★ Led the N.L. in walks four times
- ★ Surpassed 30 homers in four straight seasons
- ★ Hit 20 or more homers 11 times
- ★ Won five Gold Gloves
- ★ Played in at least 154 games in 11 straight seasons

MAJOR LEAGUE TOTALS

G	AB	H	BA	2B	3B	HR	R	RBI	SB
2,243	8,143	2,254	.277	365	67	342	1,138	1,331	35

MIKE SCHMIDT

Although Mike Schmidt had planned to continue his record-setting career with another season of active duty in 1989, he reluctantly retired in midseason. Amidst a flourish of media attention, Schmidt said farewell to the Phillies fans who have long considered him a living legend. In 1983, in a special team centennial celebration, nearly 20,000 fans voted Schmidt the "Greatest Phillies Player" of all time.

Few of those fans would have cast those votes for Schmidt after the 1973 season. They would have laughed at anyone who predicted that Schmidt could hit 542 homers (the seventh-highest total in history). In fact few people would have believed he'd survive in the major leagues. The Phillies had high hopes for Schmidt and had made him a second-round draft selection in June 1971. He had been a college All-American at Ohio University, where he earned a bachelor's degree in business. Schmidt had little success in a half-season with the Phillies minor league affiliate in Reading in 1971, hitting just .211, but he prospered in Eugene in 1972, posting a .291 average with 26 home runs and 91 RBI. When he appeared in 13 games for Philadelphia near the end of the season, he batted just .206.

Schmidt started his historic home run quest with his first four-bagger in the majors on September 16, 1972: a three-run shot off Montreal's Balor Moore. In 1973 Schmidt was Philadelphia's starting third baseman. He hit 18 homers but batted a paltry .196 and fanned 136 times in only 367 at-bats.

Finally, the faith the Phillies had invested in Schmidt began to pay off. In 1974 he won his first National League home run crown with 36 blasts. He drove in 116 runs and pumped his average up to a healthy .282.

Prior to 1988 Schmidt never fell below 21 homers or 78 RBI in one season (both totals coming in a subpar 1978). His career highs in home runs and RBI came in 1980, with 48 dingers and 121 RBI. Those league-leading totals were a prelude to a .381 performance (3 homers and 7 RBI) in the 1980 World Series win over the Kansas City Royals. Schmidt was named National League Most Valuable Player, National League Player of the Year, and World Series Most Valuable Player for his efforts. Schmidt, Stan Musial, and Roy Campanella are the only players who have won three league Most Valuable Player awards in their careers.

Schmidt gained lasting fame through his many home runs. Only Hank Aaron and Willie Mays hit more National League round-trippers than Schmidt. He topped 30 homers on 13 occasions—the same number of seasons that Babe Ruth had turned the trick. Schmidt surpassed the 35-homer barrier 11 times—as many times as Aaron had (Ruth managed to do it a record 12 times). Only Ruth won more league home run titles than Schmidt. Ruth led the American League nine times, while Schmidt paced the National League eight times. Schmidt holds the record for most career home runs by a third baseman. He homered in each National League Park at least once in 1979. Prior to 1989 Schmidt had hit 263 of his homers at Philadelphia's Veterans' Stadium, ranking fourth on the all-time list for homers in one ballpark. He's tied at 44 (with Willie McCovey) for eighth in multiple-homer games.

Schmidt was not a one-dimensional star all those years. The longtime third sacker also broke National League records for career double plays, assists, and total chances. Though he did not finish the 1989 season, he still broke the N.L. record for most lifetime seasons at third base—17—a mark once held by Pie Traynor, Stan Hack, and Eddie Mathews. In addition the National League honored Schmidt with ten Gold Gloves during his career.

Pride and a lucrative contract convinced Schmidt not to retire after the 1988 season, though the longtime star had achieved so many records in 1987 and 1988 that he didn't have many statistical milestones to shoot for. He had also struggled with a torn rotator cuff in 1988. Yet Schmidt felt he would be retiring on a sour note, since all of his offensive totals had withered. So he underwent off-season surgery and decided to prove he could still perform well as his 40th birthday loomed near. To prompt his return the Phillies presented Schmidt with a unique contract that awarded him $500,000, with a $500,000 bonus if he was on the roster after May 15, and another $500,000 if he was still there after August 15.

Schmidt collected the May 15 longevity bonus and had a half-dozen homers by early May. The Phillies favorite quickly realized, however, that he was not playing the game to his full potential and decided to call it quits by early summer. Schmidt tearfully bade farewell to his fans and his team during a prepared statement to the press—perhaps the only tender moment in the otherwise turbulent 1989 season.

CAREER HIGHLIGHTS
MICHAEL JACK SCHMIDT

Born: September 27, 1949 Dayton, OH
Height: 6'2" **Weight:** 195 lbs. **Batted:** Right **Threw:** Right
Third baseman: Philadelphia Phillies, 1972-89.

★ Ranks third in N.L. history in home runs
★ Topped the N.L. in home runs seven times
★ Holds the record for most career home runs by a third baseman
★ Won ten Gold Gloves
★ Named to six Silver Slugger teams
★ Played in 11 All-Star games (eight as a starter)

MAJOR LEAGUE TOTALS

G	AB	H	BA	2B	3B	HR	R	RBI	SB
2,404	8,352	2,234	.267	408	59	548	1,506	1,595	174

Mike Schmidt hit a career high of 48 home runs during his phenomenal 1980 season. His Phillies fought their way to the World Series that year, beating the Royals in six games. Schmidt hit .381 in Series play and belted 3 homers.

RED SCHOENDIENST

One of the newest inductees into the Baseball Hall of Fame, Red Schoendienst, was mistaken for a batboy applicant when he reported for minor league duty in 1943.

Schoendienst (pronounced SCHAIN-deenst) was a red-haired (hence his nickname), freckle-faced shortstop who signed with the Cardinals at age 19 in 1942. He attended a Sportsman's Park tryout in St. Louis to see a night game against the Dodgers. However, the Cardinals scouts liked his potential and offered him a $75-per-month contract. As a youth in the Civilian Conservation Corps, he damaged his vision when he got a staple lodged in his left eye. This ruled him out of military service, but he became a civilian clerk at Scott Air Force base. Because he had difficulty seeing with his bad eye while batting from the right against righthanders, he became one of the game's finest switch-hitters.

Schoendienst played his 1942 debut season in the minors at Union City and Albany, and he began his 1943 campaign with Lynchburg of the Piedmont League. After just nine games, he was hitting a blistering .472 and was promoted to Rochester of the International League, which was managed by former "Gashouse Gang" member Pepper Martin. When Schoendienst tried to enter the clubhouse, Martin shooed him away, thinking that he was a youngster wanting to be the team's new batboy. When Schoendienst insisted that he was a real minor leaguer, Martin moaned out load that he was getting babies to make up his roster.

The Illinois native served the Cardinals in several positions during his first few seasons in the bigs. He opened the 1945 season as the Cardinals left fielder, hitting .278 with 1 homer and 47 RBI. He led the league with 26 stolen bases. In 1946 Cardinals second baseman Lou Klein jumped his contract to play in the Mexican League, so Schoendienst had a new position. Because he was brought up as a shortstop in the minor leagues, the conversion wasn't traumatic. In 1946 Schoendienst led the Cardinals to a world championship. He had the top fielding percentage in the league for second sackers, and he hit .281.

While providing steady defense, Schoendienst gained the reputation as a surprising clutch hitter. He batted above .300 from 1952 through 1954. His finest outing at the plate was in 1953, when he registered career highs in

home runs (15), RBI (79), average (.342—only 2 points behind league leader Carl Furillo), and runs scored (107). To top it all off, Schoendienst was first in the senior circuit in putouts, assists, double plays, and fielding percentage.

Despite spending most of his career in St. Louis, Schoendienst saw more World Series action as a member of the Milwaukee Braves. He became the team's second baseman after being acquired from the Giants on June 15, 1957, for Bobby Thomson, Ray Crone, and Danny O'Connell. He hit .278 when the Braves won the 1957 world championship over the Yankees. In 1958 he hit .300 during the postseason when the Yanks turned the tables.

Schoendienst was the hero of the 1950 All-Star game played at Chicago's Comiskey Park. The National League won the game 4-3 with a 14th-inning homer from an unlikely home run hitter. Facing lefty reliever Ted Gray of the Detroit Tigers, Schoendienst hit from the right side and blasted an early offering into the left field stands for the

game-winning hit. The fleet switch-hitter was a ten-time All-Star and was named to *The Sporting News* All-Star team five times.

Schoendienst made one of baseball's greatest comebacks in 1960. He was diagnosed with tuberculosis after Milwaukee's 1958 World Series. In February 1959 part of Schoendienst's right lung was removed in surgery. He came back to hit .257 in 68 games for the Braves before returning to St. Louis to finish his career.

A whole new generation who may be unfamiliar with the accomplished infielder knows Schoendienst as a Cardinals manager. From 1961 to 1963 he served as a Cardinals player/coach. He piloted the Cardinals from 1965 to 1976 and then for one return engagement in 1980. While managing the Cardinals, Schoendienst led the team to National League pennants in 1967 and 1968 and to a world championship against the 1967 Boston Red Sox. The Associated Press named him National League Manager of the Year on both occasions. His teams finished in second place in 1971, 1973, and 1974. In 1973 and 1974 the Cardinals missed a division pennant by just one and a half games. Schoendienst moved to Oakland for 1977 and 1978 to become an Athletics coach. He then rejoined the Cardinals as a coach. In 1980 when manager Whitey Herzog became team general manager on a trial basis, Schoendienst regained the managerial throne temporarily for the rest of that season. No man, not even Herzog, has surpassed Schoendienst's 13-year reign as the Redbirds skipper. In that time he compiled a record of 1,028 wins and 944 losses.

CAREER HIGHLIGHTS
ALBERT FRED SCHOENDIENST

Born: Febraury 2, 1923   Germantown, IL
Height: 6'0"   **Weight:** 170 lbs.   **Batted:** Both   **Threw:** Right
Second baseman: St. Louis Cardinals, 1945-56, 1961-63; New York Giants, 1956-57; Milwaukee Braves, 1957-60. Manager: St. Louis Cardinals, 1965-76, 1980.

- ★ Led the N.L. in stolen bases in 1945
- ★ Played in three World Series
- ★ Topped the N.L. with 22 pinch hits in 1962
- ★ Led the N.L. with 200 hits in 1957
- ★ Elected to the Hall of Fame in 1989
- ★ Won N.L. pennants in 1967 and 1968 as Cardinals manager

MAJOR LEAGUE TOTALS

G	AB	H	BA	2B	3B	HR	R	RBI	SB
2,216	8,479	2,449	.289	427	78	84	1,223	773	89

Recently elected to the Hall of Fame, Red Schoendienst proved his merit in 1960 when he staged a triumphant comeback. Schoendienst, who had been diagnosed with tuberculosis, returned to play ball after having a lung removed.

TOM SEAVER

icknamed "Tom Terrific" (after the superhero cartoon character) while with the New York Mets, Tom Seaver was the keystone of the Mets pitching staff for almost ten years. Named Rookie of the Year in 1967 when he was a 16-game winner for the Mets, Seaver went on to achieve extraordinary statistics during his 20 years in the major leagues.

Seaver wasn't a high school sports star hounded by professional teams. Following service as a U.S. Marine, Seaver attended the University of Southern California. The Atlanta Braves were very close to bringing Seaver into the fold in 1966 when they offered him an estimated signing bonus of $40,000. The contract was canceled by the Commissioner of Baseball, William Eckert, on a technicality involving Seaver's amateur status as a college player. When the National Collegiate Athletic Association ruled that Seaver had lost his amateur status by accepting the Braves offer, the young hurler stood in no-man's land. However, the baseball commissioner ruled that any team that matched the Braves former offer could have Seaver. In a specially arranged lottery, the Mets won the rights to Seaver and gave him a $50,000 bonus for signing a contract.

Seaver was a Mets star for ten seasons. His award-winning rookie season included 16 wins. When the "Miracle Mets" won the 1969 World Series, Seaver led them with a league-leading 25-7 season. He won 19 games in 1973, leading the Mets to another National League pennant. After four 20-win seasons (1969, 1971, 1972, and 1975), Seaver was traded in mid-1977 after disagreeing with the team ownership. The Reds gave up Steve Henderson, Pat Zachry, Doug Flynn, and Dan Norman in return for Seaver. As a Red, Seaver led the National League with a stunning 14-2 record during the strike-shortened season of 1981. He won a total of 75 games in five and a half seasons in Cincinnati.

After a disastrous 1982 season, which included a career-low 5-13 record, Seaver was dealt back to the Mets on December 16, 1982, for Charlie Puleo, Lloyd McClendon, and Jason Felice. His return was celebrated by New York fans, and it appeared likely that, at age 39, he'd finish out his career at Shea Stadium. However, the Chicago White Sox, who had lost pitcher Dennis Lamp to the Toronto Blue Jays through free agency, noticed that

the Mets had not protected Seaver's name in the reentry draft. The White Sox drafted Seaver from the Mets roster to boost their fragile pitching staff. Seaver went off to the Windy City and spun two consecutive winning seasons. In 1984 he led Chicago with a 15-11 record. The following season Seaver won 16 games.

On June 29, 1986, the White Sox traded Seaver to the Boston Red Sox for infielder/outfielder Steve Lyons. Seaver won 5 games for Boston against 7 losses. Nostalgic fans were excited about Seaver's chance to appear in one more postseason battle when the Red Sox seemed guaranteed of winning the pennant. However, Seaver went down with a knee injury and wasn't activated for either the American League Championship Series or the World Series. After being released by the Red Sox after the 1986 campaign, Seaver

signed on for a third stint with the Mets early in the 1987 season. After being shelled in an exhibition game, however, he announced his retirement.

For his distinguished career, Seaver racked up an impressive array of accomplishments. He's one of only 19 players in history to earn 300 wins. Seaver ranks 15th, tied with 19th-century pitcher Mickey Welch. His 3,640 strikeouts are third best, with only Nolan Ryan and Steve Carlton earning more. The big righthander earned 200 or more strikeouts during ten seasons, including nine seasons in a row (from 1968 to 1976). Seaver earned 61 career shutouts, the seventh-best total in baseball. His only shortcoming was a 1-2 record during the 1969 and 1973 World Series.

Seaver's career statistics are certainly Hall of Fame caliber. He should be a first-ballot selection when he becomes eligible for enshrinement in 1992. Meanwhile, Seaver is making use of the public relations degree he earned at USC in 1974. He has been active in TV broadcasting since he started doing some weekend sports reports for a New York station in 1975. Since then, he has served as a color commentator for numerous sporting events, including the World Series and some golf tournaments. He first gained national attention as a broadcaster hosting a syndicated show called "Greatest Sports Legends." Despite his varied experience in television, Seaver faced a huge challenge in 1989. He was slated to replace the best-known player-turned-broadcaster, Joe Garagiola, who had been a fixture on NBC-TV's "Game of the Week" broadcasts for nearly three decades.

CAREER HIGHLIGHTS
GEORGE THOMAS SEAVER

Born: November 17, 1944   Fresno, CA
Height: 6'1"   **Weight:** 195 lbs.   **Batted:** Right   **Threw:** Right
Pitcher: New York Mets, 1967-77, 1983; Cincinnati Reds, 1978-82; Chicago White Sox, 1984-86; Boston Red Sox, 1986.

- ★ Named N.L. Rookie of the Year in 1967
- ★ Won three league ERA titles
- ★ Pitched in three World Series
- ★ Won the Cy Young award in 1969, 1973, and 1975
- ★ Posted five 20-win seasons
- ★ Ranks seventh in career shutouts with 61
- ★ Member of the 300-win club
- ★ Has the third-highest strikeout total in history

MAJOR LEAGUE TOTALS

G	IP	W	L	Pct.	SO	BB	ERA
656	4,782	311	205	.603	3,640	1,390	2.86

Tom Seaver returned to the Mets for the 1983 season, and fans assumed he'd finish his career there. But the White Sox noticed that the Mets had not protected Seaver's name in the reentry draft, so the Sox lifted the famed hurler from the Mets roster.

JOE SEWELL

While Joe Sewell may not have been the greatest hitter in baseball history, statistics back up the claim that he was the most disciplined hitter of the 20th century. Never before or since has a player struck out as seldom as Sewell, who fanned just 114 times in a 14-year career.

Sewell's microscopic strikeout total seems even more incredible in light of today's free-swinging hitters. Many contemporary players, who often strike out more than 114 times in one season, can only dream of Sewell's bat control. While playing with the Cleveland Indians and New York Yankees, Sewell never struck out more than 20 times in one season. Only in his first four seasons did Sewell have more than ten Ks. In his last 1,864 plate appearances, stretched over the final four seasons of his career, Sewell had just 18 strikeouts. Sewell was no wimpy singles hitter who never came close to a homer, either. He belted 49 four-baggers during his career, including a career high of 11 dingers in 1932 (when he had just 3 strikeouts in 124 games).

The Alabama native started his pro career in 1920 at age 21 with New Orleans. One of the saddest accidents in major league history gave Sewell his first chance with the Cleveland Indians. He got an unexpected call-up to the Tribe when their star shortstop, Ray Chapman, died after being beaned with a pitch from Carl Mays. Sewell played in 22 games and batted .329 during his emergency debut. Interestingly, he had batted only .289 in 92 games with New Orleans. Even though he wasn't technically eligible for World Series play because he had joined the team at such a late date, his inclusion was allowed by Dodgers owner Charlie Ebbets because the Indians claimed that they had no other shortstop to use after Chapman's untimely death. When he was inserted into the lineup, Sewell batted .174 with 4 hits in the competition. In 1921 Sewell started a momentous achievement with the Indians by putting together a streak of 1,103 consecutive games played. The streak is the sixth-longest in baseball history.

Prior to his year at New Orleans, Sewell had played college football and basketball at the University of Alabama. Eventual Cubs star Riggs Stephenson was also on the Crimson Tide team that year. Sewell had taken a year out for military service before he started his memorable career. He had also graduated with a Bachelor of Science degree in

1920. Before Sewell found his true calling on a baseball field, he had considered studying medicine.

Sewell put together some impressive achievements with Cleveland. He maintained his reputation as an outstanding glove man every season. At the plate he was a perennial .300 hitter. In 1923 and 1924 Sewell had totals of 109 and 104 RBI.

After spending 11 years with the Indians, Sewell was a New York Yankee for his last three seasons. Although the team obtained him as a backup third baseman, a return to form in 1931 helped Sewell land a starting job with the Bronx Bombers. In his second of three years with the Yankees, Sewell got his first chance to appear in a World Series for the Bronx Bombers. In four games he had 5 hits, including 4 runs scored and 3 RBI. His accomplishments during the '31 season included a .302 average and a personal best of 102

runs scored. During 1932 and 1933, Sewell's final two seasons in the majors, he had career-low batting averages of .272 and .273—impressive for any other player.

Sewell finished his 1,903-game career with a .312 batting average. He rapped out 2,226 total hits, which included 436 doubles, 68 triples, and 49 homers. The sweet-swinging southerner scored 1,141 runs and drove in 1,053. Basestealing was a secondary part of Sewell's offensive game plan. However, he did have some speed and stole 74 bases in his lifetime. Only twice did Sewell rack up more than 10 steals in a single season. Sewell's team dedication is evident in his career on-base percentage of .391. He drew 843 bases on balls in his lifetime and was hit by pitches 79 times. The master batsman's bat was well-suited for sacrifice hits, and Sewell had 275 for his career.

Sewell's brother Luke was a catcher for 20 years and a manager for another 10 (guiding the St. Louis Browns to a 1944 league title). The two brothers played together on the Indians from 1921 through 1930. Another brother, Tommy, made one pinch-hitting appearance for the 1927 Chicago Cubs.

Following his retirement as a player, Joe Sewell coached for the Yankees through 1935. He scouted for the Cleveland Indians throughout the 1950s and then retired to operate a hardware store in Alabama. He became head baseball coach at the University of Alabama in 1964 and led the team to one Southeastern Conference title in 1968.

In 1977 Sewell finally got his place in the Hall of Fame, 44 years after he stopped playing.

CAREER HIGHLIGHTS
JOSEPH WHEELER SEWELL

Born: October 9, 1898   Titus, AL
Height: 5'6"   **Weight:** 155 lbs.   **Batted:** Left   **Threw:** Right
Shortstop, third baseman: Cleveland Indians, 1920-30; New York Yankees, 1931-33.

* ★ Led the A.L. in doubles in 1924
* ★ Batted .300 or above ten times
* ★ Struck out just 114 times in a 14-year career

* ★ Topped 100 RBI twice
* ★ Played in two World Series
* ★ Elected to the Hall of Fame in 1977

MAJOR LEAGUE TOTALS

G	AB	H	BA	2B	3B	HR	R	RBI	SB
1,903	7,132	2,226	.312	436	68	49	1,141	1,053	74

Slugger Joe Sewell struck out only 114 times during his entire 14-year career. In 1926 he supposedly had an "off" year when he fanned just six times, twice more than he had in 1925. In 1929 he played in 115 consecutive games without striking out.

ROY SIEVERS

The first American League player to receive the Rookie of the Year award played with the second-rate 1949 St. Louis Browns. Roy Sievers was 22 years old at the time and was signed straight out of high school by the Browns, who really had to hustle to get him away from the St. Louis Cardinals. (Both teams saw the publicity potential in having a home-grown star.)

Sievers was introduced to baseball by his American Legion coach Walter Shannon, who also was a Cardinals scout. But the Browns, even with their lower standings, were more anxious to gamble on promising prospects. They were willing to wait for Sievers until his three-year stint in the U.S. Army was over.

Sievers first wore a baseball uniform for pay in 1947, as a utility man and pitcher for the Class-A team in Hannibal. It was a year, Sievers later said, he wished he had been in the bigs, as he led the league in hits (159), homers (34), RBI (141), and runs scored (121). His average was .317, and he even had 5 triples.

On opening day Sievers was in St. Louis, keeping the bench warm for nine innings. After the team posted a seven-game losing streak, Sievers made his official debut. In a doubleheader he clouted 4 hits in 6 plate appearances, driving in 3 runs. Even though his team lost both of these games, Sievers was a ray of hope. He was a righthanded antidote to a Browns lineup too heavy with lefties. Sievers just got better as his rookie season progressed, ending with 144 hits, 28 doubles, 16 home runs, 91 RBI, and a .306 batting average.

Brownie trainer Bob Bauman may deserve some credit for this Rookie of the Year's exemplary performance, since he placed a bottle labeled "hit pills" in the locker room that season. The medicine didn't seem to work for anyone but Roy, however.

An effort to get Sievers to hit to right field in 1950 resulted in a nasty case of the sophomore jinx, and even Bauman's pills were no cure. Sievers' slump continued into 1951, when it was augmented by a painful shoulder separation—a result of a diving catch.

He played in only 31 games in 1951 and in just 11 in 1952. Surgery helped heal Sievers for a 1953 comeback, which was limited to 92 games. He posted a .270 average—the best since his spectacular rookie season. Sievers had feared the injury would end his career. Saved by medical science, he worked hard to improve, taking manual labor jobs in the off-season to keep his muscles toned. His hitting had seemed unaffected from the start, but he had to work hard to regain defensive control. Opposing runners were quick to take advantage of Sievers' weakened arm; Sievers was quick to show them the error of that assumption.

In a bright 17-year career, the peak came in 1957. Sievers had been engaged in battle from the top of the season, racing not only Ted Williams, but also Mickey Mantle, for the title of home run king. In the last two weeks Sievers pulled ahead to end with 42 dingers, the only member of the trio to top 40 that year. It was a career-best mark, as was his league-leading 114 RBI. He nearly matched the effort with 39 homers the following year. In 1957 a home crowd of 17,826 at Washington D.C.'s Griffith Stadium turned out for "Roy Sievers Night," which included a special pre-game ceremony to honor the hardworking slug-ger. He was showered with gifts and praise for his league-leading homer chase. The "1958 Official Baseball Guide" published by *The Sporting News* contains a photo of a grinning Vice President Richard M. Nixon shaking the hand of Sievers on that special night. Sievers is trying to hold back tears as he thanks Nixon and the crowd.

The Washington Senators pulled one of the greatest trades of the 1950s when they picked up Sievers from the Baltimore Orioles (who had been the Browns only one year earlier) in exchange for Gil Coan on February 18, 1954. Sievers served time with the Senators from 1954 through 1959. He was a member of the Chicago White Sox in 1960 and 1961, playing full-time first base for his new team. Chicago gave up Earl Battey, Don Mincher, and $150,000 to obtain the veteran. The Phillies used Sievers in the same role in 1962 through early 1964. Philadelphia sold Sievers back to his old team, the Senators, in mid-1964. He retired after the 1965 season.

It is as a Senator that Sievers is most often remembered. He slammed 2 homers off Yankee ace Whitey Ford in the movie version of the musical *Damn Yankees*. Sievers says he's still amused at the sight of himself slugging those homers—filmed during an actual game—followed by a closeup shot of movie star Tab Hunter running the bases.

Roy Sievers career almost ended when he was sidelined by a separated shoulder. The injury—the result of a diving catch—was corrected with surgery plus Sievers' own efforts toward recovery.

CAREER HIGHLIGHTS
ROY EDWARD SIEVERS

Born: November 18, 1926 St. Louis, MO
Height: 6'1" **Weight:** 195 lbs. **Batted:** Right **Threw:** Right
Outfielder, first baseman: St. Louis Browns, 1949-53; Washington Senators, 1954-59, 1964-65; Chicago White Sox, 1960-61; Philadelphia Phillies, 1962-64.

★ Named A.L. Rookie of the Year in 1949
★ Led the league with 42 homers and 114 RBI in 1957
★ Drove in 90 or more runs eight times
★ Hit at least 19 homers for ten consecutive seasons

MAJOR LEAGUE TOTALS

G	AB	H	BA	2B	3B	HR	R	RBI	SB
1,887	6,387	1,703	.267	292	42	318	945	1,147	14

AL SIMMONS

Al Simmons was the classic example of a great hitter who didn't look like one. Simmons had such an unusual batting stance that when he reported to the Philadelphia Athletics for his 1924 rookie season, veterans laughed at his practice swings. But Manager Connie Mack knew better. The A's skipper had brought Simmons up because in two minor league seasons the Milwaukee native had hit .360 and .398.

Simmons was born Aloys Szymanski to Polish immigrants, but later changed his name to Aloysius Simmons. Growing up in Wisconsin, he started playing semipro ball at an early age. It wasn't until age 21 that he got his first professional job with the Milwaukee Brewers of the American Association. The Brewers started him out with Aberdeen of the Dakota League, where he hit .364 with 10 home runs in his first 99 games. He returned to Milwaukee to close out the season. After another hitting slump, he was sent to Shreveport of the Texas League, where he batted .360 with 12 homers. In his final 24 games with Milwaukee, he pumped his average up to .398. The Brewers, however, sold him to the A's. Despite Simmons' two years of success, the Wisconsin team mistakenly thought that he couldn't last in pro ball with such an unorthodox batting style.

After hitting .308 in his rookie year with Philadelphia, the 5-foot-11, 190-pound righthander exploded for a .384 mark his sophomore season. Nobody ever laughed at his odd batting stance again. Luckily, Mack had ignored the many suggestions that he alter Simmons' hitting approach. The slugger was dubbed "Bucketfoot Al" for his unusual style—which was characterized by pointing his left foot toward third base as he faced the pitcher.

Simmons compiled a .334 lifetime batting average, finishing his career with 307 home runs and 2,927 hits. In each of his first 11 seasons, Simmons batted over .300 and had more than 100 RBI. Nine times in his 20-year career he batted over .340. He won back-to-back American League batting crowns in 1930 and 1931, when he recorded marks of .381 and .390. He batted a career high of .392 in 1927 but lost the batting title to Harry Heilmann, who slapped the ball at a .398 clip. Simmons was the league's Most Valuable Player in 1929, when he hit .365 with 34 home runs and a league-leading 157 RBI.

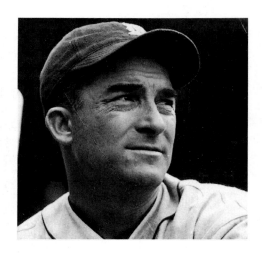

Simmons played his first nine seasons with the Philadelphia A's, leading them to three straight pennants from 1929 to 1931. Simmons had his best year during the team's three-year domination of the American League in 1930. He led the league with 152 runs and achieved another personal best with 165 RBI. His run-producing hits still didn't lead the league; that honor belonged to New York Yankee Lou Gehrig, who knocked in 174 tallies.

Because no All-Star games existed until 1933, Simmons had been a star in the American League for several years before he got to show his talent nationally in the World Series. He certainly was no disappointment. The Athletics whipped the Chicago Cubs in five Series games. Simmons scored the winning run in the crucial fifth game with a ninth-inning double. Teammate Bing Miller doubled him in for the final difference in the team's 3-2 win. Simmons finished the Series with 6 hits, 6 runs scored, and 5 RBI for a .300 average.

The Athletics defended their world championship in 1930 against the St. Louis Cardinals, defeating their National League rivals in six games. Simmons was the leading hitter on the victorious A's team. In fact Simmons' .364 average topped all World Series starters. He clubbed 8 hits, 2 homers, and 4 RBI and scored 4 runs. While the Cardinals edged the A's in seven games in the 1931 World Series, Simmons did his best to reverse the outcome. His key hit in the Series was a first-inning RBI double that staked George Earnshaw to an important early lead before he blanked St. Louis 3-0, tying the Series at two games apiece. The Series loss may have overshadowed Simmons' fine performance during the regular season. Besides winning another batting title, he had socked 22 homers and 128 RBI.

Simmons had a banner year in 1932. He was in the second year of a three-year, $100,000 contract, which was considered big money in those days. The Wisconsin native earned every penny of it, too. Simmons whacked a league-best 216 hits for a .322 batting average. His power totals soared to 35 home runs and 151 RBI. He was rewarded with a trade to the Chicago White Sox on September 28, 1932. The Sox gave up Jimmy Dykes and Mule Haas, but the most crucial part of the trade was the inclusion of $100,000 by the Chicago White Sox. Mack had become financially strapped during those Depression-era years and had started dumping high-salaried players in exchange for much-needed cash and inexpensive rookies.

Simmons retired in 1943. He was elected to the Hall of Fame in 1953.

CAREER HIGHLIGHTS
ALOYSIUS HARRY SIMMONS

Born: May 22, 1902   Milwaukee, WI   **Died:** May 26, 1956
Height: 5'11"   **Weight:** 190 lbs.   **Batted:** Right   **Threw:** Right
Outfielder: Philadelphia Athletics, 1924-32, 1940-41, 1944; Chicago White Sox, 1933-35; Detroit Tigers, 1936; Washington Senators, 1937-38; Boston Braves, 1939; Cincinnati Reds, 1939; Boston Red Sox, 1943.

★ Won ten batting titles
★ Played in four World Series
★ Had 200 or more hits five years in a row
★ Selected as A.L. MVP in 1929
★ Has 190 or more hits for eight seasons
★ Elected to the Hall of Fame in 1953
★ Drove in 100-plus runs for 12 of his first 13 seasons

MAJOR LEAGUE TOTALS

G	AB	H	BA	2B	3B	HR	R	RBI	SB
2,215	8,759	2,927	.334	539	149	307	1,507	1,827	87

Al Simmons was discovered by the legendary manager of the Philadelpha A's, Connie Mack. During the Depression, when the A's were financially strapped, Mack was forced to sell his talented slugger to the White Sox just after Simmons' banner year of 1932.

TED SIMMONS

Ted Simmons was one of the best-hitting catchers in baseball history. Simmons (nicknamed "Simba" for his long lionlike mane of hair) batted over .300 in seven seasons, and he drove in at least 80 runs in ten seasons.

Simmons' talent became evident early, when he began switch-hitting at the age of 13. He was an all-league high school basketball player and was named Most Valuable Player on the diamond. He was offered scholarships from five different universities to play on the gridiron. Instead, Simmons landed a $50,000 bonus for signing with the St. Louis Cardinals. He was their first pick in the free-agent draft of June 1967.

In the off-season Simmons continued his schooling, majoring in speech and radio. Even while a major leaguer, he held a St. Louis banking job when away from the field. His ability to master a diversity of tasks served him well in a career that required him to serve in up to five positions: catcher, first baseman, third baseman, outfielder, and designated hitter. Simmons is best known for working behind the plate, and he has set most of his major league records from that position.

After Simmons spent almost three years in the minors, the Cardinals sent him up in one of two test balloons. Finishing the last two games of the 1968 season in the bigs, he still maintained his minor league average of .331, even improving it by 2 points. He ended the next fall with five games in St. Louis. He missed spring training due to military service, rejoining Tulsa in May. After only 15 games he was in the majors to stay, totaling a .990 fielding average.

During his official rookie season of 1971, military service again caused an absence—three weeks in the middle of the season. Simmons made the most of his 133 games, with a .304 average and 77 RBI. He posted the first of seven .300-plus averages of his career and caught a no-hitter for the mighty Bob Gibson.

In 1972 and 1973 Simmons led N.L. catchers in putouts, assists, and total chances. He appeared in his first of five All-Star games in 1973. The next year he reached the 20-homer, 100-RBI plateau for the first time in his career. In 1975 he hit a career-high .332, setting a National League mark with 188 hits by a catcher. By 1976 he got his 1,000th career hit.

Simmons was an All-Star in 1977

and the following year—when he slugged a career-best 40 doubles. In 1979 he had a career-high 26 homers—and a broken left wrist. In a blockbuster trade following the 1980 season, Simmons, Rollie Fingers, and Pete Vuckovich were shipped in December to the Milwaukee Brewers for Lary Sorenson, Dave LaPoint, Sixto Lezcano, and David Green.

Despite free agency in 1983, the Brew Crew hung onto Simba, and why not? His near flawless fielding had led the loop in 1982 (.995), and in 1983 he posted a .308 average.

In 1984, for the first time in his career, Simmons spent no time behind the plate, playing at first and third base instead. He established American League records for the longest errorless game and the most innings played by a first baseman in one day (a 25-inning marathon that lasted into the wee hours of the morning of May 9).

Surprisingly, his hitting suffered

when he didn't catch. Behind the plate in 1985, his average and homers rejuvenated. But his plate appearances were declining with his 1986 acquisition by the Braves. His new function was to bolster the bench. This he accomplished with style, with 1 RBI for every 5 at-bats and a June game-winning grand slam—the second by a pinch hitter in Atlanta history. Until his retirement Simmons remained what he had always been: a careful, dangerous fastball hitter; a conservative baserunner; and a dedicated team member. His final assistance to the Braves was his personal coaching of pitcher Zane Smith, who blossomed under the veteran's guidance in 1987.

While Simmons never matched the power output of Johnny Bench, he was a pure-hitting backstop with defensive savvy. He'll be eligible for Hall of Fame consideration starting in 1994.

After 22 years as a respected catcher and master batsman, Simmons embarked upon the 1989 season with a job in the St. Louis Cardinals front office. In the town where he has made his home for years, Simmons is now director of player development.

Having spent most of his major league time as a catcher, Simmons should be able to spot talent. Primarily, however, Simmons is good for the job because he has been there.

Until he retired, Ted Simmons remained a careful but dangerous fastball hitter, a conservative baserunner, a hard-hitting backstop, and a dedicated team player. He will be eligible for Hall of Fame consideration in 1994.

CAREER HIGHLIGHTS
TED LYLE SIMMONS

Born: August 9, 1949   Highland Park, MI
Height: 5'11"   **Weight:** 193 lbs.   **Batted:** Both   **Threw:** Right
Catcher, first baseman: St. Louis Cardinals, 1968-80; Milwaukee Brewers, 1981-83; Atlanta Braves, 1986-88.

- ★ Named to eight All-Star teams
- ★ Ranked eighth in lifetime games caught
- ★ Held the N.L. record for home runs by a switch-hitter
- ★ Played in the 1982 World Series
- ★ Led N.L. catchers in assists twice
- ★ Hit both right- and lefthanded homers in one game three times

MAJOR LEAGUE TOTALS

G	AB	H	BA	2B	3B	HR	R	RBI	SB
2,456	8,680	2,472	.285	483	47	248	1,074	1,389	21

GEORGE SISLER

George Sisler batted over .400 two times, finished his career with a lifetime batting average of .340, and was regarded as one of the best-fielding first basemen in baseball during his time. Not bad for a player who reported to his first major league training camp as a pitcher.

Sisler, at 5-feet-11 and 170 pounds, was a natural athlete who first attracted pro scouts while playing ball at the University of Michigan under Coach Branch Rickey. Sisler was primarily a pitcher, but he demonstrated such hitting prowess that Coach Rickey began using him as an outfielder between starts. After graduation Sisler signed with the St. Louis Browns and made his major league debut in 1915. The Browns couldn't decide where they needed him most.

In his rookie season Sisler appeared in 81 games and split his time between pitching, playing the outfield, and patrolling first base. As a hurler Sisler won 4 and lost 4 that year, logging 6 complete games. However, the team valued his batwork so much that the Browns found him an every-day starting position. When his extraordinary batting skills had convinced the Browns to put the lefthander in the lineup on a daily basis, Sisler was made a full-time first baseman. Even later in his career he was still occasionally called on to take the mound for an inning or two of relief. His career pitching stats (in 24 games) include 5 wins, 6 losses, 3 saves, a 2.35 ERA, 9 complete games, and 1 shutout.

It was as a hitter and first baseman that Sisler found his place in the record books. In 1920 he enjoyed one of the greatest seasons a hitter has ever known—a major league record of 257 hits, 49 doubles, 18 triples, 19 home runs, 122 RBI, 137 runs scored, 42 stolen bases, and a .407 batting average that won him his first of two hitting crowns. Two years later he had a 41-game hitting streak on his way to 246 total hits and an amazing .420 batting mark. His average was the eighth highest ever recorded in baseball history. The Ohio native became the first winner of the newly created Most Valuable Player award in the American League in 1922.

Sisler's arrival in the American League rearranged baseball history in another way, too. As a minor Sisler is said to have signed a contract with Akron of the Ohio-Pennsylvania League. Akron sent his contract to the Columbus team, and Pittsburgh of the Federal League bought up Sisler's contract. Meanwhile, Sisler's father had signed him up to play with the St. Louis Browns. Young Sisler wanted to play with the Browns, where his old college coach Branch Rickey was business manager. The contract mix-ups were settled by the old three-member National Commission, who ruled in favor of the American League Browns.

During the first half of his career, Sisler compiled some of the most impressive batting statistics in the history of the game. Although in his first eight seasons he averaged .367, his lifetime numbers would have been even higher had a bad sinus condition not affected his vision—forcing him to miss the entire 1923 season. Sisler returned to the Browns in 1924 and was named player/manager, serving the team through 1926. His best success as a manager came with the 1925 Browns, who finished the season in third place with 82 wins and 71 losses. Sisler's totals in three years of major league managing included 218 wins and 240 losses for a .475 winning percentage.

Sisler was sold to the Washington Senators before the 1928 season for $25,000. He batted just .245 there and was sold to the Boston Braves for $7,500. Although he never regained his previous form, Sisler had three straight .300-plus seasons for the National Leaguers—the best was his 1929 campaign, when he batted .326 with 205 hits, 2 homers, and 79 RBI. His final season was as player/manager for Shreveport of the Texas League. There he hit .287 in 70 games before retiring as a player.

Sisler had two sons who played in the major leagues. Dick Sisler was a first baseman/outfielder for eight years, gaining fame as a member of the 1950 Philadelphia Phillies. Dave Sisler pitched for seven years during the 1950s, earning 38 lifetime wins and 29 saves.

George Sisler was a hitting coach for the Brooklyn Dodgers in 1943 and 1946 through 1950. He took over a similar job in Pittsburgh, which he held from 1951 to 1966. Sisler earned his membership in the Hall of Fame in 1939. He died two days after his 80th birthday in 1973 in St. Louis, the town he had starred in for so many years.

During his rookie season, George Sisler was tried as a hurler. Though he split his 8 decisions, one was a 2-1 victory over Walter "The Big Train" Johnson. In Sisler's only game against Detroit, Ty Cobb remained hitless in 5 attempts.

CAREER HIGHLIGHTS
GEORGE HAROLD SISLER

Born: March 24, 1893 Manchester, OH **Died:** March 26, 1973
Height: 5'11" **Weight:** 170 lbs. **Batted:** Left **Threw:** Left
First baseman: St. Louis Browns, 1915-27; Washington Senators, 1928; Boston Braves, 1928-30. Manager: St. Louis Browns, 1924-26.

★ Won two A.L. batting titles
★ Topped 200 hits six times
★ Established a major league record with 257 hits in 1920

★ Batted over .400 twice
★ Elected to the Hall of Fame in 1939
★ Led the A.L. in stolen bases four times

MAJOR LEAGUE TOTALS

G	AB	H	BA	2B	3B	HR	R	RBI	SB
2,055	8,267	2,812	.340	425	164	101	1,284	1,175	375

ENOS SLAUGHTER

Enos "Country" Slaughter was a player from the old school—a tough, hustling competitor who played baseball for the sheer love of the sport, doing whatever was necessary to score a run. During Slaughter's final season in baseball, one writer observed, "If he ever runs out of gas, there won't be any more like him." The statement proved to be prophetic—when Slaughter retired after his 1959 season with the Milwaukee Braves, an era of baseball retired with him.

Slaughter was signed by the St. Louis Cardinals in 1934. A sportswriter had spotted Slaughter playing ball on a North Carolina semipro team and had contacted scouts with the Redbirds. Slaughter refined his batting skills by cutting down on strikeouts during his three years in the minor leagues. In 1937 with Columbus of the American Association, Slaughter won the loop minor league batting crown with a .382 mark. He beat Don Padgett out of a job and became St. Louis' starting right fielder in 1938. During his rookie season, he hit .276 with 8 homers and 58 RBI in 112 games.

In his sophomore season of 1939, Slaughter batted .320. His 52 doubles (a career high) led the National League. His homer total climbed to 18 in 1940, when he batted .306. When Stan Musial joined the Cardinals at the end of the 1941 season, the team was becoming one of the strongest in the league. Slaughter racked up 13 homers, 98 RBI, and a .318 average to complement league-leading totals of 188 hits and 17 triples.

The Cardinals beat the favored Yankees in four out of five games in the 1942 World Series. In the second game Slaughter doubled in the eighth inning and scored on a single by Musial for the winning run. In the top of the ninth Slaughter squelched a Yankee rally by throwing out a runner trying to go from first to third on a single. In the decisive fifth game Slaughter contributed a solo homer in the Redbirds 4-2 win. For the Series Slaughter batted .263.

For the next three seasons, Slaughter was busy with military service in the Air Corps. Because he worked as a physical education instructor and played many exhibition games against other branches of the service, Slaughter stayed in good shape for his 1946 return to the Cardinals. In a career-high 156 games, Slaughter was better than ever for St. Louis. He hit career highs in homers (18) and RBI (a league-best 130).

The North Carolina native earned a lasting place in baseball history during the 1946 World Series. The Cards beat the Boston Red Sox in seven games as Slaughter hit .320. In one game he scored the winning run in the eighth inning after starting the rally with a single. Slaughter broke with the pitch to steal second when Harry "The Hat" Walker was at the plate. Walker singled to left center, and Slaughter kept on going around the bases in what's known as the "Mad Dash." Startled Red Sox shortstop Johnny Pesky took the cutoff throw from the outfielder and hesitated before throwing home. Running all the way, Slaughter slid in easily with the winning run. Slaughter later said he thought he could have scored on Sox outfielders earlier in the Series but hadn't challenged their arms. He told Cardinals manager Eddie Dyer that he wouldn't pass up another opportunity to

score, and he made the most of every chance.

Slaughter also hustled in the outfield (the only position he ever played in the majors); twice he topped the league in assists and double plays. In 1953, his last year in the Cardinals outfield, he led the loop with a .996 fielding percentage. His lifetime fielding percentage was .980.

Besides compiling a .300 lifetime average, the hustling veteran had an array of other impressive accomplishments in his 19 major league seasons. During his first 13 years in St. Louis, Slaughter gained solid footholds in several of the team's all-time offensive categories. Only Lou Brock and Stan Musial have surpassed Slaughter's 1,751 games. He ranks second in RBI with 1,148 (trailing only Stan Musial); third in Cardinal triples (135); fourth in at-bats (6,775), runs (1,071), hits (2,064), and total bases (3,138); and eighth in home runs (146). His average doesn't reflect the uncanny ability he displayed in making constant contact with pitches. Slaughter struck out just 538 times in his career. He appeared in ten All-Star games and played for five World Series teams (four of them world champions). If Slaughter hadn't lost three vital years to military service, he might have come much closer to 3,000 career hits and gained more immediate recognition in Cooperstown.

After coaching baseball at Duke University from 1961 to 1977, Slaughter retired to Roxboro, N.C., where he operates a tobacco plantation. He was elected to the Hall of Fame in 1985—more than a quarter of a century after he showed baseball fans the true meaning of the word hustle.

CAREER HIGHLIGHTS
ENOS BRADSHER SLAUGHTER

Born: April 27, 1916   Roxboro, NC
Height: 5'10"   **Weight:** 180 lbs.   **Batted:** Left   **Threw:** Right
Outfielder: St. Louis Cardinals, 1938-53; New York Yankees, 1954-55, 1956-59; Kansas City Athletics, 1955-56; Milwaukee Braves, 1959.

* ★ Compiled a .300 lifetime batting average
* ★ Played in five World Series
* ★ Played in 10 straight All-Star games, batting .381
* ★ Batted over .300 in 10 seasons
* ★ Elected to the Hall of Fame in 1985
* ★ Scored the winning run with his famous "Mad Dash" in the 1946 World Series

MAJOR LEAGUE TOTALS

G	AB	H	BA	2B	3B	HR	R	RBI	SB
2,380	7,946	2,383	.300	413	148	169	1,247	1,304	71

Enos Slaughter summed up his life in baseball, "A guy got in my way, I run over him. If they knocked me down at the plate, I said nothin'. You can't steal first base but if they hit me, I'm on first. And if you don't get on first, you can't score a run."

LEE SMITH

Baseball fans with an eye for finesse may have noticed a change in Boston Red Sox reliever Lee Smith. For much of his 14 years in professional ball, the righthander was a fireballer. His fastball would chew a path across the outside of home plate, while Smith recovered from the aftershock of his release.

This was five years ago, when Smith's heater flared at close to 100 mph. Still clocked at more than 90, his heat has nonetheless cooled, and like so many players who suddenly find themselves in their thirties, Smith has been forced to develop a second pitch, work on his curve and his change-up, and acquire some finesse. In short, the thrower has become a pitcher. And while Smith the thrower probably wouldn't have lasted much past his thirtieth birthday, Smith the pitcher may have another good decade in that right arm of his.

The first decade of Smith's career was memorable but unpredictable. Smith's 234 saves as of 1989 rank him among the top 10 relievers in history, and it's easy to forget that Smith needed six years to become an overnight success.

It's no wonder the Cubs nurtured Smith in their farm system for almost six years. He had been selected in the second round of the 1975 free-agent draft fresh from high school, where he had posted a 7-1 mark with an 0.95 ERA his senior year. The 6-foot-5 Smith had also been an All-State selection as a basketball player. Smith took two years to earn a winning season in the minors. At Pompano Beach in 1977, Smith was 10-4 as a starter. In 1979, his second season with Midland, Smith won 9 games. However, the Louisiana native's ERA was above 4.00 for a fourth straight year, and his walks still outnumbered his strikeouts. In 1980, his sixth minor league season, Smith found his calling in his new role as a reliever. He saved 15 games and won 4 more before getting his long-awaited call-up from the Cubs. In 18 games in Chicago, Smith went 2-0 in 22 innings.

Once bullpen ace Bruce Sutter was traded from the Cubs stable, Smith inherited the role of team stopper. He made 40 relief appearances in 1981, recording a 3-6 record with 1 save. All 3 of Smith's wins happened at Wrigley Field. Smith, at age 24 and with only 1 major league save, was at a career crossroads in 1982. If he didn't succeed

in his new role, he couldn't very well start over again in the minors. But succeed he did, with 17 saves and 2 wins in 72 appearances with a 2.69 ERA. His earlier control problems were gone. He struck out 93 in 117 innings, compared to just 37 bases on balls. During the last three months of 1982, only 4 earned runs were scored off the Cub flamethrower. Smith even got his first hit that year—a home run off Atlanta Braves knuckleballer Phil Niekro.

Smith shared Fireman of the Year honors with Philadelphia's Al Holland in 1983. He earned a league-leading 29 saves along with 4 wins and a 1.65 ERA. Smith only blew 3 save opportunities all season long, while batters hit just .194 against him. He got his first All-Star nod in 1983.

Back-to-back seasons of 33 saves came in 1984 and 1985. Smith won a career high of 9 games in 1984 and got at least 1 save off of every club. The Cubs shocked the baseball world by winning the Eastern Division pennant in 1984, partly because of Smith's clutch

relief. The Padres stopped the Cubs from World Series contention in the National League Championship Series. Smith got 1 save in the N.L.C.S. but suffered a fourth game loss on a two-run homer by Steve Garvey that won the game. Smith increased his save totals from 31 in 1986 to a personal best of 36 in 1987.

On December 8, 1987, the Cubs traded Smith to the Boston Red Sox for hurlers Al Nipper and Calvin Schiraldi. For the Cubs the trade was a major disappointment. Schiraldi missed nearly a month on the disabled list and finished with a 9-13 mark. Nipper, meanwhile, won just 2 games and was released after the 1988 season ended.

Smith, however, became the motivating presence that gained Boston the division title—adding 4 wins, 29 saves, and 96 strikeouts in 83.2 innings to Boston's title drive. Smith was able to pitch in two A.L. Championship Series games agains the Oakland A's, but the Sox weren't staking him to his usual leads to protect in the late innings. As a result, Smith would up 0-1 with an 8.10 ERA.

The Red Sox and Smith aren't through yet, however. The towering relief specialist seems to have found a new lease on life in the American League, and he should be bailing Boston out of jams for many years to come.

As relief pitcher Lee Smith approached thirty, his fastball—once clocked at close to 100 mph—began to slow down. The competent hurler adjusted by developing his curveball and a change-up.

CAREER HIGHLIGHTS
LEE ARTHUR SMITH

Born: December 4, 1957   Jamestown, LA
Height: 6'5"   **Weight:** 220 lbs.   **Bats:** Right   **Throws:** Right
Pitcher: Chicago Cubs, 1980-87; Boston Red Sox, 1988-89.

- ★ Topped the N.L. with 29 saves in 1983
- ★ Won the 1987 All-Star game
- ★ Shared *The Sporting News* Fireman of the Year award in 1983
- ★ Earned 30 or more saves in four seasons
- ★ Appeared in two All-Star games
- ★ Participated in two League Championship Series

MAJOR LEAGUE TOTALS

G	IP	W	L	Pct.	SV	SO	BB	ERA
586	835	50	57	.467	234	836	334	2.96

515

OZZIE SMITH

The Wizard of Oz of children's literature made everything look easy. So does the Wizard of the baseball world—Ozzie Smith. He fields almost flawlessly at shortstop, switch-hits with surprising ability, and steals with deceptive ease. He even has a name outside the ballpark as a decent, upstanding, and well-dressed guy.

Exactly how much of this success is talent and how much is hard work, the world may never know. All that matters is that Smith keeps producing year after year. The exuberance that the Redbirds long-time shortstop has brought to the game is worth its weight in Gold Gloves. He is as famous for his nasty double plays as he is for his joyous pre-game backflips as he emerges from the dugout and trots out to his position in the field. The Cardinals management prohibits Smith's pre-game ritual now, in order to prevent unnecessary injury, but the exuberant Oz still sneaks one in on special occasions—championships and the like—and has taught his son Ozzie, Jr. the trick on a trampoline.

Despite his now legendary sleight of hand on the field, Smith was not exactly a whiz kid. This was a matter of choice; he did not sign a pro contract until age 22 because he wanted to finish college first. The San Diego Padres picked him up in the fourth round of the June 1977 draft, and he finished that year with Walla Walla. His Northwest League bests came in at-bats (287), runs (69), assists (254), double plays (40), stolen bases (40), and fielding percentage.

Ozzie started 1978 as San Diego's regular shortstop. In 159 games he attracted attention with his 40 stolen bases, his league-leading 28 sacrifice hits, and his second-place finish in Rookie of the Year balloting. He began work on a set of statistics that seemed miraculous. He registered 548 assists—the first of a record eight seasons he'd tally 500 or more assists at shortstop. He improved his fielding average and continued to do so until he broke the record for shortstops by leading the loop for six seasons. One of the greatest plays of Smith's career came against Atlanta in April. When Jeff Burroughs scorched a grounder up the middle, Smith dived to his left. As the ball bounced up, he grabbed it barehanded and threw the Braves slugger out at first.

Smith fanned only once in every 17.54 at-bats and led National League shortstops in 1979 with 555 assists. He batted only .230 in 1980 but gained

fame by winning his first Gold Glove. Smith also stole 57 bases, making him and Padres Gene Richards and Jerry Mumphrey the first trio of teammates in National League history to have 50 steals apiece in a single season. In 1981 Smith played his last year in San Diego. Playing in every game of the season, he led the league in at-bats and three defensive categories. His February 11, 1982, trade to the Cardinals for Garry Templeton benefited both Smith and St. Louis. Smith hadn't been happy with his pay in San Diego.

Smith played so well that the Cardinals signed him to a four-year contract extension worth over $8.7 million in 1985. He hit .276 that year with a career-high 6 homers. His home run in game five of the League Championship Series (his first in more than 3,000 lefty at-bats) gave the Cards a 3-2 win against the Dodgers. His 1987 season—with a .303 average, a career-

high 182 hits, and 75 RBI—placed him second in the league's Most Valuable Player balloting. In 1988 Smith matched a career high with 57 steals. However, he slumped (as did most of the Cardinals) to .270 after his previous .300-plus performance in 1987. Smith did continue his fielding mastery by winning his ninth Gold Glove in a row. Although Smith's shoulder isn't what it used to be, he compensates for any lost ability by a cunning sense of timing and a style of throwing that doesn't unduly torture his arm.

Smith's outgoing off-the-field personality will provide him with a bright future once his baseball days are over. He has already earned national attention with his biography, called *Wizard*. In 1987 a video company produced a documentary on Smith's life called *Ozzie—The Movie*. Smith (along with such personalities as TV show host Johnny Carson) was named one of the ten best-casually-dressed men in 1982 by a panel of California fashion experts. His latest contract calls for him to receive primary consideration for a wholesale beer distributorship from the Busch family (who own the Cardinals as well).

Smith already ranks third in Cardinals history in games played at shortstop and in career stolen bases. He may never pump his career batting average up past .300, but he's going to surpass the impressive 2,000-hit barrier maybe as quickly as 1991. Regardless of his future hitting accomplishments, Smith's ticket to a future Hall of Fame membership will be earned with his amazing defense, which ranks him as one of the best in baseball history.

CAREER HIGHLIGHTS
OSBORNE EARL SMITH

Born: December 26, 1954   Mobile, AL
Height: 5'11"   **Weight:** 150 lbs.   **Bats:** Both   **Throws:** Right
Shortstop: San Diego Padres, 1978-81; St. Louis Cardinals, 1982-89.

★ Won nine straight Gold Gloves
★ Set an N.L. record for a six-game championship series with a .435 average and 10 hits in 1985
★ Has a cumulative .469 batting average for N.L.C.S. play in 1982 and 1985

★ Played in three World Series
★ Tied a major league record by leading the N.L. in fielding percentage for four straight years
★ Fielded a record 500-plus assists at shortstop for eight seasons

MAJOR LEAGUE TOTALS

G	AB	H	BA	2B	3B	HR	R	RBI	SB
1,783	6,507	1,668	.256	276	51	18	849	550	432

Defensive mastermind Ozzie Smith has already won nine straight Gold Glove awards. He fielded a record 500-plus assists at shortstop for eight seasons and tied a major league record by leading the N.L. in fielding percentage for four straight years.

REGGIE SMITH

Reggie Smith has to be one of the most overlooked stars of the 1970s. He spent a total of 17 years as a hard-hitting outfielder with four teams: the Boston Red Sox, the St. Louis Cardinals, the Los Angeles Dodgers, and the San Francisco Giants. He demonstrated a talent for switch-hitting home runs that was rivaled only by Mickey Mantle.

Smith went to Centennial High School in Compton, California, earning All-State honors in football (as a quarterback and halfback) and in baseball. He even threw with either hand during his days as a prep school athlete. His teammates then included Bobby Tolan, Bob Watson, and pitcher Don Wilson. The Houston Astros invited Smith to nearby Dodger Stadium for a tryout during his senior year of 1963. The tryout was held on the field before the game with the Astros and Dodgers. Smith didn't get a contract out of the audition, but he did keep one lasting memory. "I was just a kid trying to make the best impression I could," he said. "I was throwing as hard as possible on the sidelines when one throw got away from me. Sandy Koufax was hitting fungoes to the outfielders and my throw missed his head by less than three inches."

The Louisiana-born Smith was signed as a shortstop by the Minnesota Twins organization, then was drafted by the Boston Red Sox. During his first season in 1963, Smith played for Wytheville of the Appalachian League. The strong-armed youngster led all shortstops with 41 errors, but he was also tops in the league with 146 assists. In 1964 with Waterloo of the Midwest League, Smith divided his time between third base and the outfield. His hitting improved to 15 homers and 60 RBI with a .318 average. He proved his major league worthiness in 1966 in Toronto with a banner year, winning the International League batting title with a .320 effort. Smith continued to strengthen his long-ball prowess, achieving 30 doubles, 9 triples, 18 homers, and 80 RBI. He spent six games with the Red Sox near the season's end.

Smith's official rookie season came in 1967—an opportune time for the BoSox, as they won their first American League pennant in more than two decades, partly because of the offensive punch added by Smith's presence. In 158 games Smith stroked 15 homers and 61 RBI, batting .246. The Red Sox lost a tough seven-game battle to the St. Louis Cardinals in the World Series. In his first post-season action, Smith hit .250. Of his 6 hits, 1 was a double and 2 were homers. Despite his success, he was nosed out of the Rookie of the Year award by another promising Minnesota Twins newcomer named Rod Carew.

The next season Smith poked a league-leading 37 doubles to complement his .265 average. Smith bloomed as a hitter in 1969, posting 25 homers, 93 RBI, and a .309 record. He got his first of seven All-Star game invitations that year. His average stayed above .300 in 1970, but dipped a bit in 1971. The drop was more than compensated for by Smith's 30 homers and 96 RBI. His 33 doubles gave him his second league lead in two-base hits. Although he hit 21 home runs in 1972 and in 1973, batting .303 that latter season, Smith was traded with pitcher Ken Tatum to the St. Louis Cardinals in exchange for Rick Wise and Bernie Carbo on October 26, 1973. Smith hit above .300 during both of his two full seasons in St. Louis. He had a career high of 100 RBI in 1974. His 23 homers in 1974 and 19 in 1975 were team highs for the Redbirds.

The Dodgers obtained Smith in mid-1976, giving the Cardinals catcher Joe Ferguson and two minor leaguers. He finished out 1976 in Los Angeles, hitting 10 homers and 26 RBI in 65 games. Smith's sterling season in 1977 led the Dodgers all the way to the World Series. He hit a career-high 32 home runs that season, batting .307. Although the Dodgers lost the World Series to the Yankees, Smith paced his team with 3 homers and 5 RBI. He hit 29 dingers with 93 RBI and a .295 average in 1978. An injured shoulder required surgery in 1979 and cut the rest of his career short. Even though he became a free agent and hit 18 homers with the Giants in 1982, Smith's abilities had dwindled after the injury. He ended his career after a brief stint in the Japanese League.

Smith's career statistics include 2,020 hits in 1,987 games for a .287 average. Of those hits, 363 were doubles, 57 were triples, and 314 were home runs. Smith drove in 1,092 runs in his 17 years in the majors, scoring 1,123 runs of his own. His career slugging percentage is .489. He spent 1,668 games in the outfield and played 186 games at first base. Brief appearances at third base, second base, and designated hitter round out Smith's career. Smith's 314 homers are ranked second in history for switch-hitters—behind only Mickey Mantle. Without a great deal of fanfare, Smith handled both offensive and defensive tasks with grace.

CAREER HIGHLIGHTS
CARL REGINALD SMITH

Born: April 2, 1945   Shreveport, LA
Height: 6'0"   **Weight:** 180 lbs.   **Batted:** Both   **Threw:** Right
Outfielder, first baseman: Boston Red Sox, 1966-73; St. Louis Cardinals, 1974-76; Los Angeles Dodgers, 1976-81; San Francisco Giants, 1982.

★ Topped the .300 mark in seven seasons
★ Had double-figure homer totals in each of his 15 full seasons
★ Played in four World Series, hitting 6 homers
★ Led the A.L. in doubles twice
★ Hit 20-plus homers eight times (including six seasons in a row)
★ The second-greatest switch-hitting homer hitter in history

MAJOR LEAGUE TOTALS

G	AB	H	BA	2B	3B	HR	R	RBI	SB
1,987	7,033	2,020	.287	363	57	314	1,123	1,092	137

Though Reggie Smith batted over .300 in seven seasons, belted over 20 homers in eight seasons, and was the second-greatest switch-hitting homerun slugger in baseball, he has been largely overlooked by historians and fans.

DUKE SNIDER

It was an argument that began in the early 1950s and lasted for years: Which New York center fielder was the best in baseball? Was it the Yankees Mickey Mantle, the Giants Willie Mays, or the Dodgers Duke Snider?

Of course the debate was never settled. Even though Mantle and Mays gained a slight edge in fame because their careers lasted longer than Snider's did, all three are enshrined today in the Baseball Hall of Fame. Actually, Snider accomplished something neither Mays nor Mantle could match: The Brooklyn star clubbed 40 or more home runs for five straight seasons. From 1953 to 1957 Snider was the premier slugger in the National League. During his 18 years in the major leagues, the Duke hit a total of 407 home runs and is the all-time leader among the Dodgers.

Snider batted .300 or better on seven occasions and finished his career with a .295 lifetime average. He was also a graceful center fielder who had an exceptionally strong and accurate throwing arm. The Dodgers superstar played in six World Series, establishing National League records for most home runs (11) and most RBI (26) in postseason competition. In 1955, when the Brooklyn Dodgers won their only world championship, Snider was at the forefront. He hit 2 homers in the fifth game to give Brooklyn a 5-3 victory. Snider finished the Series with 4 homers, 5 runs scored, 8 hits, and a .320 average.

Snider, who was given the nickname "Duke" as a youngster, was signed to a minor league contract with the Dodgers organization as soon as he graduated from high school in 1944. The Dodgers gave Snider a signing bonus of only $750. His pro baseball career (after just one minor league season) was interrupted by a stint in the U.S. Navy during World War II (including nearly an entire year on a submarine). After the war Snider played in only 40 games before he was sent back down to the minors. After playing part of the 1948 season with Montreal of the International League, Snider was brought to Brooklyn to become the Dodgers starting center fielder in 1949. Carl Furillo moved from center field to right field to accommodate the talented newcomer. In his first full season Snider batted .292 with 23 home runs and 92 RBI for the 1949 club. When his hair turned gray early in his career, Snider was dubbed "The Silver Fox."

Few people remember that Snider almost won the pennant for the Brooklyn Dodgers in 1950, except that the Philadelphia Phillies "Whiz Kids" team notched a last-day win over the favored Brooklynites. With Cal Abrams on second base in the ninth inning and the score tied 1-1, Snider was at bat. Phillies center fielder Richie Ashburn had crept in close to second base to back up a possible pickoff play. Hurler Robin Roberts missed the sign, pitching instead to Snider. The Duke drove a sharp single to center. This would have been the game-winning (and pennant-winning) RBI, except that the drawn-in, out-of-position Ashburn was close enough to throw out Abrams trying to score. A 10th-inning homer by Dick Sisler won the pennant for the Phils.

While Snider was Brooklyn's offensive spark plug in the 1950s, his best seasons came in 1953 through 1956. In those first three years Snider topped the league in runs scored (including a career high of 132 in 1953). His homer

totals stayed above 40 during those seasons, including a league-best 43 in 1956. The year before, Snider won his only RBI crown with a personal best of 136 tallies.

Snider appeared on a part-time basis in the 1959 World Series, when the Los Angeles Dodgers beat the Chicago White Sox. Snider had a two-run homer in the Series, but he hit just .200. He also injured a knee, which helped shorten his career. Snider was limited to just 101 games in 1960 (hitting .243 with 14 home runs). A broken elbow in 1961 further plagued his offense. After Snider's short seasons in 1961 and 1962, the Dodgers sold their beloved slugger to the New York Mets. The Mets, started in 1962, were one of the worst teams in baseball. Adding Snider gave them some class and hopes of boosting attendance, if not winning a few games. Snider was a rare bright spot in the team's gloom. He played in 129 games—the most he had logged since 1957. Snider hit .243 with 14 homers and 45 RBI. The Duke finished his career in 1964 with the San Francisco Giants, the team he battled for years in those celebrated New York crosstown rivalries. Snider hit .210 as a pinch hitter and backup outfielder.

Following his retirement as a player, Snider became involved in several business ventures, including an avocado ranch. The California native served three years as a minor league manager, then scouted for the Dodgers and Padres. He became known to a whole new generation of fans by serving as a broadcaster for the Montreal Expos starting in the mid-70s. Snider was elected to the Hall of Fame in 1980.

CAREER HIGHLIGHTS
EDWIN DONALD SNIDER

Born: September 19, 1926 Los Angeles, CA
Height: 6'0" **Weight:** 180 lbs. **Batted:** Left **Threw:** Right
Outfielder: Brooklyn Dodgers, 1947-57; Los Angeles Dodgers, 1958-62; New York Mets, 1963; San Francisco Giants, 1964.

★ Batted .300 or better seven times

★ Hit 40 or more homers for five straight seasons

★ Topped the N.L. in runs scored three years running

★ Elected to the Hall of Fame in 1980

★ Collected 26 RBI and 11 home runs in World Series play

★ Led the N.L. in slugging percentage twice

MAJOR LEAGUE TOTALS

G	AB	H	BA	2B	3B	HR	R	RBI	SB
2,143	7,161	2,116	.295	358	85	407	1,259	1,333	99

Among his other accomplishments, Duke Snider was a remarkable postseason player. In 36 World Series games, Snider belted 11 home runs, racked up 26 RBI, and had a .594 slugging percentage.

WARREN SPAHN

itcher Warren Spahn didn't win his first contest in the majors until he was a 25-year-old rookie in 1946, but he went on to record 363 victories—more than any other left-hander.

For most of his career, which began when the Braves were still in Boston, Spahn was the most consistent, dependable hurler in baseball. He won 20 or more games 13 times, a record surpassed only by the immortal Cy Young. He led the league in victories eight seasons, including an amazing stretch from 1957 to 1961 when he topped the circuit five years in a row. He was a model of durability who led the league in complete games eight times. He pitched a no-hitter at age 39 and another at age 40. At age 42, in 1963, the big lefthander was still throwing hard enough to compile a record of 23 wins and 7 losses, with 22 complete games and a 2.60 ERA.

Perhaps none of this is surprising if the biographical information available on "Spahnie" is true. He had an idyllic childhood, encouraged every step of the way by his father. A wallpaper salesman, Edward Spahn played catch with Warren every spare moment. When taking his son to a professional game, he would draw the youngster's attention to the individual and team strategies being effected, encouraging the lad to try such mechanisms on his sandlot teams. Under his father's persistent tutelage, Spahn soon found himself playing on his dad's amateur team, digging his spikes into the ground so the force of the ball wouldn't knock him down.

Spahn's initial inclination was for first base, but even in high school he found himself outmatched. When he switched to pitching, no one could touch him, and by age 19 he was on the road to the majors. The Boston Braves signed him in 1940; that year he had a 2.73 ERA and struck out 62 in 66 innings.

The next year in Evansville, Spahn went 19-6 and posted the incredible ERA of 1.83. At the end of 1942 he received his call-up. After four games he was drafted into military service.

Wounded by shrapnel (which he described as "a scratch on the foot"), Spahn received both a Purple Heart and a Bronze Star. He was quoted as saying that he got the award only because "all of the officers were killed."

Spahn returned to baseball in 1946 as if he had never been away, earning a 2.93 average that year and a 21-win season the next. This was the first of

three such winning seasons, and Spahn's prowess led the Braves to an unsuccessful bid for the world crown in 1948. Even so, the contributions of Spahn and the Braves only other star pitcher, Johnny Sain, led their teammates to create the hopeful chant, "Spahn, Sain, and two days of rain."

The feared lefty had only one losing season from 1946 to 1963. In 1952 Spahn began to lose the "stuff" off his fastball. To add fuel to the fire, the Braves management was threatening to relocate, which distressed all of the players. Spahn dealt with what was under his control and acquired new pitches to complement his fading fastball. Pitching "every game like a no-hitter" and always throwing to "the two inches on each side of the plate," Spahn expanded his knowledge of batters and waged psychological guessing games, teasing them into becoming "hungry hitters."

Spahn was a good-hitting pitcher who was occasionally used as a pinch hitter. In 1958, when the Milwaukee Braves won their second of two consecutive National League pennants, Spahn's .333 batting average (36 hits in 108 at-bats) was the highest on the club. He earned a lifetime average of .194 with 363 hits and 35 home runs.

The durable hurler amassed some impressive lifetime totals. Beside his lifetime wins (fifth highest in history) and numerous 20-win seasons, Spahn racked up 63 career shutouts, which rank sixth on the all-time list. He led the league in innings pitched four times and hurled 5,246 frames in his career (seventh best in history). He logged 382 complete games in 665 starts and finished with 29 career saves. Adding his saves and wins together, that means that Spahn played a part in nearly 400 wins during his career. His win totals would be far above the 400 mark if he hadn't been forced to delay his career for three years due to military service during World War II.

Spahn was elected to the Hall of Fame in 1973 while he was a pitching coach for the Cleveland Indians. His post-career activities included managing Tulsa from 1967 to 1970 and capturing the 1968 championship of the Pacific Coast League. After one year of scouting and minor league coaching for the Cardinals, Spahn spent two years with the Indians (1972-73). His last year in baseball was 1978, when he coached a minor league team for the California Angels. He has since devoted himself to Oklahoma cattle ranching and perfecting his swing on the golf course.

CAREER HIGHLIGHTS
WARREN EDWARD SPAHN

Born: April 23, 1921   Buffalo, NY
Height: 6'0"   **Weight:** 172 lbs.   **Batted:** Left   **Threw:** Left
Pitcher: Boston Braves, 1942-50; Milwaukee Braves, 1953-64; New York Mets, 1965; San Francisco Giants, 1965.

★ Won the Cy Young award in 1957
★ Earned four league strikeout crowns
★ Pitched in three World Series
★ Won 363 games—more than any other lefthander

★ Was a 20-game winner 13 times
★ Earned three N.L. ERA crowns
★ Elected to the Hall of Fame in 1973
★ Led the N.L. in complete games and wins eight times

★ Set an N.L. record for home runs by a pitcher with 35

MAJOR LEAGUE TOTALS

G	IP	W	L	Pct.	SO	BB	ERA
750	5,246	363	245	.597	2,583	1,434	3.08

Warren Spahn won more games than any other lefthand hurler. He won the Cy Young award when he was 36 and pitched a 23-7 season at age 42. Stan Musial once said, "I don't think Spahn will ever get into the Hall of Fame. He'll never stop pitching."

TRIS SPEAKER

Tris Speaker was such a tremendous center fielder that even though he finished his career with a .344 lifetime batting average, baseball historians invariably mention his defensive skills first. It's easy to see why he was among the first three outfielders elected to the Hall of Fame—preceded only by Babe Ruth and Ty Cobb.

Speaker played so shallow in center field that he almost dared batters to try to hit one over his head. Each time a batter hit, he would race back to make the catch. That unique talent, combined with his strong arm, made him the best defensive center fielder of his era.

Known as the "Gray Eagle," Speaker was raised on the plains of Texas. As a ten-year-old boy he was thrown from a bronco, badly breaking his right arm and his collarbone. To compensate for the injuries, the naturally right-handed Speaker batted and threw left for the rest of his days.

Speaker came up to the Boston Red Sox in 1907. By 1909 he was the Red Sox starting center fielder. He was obtained by the Red Sox from Houston of the Texas League in 1907 at the bargain price of $400. Speaker began his pro career as a pitcher because lefties were valued even back then. During his first season with Cleburne of the North Texas League in 1906, he lost 6 straight without a single victory. After his last setback (a 22-4 loss), everyone knew Speaker's future was at another position.

During his 19 full seasons in the majors, Speaker only once failed to bat over .300. In 11 of those years he batted over the .340 mark, 5 times topping .380. Ty Cobb had won nine batting titles in a row; it was Speaker who finally broke his streak with a league-leading .386. He won the American League Most Valuable Player award (then called the Chalmers award, because an automobile made by that company was presented to each year's winner) in 1912, when he collected 222 hits on his way to a .383 batting mark. Led by Speaker the Red Sox won world championships in 1912 and 1915. Speaker topped the 1912 Sox with a .300 World Series batting average, which included 9 hits, 4 runs scored, and 2 RBI. The Red Sox won the 1915 World Series quietly, earning three 2-1 wins and a 5-4 clinching victory. Speaker hit .294 with 5 hits to help earn the championship.

The Red Sox had one of the swiftest, hardest-hitting outfields in baseball, with

Speaker flanked by Harry Hooper and Duffy Lewis. Probably in a derivation of his last name, Speaker earned "Spoke" as another nickname. When Speaker objected to having his pay cut by the Red Sox after the 1915 World Series win, he was traded to the Cleveland Indians for "Sad Sam" Jones, Fred Thomas, and $55,000.

The native Texan played with the Indians from 1916 to 1926. In 1919 he became a player/manager for the Tribe. Just one year later he sparked the team to a world championship against the Brooklyn Dodgers. During the regular season Speaker hit a blistering .388 with a league-leading 50 doubles, 8 home runs, 107 RBI, and 137 runs scored. He drew 97 bases on balls but struck out just 13 times in 552 at-bats. (During his entire career, Speaker struck out just 220 times.) In the World Series, the Indians defeated Brooklyn 5-2. Speaker hit .320 in the affair, winning the sixth game 1-0 on a sixth-inning RBI single. As a manager, Speaker piloted his team to second-place finishes in both 1921 and 1926. He finished his managerial career with a 616-520 record in eight seasons.

Speaker's pro career ended with a two-year stint as a player/manager with Newark of the International League. Even past age 40, Speaker could still hit with gusto. In 1929 he batted .355 in 48 games. His final average in 1929 was .419 in 11 games. In 1931 he served as a baseball broadcaster for a Chicago radio station, becoming one of the first ex-players to share his years of experience with fans. In 1932 he became part-owner and manager of the Kansas City franchise in the American Association.

When Speaker retired in 1928, he had accumulated 3,514 hits, including a record 793 doubles—still tops on the all-time list. His record of 448 assists, 7,461 chances accepted, and 6,794 putouts is still the best among all American League outfielders. Only Ty Cobb, Willie Mays, and Hank Aaron played more games in a major league outfield than Speaker. Speaker holds one of the most incredible records in defensive history: 139 double plays, 32 more than Cobb, the only other outfielder ever to "turn two" more than 100 times in a career.

Tris Speaker holds one of the most amazing records in baseball history. He participated in 139 double plays—32 more than Ty Cobb—during his 19 full seasons in the major leagues.

CAREER HIGHLIGHTS
TRISTAM E SPEAKER

Born: April 4, 1888 Hubbard, TX **Died:** December 8, 1958
Height: 6'0" **Weight:** 193 lbs. **Batted:** Left **Threw:** Left
Outfielder: Boston Red Sox, 1907-15; Cleveland Indians, 1916-26; Washington Senators, 1927; Philadelphia Athletics, 1928. Manager: Cleveland Indians, 1919-26.

★ Led the league with 130 RBI in 1923
★ Batted over .300 in 18 seasons
★ Played in three World Series
★ Holds the record for assists and putouts by an A.L. outfielder
★ Led the A.L. in hits twice
★ Led the A.L. in batting in 1916
★ Elected to the Hall of Fame in 1939
★ Holds a major league record with 793 career doubles

MAJOR LEAGUE TOTALS

G	AB	H	BA	2B	3B	HR	R	RBI	SB
2,789	10,207	3,514	.344	793	223	117	1,881	1,528	433

WILLIE STARGELL

One of the most popular players to ever wear a Pirates uniform, Willie Stargell played 21 seasons for Pittsburgh, providing the power that led to six division titles and two world championships.

Stargell made his debut in the majors in 1962. He grew up in California and attended Santa Rosa Junior College, playing for the collegiate team briefly before signing with the Pirates by way of a $1,200 bonus. Previously, he had served four years in the Pirates minor league organization, where he showed constant improvement. In 1961 with Asheville of the Sally League, Stargell blasted 22 homers and 89 RBI, batting .289. The next season with Columbus of the International League, he smacked 27 home runs and 82 RBI to complement a .276 batting average. By season's end he earned a ten-game debut with Pittsburgh. His official rookie season came in 1963. In 108 games playing both as an outfielder and first baseman, Stargell batted .243 with 11 homers and 47 RBI.

One of the most significant seasons Stargell had came in 1979, his 18th year with the Pirates. By then Stargell was called "Pops" by the younger players, who often turned to him for guidance. During Pittsburgh's 1979 world championship season, Stargell was the father figure who united his team into a family. The team even adopted Sister Sledge's hit tune "We Are Family" as their theme song. The record was constant background music in the Pirates locker room as Stargell went through his postgame ritual of handing out tiny gold stars to reward outstanding individual performances by his teammates. The players displayed their gold stars proudly on their caps, and many of the team members looked like decorated war veterans. With Stargell as their captain, the Pirates played with enthusiasm down the stretch and into the World Series.

Stargell was rewarded for his contributions by winning a share of the 1979 Most Valuable Player award for the National League. That year the award was given jointly to Stargell and St. Louis Cardinal Keith Hernandez. Stargell was honored as much for his intangible contributions as he was for his on-field performance. His 32 home runs were only the fifth highest in the National League in 1979, and that was the only offensive category in which he finished in the top five.

The Oklahoma native was fresh in the minds of baseball writers after his memorable achievements in postseason play. Stargell won the first game of the National League Championship Series against the Cincinnati Reds with an 11th-inning three-run homer. In the three-game sweep of the Reds, Stargell batted .455 with 2 homers and 6 RBI. When the Pittsburgh "family" faced the Baltimore Orioles in the World Series, a seven-game battle ensued. The Pirates, after trailing in the Series three games to one, battled back to win the Series. In the seventh game the Pirates trailed 1-0 before a two-run homer by Stargell put the team on top to stay. He was awarded Most Valuable Player honors in both the Championship Series and the World Series. His 1.182 slugging percentage in the N.L.C.S. established a record, as did his 7 long hits and 25 total bases in the World Series.

Stargell also had a banner season in 1971, leading the Pirates to their first world championship against the Orioles. That year he hit .295 with a league-leading 48 home runs and 125 RBI. In the World Series Stargell managed just 5 hits for a .205 average. Probably the best all-around season of Stargell's career came in 1973, when he led the senior circuit in home runs (44), doubles (43), RBI (119), and slugging percentage (.646).

The 6-foot-2 power slugger finished his career in 1982. His lifetime totals include 475 homers (tying Stan Musial on the all-time list), 1,540 RBI, 2,232 total hits, and a .282 batting average. The Pirates' record book looks like Stargell and former Pirate slugger Ralph Kiner split it down the middle. While Kiner was the team's most notable righthand power hitter, Stargell gets the nod from the left side. Stargell's home runs, RBI, and extra-base hits (953) are all team records. His home run totals are obscured by his many years in Pittsburgh's cavernous Forbes Field. The lefthand powerhouse is remembered in the Steel City for slugging 7 homers out of the huge stadium. Stargell's tape-measure blasts weren't limited to home games. He's the only player ever to hit a ball out of Dodger Stadium. Stargell did it twice, hitting a 506-foot shot in 1969 and a 470-foot dinger in 1973.

In 1988 Stargell became the 17th player in history to be elected into the Hall of Fame during his first year of eligibility. Stargell served as an Atlanta Braves coach with his old Pittsburgh manager Chuck Tanner from 1986 to 1988. The Pirates honored Stargell in 1982, the year he retired, by retiring his uniform number (8). He was the fifth player in Pirates history to earn the distinction.

CAREER HIGHLIGHTS
WILVER DORNEL STARGELL

Born: March 6, 1940 Earlsboro, OK
Height: 6'2" **Weight:** 188 lbs. **Batted:** Left **Threw:** Left
First baseman, outfielder: Pittsburgh Pirates, 1962-82.

- ★ Shared the N.L. MVP award in 1979
- ★ Drove in 100-plus runs five times
- ★ Named N.L. Comeback Player of the Year in 1978
- ★ Led the N.L. in homers twice
- ★ Played in seven All-Star games
- ★ Elected to the Hall of Fame in 1988

MAJOR LEAGUE TOTALS

G	AB	H	BA	2B	3B	HR	R	RBI	SB
2,360	7,927	2,232	.282	423	55	475	1,195	1,540	17

In 1979 Willie Stargell shared N.L. MVP honors with Rickey Henderson. Though Stargell's stats were not remarkable, the award honored his role as team leader. With his encouragement and example, the Pirates pushed their way to the World Series.

RUSTY STAUB

If a prerequisite for fame as a major league baseball player is a snappy nickname, Daniel Joseph Staub was blessed almost from birth. When he was born in New Orleans, Louisiana, on April 1, 1944, nurses at the hospital dubbed the child "Rusty" for his auburn hair. While many athletes have to find big league fame before getting a notable label, Staub got the nickname first and then the fame.

Staub was the type of dependable ballplayer who performed solidly and consistently year after year, without fanfare and out of the spotlight. After his career was over, though, the record books showed that Staub was a great ballplayer.

Staub is one of just a dozen players who performed in the major leagues for 23 or more seasons. During his career, which spanned from 1963 through 1985, he stroked 2,716 base hits, including 499 doubles and 292 home runs. He drove in 1,466 baserunners and scored 1,189 times himself. He batted over .300 five times, including a .333 mark in 1967, and he finished his long career with a .279 lifetime batting average. He is the only major leaguer in history to gain more than 500 hits with four different ballclubs. Staub even shares a record with the immortal Ty Cobb—they are the only two players in history to hit home runs before their 20th and after their 40th birthdays.

Toward the end of his career with the New York Mets, Staub served primarily as a pinch hitter. He was the best batsman off the bench that any team could wish for. Just knowing that Staub might make a late-inning plate appearance seemed to intimidate opponents of the Mets. Staub's lifetime pinch-hitting average was .279. In 1983 Staub collected 24 pinch hits in 81 at-bats (for a .296 average). He fell just one shy of the single-season mark for pinch hits, but he tied a major league record with 25 pinch-hit RBI. His 18 pinch hits and 18 RBI led the National League for the second straight year in 1984. In 1985, his final season, Staub topped the Mets with 11 pinch hits. His 100 career pinch hits rank him 11th on the all-time list.

Staub, who spent just two seasons in the minors, played in his first major league game with the Houston Colt .45s in 1963 at the age of 19. He shuttled between first base and the outfield with Houston, then was traded to the Montreal Expos in 1969. There he became a national hero. Fans called him "Le Grande Orange" in tribute to his reddish hair and his success in Canada. He batted .302 with 29 homers and 79 RBI in 1969, then knocked in 94 runs with the aid of 30 round-trippers in 1970.

Staub served two terms with the Mets, the first coming in 1972 through 1975. New York traded Tim Foli, Ken Singleton, and Mike Jorgensen to obtain Staub on April 5, 1972, from the Montreal Expos. Staub had an average debut season in the Big Apple. In 1973 Staub and all his teammates played beyond all expectations and quietly snatched the Eastern Division title with an 82-79 record. Staub batted .279 with 15 home runs and a team-leading 76 RBI. In the outfield Staub was at his best, leading the league with 5 double plays. Although he made 7 errors, he gunned down 17 baserunners during the season. In the 1973 League Championship Series, he had just 3 hits (for a .200 batting average), but each hit was a home run. He led the Mets with 5 RBI as the team scrambled out of the five-game N.L.C.S. and advanced to the World Series against the Oakland A's. The Louisiana native led all regulars from both teams with 11 hits and a .423 batting average in the seven-game affair. He single-handedly won the fourth game for the Mets 6-1 with a three-run homer, 3 singles, and 5 RBI.

Staub hit 19 homers in both 1974 and 1975. In the latter season he surpassed 100 RBI for the first time. The Detroit Tigers obtained Staub prior to the 1976 season for hurler Mickey Lolich. In Detroit Staub got his first idea of what professional pinch hitting was like from his full-time duty as a designated hitter. Staub was named as a starter to the American League All-Star team for his banner 1976 debut in the junior circuit. He ended the season with 15 homers, 96 RBI, and a .299 average. Working exclusively as a designated hitter in 1977, Staub clubbed 22 homers and 101 RBI. He hadn't cleared the 20-homer barrier since 1970. The American League voted Staub Outstanding Designated Hitter in 1978, when he appeared in all 162 games, batting .273 with 24 homers and a personal best of 121 RBI.

Since his retirement as a player, Staub has become a successful restauranteur. He has also served the Mets as a spring training instructor and scout. In 1989 he broadcasted Mets games for a cable TV outlet. In 1986 he and Bud Harrelson became the first players to be elected into the Mets Hall of Fame.

CAREER HIGHLIGHTS
DANIEL JOSEPH STAUB

Born: April 1, 1944   New Orleans, LA
Height: 6'2" **Weight:** 190 lbs.   **Batted:** Left   **Threw:** Right
First baseman, outfielder: Houston Colt .45s/Astros, 1963-68; Montreal Expos, 1969-71, 1979; New York Mets, 1972-75, 1981-85; Detroit Tigers, 1976-79; Texas Rangers, 1980.

* Named to six All-Star teams
* Reached double digits in homers 13 times
* Played in the major leagues for 23 seasons

* Led the N.L. in doubles in 1967
* Batted .423 (11 for 26) in the 1973 World Series
* Hit major league homers before his 20th and after his 40th birthday

MAJOR LEAGUE TOTALS

G	AB	H	BA	2B	3B	HR	R	RBI	SB
2,951	9,720	2,716	.279	499	47	292	1,189	1,466	47

Rusty Staub was a member of the original Montreal Expos. Canadian fans, ecstatic to have a major league team, dubbed Staub "le Grande Orange" because of his red hair. Staub was so enthusiastic about the Expos, he took French lessons.

RIGGS STEPHENSON

Few people would claim that Riggs Stephenson was the greatest hitter who ever lived. After all, his 14-year career featured only six seasons with more than 100 games played. Because of a bad throwing arm from a childhood accident, Stephenson was never in great demand as a major leaguer. (In those days, defense was a main ingredient on any team.) But when he did play, Stephenson could really hit up a storm.

Stephenson could have been a great designated hitter; however, in the 1920s he needed a full-time position in the field, too. Although he was a banner hitter—as high as .371 in part-time duty in 1924—he couldn't stick in the starting lineup because of his throwing problems. He was sent to the minors in 1925 to learn how to play the outfield. It was there that he was plucked off the Indianapolis roster the following year.

Aside from his final part-time season with the Chicago Cubs in 1934, Stephenson was a perennial .300 hitter. He didn't get a full-time starter's job with a team until 1927 at the age of 29. Once he did get in the starting lineup, his batting average soared. Hall of Fame manager Joe McCarthy took over the reins of the Chicago Cubs in 1926. Having seen Stephenson play ball back in the minors, he tried to convert him from second base to the outfield. McCarthy liked what he saw and insisted that the Cubs acquire the 185-pounder as a starter.

Stephenson didn't disappoint his new skipper. He batted above .300 for the next eight seasons; his lowest average from 1926 to 1933 was .319. With Stephenson in left, Kiki Cuyler in right field, and Hack Wilson in center, the Cubs had one of the most offensively potent outfield trios in baseball history. Stephenson batted in the fifth position on a team that featured the likes of first baseman Charlie Grimm, second baseman Rogers Hornsby, and catcher Gabby Hartnett. The media dubbed the club the "North Side Murderers' Row."

After batting .338 in 1926, the first year the Cubs discovered the 28-year-old outfielder, Stephenson increased his success at the plate in 1927. He played in 152 games, hitting .344 (his highest average thus far) with a league-leading 46 doubles. Stephenson collected career highs in games, doubles, and runs scored (110). Under McCarthy, Stephenson prospered as a hitter, and the Cubs flourished as National League contenders. In 1928 Stephenson batted

.324. He hit 8 home runs and had 90 RBI. As usual Stephenson maintained his traditional 2-to-1 ratio of walks versus strikeouts.

In 1929 the Cubs won the National League pennant. A career-best season by Stephenson was one reason why the Cubs finished at the top of their league that year. He batted .362 that year, finishing fifth in the National League batting race behind champion Lefty O'Doul of Philadelphia, who hit a league-leading .398. He had never before matched his previous totals of 17 home runs and 110 RBI. His slugging percentage mushroomed to .562. Stephenson was active on the base paths as well, scoring 91 runs and stealing a personal best of 10 bases.

The Cubs were defeated in that year's World Series by the Philadelphia Athletics in five games. Stephenson had an admirable Series effort, batting .316 with 6 hits, 3 runs scored, and 3 RBI. With the whole Cub team batting a combined .249, Stephenson's mark looks even better.

Although the 1932 Chicago Cubs won another league pennant, they had

less success against the American League rival New York Yankees than they did with their 1929 opponents. The mighty Bronx Bombers shelled the Cubs in four straight games, winning by scores of 12-6, 5-2, 7-5, and 13-6. Stephenson was a rare bright spot in the Cubs' postseason gloom. He batted .444 against New York, getting 8 hits in 18 at-bats, with 4 RBI and 2 runs scored.

Injuries started catching up with Stephenson in 1933. He got into just 97 games and batted .329 with 4 home runs and 51 RBI. In 1934 a hobbled Stephenson appeared in only 38 games before calling it quits. His average plummeted to .216, and he had no homers and just 7 RBI.

Stephenson's major league totals include 1,515 hits in 1,310 games for a career batting average of .336. His batting mark is the 18th-highest lifetime total in baseball history. Of his total hits, 321 were doubles and 54 were triples. A tribute to Stephenson's keen batting eye is his lifetime strikeout totals. He struck out just 247 times in 4,508 official at-bats, but he drew 494 bases on balls.

Stephenson was active in organized baseball through 1939. He spent the 1935 season at Indianapolis in the American Association. In Birmingham during the next two seasons, he served as player/manager and accumulated winning records. After a year managing Helena, Montana, and another season at Montgomery, Alabama, Stephenson left pro baseball.

Stephenson returned to his native state of Alabama for his retirement years. He died of heart failure in Tuscaloosa, Alabama, on November 15, 1985, at the age of 87.

CAREER HIGHLIGHTS
JACKSON RIGGS STEPHENSON

Born: January 5, 1898 Akron, AL **Died:** November 15, 1985
Height: 5'10" **Weight:** 185 lbs. **Batted:** Right **Threw:** Right
Outfielder, second baseman: Cleveland Indians, 1921-25; Chicago Cubs, 1926-34.

* ★ Led the N.L. in doubles in 1927
* ★ Drove in a career high of 110 runs in 1929
* ★ Batted over .300 in 12 seasons
* ★ Had a .407 batting average as a pinch hitter in 1930
* ★ Hit .367 for the 1930 Cubs

MAJOR LEAGUE TOTALS

G	AB	H	BA	2B	3B	HR	R	RBI	SB
1,310	4,508	1,515	.336	321	54	63	714	773	54

The Chicago Cubs flourished after acquiring Riggs Stephenson in 1926. The Cubs had
been in the cellar the previous year, but with Stephenson's powerful bat, they steadily
improved. In 1929 they won the N.L. pennant.

MEL STOTTLEMYRE

Mel Stottlemyre has been making baseball in New York City exciting for more than a quarter of a century. He has had the luck and the talent to participate in the game from many different vantage points.

He has served both leagues—as a pitcher for the American League Yankees and as a pitching coach for the National League Mets. His ability to adapt to the rigors of coaching is surprising, because his own solid playing career ended with a rotator cuff injury. Now he coaches others to be masters of no hits, low hits, shutouts, and saves.

His career is not the sort to raise eyebrows, because Stottlemyre was a picture of consistency. He turned in 3 to 4 shutouts a year without batting an eye. He could be counted on for well over 100 strikeouts in a season, along with well under 100 walks. He even clouted 7 home runs in his career and posted a .200 or higher batting average twice.

He signed his first pro contract in 1961, at the age of 20. During his first season with Harlan in the Appalachian League, he had 5 wins and 1 loss for an .833 winning percentage. In eight games, his ERA was a tidy 3.12. He had 61 strikeouts (and just 15 bases on balls) in 49 innings, posting a 4-to-1 ratio of Ks-to-walks.

In 1962 he was with Greensboro of the Carolina League. Stottlemyre led the league in innings pitched with 241, and he won 17 and lost 9. His ERA was down to 2.50. Stottlemyre struck out 190 opposing hitters, the highest strikeout total he'd ever post in a single season. In 1963 Richmond of the Triple-A International League welcomed him, and he hurled for a 7-7 record with a 4.05 ERA. Still with Richmond in 1964, Stottlemyre was 13-3 and carved his ERA to an all-time low of 1.42. His 6 shutouts were tops in the circuit. He was named Minor League Player of the Year by *The Sporting News* and was the International League Most Valuable Pitcher.

Stottlemyre was called up to New York for a 13-game tryout late in the 1964 season. He continued on his tear, with 9 wins and 3 losses for the New York Yankees, compiling a .750 winning percentage and a 2.06 ERA in 96 innings of work.

The Bronx Bombers claimed the American League pennant that year with young Stottlemyre's assistance. He appeared in three of the seven closely fought World Series games against the St. Louis Cardinals. He took game two

with a complete-game effort, allowing only 3 runs and 7 hits throughout. The 6-foot-1 rookie successfully battled St. Louis ace Bob Gibson. Stottlemyre's Yankees staged a four-run ninth-inning rally to claim an 8-3 victory. Stottlemyre appeared again four days later in game five. This time Gibson went the distance while Stottlemyre lasted just seven innings, leaving the game with a 2-0 deficit. The Cardinals touched Yankee pitching in extra innings for a 5-2 win. He was active three days later in game seven, starting and pitching four innings. In the fourth inning the Cardinals mounted a three-run outburst. After Stottlemyre left the game, St. Louis upped the final score to 7-5, taking the title away from the once proud American Leaguers. Stottlemyre's ERA for the Series was 3.15. In 20 total innings, he gave up 18 hits while walking 6 and striking out 12.

The Yankees were happy enough with Stottlemyre's previous performance to use him more than any other pitcher in the junior circuit in 1965. With 291 innings Stottlemyre posted his first 20-win season, losing 9 and striking out 155 (the most he ever struck out in the big leagues). He led the American League with 18 complete games that year and was named as a pitcher on *The Sporting News* American League All-Star team.

Stottlemyre, a three-time 20-game winner, pitched in seven opening-day games with the Yankees. He finished his career with a record of 164-139.

One of Stottlemyre's most lasting achievements in baseball happened off the field. He has inspired two of his sons, both righthand pitchers, to try to follow his path to glory. Mel Jr. is on the 40-man roster for the Kansas City Royals. Todd is on the 40-man roster for the Toronto Blue Jays. The elder Stottlemyre was the pitching coach on the major league All-Star team that toured Japan in 1986. He currently runs Stottlemyre Athletic Stores in Washington State and is a member of the Sports Committee for the Leukemia Society of America. Most impressively, Stottlemyre has helped mold the Mets pitching staff into one of the strongest hill corps of the 1980s.

Though Missouri native Mel Stottlemyre did not enjoy a lengthy career, he managed to throw 40 shutouts and pitch three 20-win seasons. The righthand hurler also set an A.L. record with 272 consecutive starts.

CAREER HIGHLIGHTS
MELVIN LEON STOTTLEMYRE

Born: November 13, 1941   Hazelton, MO
Height: 6'1" **Weight:** 178 lbs.   **Batted:** Right   **Threw:** Right
Pitcher: New York Yankees, 1964-74.

- ★ Threw 40 shutouts during his career
- ★ Set an A.L. record with 272 consecutive starts (since surpassed by Tiger John Morris)
- ★ Selected for five A.L. All-Star teams
- ★ Totaled three 20-win seasons

MAJOR LEAGUE TOTALS

G	IP	W	L	Pct.	SO	BB	ERA
360	2,662	164	139	.541	1,257	809	2.97

DARRYL STRAWBERRY

As the decade of the '80s began, the Miracle Mets were just a footnote in the New York team's proud history. The once perennial contenders of the late 60s and early 70s had faded into the annals of the National League. No longer miraculous, the Mets needed a miracle.

One of the team's loudest prayers had to be for a home run hitter. The 1982 club finished in last place in the Eastern Division even though Met Dave Kingman led the league with 37 round-trippers. He was a defensive liability and an unhappy camper who would be dropped from the roster after one more season. Outfielder George Foster was there, but he was just a ghost of his former self after hitting 13 homers in 1982.

Enter Darryl Strawberry—a tall, thin youngster full of purebred power. The lanky outfielder was dubbed "The Straw Man." However, he appeared to be the savior the Mets were dreaming of. With a unique combination of speed and muscle, Strawberry gave the Mets offensive credibility.

Strawberry made his debut in 1983 in New York, one year before the arrival of another miraculous rookie—pitcher Dwight Gooden. Strawberry's call-up was celebrated enthusiastically by a city hungry for a winning season, since the touted minor league veteran had clubbed a league-leading 34 home runs in 1982 for Jackson and had batted .333 in just 16 games with the Triple-A Tidewater team.

Strawberry's first major league at-bat was against the Cincinnati Reds man-eating hurler Mario Soto, who made short work of the Mets new kid. The aftershock left Strawberry scared hitless for a week and nearly hitless for a month afterward.

He was benched one month after his call-up and taken under the ample wing of Jim Frey, then a New York coach (now in the Chicago Cubs front office). Frey advised him on individual pitchers' peculiarities and also encouraged Strawberry's natural instincts as a power hitter, convincing him that striking out was no disgrace.

Strawberry returned to bat .313 over the last 54 games of the season. His season's end mark was .257, and through 1989 he had yet to close anywhere close to .300. Perhaps he never will, but with his youth and the strength of his numbers, who cares? The 27-year-old has hit more than 25 home runs yearly since his promotion, posting 39 homers in 1987 and leading the league with that number in 1988. In each of these two seasons, he also topped 100 runs and 100 RBI, besting the circuit in 1988 with his .545 slugging percentage. His base larcenies have always come in double digits, with a to-date high of 36 in 1987. Strawberry shows promise of putting his homers and steals together to become an eventual "40/40" man.

His natural ability and serious approach to the unfamiliar role of "public figure" left both fans and media unprepared for the yo-yo-like qualities of Strawberry's figures. His fielding average has been in the .970s for the past three years, but he occasionally throws too high or to the wrong base. He'll go days (or weeks) with dismal batting before suddenly going on a tear. He doesn't always hit well when there are runners on base. Yet when the heat is really on, Strawberry does come through.

He has been through two League Championship Series, one World Series, and five All-Star games without an error in the field. He notched a solo homer in the 1986 Series, and in the 1988 League Championship Series he batted .300 with 6 RBI.

He has been getting better every season—taking more walks and improving his once negligible power against lefthand pitchers. In 1984 the 1983 Rookie of the Year was treated to a "Strawberry Sunday" at Shea Stadium, where thousands of ice-cream-eating fans watched him receive his award.

At the beginning of that season, teammate Mookie Wilson had observed that, as a rookie, Strawberry had wanted "to do everything by himself." Wilson added that if Mets pitching improved, "watch out for us in '85." His prediction was entirely correct. In 1985 New York was second in its division; in 1986 it was first. The next year it was second again; the year after, first.

Strawberry once said that he has been able to lead by example. Many of his best examples are from the story of his life. He had been a baseball-zoned young man coached by neighbors who replaced his estranged father. He was a "skinny, frail" scholarship winner who pumped iron to better his game. He grew into a lonely young player who called home collect every day of his first minor league season. He has changed his running style and his batting style. He has learned to handle the press, and has told them he wants the game to stay fun.

Let's hope that it does, because if Strawberry's having fun, we're all in for a good time.

CAREER HIGHLIGHTS
DARRYL EUGENE STRAWBERRY

Born: March 12, 1962 Los Angeles, CA
Height: 6'6" **Weight:** 190 lbs. **Bats:** Left **Throws:** Left
Outfielder: New York Mets, 1983-89.

* Named Rookie of the Year in 1983
* Drove in 90-plus runs four times
* Batted .300 in the 1988 N.L. Championship Series
* Led the N.L. with 39 homers in 1989
* Appeared in the 1986 World Series
* Played in his sixth straight All-Star game in 1989

MAJOR LEAGUE TOTALS

G	AB	H	BA	2B	3B	HR	R	RBI	SB
957	3,361	875	.260	169	29	215	570	625	176

Home run slugger Darryl Strawberry continued his assault on the ball in 1989 with a season total of 29 home runs. Strawberry led the N.L. in home runs in 1988 with 39, the same number he had belted a year earlier.

BRUCE SUTTER

Call him Bruce, even though his name is Howard. Like kung-fu legend Bruce Lee, relief artist Bruce Sutter always comes back for one more battle—no matter how high the obstacles are stacked against him.

He missed a chunk of the 1985 season with shoulder problems, which multiplied into a four-month absence in 1986. His third surgery, to correct a torn rotator cuff in 1987, took him out of commission for that entire season. He started the 1988 campaign a reconstructed man, with a new shoulder and a new knee. "Bionic Bruce" was 35 years old.

In professional baseball being 35 often means you're on your last leg. Unfortunately for righty Sutter, he is on his last arm, too. Yet he made a comeback in 1988. Despite his 1-4 record and 4.76 ERA, Sutter notched 14 saves. He saved the best for last; his 14th save put his lifetime total up to 300, making him third on the all-time list.

The righthander's split-fingered fastball is still intact despite the surgery. Sutter is an unrefuted master of the sharp-sinking "pitch of the 1980s." Sutter could be called the reliever of the 80s. Most of those years have been good ones for Sutter. He was originally selected by the Washington Senators in the 21st round of the free-agent draft in June 1970, when he was only 16 years old. He passed on the chance, instead signing with the Cubs as a minor league free agent in 1971. He labored in the Cubs farm system for four years, tying for the Texas League lead with 13 saves in 1975. For three of his minor league seasons, Sutter's ERA remained at 1.50 or less.

He made his debut with the Cubs on May 9, 1976, in one frame of relief. He finished the year with 10 saves, 6 wins, 73 Ks in 83 innings, and a 2.71 ERA.

Sutter's success snowballed. In 1977 his ERA plummeted to 1.35, his saves went into orbit at 31, and for the first time he whiffed more than 1 batter per inning (129 in 107 IP). On September 9, in a game against Montreal, he set a record as he fanned 6 consecutive players and struck out the side on just 9 pitches. With 1.2 innings of hitless relief, he won the All-Star game that season.

If his 1977 stats were memorable, his 1979 stats were breathtaking. Named Cy Young award winner, *The Sporting News* Fireman of the Year, and a National League All-Star, Sutter

backed up his awards with monumental accomplishments: 37 saves, 6 victories, a second All-Star game victory, and a 2.23 ERA in 62 games. For the last of three consecutive years, he topped the 100-strikeout plateau (at 110) with more than 1 K per inning. Sutter, who had previously won a large salary arbitration and had irked the team ownership, was traded to the St. Louis Cardinals for third baseman Ken Reitz, first baseman Leon Durham, and Tye Waller on December 22, 1980.

Starting in 1979 Sutter led the National League in saves for four straight years. Sutter played a major role in the 1982 world championship earned by the Cardinals. During the regular season he had 38 saves and 9 victories (playing a part in more than half of the team's wins). His ERA was only 1.54. In the 1982 National League Championship Series against Atlanta, he had a win and a save, allowing just 1 hit and no runs in 4.1 innings of work.

In the seven-game World Series against the Milwaukee Brewers, Sutter had 1 victory and a pair of saves. In 1984 Sutter achieved a National League record with 45 saves for the Cardinals.

On December 7, 1984, Sutter signed a big-money six-year deal with the Atlanta Braves. In 1985 he claimed his ninth straight 20-save season—the longest streak in baseball history. Even with time on the injury list, he was personally responsible for almost half of Atlanta's wins. However, his shoulder problems were showing, as his ERA soared to 4.48.

Sutter was used sparingly in 1988, seldom pitching in consecutive games. He still proved to be attentive defensively and effective on pickoff moves. His competitiveness remained, as he fanned 40 in 45 innings.

A reinjured rotator cuff greeted Sutter in 1989 spring training. The Braves started Sutter on the 60-day disabled list, hoping that the courageous veteran could make one more comeback. Their hopes were dashed, however, as Sutter announced his retirement at the end of the 1989 season. Despite the injuries that prevented a longer career, Sutter's varied achievements should gain him eventual membership in the Hall of Fame.

Bruce Sutter made a successful comeback to the Atlanta Braves pitching staff in 1988 after missing two seasons because of an injury. The comeback was short-lived, however, as Sutter retired in 1989.

CAREER HIGHLIGHTS
HOWARD BRUCE SUTTER

Born: January 8, 1953   Lancaster, PA
Height: 6'2"   **Weight:** 190 lbs.   **Batted:** Right   **Threw:** Right
Pitcher: Chicago Cubs, 1976-80; St. Louis Cardinals, 1981-84; Atlanta Braves, 1985-88.

- ★ Won the 1979 Cy Young award
- ★ Set an N.L. record with 45 saves in '84
- ★ Made a successful 1988 comeback after missing nearly two seasons due to injury
- ★ Has a 2-0 mark in four All-Star games
- ★ Led the N.L. in saves five times
- ★ Struck out six consecutive batters in 1977

MAJOR LEAGUE TOTALS

G	IP	W	L	Pct.	SV	SO	BB	ERA
661	1,040	68	71	.489	300	861	309	2.84

DON SUTTON

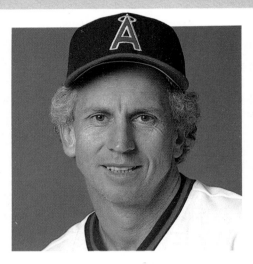

In 1988 Don Sutton's distinguished career finished its trip around the bases. Although the journey had taken nearly a quarter of a century to complete, Sutton ended where he had begun—with the Los Angeles Dodgers.

When the California Angels let him go in 1987, Sutton was 43 years old and already musing about a front office position with a team or a future in sports broadcasting. But the Dodgers offered him a spot, and Sutton found it hard to resist notching an additional year wearing Dodger Blue, making his total service to the Los Angeles team 16 years.

Some of those years were stupendous: 1969, with Sutton's career-high 217 strikeouts; 1972, when his major league ERA shrank to an all-time low of 2.08 while he compiled a record of 19 wins and 9 losses with a .679 winning percentage; 1976, when he registered 21 wins for the first and only time in his career; or 1980, his farewell to the Blue Crew with a loop-leading ERA of 2.21.

Some years, even with strong Dodger teams behind him, were horrendous: From 1966 to 1969 Sutton lost 13 straight games to the Chicago Cubs, setting an all-time record; in 1968 he tied for the N.L. lead in balks—a paltry three—laughable by modern standards; and in 1980, before his Dodger curtain call, Sutton established a record for most consecutive homers allowed within an inning.

These negative stats give Sutton human qualities, but they don't begin to show the full accomplishments of his career. Sutton lasted in the major leagues for 23 years with the assistance of determination and hard work. For 19 of his 23 seasons, Sutton posted winning records. Year by year, with little fanfare, Sutton marched slowly to 300 victories. In addition he holds the records for the most years and the most consecutive years with 100 or more strikeouts (21). He tied the modern National League record for most one-hit games in a lifetime (5). He has started eight World Series games in four different series. Sutton also has a 1-0 mark in All-Star competition. He won the 1977 contest by pitching three scoreless innings, allowing only 1 hit while striking out 4.

Sutton's finest year in postseason play came in 1974. The Alabama native earned his tenth straight win of the season with a 3-0 win in the opening game of the National League Championship Series against the Pittsburgh Pirates. Sutton personally clinched the National League pennant for the Dodgers with eight strong innings in the decisive fourth game. In eight innings he gave up only 3 hits (one a solo homer by Willie Stargell) as the Dodgers rolled to a 12-1 win. The Oakland A's beat the Dodgers in a five-game World Series. Sutton won the team's only game with an eight-inning effort in game two.

Sutton helped the Dodgers return to the World Series in 1977. He was 14-8 during the regular season. In the National League Championship Series he won the second game against Philadelphia with a nine-hit 7-1 victory. In the World Series against the Yankees, the Dodgers were toppled in six games. Sutton had a fine Series, pitching seven strong innings in the first game (but leaving in a 2-2 tie, thus getting no decision). In game five Sutton submitted a complete-game win in a 10-4 slugfest.

Following the 1980 season Sutton became a free agent. When asked about his long-time faithfulness to the Dodgers, Sutton jokingly replied, "I'm the most loyal player money can buy." The Houston Astros signed Sutton to a three-year, $1.2 million contract. He was traded to the Milwaukee Brewers in late 1982 and helped pitch the team to its first American League pennant. Sutton had one of the team's Championship Series wins against the Angels. In 1985 and 1986 with Oakland and then the California Angels, Sutton earned consecutive 15-win seasons, his best effort since 1978. On June 18, 1986, Sutton won his 300th career game against the Texas Rangers.

His final season back with the Dodgers ended on a sad note. After going 3-6, he was on the disabled list from June 29 to August 9. Sutton was given his unconditional release on August 10. He was cut in order to make room on the roster for rookie pitcher Ramon Martinez. Two days later Sutton's mother was killed in a car accident.

Sutton finished his career with 324 victories. He was the 19th player in history to attain the coveted 300-win plateau. Sutton ranks fourth in career strikeouts (3,574), trailing only Nolan Ryan, Steve Carlton, and Tom Seaver. He is ranked in the top ten in virtually every all-time Dodger pitching category. Sutton has the top spot on the Dodger lists in wins, games, starts, strikeouts, shutouts, and innings pitched. He has bested both Hall of Fame teammates Don Drysdale and Sandy Koufax in these categories, which says something about Sutton's chances of making it to Cooperstown. He'll be eligible for Hall of Fame induction in 1994.

CAREER HIGHLIGHTS
DONALD HOWARD SUTTON

Born: April 2, 1945   Clio, AL
Height: 6'1"   **Weight:** 190 lbs.   **Batted:** Right   **Threw:** Right
Pitcher: Los Angeles Dodgers, 1966-80, 1988; Houston Astros, 1981-82; Milwaukee Brewers, 1982-84; Oakland Athletics, 1985; California Angles, 1985-87.

- ★ Pitched in four World Series
- ★ Belongs to the exclusive 300-win circle
- ★ Held a record with 100-plus strikeouts for 21 seasons
- ★ Has a 1-0 mark in four All-Star games
- ★ Had 200-plus strikeouts for five seasons
- ★ Shares an N.L. record for pitching five no-hitters

MAJOR LEAGUE TOTALS

G	IP	W	L	Pct.	SO	BB	ERA
774	5,282	324	256	.559	3,574	1,343	3.26

Don Sutton, who spent his glory years with the Los Angeles Dodgers, set team records in wins, games, starts, strikeouts, shutouts, and innings pitched. Sutton won 324 games in his career and pitched 100-plus strikeouts for 21 seasons.

KENT TEKULVE

Early in the 1989 season Cincinnati Reds reliever Kent Tekulve attained and left behind the all-time major league record for appearances as a pitcher. Hoyt Wilhelm had held the record at 1,018 for well over a decade. By the end of 1988, however, Tekulve was hot on his heels with 1,013 appearances. His quest for the record was only temporarily sidetracked when the Phillies released Tekulve at the conclusion of the 1988 season.

Because of his longevity, it is no surprise that Tekulve's role has changed from long stopper to middle relief. He appears in an average of 70 games per year but seldom for much more than an inning per game. His lifetime save totals put him near the top of the all-time list of major league save-masters.

Of course stats like that don't come easily. They came even less easily to Tekulve, who began his minor league career at the age of 22, after completing a bachelor's degree in physical education.

He was signed as a free agent in July 1969 by the Pittsburgh Pirate organization. He had time for nine games with Geneva of the New York-Penn League before the season ended and made good with 6 wins, 2 losses, and a 1.70 ERA. Despite these promising figures, Tekulve embarked on a career as a reliever; in 1970 he won only 10 decisions in 41 games, for a .400 percentage. His ERA was a healthy 1.94, however, until his winning season of 1971 with Salem of the Carolina League. His 3.48 ERA was offset by his 11-5 record.

Tekulve's time in the minors stretched into a seemingly infinite twilight zone, his statistics bouncing like ping-pong balls and dropping just as fast. Time at Sherbrooke and Charleston in 1972 produced a rise, then a steep drop in performance. Thus, all of 1973 was devoted to Sherbrooke, with encouraging results: league highs in games (57), wins (12), and winning percentage (.750), and all-time personal bests in strikeouts (89) and ERA (1.53).

The shift to Charleston came much more smoothly in 1974, with Tekulve maintaining a winning percentage and adding nominally to his ERA (2.25).

It had been five years since Tekulve entered organized baseball. He toiled yet another season in the Pirates minor league system with Charleston in 1974, pitching 35 more games with the Triple-A team. His constant improvements and his never waning determination finally got him a long-awaited debut with the Pittsburgh Pirates. In nine games he was 1-1 with a bloated 6.00 ERA. It was back to Charleston for a seventh season. His 1.77 ERA set the tone of another fine minor league season. Finally, at age 28, Tekulve was in the major leagues to stay. He finished the 1975 season in Pittsburgh, hurling in 34 games. He won 1 game, saved 5 others, and posted a 2.25 ERA.

Tekulve was ready to make his long-awaited mark in the majors. Using his distinctive submarine delivery, a low-slung motion that looks as though he popped out of a hole in the pitching mound, Tekulve became one of the busiest hurlers in baseball. His appearances climbed from 64 in 1976 to 72 in 1977. He led the National League in games pitched in 1978 and 1979 with respective totals of 91 and 94. From 1977 through 1979 he won a total of 28 games. After just 7 saves in 1977, he tallied career highs of 31 saves in the next two seasons.

The Pirates marched straight to the 1979 World Series with the aid of Tekulve's sure-fire relief. Pittsburgh nipped the Baltimore Orioles in seven hard-fought games. Tekulve got his first save in game two with a one-inning stint of scoreless relief. The Orioles tagged Tekulve with a loss in the fourth game, but the bespectacled pitcher got his revenge in the final two games of the Series. He tossed three shutout innings of relief in game six and nailed down the world championship with 1.2 innings of work to close out the seventh-game victory. In five appearances Tekulve had a 2.89 ERA in 9.1 innings of work. His 3 saves set a new World Series record.

Pittsburgh traded Tekulve to the Philadelphia Phillies in exchange for reliever Al Holland and minor leaguer Frankie Griffin on April 20, 1985. He proved that the Pirates were a bit hasty in shipping him out. In 1986, his first full season in Philadelphia, he won 11 games and saved 4 others. Tekulve, at age 40, led the National League for the fourth time in games pitched with 90 appearances in 1986.

The Phillies, hoping to revitalize their club for 1989, released Tekulve in favor of younger talent. The Cincinnati Reds quickly snapped up the free agent, who was born in Cincinnati, on March 5, 1947. But after a dismal 1989 season, Tekulve hung up his spikes. Whether or not he ever makes it to Cooperstown, Tekulve will be remembered as an exciting record-breaking hurler.

CAREER HIGHLIGHTS
KENTON CHARLES TEKULVE

Born: March 5, 1947   Cincinnati, OH
Height: 6'4"   **Weight:** 190 lbs.   **Batted:** Right   **Threw:** Right
Pitcher: Pittsburgh Pirates, 1975-85; Philadelphia Phillies, 1985-88; Cincinnati Reds, 1989.

* Holds major league record for most games pitched in relief
* Had consecutive seasons of 31 saves in 1978 and 1979
* Led the N.L. in appearances four times
* Holds N.L. record for most lifetime games finished
* Earned a record three saves in the 1979 World Series
* Named to 1980 All-Star team

MAJOR LEAGUE TOTALS

G	IP	W	L	Pct.	SV	SO	BB	ERA
1,013	1,384	94	87	.519	183	748	468	2.77

Kent Tekulve retired after the 1989 season, but not before he broke Hoyt Wilhelm's long-standing record of 1,018 lifetime appearances as a pitcher. Tekulve also holds the record for most games pitched in relief and most games finished.

BILL TERRY

Bill Terry, the last National Leaguer to bat over the magic .400 mark, almost gave up the game before ever making it to the majors. He was 27 years old when he became the New York Giants regular first baseman in 1925, but he quickly established himself as one of the top hitters in the league. During the four-year period from 1929 to 1932, Terry batted at a .368 clip, and youngsters everywhere were copying his stance and idolizing this soft-spoken hero.

Terry began his professional career in 1915 as a pitcher in the Georgia-Alabama League and after a season there moved to Shreveport of the Texas League. After stagnating in Texas for two years, Terry left organized ball in favor of a business career with an oil company in Memphis, where he continued on in semipro baseball for four years.

It was there that he was discovered and signed by Giants manager John McGraw, who was alerted to Terry while on his annual trip to Memphis. Terry batted .336 and .377 in two years in Toledo of the American Association before McGraw brought him up to the Giants.

Terry batted over the .300 mark in nine straight subsequent seasons. Six times he collected more than 200 hits, including his 1930 MVP year, when he rapped out 254 base hits on his way to a .401 batting average, the last time anyone batted over .400 in the senior circuit. Terry first faced World Series competition in 1924. He platooned at first base with George "High Pockets" Kelly (the man Terry would eventually replace as the Giants starting first sacker). In just 14 at-bats, Terry had 6 hits, including 1 triple, 1 homer, and 3 runs scored.

Terry's first shining season came in 1927. Firmly embedded in the starting lineup, the man known as "Memphis Bill" hit .326 with 20 home runs and 121 RBI. He also scored 101 runs. It was the first of six consecutive campaigns in which the 6-foot-1, 200-pound first baseman would pass the 100 mark in both runs and RBI. While Terry was never a concentrated power hitter, he still racked up five double-digit efforts in the homer department. During the 1930 season he achieved career highs of 129 RBI and 139 runs scored. His best year for four-baggers came in 1932, when he went deep 28 times. Terry's biggest accomplishment was the contact he made at the plate. He was

tough to strike out, fanning just 449 times in 14 years.

McGraw stepped down from his managerial post in the middle of the 1932 season after holding the same job for 29 years. Before leaving he named Terry as the new Giants skipper. So Terry pulled double duty, serving as both major league manager and starting first baseman.

As a manager Terry led his troops to three pennants in five years. The Giants were National League champions in 1933, 1936, and 1937. In nine years as manager, he had four teams that won 90 or more games. Terry's career managerial record was 823 wins versus 661 losses for a .555 winning percentage. In his first full year as Giants manager in 1933, the team did a dramatic turnaround. Only one year before the team was stuck in sixth place under Terry, with a 55-59 record. However, in

1933 the Giants won 91 and lost 61. That year Terry batted .322 with 6 homers and 58 RBI. He was 4 of 6 as a pinch hitter.

When the Giants moved to the World Series to pummel the Washington Senators in five games, Terry was a major factor in the team's championship. Not only did he provide strong leadership, but he swung a strong bat. Terry hit .273 in the Series with 6 hits, 1 homer, and 3 runs scored. His home run in the fourth game meant the difference in New York's 2-1 victory.

Terry was beaten by two games in the 1934 pennant race by the Brooklyn Dodgers. He was teased all season long about the comments he had made to newspapers in the spring. When asked if he was concerned about the ability of the crosstown rivals, Terry had responded mockingly, "Brooklyn? Is Brooklyn still in the league?" The Dodgers made him eat the words.

The Giants lost to the New York Yankees in the 1936 and 1937 World Series. Terry hit .240 in the 1936 fall classic (with a game-winning sacrifice fly) but didn't appear in 1937.

In his 14-year career Terry collected 2,193 hits (154 of them home runs) and compiled a .341 lifetime batting average. He still holds the Giants team record for highest batting average (.401), most hits (254), and most runs scored in a season (139 in 1930). On the Giants all-time list, he still ranks in the top ten for every offensive category except stolen bases. His uniform number (3) was retired by the team, making him one of only eight team members in history to receive such an honor.

Terry received the ultimate honor in 1954, election to the Baseball Hall of Fame.

CAREER HIGHLIGHTS
WILLIAM HAROLD TERRY

Born: October 30, 1898 Atlanta, GA **Died:** January 9, 1989
Height: 6'1" **Weight:** 200 lbs. **Batted:** Left **Threw:** Left
First baseman: New York Giants, 1923-36. Manager: New York Giants, 1932-41.

* Batted a league-leading .401 in 1930
* Hit .300 or better for 11 seasons
* Led the Giants to three World Series as player/manager
* Last N.L. player to hit .400
* Had 200 or more hits six times
* Elected to the Hall of Fame in 1954

MAJOR LEAGUE TOTALS

G	AB	H	BA	2B	3B	HR	R	RBI	SB
1,721	6,428	2,193	.341	373	112	154	1,120	1,078	56

Bill Terry's reputation for being blunt did not always make him popular with the press. But his reputation as player/manager for the N.Y. Giants was unblemished; he led his team to three pennants and one world championship.

SAM THOMPSON

A good many rookie players burst upon the scene, but very few make their big debut bursting at the seams. Outfielder Sam Thompson set such a precedent with his 1885 premiere. At 6-foot-2 and 207 pounds —far and away larger than most men of that era—Thompson could not be fitted properly with a uniform in time for his first appearance with the Detroit Wolverines of the National League. Ripping a triple in his first plate appearance, his trousers followed suit as he rounded second base. At season's end, however, his .303 batting average proved he was no flash in the pan.

Dubbed "Big Sam" as well as "The Marvel," Thompson was a prolific home run hitter in the difficult dead-ball era. In 1906 he stepped out of his seven-year retirement from the major leagues to play eight games with the Detroit Tigers at the age of 46. While the decimated Tigers were running low on healthy players and needed all the help they could get, critics accused the team of staging a publicity stunt to sell more tickets. Thompson, however, had 7 hits in his eight starts along with 1 triple, 4 runs scored, and 3 RBI, which isn't bad for any player after a seven-year absence from the majors.

From 1900 until 1907 Thompson played for the Detroit Athletic Club, often sparking enough interest to outdraw the attendance of the crosstown Tigers. He remained unflappingly loyal to his adopted city even after his retirement, attending games regularly and hosting a 1907 player reunion for his old Wolverine teammates.

Thompson's chance to shine came quickly, as he played less than two seasons of minor league baseball before joining Detroit. After serving with Evansville of the Northwest League in 1884 and Indianapolis of the American Association for most of 1885, he joined the Wolverines after his Indianapolis manager got the job in Detroit. He progressed up the ladder of success rapidly and easily. Playing part-time in 1885 in just 63 games, Thompson had 7 home runs and 44 RBI. He batted .310 in his sophomore year, with 156 hits, including 8 homers and 89 RBI.

His third year was indeed charmed, as Thompson paced the National League's offense in at-bats (545), hits (203), triples (23), RBI (166—the 12th-highest total in baseball history), batting average (.372), and slugging percentage (.571). Thompson was an aggressive outfielder who plowed through the low

fences in Detroit's home park to make difficult catches. The cannon-armed fly-hawker was the first player of his day to throw all the way from the outfield to home plate on the bounce.

The Wolverines became defunct in 1888, but Thompson lived on with the National League's Phillies, two times leading the league in homers (20), doubles (41), hits (222), and at-bats (600, just below his all-time mark of 609). His 165 league-leading RBI in 1895 with the Phillies came just one notch below his personal best of 166 set eight years earlier. In 1895 his slugging percentage of .654 was close on the heels of his .686 mark set just the previous year.

Although the big lefty took a batting title only once, he topped that winning mark on two occasions, with .392 in 1895 and .407 in 1894.

Thompson's initial retirement at age 38 had been somewhat involuntary, as he was bothered with an ailing back. His trademark hunched stance in the batter's box may have aggravated the problem.

When the 46-year-old played his final eight-game stint with the Tigers in 1906, he was cheered by a full house of fans. He rewarded them with a triple and 2 RBI. Although he was baffled by a newfangled pitch called a spitter, he still kept up with younger outfielders Ty Cobb and Sam "Wahoo" Crawford.

Thompson finished his career with 1,979 hits in 1,407 games for a .331 batting average. His hits included 340 doubles and 160 triples, along with 1,299 RBI and 1,256 runs scored. Thompson's lifetime slugging percentage was a cool .505. He racked up 229 lifetime stolen bases and amassed nearly twice as many bases on balls (450) as strikeouts (226).

Thompson, when not around a baseball diamond, spent his later years as a real estate agent in the Detroit area. He enjoyed the status of a local hero until his death in 1922. More than a half century later, the Hall of Fame posthumously inducted the gifted outfielder.

One of the most popular players to ever play in Detroit, Sam Thompson was also one of the greatest. His ratio of RBI to games played is the best of all-time, and he compiled a .331 batting average with only 226 strikeouts in his career.

CAREER HIGHLIGHTS
SAMUEL LUTHER THOMPSON

Born: March 5, 1860 Danville, IN **Died:** November 7, 1922
Height: 6'2" **Weight:** 207 lbs. **Batted:** Left **Threw:** Left
Outfielder: Detroit Wolverines, 1885-88; Philadelphia Phillies, 1889-98; Detroit Tigers, 1906.

★ Hit a career high of .407 in 1894
★ Won two N.L. home run titles, in 1889 and 1895
★ Knocked in 166 runs in only 118 games in 1887
★ Led the league in hitting in 1887

★ Batted above .300 nine times
★ Earned two RBI crowns with 166 and 165 runs batted in
★ Generally regarded as the top pre-1900 slugger
★ Elected to the Hall of Fame in 1974

MAJOR LEAGUE TOTALS

G	AB	H	BA	2B	3B	HR	R	RBI	SB
1,407	5,984	1,979	.331	340	160	127	1,256	1,299	229

LUIS TIANT

Luis Tiant, one of the last of the Cuban-born major leaguers, got his start playing with the Mexico City Tigers in the Mexican League. Playing his first professional season in 1959, he launched his baseball career with a truly terrible record of 5 wins and 19 losses with an ERA of 5.92. It was not the kind of season typical of the hard-throwing righthander who later went on to record 229 wins in the big leagues.

Fortunately Tiant was invited back to Mexico City and pitched for the Tigers two more seasons before playing minor league ball in the United States. In 1960 Tiant topped the Mexican League with a 17-7 mark and .708 winning percentage. His first two years were marked by wildness, as he produced more bases on balls than strikeouts (including a league high of 124 walks in 1961). His ERA was 5.78 his first year and 4.65 in his sophomore campaign. After a 12-9 record with Mexico City in 1961 (with a 3.78 ERA and 141 strikeouts), he signed a contract with the Cleveland Indians organization.

Tiant played for a number of teams in the Tribe's system, including Jacksonville of the Interstate League, Charleston of the Eastern League, Burlington of the Carolina League, and finally Portland of the Pacific Coast League. Tiant's 1963 campaign included a record of 14 wins and 9 losses, with a no-hitter against Winston-Salem on May 7. Tiant led the Carolina League with 207 strikeouts. When he reached the Pacific Coast League in 1964, Tiant tallied a snappy 15-1 record in 17 games. Besides his league-high performance of .938, Tiant lowered his once flabby ERA to 2.04. His permanent call-up came in mid-1964.

Once he reached the Cleveland Indians, Tiant quickly proved he could pitch on the major league level. In his first big league appearance the rookie pitched a shutout against the New York Yankees, then went on to record 10 wins against 4 losses. While Tiant was indeed a big league rookie, he was no longer a youngster. The Cuban hurler was 23 years old and had been active in organized baseball for five years.

Tiant's first big success was a 21-9 outing with the 1968 Cleveland Indians. Later with the Boston Red Sox, he won 20 and 22 games during the 1973-74 seasons. In the 1975 World Series, he won two of Boston's three victories against the triumphant Cincinnati Reds. He opened the Series with a 5-hit win

in game one. On three days rest he hurled a complete-game victory in the fourth game. He tried to win the sixth game as well, but got a no-decision after seven innings of work.

One of the most memorable elements in Tiant's style was his unusual windup. Ever-changing, his pitching motion spun the hurler around like a reversing corkscrew. Often he seemed to look skyward before he delivered. Sidearm, three-quarters, it didn't matter. Tiant had an assortment of pitches he could serve up in a variety of ways. Because he sometimes seemed to turn his back to the mound, he was able to baffle runners thinking about stolen bases. His odd contortions were surprisingly effective in holding runners on base. Umpires found it difficult to make balk calls against Tiant, because his motion always changed.

Tiant's lifetime pitching totals, stretched across 19 major league seasons, include 229 wins and 172 losses. To date more than a half-dozen Hall of Famers have won fewer games than Tiant did. He's tied for 50th place on

the all-time winner's list. While Tiant never won any league strikeout crowns, he finished his career with 2,416 Ks, versus just 1,104 bases on balls. Three times in his career he led the league in shutouts, and he racked up a grand total of 49 no-run games. Tiant surpassed 196 innings pitched in ten different seasons, including a personal best of 311 frames in 1974.

One of Tiant's most overlooked talents may have been his hitting. Although he had a lifetime batting average of .164 (before the designated hitter rule overtook the American League in 1973), Tiant had 84 career hits, including 5 home runs.

It shouldn't be surprising that Tiant's Hall of Fame-quality stats didn't bring him more attention with baseball writers in 1988, his first year of eligibility for the Hall. He received 47 votes. He wasn't an instant winner of the balloting, mostly because the recent focus directed to new members has been toward non-pitching stars. With the glut of famous pitchers who are becoming eligible for the HOF in the next five years, Tiant may have to wait a few years before he gets his chance.

But don't count Tiant out of Cooperstown yet. Once the Hall runs out of its current stock of homer-hitting candidates, Tiant's years of excellence will have to be rewarded.

It looked like Luis Tiant's career was over after only five years in the majors, but Boston gave him another chance. In 1972 he led the league with a 1.91 ERA and was named Comeback Player of the Year.

CAREER HIGHLIGHTS
LUIS CLEMENTE VEGA TIANT

Born: November 23, 1940   Marianao, Cuba
Height: 6'0"   **Weight:** 180 lbs.   **Batted:** Right   **Threw:** Right
Pitcher: Cleveland Indians, 1964-69; Minnesota Twins, 1970; Boston Red Sox, 1971-78; New York Yankees, 1979-80; Pittsburgh Pirates, 1981; California Angels, 1982.

★ Won 20 or more games four times
★ Had the best ERA in the A.L. twice
★ Earned 49 career shutouts

★ Won 2 games in the 1975 World Series
★ Led the A.L. in shutouts three times
★ Hurled 187 complete games

MAJOR LEAGUE TOTALS

G	IP	W	L	Pct.	SO	BB	ERA
573	3,486	229	172	.571	2,416	1,104	3.30

JOE TINKER

It's only appropriate that when shortstop Joe Tinker was elected to the Baseball Hall of Fame over 40 years ago, he was accompanied by his two famous teammates—second baseman Johnny Evers and first baseman Frank Chance. Together, the Chicago Cubs trio of "Tinker to Evers to Chance" was the most famous double-play combination in the history of baseball, a fact that was acknowledged by baseball fans long before the special Hall of Fame Veterans Committee decided in 1946 that the three great infielders should enter Cooperstown as a group.

It was at the end of the 1902 season that the trio played their first game together. Of the three, first baseman Frank Chance had been the first to arrive in Chicago some four years earlier. Tinker came at the start of the 1902 season, and when Johnny Evers was called up to the Cubs that September, the trio was complete. Baseball historians say that the first of many double plays from Tinker to Evers to Chance occurred on September 15, 1902.

The famous double play combination remained together for ten years. In 1913 Chance went to the New York Yankees, where he finished his career in 1914, while Tinker was traded to the Cincinnati Reds. Tinker stayed one season before he jumped ship and joined the Chicago Whales of the outlaw Federal League as a player/manager, becoming the first big-name player to make the move. He held the job for the 1914 and 1915 seasons, assembling impressive records as a skipper. The 1914 Whales finished second in their division with a record of 87 wins and 67 losses. The following season Tinker's Whales took first place with an 86-66 mark. Winning must have been a refreshing change for the scrappy Tinker since he was a player/manager for the Cincinnati Red Stockings in 1913 and his team had a mediocre season in seventh place, winning 64 games and dropping 89.

Peace was restored to the major leagues in 1916, so Tinker rejoined his Chicago Cubs for a final season. Although he wanted both to manage and play in 1916, he appeared in just seven games, getting 1 hit in ten plate appearances. As a manager he had similar misfortunes. The Cubs finished in fifth place with a 67-86 outcome. Tinker's grand totals as a manager included 304 wins and 308 losses for a .497 winning percentage.

In a 15-year career Tinker relied more on his glove than his bat to earn his way to Cooperstown. Only once did he bat over .300 (during his 1913 season in Cincinnati), retiring with a .262 lifetime average. Tinker became a hero in 1908 when the Cubs and the New York Giants were locked in a tie for first place and had to replay an earlier game that had ended with an even score. With the pennant on the line, Tinker ripped a triple off the Giants Christy Mathewson to win the game and give his Cubs the National League title. The light-hitting Tinker surprised everyone in the second game of the World Series against the Detroit Tigers by clubbing a two-run homer. His eighth-inning blast was the key to a six-run rally that beat the Bengals 6-1.

Tinker's cumulative batting average for four World Series appearances is .235. Tinker managed just 3 hits and 4 runs scored in the 1906 Series (won by the White Sox in six games), batting .150. The Cubs chalked up their second straight National League pennant in 1907, sweeping the Detroit Tigers in four consecutive games. Although Tinker was first on the Cubbies in runs scored (with 4), he had just 2 hits in four games for a .154 average.

Tinker was one of the most accomplished shortstops of the early 20th century. He ranks 15th in history with 10,241 putouts and is 14th on the all-time list with 5.9 chances per game. He is 15th in career assists with 3.4 per game. The Kansas native was a league leader in fielding percentage five times during his career.

While offense was never Tinker's strong suit, he does hold the all-time Cubs record for most triples by a right-hand hitter (93) and is second to teammate Chance in lifetime stolen bases (336, to Chance's 404 steals). In his entire career, Tinker played in 1,804 games, collecting 1,687 hits, 263 doubles, 114 triples, 31 home runs, and 782 RBI. His stolen base totals stayed in double digits for the first 13 years of his career, climbing as high as 41 in 1904.

Following his retirement as a player, Tinker was president and manager of the Columbus franchise in the American Association through 1920. During his career Tinker was a hit performer when he took to the vaudeville circuit (performing a baseball-related routine, of course). The Cincinnati Reds named their spring training home Tinker Field, partially because the former star had helped finance the baseball complex. He became successful investing in Florida real estate in the 1920s and died there in 1948, two years after his Hall of Fame election.

CAREER HIGHLIGHTS
JOSEPH BERT TINKER

Born: July 27, 1880 Muscotah, KS **Died:** July 27, 1948
Height: 5'9" **Weight:** 175 lbs. **Batted:** Right **Threw:** Right
Shortstop: Chicago Cubs, 1902-12, 1916; Cincinnati Red Stockings, 1913; Chicago Whales (Federal League), 1914-15. Manager: Cincinnati Red Stockings, 1913; Chicago Whales, 1914-15; Chicago Cubs, 1916.

★ Played in four World Series
★ Was part of the famous Tinker-to-Evers-to-Chance double-play combination
★ Elected to the Hall of Fame in 1946
★ Led the N.L. in fielding percentage four times
★ Stole 20-plus bases during each of his first 11 seasons

MAJOR LEAGUE TOTALS

G	AB	H	BA	2B	3B	HR	R	RBI	SB
1,804	6,434	1,687	.262	263	114	31	774	782	336

Immortalized as part of the Tinker to Evers to Chance double-play combination, Joe Tinker should be best remembered for his outstanding fielding. He led N.L. shortstops five times in fielding average, in assists twice, and in putouts twice.

JOE TORRE

The youngest of five children, hard-hitting utility man Joe Torre was once described by his first-sacker brother, Frank, as "an accident." Joe was, indeed, an accident waiting to happen, and he was waiting for major league pitchers.

Joe's pursuit of big league competition began almost the day he was born to Milwaukee Braves scout Joseph Paul Torre, Sr., in Brooklyn. Elder brother Frank started playing with the Braves in 1956, about the time Joe Jr. made a name for himself as a star third sacker at a private prep school.

Visiting Frank when the Braves played at nearby Ebbets Field, the 16-year-old Joe (then 5-foot-10 and 240 pounds) was crushed when Frank referred to him as "Fat Boy." Joe didn't speak to his elder brother for a year. But the lesson Frank had hoped to instill sank in when Joe Jr. graduated from high school in 1959 without a single offer to play professional baseball.

Joe had never wanted to do anything but play ball. Now the brother he had resented came to his rescue by telling him to try again as a catcher. Catchers, Frank maintained, weren't expected to run well. So even with his outsized girth, Joe would have an outside chance, if he could hit the ball.

That he could. Signed with the Braves in August 1959, Joe finished his 1960 minor league season with 16 homers, 74 RBI, a league-best .344 batting average, and a .987 fielding average (the best among catchers in the Northern League). In May of 1961 he was called up from Louisville (where he was batting .342) to substitute for injured Braves catcher Del Crandall. Receiving for the wizard-like Warren Spahn, Torre later admitted to being terrified—until he caught his first pop-up. In that doubleheader he went on to hit a single, a double, and a home run and then threw out three would-be basestealers.

A solid career as a utility man began, with Torre placing second in Rookie of the Year balloting. Torre posted solid statistics for the next two seasons while roaming the infield and outfield. His patience paid off at the end of 1963 when Crandall was traded and Torre became the Braves starting catcher.

He took over with a cool control that belied his 22 years. Torre's fielding average of .995 bested all other catchers in the league. He became the first backstop in almost ten years to bat over .300 (.321), top 100 runs (109), and

clout 20 home runs. He was selected for his first of nine National League All-Star teams. He caught the entire game that year. Upon the Braves 1966 move to Atlanta, Torre walloped three dozen homers and 101 runs and averaged .315 at the plate. But hard times were at his heels: a beanball that broke three bones, smashed the roof of his mouth, and caused temporary vision loss; a divorce; a child with a birth defect; and player-management friction, with Torre serving as go-between (as the players' representative).

These problems were magnified when Torre asked for a higher salary, as well as an apology for comments made by management concerning his team spirit (a point of great pride with Torre). He was traded to St. Louis for Orlando Cepeda in 1969. Torre later called the experience "being reborn."

The stress of Braves battles left their mark, and in 1970 Torre embarked on a high-protein diet that got his weight

close to 200 pounds—not so bad on a 6-foot-1 frame. His average jumped from .289 the previous year to .325 in 1970. Despite his well-known slowness on the base paths, Torre proudly legged out an infield safety for his 200th hit of the season.

The greatest season of Torre's career came in 1971, when he was named the league's MVP. He hit .363 to win his only batting title. Some baseball writers speculated that Torre would have exceeded the magic .400 mark if he had been speedy enough to bunt and run out infield hits. Despite his lack of speed, Torre was tops in the senior circuit with 230 hits and 137 RBI. Part of his success stemmed from getting a new full-time position: third base. The Cardinals correctly assumed that Torre could concentrate better on his own hitting if he wasn't immersed in catching duty. Also the team wanted to preserve Torre's legs. He led the league in putouts at his new position. Torre was entertaining to watch at the hot corner. Before every pitch, he'd go into a bent-knee stoop to get into position for grounders.

The Brooklyn native served the next two years as the Cardinals starting first baseman. He lost his job to rookie Keith Hernandez and was traded to the New York Mets before the 1975 season for pitcher Ray Sadecki and Tommy Moore. Torre retired in early 1977.

He managed his hometown Mets from 1977 to 1981, but his clubs never finished better than fifth. Torre fared better as Atlanta's manager from 1982 to 1984, earning a division title and two second-place finishes. Since 1985 Torre has been a TV broadcaster for California Angels' games.

CAREER HIGHLIGHTS
JOSEPH PAUL TORRE

Born: July 18, 1940   Brooklyn, NY
Height: 6'1"   **Weight:** 212 lbs.   **Batted:** Right   **Threw:** Right
Catcher, first baseman, third baseman: Milwaukee Braves, 1960-65; Atlanta Braves, 1966-68; St. Louis Cardinals, 1969-74; New York Mets, 1975-77. Manager: New York Mets, 1977-81; Atlanta Braves, 1982-84.

- ★ Elected to nine All-Star teams
- ★ Won the 1971 batting title
- ★ Drove in 100-plus runs five times
- ★ Won 1971 N.L. MVP award
- ★ Earned a career-high 230 hits in 1971
- ★ Had 20 or more homers six times

MAJOR LEAGUE TOTALS

G	AB	H	BA	2B	3B	HR	R	RBI	SB
2,209	7,874	2,342	.297	344	59	252	996	1,185	23

In 1969 Joe Torre was traded to the St. Louis Cardinals and placed full-time at third base—which spurred him to lead the N.L. in batting with .363, in hits with 230, and in RBI with 137. He was named the league's MVP.

ALAN TRAMMELL

lan Trammell played the 1987 season as though he wanted to be the American League's Comeback Player of the Year. He knew just how, because he'd been there only four years before. In 1983 he had hammered his batting average to .319, an increase of 61 points. Trammell went on to spark his Tigers to a 1984 World Series celebration, clouting not 1, but 2 two-run homers in the decisive game three.

After another breathtaking year in 1984, Trammell's batting ebbed to the middle .200s, and his usually fine fielding fell away, too. Then in the spring of 1987 he blossomed again, slamming a career-high .343 the year before his 30th birthday, with a personal-best 28 home runs. Amazingly, he was nosed out of the batting title, yet he seemed once again the slugger of old, providing the durable, dependable defense needed for a team of perennial champs.

Trammell was drafted out of high school by Detroit in the second round of the 1976 selection process. He split that first pro year between rookie class ball and the Tigers Double-A farm team at Montgomery in the Southern League. In 1977 he hit .291 for Montgomery, with a league-leading 19 triples, copping the league's Most Valuable Player award and earning a September trial with the parent club. He hit only .186 (all singles) with the Tigers in 19 games.

In need of a solid player up the middle, the Tigers decided to give Trammell the starting shortstop job in 1978, and he's been posted there ever since. He and Lou Whitaker have formed the longest-running double-play combination in baseball history; they played together 12 years in 1989. Trammell worked his batting average up to an even .300 in 1980 and then suffered a pair of back-to-back .258 seasons that set the stage for his 1983 comeback.

The following year, as the Tigers blazed their way to the Series, Trammell maintained a .314 average with 14 home runs, despite losing the entire month of July to an injury. His postseason play made it seem as if he'd never missed a day, as the Tigers swept the Royals and Trammell batted .364. He sparked the Bengals in the opening game of the American League Championship Series with a triple, a solo home run, and 3 RBI.

In World Series play he tied major league records for most hits in a five-game series (9) and for single-handedly acquiring all of his team's runs in a game (4). His latter record-tying effort came in the fourth of five games against the San Diego Padres. He belted a pair of two-run round-trippers to lead his Tigers to a 4-2 victory. In the Series opener Trammell's first-inning RBI single, which drove in infield partner Whitaker, amounted to the winning run of the Tigers' 3-2 victory.

Before the Series was finished, Trammell owned a .450 batting average. He led all players from both teams in hits (9) and runs scored (5) while driving in a total of 6 runs. He won a new car by being named World Series Most Valuable Player.

Throughout the 80s the lean middleman came into his own as a basestealer, averaging 14 a year, peaking with 30 in 1983, and slowing to 7 in 1987 due to a month-long injury.

Trammell's most serious layoff came in 1984, when he missed one month of play and then underwent shoulder surgery after his Series victory. Known for some time as one of the premier active clutch hitters, he altered his stroke to accommodate the shoulder and wound up improving his already sound power hitting and average. He learned to compensate for his weakened throwing arm by getting rid of the ball more quickly. He is fluid and confident in the field, attributes that overflow into his running. Though not a roadrunner, Trammell has excellent instincts on the base paths as proven by his steals when he's been healthy. He is an adept study of other players and of the ball itself and often gets an extra base simply by anticipating how well an opponent will play a given ball.

Even with his recent injuries, Trammell received Gold Gloves for his excellence on the field in both 1987 and 1988.

Trammell is a player greatly admired by his comrades but often taken for granted by the fans. His steady, exemplary statistics rarely lead the American League—surprising considering how far above the league average his batting is, whether on grass or turf, day or night. He hits for power and average, can lay down the bunt, and watches the ball so carefully that change-ups don't phase him.

The California native may not be a future home run king or batting champion, but the Detroit Tigers don't seem to mind. His determination and team leadership in the every-day lineup are the biggest contributions any star player could make.

CAREER HIGHLIGHTS
ALAN STUART TRAMMELL

Born: February 21, 1958   Garden Grove, CA
Height: 6'0"   **Weight:** 170 lbs.   **Bats:** Right   **Throws:** Right
Shortstop: Detroit Tigers, 1977-89.

- ★ Named to the A.L. All-Star team five years
- ★ Named to Silver Slugger teams in 1987 and 1988
- ★ Batted .450 in the 1984 World Series, tying two all-time records
- ★ Named to the Gold Glove team in 1980 and 1983
- ★ Named A.L. Comeback Player of the Year 1983
- ★ Has twice led the A.L. in sacrifice hits

★ Hit .343 in 1987, one of the highest averages in recent history by a shortstop

MAJOR LEAGUE TOTALS

G	AB	H	BA	2B	3B	HR	R	RBI	SB
1,689	6,143	1,759	.286	292	49	138	938	721	187

Alan Trammell is a dependable fielder who is trying to overcome injuries to be just as dependable with his bat. He has won four Gold Gloves for his fielding and narrowly missed a batting title in 1987 with a .343 batting average.

PIE TRAYNOR

ie Traynor was the complete third baseman, a dazzling fielder and consistent hitter who mastered the position so well that for a 15-year period in the 1920s and early 30s, no one played it better. Some say he was the greatest defensive third baseman of all time.

Traynor played far behind the bag, relying on his exceptional range and his strong arm, which never let him down. Nothing got past him on either side, and he was especially adept at fielding bunts and robbing batters of hits down the line. At the plate Traynor was equally effective. In a 17-year career, he compiled a .320 lifetime average, several times topping the .340 mark. His personal best came in 1930 when he batted at a .366 clip, closing out a spectacular four-year stretch during which he averaged .350.

Harold Joseph Traynor played his entire career in a Pirates uniform. He grew up playing ball on a parish school playground where a priest served double duty as umpire and coach. After the contests the priest frequently took the young athletes to a pastry shop, where Traynor ate so much pie that he earned the odd nickname that stuck with him for life.

At the age of 21 Traynor signed a professional contract with Portsmouth of the Virginia League, where he played the 1920 season. The following year he advanced to Birmingham of the Southern League and then was called up to Pittsburgh to join the Pirates for a few games. By 1922 Traynor was a fixture at third base. Few people remember that the Pirates originally tried Traynor as a shortstop.

One of Traynor's finest seasons was in 1925, when he helped the Pirates gain their first world championship since 1909. The Pirates finished the regular season with a 95-58 record and went on to topple the Washington Senators in the World Series. In the seven-game series Traynor batted .346 with 9 hits (including 2 triples and a homer), 4 RBI, and 2 runs scored. True to form, he played seven games of errorless baseball against the American League opposition. Traynor's totals during the regular season included 6 homers, 106 RBI, 114 runs scored, and a .320 batting average. He was spectacular in the field that year, leading the senior circuit in putouts (226), assists (303), double plays (41), chances per game (3.7), and fielding percentage (.957).

In 1927 the Pirates regained their National League Championship, only to be swept by the "Murderers' Row" New York Yankees team in the World Series. Traynor hit .342 during the regular season with 5 home runs and 106 RBI. Teammate Paul Waner won the National League batting title that year with a .380 mark. There is a story that Waner's and Traynor's success can be traced to the same bat. They found a bat cast off by Tim Hendryx, a little-known American League outfielder. The Pirate teammates shared the bat all season, and the lucky lumber helped them all the way to a National League pennant.

When Traynor's brilliant playing career started winding down in 1934, he was named Pittsburgh's manager, a position he held for six years until Frankie Frisch took over after a disappointing 1939 season. From 1935 through 1938 Traynor's Pirates were a competitive team in the National League. The Bucs finished fourth in 1935 and 1936, third in 1937, and second in 1938. While the 1936 team had 84 wins, the other three squads won 86. In 1938 the Chicago Cubs beat out the Pirates for the pennant by just three victories. Traynor's lifetime managerial record included 457 wins and 406 losses for a .530 winning percentage. Traynor remained in Pittsburgh as a Pirates radio broadcaster for more than two decades.

As a hitter Traynor had only 58 home runs but still drove in 1,273 runs. He finished his career with 2,416 hits, which included 371 doubles and 164 triples. Traynor was an excellent contact hitter. He struck out just 278 times in his career, never more than 28 times a season. In 1926 Traynor fanned just 14 times in 574 times at bat! Although he was past his prime when the All-Star game was originated in 1933, Traynor still was honored with invitations to play in the first two annual contests.

Traynor ranks in the Pirates all-time top ten in many categories, including games, at-bats, runs, hits, singles, doubles, triples, total bases, RBI, extra-base hits, batting average, and stolen bases. Pirate third sackers of the past 50 years have paled in comparison to Traynor. The only one to even approach Traynor's longevity at the hot corner was Richie Hebner. Hebner played in 1,053 games, far fewer than Traynor's 1,864.

Traynor ranks fifth among all third basemen in career putouts (2,291), 11th in chances (6,140), and 15th in double plays (308). He was elected to the Hall of Fame in 1948. When he died in 1972, the Pirates posthumously honored their great third sacker by retiring his uniform number (20). Only eight former Pirates have received such an honor.

CAREER HIGHLIGHTS
HAROLD JOSEPH TRAYNOR

Born: November 11, 1899 Framingham, MA **Died:** March 16, 1972
Height: 6'0" **Weight:** 170 lbs. **Batted:** Right **Threw:** Right
Third baseman: Pittsburgh Pirates, 1920-37. Manager: Pittsburgh Pirates, 1934-39.

- ★ Batted over .300 in ten seasons
- ★ Uniform number retired by Pirates
- ★ Compiled a .320 lifetime batting average

- ★ Played in two World Series
- ★ Elected to the Hall of Fame in 1948
- ★ Never struck out more than 28 times a season

MAJOR LEAGUE TOTALS

G	AB	H	BA	2B	3B	HR	R	RBI	SB
1,941	7,559	2,416	.320	371	164	58	1,183	1,273	158

Pie Traynor's range at third base was all-encompassing. A sportswriter once wrote, "He doubled down the left field foul line, but Traynor threw him out." Traynor also helped his team with a lifetime .320 batting average.

FERNANDO VALENZUELA

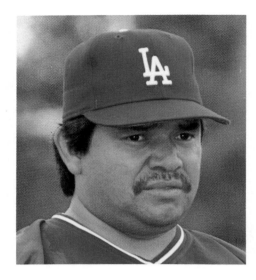

Life sometimes seems like a roller coaster ride: The highs and lows are not very far apart. Fernando Valenzuela knows all about it. He was an amazing and exciting pitcher for the Dodgers for six years; now he is struggling to regain what he lost after having undergone shoulder reconstruction. If pure talent has anything to do with it, fans should see Valenzuela back as a premier hurler.

Valenzuela burst upon the scene in 1981 and became the first player ever to snag both Rookie of the Year and Cy Young awards simultaneously. He set National League highs in innings pitched (190) and strikeouts (180) and pitched 36 straight scoreless innings and 8 shutouts, tying a rookie record set in 1913. The following year he won 19 games, starting a career-high 37 games.

Here was a pitcher who seemed to have everything; he was a young left-hander, with five different pitches and an uncanny pick-off move, and he was an exceptional fielder and an acceptable batsman to boot. In 1985 Valenzuela posted a career-best 2.45 ERA. In 1986 he cleared the 20-win mark with a 21-11 season. Yet only two years after that "Nando" (as he's called by young Dodger fans) was forced to sit and watch his Dodgers make their frenzied way to a World Series championship. Still rehabilitating with a reconstructed shoulder muscle, he saw a boy wonder named Orel Hershiser (actually two years his senior) become the pitching sensation of the Series and the baseball world.

Some critics blame Blue Crew manager Tommy Lasorda for Valenzuela's troubles. He worked the youngster hard, especially during his sophomore season, when Valenzuela logged a whopping 285 innings. In 1987 and 1988 (when he appeared in 24 games before going on the disabled list for the first time on July 31) his wins declined while his ERA rose and lodged at around 4.00.

Valenzuela was discovered pitching in the Mexican Leagues in his professional rookie season of 1978. The Dodgers purchased Valenzuela from Yucatan of the Mexican League on July 6, 1979. After pitching three games in 1980 for the Dodgers Lodi affiliate, he spent most of the 1980 season at San Antonio. There he was 13-9 with 11 complete games and 4 shutouts. On September 10 the Dodgers brought him up to stay. That first year Valenzuela (as a reliever) didn't give up a run in 10 games and 17.2 innings. Counting his shutouts at San Antonio, the gifted lefty had thrown 52.2 consecutive innings of scoreless baseball. His 16 strikeouts were another highlight in his brief debut.

When teammate Jerry Reuss was ailing and couldn't answer the call as the Dodgers opening-day pitcher, the rookie sensation got the chance. Valenzuela succeeded, tossing a five-hit shutout win against the Houston Astros. His season began with 8 straight wins (running his consecutive win total to 10, counting 1980), including 7 complete games and a 0.50 ERA. By season's end Valenzuela led the majors in strikeouts (180), complete games (11), shutouts (8), and innings pitched (192.1). He also racked up 36 straight scoreless innings, another N.L. best. The only reason his totals weren't higher was the 1981 players' strike. In the 1981 N.L. division play-offs, Valenzuela won game four with a four-hitter. He pitched well in the opener, allowing only 1 run in 8.1 innings before leaving with the score tied. When the Dodgers advanced to the N.L. Championship Series, Valenzuela won the decisive fifth game 2-1 on a three-hit masterpiece. The Dodgers needed six games to take a world championship from the New York Yankees. Despite giving up 9 hits and 7 walks, Valenzuela won the third game of the Series 5-4.

The southpaw was 19-13 in his sophomore season, finishing third in the Cy Young balloting. He started a career-high 37 games that year and was second in the league in wins. In 1983 Valenzuela won 15 games and was second in the league with 4 shutouts. He had a losing record in 1984 but still finished second in the league in strikeouts and innings pitched and had 12 complete games. Valenzuela's winningest season came in 1986. He was 21-11 (a league best), leading the majors with a career high of 20 complete games. In the All-Star game he tied Carl Hubbell's record by striking out 5 consecutive batters.

Even if Valenzuela doesn't rebound to his former glory, he'll still be long remembered by baseball fans everywhere.

Being named the Rookie of the Year and winning the Cy Young award in 1981 are highlights of Fernando Valenzuela's career. Because of a reconstructed shoulder muscle in 1988, Valenzuela is battling to regain his former glory.

CAREER HIGHLIGHTS
FERNANDO ANGUAMEA VALENZUELA

Born: November 1, 1960   Navoja, Mexico
Height: 5'11"   **Weight:** 202 lbs.   **Bats:** Left   **Throws:** Left
Pitcher: Los Angeles Dodgers, 1980-89.

★ Named the N.L. Rookie of the Year in 1981

★ Named to six N.L. All-Star teams as of 1988

★ Led the N.L. in complete games three times

★ Won the Cy Young award in 1981 as a rookie

★ Had 7 game-winning RBI as of 1988

★ Was 1-0 in the 1981 World Series

MAJOR LEAGUE TOTALS

G	IP	W	L	Pct.	SO	BB	ERA
298	2,144	128	103	.554	1,644	838	3.20

DAZZY VANCE

Arthur Charles Vance was a fastball hurler who won 197 games in a 16-year career that didn't start in earnest until he was 31. While baseball beat writers often called Vance "The Dazzler" for his pitching success, his nickname derives more from his status as a late bloomer. Vance earned his moniker as a child due to a flowery Midwestern expression of his day, "Ain't that a daisy." Young Vance, mocking a cowboy, mispronounced the word daisy as "dazzy"; hence the nickname.

Vance was signed to a minor league contract in 1912 with Red Cloud of the Nebraska State League; he won 11 and lost 15. The strapping righthander progressed in the league, claiming a 17-4 mark with Hastings in 1915. He was bought by the Pittsburgh Pirates, who used him in one game, which he lost. The New York Yankees tried Vance, but he was defeated in all three of his decisions. Vance was battered in two appearances with the Yanks in 1918, getting tagged with an 18.00 ERA after just two innings of work.

After that the unlucky hurler became a well-traveled minor leaguer, bouncing from team to team. His many stops included Columbus, Toledo, Memphis, Sacramento, and New Orleans. He was in the minors for ten years, trying to cope with nagging arm problems. After winning 21 games in the Southern League in 1921, he returned to the major leagues. When he finally came up to Brooklyn to stay in 1922, the tall righthander had pitched a total of only 32 major league innings and had yet to win a game. Vance finally recorded his first big league win ten years after his career began, as a 31-year-old rookie with the Dodgers.

Starting fresh at the age of 31, Vance strung together a dozen outstanding years, finishing his career with 197 wins which led to his induction into the Baseball Hall of Fame in 1955. He did it after getting the latest start of any Hall of Famer on record, and he did it with a blazing fastball. One player honored Vance and his fastballs by saying, "He could throw a creampuff through a battleship."

Vance led the league in strikeouts an amazing seven years in a row. Twice he topped the circuit in victories. He won a career-high 28 games in 1924—when he won 15 in a row and took the National League Most Valuable Player award. He came back with 22 wins the next season, and he edged out Rogers

Hornsby for MVP honors, which was quite a feat considering that Hornsby had hit a scorching .424 that year.

In his prime he was the highest-paid pitcher in baseball, earning $20,000 in 1928 and $25,000 in 1929. When Vance went 14-13 in 1929 his salary was cut to $20,000. His pay climbed by $3,000 when he won 17 games in 1930. The Dodgers gave Vance only $17,000 in 1932 due to his 11-13 record. Unlike today's players, who have the comfort of long-term contracts, the players of Vance's era had to contend with strong-willed owners willing to reward their players only for their previous year's accomplishments. Despite the pay cuts Vance had far outdistanced most of his pitching contemporaries in salary for several years, so the salary adjustments were probably not very traumatic.

Because Vance pitched for a topsy-turvy Dodgers club that never maintained any winning consistency, the Iowa native didn't get into a World Series until the end of his career. As a member of the 1934 St. Louis Cardinals, Vance had one relief outing in the Series versus the Detroit Tigers. Vance relieved starter Tex Carleton, hurling 1.1 innings of scoreless middle relief. He was still sharp at age 43, getting 3 of his 4 outs via strikeouts. The Cards lost the game 10-4 but won the Series in seven games.

Had Vance not spent so much time in the minor leagues he might be remembered as one of baseball's greatest pitchers ever. He could have had at least another six seasons to improve his already impressive lifetime totals. As his career stats stand, Vance achieved remarkable success considering his late beginning in the major leagues. Vance won 197 games out of 442 starts. He logged 31 career shutouts, leading the league in that department four times. His career ERA was 3.24, but he was first in the category three times: in 1924 (2.16), in 1928 (2.09), and in 1930 (2.61). Vance joined the exclusive circle of no-hit pitchers with a 1-0 gem against the Philadelphia Phillies in 1924. In 1925 against the Cardinals he racked up 17 strikeouts in ten innings.

Due to his abbreviated career, he had to wait some two decades before being recognized with membership in the Baseball Hall of Fame.

His long arms (an 83-inch reach) and his high-kick windup propelled Dazzy Vance's fastballs past many batters. He wore tattered sleeves to confuse batters, but his pitching alone would have done the job.

CAREER HIGHLIGHTS
CLARENCE ARTHUR VANCE

Born: March 4, 1891 Orient, IA **Died:** February 16, 1961
Height: 6'2" **Weight:** 200 lbs. **Batted:** Right **Threw:** Right
Pitcher: Pittsburgh Pirates, 1915; New York Yankees, 1915, 1918; Brooklyn Dodgers, 1922-32, 1935; St. Louis Cardinals, 1933-34; Cincinnati Reds, 1935.

★ Elected to the Hall of Fame in 1955
★ Led the N.L. in strikeouts seven consecutive seasons
★ Was first in the N.L. in shutouts four times
★ Paced the N.L. in complete games twice
★ Hurled a no-hitter against the Phillies in 1924
★ Topped the league in ERA three times

MAJOR LEAGUE TOTALS

G	IP	W	L	Pct.	SO	BB	ERA
442	2,967	197	140	.585	2,045	840	3.24

ARKY VAUGHAN

Arky Vaughan batted over the .300 mark in 11 of his 12 full seasons. During his first seven seasons he batted at a .357 clip. Even more importantly, he became the best Pirate shortstop since the days of Honus Wagner.

Vaughan compiled a lifetime batting average of .318, which ranks second among Hall of Fame shortstops behind Wagner himself. In 1935 Vaughan led the National League with a lofty .385 batting average, a mark that has not been topped by any National Leaguer since. Throughout his 14-year career in the major leagues, Vaughan struck out fewer than 20 times a season on the average, and three times in a row he led the league in bases on balls. His hitting skills were enough to make him a favorite with fans, but he added to his popularity by being a dependable fielder and an excellent baserunner who paced the league with 20 stolen bases in 1943.

Vaughan compiled some amazing statistics during the 1930s and early 1940s, but he was overlooked by the Hall of Fame for many years. Although he was eligible to be elected by the baseball writers as early as 1953 and remained on the ballot well into the 1960s, it wasn't until 1985 that the oversight was finally corrected by the special Veterans Committee. Vaughan was inducted posthumously; he had drowned in 1952 at the age of 40 while on a fishing trip to California.

Joseph Floyd Vaughan was born in Arkansas, which is how he got the nickname Arky, but he grew up in California. Vaughan played professional ball for the first time in 1931, with Wichita of the Western League. Art Griggs, the Wichita manager, lived in California and had spotted Vaughan playing high school baseball in the area. He invited the young man to spring training with the Pirates. Because of his speed Vaughan won Pittsburgh's attention, and a contract followed. He batted .338 with 21 home runs, 81 RBI, and a league-leading 145 runs scored at Wichita. His achievements in the Texas League included getting 9 straight hits during the season and stealing 3 bases in one game. Vaughan opened the 1932 campaign as the Pittsburgh Pirates starting shortstop. His rookie season consisted of a .318 average with 4 homers, 61 RBI, and 10 stolen bases. He remained in Pittsburgh for the next ten seasons, and his batting average never dipped below the .300 mark.

It was inevitable that any Pittsburgh

shortstop would be compared to the great Honus Wagner. Vaughan had Wagner to thank for his success on the Pirates because "The Flying Dutchman" became Vaughan's personal tutor. Wagner, then a Pirates coach, even roomed with Vaughan during Pirate road trips. While he could never make Vaughan a great fielder, he instilled confidence and aggressiveness in his prize pupil at the plate.

Vaughan played in seven All-Star games during his career. In 1941 he became the first player in the history of the midseason classic to hit 2 homers in one game. Although Vaughan drove in 4 runs for the National Leaguers, the American League won the game on a ninth-inning homer by Ted Williams.

In 1941 the Pirates were aching to build a winning franchise. That meant making any kind of sacrifice, even trad-

ing stars like Vaughan for young players. They sent the Arkansas native to the Brooklyn Dodgers on December 12 in exchange for four players: Pete Coscarart, Luke Hamlin, Babe Phelps, and Jimmy Wasdell. Vaughan took over third base for Cookie Lavagetto that first year, hitting .277 with 2 homers and 49 RBI. Moving back to his usual position of shortstop, Vaughan subbed for team captain Pee Wee Reese, who was serving military duty during those war years. In 1943 Vaughan was first in the National League with 20 stolen bases, which was a personal best. Never before had he topped 14 steals in a year. His average climbed to .305, and he was first in the league with 112 runs scored. Vaughan temporarily retired in 1943 (despite leading the league in runs scored and stolen bases) mainly because of a dispute with Dodger manager Leo Durocher. When Durocher was suspended in 1947, Vaughan came back to the team. Vaughan's final two seasons in Brooklyn consisted of pinch-hitting and backup infielder roles. He batted 10-for-26 as a pinch hitter in 1947 and had a final batting average of .325 in 64 games. Vaughan participated in his first World Series that year, only to see his Dodgers beaten by the New York Yankees in seven games. Vaughan appeared in three games in the Series and had two pinch-hit opportunities. He doubled for his first at-bat and walked for the second.

Vaughan was released by the Dodgers following the 1948 season. In 1949 he played with the San Francisco Seals of the Pacific Coast League before retiring as a player. His career stats include a .318 average, 2,103 hits, 118 stolen bases, 356 doubles, 128 triples, and 1,173 runs scored.

CAREER HIGHLIGHTS
JOSEPH FLOYD VAUGHAN

Born: March 9, 1912 Clifty, AR **Died:** August 30, 1952
Height: 5'11" **Weight:** 175 lbs. **Batted:** Left **Threw:** Right
Shortstop: Pittsburgh Pirates, 1932-41; Brooklyn Dodgers, 1942-43, 1947-48.

★ Batted at a .300 clip 12 times
★ Was the last N.L. batter to hit as high as .385 (in 1935)
★ Named N.L. MVP in 1935
★ Won the N.L. stolen base title in 1943
★ Topped the N.L. in triples three times
★ Elected to the Hall of Fame in 1985

MAJOR LEAGUE TOTALS

G	AB	H	BA	2B	3B	HR	R	RBI	SB
1,817	6,622	2,103	.318	356	128	96	1,173	926	118

Arky Vaughan was known for his fine hitting and fielding, as well as for his honesty and integrity. In 1943 Vaughan handed in his uniform because he believed that Leo Durocher had unfairly suspended another player.

MICKEY VERNON

Few people today remember "the Sometime Splinter," a tall gangly slugger who twice hijacked the A.L. batting title from Boston Red Sox immortal Ted Williams.

Mickey Vernon had several reasons for what many see as his unfulfilled potential. He seldom played for a winning team—although the Washington Senators were not disgraceful during his tenure. He was also frequently injured, so his career was marked by high highs and low lows. Vernon attributed both his good seasons and his bad ones to simple luck—which is not to say he didn't play hard.

Some of Vernon's claims to fame were merely incidental. Although 20-year careers are not uncommon in the major leagues, Vernon's service just happened to date from 1939 to 1960, making him one of those rare athletes who played major league baseball in four different decades.

It is also not unusual for U.S. presidents to be sports fans, even to rub elbows occasionally with their favorite field heroes. But when President Dwight D. Eisenhower was quoted in newspapers as saying that his favorite player was Mickey Vernon, no one knew just why Ike liked Mike. Perhaps he admired Vernon's fighting spirit: After returning from two years of World War II naval service (battling seasickness all the way), Vernon posted a career-high hitting mark, taking the 1946 title with a .353 average. He played with pain until an appendix operation brought relief and upped his already respectable stats. Once Vernon played an entire season with an infected buttock (the result of a fishing accident) without telling anyone the reason for his altered swing. Perhaps Ike liked the pluck that Vernon displayed in bouncing back from one of his worst seasons in 1952, when he had a .251 average and 10 home runs, to a 1953 effort of 15 round-trippers, 205 hits, 115 RBI, and league leads in doubles (43) and average (.337). He risked losing the stats that would have given him the batting crown (which went to Cleveland's Al Rosen) because he insisted on playing in the last game of the season rather than sitting it out. Inspired by Ted Williams' 1941 performance, he said, "I either want to win it swinging or lose it swinging."

Starting in the minors in 1937, the 19-year-old Vernon was a slugger from the start, posting .300-plus seasons in 1938 and 1939. He finished 1939 and 1940 with the Washington Senators, after the St. Louis Browns relinquished his option due to a full infield staff.

Vernon's two batting titles came seven years apart. His first was a league-leading .353 average in 1946 with 8 homers and 85 RBI. Vernon topped Williams by 11 percentage points in the batting race. The 6-foot-2, 170-pound Vernon was first in the league with 51 doubles and third in total bases with 298. Vernon was considered one of the league's finest fielders at first base. The on-again, off-again nature of Vernon's play is evident from the stats he amassed before and after his first batting championship. From 1941 to 1943 Vernon's average sank from .299 to .271 to .268. His hit totals ranged from a high of 168 in 1942 to 148 in 1943. He served in the Navy in 1944 and 1945, then returned to baseball in 1946 and won the batting title. Perhaps Vernon was one of the few players to benefit from missed playing time while in the military.

After 1946 Vernon's statistics tailspinned again. His average dropped 88 points, down to .265 in 1947, but he still drove in 85 runs. Vernon struggled more in 1948, batting only .242 with 3 homers and 48 RBI in 153 games. The Indians traded Vernon and Early Wynn to the Washington Senators on December 14, 1948, for Eddie Robinson, Joe Haynes, and Eddie Klieman.

Vernon batted .291 in his first full year with the Tribe. The Senators reobtained Vernon early in the 1950 season in exchange for Dick Weik. He finished the season in Washington with a .306 average. In 1951 he hit 9 home runs and 87 RBI and had a .293 average. His seesaw success produced a subpar .251 batting mark in 1952. The hard-swinging lefty gained his second hitting title in 1953, amassing a .337 average and leading the league with 43 doubles. Vernon knocked in a career high of 115 runs and paced A.L. first basemen in double plays for the second of three seasons.

After retiring Vernon managed the Senators to ninth- and tenth-place finishes in 1961 and 1962 before being replaced by Gil Hodges. Besides managing minor league teams for six seasons, Vernon was a coach for the St. Louis Cardinals, Pittsburgh Pirates, and Montreal Expos. He later served as a scout for the New York Yankees.

Mickey Vernon was one of the few players to benefit from missing playing time due to military service in WW II. After returning from the Navy in 1946, Vernon won the A.L. batting crown with a .353 average.

CAREER HIGHLIGHTS
JAMES BARTON VERNON

Born: April 22, 1918   Marcus Hook, PA
Height: 6'2"   **Weight:** 170 lbs.   **Batted:** Left   **Threw:** Left
First baseman: Washington Senators, 1939-48, 1950-55; Cleveland Indians, 1949-50, 1958; Boston Red Sox, 1956-57; Milwaukee Braves, 1959; Pittsburgh Pirates, 1960. Manager: Washington Senators, 1961-63.

- ★ Won two A.L. batting titles
- ★ Played on seven All-Star teams
- ★ Led the league in doubles three times
- ★ Drove in a career-high 101 runs in 1953
- ★ Leads A.L. first basemen in career putouts

MAJOR LEAGUE TOTALS

G	AB	H	BA	2B	3B	HR	R	RBI	SB
2,409	8,731	2,495	.286	490	120	172	1,196	1,311	137

HONUS WAGNER

istory has a way of being rewritten as time goes by. Take the story of Honus Wagner. Before 1950 children knew him as a patient coach for his beloved Pirates. But their parents remember him as a compact dynamo at shortstop. Although his arms seemed too long and his legs too short, no one was more single-minded in pursuit of success on the diamond. And no one was more successful.

After his death a baseball "tobacco card" from 1909 bearing his image was in high demand. The high price had something to do with Wagner's dedication and prowess, which was legendary in his day. But it had even more to do with the scarcity of the card since it was pulled from circulation in 1909 at Wagner's request. Today the story is that the health-minded Wagner objected to his image appearing on a card distributed with cigarettes, a lure that he felt might encourage children to smoke. Detractors have conjectured that Wagner also objected because the card was generating profit for the tobacco company but not for him. Considering that the kind-hearted Wagner was adored by the fans, had a reputation for being more than helpful to the rookies, and never acted the star, the former version is probably the true one.

John Peter Wagner started playing professional ball at age 21 in Steubenville, Ohio, in 1895. Until 1914 (when he was 40) he batted below .300 only once. In those 17 astonishing years he batted .330 or more in a dozen seasons. He led the National League in batting average eight different times and had four consecutive batting titles from 1906 to 1909. He led the loop in hits once and also tied once for that record; in runs scored he was a two-time leader; in triples he led three times; in RBI, five; in stolen bases, five; and in slugging percentage, six. His circuit leads in doubles totaled seven. He led N.L. shortstops in double plays four times and fielding average three times. His totals accounted for his reputation as an all-around baseball player. Wagner credited his fine hitting to good eyesight, perfect timing, and endless practice sessions at the plate.

One of nine children born to a Pittsburgh coal miner, Wagner learned to play every position on a sandlot with his brothers. He did, indeed, appear in the major leagues at every position save backstop, causing the highly revered manager John McGraw to comment, "I believe he could have been the number

one player at any position he might have selected."

Wagner spent the first five years of his career as a utility player and then slugged Pittsburgh into three successive pennants from 1901 to 1903. He stayed at shortstop for 16 years and, according to Branch Rickey, never asked for anything more, on the field or off. When he was coaching in his late 60s, Wagner would navigate miles of public transportation to get to the field, and he never complained. The game was all there was to him. He remained single until his forties, surrounded by dozens of pets and a wayward automobile. After hanging up his spikes, he managed his Pirates for three days but found that being able to play and explaining how to do it were two very different things. At age 43 he took up coaching baseball and basketball at Carnegie-Mellon (then Carnegie Institute of Technology) in Pittsburgh. He also served as sergeant-at-arms for the state legislature and co-owned a Pitts-

burgh sporting goods store with Pie Traynor. He returned to the Pirates as a coach in 1933 and stayed until 1951.

His German heritage and fleet performance earned him the tag of "The Flying Dutchman." He was also called "Honus" and "Hans" in deference to his heritage. He never spoke back to an umpire—or spoke to one at all. He was so exuberant on the field that he would fling handfuls of dirt along with the ball on a tight putout. He out-hit Ty Cobb with a .333 average in the 1909 World Series (which the Pirates won in seven games) and tagged out the fiery slugger so hard that he required three stitches. When Pittsburgh won the World Series that year, the winning share for Wagner and his teammates was $1,825 each. (In contrast, members of the 1971 world champion Pittsburgh Pirates received $18,165 each.)

There was never anything but the game for Wagner, and it never stopped being fun. This spirit, along with his long list of accomplishments, earned him a charter membership in the Baseball Hall of Fame in 1936. He was voted into Cooperstown directly after Ty Cobb and right before Babe Ruth.

Some may argue about who is the best ball player of all time, but there is little doubt who told the biggest stories. Honus Wagner once said that a dog ran onto the field and grabbed the ball so he had to throw the dog and ball to first for the out.

CAREER HIGHLIGHTS
JOHN PETER WAGNER

Born: February 24, 1874 Mansfield, PA **Died:** December 6, 1955
Height: 5'11" **Weight:** 200 lbs. **Batted:** Right **Threw:** Right
Shortstop: Louisville Colonels, 1897-99; Pittsburgh Pirates, 1900-17. Manager: Pittsburgh Pirates, 1917.

- ★ Batted .300-plus for 17 straight years
- ★ Was first in the league in doubles seven times
- ★ Led the league in stolen bases five times
- ★ Won eight batting titles
- ★ Elected to the Hall of Fame as a charter member in 1936
- ★ Played in two World Series

MAJOR LEAGUE TOTALS

G	AB	H	BA	2B	3B	HR	R	RBI	SB
2,792	10,430	3,415	.327	640	252	101	1,736	1,732	722

BOBBY WALLACE

Most Hall of Famers are remembered for their offensive heroics: how many homers they hit or how many victories they posted. Because Bobby Wallace, who joined the immortals of Cooperstown in 1953, was never an offensive firecracker, he is often not remembered at all. Wallace was never the type of controversial, outspoken player who anchored world championship teams. In fact he only hit .300 twice in his long career, and he never led the league in a single offensive category. Instead Wallace was honored for his fielding excellence and his longevity in the major leagues. The 5-foot-8, 170-pound workhorse lasted in the majors from 1894 through 1918, a total of 25 seasons, and he remained a high-quality contributor throughout that time. In *The Bill James Historical Baseball Abstract,* Wallace is chosen as one of the 100 greatest players of all time because of his career value, meaning the overall assistance he provided to his team throughout his career (as opposed to just a few incredible seasons).

Wallace began his professional career in 1894, when he signed his first contract with a semipro team in Franklin, Pennsylvania. Later that year he was picked up by the National League Cleveland Spiders. During that first season Wallace served as a pitcher. In four games he was 2-1 with 3 complete games. In 1895, Wallace's first full season, he improved his record to 12-14 with 22 complete games, 1 shutout, and 1 save.

Wallace had only 22 total mound appearances in 1896 because he was in the Cleveland outfield for 23 games and at first base for another. The Spiders realized that Wallace hit better than the average pitcher, so they tried him in other positions. As a pitcher, Wallace was 10-7 that year. He posted 13 complete games in 16 starts and pitched 2 shutouts while compiling a 3.34 ERA. However, his walks outnumbered his strikeouts as they had for the past two seasons. As a hitter, Wallace batted .235 with 1 home run and 17 RBI.

Wallace improved his average by exactly 100 points the next season. In 1897 he batted a career best of .335 with 4 homers, 112 RBI, and 99 runs scored. His slugging average was a personal high of .504. The Pittsburgh native kept busy as the Spiders starting third baseman, playing 130 games at the hot corner.

While his statistics dipped a bit in

1898, Wallace continued to prosper as a full-time player. He hit .270 with 3 homers, 99 RBI, and 81 runs scored. After the season's end Wallace and the entire Spiders starting lineup joined the St. Louis Cardinals in one of baseball's strangest deals. The brothers who owned the Spiders bought the club in St. Louis and moved all their best players from the Spiders roster. At that time there was no limit to the number of teams a person could own. The Spiders, without Wallace or any other talent, won only 20 out of 154 games that season and quickly folded.

Wallace played at shortstop for 100 games during his first season with the Cardinals in 1899. He batted .295 with a career-high 12 homers and 108 RBI. By 1901 he had lifted his average to .324 with 2 home runs and 91 RBI.

The slick-fielding shortstop jumped to the newly born American League in 1902 and remained there with the St. Louis Browns for the next 15 seasons. Wallace was given a no-trade contract,

and he soon became one of the highest-paid players in the American League. Throughout the first ten years of the 20th century, Wallace became the American League's resident fielding wizard. He frequently led the junior circuit in numerous defensive categories, including putouts, assists, and total chances. Even today he ranks among the top ten on the all-time defensive lists in total chances, putouts, and assists for shortstops.

In 1914 Wallace played in just 26 games. His home had caught on fire, and he was badly burned and lost all his possessions. Because he was a local hero, St. Louis Browns fans held a special day in his honor; during the game that day fans helped replace the belongings he had lost in the fire.

Wallace considered ending his career in 1915. In June of that year he attempted to become an American League umpire, but after a trial period of one year the Browns were able to convince Wallace to return to the club.

After playing in 32 games in 1918, Wallace retired. He finished with 2,309 hits in 2,382 games for a .268 batting average. He had 391 doubles, 143 triples, 34 home runs, and 1,121 RBI. Wallace served as a playing manager for the St. Louis Browns in 1911 and 1912, then managed the Cincinnati Reds for 25 games in 1937. His lifetime managerial record was 62-154 for a winning percentage of .287. He scouted for the Chicago Cubs and the Cincinnati Reds and served the Reds as a coach in 1926. Wallace remained as a Reds scout well into his eighties. He was elected to the Hall of Fame seven years before his death, which came in 1960, one day before his 87th birthday.

CAREER HIGHLIGHTS
RODERICK JOHN WALLACE

Born: November 4, 1873 Pittsburgh, PA **Died:** November 3, 1960
Height: 5'8" **Weight:** 170 lbs. **Batted:** Right **Threw:** Right
Pitcher, shortstop, third baseman: Cleveland Spiders, 1894-98. Shortstop: St. Louis Cardinals, 1899-1901, 1917-18; St. Louis Browns, 1902-16. Manager: St. Louis Browns, 1911-12; Cincinnati Reds, 1937.

★ Won 24 games as a pitcher
★ Was a perennial leader in several defensive categories at shortstop

★ Played in 25 major league seasons
★ Elected to the Hall of Fame in 1953

MAJOR LEAGUE TOTALS

G	AB	H	BA	2B	3B	HR	R	RBI	SB
2,382	8,618	2,309	.268	391	143	34	1,057	1,121	201

Bobby Wallace got into the Hall of Fame for one reason, his amazing fielding at shortstop. Wallace averaged 6.1 chances per game; only four shortstops have bettered that. He also lead in fielding percentage and assists three times.

ED WALSH

Edward Augustine Walsh was nicknamed "Big Ed" by his contemporaries in major league baseball. Although he was an average size by today's standards (6-foot-1 and 195 pounds), Walsh was one of the biggest men in the major leagues if measured in terms of a successful career.

Walsh pitched his way into the Baseball Hall of Fame by doing something that would get today's hurlers ejected—he threw spitballs. In the early part of the century the spitball was a legal pitch. Many hurlers included it in their arsenals, but none were as successful as Walsh, the acknowledged master of the spitball.

Walsh didn't throw the spitter when he started his professional career in 1902 with Wilkes-Barre of the Pennsylvania State League. During two seasons in the minors Walsh was never even exposed to the pitch, but when he was called up to the Chicago White Sox as a 23-year-old rookie in 1904, he was advised that he had better throw the wet one if he hoped to be successful in the majors.

Fortunately Walsh's roommate that year was Elmer Stricklett, a rookie who was proficient with the spitter. Stricklett taught the tricky pitch to Walsh, and soon the student was throwing it better than his teacher. One hitter claimed that Walsh's spitball was so deceptive that all a batter could see was the spit when it crossed the plate. While he had problems with his knuckleball, Walsh claimed he could control his spitter perfectly. His claims are supported by just 617 lifetime walks, compared to 1,736 strikeouts. Stricklett stayed in the major leagues just four seasons and lost more games than he won. Walsh, on the other hand, had a 14-year career in the majors that ended with 195 victories and a plaque in Cooperstown.

Walsh played all but four games of his Hall of Fame career with the Chicago White Sox. During his prime, from 1907 to 1912, the big right-hander averaged 25 wins a season. In 1908 he accomplished what very few pitchers have done: He won 40 games and lost just 15 with a magnificent ERA of 1.42. He led the league in virtually every pitching category that year, including games started (49), complete games (42), wins (40), winning percentage (.727), innings pitched (464), strikeouts (269), shutouts (11), and saves (6). Walsh was a workhorse who led the league five times in games and four times in innings pitched. His career

ERA of 1.82 still ranks at the top of the all-time list. During 1908 he twice won two games in one day, yielding only 1 run in a doubleheader against the Red Sox on September 29. Not only did his 464 innings set a modern record, but it was the second time he had exceeded 400 frames of work in a season.

Walsh was on the receiving end of a record on October 2, 1908. His White Sox were facing the Cleveland Indians and rugged veteran Addie Joss. Although Walsh yielded just 1 run to the Tribe (striking out 15), Joss was even better. He hurled a perfect game against the Sox, winning 1-0.

Walsh did his best to keep the White Sox in the 1908 pennant race, pitching the last seven games of the season. He set several endurance records that year, but his White Sox finished in third place with an 88-64 record, just one and a half games behind the pennant-winning Detroit Tigers.

The White Sox had much better success in 1906. Known as "The Hitless

Wonders," the team relied on their strong pitching staff to earn the pennant. Walsh led the ChiSox through a 19-game winning streak in August that secured the American League pennant. The team then opposed the crosstown Chicago Cubs. After the teams had split the first two Series games, Walsh hurled a two-hitter (with 12 strikeouts) to boost the Sox in game three. He finished the Series with 2 victories and 17 strikeouts, posting a 1.20 ERA. The Sox whipped the Cubs in six games to earn the world championship. That year Walsh and his teammates received World Series profit shares of $1,874 each—a big windfall for a player whose salary never exceeded $6,000.

Walsh finished his career with 195 wins and 126 losses for an admirable .607 winning percentage. His 57 career shutouts are the ninth-best total in major league history. When his 34 saves are added to his lifetime totals, Walsh participated in a grand total of 229 victories during his career.

Following his retirement as a player, Walsh served as a White Sox coach for four years and managed in the Eastern League for one. While Walsh was coaching baseball at Notre Dame University, his two sons were on the team's pitching staff. Walsh was elected to the Hall of Fame in 1946.

Ed Walsh has the lowest career ERA in history (1.82). He is the only pitcher to have led the league in ERA and losses in the same year—in 1910 his ERA was 1.27 but his team had only a .211 average and 7 home runs.

CAREER HIGHLIGHTS
EDWARD AUGUSTINE WALSH

Born: May 14, 1881 Plains, PA **Died:** May 26, 1959
Height: 6'1" **Weight:** 193 lbs. **Batted:** Right **Threw:** Right
Pitcher: Chicago White Sox, 1904-16; Boston Braves, 1917.

★ Led the A.L. with 40 wins in 1908
★ Holds a major league record with a 1.82 lifetime ERA
★ Struck out more than 250 batters in four seasons
★ Won 20 or more games four times
★ Beat the Cubs twice in the 1906 World Series
★ Set a season record for pitchers with 227 assists in 1907

★ Elected to the Hall of Fame in 1946

MAJOR LEAGUE TOTALS

G	IP	W	L	Pct.	SO	BB	ERA
430	2,965	195	126	.607	1,736	617	1.82

LLOYD WANER

While Hollywood's Warner Brothers were famous for making movies, Pittsburgh's Waner Brothers were famous for winning baseball games. Brothers Paul and Lloyd Waner patrolled the Pirates outfield together for 14 seasons between 1927 and 1940. Known as "Big Poison" and "Little Poison," both Waners were complete ballplayers who could hit, run, and field. When their playing days were over, both brothers found themselves in the Hall of Fame.

Lloyd, Little Poison, was only a shade shorter and a few pounds lighter than his brother; but he was three years younger and had arrived in the majors a year later. Growing up on a farm near the small town of Harrah, Oklahoma (just outside of Oklahoma City), the youngest Waner said he got his first baseball experience by batting corncobs with a hoe handle. He attended McLoud High School, then received a teaching certificate from the East Central Teachers College in Ada, Oklahoma.

Lloyd's start in pro baseball was not an auspicious one. Like his older brother, Lloyd signed his first pro contract with San Francisco of the Pacific Coast League. But, unlike Paul, he did not find immediate success. Batting just .250 in 1925, Lloyd was brought back to San Francisco for the start of the 1926 season. He was released after hitting a dismal .200 in six games.

With a little influence from Paul, who was then with the Pirates, Lloyd got another shot at pro ball with Columbia of the Sally League. Pirates owner Barney Dreyfuss didn't have to pay Lloyd any bonus money to get him to sign. Lloyd finished out the 1926 season batting at a convincing .345 clip (with 172 hits in 121 games), winning the league's Most Valuable Player award. The following year on opening day he joined Paul in the Pirates outfield.

Lloyd exploded onto the major league scene in 1927, batting .355 with a league-leading 133 runs scored. His total of 223 hits (198 of them singles) is still a record for major league rookies. During his first four seasons with the Pirates, Lloyd averaged better than .350 at the plate, and he rapped out more than 200 hits in each of his first three seasons. In 1928 he batted .335 with 221 hits. In 1929 Waner upped his totals to .353 with a career-high 234 hits (and a league-leading 20 triples). Lloyd was an excellent leadoff

hitter, setting the offensive table for teammates such as Pie Traynor, Dick Bartell, Adam Comorosky (who led the team in RBI), and older brother Paul—all RBI specialists. That year the Pittsburgh offensive machine was in high gear, with Lloyd scoring a career-high 134 runs. He was on pace to gain 200-plus hits for a fourth consecutive year in 1930 when he was sidelined by an appendectomy 68 games into the season. Fully recovered, Waner returned in 1931 to bang out a league-leading 214 base hits. Much of Waner's batting success was attributed to his amazing speed, particularly when running to first base. He was also one of the most difficult players in history to strike out.

Lloyd had his only World Series experience in 1927 against the New York Yankees team dubbed "Murderers' Row" for their heavy hitters. The youngest Waner did some of his own heavy hitting though. He batted .400 with 6 hits (including a double and a triple) and 5 runs scored. Unfortunately, the Waners and teammates were ham-

mered by the Bronx Bombers in four straight contests.

Donnie Bush, Waner's first manager, was the person who gave him the most assistance early in his career. In 1927 Bush had so much confidence in Lloyd that he moved resident center fielder Kiki Cuyler to make room for his new prize pupil.

Besides his Little Poison moniker, Lloyd was also given the nickname "Muscles." Lloyd once said that he attributed much of his success to his wrist muscles, which helped him get around on pitches quickly.

Waner's lifetime totals include a .316 average, 2,459 hits, and 1,201 runs scored. He ranks second all-time with 44.9 at-bats per strikeout. Only Roberto Clemente, Max Carey, and brother Paul played more games in a Pirate outfield than Lloyd (1,680). Even today Lloyd ranks in the Pirates top ten in games played, at-bats, runs scored, hits, singles, triples, total bases, and batting average.

After retiring from active duty, he scouted for the Pirates and the Orioles until 1956. Lloyd Waner was elected to the Hall of Fame in 1967, 15 years after his brother Paul was enshrined in Cooperstown. Lloyd retired in his native state of Oklahoma, where he died in 1982 at age 76.

Lloyd Waner was never a power hitter. In his first season, he set a rookie record with 223 hits, 198 of which were singles. Though mostly a singles hitter, his lifetime .316 average shows that he did his most important job well—getting on base.

CAREER HIGHLIGHTS
LLOYD JAMES WANER

Born: March 16, 1906 Harrah, OK **Died:** July 22, 1982
Height: 5'9" **Weight:** 150 lbs. **Batted:** Left **Threw:** Right
Outfielder: Pittsburgh Pirates, 1927-40, 1944-45; Boston Braves, 1941; Cincinnati Reds, 1941; Philadelphia Phillies, 1942; Brooklyn Dodgers, 1944.

★ Had a .316 lifetime batting average
★ Hit .400 in the 1927 World Series
★ Had four seasons of 200-plus hits

★ Batted over .300 in 13 seasons
★ Named to the 1938 All-Star team
★ Elected to the Hall of Fame in 1967

MAJOR LEAGUE TOTALS

G	AB	H	BA	2B	3B	HR	R	RBI	SB
1,993	7,772	2,459	.316	281	118	28	1,201	598	67

PAUL WANER

When Paul Waner ripped a single to center on June 19, 1942, he became only the third player in National League history to accumulate 3,000 career hits. Only the great Cap Anson and Honus Wagner had done it before. Waner was, indeed, one of the greatest hitters of his era. Fourteen times he batted over the .300 mark, six times better than .350. In eight seasons he collected more than 200 hits, and three times he led the National League in batting.

As a rookie with the Pittsburgh Pirates in 1926, Waner batted .336. The next year he won the National League Most Valuable Player award and his first batting title, hitting .380 with a league-leading 237 base hits. When younger brother Lloyd joined Paul in the Pittsburgh outfield, fans embraced the brothers from Oklahoma as heroes. Neither brother was particularly tall and they both weighed only around 150 pounds, so the Waners were thought of as hardworking "little guys." They weren't brawny home run hitters; instead, they relied on keen discipline at the plate and great speed in the field to gain their fame in the National League.

Paul was a hard-hitting speedster who led the league in triples his first two years in the majors and in doubles in two later seasons. Frequently taking extra bases, Waner piled up two-base and three-base hits during his 20-year career; his lifetime totals in both categories still rank in the top ten on the all-time list. Waner ended his productive career with 3,152 hits and a .333 career batting mark. He is still ranked in the top ten in many career categories for the Pirates, including games, at-bats, runs scored, hits, singles, doubles (tied for first with Honus Wagner at 556), triples, total bases, RBI, and extra-base hits. His lifetime average as a Pirate is a team-record .340. Combined with Lloyd's 2,459 hits, the two brothers had a record number of hits—even higher than all three DiMaggio brothers put together.

Both Waner brothers were known as excellent contact hitters, and both got their professional starts with San Francisco of the Pacific Coast League. Before starting in San Francisco, Paul Waner played ball in grammar school in Harrah, Oklahoma. Then he moved to Oklahoma City for high school. He attended East Central State College at Ada, Oklahoma; he had hoped to become a lawyer. His collegiate days were occupied with playing first base

and outfield on the college team. Upon signing his pro contract, Paul spent three seasons in the Pacific Coast League. He averaged .369, .356, and .401 before he was purchased by Pittsburgh in 1926. The San Francisco Seals, like all other minor league teams, sold the contracts of successful players to major league clubs for income. Paul's contract went untouched at $100,000, because he was so small. Teams didn't believe he had the strength to be a major league hitter.

He made believers out of the Pirates team ownership after his .401 season with 280 hits in 1925. Younger brother Lloyd joined him a year later to patrol the Pirates outfield. (Paul was instrumental in getting the Pirates to sign his brother.)

One of the noted anecdotes about the Waner brothers revolves around their only World Series appearance in

1927, versus the New York Yankees team nicknamed "Murderers' Row." After the Waners had watched the Yankees finish batting practice, all the wide-eyed Lloyd could remark to his brother was, "Gee, they're big, aren't they?" Although the Yankees swept the Bucs in four straight games, Paul hit .333 with 5 hits (including 1 double) and 3 RBI in the fall classic.

The Waners did prove to be poison for opposing pitchers, but their nicknames, "Big Poison" and "Little Poison," were actually supplied unintentionally by a New York sportswriter. He had a thick Brooklyn accent, and was actually referring to the brothers as big and little "person." Older brother Paul later confessed that he needed glasses but didn't want to wear them while playing because of his vanity. He also claimed that the ball looked larger to him when he was batting, so the glasses wouldn't have helped.

After the Pirates let Waner go in 1941, he hooked up with the Brooklyn Dodgers, Boston Braves, and New York Yankees through 1945. His best post-Pittsburgh effort came in 82 games with the Dodgers in 1943, when he batted .311. That year he succeeded in 10 of 21 pinch-hitting assignments. Following his retirement as a player, Waner managed one year in the International League. He was batting coach for the Milwaukee Braves during their 1957 world championship and for the St. Louis Cardinals in 1958 and 1959. He finished his baseball career as batting coach for the Phillies from 1960 until his death. Paul Waner was elected to the Hall of Fame in 1952, and he died in Florida in 1965 at the age of 62.

CAREER HIGHLIGHTS
PAUL GLEE WANER

Born: April 16, 1903 Harrah, OK   **Died:** August 29, 1965
Height: 5'9" **Weight:** 153 lbs.   **Batted:** Left **Threw:** Left
Outfielder: Pittsburgh Pirates, 1926-40; Brooklyn Dodgers, 1941, 1943-44; Boston Braves, 1941-42; New York Yankees, 1944-45.

- ★ Batted .300-plus 14 times
- ★ Had eight seasons of 200-plus hits
- ★ Led the N.L. in batting three times
- ★ Ranks ninth in career doubles and tenth in career triples

- ★ Played in the 1927 World Series
- ★ Named to four All-Star teams
- ★ Elected to the Hall of Fame in 1952
- ★ Became the third N.L. player to reach 3,000 hits

MAJOR LEAGUE TOTALS

G	AB	H	BA	2B	3B	HR	R	RBI	SB
2,549	9,459	3,152	.333	603	190	113	1,626	1,309	104

A small man, Paul Waner showed the baseball world that big talent can come in small packages. Waner was a line drive hitter, who led his league in doubles and triples twice. He also led the N.L. in batting average three times.

BOB WELCH

Accomplished Oakland Athletics power pitcher Bob Welch is often said to have perfect delivery. His warp-speed fastball and beefed-up curveball made their debuts in the American League in 1988, giving notice that the veteran righthander plans to continue his career as one of baseball's consistent winners.

Bad luck and assorted injuries stopped Welch from winning 20 games a season in his first 11 years, but don't let that fool you. Eight times in his career Welch has won 13 or more games in a season. His 17 wins in his first season with Oakland in 1988 was a career high, which he matched in '89.

When the A's, Mets, and Dodgers hooked up in a three-way trade on December 11, 1987, Welch was one of the principals. Because the Dodgers had been without a solid starting shortstop since the retirement of Bill Russell, the team went to great lengths to get Alfredo Griffin from Oakland—sacrificing pitchers Matt Young, Jack Savage, and Welch to get Griffin and reliever Jay Howell. Immediately the skeptics spoke up. Was Welch too much to give? Would the A's be big winners in the trade?

Ultimately both teams benefited, and in 1988 they faced off in the World Series. The postseason appearance must have been a personal triumph for Welch, who got to show his former teammates what he had achieved with his new team. His 17-9 record trailed only team ace Dave Stewart, and his 36 starts were second highest in the league behind Stewart's 37. Welch also had career highs in strikeouts (158) and innings pitched (245).

Welch's success was obscured in the World Series by his traditional lack of luck. Because the A's bats were dormant throughout the entire five games, Welch was only given 1 run to work with. He left after five innings in the third game, when he yielded just 1 Dodger run on 6 hits. He struck out 8 Dodgers in five innings while walking 3. Welch got no decision in the game, which ended in a 2-1 win for the Dodgers.

The World Series duel of 1988 brought back memories of Welch's major league debut, a classic baptism by fire. Before attending Eastern Michigan University, the Detroit native was selected by the Chicago Cubs in the 14th round of the 1974 draft. Three years later he signed with the Los Angeles Dodgers after they selected him in the

first round. His 14 appearances that season with Double-A San Antonio were unremarkable: He had 4 wins, 5 losses, and a 4.44 ERA. However, his 56 strikeouts in 71 innings held a promise that was fulfilled in a special Arizona fall training camp, where he went 5-1 and fashioned a 1.72 ERA, winning the John Carey award as the most improved Dodger. The improvements held the following year. After 11 games in Triple-A Albuquerque, he had 5 wins, 1 loss, and a 3.78 ERA. On June 19 the 21-year-old went to Los Angeles, where he acquired a win and a save in just four days. Joining the starting rotation on August 5 for the ailing Rick Rhoden, Welch blanked the Giants, sparking and aiding a seven-game Dodgers winning streak. His fine 2.03 ERA in 23 games landed the team in a successful pennant race. His four-hit win against the Padres on September 24 clinched the Western Division title for Los Angeles and gave him a total of 3 shutouts for the season.

The remarkable rookie won one game of the National League Championship Series against the Philadelphia Phillies. Welch logged 4.1 innings of relief in the N.L.C.S. opener, allowing just 2 hits and 1 run while striking out 5 and walking none. He made three relief appearances in his team's unsuccessful World Series bid against the Yankees. His brief glory came in game two when he struck out Reggie Jackson to earn a save.

Welch had a sore arm in his sophomore campaign of 1979, which limited his effectiveness and innings pitched. Working in relief for half the season, the big righthander was 5-6 with 5 saves. Welch made a dramatic comeback in 1980. Before spring training began he entered an alcohol rehabilitation treatment facility. He began the season stronger than ever, winning 9 of his first 12 decisions and getting a spot on the National League All-Star roster. Welch earned a 14-9 record that year. A bone spur in Welch's elbow slowed down his progress in 1981. He won 9 games in 23 starts. During the postseason Welch was moved to the bullpen but had little success in the N.L.C.S. or World Series (although the Dodgers finally beat the Yankees in six games).

Based on his 1989 performance (17-8, with a 3.00 ERA), Welch still has lots of talent to offer the A's. He's still tough on righthand batters, and he has maintained his good follow-through, which has made him one of baseball's best fielders. Runners who do get on base discover that Welch's pickoff move has few equals. If the A's continue to give their veteran offensive support, Welch could be a dominant force in the A.L. for years to come.

CAREER HIGHLIGHTS
ROBERT LYNN WELCH

Born: November 3, 1956 Detroit, MI
Height: 6'3" **Weight:** 193 lbs. **Bats:** Right **Throws:** Right
Pitcher: Los Angeles Dodgers, 1978-87; Oakland A's, 1988-89.

* Earned a career-high 17 wins in 1988
* Tied for the N.L. lead in shutouts in 1987
* Struck out Reggie Jackson to earn a World Series save in 1978
* Played on the 1980 All-Star team
* The sixth-winningest L.A. Dodger in history
* Appeared in six L.C.S. and four World Series

MAJOR LEAGUE TOTALS

G	IP	W	L	Pct.	SO	BB	ERA
361	2,276	149	103	.591	1,587	724	3.18

*In only two years with the Oakland A's, Bob Welch has twice been to the World Series.
His near-perfect delivery, incredible fastball, improved curveball, and deadly pickoff move
make him a formidable opponent and an asset for Oakland.*

ZACK WHEAT

Zack Wheat, the hard-hitting outfielder, was a favorite of Brooklyn Dodgers fans. Playing in the deadball era, he was adept with both the bat and the glove, and registered more playing time in a Dodgers uniform than any player in that team's long history.

Nicknamed "Buck" to go with his last name, Wheat got his professional start playing with Shreveport of the Texas League in 1908. A year later he advanced to Mobile of the Southern Association, where, despite a rather dismal .246 batting average, he was impressive enough to be added to the Brooklyn roster at the end of the season. Maybe it was beginner's luck, but Wheat had more success hitting major league pitching than he had in the minor leagues, as evidenced by his first-year .304 batting average. It was the first of 14 seasons that he would hit better than .300 for the Dodgers.

A brilliant outfielder, Wheat showed quickness, intelligence, and a great throwing arm on defense. He tallied an average of 15 outfield assists per season and participated in 54 double plays, while posting a career fielding percentage of .966. Dodgers general manager Branch Rickey once said that Wheat was the finest outfielder the team ever had. Manager Casey Stengel ranked the Dodger great behind only Stan Musial on his all-time player list. Wheat was also an exciting cleanup hitter and a speedy baserunner. He quickly developed into one of the best all-around competitors of the day, as popular with fans in Brooklyn as Babe Ruth was with fans in the Bronx. Unlike the hulking Ruth, Wheat was surprisingly small for such a versatile athlete. He was 5-foot-10 and weighed 170 pounds and wore only a size 5½ shoe.

Wheat was a terror at the plate, eight times batting over .320. For two straight seasons, 1923 and 1924, Wheat hit at an identical .375 clip and then followed it up with a .359 average the next year. The only year he won the National League batting title was in 1918, when he hit .335. He banged out a total of 2,884 hits in his career and was only one good season away from the magic 3,000-hit plateau when he retired. Wheat spent his final year in baseball with Connie Mack's Philadelphia Athletics—his only season out of a Dodgers uniform. Wheat ended his baseball career after playing in 1928 with the Minneapolis Millers of the American Association. In his tenure with Brooklyn, the team won two

National League pennants, in 1916 and 1920, but never won a World Series. But Wheat made things interesting in the fall classic with a .333 batting average, and his 10 hits topped players from both teams. During Wheat's 18 years in Brooklyn, 14 of the Dodger teams were second-division squads winding up from fifth to seventh place in the National League. Thus Wheat's hitting was a bright spot for several gloomy Dodger clubs.

When the baseball became more lively in the early 1920s, Wheat began pounding the horsehide even harder. He had always been a line-drive hitter, but with the added zip in the baseball, his "frozen ropes" started falling in for hits even more often. The birth of the "rabbit" ball was reflected in Wheat's stats. In 1921 he slugged 14 home runs (5 more than any previous year) with 85 RBI. In 1922 Wheat walloped career highs of 16 round-trippers and 112 RBI. He played in just 98 games in 1923 but rebounded for more long-ball hitting in 1924 with 14 homers and 97 RBI. He socked 14 more homers in

1925 along with 103 RBI. This seems like more than coincidence: Wheat had played 12 years with the Dodgers before gaining the gift of power. Unlike many hitters, who feasted on nothing but fastballs, Wheat loved to hit curves. Christy Mathewson was one of Wheat's favorite pitchers to bat against, because he could handle the breaking pitches from "Big Six."

Wheat was one of baseball's most tireless performers. He was injured in 1917 and played in just 109 games; and in 1923 he staged a prolonged contract holdout and saw action in just 98 contests. Aside from those two seasons, Wheat was a mainstay in the Dodgers outfield. He still holds the all-time club record for most games (2,322) and most at-bats (8,859). His lifetime totals include 132 home runs, 1,248 RBI, and 1,289 runs scored. His 172 triples are another Dodger record and rank 23rd in history (tying with Tommy Leach). Wheat's 205 stolen bases are seventh on the all-time Dodger list.

Following his retirement as a player, Wheat turned to farming, worked as a police officer in Kansas City, and then ran a fishing resort in the Missouri Ozarks before he retired. In 1959, more than three decades after his retirement, the Hall of Fame finally honored Wheat for his achievments by inducting him. He died at age 83 in 1972.

Zack Wheat was a fixture in left field at Ebbets Field in Brooklyn for eighteen years. A curveball hitter, Wheat batted over .300 fourteen times but only won the N.L. batting crown once—in 1918 with a .335 average.

CAREER HIGHLIGHTS
ZACHARY DAVIS WHEAT

Born: May 23, 1888 Hamilton, MO **Died:** March 11, 1972
Height: 5'10" **Weight:** 170 lbs. **Batted:** Left **Threw:** Right
Outfielder: Brooklyn Dodgers, 1909-26; Philadelphia Athletics, 1927.

* Compiled a .317 batting mark
* Won the N.L. batting title in 1918
* Ranks first in career hits among all Dodgers
* Batted over .300 in 14 seasons
* Played in two World Series
* Elected to the Hall of Fame in 1959

MAJOR LEAGUE TOTALS

G	AB	H	BA	2B	3B	HR	R	RBI	SB
2,410	9,106	2,884	.317	476	172	132	1,289	1,248	205

LOU WHITAKER

After watching even one Detroit Tigers game, it's easy to understand why their second baseman is called "Sweet Lou." Lou Whitaker's youthful face and diminutive form, combined with his agility at second base, swift arm, and basestealing prowess, make him a fan favorite.

Whitaker is also an aggressive power hitter who has posted double-digit homer totals for the past eight years (peaking at 28 in 1989), and he hasn't brought in fewer than 55 RBI since 1982. Unfortunately an off-field knee injury took him out of the 1988 season in early September, and the symptoms have been evident for some time. His batting average and power stats had been dropping over the past few years, though his 1989 performance of 28 homers and 85 RBI betters any of his previous power stats. He has had to rely more and more on his exceptional eye and patience. While he may have slowed down a bit in the infield in recent years, he still succeeds with his glove through determination, and he wisely plays hitters in the proper locations.

The Brooklyn native began his career at 18, when he was drafted by the Tigers. Although signed in June of 1975, Whitaker got in 42 games before the season's end. The following season he was the Florida State League Most Valuable Player, and small wonder: He led in many offensive and defensive categories, with 30 double plays, 99 putouts, 267 assists, a .924 fielding average, and 70 runs scored.

Although he bettered each of those categories (save double plays) the following year in the Southern League, only his 81 runs brought top honors. (These high marks were accomplished in 17 fewer games than before, due to a two-week disability listing.) His assists rose to 285, his fielding to .970, and his putouts more than doubled to 208. Whitaker rose out of the minors, finishing 1977 with 11 games in Detroit. In that short time he put out 17 with no errors, stole 2 bases, and batted .250.

In the spring of 1978 Sweet Lou was the Tigers starting second baseman, a role he has held through the 1989 season. His quick reflexes and excellent contact were used in the leadoff position for many years. (Lately he has been batting number three, and in 1988 his average rose for the first time in five years.) In 1978 Whitaker set the tone for his many seasons of accomplishments by becoming the A.L. Rookie of

the Year, beating out Paul Molitar and teammate Alan Trammell, among others. The Brooklyn boy managed 138 hits that year in 139 games but belted only 3 homers. He racked up 58 RBI and was responsible for 71 runs and 7 stolen bases.

The next season he spent two weeks on the disabled list, but he still raised his batting and fielding averages. He swiped 20 bases, a personal best. His 340 putouts were also a personal best. He faltered slightly during the 1980 season as his statistics slipped in almost every category, but in 1981 he had a league-leading 354 assists. This was a prelude to 1982, when he led the American League with personal bests in fielding average (.988) and assists (470). He also clobbered his first season of double-digit homers (15), and he inflated his batting average to .286. His

average kept rising until it reached .320 in 1986, his best ever. No other American League second sacker came close to Whitaker in chances (811) or double plays (120) in 1982. But Whitaker had to wait one more year before catching up to Frank White, who monopolized the Gold Glove award for second basemen for six years from 1977 to 1982.

Whitaker's bat became active in the 1983 season, as the still young second sacker tallied 206 hits and 40 doubles.

Whitaker has likewise acquitted himself well in Series play, appearing in eight World Series games in the 1984 and 1987 seasons. In 1984 the Tigers were victorious in the World Series. Whitaker tied a record with 5 runs in a five-game Series. He has never committed an error in postseason play.

Together with shortstop Alan Trammell, Whitaker has helped solidify the Tigers keystone combination for more than a decade. Whitaker has been a consistent, all-around performer for Detroit and has the talent to keep them in pennant contention for the next few seasons.

Lou Whitaker has been with the Detroit Tigers his whole major league career, and he is one of the players who has helped the Tigers to their two World Series appearances. In 1984 the Tigers were successful in their Series bid, and Whitaker tied a record with 5 runs in a five-game Series.

CAREER HIGHLIGHTS
LOUIS RODMAN WHITAKER

Born: May 12, 1957 Brooklyn, NY
Height: 5'11" **Weight:** 160 lbs. **Bats:** Left **Throws:** Right
Second baseman: Detroit Tigers, 1977-89.

- ★ Won the A.L. Rookie of the Year award in 1978
- ★ Batted .278 in the 1984 World Series
- ★ Played in two A.L. Championship Series
- ★ Named to the Gold Glove team in 1983 through 1985
- ★ Played in four All-Star games
- ★ Named to the Silver Slugger team in 1983, 1984, 1985, and 1987

MAJOR LEAGUE TOTALS

G	AB	H	BA	2B	3B	HR	R	RBI	SB
1,695	6,221	1,719	.276	279	58	149	965	721	116

HOYT WILHELM

oyt Wilhelm was the first extremely successful long-term relief pitcher in baseball. Beginning his career in 1952, Wilhelm established major league records for games pitched (1,070) and relief wins (123) by the time he retired 21 years later. Although the save wasn't an official record category until 1969, baseball researchers have determined that Wilhelm would have earned 227 saves during his career, ranking him fifth on the all-time list. His statistics are incredible considering that he didn't make his major league debut until he was 28 years old.

Wilhelm was extremely effective during his first season, when he played with the New York Giants. He notched 15 wins in relief with 11 saves and only 3 losses. He led the National League with a winning percentage of .833, an ERA of 2.43, and an amazing 71 appearances. He paced the senior circuit in appearances again in 1953 with 68, winning 7 games and saving 15. In 1954 Wilhelm's record was a sparkling 12-4 with 7 saves; he worked exclusively in 57 relief outings. The Giants won the National League pennant that season and subsequently whipped the highly favored Cleveland Indians in the World Series. In the third game of the World Series Wilhelm relieved shaky starter Ruben Gomez, who early in the game was getting battered by Indian hitters. Wilhelm unveiled his knuckler and retired 5 straight batters.

The Giants traded Wilhelm in 1957 to the St. Louis Cardinals in exchange for first baseman Whitey Lockman. On September 21 the Cardinals sold him to Cleveland. It looked like Wilhelm's future might be in jeopardy when he failed to stick with the Indians for an entire season. The Baltimore Orioles rescued Wilhelm from nowhere, picking him up on waivers, and he stayed there from 1958 through 1962.

Wilhelm received three All-Star invitations while with the Orioles. In his first year in Baltimore he won his second ERA title with a 2.19 effort, becoming one of the few pitchers in history to lead both leagues in ERA. The 1960s became Wilhelm's decade. Every year fans talked about Wilhelm's advancing age; but every year the tobacco-chewing moundsman added a few more saves to his ever-growing total. From 1961 until his 1972 retirement, Wilhelm had double-digit save totals in 9 of 12 campaigns.

Wilhelm had one of his finest seasons when he went back to the bullpen in

1962, his final season with the Orioles. After three seasons in the starting rotation, Wilhelm got back into the relief groove with 15 saves, 7 wins, and a 1.94 ERA. The O's put Wilhelm on the trading block after the season, and on January 14, 1963, Wilhelm, Dave Nicholson, Ron Hansen, and Pete Ward went to the ChiSox in exchange for shortstop Luis Aparicio and outfielder Al Smith.

Wilhelm had some of his best years in the Chicago bullpen. He posted three straight years of 20 or more saves from 1963 through 1965. The big righty kept his ERA under 2.00 for five consecutive seasons, while his appearances were just as impressive: 55 in 1963, 73 in 1964, 66 in 1965, 46 in 1966, 49 in 1967, and 72 in 1968.

The North Carolina native pitched for nine different teams in 21 years, making him one of baseball's most traded players of the 1950s and 1960s.

When he finally retired in July of 1972, he was five days short of his 49th birthday. The original relief specialist was able to pitch so long and so effectively because he relied almost exclusively on the knuckleball. He first heard about the pitch in 1939 while listening to radio broadcasts of Senators games. The announcers talked about pitcher Dutch Leonard's famous "butterfly" pitch, now known as a knuckleball. Wilhelm learned to throw the knuckler at age 16, when a newspaper ran a how-to article about the pitch. Part of the beauty of Wilhelm's "out" pitch was that it required little physical effort compared to other pitches, such as a fastball or slider. Wilhelm's effortless delivery and trick pitch prolonged his career for more than two decades.

Although primarily a relief pitcher, Wilhelm was used by the Baltimore Orioles in a starting capacity on several occasions in the late 1950s and early 1960s. In 1958 Wilhelm started four games for the Orioles, and in one of his starts he pitched a no-hitter. Throwing just 99 pitches, nearly all of them knuckleballs, Wilhelm recorded a 1-0 no-hit victory over the New York Yankees.

In his career, Wilhelm had a record of 143 wins, 122 losses, 20 complete games, and 5 shutouts in 1,070 games started. When you combine Wilhelm's career victories and saves, he was partially responsible for 370 victories.

Wilhelm served as a New York Yankees minor league coach after his retirement. He became the first relief pitcher ever represented in the Hall of Fame when he was inducted in 1985.

CAREER HIGHLIGHTS
JAMES HOYT WILHELM

Born: July 26, 1923   Huntersville, NC
Height: 6'0"   **Weight:** 190 lbs.   **Batted:** Right   **Threw:** Right
Pitcher: New York Giants, 1952-56; St. Louis Cardinals, 1957; Cleveland Indians, 1957-58; Baltimore Orioles, 1958-62; Chicago White Sox, 1963-68; California Angels, 1969; Atlanta Braves, 1969-70, 1971; Chicago Cubs, 1970; Los Angeles Dodgers, 1971-72.

★ Pitched a no-hitter against the Yankees in 1958
★ Hit a home run in his first major league at-bat and never hit another

★ Established a major league record by pitching in 1,070 games
★ Elected to the Hall of Fame in 1985

MAJOR LEAGUE TOTALS

G	IP	W	L	Pct.	SV	SO	BB	ERA
1,070	2,253	143	122	.540	227	1,610	778	2.52

Hoyt Wilhelm is the first relief pitcher to be inducted into the Hall of Fame. Wilhelm owes his fame and his longevity to his knuckleball, which he popularized and used almost to the exclusion of his other pitches.

BILLY WILLIAMS

The City of Chicago rejoiced when Cubs favorite Billy Williams, the most productive lefthand slugger in the club's history, was inducted into the Baseball Hall of Fame in 1987. It was the culmination of a great major league career that stretched from 1959 to 1976. Williams appeared in only a few games in 1959 and 1960 and so was technically still a rookie in 1961 when he became the Cubs full-time left fielder. He batted .278 that year with 25 home runs and 86 RBI to capture the N.L. Rookie of the Year award.

Williams did not miss a single game between September of 1963 and September of 1970—a remarkable string of 1,117 straight games, which was broken by Steve Garvey's 1,207 games.

Chicago Cubs hitting coach Rogers Hornsby was one of the first big influences on Williams' career. Because he spent nearly four complete seasons in the minor leagues, Williams had lots of tutoring before he became a full-time Cub in 1961. Former Cub general manager Bob Kennedy was instrumental in coaching Williams on defense during his early years. Williams was a well-traveled minor leaguer with stops in Ponca City, Pueblo, Burlington, San Antonio, Fort Worth, and Houston. One of his best minor league seasons came in Houston (of the American Association) in 1960, where he batted .323 with 26 homers and 80 RBI.

Williams was a model of consistency for the Cubs throughout the 1960s. In 1964 he registered his highest average to date at .312, along with 33 home runs and 98 RBI. In the 1964 All-Star game Williams hit 1 of 3 homers that led the National League to a 7-4 win over the junior circuit.

Williams hit .300 or better five times during his career; he had 14 seasons with 20 or more homers, ten seasons with more than 90 RBI, and nine seasons of more than 90 runs scored. Williams finished second in the Most Valuable Player balloting twice during his distinguished career, but he was edged out both years by Cincinnati catcher Johnny Bench, whose Reds won the National League pennant both years. (Traditionally, players on winning teams get preference in postseason awards.) Williams was, however, honored by *The Sporting News* as the Player of the Year for his amazing 1972 campaign.

In that season he won his first and only National League batting crown

with a .333 average. His slugging percentage also topped the National League at .606. His 37 homers finished 3 behind league-leader Bench at 40. Williams knocked in 122 runs, again just 3 behind the league-leading Bench. If Williams had earned just 4 more homers and 4 additional RBI, he would have been the first triple crown winner in the senior circuit since Joe Medwick accomplished the feat in 1937.

This wasn't even Williams' greatest season. That had occurred two years earlier, in 1970. During that momentous season Williams racked up remarkable stats, including a league-leading 205 hits, 42 homers, a career-best 6.6 home run percentage, a league-high 373 total bases, a league-best 137 runs scored, 129 RBI, and a .322 batting average. He finished second in the league in RBI, second in homers, and fourth in average.

Even superstars don't have guaranteed jobs, as Williams painfully found out on October 23, 1974. The Cubs ownership was cutting the budget and

bringing in younger, more inexpensive players. So Williams was sent to the Oakland A's in exchange for pitchers Bob Locker and Darold Knowles and infielder Manny Trillo.

The trade to Oakland put Williams in a designated hitter's role for two seasons. In 1975 he had his best year with the A's, batting .244 with 23 home runs and 81 RBI in 155 games. The Athletics, meanwhile, continued their domination of the American League Western Division with yet another pennant. Williams narrowly missed getting his first World Series appearance when the A's were defeated by the Boston Red Sox in the A.L. Championship Series. Williams was hitless in eight postseason at-bats.

Williams retired after 18 major league campaigns, and he remains one of the greatest sluggers in the history of Cubs baseball. His 392 home runs are the most career four-baggers by any Cub lefthand hitter. He also holds team marks for lefthanders in total hits, doubles, extra-base hits, RBI, and slugging percentage. Additionally, no Cub has ever scored more career runs than Williams.

After his retirement Williams served as the Cubs hitting instructor and first base coach from 1978 to 1982. He spent the next three seasons coaching with the Oakland A's before returning to the Cubs in 1986. After serving as a hitting coach in 1986 and 1987, Williams moved to the team's front office in 1988, where he became a special player consultant. The Cubs have retired Williams' uniform number (26), making him one of only two players in Chicago history (the other was Ernie Banks) to receive the honor.

CAREER HIGHLIGHTS
BILLY LEO WILLIAMS

Born: June 15, 1938   Whistler, AL
Height: 6'1"   **Weight:** 175 lbs.   **Batted:** Left   **Threw:** Right
Outfielder: Chicago Cubs, 1959-74; Oakland Athletics, 1975-76.

★ Named the N.L. Rookie of the Year in 1961
★ Hit 20 or more homers 14 times
★ Won the 1972 batting title with a .333 average

★ Established an N.L. record by playing in 1,117 consecutive games
★ Led the N.L. in hits and runs in 1970
★ Elected to the Hall of Fame in 1987

MAJOR LEAGUE TOTALS

G	AB	H	BA	2B	3B	HR	R	RBI	SB
2,488	9,350	2,711	.290	434	88	426	1,410	1,475	90

Billy Williams was a shining light in a disappointing era for Chicago Cubs fans. In 1972 Williams won the N.L. batting crown with a .333 average, 37 homers, and 122 RBI. He came 4 homers and 4 RBI away from winning the triple crown.

TED WILLIAMS

ed Williams had plenty of nicknames. "The Splended Splinter" may have been as much a tribute to his tall, gaunt frame as to his mythic ability to shatter a bat in quest of a home run. "Thumper" was direct homage to his hitting prowess. "Teddy Ballgame" quite simply demonstrated that Williams and the game were one and the same. Two more monikers also define Ted Williams: "The Kid" and "The Big Guy." Never since has a player shown such unabashed determination, denied it so loudly, or carried on such a love/hate affair with his fans.

Williams was quite a personality. Comtemporary writers dryly commented on Williams' frequent demonstrations of his ability to "spit to all fields." His verbal brawls with the press on and off the diamond only served to further endear him to fans—and some writers as well.

Williams' career began in 1936 when the 17-year-old Kid signed with the newly organized San Diego Padres of the Pacific Coast League. Few fans are aware that his debut batting average was .285. Yet Williams himself is the last person to claim that his .344 lifetime average (including one full season at .406) was the result of natural talent. He made a serious study of hitting, and little else, throughout his life: while growing up with his workaholic mother, during his two seasons in the minors, and throughout his big league career. Even in 1959 the intimidating veteran could take strikes off a newcomer, analyzing the pitcher's windup, change-up, and delivery until something clicked and he smashed a home run.

For all this, Thumper was a notorious pull hitter, so much so that opposing Cleveland manager Lou Boudreau created "The Williams Shift," soon a standard on every American League team. Oddly, Williams' amazing power only once led the BoSox to a World Series. In Boston's 1946 Series bid, the same year Boudreau shifted the bulk of his fielders to right field (Williams' field of choice), Williams played poorly in the postseason. The Cardinals stopped Boston in seven games, and Williams had just 5 hits for a .200 average.

Even with the opposing outfielders stacked like sardines against him, Williams would seldom bunt. He did learn to hit to the opposite field, but always grudgingly. The opposing team's defensive tactics were not as detrimental to his lifetime stats, however, as the pitchers' tendency to throw around him.

He also lost five seasons as a pilot in World War II and Korea.

Nevertheless, Williams' lifetime stats lead the BoSox and often place him second or third in major league history. He only once batted below .300 in the majors. In his short seasons of 1952 and 1953 he hit .400 and .407.

Williams claimed the major league triple crown not just once, which would be amazing enough, but twice, in 1942 and 1947. Neither time did his feat earn him the Most Valuable Player award, probably because he had such an uneven relationship with the national press. Indeed, his three marriages and subsequent divorces received as much coverage as his on-field antics. Williams himself fueled the fire, claiming that he prolonged his career only so he could keep up his alimony payments.

Such comments belied his year-round dedication to the game. (He always kept in shape in the off-season by hunting and fishing.) Still, after bringing his .254 average in 1959 up to a .316 mark in 1960, the 42-year-old superstar hung up his spikes while they were still sharp. His stunning career statistics include 521 homers (the tenth-highest total ever), the sixth-best batting average at .344, and an incredible .634 slugging percentage (ranking second on the all-time list). One little-known accomplishment on Williams' resume is his 2,019 bases on balls, the second-highest total ever. He drew 90 or more walks 14 times and led the league in free passes on eight occasions.

A frustrating four-year career managing the Washington Senators (which became the Texas Rangers in 1972) began when Williams led the Senators to a surprising 86-76 record and a fourth-place finish in 1969, but the team floundered the following three years. Williams ended his managerial career with a 273-364 record.

The 18-time All-Star knew no bounds to his competitiveness. In 1950, when Williams was playing left field during the All-Star game at Chicago's Comiskey Park, he fractured his left elbow crashing into the left field wall during a first-inning catch. Despite the pain, he stayed in the game until the ninth inning. Although he played in just 19 more games that season, he finished with 28 homers, 97 RBI, and a .317 average.

CAREER HIGHLIGHTS
THEODORE SAMUEL WILLIAMS

Born: August 30, 1918 San Diego, CA
Height: 6'3" **Weight:** 205 lbs. **Batted:** Left **Threw:** Right
Outfielder: Boston Red Sox, 1939-60. Manager: Washington Senators, 1969-71; Texas Rangers, 1972.

* Selected as the A.L. MVP in 1946 and 1949
* Is second only to Babe Ruth in career walks
* Was the last batter to hit over .400
* Won seven batting titles
* Has a career slugging average of .634, the second highest in baseball history to Babe Ruth
* His career on-base percentage of .483 is the highest in history
* Has the tenth-best home run total of all-time
* Won two triple crowns
* Elected to the Hall of Fame in 1966
* Is the only player to win a batting title after age 40

MAJOR LEAGUE TOTALS

G	AB	H	BA	2B	3B	HR	R	RBI	SB
2,292	7,706	2,654	.344	525	71	521	1,798	1,839	24

Ted Williams was a competitive player who is either the best or the second best (Babe Ruth being the other) hitter of all time. Williams earned two triple crowns, in 1942 and 1947, and a lifetime .344 batting average.

VIC WILLIS

Major league history is dotted with gifted players who've been surrounded by mediocre teams. No matter how great these stars were, their talents were hidden by the constant struggles of their so-so clubs. Notable Hall of Famers who have suffered this fate include Pittsburgh Pirates star Ralph Kiner, Chicago White Sox spark plug Luke Appling, and Chicago Cubs greats Ernie Banks and Billy Williams.

But no player has had the misfortune of Vic Willis, a talented moundsman who pitched in 13 major league campaigns. Despite his many accomplishments, history has remembered Willis for one thing: losses. No pitcher since 1900 has had more single-season losses than Willis. He endured 29 league-leading defeats with the 1905 Boston Braves. Willis wasn't alone in the loss column that year, however. Boston had a record four 20-game losers on its staff that season. The Braves lost 103 games, winning only three more games than the last-place Brooklyn Dodgers. Willis had a respectable 3.21 ERA that year and completed 36 of the 41 games in which he pitched.

After graduating from high school in Wilmington, Delaware, Willis began his pro career in the Pennsylvania State League with Harrisburg in 1895. His first success came in 1896, when he won 10 games. In 1897 he was a 21-game winner with Syracuse in the Eastern League. Then, at the age of 22, he got his first chance in the big leagues with the Boston Braves in 1898.

Willis was an immediate success with the Braves. He won 24 games in his first season, then went 27-8 with a league-leading 5 shutouts in his sophomore season. He had an amazing .771 winning percentage and logged 35 complete games in 38 appearances. The Delaware native fell on hard times at the turn of the century. His 1900 record was 10-17 with a 4.19 ERA. Willis pitched in just 33 games that season, the fewest in his career.

Willis made a dazzling comeback in 1901. He went 20-17 with a 2.36 ERA. In 38 starts Willis needed relief help only three times. His 6 shutouts were tops in the N.L. The following season Willis became the senior circuit's workhorse, winning 27 games and losing 20 (which unfortunately led the league). His 2.20 ERA reflected his constant success throughout the season.

But as the Braves faltered, so did Willis. His record plummeted during the next three seasons. He was 12-18 in

1903, 18-25 in 1904, and 12-29 in 1905. During the latter two years he led the league in losses. It's easy to see why he would have felt relieved when he was traded to the Pittsburgh Pirates on December 15, 1905, for Dave Brain, Del Howard, and Vive Lindaman.

Willis had four fine seasons with the Bucs. He was 23-13 in 1906, 21-11 in 1907, 23-11 in 1908, and 22-11 in 1909. His final 20-game season helped the Pirates win the National League pennant. Although the Pirates beat the Detroit Tigers in a seven-game World Series in 1905, Willis suffered a loss after starting the sixth game.

In 1910 Willis was sold to St. Louis by the Pirates. Unhappy with being traded from his native East Coast all the way to St. Louis in 1910, Willis stayed only one season with the Redbirds. He won 9 and lost 12 in 33 games, compiling a 3.35 ERA along with 12 complete games and 3 saves. Willis retired at the relatively young age of 34 and returned to his home state of Delaware.

Willis was 247-204 with a 2.63 ERA in 513 games in his career. Twelve times he won in double figures. Out of 471 starts he logged 388 complete games and 50 shutouts. In 3,997 innings of work he struck out 1,651 and walked 1,212. Eight times in his career Willis topped the 300-inning barrier. The lanky righthander had a sterling record in relief during his time in the majors. His cumulative record out of the bullpen was 13-3 with 10 saves. As a hitter, Willis fared adequately. He batted just .166 lifetime, but he had 248 career hits and 1 home run.

On the Braves all-time list, Willis ranks fourth in strikeouts with 1,161, fifth in innings pitched with 2,575, and fifth (tied with Tommy Bond) in wins at 149. Even though he spent just eight seasons in a Braves uniform, Willis rates close to Warren Spahn, Phil Niekro, and Kid Nichols as one of the greatest Braves hurlers in history.

Following his retirement, Willis was a hotel proprietor in Newark, Delaware. He died in 1947 at the age of 70.

Many historians are puzzled as to why Willis never has been seriously considered for baseball's Hall of Fame. Perhaps his two horrendous losing seasons and his lack of World Series exposure make him an unknown quantity with the Veterans Committee. However, Willis may someday get enshrinement in Cooperstown. His 247 career wins tie him with Hall of Famer Joe McGinnity for 37th place on the all-time list. More than a dozen Hall of Fame members won fewer games than Willis did. The facts speak clearly: Willis may not be well known, but he is one of baseball's most successful hurlers.

CAREER HIGHLIGHTS
VICTOR GAZAWAY WILLIS

Born: April 12, 1876 Cecil Co., MD **Died:** August 3, 1947
Height: 6'2" **Weight:** 185 lbs. **Batted:** Right **Threw:** Right
Pitcher: Boston Braves, 1898-1905; Pittsburgh Pirates, 1906-09; St. Louis Cardinals, 1910.

★ Won 20 or more games seven times
★ Earned the N.L. strikeout title in 1902
★ Led the league in shutouts on two occasions
★ Pitched a career-high 410 innings in 1902
★ Topped the league in complete games twice
★ Lost a 20th-century record 29 games in 1905

★ Pitched in the 1909 World Series

MAJOR LEAGUE TOTALS

G	IP	W	L	Pct.	SO	BB	ERA
513	3,997	247	204	.548	1,651	1,212	2.63

Though leading the league in losses in 1904 and 1905, Vic Willis also had seven seasons of winning 20 or more games. He set a modern day record of 45 complete games in 1901, and he had 388 complete games and 50 shutouts in his career.

MAURY WILLS

aury Wills made his major league debut with the Los Angeles Dodgers in 1959 and quickly established himself as baseball's premier basestealer and one of the top shortstops in the National League.

An overnight success? Only if you don't count his eight seasons in the minor league system after graduating from high school in 1950. Wills had received offers of football scholarships from nine different colleges but opted to hitchhike from his hometown of Washington, D.C., to Maryland for a tryout with the New York Giants. He had dreamed of this moment from the time he was little and played sandlot ball with a paper-sack mitt (because his family could not afford a real glove). The many years of visualizing success paid off. In his tryout Wills struck out 21 consecutive batters. The Giants were impressed, but they rejected him because they couldn't imagine a 155-pound pitcher. The story was the same with the Brooklyn Dodgers, yet Wills received a contract, because he outsprinted everyone else.

The following spring at training camp Wills noticed an overflow of pitchers, a dearth of infield staff, and no second basemen at all. He wisely chose this position, and after one season of flexing his considerable arm muscles he was promoted to shortstop.

It took time to learn an entirely new position. By 1955 Wills was still batting only .202 and was demoted to a lower minor league classification. But his brief periods of despair were overshadowed by his long-lasting desire to play ball.

In 1956 Pueblo manager Ray Hathaway appointed Wills team captain. This act of faith inspired Wills to a .302 average, with 34 stolen bases. Wanting to put Wills' speed to use on the base paths, Hathaway turned the former hurler into a hacker so that he'd be in a position to steal. Wills was an attentive student; he quickly learned switch-hitting from Bobby Bragan in Spokane. Even so, Wills was sold in 1958 to Detroit, but they promptly asked for a refund. A Dodger once more, Wills batted .313 in 48 games with 25 base larcenies. His long-awaited debut came in late 1959, and Wills was an instant hit with his daring baserunning, hit-and-run expertise, and drag-bunting. Wills sparked the Dodgers to a World Series win against the White Sox.

Just as Luis Aparicio had restored the running game in the American League, Wills did the same in the senior circuit. Wills won six straight league stolen base titles in 1960-65. Manager Walter Alston had given his star sprinter a free reign on the base paths, which resulted in a record 104 steals in 165 games in 1962, surpassing the immortal Ty Cobb's 96 steals in 156 games. The switch-hitter had a .299 average, 208 hits, and 130 runs that year, making him the league's MVP choice.

Other awards showered upon the 30-year-old were AP's Athlete of the Year, *Sport* magazine's Man of the Year, and a second consecutive Gold Glove. He also earned the nickname "Mouse" for his size and speed.

Wills later expressed regret that he didn't try for even more stolen bases in that shining season, perhaps because he neared those numbers only once afterward (94 in 1965, his sixth straight league steal lead). But Wills was troubled after 1962 with knee and leg injuries. After 1965 his larcenies declined yearly, never reaching above 52 and dropping to a single swipe in his final year. Never

a power hitter (with only 20 career homers), Wills accomplished his 586 career stolen bases with a record number of short hits; he led the league in singles four times, in at-bats twice, and in triples once.

Wills played in four World Series during his first eight major league seasons. In 1965 the Dodgers beat the Twins in seven Series games. The scrappy shortstop paced the winners with 11 hits for a .367 average. His cumulative postseason records include 19 hits in four fall classics for a .244 average. Wills swiped 6 bases during his postseason play.

Wills was traded in late 1966 to the Pirates for Bob Bailey and Gene Michael. After two seasons the Expos picked him up in the expansion draft, trading him back to the Dodgers with Manny Mota in mid-1969. Wills remained in L.A. for the rest of his career. After two unsuccessful seasons managing the Seattle Mariners in 1980 and 1981 (he was only the third black manager in baseball history), he took a job in the Dodgers community services department.

The major leagues still had a Wills in its infield through 1982. Elliot "Bump" Wills, Maury's son, played with the Texas Rangers and Chicago Cubs from 1977 through 1982.

Maury Wills was the first ballplayer to break 100 steals in the 20th century, and in the process he brought back the running game to the N.L. He lead the league in stolen bases for six straight seasons.

CAREER HIGHLIGHTS
MAURICE MORNING WILLS

Born: October 2, 1932   Washington, D.C.
Height: 5'11"   **Weight:** 170 lbs.   **Batted:** Both   **Threw:** Right
Shortstop: Los Angeles Dodgers, 1959-66, 1969-72; Pittsburgh Pirates, 1967-68; Montreal Expos, 1969. Manager: Seattle Mariners, 1980-81.

★ Selected N.L. MVP in 1962
★ Played in four World Series
★ Led the N.L. in stolen bases for six straight seasons
★ Compiled 586 stolen bases
★ Won two Gold Glove awards
★ Set a record for single-season steals with 104 in 1962

MAJOR LEAGUE TOTALS

G	AB	H	BA	2B	3B	HR	R	RBI	SB
1,942	7,588	2,134	.281	177	71	20	1,067	458	586

HACK WILSON

At 5-foot-6 and 190 pounds, Hack Wilson looked more like a fire hydrant than a ballplayer. When he reported to the New York Giants for his 1923 rookie season, the equipment manager couldn't even find a uniform to fit him. According to one often told story, the young outfielder was given an extra outfit belonging to manager John McGraw, who at 5-foot-6 and a paunchy 160 pounds looked a little like a fire hydrant himself.

Bulging out of his ill-fitting uniform, Wilson looked like his body was put together with parts left over from other ballplayers. He had muscular arms, broad shoulders, and a huge chest that dropped into a more-than-ample abdomen. His massive upper body was supported by stubby legs and tiny feet.

Wilson was given the nickname "Hack" by a teammate, who said he looked like Hack Miller, a Chicago Cubs outfielder who was the son of a circus strongman. Many people believed he earned the nickname for the ferocious hacks he'd take at pitches.

Never advancing past the sixth grade, Wilson spent his childhood working. First he served as a printer's assistant for $4 a week. Two years later he was laboring in the Baldwin, Pennsylvania, locomotive works. He worked in shipyards and steel mills before getting his first shot to play baseball in 1921, with Martinsburg of the Blue Ridge League for $175 a month. The burly youngster was slated as a catcher due to his husky frame. However, he broke his leg during the first game trying to score. Because of the injury he was moved to a less strenuous position in the outfield. Wilson's average kept growing every year. In 1922 he batted .366. The following season with Portsmouth of the Virginia League, Wilson batted .388 with 19 home runs. While other scouts didn't like Wilson's shortness, the small but scrappy McGraw thought he'd fit in on his Giants team. In 1924 Wilson batted .295 with 10 homers and 57 RBI. In the 1924 World Series (which the Giants lost to the Washington Senators) Wilson hit .233 with 7 hits and 3 RBI. When his average dropped to .239 the following season, he was demoted to Toledo of the American Association. When he went to the minors the Giants left their stocky slugger unprotected, and he became available to other teams. The Chicago Cubs drafted Wilson and put him to work immediately during the 1926 season.

The Pennsylvania native played only ten full seasons in the big leagues, but he crammed 266 home runs and 1,062 RBI into his short career. He led the league in home runs for four years; twice he was the league leader in RBI. In 1930 he hit .356 and compiled a league-record 56 home runs and a major league mark of 190 RBI. Both records stand today. Today's fans might assume that Wilson's impressive numbers would have won him the triple crown, but he didn't even finish in the top five in batting average that season. New York's Bill Terry ran away with the batting title, hitting .401. Wilson's slugging average was the highest in the league, however, at .723.

Wilson wasn't a one-season wonder. He drove in 100-plus runs for the Cubs from 1926 through 1930. His season homer totals climbed yearly: 21 in 1926, 30 in 1927, 31 in 1928, and 39 in 1929. He led the Cubs to the 1929 National League pennant by racking up 159 RBI and a .345 average. Although he had 8 hits in the five-game Series, writers made Wilson the Cub scapegoat for the Series loss to the Philadelphia Athletics. He was highly criticized for losing two fly balls in the sun, which helped the A's win the fourth game 10-8 on unearned runs.

A tough competitor who frequently swung with his fists as well as his bat, he once punched out one of his own teammates in a fight over a clubhouse card game. At one time Wilson even considered a professional boxing career during the off-season, but the idea was rejected by the baseball commissioner.

Throughout his life Wilson was a brawling, hard-drinking free spirit and a celebrated after-hours reveler. But the fast living shortened Wilson's career. After his baseball career ended in 1934, Wilson's personal life went downhill. He tried opening his own tavern but had little luck there or in several other jobs. His years of drinking caught up with him and he died of internal hemorrhaging at the age of 48. The future Hall of Famer died penniless; friends passed the hat to pay for the funeral.

Due to his controversial behavior during his playing days, many baseball writers weren't anxious to see Wilson enter the Hall of Fame. After prolonged public campaigning by his fans, Wilson finally gained his place among the Cooperstown elite, some three decades after his death.

Hack Wilson's tempestuous lifestyle shortened his playing career, but he still managed to pack a lot of talent into his few short years. Wilson led the N.L. in homers four times and set the N.L. record with 56 in 1930.

CAREER HIGHLIGHTS
LEWIS ROBERT WILSON

Born: April 26, 1900   Elwood City, PA   **Died:** November 23, 1948
Height: 5'6"   **Weight:** 190 lbs.   **Batted:** Right   **Threw:** Right
Outfielder: New York Giants, 1923-25; Chicago Cubs, 1926-31; Brooklyn Dodgers, 1932-34; Philadelphia Phillies, 1934.

- ★ Led the N.L. in homers four times
- ★ Drove in 100-plus runs six times
- ★ Clubbed an N.L. record of 56 homers in 1930
- ★ Batted .300 or better five times
- ★ Elected to the Hall of Fame in 1979
- ★ Held a major league record with 190 RBI

MAJOR LEAGUE TOTALS

G	AB	H	BA	2B	3B	HR	R	RBI	SB
1,348	4,760	1,461	.307	266	67	244	884	1,062	52

WILLIE WILSON

Switch-hitting power fielder Willie Wilson is a Kansas City Royals tradition in center field. While Amos Otis was the resident center fielder for the team throughout the 1970s, Wilson is the foundation of Royals lineups during the 1980s. Blazing speed has kept Wilson in the American League forefront for 11 seasons. At bat, on the base paths, and in the field, the Royals speedster has used his quickness to become a star.

A first-round draft pick by the Kansas City Royals in 1974, Wilson signed for $90,000 and immediately went to work in the minor leagues. In his first pro season with Sarasota in 1974, Wilson won the league's stolen base title with 24. His average was a modest .252 due to 51 strikeouts in 155 at-bats. Advancing to Waterloo in 1975, Wilson again excelled in stolen bases and strikeouts. His 8 homers, 73 RBI, and league-leading 132 hits brought him a .272 average. He led the league with 76 steals, the second time he led the league in two pro seasons. But Wilson whiffed 99 times, keeping his average somewhat low. With Jacksonville in 1977 Wilson batted .253 and swiped 37 more bases. Letting him bypass Triple-A ball, the Royals called up the young speed merchant for a 12-game audition. The reviews were mixed at best; he had just 1 hit in six plate appearances. His two stolen bases were the best result of his brief call-up.

Wilson served his time with Triple-A Omaha in 1977, where he hit .281, was named to his third minor league All-Star team in four seasons, and broke the American Association mark for stolen bases with 74. The previous record had stood for 56 years. When Wilson returned to Kansas City to conclude the season with a 13-game trial, he was a changed hitter. This time he rapped out a .324 average (12 hits in 34 at-bats), highlighted by 8 stolen bases.

Wilson was ready for major league action, but he played in just 127 games in 1978 due to the presence of starting center fielder Amos Otis. Although Wilson led the Royals with 46 stolen bases, his hitting suffered. His .217 average did little for his struggle to become an every-day player. Starting outfielder Al Cowens broke his jaw, and Wilson finally got a chance at full-time duty in 1979. Once Wilson got into the starting lineup, he earned a regular job. Wilson pilfered 83 bases, setting a team record and leading the American

League. At the plate Wilson hit .315 in 154 games. His speed earned him 13 triples, the first of six seasons in which he'd gain 10 or more three-base hits.

In 1980 Wilson had the finest season of his career, leading the league in three categories: at-bats (705), runs scored (133), and hits (a career-high 230). Wilson matched Garry Templeton's 1979 record by gaining at least 100 hits as a lefthand hitter and 100 from the right side. No American League switch-hitter had ever had as many hits in one season. A record-setting 32 consecutive stolen bases and a Gold Glove for fielding excellence (his first) highlighted Wilson's accomplishments. Wilson batted .308 in the American League Championship Series against New York but then suffered through an awful World Series, hitting .154 with 12 strikeouts. The Phillies downed the Royals in the six-game contest.

In 1981 Wilson batted .303 in 102 games (due to the strike-shortened season). The Royals played the Oakland A's in a special divisional playoff, only to lose three straight games. The following season Wilson won the league batting title with a .332 mark. Despite missing 25 games in April with a pulled hamstring, Wilson stole 37 bases and led the league with 15 triples.

Wilson played a big part in Kansas City's first world championship in 1985. He batted .278 (with a league-best 21 triples) and stole 43 bases. In a seven-game A.L.C.S. with Toronto, Wilson tallied a .310 average with 9 hits. When the Royals faced their cross-state rivals, the St. Louis Cardinals, in the 1985 World Series, Wilson avenged his woeful performance in the fall classic in 1980. Against the Cardinals, Wilson hit .367 with 11 hits, 3 RBI, and 3 stolen bases as the Royals whipped the Cardinals in seven games.

Wilson is showing the same signs of slowing down that most veterans exhibit. He hasn't hit .300 since 1984, and his strikeouts climbed to a career-high 106 in 1988. Still, he remains one of the American League's best glove men in center field. In 1988 his 34 stolen bases put him over 30 steals a season for the 11th straight year. He will probably never catch Rickey Henderson, but Wilson already ranks in the top ten in lifetime steals (with 588). Willie Wilson may never gain a spot in the Hall of Fame, but he'll be remembered as one of the American League's most exciting players of the 1980s and as a prime ingredient in many Royals pennant wins.

CAREER HIGHLIGHTS
WILLIE JAMES WILSON

Born: July 9, 1955   Montgomery, Alabama
Height: 6'3"   **Weight:** 190 lbs.   **Bats:** Both   **Throws:** Right
Outfielder: Kansas City Royals, 1976-89.

★ Named to A.L. All-Star team in 1982 and 1983

★ Named to *The Sporting News* A.L. Gold Glove team in 1980

★ Led the A.L. in triples for 5 seasons

★ Named to *The Sporting News* A.L. Silver Slugger team in 1980 and 1982

★ Held the A.L. record for most hits by a switch-hitter with 230 in 1980

★ Led A.L. in batting in 1982

★ Held the A.L. record for highest lifetime stolen base percentage in 300 or more attempts with .841

MAJOR LEAGUE TOTALS

G	AB	H	BA	2B	3B	HR	R	RBI	SB
1,672	6,492	1,879	.289	228	130	38	1,011	467	588

Willie Wilson has been a solid performer for the Kansas City Royals and has led them to
one world championship, two pennants, and almost yearly divisional championships.
Wilson's 588 lifetime stolen bases are part of the Royal's winning ways.

DAVE WINFIELD

Dave Winfield was one of the most sought-after athletes of the early 1970s. The Baltimore Orioles wanted to draft him in 1969, straight out of high school. After Winfield's four years of exhibiting his various athletic talents at the University of Minnesota, more contenders for his services emerged (especially after he became an All-American in baseball in 1973). Winfield was a first-round draft pick of the San Diego Padres. Football's Minnesota Vikings made him a 17th-round choice in the NFL draft. The Atlanta Hawks chose Winfield in the 50th round of the NBA draft. He was chosen by the Utah Jazz in the sixth round of the now-defunct American Basketball Association draft.

Among his many suitors, Winfield chose the Padres, partly due to San Diego's $100,000 signing bonus and an automatic berth in the Padres starting lineup—no minor leagues, no dues to pay. The multitalented athlete gave the Padres no reason to regret their whirlwind courtship.

For five years Winfield worked diligently at his statistics, which started out respectably and continued to improve. His rookie batting average was .277 with 3 homers and 12 RBI. His 65 putouts and 3 errors at first base and the outfield earned him a .957 fielding average. Full-time outfield work followed in 1974, as well as an increase in games and an unfortunate increase in errors. Leading the league with 12 miscues, Winfield still improved his fielding by 3 points. His real redemption came by way of 20 homers and 75 RBI.

The 1975 season mirrored Winfield's sophomore campaign. He hit .267 with 15 homers and 76 RBI. He celebrated the bicentennial in 1976 by improving his batting average to .283. Missing 25 games that year hurt Winfield's power totals. In the field Winfield led the league with 15 assists, made 304 putouts, and boosted his fielding average to .982. The big Minnesotan stole a career-high 26 bases that year.

Winfield broke loose with 25 homers and 92 RBI in 1977. His sixth and seventh seasons in 1978 and 1979 featured identical .308 averages and respective totals of 24 and 34 homers. His RBI totals zoomed from 97 to a league-leading 118. His fielding kept improving too, and a Gold Glove resulted in 1979, his first of seven. Winfield has not become famous through his patience. His habits at the plate are well known; he chases a lot of bad pitches, even after 16 years. No one's better at out-guessing a pitcher though, and when Winfield connects, watch out. Pitchers knew this by the end of 1979, and he received 24 intentional bases on balls that season. Winfield's impatience shows occasionally in the outfield, too. Many of Winfield's errors are due to his strong throwing arm: The ball sometimes ends up at the wrong base.

Temperance is his on the base paths, though. The large slugger makes tracks with seemingly little effort. Aggressive and capable of 20-plus steals in his prime, Winfield can still produce in double digits. He has played in an astonishing 12 All-Star games, setting a record for most lifetime All-Star doubles (7) and tying records for most at-bats in one game (5) and most consecutive All-Star games with at least one hit (7).

Winfield concluded his stint with the Padres in 1980. His final season in San Diego consisted of 20 homers, 87 RBI, and a .273 average. Winfield was the chief topic of league discussions following the season. When Winfield became a free agent, teams saw him as a quick fix for a losing club. The New York Yankees finally snared the high-demand star with a ten-year contract for $13 million. This made him baseball's highest-paid player at the time. Winfield had asked the Padres for a ten-year pact with a promise that the team would not be sold without Winfield's consent.

In New York Winfield became successful on the field and controversial out of uniform. He wrote an autobiography in 1988, which offered frank insights about teammates and unbridled criticism of Yankees owner George Steinbrenner. Steinbrenner responded to the book with threats to trade the longtime star. Winfield and his boss had dueled verbally before. Suits and countersuits flew when Winfield accused Steinbrenner of reneging on an agreement to donate to the charitable foundation Winfield had formed while in San Diego. Steinbrenner countersued, alleging that charitable funds were misspent.

Winfield has not let any off-field controversy affect his on-field work. As early as 1982 he established himself as one of the junior circuit's biggest homer threats. He hit 37 dingers in 1981 and 32 in 1982. In his first eight years he was under 19 homers just once. Since 1982, his low for RBI has been 97 and he batted .340 in 1984.

The 1989 season began darkly for Winfield. A herniated disk put him on the 60-day disabled list before the season began. His back problems put him on the bench for the entire season. When players reach Winfield's age, any injury can end a career. Regardless of his future, his past achievements give him a chance at a future spot in the Baseball Hall of Fame.

CAREER HIGHLIGHTS
DAVID MARK WINFIELD

Born: October 3, 1951 St. Paul, MN
Height: 6'6" **Weight:** 220 lbs. **Bats:** Right **Throws:** Right
Outfielder: San Diego Padres, 1973-80; New York Yankees, 1981-89.

- ★ Played in 12 All-Star games
- ★ Named to the Silver Slugger team from 1981 through 1983
- ★ Led the N.L. in RBI in 1979
- ★ Won seven Gold Gloves
- ★ Established a record with five All-Star doubles
- ★ Drove in 100 or more runs in seven seasons

MAJOR LEAGUE TOTALS

G	AB	H	BA	2B	3B	HR	R	RBI	SB
2,269	8,421	2,421	.287	412	74	357	1,314	1,438	209

An amazing athlete, Dave Winfield was courted by basketball and football teams.
Winfield never played in the minors and was successful almost from his first game.
Winfield has won seven Gold Gloves and has a .287 career average.

JOE WOOD

Long before Babe Ruth interrupted his brilliant pitching career to become the Sultan of Swat, another pitcher had already done the same, but under very different circumstances. Certainly Babe Ruth's debut in baseball was far different from that of Smokey Joe Wood.

Wood was a modest, shy man, and he hesitated to talk about his professional debut, but after finally admitting to it, he maintained that the great Rogers Hornsby had also started out on a Bloomer Girls team. Smokey Joe, named for the great balls of fire he threw, was 17 and a player on a highly competitve local Kansas team when the Bloomer Girls barnstormed the place, losing a game to Wood and his teammates. To his surprise, their manager asked Joe to play the final three weeks of the tour; only half of the team was actually female, as Wood later learned. Wood joined on the condition that he would not have to wear a wig. He was told that his baby face precluded the need.

Wood always considered the next year as his true debut, when his father accompanied him to his minor league home in Hutchinson, Kansas. He recalled winning about 20 games and striking out about 200 batters.

When Wood made it to the pros with Boston, he proved to be a superlative and prolific pitcher. In 1911, at the age of 21, the righthander fashioned a 23-17 mark, struck out 231 batters, and hurled a no-hitter. The following year he won 34, lost only 5, and earned 3 favorable World Series decisions. On his way to that glorious day, he had won 16 consecutive regular season games (matching the American League record), notched 10 shutouts, and sculpted an ERA of 1.91.

Age 22 is a heady time to have your dreams come true and the world at your feet. It's also a bad time to have all that you've worked for taken away. When Smokey Joe was 23, he slipped on a wet grassy infield while going in for a bunt. In his fall he broke the thumb on his pitching hand. Perhaps something else was injured as well but passed undetected; the injury was to cause him lifelong pain. Or perhaps it was all caused by a career started too soon and executed too hard. All that Smokey Joe knew was that after that fall, he could not throw a ball without excruciating pain in his shoulder and arm.

In spite of the pain Wood pitched through the 1915 season and pitched

with everything he had. He led the league in ERA (1.49), and he won 15 and lost 5. He only pitched for half seasons, because it took him up to three weeks to recover after pitching a single game. If he pitched more than three innings, he could not raise his arm.

By 1916 he was out for the entire season, trying to nurse the arm back. During that year out the frustration built, and Wood examined his career long and hard. In 1912 he had won an incredible 34 games—and batted an even more incredible .290. He didn't believe his career should have to end because of his injury.

The Red Sox had promised him a free rein in career decisions, and Wood opted to go to the Indians where his friend (and longtime roommate) Tris Speaker played. The Indians paid $15,000 for him. (This was twice as much as Wood says he was paid annually by either team, before and after his brilliant 1912 season.) Wood took spring training with the Indians to prove

he could do more than pitch. In 1918, with the teams weakened by the loss of men to WWI, Wood was back in the lineup as an outfielder.

That year he was part of the longest game ever played at the Polo Grounds, a 19-inning battle against the Yankees that Wood won with a tie-breaking homer. It was the same field, he remembered, where just six years before he had pitched two World Series wins. It had taken six years to prove—to himself as well as to others—that he was "a ball player, not just a pitcher."

After his playing days, he spent two full decades coaching the Yale University team, ending with a composite record of 283-228-1. He maintained his playing day salary and was content to work close to home. It had caused him some distress when he was playing to return from a road trip and find that his toddlers didn't know him. After retiring from Yale he and his brother opened a golf course in Hollywood, and it was here that Wood made enough to retire comfortably. He was a golfer until late in life, but the bad arm troubled him until the day he died, at age 95.

Wood played with some of the greatest players in baseball history: Walter Johnson, Christy Mathewson, Babe Ruth, and Ty Cobb. He would not have admitted it himself, but his own name also belongs on this list of all-time greats.

Starting as a pitcher, Smokey Joe Wood ended his career "as a ballplayer, not just a pitcher" when an injury sent him to the outfield. He once hit a game-winning homer in the same park where he had pitched two World Series wins.

CAREER HIGHLIGHTS
HOWARD ELLSWORTH WOOD

Born: October 25, 1889 Kansas City, MO **Died:** July 27, 1985
Height: 5'11" **Weight:** 180 lbs. **Batted:** Right **Threw:** Right
Pitcher: Boston Red Sox, 1908-15; Cleveland Indians, 1917, 1919-20. Outfielder: Cleveland Indians, 1918-22.

- ★ Made his debut in 1906 with the Kansas City Bloomer Girls
- ★ Pitched a no-hitter on July 29, 1911, at age 22
- ★ Won three World Series games in 1912
- ★ Won 16 consecutive decisions in 1912
- ★ Batted .283 in his last four years as an outfielder

MAJOR LEAGUE TOTALS

G	IP	W	L	Pct.	SO	BB	ERA
225	1,438	116	57	.671	989	421	2.03

EARLY WYNN

In a career that spanned four decades, Early Wynn compiled 300 victories while pitching for the Washington Senators, Cleveland Indians, and Chicago White Sox. His 23 consecutive years in the American League—from 1939 to 1963—is a record for pitchers, too.

Wynn was a 20-game winner five times during his career, and 10 times he won 17 or more. His highest win total occurred in 1954, when he led the circuit with a 23-11 record. In 1959, at the age of 39, Wynn led the league again with 22 victories to capture the Cy Young award, and he led the Chicago White Sox to the American League pennant.

As his career was winding down, Wynn set his sights on 300 career wins, a goal he very much hoped to achieve. When the White Sox released him after a dismal 7-15 year in 1962, it appeared that the righthand hurler was going to end his career just 1 game shy of his goal. Wynn had 299 victories to his credit but no team to play for. The 1963 season started without him, but Wynn kept himself in shape, hoping some major league team would call. Finally his former club, the Cleveland Indians, offered Wynn the chance he wanted in June. The 43-year-old hurler started just 5 games for the Indians, but it was enough to get him the 1 victory he needed. His 300 wins helped him win election to Cooperstown in 1971. Wynn was the 14th pitcher in baseball history to win that many games.

The Alabama native had the honor of pitching in two World Series during his career. With the 1954 Cleveland Indians (they won a record 111 games that year), Wynn lost his only decision after pitching seven innings against the San Francisco Giants. Wynn wasn't alone in his suffering as the Giants swept the Tribe in four straight games that year. In 1959, as a member of the Chicago White Sox, Wynn had more luck. He was 1-1 in 3 starts. He threw 7 shutout innings in the opening game of the Series, as the "Go Go" White Sox whipped the Los Angeles Dodgers 11-0.

The Chicago White Sox picked up Wynn from the Cleveland Indians with Al Smith in a trade that sent Minnie Minoso and Fred Hatfield to Cleveland on December 4, 1957. Although Wynn had a losing record in 1958 with Chicago (winning 14 and losing 16), he won his second consecutive strikeout title with 179 Ks. Wynn bounced back

in 1959 with one of his most productive seasons. That year, his 22nd season in professional baseball, he won his first and only Cy Young award. At age 39 he served as the ace of the pitching staff for the ChiSox. He won 22 and lost 10, leading the loop with 256 innings pitched and 119 bases on balls and a tidy 3.16 ERA.

Wynn was competitive in all aspects of the game, even hitting. He had a lifetime average of .214 (with 365 total hits—ranking tenth among pitchers), while hitting 17 homers (19th overall among pitchers) and 173 RBI.

One of baseball's most famous and most quoted comments belongs to Early Wynn. Wynn was a well-known brushback artist who would throw extremely close to batters to keep them from crowding the plate. Once a reporter sarcastically asked Wynn if he'd brush back his own grandmother. "Only if she dug in," he replied laconically.

Wynn's lifetime totals include 300

wins and 244 losses in 691 appearances. He never had amazing control as evidenced by his 1,775 walks—fifth highest on the all-time list. He won his fame for his durability. He started 612 games in his career (leading the league five times) and registered 290 complete games. For 14 seasons he hurled in at least 200 innings. He logged 49 career shutouts. After only nine years with the Indians, Wynn still ranks among the top ten in eight different all-time categories for Cleveland hurlers. The Alabama native earned 164 of his 300 career wins in a Cleveland uniform. Critics who say Wynn accomplished his goal simply by hanging on to his career years after his prime haven't fully studied his marks. Besides his career wins, Wynn added 15 saves to his stats during those 23 years, making him partly responsible for even more victories.

Wynn's baseball career didn't end once he hung up his glove. From 1964 through 1966 he served as the Indians pitching coach. Wynn was the pitching coach for the Minnesota Twins from 1967 to 1969, and his influence was immediately seen. The Twins pitching staff, in the tradition of Wynn, led the league with 58 complete games and 396 walks. After spending the next three years as a minor league manager, Wynn became a broadcaster for the Toronto Blue Jays and later the White Sox.

Even in retirement Wynn has shown the same outspoken aggressiveness that made him a major league winner. He has repeatedly criticized baseball's pension system and has campaigned vigorously to raise funds for older retirees. He displays the same zeal now that he exhibited on big league pitching mounds for nearly a quarter of a century.

CAREER HIGHLIGHTS
EARLY WYNN

Born: January 6, 1920   Hartford, AL
Height: 6'0"   **Weight:** 220 lbs.   **Batted:** Both   **Threw:** Right
Pitcher: Washington Senators, 1939-48; Cleveland Indians, 1949-57, 1963; Chicago White Sox, 1958-62.

★ Won 300 games during a 23-year career
★ Won the Cy Young award in 1959
★ Pitched in two World Series
★ Once held the longevity record for pitchers
★ Won 20 or more games five times
★ Elected to the Hall of Fame in 1971

MAJOR LEAGUE TOTALS

G	IP	W	L	Pct.	SO	BB	ERA
691	4,566	300	244	.551	2,334	1,775	3.54

Early Wynn started out an erratic pitcher but ended one of the most successful pitching careers of all time in 1963 as the 14th 300-game winner in history. His career spanned four decades, and he logged 290 complete games.

CARL YASTRZEMSKI

When 21-year-old Carl Yastrzemski joined the Boston Red Sox in 1961, he had some enormous shoes to fill; those of the "Splendid Splinter," left fielder Ted Williams, the greatest hitter in modern baseball.

Even die-hard Sox fans expected the over-sized spikes to trip up the rookie. Instead, "Yaz" took two giant steps and forced a legacy of his own in 23 big league seasons. He didn't shake Ted's shadow overnight—in fact, it was 1963 before Yaz's minor league potential showed itself in the bigs.

Growing up on a New York farm and playing semipro baseball, young Yaz was an all-around athlete, setting a Long Island high school basketball record in 1957 with 628 points. On his high school baseball team he played both pitcher and catcher as well as outfielder, raising scouts' eyebrows with a .506 batting average.

It's no wonder that many major league teams competed for his services when he graduated from high school in 1957. The BoSox made him a comprehensive offer: a $100,000 bonus plus a baseball scholarship to Notre Dame.

Who could ask for anything more? A young man with big dreams and an even bigger bat could. After two years of hitting the books, Yaz was longing to hit grand slams instead. He spent his first year (1959) in Raleigh at second base and shortstop—the first and last time he'd play either of those positions. Even so, he was the Carolina League's MVP and led the circuit in seven categories, including batting average (.377), putouts (.255), errors (45), and fielding average (.923). Ironically, the fielding mark would become an all-time low for Yaz, who would soon become a master of playing caroms off Fenway Park's "Green Monster."

Although his second minor league year was not quite as stellar as his first, Yaz maintained high standards. When Williams stepped down, Yaz was sent to the plate.

He admitted in later years that the pressure was tough, with pitchers treating him with kid gloves from the start. Yaz worked closely with manager Pinky Higgins to reshape his stance out of its acquired crouch. Confidence and contact returned. By 1963 Yaz was leading the loop in offensive categories once held by Williams: hits (183), doubles (40), and batting average (.321). He was named to his first of 18 All-Star teams, three of which he would not appear in due to injury.

Yaz did not resent the challenge of growing out of Williams' shadow, partly because Williams helped him. Yaz credited "Teddy Ballgame" with correct assessments of his early slumps; and he credits manager Dick Williams, who took over in 1967, with being a man who could move mountains.

The Red Sox moved in 1967, with Yaz at the head of the class. Williams called Yaz "phenomenal" that year. Winning the triple crown, a feat no player has achieved since, Yaz became American League and Major League Player of the Year. His numerous league-leading stats, including home runs (a career high of 44) and batting average (.326), paced the Red Sox to a seven-game World Series battle. Yaz would bat .400 in the postseason (with 2 opening-game homers and a sixth-game shot), recording nary an error, a fielding performance he was to repeat in 1975 in another World Series bout. This time against Cincinnati, he more than doubled his 1967 putouts (16) in 1975 with 35, leaving no doubt as to

why he possessed seven Gold Glove awards.

In 1969 and 1970 the Boston belter notched a pair of 40-homer seasons and belted a personal-best batting average of .329 in 1970. He had no trouble giving pitchers the business on the field: In 1966, amid his stellar season, Yaz completed his business degree at Merrimack College.

At age 44, after toting up a list of accomplishments, awards, and record-breaking stats that print out longer than a regulation bat, Carl Yastrzemski made his farewell tour of the American League. The veteran proved he still had talent, as evidenced by his 10 homers, 56 RBI, and .266 batting average. His son spent some time in the minors in the 1980s, not long after the senior Yaz hung up the glove.

Yaz had many memorable moments in his distinguished career. On September 12, 1979, Yaz laced an eighth-inning single off New York hurler Jim Beattie for his historic 3,000th hit before an adoring home crowd in Boston. Who would have thought that the same free-swinging rookie who singled off Kansas City Athletics pitcher Ray Herbert during his first at-bat on opening day in 1961 would achieve such an awesome record some two decades later?

Yaz was elected to the Hall of Fame in 1989—his first year of eligibility.

Ted Williams called Carl Yastrzemski the greatest player who ever lived—but just for the month of September 1967. He almost helped capture the pennant for Boston, winning the triple crown and MVP award in the process.

CAREER HIGHLIGHTS
CARL MICHAEL YASTRZEMSKI

Born: August 22, 1939   Southampton, NY
Height: 5'11"   **Weight:** 175 lbs.   **Batted:** Left   **Threw:** Right
Outfielder: Boston Red Sox, 1961-63.

* Selected as the A.L. MVP in 1967
* Won the triple crown in 1967
* Led the A.L. in hitting three times
* Hit 40 or more homers three times
* Played in two World Series
* Elected to the Hall of Fame in 1989
* Led the A.L. in doubles three times and in walks twice

MAJOR LEAGUE TOTALS

G	AB	H	BA	2B	3B	HR	R	RBI	SB
3,308	11,988	3,419	.285	646	59	452	1,816	1,844	168

CY YOUNG

When major league baseball decided in 1956 to start honoring the finest pitcher in the game each season, the award was named for Cy Young, a name that was synonymous with quality pitching.

To fans it must have seemed a natural enough choice. Over a 22-year career, the durable Young compiled pitching records that will probably never be matched. His 511 victories are so far out in front on the all-time win list that the second-place Walter Johnson trails by 95 games. Young also ranks first in complete games with 749, and in innings pitched with 7,357. Despite his many wins, he led his league in victories only five times: twice in the National League (with 34 in 1893 and 35 in 1895) and three times in the American League with Boston from 1901 through 1903 (with respective win totals of 33, 32, and 28). Young was a pitching workhorse throughout his career, hurling relief stints in between starts.

Young played just one season of minor league ball; for Canton of the Tri-State League. He came up to Cleveland in 1890. It's said that early in his career, while Young was warming up one day by throwing against a wooden outfield fence, someone observed that it looked like a cyclone had hit it. A nearby baseball writer supposedly overheard the remark and shortened it to "Cy," deeming it an appropriate nickname for the hard-throwing righthander.

Young's brilliant career spanned from 1890 to 1911 and included five teams in two leagues. The 6-foot-2, 210-pound country boy won 20 or more games for an incredible 15 seasons. He got started with the Cleveland Spiders in 1890, finishing with an average 9-6 mark. In 1891 Young reeled off 27 triumphs amid 22 defeats. He followed with a career-high 36 wins in 1892, leading the National League with 9 shutouts and a 1.93 ERA. Young would win at least 19 games each season until 1905 with Boston (when he fell to 18 wins). The other players called him "Farmer" because he had grown up in rural Ohio and still spent time there during the off-season. One of the most impressive records Young harvested in his career was a string of 44 consecutive scoreless innings.

In 1903 Young sparked his Boston club to the American League pennant. For the third consecutive year, Young was the leading winner in the new league, with 28 victories against just 9 losses. He was tops in the American

League in winning percentage (.757), complete games (34), innings pitched (342), shutouts (7), and saves (2). Boston (then called the Pilgrims or Puritans) beat Pittsburgh five games to three in the first N.L.-versus-A.L. matchup. Young won 2 games and lost 1 in three Series starts. In the opener the Pirates nicked Young for 12 hits and 7 runs in a 7-3 loss. Two days later Young pitched seven innings of relief in Pittsburgh's 4-2 triumph. Young was more successful as a starter in game five, scattering 6 hits during an 11-2 win. On one day of rest Young returned to stymie the Pirates again. Boston whipped their National League rivals 7-3 thanks to a third complete game from the big righthander. For his 34 innings pitched in the historic first Series, Young had a 1.59 ERA. He struck out 17 and walked just 4, typical of the control master.

During the following season Young accomplished his first perfect game. He later said that his 1904 perfect game against the Philadelphia Athletics was one of his fondest memories from his long career. It was the first no-hitter ever in the junior circuit. During the game only 6 balls were hit to the outfield. The entire game took one hour and 23 minutes.

During his career Young gave much credit for his success to catcher Lou Criger. Young pitched exclusively to Criger while in St. Louis. When Young was traded to Boston, he wanted Criger there too. Together they formed one of the greatest batteries of the early 20th century.

Young was a decent batter during his day, and many times he helped his own cause with the bat. He hit 18 career home runs and had 623 total hits for a .210 average.

The Ohio native continued to pitch until he was 44 years old, and although he retired after the 1911 season, his throwing still wasn't affected. He could still throw as hard as ever and had added a spitball and curves to his assortment of pitches. But he was no longer able to field the position adequately, due to his slowness in getting off the mound. "My arm is as good as the day I came into the majors," he explained, "but I'm too portly to get about. When the third baseman has to start doing my work, it's time for me to quit." In his last game he lost a 1-0 decision. Upon his retirement he went back to his farm near Peoli, Ohio, and continued the same hardworking life he had known before he became a baseball immortal. His last involvement with baseball was in 1907, when he managed the Red Sox to a 3-3 record in six games. Young was elected to the Hall of Fame in 1937. He died at age 88 in 1955.

CAREER HIGHLIGHTS
DENTON TRUE YOUNG

Born: March 29, 1867   Gilmore, OH   **Died:** November 4, 1955
Height: 6'2"   **Weight:** 210 lbs.   **Batted:** Right   **Threw:** Right
Pitcher: Cleveland Spiders, 1890-98; St. Louis Cardinals, 1899-1900; Boston Red Sox, 1901-08; Cleveland Indians (then known as the Naps), 1909-11; Boston Braves, 1911. Manager: Boston Red Sox, 1907.

★ Pitched three no-hitters
★ Threw a record 749 complete games
★ Elected to the Hall of Fame in 1937
★ Hurled 76 shutouts
★ Earned 30 or more wins for five seasons
★ Won 21 games in 1908 at the age of 41
★ Won a record 511 games in the major leagues

MAJOR LEAGUE TOTALS

G	IP	W	L	Pct.	SO	BB	ERA
906	7,357	511	315	.619	2,803	1,217	2.63

Cy Young won 20 games in 16 seasons—14 of those winning years were consecutive. He was a control pitcher who led the league in fewest walks and most strikeouts eleven times, and once went 20 innings without walking a batter.

ROBIN YOUNT

The Milwaukee Brewers superstar Robin Yount was the third player selected in the first round of the free-agent draft in June 1973. He was just 18 years old when he became the Brewers regular shortstop in 1974. At the time he was the youngest player in the major leagues.

Although the media had a field day reporting about Robin the boy wonder, he had an unspectacular rookie year. Yount hit just .250 with 3 homers and 26 RBI in 107 games. His fielding average was .962 as he quickly learned the rigors of playing shortstop in the bigs. In his sophomore year his fielding average dropped still further to .939, and he posted his first league lead with 44 errors. At the plate Yount improved slightly with a .267 average, 8 home runs, and 52 RBI. Things were looking up in 1976. Splitting time between shortstop and the outfield, he led the league in games (161), putouts (290), total chances (831), and double plays (104). Yount didn't exceed that putout total until 1986.

Playing shortstop on a full-time basis in 1977 set an eight-year trend for Yount. His average climbed to .288. In 1978 he started to show a little of his full potential when, despite five weeks on the disabled list, he improved his batting average to .293 and more than doubled his home run total of the year before. Newlywed Yount held out for a high-octane multiyear contract in 1978, threatening to quit the game and play professional golf instead. Despite his nomination to *The Sporting News* All-Star team in 1978, the Brewers weren't prepared for Yount's season-long slump in 1979. In spite of a career-high 517 assists, his batting average slumped to .267 and his fielding to .969.

The 1980s held more promise for the multitalented Brewer. He started out with a rejuvenated batting average of .293 and a league lead in doubles with 49. He also achieved double digits in home runs for the first time, almost tripling his previous year's output with 23 blasts. In 1981 Yount led league shortstops in fielding with a .985 fielding average, making fewer that 10 errors for the first time ever. He wouldn't match that achievement for four more years. As a hitter Yount fared adequately with a .273 batting mark, 10 homers, and 49 RBI.

Yount first reached possible superstardom in 1982, rallying the Brewers to their first-ever American League pennant. In an amazing offensive display,

Yount batted .331, drove home 114 RBI, and smashed 29 home runs. He led the league in slugging percentage (.578), total bases (367), hits (210), and doubles (46), and was among the leaders in virtually every offensive category. It was Yount's first Gold Glove year. He was first in assists with 489, his second-best career mark. The Brewers shortstop was the runaway choice for the American League MVP award that year. Milwaukee faced the California Angels in the A.L. Championship Series, beating the Halos in five games. Yount hit .250 in the A.L.C.S. with 4 hits. The Brew Crew advanced to the World Series against the pride of the National League, the St. Louis Cardinals. In game five of the Series, Yount became the first player in Series history to have two four-hit games. He highlighted game five, which the Brewers won by a 6-4 margin, with his first World Series homer. In the Series he batted .414 with 12 hits and 6 RBI, leading all

World Series regulars in batting average. The postseason awards garnered by Yount included *The Sporting News* 1982 Player of the Year and a spot on *TSN's* All-Star and Silver Slugger teams.

Following Milwaukee's glory year of 1982, Yount has continued to be an offensive mainstay in suds city. He has averaged 150 hits per season since his sophomore year. Starting in 1982 Yount's average has stayed near the .300 mark each season. His homer totals have been in double digits every year except 1986, when he was recovering from shoulder surgery. The surgery is what prompted Yount's full-time move from shortstop into the outfield. He could still cover lots of ground, but the team was concerned about preserving his throwing arm. Yount's arm isn't what it used to be, but he has a quick release and uses intelligence to make up for any physical shortcomings. He normally finds the cutoff man, throws to the right base, and gets a good start on balls hit his way.

As a hitter Yount is very patient at the plate. He has wide-ranging power and can fight off a variety of tough pitches. He has become an older-but-wiser baserunner since leaving shortstop. Yount earned a career high of 22 steals in 1988 and had 226 lifetime swipes to his credit at the end of the 1989 season.

Robin Yount became one of the youngest players to earn 2,000 career hits when he accomplished that feat at age 30 in 1986. He could also be the youngest ever to top 3,000 hits and could earn a ticket to the Hall of Fame if he passes that elusive mark.

CAREER HIGHLIGHTS
ROBIN YOUNT

Born: September 16, 1955 Danville, IL
Height: 6'0" **Weight:** 165 lbs. **Bats:** Right **Throws:** Right
Shortstop, outfielder, designated hitter: Milwaukee Brewers, 1974-89.

* Named A.L. MVP in 1982
* The first player in history to have 4 or more hits in two World Series games
* Has hit in double figures for home runs nine times
* Batted .414 in the 1982 World Series
* Tied for the 1988 league lead in triples with 11
* Became the youngest regular player in A.L. history at age 18 in 1974
* Hit .300 or better six times

MAJOR LEAGUE TOTALS

G	AB	H	BA	2B	3B	HR	R	RBI	SB
2,291	8,907	2,602	.292	481	111	208	1,335	1,084	226

Robin Yount started out with a reliable glove, but has been working hard at making his batting even more reliable. His 1989 season is evidence of his ability: He led his team with a .318 batting average and 103 RBI.

HALL OF FAME ROSTER

Name	Career Dates	Year Selected
First Basemen		
Anson, Cap	1876-1897	1939
Beckley, Jake	1888-1907	1971
Bottomley, Jim	1922-1937	1974
Brouthers, Dan	1879-1904	1945
Chance, Frank	1898-1914	1946
Connor, Roger	1880-1897	1976
Foxx, Jimmie	1925-1945	1951
Gehrig, Lou	1923-1939	1939
Greenberg, Hank	1930-1947	1956
Kelly, George	1915-1932	1973
Killebrew, Harmon	1954-1975	1984
Leonard, Buck	1933-1950	1972
McCovey, Willie	1959-1980	1986
Mize, Johnny	1936-1953	1981
Sisler, George	1915-1930	1939
Stargell, Willie	1962-1982	1988
Terry, Bill	1923-1936	1954
Second Basemen		
Collins, Eddie	1906-1930	1939
Doerr, Bobby	1937-1951	1986
Evers, Johnny	1902-1929	1939
Frisch, Frankie	1919-1937	1947
Gehringer, Charlie	1924-1942	1949
Herman, Billy	1931-1947	1975
Hornsby, Rogers	1915-1937	1942
Lajoie, Nap	1896-1916	1937
Robinson, Jackie	1947-1956	1962
Schoendienst, Red	1945-1963	1989
Shortstops		
Aparicio, Luis	1956-1973	1984
Appling, Luke	1930-1950	1964
Bancroft, Dave	1915-1930	1971
Banks, Ernie	1953-1971	1977
Boudreau, Lou	1938-1952	1970
Cronin, Joe	1926-1945	1956
Jackson, Travis	1922-1936	1982
Jennings, Hugh	1891-1918	1945
Lloyd, John Henry	1905-1931	1977
Maranville, Rabbit	1912-1935	1954
Reese, Pee Wee	1940-1958	1984
Sewell, Joe	1920-1933	1977
Tinker, Joe	1902-1916	1946
Vaughan, Arky	1932-1948	1985
Wagner, Honus	1897-1917	1936
Wallace, Bobby	1894-1918	1953
*Ward, Monte	1878-1894	1964
Third Baseman		
Baker, Frank	1908-1922	1955
Collins, Jimmy	1895-1908	1945
Dandridge, Ray	1833-1948	1987
Johnson, Judy	1921-1938	1975
Kell, George	1943-1957	1983
Lindstrom, Fred	1924-1936	1976
Mathews, Eddie	1952-1968	1978
Robinson, Brooks	1955-1977	1983
Traynor, Pie	1920-1937	1948
Left Fielders		
Brock, Lou	1961-1979	1985
Burkett, Jesse	1890-1905	1946
Clarke, Fred	1894-1915	1945
Delahanty, Ed	1888-1903	1945
Goslin, Goose	1921-1938	1968
Hafey, Chick	1924-1937	1971
Irvin, Monte	1938-1956	1973
Kelley, Joe	1891-1908	1971

Name	Career Dates	Year Selected
Left Fielders *(continued)*		
Kiner, Ralph	1946-1955	1975
Manush, Heinie	1923-1939	1964
Medwick, Joe	1932-1948	1968
Musial, Stan	1941-1963	1969
O'Rourke, Jim	1876-1904	1945
Simmons, Al	1924-1944	1953
Wheat, Zack	1909-1927	1959
Williams, Billy	1959-1976	1987
Williams, Ted	1939-1960	1966
Yastrzemski, Carl	1961-1983	1989
Center Fielders		
Averill, Earl	1929-1941	1975
Bell, Cool Papa	1922-1946	1974
Carey, Max	1910-1929	1961
Charleston, Oscar	1915-1950	1976
Cobb, Ty	1905-1928	1936
Combs, Earle	1924-1935	1970
DiMaggio, Joe	1936-1951	1955
Duffy, Hugh	1888-1906	1945
Hamilton, Billy	1888-1901	1961
Mantle, Mickey	1951-1968	1974
Mays, Willie	1951-1973	1979
Roush, Edd	1913-1931	1962
Snider, Duke	1947-1964	1980
Speaker, Tris	1907-1928	1937
Waner, Lloyd	1927-1945	1967
Wilson, Hack	1923-1934	1979
Right Fielders		
Aaron, Hank	1954-1976	1982
Clemente, Roberto	1955-1972	1973
Crawford, Sam	1899-1917	1957
Cuyler, Kiki	1921-1938	1968
Flick, Elmer	1898-1910	1963
Heilmann, Harry	1914-1932	1952
Hooper, Harry	1909-1925	1971
Kaline, Al	1953-1974	1980
Keeler, Willie	1892-1910	1939
*Kelly, King	1878-1893	1945
Klein, Chuck	1928-1944	1980
McCarthy, Tommy	1884-1896	1946
Ott, Mel	1926-1947	1951
Rice, Sam	1915-1935	1963
Robinson, Frank	1956-1976	1982
Ruth, Babe	1914-1935	1936
Slaughter, Enos	1938-1959	1985
Thompson, Sam	1885-1906	1974
Waner, Paul	1926-1945	1952
Youngs, Ross	1917-1926	1972
Catchers		
Bench, Johnny	1967-1983	1989
Berra, Yogi	1946-1965	1972
Bresnahan, Roger	1897-1915	1945
Campanella, Roy	1948-1957	1969
Cochrane, Mickey	1925-1937	1947
Dickey, Bill	1928-1946	1954
Ewing, Buck	1880-1897	1946
Ferrell, Rick	1929-1947	1984
Gibson, Josh	1930-1946	1972
Hartnett, Gabby	1922-1941	1955
Lombardi, Ernie	1931-1947	1986
Schalk, Ray	1912-1929	1955
Pitchers		
Alexander, Grover	1911-1930	1938
Bender, Chief	1903-1925	1953

Name	Career Dates	Year Selected
Pitchers (continued)		
Brown, Mordecai	1903-1916	1949
Chesbro, Jack	1899-1909	1946
Clarkson, John	1882-1894	1963
Coveleski, Stan	1912-1928	1969
Dean, Dizzy	1930-1947	1953
DiHigo, Martin	1923-1945	1977
Drysdale, Don	1956-1969	1984
Faber, Red	1914-1933	1964
Feller, Bob	1936-1956	1962
Ford, Whitey	1950-1967	1974
Galvin, Pud	1879-1892	1965
Gibson, Bob	1959-1975	1981
Gomez, Lefty	1930-1943	1972
Grimes, Burleigh	1916-1934	1964
Grove, Lefty	1925-1941	1947
Haines, Jess	1918-1937	1970
Hoyt, Waite	1918-1938	1969
Hubbell, Carl	1928-1943	1947
Hunter, Jim	1965-1979	1987
Johnson, Walter	1907-1927	1936
Joss, Addie	1902-1910	1978
Keefe, Tim	1880-1893	1964
Koufax, Sandy	1955-1966	1972
Lemon, Bob	1941-1958	1976
Lyons, Ted	1923-1946	1955
Marichal, Juan	1960-1975	1983
Marquard, Rube	1908-1925	1971
Mathewson, Christy	1900-1916	1936
McGinnity, Joe	1899-1908	1946
Nichols, Kid	1890-1906	1949
Paige, Satchel	1926-1965	1971
Pennock, Herb	1912-1934	1948
Plank, Eddie	1901-1917	1946
Radbourn, Charles	1880-1891	1939
Rixey, Eppa	1912-1933	1963
Roberts, Robin	1948-1966	1976
Ruffing, Red	1924-1947	1967
Rusie, Amos	1889-1901	1977
Spahn, Warren	1942-1965	1973
Vance, Dazzy	1915-1935	1955
Waddell, Rube	1897-1910	1946
Walsh, Ed	1904-1917	1946
Welch, Mickey	1880-1892	1973
Wilhelm, Hoyt	1952-1972	1985
Wynn, Early	1939-1963	1972
Young, Cy	1890-1911	1937

*Played more than one position for much of his career.

Name		Year Selected
Managers		
Alston, Walter		1983
Harris, Bucky		1975
Huggins, Miller		1964
Lopez, Al		1977
Mack, Connie		1937
McCarthy, Joe		1957
McGraw, John		1937
McKechnie, Bill		1962
Robinson, Wilbert		1945
Stengel, Casey		1966

Umpires		
Barlick, Al		1989
Conlan, Jocko		1974
Connolly, Tom		1953
Evans, Billy		1973
Hubbard, Cal		1976
Klem, Bill		1953

Pioneers and Executives		
Barrow, Ed		1953
Bulkeley, Morgan		1937
Cartwright, Alexander		1938

Name	Year Selected
Pioneers and Executives (continued)	
Chadwick, Henry	1938
Chandler, Albert	1982
Comiskey, Charles	1939
Cummings, Candy	1939
Frick, Ford C.	1970
Giles, Warren	1979
Griffith, Clark	1946
Harridge, Will	1972
Johnson, Ban	1937
Landis, Kenesaw	1944
MacPhail, Larry	1978
Rickey, Branch	1967
Spalding, Al	1939
Weiss, George	1971
Wright, George	1937
Wright, Harry	1953
Yawkey, Tom	1980

Ford C. Frick Award (Broadcasters)	
Allen, Mel	1978
Barber, Red	1978
Brickhouse, Jack	1983
Buck, Jack	1987
Canel, Eli (Buck)	1985
Caray, Harry	1989
Elson, Bob	1979
Gowdy, Curt	1984
Harwell, Ernie	1981
Hodges, Russ	1980
Nelson, Lindsey	1988
Prince, Bob	1986
Scully, Vin	1982

J.G. Taylor Spink Award (Sportswriters)	
Addie, Bob	1981
Broeg, Bob	1979
Broun, Heywood	1970
Brown, Warren	1973
Burick, Si	1982
Carmichael, John	1974
Cobbledick, Gordon	1977
Daniel, Dan	1972
Drebinger, John	1973
Dryden, Charley	1965
Fullerton, Hugh	1964
Graham, Frank	1971
Holmes, Tommy	1979
Hunter, Bob	1988
Isaminger, James	1974
Kaese, Harold	1976
Kelly, Ray	1988
Kieran, John	1973
Lang, Jack	1986
Lardner, Ring	1963
Lawson, Earl	1985
Lewis, Allen	1981
Lieb, Fred	1972
McGuff, Joe	1984
Meany, Tom	1975
Mercer, Sid	1969
Munzel, Edgar	1977
Murnane, Tim	1978
Murray, Jim	1987
Povich, Shirley	1975
Reichler, Joe	1980
Rice, Grantland	1966
Richman, Milton	1980
Runyon, Damon	1967
Salsinger, H.G.	1968
Smith, Ken	1983
Smith, Red	1976
Stockton, J. Roy	1972
Young, Dick	1978

CY YOUNG AWARD WINNERS
(one selection 1956-66)

National League

1956 Don Newcombe, Brooklyn (RH)
1957 Warren Spahn, Milwaukee (LH)
1960 Vernon Law, Pittsburgh (RH)
1962 Don Drysdale, Los Angeles (RH)
1963 Sandy Koufax, Los Angeles (LH)
1965 Sandy Koufax, Los Angeles (LH)
1966 Sandy Koufax, Los Angeles (LH)
1967 Mike McCormick, San Francisco (LH)
1968 Bob Gibson, St. Louis (RH)
1969 Tom Seaver, New York (RH)
1970 Bob Gibson, St. Louis (RH)
1971 Ferguson Jenkins, Chicago (RH)
1972 Steve Carlton, Philadelphia (LH)
1973 Tom Seaver, New York (RH)
1974 Mike Marshall, Los Angeles (RH)
1975 Tom Seaver, New York (RH)
1976 Randy Jones, San Diego (LH)
1977 Steve Carlton, Philadelphia (LH)
1978 Gaylord Perry, San Diego (RH)
1979 Bruce Sutter, Chicago (RH)
1980 Steve Carlton, Philadelphia (LH)
1981 Fernando Valenzuela, L.A. (LH)
1982 Steve Carlton, Philadelphia (LH)
1983 John Denny, Philadelphia (RH)
1984 Rick Sutcliffe, Chicago, (RH)
1985 Dwight Gooden, New York (RH)
1986 Mike Scott, Houston (RH)
1987 Steve Bedrosian, Philadelphia (RH)
1988 Orel Hershiser, Los Angeles (RH)

American League

1958 Bob Turley, New York (RH)
1959 Early Wynn, Chicago (RH)
1961 Whitey Ford, New York (LH)
1964 Dean Chance, Los Angeles (RH)
1967 Jim Lonborg, Boston (RH)
1968 Denny McLain, Detroit (RH)
1969 Mike Cuellar, Baltimore (LH)
       Denny McLain, Detroit (RH)
1970 Jim Perry, Minnesota (RH)
1971 Vida Blue, Oakland (LH)
1972 Gaylord Perry, Cleveland (RH)
1973 Jim Palmer, Baltimore (RH)
1974 Jim Hunter, Oakland (RH)
1975 Jim Palmer, Baltimore (RH)
1976 Jim Palmer, Baltimore (RH)
1977 Sparky Lyle, New York (LH)
1978 Ron Guidry, New York (LH)
1979 Mike Flanagan, Baltimore (LH)
1980 Steve Stone, Baltimore (RH)
1981 Rollie Fingers, Milwaukee (RH)
1982 Pete Vuckovich, Milwaukee (RH)
1983 LaMarr Hoyt, Chicago (RH)
1984 Willie Hernandez, Detroit (LH)
1985 Bret Saberhagen, Kansas City (RH)
1986 Roger Clemens, Boston (RH)
1987 Roger Clemens, Boston (RH)
1988 Frank Viola, Minnesota (LH)

MOST VALUABLE PLAYER AWARD

National League	American League
Chalmers Award, 1911-14	
1911 Frank Schulte, Chicago (RF)	1911 Ty Cobb, Detroit (CF)
1912 Larry Doyle, New York (2B)	1912 Tris Speaker, Boston (CF)
1913 Jake Daubert, Brooklyn (1B)	1913 Walter Johnson, Washington (P)
1914 Johnny Evers, Boston (2B)	1914 Eddie Collins, Philadelphia (2B)
League Awards, 1922-29	
1922 No Selection	1922 George Sisler, St. Louis (1B)
1923 No Selection	1923 Babe Ruth, New York (RF)
1924 Dazzy Vance, Brooklyn (P)	1924 Walter Johnson, Washington (P)
1925 Rogers Hornsby, St. Louis (2B)	1925 Roger Peckinpaugh, Washington (S)
1926 Bob O'Farrell, St. Louis (C)	1926 George Burns, Cleveland (1B)
1927 Paul Waner, Pittsburgh (RF)	1927 Lou Gehrig, New York (1B)
1928 Jim Bottomley, St. Louis (1B)	1928 Mickey Cochrane, Philadelphia (C)
1929 Rogers Hornsby, Chicago (2B)	1929 No Selection
Baseball Writers Association of America, 1931-Present	
1931 Frankie Frisch, St. Louis (2B)	1931 Lefty Grove, Philadelphia (P)
1932 Chuck Klein, Philadelphia (RF)	1932 Jimmie Foxx, Philadelphia (1B)
1933 Carl Hubbell, New York (P)	1933 Jimmie Foxx, Philadelphia (1B)
1934 Dizzy Dean, St. Louis (P)	1934 Mickey Cochrane, Detroit (C)
1935 Gabby Hartnett, Chicago (C)	1935 Hank Greenberg, Detroit (1B)
1936 Carl Hubbell, New York (P)	1936 Lou Gehrig, New York (1B)
1937 Joe Medwick, St. Louis (LF)	1937 Charlie Gehringer, Detroit (2B)
1938 Ernie Lombardi, Cincinnati (C)	1938 Jimmie Foxx, Boston (1B)
1939 Bucky Walters, Cincinnati (P)	1939 Joe DiMaggio, New York (CF)
1940 Frank McCormick, Cincinnati (1B)	1940 Hank Greenberg, Detroit (1B)
1941 Dolph Camilli, Brooklyn (1B)	1941 Joe DiMaggio, New York (CF)
1942 Mort Cooper, St.Louis (P)	1942 Joe Gordon, New York (2B)
1943 Stan Musial, St. Louis (LF)	1943 Spud Chandler, New York (P)
1944 Marty Marion, St. Louis (SS)	1944 Hal Newhouser, Detroit (P)
1945 Phil Cavarretta, Chicago (1B)	1945 Hal Newhouser, Detroit (P)
1946 Stan Musial, St. Louis (1B)	1946 Ted Williams, Boston (LF)
1947 Bob Elliott, Boston (3B)	1947 Joe DiMaggio, New York (CF)
1948 Stan Musial, St. Louis (LF)	1948 Lou Boudreau, Cleveland (SS)
1949 Jackie Robinson, Brooklyn (2B)	1949 Ted Williams, Boston (LF)
1950 Jim Konstanty, Philadelphia (P)	1950 Phil Rizzuto, New York (SS)
1951 Roy Campanella, Brooklyn (C)	1951 Yogi Berra, New York (C)
1952 Hank Sauer, Chicago (LF)	1952 Bobby Shantz, Philadelphia (P)
1953 Roy Campanella, Brooklyn (C)	1953 Al Rosen, Cleveland (3B)
1954 Willie Mays, New York (CF)	1954 Yogi Berra, New York (C)
1955 Roy Campanella, Brooklyn (C)	1955 Yogi Berra, New York (C)
1956 Don Newcombe, Brooklyn (P)	1956 Mickey Mantle, New York (CF)
1957 Henry Aaron, Milwaukee (RF)	1957 Mickey Mantle, New York (CF)
1958 Ernie Banks, Chicago (SS)	1958 Jackie Jensen, Boston (RF)
1959 Ernie Banks, Chicago (SS)	1959 Nellie Fox, Chicago (2B)
1960 Dick Groat, Pittsburgh (SS)	1960 Roger Maris, New York (RF)
1961 Frank Robinson, Cincinnati (RF)	1961 Roger Maris, New York (RF)
1962 Maury Wills, Los Angeles (SS)	1962 Mickey Mantle, New York (CF)
1963 Sandy Koufax, Los Angeles (P)	1963 Elston Howard, New York (C)
1964 Ken Boyer, St. Louis (3B)	1964 Brooks Robinson, Baltimore (3B)
1965 Willie Mays, San Francisco (CF)	1965 Zoilo Versalles, Minnesota (SS)
1966 Roberto Clemente, Pittsburgh (RF)	1966 Frank Robinson, Baltimore (RF)
1967 Orlando Cepeda, St. Louis (1B	1967 Carl Yastrzemski, Boston (LF)
1968 Bob Gibson, St. Louis (P)	1968 Denny McLain, Detroit (P)
1969 Willie McCovey, San Francisco (1B)	1969 Harmon Killebrew, Minnesota (3B)
1970 Johnny Bench, Cincinnati (C)	1970 Boog Powell, Baltimore (1B)
1971 Joe Torre, St. Louis (3B)	1971 Vida Blue, Oakland (P)
1972 Johnny Bench, Cincinnati (C)	1972 Richie Allen, Chicago (1B)
1973 Pete Rose, Cincinnati (LF)	1973 Reggie Jackson, Oakland (RF)
1974 Steve Garvey, Los Angeles (1B)	1974 Jeff Burroughs, Texas (RF)
1975 Joe Morgan, Cincinnati (2B)	1975 Fred Lynn, Boston (CF)
1976 Joe Morgan, Cincinnati (2B)	1976 Thurman Munson, New York (C)
1977 George Foster, Cincinnati (LF)	1977 Rod Carew, Minnesota (1B)
1978 Dave Parker, Pittsburgh (RF)	1978 Jim Rice, Boston (LF)
1979 Keith Hernandez, St. Louis (1B)	1979 Don Baylor, California (DH)
Willie Stargell, Pittsburgh (1B)	
1980 Mike Schmidt, Philadelphia (3B)	1980 George Brett, Kansas City (3B)
1981 Mike Schmidt, Philadelphia (3B)	1981 Rollie Fingers, Milwaukee (P)
1982 Dale Murphy, Atlanta (CF)	1982 Robin Yount, Milwaukee (SS)
1983 Dale Murphy, Atlanta (CF)	1983 Cal Ripken, Baltimore (SS)
1984 Ryne Sandberg, Chicago (2B)	1984 Willie Hernandez, Detroit (P)
1985 Willie McGee, St. Louis (CF)	1985 Don Mattingly, New York (1B)
1986 Mike Schmidt, Philadelphia (3B)	1986 Roger Clemens, Boston (P)
1987 Andre Dawson, Chicago (RF)	1987 George Bell, Toronto (LF)
1988 Kirk Gibson, Los Angeles (LF)	1988 Jose Canseco, Oakland (RF)